CB062746

Tribute to Ruben Aldrovandi

Tribute to Ruben Aldrovandi

F. Caruso, J. G. Pereira, A. Santoro

Editors

Copyright © 2024 Editors
1ª Edição

Direção editorial: Victor Pereira Marinho e José Roberto Marinho

Capa: Fabrício Ribeiro
Projeto gráfico e diagramação: Francisco Caruso

Edição revisada segundo o Novo Acordo Ortográfico da Língua Portuguesa

Dados Internacionais de Catalogação na publicação (CIP)
(Câmara Brasileira do Livro, SP, Brasil)

Tribute to Ruben Aldrovandi / F. Caruso, J. G. Pereira, A. Santoro editors. –
São Paulo: Livraria da Física, 2024.

Vários autores.
ISBN 978-65-5563-418-1

1. Artigos - Coletâneas 2. Homenagem 3. Homens - Biografia 4. Professores - Biografia
I. Caruso, F. II. Pereira, J. G. III. Santoro, A.

24-190629   CDD-371.10092

Índices para catálogo sistemático:
1. Professores : Biografia 371.10092

Eliane de Freitas Leite - Bibliotecária - CRB 8/8415

Todos os direitos reservados. Nenhuma parte desta obra poderá ser reproduzida sejam quais forem os meios empregados sem a permissão da Editora.
Aos infratores aplicam-se as sanções previstas nos artigos 102, 104, 106 e 107 da Lei Nº 9.610, de 19 de fevereiro de 1998

LF EDITORIAL
Editora Livraria da Física
www.livrariadafisica.com.br
(11) 3815-8688 | Loja do Instituto de Física da USP
(11) 3936-3413 | Editora

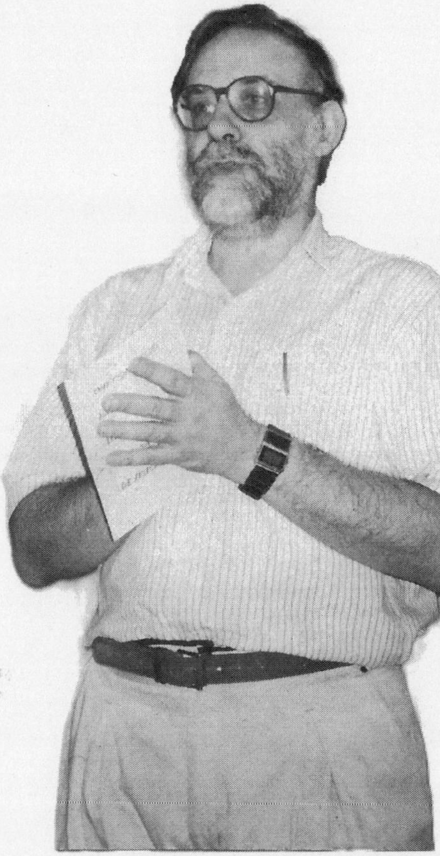

**Caminante, no hay camino,
se hace camino al andar.**

**Wanderer, there is no path,
the path is made by walking.**

Antonio Machado, Spanish poet

Authors & Affiliations

Vanessa C. de Andrade

Instituto de Física, Universidade de Brasília, Brasília, Brazil.

Henrik Aratin

Department of Physics, University of Illinois at Chicago, Chicago, USA.

Adriana V. Araujo

Departamento de Matemáticas, Universidad Sergio Arboleda, Bogotá, Colombia.

Ana Lucia Barbosa

São Paulo, Brazil.

Mario W. Barela

Instituto de Física Teórica, Universidade Estadual Paulista, São Paulo, Brazil.

Francisco Caruso

Centro Brasileiro de Pesquisas Físicas (CBPF). Also at Universidade do Estado do Rio de Janeiro (UERJ). Membro titular da Academia Brasileira de Filosofia e do Pen Clube do Brasil.

Luíz C. B. Crispino

Programa de Pós-Graduação em Física, Universidade Federal do Pará, Belém, Brazil. Also at Departamento de Matemática da Universidade de Aveiro and Centre for Research and Development in Mathematics and Applications (CIDMA), Campus de Santiago, Aveiro, Portugal.

Rodrigo R. Cuzinatto

Instituto de Ciência e Tecnologia, Universidade Federal de Alfenas, Poços de Caldas, Brazil.

Júlio C. Fabris

Núcleo Cosmo-UFES & Departamento de Física, Universidade Federal do Espírito Santo, Vitória, Brazil. Also at National Research Nuclear University, Moscow Engineering Physics Institute, Moscow, Russia.

Luíz A. Ferreira

Instituto de Física de São Carlos, Universidade de São Paulo (USP), São Carlos-SP, Brazil.

Diógenes Galetti

Instituto de Física Teórica, Universidade Estadual Paulista, São Paulo, Brazil.

Evelise Gausmann

Rio Grande, Brazil.

José F. Gomes

Instituto de Física Teórica, Universidade Estadual Paulista, São Paulo, Brazil.

José A. Helayël-Neto

Centro Brasileiro de Pesquisas Físicas (CBPF), Rio de Janeiro, Brazil.

Friedrich W. Hell

Institute for Theoretical Physics, University of Cologne, Cologne, Germany.

Richard Kerner

LPTMC Sorbonne-Université, Paris, France.

Martin Krššak

Faculty of Mathematics, Physics and Informatics, Comenius University, Bratislava, Slovak Republic. Also at School of Astronomy and Space Science, University of Science and Technology of China, Hefei, Anhui, China.

Luiz C. S. Leite

Instituto Federal do Pará, Campus Altamira, Pará, Brazil.

Gabriel V. Lobo

Instituto de Física Teórica, Universidade Estadual Paulista, São Paulo, Brazil.

Diego F. López

Department of Mathematics and Statistics, Dalhousie University, Halifax, Canada.

Miguel A. Manna

Université Montpellier, Laboratoire Charles Coulomb, Montpellier, France.

Léo G. Medeiros

Escola de Ciência e Tecnologia, Universidade Federal do Rio Grande do Norte, Lagoa Nova, Natal, Brazil.

João P. Melo

Centro Brasileiro de Pesquisas Físicas (CBPF), Rio de Janeiro, Brazil.

Eduardo M. de Morais

Independent Researcher, Poços de Caldas, Brazil.

Adriano A. Natale

Instituto de Física Teórica, Universidade Estadual Paulista, São Paulo, Brazil.

Sérgio F. Novaes

Instituto de Física Teórica, Universidade Estadual Paulista, São Paulo, Brazil.
Also at Advanced Institute for Artificial Intelligence (AI2), São Paulo, Brazil.

Mario Novello

Centro de Estudos Avançados de Cosmologia (CEAC), Centro Brasileiro de Pesquisa Físicas (CBPF), Rio de Janeiro, Brazil.

Yuri N. Obukhov

Theoretical Physics Laboratory, Nuclear Safety Institute, Russian Academy of Sciences, Moscow, Russia.

Marco A. A. de Paula

Programa de Pós-Graduação em Física, Universidade Federal do Pará, Belém, Pará, Brazil.

José G. Pereira

Instituto de Física Teórica, Universidade Estadual Paulista, São Paulo, Brazil.

Bruto M. Pimentel

Instituto de Física Teórica, Universidade Estadual Paulista, São Paulo, Brazil.

Vicente Pleitez

Instituto de Física Teórica, Universidade Estadual Paulista, São Paulo, Brazil.

Pedro J. Pompeia

Departamento de Física, Instituto Tecnológico de Aeronáutica, São José dos Campos, Brazil.

Roldão da Rocha

Center of Mathematics, Federal University of ABC, Santo André, Brazil.

José E. Rodrigues

Departamento de Física, Universidade Estadual Paulista, Guaratinguetá, Brazil.

Johan R. Salazar

Instituto de Física Teórica, Universidade Estadual Paulista, São Paulo, Brazil.

Alberto Santoro

Instituto de Física, Universidade do Estado do Rio de Janeiro, Rio de Janeiro, Brazil.

Carlos A. Savoy

Institut de Physique Théorique, Université Paris Saclay, Gif-sur-Yvette, France.

Julio M. H. da Silva

Departamento de Física, Universidade Estadual Paulista, Guaratinguetá, Brazil.

Alfredo T. Suzuki

Department of Physics, La Sierra University, Riverside, USA.

Júnior D. Toniato

Departamento de Química e Física & Núcleo Cosmo-UFES, Universidade Federal do Espírito Santo, Alegre, Brazil.

Paulo A. F. da Veiga

Departamento de Matemática Aplicada e Estatística, Universidade de São Paulo (USP), São Carlos, Brazil.

Abraham H. Zimerman

Instituto de Física Teórica, Universidade Estadual Paulista, São Paulo, Brazil.

Preface

As a professor at Instituto de Física Teórica (IFT), Ruben Aldrovandi influenced and motivated several generations of students to pursue a career in theoretical physics, particularly gravitation and cosmology. With his charism, enhanced by the inseparable pipe, and with his romantic view of scientific research, Ruben captivated many students.

Besides his academic legacy, Ruben played important administrative roles at both IFT and Fundação IFT, the maintainer of the institute. He spent many years as the Scientific Director of the Instituto and a member of the Fundação board of trustees, having held the positions of vice president and president of that board.

When the federal funding agency Finep decided it would no longer support the Instituto, Ruben led the search for a solution, which took quite some time. In the late nineteen-eighties, such a search eventually culminated with an agreement between Fundação IFT and the Universidade Estadual Paulista (UNESP), according to which the Institute would be incorporated into UNESP. Despite being transferred to UNESP, it was agreed that Fundação IFT would continue to lodge the Institute on its premises.

With the moving of IFT to the newly constructed UNESP Campus at Barra Funda in 2009, the Foundation and the Institute dissociated and began to chart their destinies independently. One can safely say that Ruben played a crucial role in both IFT and Fundação IFT, which wouldn't be what they are today without Ruben's interventions.

The purpose of the present book, which is made up of articles and testimonies, is to pay tribute to the academic, administrative, and scientific legacy of Ruben Aldrovandi. The contributing authors have various relationships with him: students who attended his classes, students who graduated under his supervision, and post-doctor researchers who worked under his supervision. It also includes old friends, colleagues, collaborators, and researchers who share the same scientific interests with him.

This preface wouldn't be complete without a few words concerning Ruben as a scientist. The main characteristic of Ruben's work was the focus on fundamental questions, an attitude that frequently required him to leave the mainstream of physics. Although his research concentrated mainly on theoretical physics, Ruben had a broad view of physics and recognized the value of other research areas. He was an enthusiast of experimental high-energy physics and considered the possibility of creating a group in this area while he was the institute's scientific director.

Ruben was an autonomous and critical thinker. Permanently oblivious to fads, he preferred to forge his own path. His research work was motivated solely by the pleasure of exploring new ideas and his love of science. Furthermore, his introverted personality has kept him away from the holophotes. Physics would undoubtedly benefit from more scientists like Ruben.

The Editors

Acknowledgements

The editors warmly thank the authors who contributed to the present volume honoring Ruben Aldrovandi. Without their efforts and time, this book wouldn't come to life.

This book wouldn't be possible without the support of Fundação Instituto de Física Teórica. The editors thank the Foundation direction, particularly Prof. Gerson Francisco.

Summary

SCIENTIFIC REPORTS   1

1 An overview of field theories of gravity   3
    1.1 Introduction 4
    1.2 The main framework 4
    1.3 Scalar gravity 10
    1.4 Spinor theory of gravity 23
    1.5 Tensor theory 28
    1.6 Final comments 32

2 De Sitter-invariant approach to cosmology   37
    2.1 Introduction 38
    2.2 Minkowski and de Sitter as quotient spaces 40
    2.3 De Sitter-invariant general relativity 41
    2.4 De Sitter-invariant Friedmann equations 46
    2.5 Some physical implications 48
    2.6 Final remarks 53

3 Effects of new physics on the standard model: parameters and vice versa   57
    3.1 Introduction 58
    3.2 Examples in the standard model construction 58
    3.3 Patterns to avoid in the beyond standard model phenomenology . . . 60
    3.4 Examples in classical physics 63
    3.5 Conclusions 64

4 Symmetry breaking and confinement in supersymmetric gauge field theories   67
    4.1 Supersymmetry: what for? 68
    4.2 Spontaneous gauge symmetry breaking 70
    4.3 Confinement and t' Hooft anomaly condition 72
    4.4 Final remarks 76

5 A natural QCD infrared cutoff   79
    5.1 Introduction: Dynamical gluon mass generation 80
    5.2 Phenomenology with dynamically massive gluons 81

	5.3	Dynamical perturbation theory	84
	5.4	Final remarks	85

6 Describing paths on discrete and finite quantum phase spaces 89
    6.1 A brief review of Schwinger's operator bases 90
    6.2 Discrete and finite quantum phase spaces 92
    6.3 A brief review of q-objects 95
    6.4 Discrete phase spaces and the q-algebra 96

7 Scalar-tensor gravity in Lyra geometry 105
    7.1 Introduction 106
    7.2 Lyra geometry 107
    7.3 Lyra spacetime 111
    7.4 Lyra scalar-tensor gravity 112
    7.5 Lyra-Schwarzschild solution 115
    7.6 Final remarks 118

8 Braid groups, translation operators and symmetry of Painlevé type equations 121
    8.1 Introduction 122
    8.2 Translations for $A_2^{(1)}$ 123
    8.3 Translation operators of $A_3^{(1)}$ affine Weyl group 126
    8.4 Comments on uniqueness of the square-roots of the product of translations and long term goals of the project 131

9 Inflationary dynamics in modified gravity models 135
    9.1 Introduction 136
    9.2 Fundamentals of the proposed modified gravity models 138
    9.3 Inflation on the FLRW background 139
    9.4 Final remarks 147

10 The Miles' theory of surface wind-waves in finite depth: a predictive physical model in coastal regions 153
    10.1 Introduction 154
    10.2 Wind generated surface waves: the linear regime 156
    10.3 Young-Donelan field experiments on growth of surface wind-waves in finite depth 161
    10.4 Conclusions 167

11 Field propagators in the interpolating angle and their limiting cases for instant form dynamics (IFD) and light-front dynamics (LFD) 171
    11.1 Introduction 172
    11.2 Feynman propagator 174
    11.3 The fermion propagator in the IFD limit 185

    11.4 Conclusion 189

12 Local versus global subtleties of projective representations   191
    12.1 Introduction 192
    12.2 Basic background 193
    12.3 Local exponents and differentiability 194
    12.4 Considerations about the local group and extensions 198
    12.5 A glance at characterizations coming from algebraic topology 201
    12.6 Concluding remarks 203

13 Teleparallelism, gauge theory and anholonomy: Utiyama's approach.   205
    13.1 Introduction 206
    13.2 Utiyama's approach to gauge theory 208
    13.3 The translation group 210
    13.4 Geometrical interpretation 214
    13.5 Final remarks 216

14 The beauty of self-duality   219
    14.1 Introduction 220
    14.2 Multi-field kinks in $(1+1)$-dimensions 223
    14.3 Lumps in $(2+1)$-dimensions 229
    14.4 Monopoles in $(3+1)$-dimensions 231
    14.5 Skyrmions in $(3+1)$-dimensions 233
    14.6 Instantons in four Euclidean dimensions 237

15 Introducing braids, knots, and links   241
    15.1 Introduction 242
    15.2 Braids and braid groups 245
    15.3 Identical particles 252
    15.4 Artin classical braids 254

16 On Yang-Mills stability bounds and finiteness of the free energy   265
    16.1 Introduction and the model 266
    16.2 Our Main Results and Some Steps of the Proofs 270
    16.3 Conclusions 277

17 Nonmetricity and hypermomentum: on the possible violation of Lorentz invariance   281
    17.1 Introduction 282
    17.2 General relativity 283
    17.3 Metric-affine geometry of spacetime 284
    17.4 Gauge theories of gravitation as a unifying framework .. 285
    17.5 Possible violation of Poincaré-Lorentz invariance 286

17.6 Hyperfluid controlled by the energy-momentum and the hyper-momentum laws 287
17.7 Conclusions and outlook 289

18 Agglomeration of local structures as a model of glass formation   **297**
18.1 Stochastic agglomeration model 298
18.2 The alkali-borate glasses 303
18.3 The Volterra approach 310

19 Re-assessing properties of Dirac's equation in presence of Lorentz-symmetry violation   **323**
19.1 Intuitive and general aspects of Lorentz-symmetry violation 324
19.2 Some aspects of the QED fermionic sector in the SME 328
19.3 The special case with vanishing $R_\mu \gamma^\mu \gamma_5$ 331
19.4 Concluding comments 340

20 Geodesic analysis, absorption and scattering in the static Hayward spacetime   **343**
20.1 Introduction 344
20.2 Hayward spacetime 345
20.3 Geodesic analysis 347
20.4 Partial-wave analysis 351
20.5 Results 354
20.6 Final remarks 362

21 On alternative (or modified) theories of gravity   **369**
21.1 At that time... 370
21.2 The variation of the fundamental constants 371
21.3 Scalar tensor theories: some curiosities in the Brans-Dicke case 374
21.4 The cosmological constant: a problem? 380
21.5 Unimodular Gravity 384
21.6 Final remarks 388

22 Teleparallel gravity, covariance and their geometrical meaning   **393**
22.1 Introduction 394
22.2 Einstein's teleparallelism and its revival 395
22.3 Metric-affine approach to teleparallel geometries 399
22.4 Einstein's teleparallelism and teleparallel gravity 404
22.5 Geometrical significance of teleparallelism 407
22.6 Conclusions 410

23 The geopolitics of artificial intelligence: navigating towards an enlightened tomorrow — 419
- 23.1 Introduction — 420
- 23.2 The new geopolitical landscape — 421
- 23.3 Economic implications of AI — 423
- 23.4 Ethical and societal considerations — 424
- 23.5 The path forward: a Brazilian roadmap — 426
- 23.6 Conclusion — 430

24 Necessary steps for looking at time as multidimensional — 433
- 24.1 Introduction — 434
- 24.2 Prelude to an one-dimensional time — 434
- 24.3 More than three space dimensions was not acceptable in the Classical Greek Philosophy — 436
- 24.4 New speculations about the fourth dimension — 437
- 24.5 Kant's conjecture and beyond — 438
- 24.6 The new background of non-Euclidean geometries — 441
- 24.7 The fourth dimension as time-like component of the new space-time concept in Physics — 443
- 24.8 The role of metric space in the problem of space-time dimensionality — 447
- 24.9 Giambiagi and Bolini on multidimensional time — 450
- 24.10 Concluding remarks — 451

PERSONAL TESTIMONIES — 459

1 O casarão da rua Pamplona — 461

2 Ruben: O início de uma grande amizade — 465

3 Lembranças / Remembrances — 471

4 Some Words of Gratitude — 473

5 A personal tribute to Ruben — 475

6 Breves palavras sobre o professor Ruben Aldrovandi — 477

7 Ruben Aldrovandi: the French Connection — 481

8 Ruben: a personal tribute — 485

9 Ruben: uma pequena biografia — 487

SCIENTIFIC REPORTS

1
An overview of field theories of gravity

M. Novello, J. D. Toniato

Abstract: In the general relativity theory the basic ingredient to describe gravity is the geometry, which interacts with all forms of matter and energy, and as such, the metric could be interpreted as a true physical quantity. However the metric is not matter nor energy, but instead it is a new dynamical variable that Einstein introduced to describe gravity. In order to conciliate this approach to the more traditional ones, physicists have tried to describe the main ideas of GR in terms of standard conceptions of field theory. In this sense, curved metrics are seen as a dynamical variable emerging from a more fundamental field which lies upon a flat Minkowski spacetime. This was made by the hypothesis that the metric tensor may be written as $g_{\mu\nu} = \eta_{\mu\nu} + h_{\mu\nu}$ where the tensor $h_{\mu\nu}$ was interpreted either in terms of a spin-2 or constructed in terms of other fields. We review some proposals that were suggested in the treatment of gravity in terms of scalar, spinor and tensor fields configurations.

1.1 Introduction

This review treat the different possibilities for describing gravitation in terms of a field theory and intends to show the relevance of these theories in the understanding of gravitational phenomena. Interestingly, only the scalar field had a first version prior to the theory of general relativity (GR). Yet it was a rather simplistic version. Nevertheless, after the recognition of the importance of the modification of the metric of space-time made by Einstein several proposals to represent gravitational interaction in terms of modified geometry appeared using a scalar field to build an effective metric.

Although such a formulation of an effective metric has only developed in the last few decades, we can no doubt point to Gordon's proposal in 1923 as the original source of this idea [1]. Indeed, in the analysis of the propagation of electromagnetic waves in moving dielectrics, Gordon remarked that if one changes the geometry of the space-time in the domain of the propagation of a wave, the characterization of the motion can be described in a similar way as in the empty space, that is, the wave propagates through geodesics of this effective metric. At the first times this method of the effective geometry was used only for the propagation of waves. Later on, it was realized that it can be used formally to describe the dynamics of distinct formulations of non-linear field theories, as it will be discussed here.

This manuscript is organized as follows. In section 1.2 we provide an overview of the origins and developments of the effective metric for different kinds of force, including gravity. Section 1.3 deals with the early proposals for scalar theories of gravity and with the recent developments of a scalar theory within an effective metric framework. In section 1.4 a spinor theory of gravity is presented, as well as an unified treatment of gravity and Fermi (weak) interaction. Section 1.5 discuss the tensorial formulations, from the simplest reproduction of general relativity by Feynmann and collaborators to the most recent approaches. We conclude in Section 1.6 with some comments on these alternative field theories of gravity.

1.2 The main framework

Although general relativity is usually presented in the framework of Riemannian geometry, it is possible to fully describe the exact Einstein's theory of gravity in terms of a spin-2 field propagating in an arbitrary background spacetime (see, for instance, Refs. [2, 3]). The main idea can be summarized as follows. Consider a flat Minkowski background (just to simplify our exposition) endowed with a metric $\eta_{\mu\nu}$. In a Lorentzian coordinate system the metric of the background takes the standard constant expression. We may allow for general coordinates; the curvature tensor however vanishes,

$$R^{\alpha}{}_{\beta\mu\nu}(\eta_{\varepsilon\sigma}) = 0. \tag{1.1}$$

In a Galilean coordinate system the metric of the background can assume standard constant expression. From now on $\eta_{\mu\nu}$ are the component (not necessarily constant) of the Minkowski metric in general coordinates. Then one introduces a symmetric second order tensor $h_{\mu\nu}$ and writes

$$g_{\mu\nu} = \eta_{\mu\nu} - h_{\mu\nu}. \tag{1.2}$$

This binomial form is an exact expression for the metric $g_{\mu\nu}$. Note however that its inverse, the contravariant tensor $g^{\mu\nu}$, is not in general a binomial form but, instead, it is an infinite series,

$$g^{\mu\nu} = \eta^{\mu\nu} + h^{\mu\nu} - h^{\mu\alpha} h_\alpha{}^\nu + \ldots \tag{1.3}$$

There are two main postulates founding general relativity: i) The background Minkowski metric is not observable. Matter and energy interact gravitationally only through the combination $\eta_{\mu\nu} - h_{\mu\nu}$ and its derivatives. Any test body in a gravitational field moves along a geodesic relative to the metric $g_{\mu\nu}$; ii) The dynamics of gravity is described by an equation relating the contracted curvature tensor $R_{\mu\nu}$ to the stress-energy tensor of matter.

In other words general relativity assumes the hypothesis that gravity may be interpreted as nothing but a modification of the geometry of the underlying spacetime and the spacetime metric satisfies a dynamical equation that controls the action of matter on the modifications of the geometry. Although the first hypothesis have already demonstrated its success in describing a large number of phenomena, the second hypothesis has a more restrict support, it has a less sound acceptance. Indeed, it is well known the existence of a profuse number of models which modifies GR dynamics. Here we concentrate in those theories that describe the dynamics of the geometry as a consequence of other interactions due to non-gravitational process.

1.2.1 Binomial metrics

Recently, interest has grown in the study of a specific hypothesis that dynamical processes can be satisfactory described as a consequence of the modification in the geometric structure of spacetime. It is clear that, for GR specifically, there is a natural motivation once gravity is taken as an universal form of interaction. But in effective theories, the spacetime metric arises as a result of the dynamical equations of non-gravitational fields. The features of this procedure has been analyzed in the context of propagation of linear waves [92] and to nonlinear theories [5].

The method is based on writing the spacetime metric in the form of Eq. (1.2) which gives, automatically, an infinite series for its contravariant version, as in Eq. (1.3). Thus, the usage of the same GR approach deals with serious difficulties. Alternatively, one can implement a novel interpretation and understand the theory as a spin-2 field propagating in a flat background. Meanwhile, one could also to consider the conditions under which the contravariant metric results in a binomial form as well.

Considering the metric structure, defined as

$$g_{\mu\nu} = a\eta_{\mu\nu} + b h_{\mu\nu}. \tag{1.4}$$

If $h_{\mu\nu}$ satisfies the closure relation below,

$$\eta^{\alpha\beta} h_{\mu\alpha} h_{\beta\nu} = m \eta_{\mu\lambda} + n h_{\mu\lambda}. \tag{1.5}$$

then the contravariant metric, $g^{\mu\nu}$, will also have a binomial form,

$$g^{\mu\nu} = \alpha \eta^{\mu\nu} + \beta h^{\mu\nu}, \tag{1.6}$$

where $h^{\mu\nu} = \eta^{\mu\alpha}\eta^{\nu\beta} h_{\alpha\beta}$ and

$$\alpha = \frac{a+bn}{a(a+bn)-mb^2}, \quad \beta = \frac{-b}{a(a+bn)-mb^2}. \tag{1.7}$$

1.2.2 Newtonian attractions

Let us face the first main proposal of general relativity, that is: is it possible to eliminate the acceleration induced on an arbitrary body A by a gravitational field using a convenient modification of the metric associated to the spacetime where A is propagating? We know the answer of general relativity: all gravitational effects are equivalently described in terms of the universal metric modification of the geometry of the spacetime. Notwithstanding, let us show how the answer can be found in other approach. Note however that this must not be considered as an a priori once one could well make other kind of convention to ascribe specific metrics to different events. If we accept this point of view then, each interaction, each event, each process requires a particular modification of the metric environment in such a way that one can eliminate any kind of force by just a modification of the metric in which a body moves in such a way that it is interpreted as a free body. In other words, the metric becomes just a convention to eliminate the force that drives the motion of the body.

The main direct consequence of this is that, contrary to the principles of general relativity, those metrics do not need any additional constraint that should be interpreted as its dynamics. The very fact that GR assumes that the universality of gravity is the origin to accept its geometric interpretation and, once this modification of the geometry is universal, completely independent of any particular process, it makes almost obligatory the existence of a particular dynamics for the metric. On the other hand, in the treatment of other forces, once each process has its own particular metric, in which the body movement is interpreted as inertial, there is no extra dynamics for the geometry: its characterization depends on the interaction.

A classical example is that of a photon propagating inside a moving dielectric, which may acquires an acceleration. In 1923 Gordon showed that it is possible to describe photon's path as a geodesics over a modified metric [1]. This means that a change in the geometry can eliminate the acceleration felt by the photon. The interest on this description is that it allows its generalization for any kind of accelerated path, independently of the origin of the force and for any kind of massive or massless particle. Let us show the nature of this procedure by considering the simple case of an accelerated motion in flat Minkowski spacetime, when the acceleration is the gradient of a scalar function,

$$a_\mu = \partial_\mu \Phi, \tag{1.8}$$

with Φ an arbitrary scalar field.

Using the freedom in the definition of the four-vector we set $\eta_{\mu\nu} v^\mu v^\nu = 1$ and thus the acceleration is orthogonal to the velocity. Let us construct for any congruence of curves the associated effective metric under the form

$$\hat{q}^{\mu\nu} = \alpha \eta^{\mu\nu} + \beta v^\mu v^\nu, \tag{1.9}$$

with α and β arbitrary (in principle) functions of Φ. The corresponding covariant expression is

$$\hat{q}_{\mu\nu} = \frac{1}{\alpha} \eta_{\mu\nu} - \frac{\beta}{\alpha(\alpha+\beta)} v_\mu v_\nu. \tag{1.10}$$

We are using the hat symbol to denote objects in the auxiliary geometry where the metric is given by $\hat{q}_{\mu\nu}$. The associated covariant derivative of an arbitrary vector S^μ, represented by a semi comma (;), is defined by

$$S^\alpha{}_{;\mu} = S^\alpha{}_{,\mu} + \hat{\Gamma}^\alpha{}_{\mu\nu} S^\nu \tag{1.11}$$

where the corresponding Christoffel symbol is given by

$$\hat{\Gamma}^\varepsilon{}_{\mu\nu} = \frac{1}{2} \hat{q}^{\mu\nu} \left(\hat{q}_{\lambda\mu,\nu} + \hat{q}_{\lambda\nu,\mu} - \hat{q}_{\mu\nu,\lambda} \right). \tag{1.12}$$

By setting $\hat{v}^\mu = \Omega^{-1} v^\mu$, and requiring that $\hat{v}^\mu$ must be normalized, one obtains that $\Omega = 1/\sqrt{\alpha+\beta}$. In order to identify this congruence generated by $\hat{v}^\mu$ and v_μ we require that Ω be constant along the motion, that is, $v^\mu \partial_\mu \Omega = 0$. The condition that makes the congruence as geodesic is provided by

$$\partial_\mu \Phi = \hat{\Gamma}^\varepsilon_{\mu\nu} v_\varepsilon v^\nu = \frac{1}{2}(\alpha+\beta) v^\alpha v^\nu \hat{q}_{\alpha\nu,\mu}. \tag{1.13}$$

Then

$$a_\mu + \frac{1}{2}\partial_\mu \ln(\alpha+\beta) = 0. \tag{1.14}$$

Thus, for any congruence Γ of accelerated curves in Minkowski spacetime driven by a potential as in (1.8), it is always possible to construct an associated auxiliary metric in the form (1.10) such that, if

$$\alpha + \beta = e^{-2\Phi}. \tag{1.15}$$

the paths of the curves become geodesics in this effective geometry.

More general situations of geometric modifications to describe accelerated motions can be found in Ref. [5]. The method exposed before is in the basis of the so called analogue models of gravity. In these models, non-gravitational phenomena (the accelerated motion) are used to mimic typical kinematic effects that occurs in curved spacetimes (free motion of test particles in the presence of gravity). Most popular of these analogue models are the artificial black holes, where the effective metric presents an event horizon-like structure. For a review on the subject, the reader can refer, for instance, to Refs. [6, 7].

In the next sections we enter in a distinct analysis where different fields, obeying a given nonlinear equation of motion, can be described in terms of modifications of the background geometry generated by themselves.

1.2.3 Effective metrics in nonlinear scalar fields

Motivated by the discussion of the previous section, we wish now to discuss the whether is possible to translate nonlinear scalar field dynamics within a Minkowski spacetime into linear field equations over an effective geometry. Consider the following nonlinear Lagrangian,

$$L = V(\Phi)\omega, \tag{1.16}$$

where $\omega \equiv \eta^{\mu\nu}\partial_\mu \Phi \partial_\nu \Phi$, as before. The field equation derived from the minimal action principle is given by,

$$\frac{1}{\sqrt{-\eta}}\partial_\mu \left(\sqrt{-\eta}\,\eta^{\mu\nu}\partial_\nu \Phi\right) + \frac{1}{2}\frac{V'}{V}\omega = 0, \tag{1.17}$$

where $V' \equiv dV/d\Phi$ and η is the determinant of $\eta_{\mu\nu}$.

The field equation (1.17) can be seen as that of a massless Klein-Gordon field propagating in a curved spacetime whose geometry is governed by Φ itself. In other words, the same dynamics can be written either in a Minkowski background or in another geometry constructed in terms of the scalar field. Following the steps established in [8], let us introduce the contravariant metric tensor $q^{\mu\nu}$ by the binomial formula

$$q^{\mu\nu} = \alpha \eta^{\mu\nu} + \frac{\beta}{\omega} \partial^\mu \Phi \partial^\nu \Phi, \qquad (1.18)$$

where $\partial^\mu \Phi \equiv \eta^{\mu\nu} \partial_\nu \Phi$ and parameters α and β are dimensionless functions of Φ. Note that the quantity w can be written in terms of its effective counterpart,

$$\Omega \equiv q^{\mu\nu} \partial_\mu \Phi \partial_\nu \Phi = (\alpha + \beta) \omega. \qquad (1.19)$$

From this expression, giving α and β we obtain Ω as function of ω and Φ.

The corresponding covariant expression of the metric, defined as the inverse $q_{\mu\nu} q^{\nu\lambda} = \delta^\lambda_\mu$, is also a binomial expression, once it satisfies the closure relation (1.5). Its coefficients can be founded by inverting expressions in (1.7),

$$q_{\mu\nu} = \frac{1}{\alpha} \eta_{\mu\nu} - \frac{\beta}{\alpha(\alpha+\beta)\omega} \partial_\mu \Phi \partial_\nu \Phi. \qquad (1.20)$$

Now we ask whether it is possible to find α and β, in such a way that the dynamics of the field (1.17) takes the form

$$\Box \Phi = 0, \qquad (1.21)$$

where $\Box$ is the Laplace-Beltrami operator relative to the metric $q_{\mu\nu}$, that is

$$\Box \Phi \equiv \frac{1}{\sqrt{-q}} \partial_\mu (\sqrt{-q} \, q^{\mu\nu} \partial_\nu \Phi). \qquad (1.22)$$

We then conclude that, given the Lagrangian $L = V(\Phi)\omega$ with an arbitrary potential $V(\Phi)$, the field theory satisfying Eq. (1.17) in Minkowski spacetime is equivalent to a massless Klein-Gordon field in the metric $q^{\mu\nu}$ provided that the functions $\alpha(\Phi)$ and $\beta(\Phi)$ satisfy the condition

$$\alpha + \beta = \alpha^3 V. \qquad (1.23)$$

It is worth to note that such an equivalence is valid for any dynamics described in the Minkowski background by a Lagrangian non linear in the kinetic term ω (see details in [9]).

Up to now, there is no relevant physical meaning associated with the effective metric $q_{\mu\nu}$. It determines a spacetime geometry from where the scalar field dynamics can be seen as a sourceless wave. The important step in the direction to attribute a physical significance to $q_{\mu\nu}$ is to determine what is its role when other fields are present. It can acquires a universal character, in the same lines as in GR, giving rise to a scalar field theory of gravity as it will be discussed in the next section.

1.3 Scalar gravity

1.3.1 Preliminary attempts

The history of the first attempts to describe gravitational phenomena with a single scalar field coincides with the history of the conception of general relativity by itself. Already in 1907, two years after the formulation of special relativity, Einstein had dedicate himself to develop a relativistic generalization of Newton's gravitational theory [10]. His ideas can be summarized as follows. Firstly, there is the natural generalization of Newtonian force to a four-vector quantity,

$$\mathcal{F}^\mu = \frac{d}{d\tau}\left(m\frac{dx^\mu}{d\tau}\right), \qquad (1.24)$$

where m is the particle mass and τ is the proper time. This last definition imposes an auxiliary condition due to the constancy of light velocity. Contracting (1.24) with the metric, and assuming that M is always a constant, one obtains the relation

$$\eta_{\mu\nu}\mathcal{F}^\mu \frac{dx^\nu}{d\tau} = 0. \qquad (1.25)$$

This condition is naturally satisfied in electromagnetism, once the electromagnetic four-force is defined as $\mathcal{F}^\mu_{em} = F^{\mu\alpha}\eta_{\alpha\beta}dx^\beta/d\tau$, and due to the anti-symmetry of Maxwell's tensor, $F^{\mu\nu}$.

For the gravitational case, the simplest way to follow is to construct the gravitational four-force from the gradient of the scalar potential Φ, and generalize Poisson's equation to a four dimensional one. Thus, one come up with the following equations,

$$\mathcal{F}^\mu_g = mc^2\partial^\mu\Phi, \qquad \Box\Phi = -\frac{4\pi G}{c^2}\rho. \qquad (1.26)$$

In the above, $\Box$ is the d'Alembert operator and ρ is the mass density distribution. Note that the scalar potential is now dimensionless. However, with the condition (1.25), one gets $d\Phi/d\tau = 0$. Such result basically implies that the gravitational force on any particle is always null, an inconsistency pointed out by Einstein and which lead him to question the compatibility between gravity and special relativity. The discussion that emerged in the following years, concerning mainly the equivalence principle and general covariance, ended up with the formulation of the general theory of relativity. The details of this enticing history can be seen, for instance, in Ref. [11]. But in the mean time, a feel other attempts to develop a scalar theory of gravity was made by Nordström.

1.3.1.1 Nordström's theories

In order to improve Einstein's developments on the relativistic generalization of Newtonian gravity, Nordström explored the idea of a variable mass [12, 13]. Equation (1.26) is then rewritten as follows,

$$m\frac{dv_\mu}{d\tau} + v_\mu \frac{dm}{d\tau} = mc^2 \frac{\partial \Phi}{\partial x^\mu}. \tag{1.27}$$

Contracting the above equation with v^μ and integrating gives the gravitational field dependence of the mass,

$$m(\Phi) = m_0 e^\Phi, \tag{1.28}$$

with m_0 a constant. Folowing that equation (1.27) return the equation of motion of test particles, namely

$$c^2 \frac{\partial \Phi}{\partial x^\mu} = \frac{dv_\mu}{d\tau} + v_\mu \frac{d\Phi}{d\tau}. \tag{1.29}$$

Although the independence of equation (1.29) with respect to the mass could suggest an agreement of this theory with the weak version of the equivalence principle, a simple case of study can reveal some inconsistencies. Consider a free fall in a static gravitational field acting only in the direction of the movement, say $\Phi = \Phi(z)$. From (1.29) one can obtain the relations

$$\frac{dV_z}{dt} = -c^2\left(1 - \frac{V^2}{c^2}\right)\frac{d\Phi}{dz}, \quad \frac{dV_x}{dt} = 0, \quad \frac{dV_y}{dt} = 0, \tag{1.30}$$

with V_i are the components of the tree-vector $\vec{V} = d\vec{x}/dt$ and t is the local time. Thus, bodies with horizontal velocities would affect the vertical free fall, which shows that Nordström model violates the equivalence principle.

Another point of criticism in the Nordström theory concerns the source of the gravitational field. The mass density ρ is a projection of the energy momentum tensor dependent on the observer,

$$\rho = T_{\mu\nu} v^\mu v^\nu, \quad \text{with} \quad T_{\mu\nu} = -\frac{2}{\sqrt{-\eta}} \frac{\delta(\sqrt{-\eta} L_m)}{\delta \eta^{\mu\nu}}, \tag{1.31}$$

and L_m is the Lagrangian function of matter fields. One thus see that the modified Poisson equation in (1.26) is not Lorentz invariant. Actually, it was Einstein that suggested that the only scalar quantity that could be source of the gravitational field is the trace of the energy momentum tensor, $T = T_{\mu\nu}\eta^{\mu\nu}$. In a second model, Nordström implemented this modification together with the argument that the theory should be nonlinear, once the energy momentum tensor should also account for the gravitational energy. As a result, the field equation and the gravitational force law are now described as follows,

$$\Box \Phi = -\frac{4\pi G}{c^4} \frac{T}{\Phi}, \quad F_g^\mu = \frac{mc^2}{\Phi} \partial^\mu \Phi. \tag{1.32}$$

The equation of motion for test particles is also modified, namely

$$c^2 \frac{\partial \Phi}{\partial x^\mu} = \Phi \frac{dv_\mu}{d\tau} + v_\mu \frac{d\Phi}{d\tau}, \qquad (1.33)$$

with the mass now having a linear dependence with the gravitational field, i.e. $m(\Phi) = m_0 \Phi$.

In 1913, Einstein described Nordström's second theory, together with his own *Entwurf* formulation, as the only ones with a satisfactory description of the gravitational interaction [14]. However, the *Entwurf* model were not a scalar theory of gravity, being the first time that Riemannian manifolds and tensor calculus were used to explore the idea of curved spacetimes as a consequence of gravity [15].[1] Both theories would satisfies basics requirements such as the equality of inertial and gravitational mass, reduction to special relativity as a limiting case and conservation of energy and momentum.

Nowadays, it is clear that Nordström's theory lacks of empirical confirmation once it cannot provide any deflection of light and it does not explain the anomalous motion of Mercury. However, at that time, there wasn't any measurement of light bending and no other theory could satisfactory explain Mercury's perihelion advance.

1.3.1.2 Einstein and Fokker reformulation of Nordström theory

Nordström second theory also have kinematic effects that are typical in metric theories of gravity: the gravitational field would alter the tick of clocks and the length of rods. Such feature indicates that Nordström scalar theory could be interpreted as spacetime theory. It was Einstein and Fokker that demonstrated this property applying the mathematical tools of tensor calculus to Nordström theory [16]. It is shown that equation of motion (1.33) describes a geodesic in a curved geometry conformal to Minkowski spacetime,

$$g_{\mu\nu} = \Phi^2 \eta_{\mu\nu}. \qquad (1.34)$$

In this case, the Ricci scalar is simply described as $R = -(6/\Phi^3)\Box\Phi$. On the other hand, the energy-momentum tensor should now be defined as a variation of matter Lagrangian with respect to the physical metric $g_{\mu\nu}$,

$$T_{\mu\nu} = -\frac{2}{\sqrt{-g}} \frac{\delta(\sqrt{-g}\, L_m)}{\delta g^{\mu\nu}}. \qquad (1.35)$$

---

[1] *Entwurf* means outline, or sketch, and it is how the 1913 paper by Einstein and Grossmann is usually known [15]. It is a short name derived from the original title *Entwurf einer verallgemeinerten relativitätstheorie und einer theorie der gravitation*.

Thus, the trace appearing in Nordström field equation [cf. (1.32)] will transform as $T \to T/\Phi^4$. Therefore, theory's dynamics can be rewritten as follows,

$$R(g) = \frac{24\pi G}{c^4} T(g). \qquad (1.36)$$

where the notation $R(g)$ and $T(g)$ is used to emphasize that both the Ricci scalar and the trace of energy-momentum tensor are constructed with the physical metric $g_{\mu\nu}$.

This formulations describes the gravitational field in a covariant and geometrical way, which guarantees the validity of the equivalence principle in its strong and weak versions. It is worth to mention that within this description of Nordström theory, the mass are no longer dependent of the gravitational field. However, spacetime would admit preferred coordinate systems in which equation (1.36) reduces to Nordström equation. Moreover, in metric (1.34), only the conformal factor has a dynamics influenced by matter and energy, but its structure cannot be changed by simply modifying the matter distribution of a system.

Even so, Einstein's work on Nordström theory was essential for him to return to the quest of finding a fully covariant theory of gravity. The outcome of his quest, the well know theory of general relativity, led to the replacement of the traditional single scalar potential of gravity in favor of the ten independent components of the spacetime metric. The history of this remarkable endeavor is depicted, for instance, in Ref. [17].

1.3.1.3 Scalar theories post general relativity

The observational and experimental success of general relativity cemented the concept that gravity is a geometrical phenomenon. Any theoretical formulation aiming to viably describe gravitational interactions should be a metric theory of gravity. In this sense, the majority of scalars theories of gravity proposed after the advent of general relativity were also metric theories of gravity. In general, those can be grouped in two classes: conformally flat theories and stratified theories.

The conformally flat class of scalar theories are formulations where the physical metric ($g_{\nu\mu}$) is generated from a scalar field (Φ) and flat metrical structure ($\eta_{\mu\nu}$) through a conformal relation, $g_{\mu\nu} = \Omega(\Phi)\eta_{\mu\nu}$. Different forms of the function $\Omega(\Phi)$ and the field equation of Φ will give rise to distinct theories. Nordström theory is an example of a conformally flat theory with $\Omega = \Phi^2$.

Stratified theories considers, besides a scalar function representing the gravitational field, a universal time coordinate t whose gradient is covariantly constant and timelike with respect to the flat background, i.e., $t_{;\mu;\nu} = 0$ and $\eta^{\mu\nu} t_{,\mu} t_{,\nu} = -1$. The function t defines a preferred reference frame in a which the spatial slices of spacetime are conformally flat. In a frame where $t_{,\mu} = \delta_\mu^0$, the physical metric is constructed according to the line element below,

$$ds^2 = g_{\mu\nu} dx^\mu dx^\nu = f(\Phi)dt^2 - h(\Phi)\eta_{ij} dx^i dx^j, \qquad (1.37)$$

with $f(\Phi)$ and $h(\Phi)$ arbitrary functions that will differ one theory from another.

Conformally flat theories cannot produce an coupling between gravity and electromagnetism since Maxwell's equations are conformally invariant. This implies that there is no light bending effect in those theories. The preferred frame idea brought within stratified theories is a way to avoid this complication. Other possibility explored to circumvent this problem is to consider light velocity dependent of gravitational field Φ (see, for instance, Ref. [18]. Notwithstanding, the effective metric formalism discussed in section 1.2 lead the way to another possibility for describing gravity through a single scalar field. The fundamentals of this scalar field theory of gravity is discussed in the next section.

1.3.2 Geometric scalar gravity

The geometric scalar gravity (GSG) was first presented in Ref. [19] and it is based upon the idea of giving an universal and gravitational meaning for the effective scalar metric discussed in previous section [cf. (1.10)]. In section 1.2, it was discussed two founding postulates of GR that determine all gravitational phenomena to be interpreted as a modification of spacetime geometry given by Einstein's equation. Although those postulates can be adjusted, the main ideas brought by them are fundamental for what is called metric theories of gravity. We start this section reviewing the postulates of Nordström-like theories of gravity, and then proceeding to the postulates of the geometric scalar gravity.

1.3.2.1 Postulates of Nordström-like theories

Nordström's second theory and its geometric reformulation by Einstein and Fokker was discussed in sections 1.3.1.1 and 1.3.1.2. We can recast any Nordström-like theory as based on the following postulates:

1. Gravity is mediated by a single massless scalar field Φ, satisfying a linear dynamics in Minkowski spacetime.

2. All kind of matter and energy interact with Φ only through a minimal coupling with the "physical" metric $g_{\mu\nu}$, which is conformal to the Minkowski metric, $g_{\mu\nu} = A^2(\Phi)\eta_{\mu\nu}$.

The hypothesis that the matter fields are minimally coupled to the physical metric $g_{\mu\nu}$ warrants the validity of the weak equivalence principle. The total action leads to the following field equations:

$$\Box\Phi = -\frac{4\pi G}{c^4} A' A^3 T, \quad \text{and} \quad T^{\mu\nu}{}_{;\nu} = 0, \qquad (1.38)$$

with $A' = dA/d\Phi$. Here the energy-momentum tensor of the non-gravitational fields, $T_{\mu\nu}$, is defined as in equation (1.35), with its trace given by $T_{\mu\nu}g^{\mu\nu}$. The covariant derivative in Eq. (19.55) is taken with respect to $g_{\mu\nu}$. The scalar curvature of the conformal geometry reads $R = -6\Box A/A^3$. By using this relation, equation (1.38) may be rewritten in the Einstein-Fokker covariant form,

$$R = \frac{24\pi G}{c^4} A'^2 T - \frac{6 A''}{A} g^{\mu\nu} \partial_\mu \Phi \partial_\nu \Phi. \qquad (1.39)$$

For $A = \Phi$, equation (1.39) recovers the original one from Nordström's second theory in the Einstein-Fokker reformulation [cf. (1.32)].

1.3.2.2 Postulates of geometric scalar gravity

As a possible way to solve the difficulties that exist in Nordström's theories due to a priori assumptions of conformal symmetry, the GSG theory explore the possibility that the physical metric be related to the Minkowski metric by a more general structure as in (1.18). This hypothesis immediately permits the coupling of the electromagnetic field to the physical metric. It is also explored more general Lagrangians for the gravitational part of the action and, in particular, modifications of the kinetic term.

Summarizing, the GSG enlarge the Nordström's family according to the following postulates:

1. Gravity is mediated by a scalar field Φ satisfying a nonlinear dynamics in Minkowski's spacetime, described by the action,

$$S_{\text{gravity}} = \frac{1}{\kappa c} \int L(\Phi, \partial_\mu \Phi) \sqrt{-\eta}\, d^4x. \qquad (1.40)$$

2. All kind of matter and energy interact with Φ only through a coupling with the physical metric $q_{\mu\nu}$, given by

$$q_{\mu\nu} = a(\Phi, \omega)\eta_{\mu\nu} + b(\Phi, \omega)\partial_\mu \Phi \partial_\nu \Phi \qquad (1.41)$$

where $\omega = \eta^{\mu\nu}\partial_\mu \Phi \partial_\nu \Phi$. Thus, the action for the matter may be written as

$$S_{\text{matter}}(\psi, q_{\mu\nu}) = \frac{1}{c} \int \sqrt{-q}\, L_m\, d^4x. \qquad (1.42)$$

with q the determinant of $q_{\mu\nu}$.

When $a = a^2(\phi)$, $b = 0$ and L is the Lagrangian of a massless Klein-Gordon field we are back to Nordström theories. It is worth to note that the coupling of matter and energy fields with a metric structure like in (1.41) have been considered in many contexts within scalar-tensor theories of gravity (see, for instance, Refs. [20, 21, 22]). They are usually called disformal gravity. Moreover, general ways to deform the spacetime has been considered to enlighten many gravitational problems and metric disformations are also embedded in this class of transformations (see [23] and the references therein). However, the GSG model seems to be the unique one where a scalar field disformally coupled is used to modify the original Nordström's idea and describe gravity in the context of a purely scalar theory.

We call a theory belonging to this family a geometric scalar theory of gravity for the obvious reason that matter interacts with gravity only through coupling to the physical metric (1.41). A general geometric scalar theory of gravity is characterized by three functions: the functions a and b characterizing the metric and the Lagrangian L of the scalar field.

1.3.3 A particular case of GSG

It is clear that functions a, b and L cannot be chosen arbitrarily, once the resulting theory must be in agreement with gravitational tests. In this section, it is discussed some basic assumptions used as a guide to propose a model within GSG.

We first note that, when $T = 0$, Nordström's theories coincide with the flat space massless Klein-Gordon theory irrespectively of the conformal factor (see Eq. (1.38)). A similar – but also distinct – feature is shared by a particular class of geometric scalar theories of gravity that in vacuum reduce to the massless Klein-Gordon equation but now w.r.t. the curved spacetime physical metric $q_{\mu\nu}$. This possibility was considered in section 1.2.3, thus, by restricting the metric structure to the particular form of (1.18), and with a Lagrangian $L = V(\Phi)\omega$, the vacuum dynamics of the scalar field take the form of a massless Klein-Gordon field, $\Box\Phi = 0$, provided that condition (1.23) holds. Therefore, contrary to the case of Nordström's theory, in the GSG approach the field equation keeps its nonlinearity and the gravitational scalar field is self-interacting.

Consider now the Newtonian correspondence principle. For simplicity, we will set units such that $G = c = 1$. Assuming the hypothesis, as in general relativity, that test particles follow geodesics relative to the metric $q_{\mu\nu}$, in the case of a static weak field configuration and low velocity motions, we have

$$\frac{d^2 x^i}{dt^2} \approx -\Gamma^i_{00} \approx -\frac{1}{2}\partial^i(\ln\alpha) = -\partial^i \Phi_N, \tag{1.43}$$

where Φ_N is the Newtonian gravitational potential. Thus, the relation between the time component of the physical metric and the Newtonian potential is given by

$$q_{00} = \frac{1}{\alpha} \approx 1 + 2\Phi_N. \tag{1.44}$$

Moreover, using that $\Box \Phi = 0$, one obtains the right (vacuum) Newtonian limit, $\nabla^2 \Phi_N = 0$. The above relation shows the linear behavior of the metric coefficient α in order to be in agreement with Newtonian limit. However, for analytical purposes, we will explore the consequences of extrapolating this relation and take into account a more general expression, namely

$$\alpha = e^{-2\Phi}. \tag{1.45}$$

To determine the dynamics of Φ in a presence of matter fields, one first vary S_{matter} with respect to the physical metric, introducing then the energy-momentum tensor. After some algebra (see Ref. [19] for details), the final form of the theory's field equation reads

$$\sqrt{V}\,\Box\Phi = \kappa\,\chi, \tag{1.46}$$

where the right hand side is simplified by the notation

$$\chi = -\frac{1}{2}\left[T + \left(2 - \frac{V'}{2V}\right)E + C^\lambda_{;\lambda}\right]. \tag{1.47}$$

$$E \equiv \frac{T^{\mu\nu}\partial_\mu\Phi\,\partial_\nu\Phi}{\Omega}, \tag{1.48}$$

$$C^\lambda \equiv \frac{(\alpha^2 V - 1)}{\Omega}\left(T^{\lambda\mu} - E\,q^{\lambda\mu}\right)\partial_\mu\Phi. \tag{1.49}$$

The symbol ";" stands for the covariant derivative with respect to the physical metric $q_{\mu\nu}$. The above equation makes clear that not only the trace of the energy-momentum tensor acts as a source for the gravitational field, but also a non-trivial coupling between the gradient of the scalar field and the complete energy-momentum tensor of the matter field. This makes possible the coupling between gravity and electromagnetism in this scalar theory.

The coupling constant κ is determined through the correspondence principle with Newton's gravitational theory. The Newtonian limit can be obtained when $T^{00} \approx \rho$, $T^{0i} \approx 0$ and $\partial_t \Phi \approx 0$, where i stands for spatial components and ρ is the matter density. Applying this approximation scheme gives the identification $\kappa = 8\pi G/c^4$.

The next task is to determine the functional dependence of β on Φ, or either the form of the potential $V(\Phi)$ once both functions are related by (1.23). To select among all possible Lagrangians of the above form we look for indications from the various circumstances in which reliable test have been performed. In this vein, one must analyze the consequences of GSG for the solar system and, in a first approximation, the requirement that vacuum and spherically solution meets Schwarzschild geometry could be a strong indication in that direction. This requirement is achieved by the following potential,

$$V(\Phi) = \frac{(\alpha-3)^2}{4\alpha^3}. \tag{1.50}$$

Details of how to obtain this result can be found in Ref. [19]. It has been shown that three charts are necessary to cover the Schwarzschild solution and that the region inside the horizon is somehow surprisingly the disformal transformation of a Euclidean metric [24].

1.3.4 Post-Newtonian analysis

The post-Newtonian analysis of a gravitational theory consists of a practical way to obtain theoretical predictions that can be confronted with observations. Essentially, it is a weak-field and slow motion approximation scheme that, at first order, it guarantees that the theory recovers Newton's gravity results and, on higher orders, introduces the departures from the Newtonian formulation. After solving the approximated field equations, the metric components are presented as a combination of Newtonian potential and several others post-Newtonian ones. Within this method, there is the parametrized post-Newtonian (PPN) formalism, a useful tool to test metric theories of gravity since it gives a physical meaning to each one of the metric coefficients appearing in the post-Newtonian expansion, i.e. the PPN parameters. Also, it extracts observational bounds for nine of the ten parameters used in the formalism (see Ref. [25] for a detailed presentation of PPN).

The GSG model considered in this review is not covered by the PPN formalism due to the non-standard potentials that appears in the expanded metric.[2] Even so, in Ref. [24] it was investigated the post-Newtonian limit of this particular GSG model and it is verified that, in a static monopole approximation, the expanded metric does fit with the general metric of the PPN formalism. Within that simplification, the possible PPN parameters that can be read off are the following ones,

$$\beta = 1, \ \gamma = 1, \ \xi = 0, \ \zeta_2 = 0, \ \zeta_3 = 0, \ \zeta_4 = -\frac{4}{3}. \tag{1.51}$$

The physical meaning of these parameters in the standard PPN formalism are the following. The γ is associated with light trajectories and it is bounded by light deflection and Shapiro time-delay effects. The latter is the one which brings

---

[2]The limitations of the PPN formalism is rather recurrent for modern alternative theories of gravity (see, for instance, the discussion in Refs. [26, 27]).

the strongest bound on that parameter, $|\gamma - 1| \lesssim 10^{-5}$. With γ constrained, β happens to be the single parameter relevant for the perihelion shift of Mercury, and the consequent bound is $|\beta - 1| \lesssim 10^{-5}$. The Whitehead parameter ξ is related with preferred-location effects and its bound comes from spin-precession measurements of millisecond pulsars, which gives $\xi \lesssim 10^{-9}$. The ζ's parameters, when different from zero, are manifestations of non conservation of total energy and momentum. The ζ_2 and ζ_3 are constrained by binary system and lunar acceleration effects, with $\zeta_2 \lesssim 10^{-5}$ and $\zeta_3 \lesssim 10^{-8}$. The ζ_4, related with matter pressure effects, is not a independent parameter due to theoretical constraints that gravity produced by kinetic energy, internal energy and pressure should satisfy, and it does not have an independent bound.

However, it is important to note that there is no guarantee that these parameters keep their original physical meaning within GSG formulation, and the direct usage of the PPN bounds is not adequate here (or in any other theory which does not fit the PPN formalism). Notwithstanding, the fact that the values of $\beta, \gamma, \xi, \zeta_2$ and ζ_3 are the same as the ones obtained in general relativity could represent a strong indication of a satisfactory description of post-Newtonian physics. A not restrictive study of the post-Newtonian equations of motion is necessary in order to confirm such expectations. The not vanishing of ζ_4 may not be viewed as inconsistent since the proper definition of gravitational energy in GSG is ambiguous. For instance, due to the non trivial relation between the scalar field source term χ, and a generic energy-momentum tensor, there is a class of symmetric tensors $t^{\mu\nu}$ which satisfies $\chi(t^{\mu\nu}) = 0$. Those tensors may have influence on the energy and momentum conservation statements while not impacting scalar field dynamics.

1.3.5 Gravitational waves

The new era of multi-messenger astronomy, with direct observations of gravitational waves (GW), brings significant improvement for testing gravitational theories. In particular, the velocity of GW in vacuum has been measured to be the same of light [28], which is consistent with the theoretical prediction from GSG, as it was shown in Ref. [29]. A weak field approximation shows that the perturbed scalar field satisfies a wave equation over Minkowski's spacetime. Such solutions yields an oscillatory behavior for the metric as GW propagating in spacetime.

Concerning the polarization states, it is well know that any metric theory of gravity can have at most six distinct polarization modes. These modes are related to the so called Newmann-Penrose quantities (NPQ), deduced from the irreducible parts of the Riemann tensor [30]. However, the theory's dynamics can reduce the number of modes by vanishing some of the NPQ. As an example, two transversal polarization modes of general relativity is due to the fact that only one of the NPQ is not identically null. Sometimes, the polarization modes are observer-dependent (which is not the case of GR), as described by the classification presented in Ref.

[31], and this happens to be the case of GSG. Once the Ricci scalar is not identically null in vacuum, one gets the most general class of the $E(2)$-classification with an always present longitudinal mode of polarization and the detection of the others five states being observer-dependent. This is a substantial distinction from general relativity.

The existence of any mode of polarization can not be extract from the recent detections of GW [32, 33]. Thus, GSG cannot be constrained in such aspect. In the future, with the increasing of network of detectors with different alignment, polarization states can be used to restrict gravitational theories. It is worth to note that $f(R)$ theories is also classified as GSG [34].

However, GSG can be constrained by observational data from pulsars through its prediction for the orbital variation of a binary system that should be caused by the loss of energy due to gravitational radiation. The discussion on how to define an energy-momentum tensor for the linear GW, following a field theoretical point of view, starts by identifying the second order vacuum field equation for the approximation scheme $\Phi \approx \phi_0 + \phi_{(1)} + \phi_{(2)}$, yielding

$$\Box_\eta \phi_{(2)} = -\frac{9-\alpha_0}{3-\alpha_0} w_{(2)}. \tag{1.52}$$

The sub-indexes indicates the order of smallness and $w_{(2)} = \eta^{\mu\nu}\partial_\mu \phi_{(1)} \partial_\nu \phi_{(1)}$ and $\Box_\eta$ is the d'Alembertian operator constructed with Minkowski metric. The right hand side of this equation contains only the derivatives of the first order field $\phi_{(1)}$, thus it can be interpreted as the source for the second order field generated by the linear waves. However, an ambiguity emerges since GSG fundamental equation includes a non trivial interaction between matter/energy and the scalar field. In other words, the above equation must be recast in similar form as in (1.46), leading to a non unique expression for the linear gravitational energy-momentum tensor. Specifically, any tensor $\Theta_{\mu\nu}$ with its second order approximation given by

$$\Theta_{(2)\mu\nu} = \frac{1}{\kappa}\left(\sigma w_{(2)} \eta_{\mu\nu} + \lambda \, \partial_\mu \phi_{(1)} \partial_\nu \phi_{(1)}\right), \tag{1.53}$$

with the constants σ and λ satisfying the relation,

$$\sigma\left(\frac{9-5\alpha_0}{3-\alpha_0}\right) - \lambda\left(\frac{2\alpha_0}{3-\alpha_0}\right) = \frac{9-\alpha_0}{\alpha_0^{3/2}}, \tag{1.54}$$

will give origin to a source term

$$\chi_{(2)}(\Theta_{\mu\nu}) = -\frac{9-\alpha_0}{2\kappa \alpha_0^{3/2}} w_{(2)}, \quad \text{and} \quad \sqrt{V_0}\Box_\eta \phi_{(2)} = \kappa \chi_{(2)}(\Theta_{\mu\nu}). \tag{1.55}$$

Thus, $\Theta_{(2)\mu\nu}$ can be interpreted as the energy-momentum tensor for the linear gravitational waves in GSG. In the above expression, α_0 is the metric coefficient calculated with the background field ϕ_0 using definition (1.45).

The ambiguity in the GW energy-momentum tensor is encoded in the constant parameter λ, and has directly consequences for a system energy-loss rate due to the emission of gravitational waves. Specifically, for a binary system, the consequent average variation in the orbital period is determined by the following expression

$$\frac{\dot{T}}{T} = \frac{3\lambda}{4} \frac{G^3 M^3}{m_1 m_2 a^4 c^5} e^2 (1-e^2)^{-7/2} \left[f^2 + \left(\frac{f^2}{4} + 4Mf + 4M^2 \right) e^2 + 2M^2 e^4 \right], \quad (1.56)$$

where m_1 and m_2 are the masses of each component of the system, a is the semi-major axis, e is the eccentricity, $M = m_1 + m_2$ and $f = 5m_1 m_2/M - 4M$ (details in Ref. [29]). The expression above for the orbital period variation depends on G, a and c the same way as occur in GR, but the mass and eccentricity dependence are rather more involved.

It is possible to use data from the PSR 1913+16 binary pulsar to constraint the theory's free parameter λ. However, although the orbital parameters of the binary system are extracted in a theory-independent way, the mass values estimation of the two bodies in the binary system are model-dependent [35]. Once that GSG has a satisfactory agreement with GR concerning Solar System tests at the first post-Newtonian order, one can use (as a first approximation) the mass values obtained in GR. Notwithstanding, deviations from the GR mass values will lead to a distinct numerical value for λ, but it would not necessarily invalidate how GSG describes the orbital period variation of binary systems. The results are $\lambda = -1.111 \pm 0.003$ and $\sigma = 3.444 \pm 0.002$ [after using condition (1.54)], which completely fixes the energy momentum tensor expression for the gravitational waves in GSG. The minus sign in λ is due to the fact that the orbital period is decreasing while the system emits gravitational waves, i.e., $\dot{T} < 0$.

1.3.6 Cosmological scenarios

Assuming the scalar field Φ depends only on time, it yields a homogeneous and isotropic geometry,

$$ds^2 = dt^2 - a(t)^2 (dx^2 + dy^2 + dz^2). \quad (1.57)$$

with the cosmological scale factor being $a = e^{\Phi}$. Because the gravitational field depends only on t, it is natural to expect that all the relevant quantities have only temporal dependence too. Assuming the material content of the universe can be modeled as a perfect fluid decomposed in terms of the cosmic observers, $v^\mu = \delta^\mu_0$, the resulting cosmological equation,

$$a|3a^2 - 1| \left(\frac{\ddot{a}}{a} + 2\frac{\dot{a}^2}{a^2} \right) = \kappa \left[3p + \left(\frac{2\rho}{3a^2 - 1} \right) \right], \quad (1.58)$$

where ρ is the matter density ($c = 1$) and p is the fluid pressure. There are therefore two regimes classified by the sign of the quantity $3a^2 - 1$, however, the

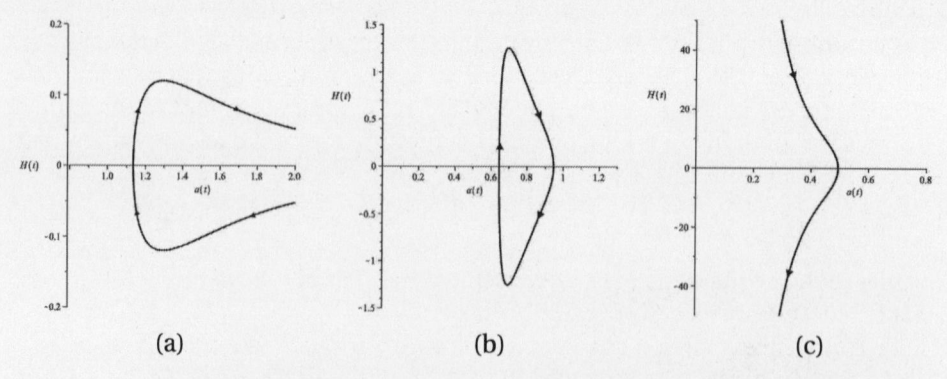

Figure 1.1: Phase diagrams for $M = 0.9\kappa\rho_0$. (a) Big Universe filled with dust ($\lambda = 0$). The universe is non singular and this property is shared with any fluid with positive λ, including radiation. (b) Big Universe cyclic scenario for negative values of λ. The figure shows the case of $\lambda = -1$ but the behavior is similar for any $\lambda < 0$. (c) Dust filled Small Universe. There is a singularity in $a = 0$ from where the evolution starts and ends after reach a maximum scale.

time evolution respects that sign and GSG cosmologies, based on a perfect fluid, are divided into two classes. We call the solutions belonging the first class (i.e. solutions such that $3a^2 > 1$) Big Universes (BU), and the solutions belonging to the the second one, Small Universes (SU). The adjective "small" makes allusion to the fact the scale factor takes values in a compact interval, but also when this occurs the spatial section is of course infinite. The existence of two classes of solution is a consequence of the choice of the potential (1.50).

For barotropic fluids, when $p = \lambda\rho$, one has $\rho = \rho_0 a^{-3(1+\lambda)}$ with ρ_0 constant. With a simple integration, both first and second time derivative of the scale factor can be written as a function of a, namely

$$\dot{a}^2 = \frac{M}{a^4} - 2\kappa\rho_0 \frac{a^{-2-3\lambda}}{|3a^2-1|}, \tag{1.59}$$

where M is a constant of integration, and

$$\ddot{a} = -2\frac{M}{a^5} + \frac{\kappa\rho_0}{a^{3(1+\lambda)}}\left[\frac{2+3\lambda}{|3a^2-1|} \pm \frac{6a^2}{(3a^2-1)^2}\right], \tag{1.60}$$

with the upper sign for BU and the lower sign being valid for SU solutions. As it should be expected, the above expression is singular at $3a^2 = 1$. However this value is unattainable because within BU (SU) $\dot{a}^2$ becomes zero at a minimal (maximum) value a_m strictly grater (smaller) than $1/\sqrt{3}$. Therefore big universes and small universes are two disjoint classes of cosmological solutions of GSG.

A qualitative analysis can be performed using equations (1.59) and (1.60) by plotting phase diagrams as shown in Figure 1.1. The left image shows the BU solution for pressureless matter ($\lambda = 0$). This universe filled with dust does not have any singular behavior and presents an accelerated phase near de bounce. At late times, the universe decelerates. Fluids with positive λ (including radiation) have a similar behavior. They all have a bounce, followed by an early accelerated phase and a final decelerated phase. The expansion last forever.

For negative values of λ it is possible to have a static solution in BU for a particular choice of M. For the others possible values of M the universe is cyclic as, for instance, the case of $\lambda = -1$, shown in Figure 1.1(b).

The SU branch includes a class of solutions, for $\lambda < 2/3$, which presents a singularity at $a = 0$. In these scenarios there is an initial big bang followed from a decelerated phase. The universe reaches its maximum scale and then stops entering in contracting phase that unavoidably ends in the singularity at $a = 0$. This case is shown in Figure 1.1(c) for $\lambda = 0$. For $\lambda > 2/3$ in SU is possible to have a static solution for a specific value of M or a cyclic and non-singular universe.

The possibility of having a bouncing for standard fluids (in BU) is quite remarkable. In Freedmann-Lemaître-Robertson-Walker (FLRW) cosmology the bouncing is possible either by non-minimal coupling with matter fields or by negative pressures. Indeed, in order to have an extremum of the scale factor $a(t)$ the expansion factor $\theta = 3\dot{a}/a$ must vanish and its derivative be positive. As it is well known, in GR the Raychaudhuri equation implies that this is possible when $(\rho + 3p)/2 < 0$. Here the situation is different: the universe always bounces for pressure values equal or greater to zero. On the other hand, GSG cosmology does not have natural mechanisms to generate a late phase of accelerated expansion of the universe if only working with ordinary matter and energy contents.

More details of background cosmological solutions in GSG can be found in Ref. [36]. A discussion of scalar perturbations, focusing on the growth of density perturbations in a matter dominated later decelerated phase was also performed in that reference. It was verified that gravitational instabilities are possible in GSG. Fortunately, they are slight different from GR, which means that the GSG cosmology can be tested separately with a properly analysis of data in this new framework.

1.4 Spinor theory of gravity

For some deep thinkers of the past certain relations between numbers of physical phenomena may suggest a more intimate connection between them. For instance the observation of the Large Number Hypothesis of Dirac. In the same vein, Stuckelberg argued that relationship of gravitational force and weak (Fermi) processes led him to propose a more deep connection between gravity and Fermi interactions.It is clear that these ideas do not prove the existence of such connections, but it permit the emergence of new ideas on physics as, for instance, in the case of Dirac, the development of the scalar-tensor theory of gravity.

The proposal to develop a theory of gravity that is based on the dynamics of spinor fields was inspired in the possible connection between gravity and the weak (Fermi) interaction based on a remark that can be made concerning the numerical values of the fundamental constants characterizing both interactions. In fact, the idea to extract motivation from such a "nomerological" argument dates back to Dirac's Large Number Hypothesis, where properties of the universe and elementary particles led him to propose the time dependence of the gravitational constant [37]. A similar analysis is performed in Refs. [38, 39] in the context of the weak and gravitational interactions, suggesting that the geometrical interpretation of the gravitational phenomena can be seen as emerging from more fundamental spinor fields. In the next sections we will review recent developments in this direction.

1.4.1 Fermi interaction and gravity: the fundamental spinors

In the case of Fermi interaction, the weak current is defined as $C_\mu = J_\mu - I_\mu$, where $J_\mu = \overline{\Psi}_g \gamma_\mu \Psi_g$ and $I_\mu = \overline{\Psi}_g \gamma_\mu \gamma_5 \Psi_g$. Thus the Lagrangian for the interaction of two fermions, Ψ_e and Ψ_n, can be written as $L_{Fermi} = g_w C_\mu^e C_n^\mu$. The use of a parity violation term (the vector minus the axial vector currents in the Fermi interaction) guides the form of fundamental vectors that are treated as the basis of the gravitational metric. Indeed, the hypothesis made in the spinor theory of gravity (STG) is based on the existence of two fundamental massless spinorial fields which are the true elementary structure of gravity. These two fields Ψ_g and Ω_g generate an effective metric which is the one dealing in general relativity. In other words, the proposal of GR that gravity deals with metric's modification of space-time has a substratum that is identified with these gravitational fermions (g-fermions).

The main ideas of the STG can be synthesized in the following sentences:

1. The geometry of general relativity is an effective representation of two physical spin-1/2 fields, called *g-fermions* and denoted by Ψ_g and Ω_g, living in the Minkowski spacetime;

2. Ψ_g and Ω_g interact via Fermi process;

3. Both fields couple with all forms of matter in an universal way;

4. This interaction can be described as a modification of the background Minkowski metric into an effective one $g_{\mu\nu}$, following the fundamental ideas of general relativity;

5. The effective metric $g_{\mu\nu}$ does not have a dynamics by its own but inherits the dynamics of the fundamental fields Ψ_g and Ω_g.

The spinorial fields Ψ_g and Ω_g they both interact universally with all kind of matter and energy only through the metric $g_{\mu\nu}$, thus following the main principle of GR. The gravitational metric $g_{\mu\nu}$ is written in terms of null vectors that can be constructed with Ψ_g and Ω_g. A combination of these vectors provide a dimensionless term $h_{\mu\nu}$,

$$h_{\mu\nu} = \ell \left[\Delta_\mu \Delta_\nu + \Pi_\mu \Pi_\nu + \varepsilon \left(\Delta_\mu \Pi_\nu + \Delta_\nu \Pi_\mu \right) \right], \tag{1.61}$$

where ℓ is a constant with dimensions of length squared and

$$\Delta_\mu = \frac{1}{\sigma \sqrt{J}} (J_\mu - I_\mu), \quad \text{with} \quad J^2 = J_\mu J^\mu, \tag{1.62}$$

$$\Pi_\mu = \frac{1}{\sigma \sqrt{j}} (j_\mu - i_\mu), \quad \text{with} \quad j^2 = j_\mu j^\mu. \tag{1.63}$$

In the above expressions $j_\mu = \overline{\Omega}_g \gamma_\mu \Omega_g$ and $i_\mu = \overline{\Omega}_g \gamma_\mu \gamma_5 \Omega_g$. The σ is a constant with dimensions of length, expected to be dependent of fundamental constants present in the weak interaction formulation, while ℓ should have influence of gravitational constant as well. Moreover, in order to satisfy the closure relation (1.5), one must have $\varepsilon^2 = 1$.

It has been explored in the literature the simpler case in which Ω_g vanishes, leading to

$$h_{\mu\nu} = \ell \Delta_\mu \Delta_\nu, \tag{1.64}$$

and a simple inspection shows that such tensor satisfies the property

$$h_{\mu\nu} \eta^{\nu\alpha} = h_{\mu\nu} g^{\nu\alpha}, \quad \text{and} \quad g^{\mu\nu} = \eta^{\mu\nu} + h^{\mu\nu}. \tag{1.65}$$

By dimensional analysis, the constant σ can be defined as $\sigma^2 = \kappa \hbar c$, where $\kappa = 8\pi G/c^4$. Thus, fixing $\ell = \kappa \hbar c$, $h_{\mu\nu}$ becomes dimensionless. It is worth to note that the Δ_μ could be simply defined to be dimensionless, but the method worked above makes usage of the connection between weak and gravitational interactions, starting with a vector depending on constants from the weak interaction realm and still getting a dimensionless tensor by combining with another quantity constructed with constants typical of the gravitational interaction.

1.4.2 The gravitational field

The fundamental spinors live in the flat Minkowski background where the metric $\gamma_{\mu\nu}$ is defined from the fundamental objects,

$$\gamma_{\mu\nu} = \frac{1}{2} (\gamma_\mu \gamma_\nu + \gamma_\nu \gamma_\mu), \tag{1.66}$$

which is a multiple of the identity of the Clifford algebra. In the case $\Omega_g = 0$ the dynamics of Ψ_g is given by the Dirac equation in arbitrary coordinate systems,

$$i\gamma^\mu \nabla_\mu \Psi_g = 0 \qquad (1.67)$$

and the internal connection contains beyond the conventional Fock-Ivanenko term an additional one,

$$\Gamma_\mu = \Gamma_\mu^{FI} + U_\mu. \qquad (1.68)$$

In STG the covariant derivative of the γ^μ is given by the Riemannian condition

$$\gamma_{\mu;\nu} = [U_\nu, \gamma_\mu] \qquad (1.69)$$

where U_μ besides to be a vector is an arbitrary object from the associated Clifford algebra. There is a simpler case where

$$U_\mu = \frac{1}{4} \gamma_\mu \gamma^\alpha U_{,\alpha} \qquad (1.70)$$

with $U_{,\alpha} = \partial_\alpha U$. The vector U_μ is driven by an external scalar field H such that $U = \varepsilon H$. This form implies the Riemannian condition for the metric, that is, $\gamma_{\mu\nu;\lambda} = 0$ and the factor $1/4$ is just for latter convenience. For the origin of this term see Ref. [39]. Note that in the case we use Euclidean coordinates, the gamma's are constant and the Christoffel symbol vanishes, as well as the Fock-Ivanenko connection. Moreover, due to the usage of only one spinor field, as well as the fact that Δ_μ is a null vector, both the determinant of $g_{\mu\nu}$ and $\eta_{\mu\nu}$ coincide. Important consequence arises in such limited framework, describing, for example, a spherically symmetric and static spacetime and a cosmological scenario (see Ref. [39]).

1.4.3 The effect of gravity on matter

Following the idea brought by general relativity, gravitational interaction is described by the substitution of the flat background by a more general structure governed by Ψ_g. To illustrate this procedure, consider the case in which matter is represented by a massless scalar field, Φ. The matter action will be

$$S_m = \frac{1}{2} \int \sqrt{-g}\, g^{\mu\nu} \partial_\mu \Phi\, \partial_\nu \Phi. \qquad (1.71)$$

Once the metric $g_{\mu\nu}$ depends on the spinor field, the variation of the total action, with respect to Ψ_g and Φ, will give, respectively

$$i\gamma^\mu \nabla_\mu \Psi_g + \kappa E_{\mu\nu} Q^{\mu\nu} \Psi_g = 0 \quad \text{and} \quad \Box \Phi = 0, \qquad (1.72)$$

with

$$E_{\mu\nu} = \Phi_{,\mu} \Phi_{,\nu} - \frac{1}{2} \Phi_{,\alpha} \Phi_{,\beta}\, g^{\alpha\beta}\, g_{\mu\nu}, \qquad (1.73)$$

being the energy-momentum tensor of the scalar field and

$$Q^{\mu\nu} = \left(\frac{g_w}{J^2}\right)^{1/4} \Delta^\mu \gamma^\nu (1-\gamma_5) - \frac{1}{2J^2} \Delta^\mu \Delta^\nu (A + iB\gamma_5), \tag{1.74}$$

with $A = \overline{\Psi}_g \Psi_g$ and $B = i\overline{\Psi}_g \gamma_5 \Psi_g$. It is worth to note that the non-linear term, $A + iB\gamma_5$, present in the dynamics of Ψ_g is not a particularity of this model. Such a term is also present in dynamical models and field theories of elementary particles (see, for instance, Refs. [40, 41, 42]).

The generalization to other forms matter is directly obtained through the usual variation of a matter action with respect to the metric $g_{\mu\nu}$, yielding

$$i\gamma^\mu \nabla_\mu \Psi_g + \kappa\, T_{\mu\nu} Q^{\mu\nu} \Psi_g = 0, \tag{1.75}$$

Given the expression of the energy-momentum tensor $T_{\mu\nu}$, this equation yields the value of Ψ_g that allows the construction of the current Δ_μ and then the metric $g_{\mu\nu}$. In this sense, it plays the same role as the equation that relates the Ricci curvature to the energy-momentum tensor in general relativity.

1.4.4 Local and global vacuum solutions

We now review some results obtained in STG for two of the simplest scenarios for gravitational theories: the geometry surround a spherically symmetric and static mass distribution; an isotropic vacuum cosmology.

For the spherically symmetric vacuum case, it is found the following line element

$$ds^2 = \left(1 - \frac{1}{S}\right) dt^2 - \left(1 - \frac{1}{S}\right)^{-1} dr^2 - r^2\, d\theta^2 - r^2 \sin^2\theta\, d\varphi^2, \tag{1.76}$$

where $S = r(a_0 - 2\lambda \log r)$. In the limit when there is no self-interaction term ($\lambda = 0$), the line element above reduces to the usual Schwarzschild form, as can be verified through Eq. (1.4.4). This suggests one to set $a_0 = 1/r_H$, with $r_H = 2m$. It is worth to note also that the limiting case where r_H goes to zero, $1/S$ vanishes and Minkowski spacetime is recovered. In conclusion, the vacuum solution of the non-interacting spinor theory reproduces the traditional Schwarzschild spacetime.

The new physics emerges when the spinors does self interact. There is an extra singular behavior of the metric when r is equal to $r_s = e^{a_0/2\lambda}$. Once the Ricci scalar at this radius is $R = 8\lambda/S^3$, one can see that it is a true singularity. This fact makes this particular non-linear solution unfeasible in general. Even so, one could use it, in certain cases, to obtain some insight of how the spinor self-interaction does modify the gravitational interaction. It could then be considered a satisfactory description of a vacuum region when the source have a radius greater than r_s. This situation can be more easily obtained in the limiting case $\lambda < 0$ and $|\lambda| \ll a_0$, where

$r_s \ll 1$. If one goes further and also assumes a weak field regime, i.e. $r \gg m$, the line element can be approximated to

$$ds^2 \approx \left(1 - \frac{2m}{r} - \frac{8\lambda m^2}{r}\ln r\right)dt^2 - \left(1 + \frac{2m}{r} + \frac{8\lambda m^2}{r}\ln r\right)dr^2 - r^2 d\Omega^2. \qquad (1.77)$$

The horizon, R_H, in this metric occurs when $S(r) = 1$, as can be seen from (1.76). The consequent equation has solution for $\lambda \neq 0$ and it is given in terms of a Lambert W function.[3] Within the limit of negative and small λ, one has

$$R_H \approx 2m\left[1 - 4|\lambda|m\ln(2|\lambda|)\right]. \qquad (1.78)$$

For completeness of this discussion, we note that if λ is positive the position of the singularity goes to higher values of the radius, i.e., $r_s \gg 1$. In the case where $\lambda \gg a_0$, one has $r_s \approx 1$ either for positive or negative values of λ. Also, the line element will be no longer a small deviation from Schwarzschild, since $S(r) \approx 2\lambda r \ln r$.

Other new result concerns the existence of an isotropic vacuum solution of the fundamental equations of STG, which reads

$$ds^2 = dt^2 - \tanh^2 t \left(dX^2 + dY^2 + dZ^2\right). \qquad (1.79)$$

This result of STG should be compared with the case of GR where in the absence of matter is not possible to find an isotropic cosmology. Moreover, one can note that, as $t \to \infty$ the solution is regular and it tends to Minkowski spacetime, in contrast with the singular behavior of Kasner metric.

1.5 Tensor theory

Although general relativity is presented as an universal modification of the metrical properties of spacetime, an alternative way to describe GR as a spin-2 field theory in the same lines as any other interaction was revived by some authors (see, for instance, Refs. [3, 2]). The idea goes back to the works of Gupta [43], Kraichnan [44] and others investigation on spin-2 field. In his book, *Lectures on Gravitation*, Feynman exposed this idea in a very simple way [45]. It was shown that a field theoretical approach of gravity should be possible and its basic ingredients should deal, besides the spin-2 field $\varphi_{\mu\nu}$ with two metric tensors: an auxiliary one $\gamma_{\mu\nu}$ – which is not observable – and an effective one, $g_{\mu\nu}$, related by $g_{\mu\nu} = \gamma_{\mu\nu} + \varphi_{\mu\nu}$.

The basic hypothesis of GR concerns the extension of the equivalence principle beyond its original domain of experimental evidence, that concerns material substance of any form, the adoption of its validity not only by matter or non-gravitational energy of any sort but also by gravity energy itself. Such an

---

[3]The Lambert W function is also called omega function or product logarithm.

universality of interaction is precisely the cornerstone that makes possible the identification of a unique overall geometry of spacetime $g_{\mu\nu}$. The properties of gravity are associated to the Riemannian curvature, which becomes then the equivalent substitute of gravitational forces. What we can learn, from the approach of Feynman et al, is that such geometric scheme is permissible but it is by no way mandatory, that is, the geometrical description of GR is nothing but a choice of representation. All observable characteristics and properties of Einstein theory can be well described in terms of a spin-2 field $\varphi_{\mu\nu}$. We emphasize that such an alternative description of GR in no way sets a restriction on it, but only enlarges its power of understanding.

From this approach it follows that contrary to a widespread belief, the field-theoretical way of treating GR appeals to a two metric structure. Furthermore, Feynman has shown that the coherence of a spin-2 theory that starts with the linear Fierz-Pauli equation, written in terms of the symmetric field $\varphi_{\mu\nu}$, in a Minkowskian spacetime requires, in a very natural way, due to the self-interaction process described above, the use of an induced metric tensor, the quantity $g_{\mu\nu}$ [46]. This is the standard procedure. Nevertheless, and just by tradition, this is not the way that Einstein theory is presented in text books.[4] This interpretation allows us to state that two-metric theories of gravity are less exotic than it is usually displayed [13]. Let us emphasize that the second metric is nothing but a convenient auxiliary tool of the theory. It is not observable and as such can be eliminated from a description made only in terms of observable quantities.

We limit our considerations here to just one single example of spin-2 field theory that can be summarized in the following statements:

- Gravity is described by a symmetric second order tensor $\varphi_{\mu\nu}$ that satisfies a non-linear equation of motion;
- Matter couples to gravity in an universal way. In this interaction, the gravitational field appears only in the combination $g_{\mu\nu} = \gamma_{\mu\nu} + \varphi_{\mu\nu}$ where $\gamma_{\mu\nu}$ is the unobservable metric of the background. In general, it is associated to flat Minkowski structure. Such tensor $g_{\mu\nu}$ acts as the true metric tensor of the spacetime as seen by matter or energy of any form.

In order to exhibit the complete covariance of the theory all quantities will be described in an arbitrary system of coordinates. In the auxiliary background geometry of Minkowski spacetime of metric $\gamma_{\mu\nu}$ the covariant derivative, represented by a semi-comma. We define a three-index tensor $F_{\alpha\beta\mu}$,

---

[4]The absence in the literature of such alternative but equivalent way to present Einstein theory of gravity seems to be the main responsible for the young students of theoretical physics to understand GR as a completely separate and different theory from any other field. In textbook presentations of GR one makes the choice of a unique geometry. This, of course, does not preclude an alternative equivalent description [2].

which we call the gravitational field, in terms of the symmetric standard variable $\varphi_{\mu\nu}$ treated as the potential to describe spin-two fields, by the expression

$$F_{\alpha\mu\nu} = \frac{1}{2}(\varphi_{\nu[\alpha;\mu]} + F_{[\alpha}\gamma_{\mu]\nu}), \qquad (1.80)$$

where $F_\alpha =$ In the expression above, the quantity F_α is the trace of $F_{\alpha\beta\mu} = F_{\alpha\mu\nu}\gamma^{\mu\nu}$, and the indices between square brackets indicates an antisymmetrization operation. From the field variables we can form the following invariants $A \equiv F_{\alpha\mu\nu}F^{\alpha\mu\nu}$ and $B \equiv F_\mu F^\mu$.[5]

1.5.1 General relativity: the field formulation

General relativity takes for granted that gravity is nothing but the fact that all existing form of energy/matter interacts through the modification of the universal geometry. However, such a view is not exclusive and it is conceivable to try to use two metrics to describe in an equivalent way all content of such theory. There is no simpler and more direct way to prove this statement than the one set forth by Feynmann. It is worth to remark that a such duplication causes no further difficulties when one realizes that the second auxiliary metric $\gamma_{\mu\nu}$ is unobservable.

Let us pause for a while and make, just for completeness, a summary of the principal features of this equivalent scheme. The theory starts with the Fierz-Pauli linear equation

$$G_{\mu\nu}^{(L)} = -\kappa\, T_{\mu\nu} \qquad (1.81)$$

in which $T_{\mu\nu}$ is the matter energy-momentum tensor and $G_{\mu\nu}^{(L)}$ is a linear tensor with respect to $\varphi_{\mu\nu}$ given by:

$$G_{\mu\nu}^{(L)} \equiv \Box\varphi_{\mu\nu} - \varphi^\alpha{}_{\mu;\alpha\nu} - \varphi^\alpha{}_{\nu;\alpha\mu} + \varphi^\alpha{}_{\alpha;\mu\nu} - \gamma_{\mu\nu}(\Box\varphi^\alpha{}_\alpha - \varphi^{\alpha\beta}{}_{;\alpha\beta}). \qquad (1.82)$$

The action for this linear theory is $S^{(L)} = \int d^4x\, \sqrt{-\gamma}(A-B)$. Since $G_{\mu\nu}^{(L)}$ is divergence-free it follows for coherence that the matter energy momentum tensor should also be divergence-free. However this is in contradiction with the fact that gravity may exchange energy with matter. To overcome such situation, one introduces an object which we call Gupta-Feynman gravitational energy tensor $t_{\mu\nu}^{(g)}$ — a cumbersome non linear expression in terms of $\varphi_{\alpha\beta}$ and its derivatives — that is to be added to the right hand side of Eq. (1.81) in order to obtain a compatible set of equations,

$$G_{\mu\nu}^{(L)} = -\kappa\left[t_{\mu\nu}^{(g)} + T_{\mu\nu}\right]. \qquad (1.83)$$

Note that, instead of using the standard procedure (as it happens in others nonlinear theories) — which in the case we examine here, asks for the introduction

---

[5]Note that, besides these invariants, it is possible to define a quantity C, constructed with the dual, that is $C \equiv F^*_{\alpha\mu\nu}F^{\alpha\mu\nu}$. We will not deal with such quantity here.

of a nonlinear functional of the invariants A and B, dealt with in the linear case — in order to obtain the dynamics of GR, one must use other functionals of the basic field $\varphi_{\mu\nu}$ which are not present in the linear case, that means, they are not displayed in terms of the invariants A and B. We do not intend to repeat here the whole procedure (see Refs. [3, 2] for more details), but only to call the reader's attention to such an unusual treatment of dealing with a nonlinear process. The origin of this approach goes back to the hypothesis of the validity of the equivalence principle for gravitational energy.

For a convenient choice of the expression of the Gupta-Feynman gravitational energy, the equation (1.83) is nothing but Einstein dynamics (see, for instance, Ref. [2]). However, another path to deal with a nonlinear extension of Fierz original model is possible, arriving at a different dynamics than in GR.

1.5.2 A non-linear Fierz extension field theory of gravity

The non-linear Fierz extension (NLFE) starts at the same point as general relativity, that is, Fierz linear theory for spin-2 field. However, instead of breaking the symmetry displayed in the linear regime, presented in the combination of invariants under the form $A-B$, as it was done in the Einstein case, it assumes that this symmetry is maintained even after the introduction of non-linearities [48]. The theory incorporates a great part of general relativity, it satisfies all standard tests of gravity and can be interpreted in the standard geometrical way like GR, as far as the interaction of matter to gravity is concerned. The most important particularity of the new theory concerns the gravity self interaction.

It is considered a more general Lagrangian function $L(U)$, with $U = A-B$. Taking the variation of the gravitational action with respect to the potential $\varphi_{\mu\nu}$, it results in the following equations of motion,

$$\left[L_U F^{\lambda(\mu\nu)}\right]_{;\lambda} = -T^{\mu\nu} \tag{1.84}$$

where L_U represents the derivative of the Lagrangian with respect to the invariant U and $T^{\mu\nu}$ is the energy-momentum tensor density of the matter contents.

A short analysis of the wave propagation description in this theory shows that it satisfies,

$$k^\mu k^\nu [\gamma_{\mu\nu} + \Lambda_{\mu\nu}] = 0, \tag{1.85}$$

where k_α represents the wave vector and

$$\Lambda_{\mu\nu} \equiv 2\frac{L_{UU}}{L_U}[F_\mu{}^{\alpha\beta} F_{\nu(\alpha\beta)} - F_\mu F_\nu]. \tag{1.86}$$

Therefore, the gravitational disturbances propagate in a modified geometry, changing the background geometry $\gamma_{\mu\nu}$, into an effective one $g_{\mu\nu}$, which depends on the energy distribution of the field $F_{\alpha\beta\mu}$. This fact shows that such a property stems from the structural form of the Lagrangian. Once the velocity of propagation of gravitational waves has been constrained to be the same as the light [28], this fact should strongly restrict the class of Lagrangian functions $L(U)$.

1.6 Final comments

The appearance of the method of the effective metric introduced by Gordon in 1923 and developed in the present century shows that the use of a Riemannian geometry, by general relativity, to describe gravity is one of many possibilities. The work of Feynmann, Grishchuk and others that used a spin-2 formulation in an unobserved space-time background has shown explicitly the similitude of the field formulation and the original metric description of general relativity.

Such field theory formulation of gravity is not restricted to a spin-2 formulation but instead can be described in terms of other structures, like a scalar or a spinor field. We have reviewed how recent advances in this direction has paved the way for new theoretical developments within the alternative gravity program, evidencing similarities and distinctions between those formulations and the paradigmatic general relativity. There is the possibility to go beyond Einstein-Nordströn's early scalar formulations of gravity. The single scalar field model shows a satisfactory description of local physics, gravitational radiation and cosmological scenarios where non-singular universes are natural solutions. A similar proposal using a non-linear spinor field satisfying Heisenberg dynamics uses the effective metric method to arrive at a gravitational theory in terms of fundamental fermion fields. This opens a new way to an unification between two different kinds of interactions, that is, gravity and the Fermi (weak) processes.

The method of effective metric and the consequent gravitational theories discussed here should also be viewed as a general framework for field theories of gravity. The theoretical models reviewed are specific cases of study within a rather much more enlarged scenario, and more general formulations still remains to be explored. In this sense, we hope that this work and the general picture here depicted can put on perspective several aspects of field formulations of alternative theories of gravity, motivating the future researches in the area.

Acknowledgements

MN would like to thank Dr. A. Hartmann for his interest and comments in a previous draft of this work, and Fundação de Amparo à Pesquisa do Estado do Rio de Janeiro (FAPERJ) for a fellowship.

Bibliography

[1] W. Gordon, *Zur lichtfortpflanzung nach der relativitätstheorie*, Ann. Phys. **72**, 421, (1923).

[2] L. P. Grishchuk, A. N. Petrov, and A. D. Popova, *Exact theory of the (Einstein) gravitational field in an arbitrary background space-time*, Comm. Math. Phys. **94**, 379 (1984).

[3] S. Deser. *Self-interaction and gauge invariance*, Gen. Rel. Gravit. **1**, 9 (1970.

[4] Jacques Hadamard, *Lectures on Cauchy's Problem in linear partial differential equations* (Mineola: Dover Publications, New York, 2003).

[5] M. Novello and E. Bittencourt, *Metric Relativity and the Dynamical Bridge: highlights of Riemannian geometry in physics*, Braz. J. Phys. **45**, 756 (2015).

[6] M. Novello, M. Visser, and G. Volovik (Eds.), *Artificial Black Holes*, (World Scientific, Singapore, 2002).

[7] V. Cardoso, L.C.B Crispino, S. Liberati, and E.S. Oliveira (Eds.), *Analogue spacetimes: the first thirty years* (Editora Livraria da Física, São Paulo, 2013).

[8] M. Novello and E. Goulart, *Beyond Analog Gravity: The Case of Exceptional Dynamics*, Class. Quant. Grav. **28**, 145022 (2011).

[9] E. Goulart, M. Novello, F. T. Falciano, and J. D. Toniato, *Hidden geometries in nonlinear theories: A Novel aspect of analogue gravity*, Class. Quant. Grav. **28**, 245008 (2011).

[10] A. Einstein, *On the relativity principle and the conclusions drawn from it*. In *The Collected Papers of Albert Einstein*, vol. 2, The Swiss Years: Writings, 1900-1909 (English translation supplement), A. Beck and Peter Havas (Eds), p. 252 (Princeton Univ. Press, Princeton, 1989).

[11] J. D. Norton, *Einstein, Nordström and the early demise of scalar, Lorentz-covariant theories of gravitation*, Archive for History of Exact Sciences **45**, 17 (1992).

[12] G. Nordström, *Relativitätsprinzip und gravitation*, Phys. Zeit. **13** 1126 (1912).

[13] G. Nordström, *Träge und schwere Masse in der Relativitätsmechanik*, Ann. Phys. **40**, 856 (1913).

[14] A. Einstein, *On the present state of the problem of gravitation*. In: *The Collected Papers of Albert Einstein*, vol. 4, The Swiss Years: Writings, 1912-1914 (English translation supplement), A. Beck and Don Howard (Eds.), (Princeton Univ. Press, Princeton, 1996) p. 198.

[15] A. Einstein, *Outline of a generalized theory of relativity and of a theory of gravitation*. In: *The Collected Papers of Albert Einstein*, vol. 4, The Swiss Years: Writings, 1912-1914 (English translation supplement), A. Beck and Don Howard (Eds.), (Princeton Univ. Press, Princeton, 1996) p. 151.

[16] Albert Einstein and Adriaan D. Fokker, *Nordström's theory of gravitation from the point of view of the absolute differential calculus*. In: *The collected papers of Albert Einstein*, vol. 4: The Swiss years: Writings 1912-1914 (English translation supplement), A. Beck and Don Howard (Eds.), (Princeton Univ. Press, Princeton, 1996) p. 293.

[17] M. Janssen and J. Renn, *Untying the knot: how Einstein found his way back to field equations discarded in the Zurich notebook*. In: *The Genesis of General Relativity*, M. Janssen, J. D. Norton, J. Renn, T. Sauer, and J. Stachel (Eds.) (Springer Netherlands, Dordrecht, 2007), p. 839.

[18] C. Page and B. O. J. Tupper, *Scalar Gravitational Theories with Variable Velocity of Light*, Month. Not. Royal Astron. Soc. **138**, 67 (1968).

[19] M. Novello, E. Bittencourt, U. Moschella, E. Goulart, J. M. Salim, and J. D. Toniato, *Geometric scalar theory of gravity*, JCAP **06**, 014 (2013). [Erratum: JCAP **01**, E01 (2014)].

[20] J. D. Bekenstein, *The relation between physical and gravitational geometry*, Phys. Rev. D **48**, 3641 (1993).

[21] J. Sakstein, *Disformal theories of gravity: from the solar system to cosmology*, JCAP **12**, 012 (2014).

[22] P. Brax and A.C Davis, *Gravitational effects of disformal couplings*, Phys. Rev. D **98**, 063531 (2018).

[23] S. Capozziello and C. Stornaiolo, *Space-time deformations as extended conformal transformations*, Int. J. Geom. Meth. Mod. Phys. **5**, 185 (2008).

[24] E. Bittencourt, U. Moschella, M. Novello, and J. D. Toniato, *More about scalar gravity*, Phys. Rev. D **93** 12, 124023 (2016).

[25] C. M. Will, *Theory and experiment in gravitational physics*, 2nd edition (Cambridge Univ. Press, Cambridge, 1993).

[26] J. D. Toniato, D. C. Rodrigues, and A. Wojnar, *Palatini $f(R)$ gravity in the solar system: post-Newtonian equations of motion and complete PPN parameters*, Phys. Rev. D **101**, 064050 (2020).

[27] J. D. Toniato and D. C. Rodrigues, *Post-newtonian γ-like parameters and the gravitational slip in scalar-tensor and $f(r)$ theories*, Phys. Rev. D **104**, 044020 (2021).

[28] B. P. Abbott et al, *Gravitational Waves and Gamma-Rays from a Binary Neutron Star Merger: GW170817 and GRB 170817A*, ApJ **848**, L13 (2017).

[29] J. D. Toniato, *The description of gravitational waves in geometric scalar gravity*, Eur. Phys. J. C **79**, 680 (2019).

[30] E. Newman and R. Penrose, *An Approach to gravitational radiation by a method of spin coefficients*, J. Math. Phys. **3**, 566 (1962).

[31] D. M. Eardley, D. L. Lee, and A. P. Lightman, *Gravitational-wave observations as a tool for testing relativistic gravity*, Phys. Rev. D **8**, 3308 (1973).

[32] B. P. Abbott et al, *Tests of General Relativity with the Binary Black Hole Signals from the LIGO-Virgo Catalog GWTC-1*, ArXiv:1903.04467.

[33] B. P. Abbott et al, *Tests of General Relativity with GW170817*, Phys. Rev. Lett. **123**, 011102, (2019).

[34] M. E. S. Alves, O. D. Miranda, and J. C. N. de Araujo, *Probing the $f(R)$ formalism through gravitational wave polarizations*, Phys. Lett. B **679**, 401 (2009).

[35] T. Damour, *Binary systems as test-beds of gravity theories*, In: *Physics of Relativistic Objects in Compact Binaries: From Birth to Coalescence*, M. Colpi, P. Casella, V. Gorini, U. Moschella, and A. Possenti (Eds.) (Springer Netherlands, Dordrecht, 2009).

[36] E. Bittencourt, U. Moschella, M. Novello, and J. D. Toniato, *Cosmology in geometric scalar gravity*, Phys. Rev. D **90**, 123540 (2014).

[37] P. A. M. Dirac, *The cosmological constants*, Nature **139**, 323 (1937).

[38] R. Onofrio, *On weak interactions as short-distance manifestations of gravity*, Modern Physics Letters A **28**, 1350022 (2013).

[39] M. Novello and A. E. S. Hartmann, *From weak interaction to gravity*, Int. J. Mod. Phys. A **36**, 2150051 (2021).

[40] W. Heisenberg, *Quantum theory of fields and elementary particles*, Rev. Mod. Phys. **29**, 269 (1957).

[41] H.-P. Dürr, W. Heisenberg, H. Mitter, S. Schlieder, and K. Yamazaki, *Zur theorie der elementarteilchen*, Zeitschrift für Naturforschung A **14**, 441 (1959).

[42] Y. Nambu and G. Jona-Lasinio, *Dynamical Model of Elementary Particles Based on an Analogy with Superconductivity. I*, Phys. Rev. **122**, 345 (1961).

[43] S. N. Gupta, *Gravitation and electromagnetism*, Phys. Rev. **96**, 1683 (1954).

[44] R. H. Kraichnan, *Special-relativistic derivation of generally covariant gravitation theory*, Phys. Rev. **98** 1118 (1955).

[45] R. P. Feynman, *Feynman lectures on gravitation*, (Addison-Wesley, Reading, 1995).

[46] M. Fierz, W. E Pauli, and P. A. M. Dirac, *On relativistic wave equations for particles of arbitrary spin in an electromagnetic field*. In *Proceedings of the Royal Society of London A*, **173**, 211 (1939).

[47] C. M. Will, *The Confrontation between General Relativity and Experiment* Living Rev. Rel. **17**, 4 (2014).

[48] M. Novello, V. A. De Lorenci, and Luciane R. de Freitas, *Do gravitational waves travel at light velocity?*, Ann. Phys. **254**, 83 (1997).

2

De Sitter-invariant approach to cosmology

A. V. Araujo, D. F. López, J. G. Pereira, J. R. Salazar

Abstract: The spacetime short-distance structure at the Planck scale is governed by a Lorentz-invariant length, known as Planck length. Since Einstein's special relativity does not admit a finite invariant length, it cannot describe the Planck scale kinematics. A possible solution to this puzzle is to replace the Poincaré-invariant Einstein's special relativity with the de Sitter-invariant special relativity. As the latter admits a finite invariant length while preserving the Lorentz symmetry, it provides a consistent description of the Planck scale kinematics. Under such replacement, general relativity changes to the de Sitter-invariant general relativity, in which the cosmological term Λ is constitutive. In this paper, the corresponding de Sitter-invariant Friedmann equations are obtained, and some implications for cosmology are presented and discussed.

2.1 Introduction

A fundamental issue of spacetime physics is the lack of a special relativity capable of describing the Planck scale kinematics. The problem is that the short-distance structure of spacetime at the Planck scale is governed by an observer-independent length given by the Planck length. Since the Poincaré-invariant Einstein's special relativity does not admit a finite invariant length, it cannot describe the Planck scale kinematics. It is then necessary to look for a special relativity that complies with the Planck scale requirements.

One of the first attempts to solve this puzzle is the so-called *doubly special relativity* [1, 2, 3, 4], a theory constructed by adding to the special relativity dispersion relation, scale-suppressed terms of higher order in the four-momentum. As these terms violate the Lorentz symmetry, the theory admits an invariant length at the Planck scale. The importance of these terms is controlled by a parameter κ, which changes the special relativity's kinematic group from Poincaré to the κ-deformed Poincaré group. Far from the Planck scale, these terms are suppressed, Lorentz symmetry is recovered, and one obtains ordinary special relativity.

A sensible alternative is to search for a special relativity that admits a finite invariant length while preserving the Lorentz symmetry. To explore such an alternative, we use the notion of locality inherent to the strong equivalence principle. According to this principle, at every spacetime point in an arbitrary gravitational field, one can define a locally inertial frame in which inertial effects precisely compensate for gravitation. Consequently, inertial forces and gravitation go out of sight, and the laws of physics reduce locally to those of special relativity, as seen from an inertial frame [5]. Note that this notion of locality differs from the usual geometric notion, according to which a curved surface can be locally approximated by a flat surface. Although this approximation is correct, it is not a physical principle and has nothing to do with the strong equivalence principle [6]. Furthermore, since the cosmological term Λ represents neither gravitation nor inertial effect, it does not interfere with the strong equivalence principle.

As quotient spaces [7], Minkowski and de Sitter are non-gravitational backgrounds for constructing physical theories. General relativity, for example, can be constructed on any of them. In either case, gravitation will have the same dynamics: only the *local* kinematics will differ. When general relativity is constructed on Minkowski, all solutions to the gravitational field equation are spacetimes that reduce locally to Minkowski, where the spacetime's local kinematics, governed by the Poincaré-invariant Einstein's special relativity, occurs. When general relativity is constructed on de Sitter, all solutions to the gravitational field equation are spacetimes that reduce locally to de Sitter,[1] where the spacetime's local kinematics, governed by the de Sitter-invariant special relativity [10, 11], occurs.

According to the geometrical structure described above, the cosmological term Λ is defined as the sectional curvature of the non-gravitational background spacetime,

$$\Lambda \sim l^{-2}, \tag{2.1}$$

with l a length parameter. The question then arises. As a sectional curvature, the cosmological term Λ must be Lorentz invariant. However, since it depends explicitly on a length parameter, it is unclear how it could be Lorentz invariant. To clarify this point, one has to distinguish between lengths and pseudo-lengths. Recall that all lengths defined in the three-dimensional Euclidian section of the background spacetime are not Lorentz invariant. For example, the squared length $(i, j, k, \cdots = 1, 2, 3)$

$$\ell^2 = g_{ij} x^i x^j, \tag{2.2}$$

is not Lorentz invariant. On the other hand, all pseudo-lengths defined in the four-dimensional background spacetime are Lorentz invariant. For example, the squared pseudo-length $(\alpha, \beta, \gamma, \cdots = 0, 1, 2, 3)$

$$s^2 = g_{\alpha\beta} x^\alpha x^\beta \tag{2.3}$$

is Lorentz invariant.

On the other hand, the de Sitter spacetime can be viewed as a hyperboloid embedded in the $(1 + 4)$-dimensional pseudo-Euclidean space with Cartesian coordinates χ^A $(A, B, C \cdots = 0, \ldots 4)$ and metric

$$\eta_{AB} = \text{diag}(+1, -1, -1, -1, -1),$$

inclusion whose points satisfy [12]

$$\eta_{AB} \chi^A \chi^B = -l^2. \tag{2.4}$$

This relation shows that the de Sitter length-parameter l is actually a pseudo-length. As such, it is Lorentz invariant, rendering the cosmological term Λ also Lorentz invariant. Thus, in order to be Lorentz invariant, *the Planck length l_P must represent the pseudo-radius of the background spacetime at the Planck scale*, which will be a de Sitter space with the Planck cosmological term

$$\Lambda_P \sim l_P^{-2}. \tag{2.5}$$

---

[1] Spacetimes that do not reduce locally to Minkowski are known since long and come under the name of Cartan geometry [8, 9].

In this case, the existence of a finite invariant pseudo-length does not clash with the Lorentz invariance, and the de Sitter-invariant special relativity provides a consistent description of the Planck scale kinematics. Note that, according to the de Sitter-invariant special relativity, Lorentz remains a symmetry at the Planck scale.

By construction, the de Sitter-invariant special relativity is a natural framework to deal with the Planck scale physics and the universe's cosmological scale. Using the corresponding de Sitter-invariant general relativity, we aim in this paper to obtain the ensuing Friedmann equations and discuss some of their implications for cosmology.

2.2 Minkowski and de Sitter as quotient spaces

Spacetimes with constant sectional curvature are maximally symmetric because they carry the maximum number of Killing vectors. Flat Minkowski spacetime M is the simplest one. Its kinematic group is the Poincaré group $\mathscr{P} = \mathscr{L} \oslash \mathscr{T}$, the semi-direct product between Lorentz $\mathscr{L}$ and the translation group $\mathscr{T}$. Algebraically, it is defined as the quotient space

$$M = \mathscr{P}/\mathscr{L}.$$

The Lorentz subgroup is responsible for the isotropy around a given point of M, and the translation symmetry enforces this isotropy around all other points. In this case, homogeneity means that all points of Minkowski are equivalent under spacetime translations. One then says that Minkowski is *transitive* under translations, whose generators are written as

$$P_\nu = \delta^\alpha_\nu \partial_\alpha, \qquad (2.6)$$

with δ^α_ρ the Killing vectors of spacetime translations.

The de Sitter space dS is also maximally symmetric, with the kinematic group given by the de Sitter group $SO(1,4)$. Algebraically, the de Sitter spacetime is defined as the quotient space

$$dS = SO(1,4)/\mathscr{L}.$$

Like Minkowski, the Lorentz subgroup is responsible for the isotropy around a given point of dS. The homogeneity, however, differs substantially. To find out the de Sitter homogeneity, let us recall that, in terms of the coordinates χ^A, the generators of infinitesimal de Sitter transformations are written as

$$L_{AB} \equiv \zeta^C_{AB} \frac{\partial}{\partial \chi^C} \qquad (2.7)$$

where
$$\zeta^C_{AB} = \eta_{AD}\chi^D \delta^C_B - \eta_{BD}\chi^D \delta^C_A \qquad (2.8)$$
are the associated Killing vectors.

In terms of the four-dimensional stereographic coordinates $\{x^\mu\}$, the ten de Sitter generators (2.7) are given by [13]

$$L_{\mu\nu} = \zeta^\alpha_{\mu\nu}\partial_\alpha \quad \text{and} \quad \Pi_\nu \equiv \frac{L_{4\nu}}{l} = \xi^\alpha_\nu \partial_\alpha, \qquad (2.9)$$

where $L_{\mu\nu}$ represent the Lorentz generators and Π_ν stand for the so-called de Sitter "translation" generators, with $\zeta^\alpha_{\mu\nu}$ and ξ^α_ν the corresponding Killing vectors.[2] In contrast to Minkowski, whose points are equivalent under spacetime translations, all points of de Sitter are equivalent under de Sitter "translations." One then say that de Sitter is transitive under de Sitter "translations."

In stereographic coordinates, the Killing vectors of the de Sitter "translations" are written as [14]

$$\xi^\alpha_\nu = \delta^\alpha_\nu - \frac{1}{4l^2}\vartheta^\alpha_\nu, \qquad (2.10)$$

where
$$\delta^\alpha_\nu \quad \text{and} \quad \vartheta^\alpha_\nu = 2\eta_{\nu\rho}x^\rho x^\alpha - \sigma^2 \delta^\alpha_\nu \qquad (2.11)$$

are, respectively, the Killing vectors of translations and proper conformal transformations. Consequently, the de Sitter "translation" generators can be recast in the form

$$\Pi_\nu = P_\nu - \frac{1}{4l^2}K_\nu, \qquad (2.12)$$

where
$$P_\nu = \delta^\alpha_\nu \partial_\alpha \quad \text{and} \quad K_\nu = \vartheta^\alpha_\nu \partial_\alpha \qquad (2.13)$$

are, respectively, the translation and proper conformal generators [15]. Equations (2.6) and (2.12) show that, whereas Minkowski is transitive under translations, the de Sitter spacetime is transitive under a combination of translations and proper conformal transformations [16].

2.3 De Sitter-invariant general relativity

We present in this section the schematic procedure to obtain the de Sitter-invariant Einstein's equation. For comparison, we first review the usual procedure to obtain the standard Einstein's equation.

---

[2]The generators Π_ν are not really translations but rotations in the planes $(4,\nu)$. Hence the quotation marks.

2.3.1 Poincaré-invariant Einstein's equation

In the case of standard general relativity, all solutions to the gravitational field equations are spacetimes that reduce locally to Minkowski. Since Minkowski is transitive under translations, a diffeomorphism in these spacetimes is defined as a local translation

$$\delta_P x^\mu = \delta_\alpha^\mu \epsilon^\alpha(x), \tag{2.14}$$

with δ_α^μ the Killing vectors of translations. From Noether's theorem, the invariance of the source Lagrangian under the diffeomorphism (2.14) yields the energy-momentum covariant conservation law

$$\nabla_\nu T^{\mu\nu} = 0 \quad \text{with} \quad T^{\mu\nu} = \delta_\alpha^\mu T^{\alpha\nu}. \tag{2.15}$$

Variation of the gravitational plus source actions under the diffeomorphism (2.14) yields the standard Einstein's equation

$$G^{\mu\nu} \equiv R^{\mu\nu} - \tfrac{1}{2} g^{\mu\nu} R = -\frac{8\pi G}{c^4} T^{\mu\nu}. \tag{2.16}$$

2.3.2 De Sitter-invariant Einstein's equation

In the case of the de Sitter-invariant general relativity, all solutions to the gravitational field equation are spacetimes that reduce locally to de Sitter. Since de Sitter is transitive under de Sitter "translations," a diffeomorphism in these spacetimes is defined as [16]

$$\delta_\Pi x^\mu = \xi_\alpha^\mu \epsilon^\alpha(x), \tag{2.17}$$

with ξ_α^μ the Killing vectors (2.10) of the de Sitter "translations." From Noether's theorem, the invariance of the source Lagrangian under the diffeomorphism (2.17) yields the covariant conservation law

$$\nabla_\nu \Pi^{\mu\nu} = 0 \quad \text{with} \quad \Pi^{\mu\nu} = \xi_\alpha^\mu T^{\alpha\nu}. \tag{2.18}$$

Variation of the gravitational plus source actions under the diffeomorphism (2.17) yields the de Sitter-invariant Einstein's equation [17]

$$\mathcal{G}^{\mu\nu} \equiv \mathcal{R}^{\mu\nu} - \tfrac{1}{2} g^{\mu\nu} \mathcal{R} = -\frac{8\pi G}{c^4} \Pi^{\mu\nu}, \tag{2.19}$$

where the Riemann tensor $\mathcal{R}^\alpha{}_{\beta\mu\nu}$ represents both the dynamic curvature of general relativity and the kinematic curvature of the background de Sitter spacetime.

2.3.3 The source of the cosmological term

Substituting the Killing vectors (2.10) in the source current $\Pi^{\mu\nu}$, it splits in the form

$$\Pi^{\mu\nu} = T^{\mu\nu} - (1/4l^2)K^{\mu\nu}, \qquad (2.20)$$

where

$$T^{\mu\nu} = \delta^\mu_\alpha T^{\alpha\nu} \quad \text{and} \quad K^{\mu\nu} = \vartheta^\mu_\alpha T^{\alpha\nu} \qquad (2.21)$$

are, respectively, the energy-momentum and the proper conformal currents [18]. Analogously to the source decomposition, the Einstein tensor $\mathcal{G}^{\mu\nu}$ splits in the form

$$\mathcal{G}^{\mu\nu} = G^{\mu\nu} - \hat{G}^{\mu\nu}, \qquad (2.22)$$

where $G^{\mu\nu}$ is general relativity's Einstein tensor and $\hat{G}^{\mu\nu}$ is the Einstein tensor of the local de Sitter spacetime. In stereographic coordinates, therefore, the de Sitter-invariant Einstein's equation (2.19) assumes the form

$$\left(R^{\mu\nu} - \tfrac{1}{2}g^{\mu\nu}R\right) - \left(\hat{R}^{\mu\nu} - \tfrac{1}{2}g^{\mu\nu}\hat{R}\right) = -\frac{8\pi G}{c^4}\left[T^{\mu\nu} - (1/4l^2)K^{\mu\nu}\right]. \qquad (2.23)$$

According to this equation, any source in spacetimes that reduce locally to de Sitter locally de Sitter spacetimes gives rise to an energy-momentum and a proper conformal current. The energy-momentum current $T^{\mu\nu}$ keeps its role as the source of general relativity's dynamic curvature, whereas the proper conformal current $K^{\mu\nu}$ appears as the source of the kinematic curvature of the local de Sitter spacetime [19].

Note that the energy-momentum current is no longer covariantly conserved. What is conserved now is the combination of energy-momentum and proper conformal currents – the source of the gravitational field equation. Note also that, whereas the gravitational part of the equation is essentially dynamic, the conformal part is purely algebraic. This difference stems from the non-propagating character of the cosmological term Λ. Taking the trace of Eq. (2.23) and identifying $G^\mu{}_\mu = -R$ and $\hat{G}^\mu{}_\mu = -\Lambda$, it reduces to

$$R - \Lambda = \frac{8\pi G}{c^4}\left[T^\mu{}_\mu - (1/4l^2)K^\mu{}_\mu\right]. \qquad (2.24)$$

2.3.4 Negative pressure from ordinary matter

We consider now a perfect fluid, whose energy-momentum tensor in co-moving coordinates is written as

$$T^\mu{}_\nu = \text{diag}(\varepsilon_m, -p_m, -p_m, -p_m), \qquad (2.25)$$

where ε_m and p_m are the matter energy density and pressure, respectively. Its trace has the form

$$T^\mu{}_\mu \equiv \delta^\mu_\alpha T^\alpha{}_\mu = \varepsilon_m - 3p_m. \tag{2.26}$$

On the other hand, the trace of the proper conformal current is

$$K^\mu{}_\mu = \vartheta^\mu_\alpha T^\alpha{}_\mu \equiv \left(2\eta_{\alpha\rho} x^\rho x^\mu - \sigma^2 \delta^\mu_\alpha\right) T^\alpha{}_\mu. \tag{2.27}$$

Since the space section of the universe is assumed to be a homogeneous space, in which all points are equivalent, one can compute the trace at any point [20]. For the sake of simplicity, one usually chooses the point $x^i = 0$, which yields $K^\mu{}_\mu = c^2 t^2 (\varepsilon_m + 3p_m)$. We can then write

$$\frac{K^\mu{}_\mu}{4l^2} = \gamma(t)(\varepsilon_m + 3p_m), \tag{2.28}$$

where

$$\gamma(t) = c^2 t^2 / 4l^2 \tag{2.29}$$

is a time-dependent dimensionless parameter. Identifying

$$\varepsilon_\Lambda \equiv \gamma(t)\varepsilon_m \quad \text{and} \quad p_\Lambda \equiv \gamma(t) p_m, \tag{2.30}$$

equation (2.28) assumes the form

$$\frac{K^\mu{}_\mu}{4l^2} = \varepsilon_\Lambda + 3p_\Lambda. \tag{2.31}$$

Using Eqs. (2.26) and (2.31), the field equation (2.24) can be recast in the form

$$R - \Lambda = \frac{8\pi G}{c^4}\left[(\varepsilon_m - 3p_m) - (\varepsilon_\Lambda + 3p_\Lambda)\right]. \tag{2.32}$$

As can be seen from Eq. (2.30), the energy densities ε_Λ and ε_m differ by the same coefficient as p_Λ differs from p_m. Consequently, p_m and p_Λ satisfy the same equation of state,

$$p_m = w\,\varepsilon_m \quad \text{and} \quad p_\Lambda = w\,\varepsilon_\Lambda, \tag{2.33}$$

with w a numerical constant. This is an expected result because ordinary matter is the source of both gravitation and dark energy. Comparing the trace (2.26) of the energy-momentum current with the trace (2.31) of the proper conformal current, we see that, even though p_m and p_Λ satisfy the same equation of state, they naturally enter the field equation (2.32) with opposite signs concerning ε_m and ε_Λ, respectively. This difference is due uniquely to the mathematical intricacies of the proper conformal current, the source of the background de Sitter spacetime – or dark energy. Therefore, in the de Sitter-invariant approach to cosmology, the source of dark energy does not need to satisfy an exotic equation of state to produce a repulsive interaction.

In the usual case of Poincaré-invariant general relativity, because the cosmological term Λ is constant, the dark energy density ε_Λ is uniformly distributed across space, independently of the matter energy-density ε_m distribution. However, in the de Sitter-invariant general relativity, these energy densities are not independent but satisfy the constraint (2.30), a property inherited from the dependence of the proper conformal current $K^{\mu\nu}$ on the energy-momentum current $T^{\mu\nu}$.

2.3.5 A hierarchy of kinematics and gravity theories

One can establish a natural hierarchy of kinematics by using the Inönü-Wigner process of Lie groups expansion and contraction [21, 22]. At the bottom of the hierarchy stands the Galilei-invariant special relativity, which governs Newtonian gravity kinematics. The Poincaré-invariant Einstein's special relativity represents a generalization of Galilei relativity for velocities near the velocity of light.

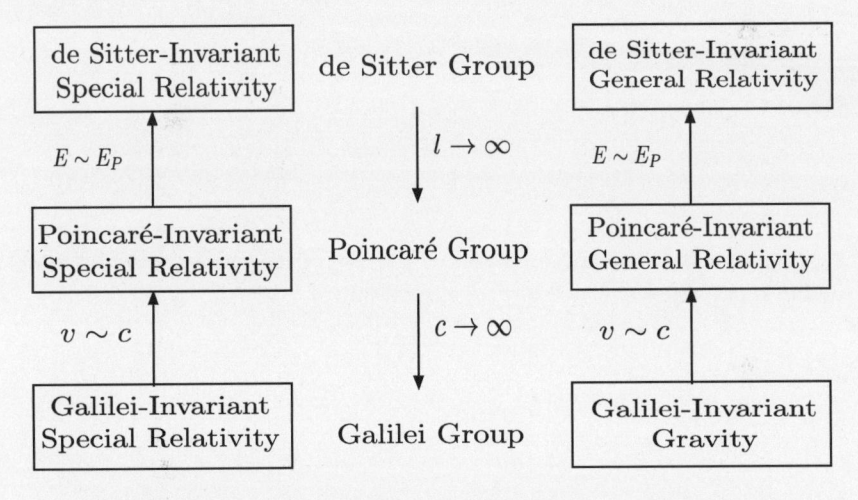

Figure 2.1: Pictorial view of the hierarchy of kinematics and gravity theories.

Accordingly, this theory gives rise to deviations concerning Galilei relativity for velocities comparable to the velocity of light. Similarly, the de Sitter-invariant special relativity may be interpreted as a generalization of Poincaré-invariant Einstein's special relativity for energies comparable to the Planck energy. Accordingly, this theory is expected to produce deviations concerning the Poincaré-invariant special relativity for energies comparable to the Planck energy and at the universe's large scale.

Conversely, the contraction limit $l \to \infty$ reduces the de Sitter-invariant special relativity to the Poincaré-invariant Einstein's special relativity. This theory reduces to the Galilei special relativity under the further contraction limit $c \to \infty$. Note that, to each special relativity, there corresponds a gravitational theory whose spacetime's local kinematics is governed by that special relativity. Figure 2.1 shows a pictorial view of the hierarchy of kinematics and the corresponding gravitational theories.

2.4 De Sitter-invariant Friedmann equations

2.4.1 FLRW metric in locally de Sitter spacetimes

The FLRW metric is constructed to comply with the cosmological principle, according to which the space section of the universe at large enough scales is assumed to be isotropic and homogeneous. There are only three possibilities: the space section can be Euclidean, spheric, or hyperbolic. Using the standard procedure, the FLRW metric is written as

$$ds^2 = c^2 dt^2 - a^2 \gamma_{ij} dx^i dx^j \tag{2.34}$$

where $a = a(t)$ is the cosmic scale factor, and

$$\gamma_{ij} = \delta_{ij} + \frac{k x_i x_j}{1 - k(x_l x^l)}, \tag{2.35}$$

with k the curvature parameter. For $k = 0, +1, -1$, the universe space section will be Euclidian, spheric, or hyperbolic, respectively.

The non-vanishing components of the Levi-Civita connection of the metric (2.34) are

$$\Gamma^0{}_{ij} = (a\dot{a}/c)\gamma_{ij}, \quad \Gamma^i{}_{0j} = (\dot{a}/ac)\delta^i_j, \quad \Gamma^i{}_{jk} = -x^i \delta_{jk}, \tag{2.36}$$

where a dot represents a derivative with respect to the cosmic time t.

2.4.2 Noether continuity equations

Recalling that $\Pi^\mu{}_\nu$ denotes the symmetric part of the tensor, the zero-component of the covariant conservation law (2.18) reads

$$\nabla_\mu \Pi^\mu{}_0 \equiv \partial_\mu \Pi^\mu{}_0 + \Gamma^\mu{}_{\rho\mu} \Pi^\rho{}_0 - \Gamma^\rho{}_{0\mu} \Pi^\mu{}_\rho = 0. \tag{2.37}$$

Separating the time and space components and noting that $\Pi^j{}_0 = \Pi_0{}^j$ vanishes due to the homogeneity of the universe space section, we obtain

$$\partial_0 \Pi^0{}_0 + \Gamma^j{}_{0j} \Pi^0{}_0 - \Gamma^i{}_{0j} \Pi^j{}_i = 0. \tag{2.38}$$

Substituting the connections (2.36) computed at $x^i = 0$, we get

$$\partial_0 \Pi^0{}_0 + 3\frac{\dot{a}}{ac}\Pi^0{}_0 - \frac{\dot{a}}{ac}\Pi^j{}_j = 0. \tag{2.39}$$

Using Eqs. (2.20) and (2.21), the components of the source current, computed at $x^i = 0$, are found to be

$$\Pi^0{}_0 = (\varepsilon_m - \varepsilon_\Lambda) \tag{2.40}$$

and

$$\Pi^j{}_j = -3(p_m + p_\Lambda). \tag{2.41}$$

Using the identifications (2.30), the conservation law (2.39) can be rewritten in the form

$$\frac{d}{dt}(\varepsilon_m - \varepsilon_\Lambda) + 3\frac{\dot{a}}{a}(\varepsilon_m - \varepsilon_\Lambda) + 3\frac{\dot{a}}{a}(p_m + p_\Lambda) = 0. \tag{2.42}$$

Assuming that the energy densities depend on the cosmic time t through the scale factor $a = a(t)$, and using the equations of state (2.33), the conservation law (2.42) becomes

$$\frac{d}{da}\left[a^3(\varepsilon_m - \varepsilon_\Lambda)\right] + 3a^2 w(\varepsilon_m + \varepsilon_\Lambda) = 0. \tag{2.43}$$

Its solution is

$$\varepsilon_m - \varepsilon_\Lambda = \beta\left(a^{-3-3w} - a^{-3+3w}\right) \tag{2.44}$$

with β an integration constant. In the contraction limit $l \to \infty$, the continuity equation (2.43) reduces to the usual expression of locally-Minkowski spacetimes

$$\frac{d}{da}(a^3 \varepsilon_m) + 3a^2 w \varepsilon_m = 0, \tag{2.45}$$

whose solution is

$$\varepsilon_m = \beta\, a^{-3-3w}. \tag{2.46}$$

2.4.3 Friedmann equations

Using the Levi-Civita components (2.36), the non-vanishing components of the Ricci tensor computed at $x^i = 0$ are found to be

$$\mathcal{R}_{00} = 3\frac{\ddot{a}}{ac^2} \tag{2.47}$$

$$\mathcal{R}_{ij} = -\frac{1}{c^2}(\ddot{a}a + 2\dot{a}^2 - 2c^2)\delta_{ij}. \tag{2.48}$$

The corresponding scalar curvature is

$$\mathcal{R} = \frac{6}{c^2}\left(\frac{\ddot{a}}{a} + \frac{\dot{a}^2}{a^2} - \frac{c^2}{a^2}\right). \tag{2.49}$$

Using these tensors in the de Sitter-invariant Einstein equation (2.19), we obtain the de Sitter-invariant Friedmann equations

$$H^2 = \frac{8\pi G}{3c^2}(\varepsilon_m - \varepsilon_\Lambda) - \frac{kc^2}{a^2} \qquad (2.50)$$

and

$$\frac{\ddot{a}}{a} = -\frac{4\pi G}{3c^2}\left[(\varepsilon_m - \varepsilon_\Lambda) + 3(p_m + p_\Lambda)\right], \qquad (2.51)$$

with $H = \dot{a}/a$ the Hubble parameter. Similarly to the ordinary Friedmann equations, taking the time derivative of equation (2.50), and using (2.51) to eliminate $\ddot{a}$, one obtains the conservation law (2.42).

The opposed signs of ε_m and ε_Λ come from their different physical effects: whereas the matter's energy density represents an attractive effect, the dark energy density represents a repulsive effect. Since the Friedmann equations are dynamic, it is natural that ε_m and ε_Λ enter the equations with opposite signs. In the de Sitter-invariant approach to cosmology, the difference $\varepsilon_m - \varepsilon_\Lambda$ is the fundamental variable for describing the universe dynamics. In other words, the balance between ε_m and ε_Λ determines how the universe evolves along with the cosmic time.[3] Note that despite ε_m and ε_Λ can evolve along with the cosmic time, they do it in such a way that the difference $\varepsilon_m - \varepsilon_\Lambda$ satisfies the Noether continuity equation (2.42).

2.5 Some physical implications

2.5.1 The topology of the universe

Considering the critical energy density $3H^2c^2/8\pi G = \varepsilon_c$, the Friedmann equation (2.50) can be rewritten in the form

$$1 = \Omega_m - \Omega_\Lambda - \frac{kc^2}{H^2 a^2}, \qquad (2.52)$$

where

$$\Omega_m \equiv \frac{\varepsilon_m}{\varepsilon_c} = \frac{8\pi G}{3H^2c^2}\varepsilon_m \quad \text{and} \quad \Omega_\Lambda \equiv \frac{\varepsilon_\Lambda}{\varepsilon_c} = \frac{8\pi G}{3H^2c^2}\varepsilon_\Lambda \qquad (2.53)$$

are, respectively, the matter and the dark-energy density parameters.

An essential feature of the de Sitter-invariant approach is that the energy densities ε_m and ε_Λ are not independent, a property inherited from the dependence of the proper conformal current $K^{\mu\nu}$ on the energy-momentum

---

[3]The negative sign of ε_Λ is a consequence of the de Sitter group, which carries a positive Λ. If the anti-de Sitter group governed the local kinematics, the sign of ε_Λ would be positive, leading to an unstable universe.

tensor $T^{\mu\nu}$, as can be seen from Eq. (2.21). This dependence establishes the constraint

$$\varepsilon_\Lambda = \gamma(t)\varepsilon_m, \tag{2.54}$$

with $\gamma(t)$ given by Eq. (2.29). Of course, the density parameters Ω_Λ and Ω_m are also related through

$$\Omega_\Lambda = \gamma(t)\Omega_m. \tag{2.55}$$

Using the Planck Collaboration values [23]

$$\Omega_\Lambda \simeq 0.69 \quad \text{and} \quad \Omega_m \simeq 0.31, \tag{2.56}$$

the present-day value of $\gamma(t)$ is

$$\gamma(t_0) \equiv \frac{\Omega_\Lambda}{\Omega_m} \simeq 2.2. \tag{2.57}$$

Consequently, the present-day value of the last term on the right-hand side of Eq. (2.52), which represents effects coming from the universe topology, is

$$-\frac{kc^2}{H^2 a^2} \simeq 1.38. \tag{2.58}$$

This relation implies that $k = -1$, pointing to a universe with hyperbolic space sections.

Note that the values (2.56) yields the relation

$$\Omega_m + \Omega_\Lambda = 1. \tag{2.59}$$

According to the Poincaré-invariant ΛCDM model, the above relation represents a dynamic equation and hints at a universe with a flat ($k = 0$) space section. Unlike the density parameters Ω_m and Ω_Λ, which represent natural constituents of the universe, the last term on the right-hand side of Eq. (2.52) does not represent a constituent of the universe. Even though it contributes to the universe dynamics, as far as the universe's inventory is concerned, only Ω_m and Ω_Λ must be considered. Since it is irrelevant to the universe's inventory whether their effects are attractive or repulsive, in the de Sitter-invariant approach, equation (2.59) is just an algebraic description of the universe's inventory without any dynamical meaning.

2.5.2 The current value of Λ

Let us pick up the conformal part of the field equation (2.24), which gives Λ in terms of the trace of the proper conformal current:

$$\Lambda = \frac{8\pi G}{c^4} \frac{K^\mu{}_\mu}{4l^2}. \tag{2.60}$$

Considering that the energy content of the present-day universe can be assumed to be preponderantly in the form of dust ($p_m = 0$), the trace of the proper conformal current computed at $x^i = 0$ is

$$K^\mu{}_\mu = \gamma(t)\varepsilon_m, \qquad (2.61)$$

where $\gamma(t)$ is a dimensionless parameter relating the dark and matter energy densities: $\gamma(t) = \varepsilon_\Lambda/\varepsilon_m$. Equation (2.60) can then be rewritten in the form

$$\Lambda = \frac{8\pi G}{c^4}\gamma(t)\varepsilon_m. \qquad (2.62)$$

Since $\gamma(t) = \varepsilon_\Lambda/\varepsilon_m$ is currently of order unity,[4] $\gamma(t) \sim 1$, we can write

$$\Lambda \sim \frac{8\pi G}{c^4}\varepsilon_m. \qquad (2.63)$$

Furthermore, as seen in Section 2.5.1, the critical energy density is also of the same order as ε_m and ε_Λ. Substituting

$$\varepsilon_m \sim \varepsilon_c = \frac{3H^2 c^2}{8\pi G} \qquad (2.64)$$

in Eq. (2.63), it yields a relation between Λ and the Hubble parameter H:

$$\Lambda \sim \frac{3H^2}{c^2}. \qquad (2.65)$$

Using the value $H \simeq 67.4$ Km/s/Mpc, the cosmological term is found to be

$$\Lambda \sim 10^{-52}\, \text{m}^{-2}, \qquad (2.66)$$

which is of the order of magnitude of the currently observed value. Besides providing an origin for Λ, the de Sitter-invariant approach to cosmology correctly determines its current order of magnitude.

2.5.3 The deceleration parameter

Together with the Hubble parameter, the deceleration parameter makes up the fundamental parameters to describe the universe's evolution. It is defined as

$$q \equiv -\frac{\ddot{a}}{a}\frac{1}{H^2} = -\frac{\ddot{a}a}{\dot{a}^2}. \qquad (2.67)$$

---

[4]In the Poincaré-invariant approach, since ε_Λ is constant and ε_m changes along the cosmic time, the condition $\varepsilon_\Lambda/\varepsilon_m \sim 1$ can only be interpreted as a coincidence [24]. However, in the de Sitter-invariant approach, where both ε_Λ and ε_m change along the cosmics time, that condition is not a coincidence but a characteristic of the de Sitter-invariant approach to cosmology.

In the ordinary case of locally Minkowski spacetimes with a cosmological constant Λ, the deceleration parameter has the form

$$q_M = \tfrac{1}{2}(1+3w)\Omega_m - \Omega_\Lambda. \tag{2.68}$$

On the other hand, using the Friedmann equations (2.50) and (2.51), the deceleration parameter in locally-de Sitter spacetimes is found to be

$$q_{dS} = \tfrac{1}{2}\big[\Omega_m(1+3w) - \Omega_\Lambda(1-3w)\big]. \tag{2.69}$$

Assuming that the present-day universe's content can be fairly described by dust ($w=0$), and using the values (2.56), the deceleration parameters are found to be

$$q_M \equiv \tfrac{1}{2}\Omega_m - \Omega_\Lambda \simeq -0.54 \tag{2.70}$$

and

$$q_{dS} \equiv \tfrac{1}{2}(\Omega_m - \Omega_\Lambda) \simeq -0.19. \tag{2.71}$$

One should remark that, although q_M and q_{dS} are formally and numerically similar, since Λ is constant in the expression for q_M and a function of the cosmic time in the expression for q_{dS}, the physical outcome of the two cases differ substantially.

2.5.4 Dimensionless coupling constants

Upon including a positive cosmological term Λ into gravitation, one adds a new repulsive interaction to spacetime physics besides the usual attractive interaction described by general relativity. Although the same field equation describes both interactions, their coupling constants differ substantially. For example, the dimensionless gravitational coupling constant for a particle of mass m is [25]

$$\alpha_G \equiv \frac{m^2}{m_P^2} = \frac{Gm^2}{\hbar c}, \tag{2.72}$$

with m_P the Planck mass. According to this expression, the strength of the gravitational interaction depends on how different the particle's mass m is concerning the Planck mass. Analogously, the dimensionless coupling constant of the interaction produced by the cosmological term Λ is

$$\alpha_\Lambda \equiv \frac{l_P^2}{l^2} \equiv \frac{\Lambda}{\Lambda_P} = \frac{G\hbar}{l^2 c^3}. \tag{2.73}$$

According to this expression, the strength of the Λ interaction depends on how different the particle's de Sitter pseudo-length is concerning the Planck pseudo-length. Even though both coupling constants depend on Newton's gravitational constant, their nature differs substantially. For example, whereas the gravitational coupling constant α_G depends on the squared mass m^2, the dark energy coupling constant α_Λ depends on the squared pseudolength l^{-2}. For comparison, let us recall that the electromagnetic fine-structure constant for a particle with electric charge q is defined as

$$\alpha_E \equiv \frac{q^2}{q_P^2} = \frac{q^2}{\hbar c}, \qquad (2.74)$$

with $q_P = \sqrt{\hbar c}$ the Planck charge. Similarly to the other interactions, the strength of the electromagnetic interaction depends on how different the particle's electric charge q is concerning the Planck charge.

2.5.5 Rescuing the local conformal transformations

Local (or proper) conformal symmetry is a broken symmetry of nature, which is expected to become an exact symmetry at the Planck scale [15]. However, as the Poincaré-invariant Einstein's special relativity does not include local conformal transformations in the spacetime kinematics, it is unclear how it could become relevant at the Planck scale. For this reason, local conformal transformation is sometimes considered the missing component of spacetime physics [26].

On the other hand, the de Sitter-invariant special relativity naturally includes the proper conformal transformations in the spacetime kinematics. Such inclusion occurs because the de Sitter group is obtained from Poincaré's by replacing translations with a combination of translations and proper conformal transformations – known as de Sitter "translations."

Note that the above inclusion does not change the dimension of the spacetime's local kinematics as Poincaré and de Sitter are ten-dimensional groups. Its unique effect is to change the local transitivity of spacetime from translations to a combination of translations and proper conformal transformations. Due to the inclusion of proper conformal transformations into the spacetime's local kinematics, it is now possible to probe its role at the Planck scale [14].

According to the de Sitter-invariant approach to physics, all Poincaré-invariant relativistic theories are incomplete because they lack the conformal sector brought about by the de Sitter-invariant approach. In particular, standard quantum mechanics is an incomplete theory and must be supplemented with a conformal sector. Recall that the completeness of standard quantum mechanics has already been questioned by Einstein, Podolsky, and Rosen [27], with their arguments known today as the EPR paradox. Due to the quantum origin of the de Sitter-invariant special relativity, we wonder if the de Sitter-invariant quantum mechanics, which incorporates a conformal sector, could somehow contribute to elucidating the EPR paradox.

2.6 Final remarks

Cosmological observations in the last decades have shown that the universe's expansion is accelerating [28, 29, 30, 31]. Since general relativity does not have a solution for a universe with accelerated expansion, it is necessary to incorporate external elements into the theory to drive the observed accelerated expansion.

In the ΛCDM model, there are two procedures for performing such inclusion. The first is to suppose the existence of a (perfect) fluid permeating the whole universe, whose energy-momentum tensor is the source of Λ. However, there are some difficulties with this procedure. To produce a repulsive effect, the fluid must satisfy an exotic equation of state not seen in any existing fluid. Furthermore, whatever is sourced by an energy-momentum current will couple to matter with the (mass-dependent) dimensionless gravitational coupling constant (2.72). The problem is that, due to its non-gravitational nature, dark energy should couple to matter with the conformal (Λ-dependent) dimensionless coupling constant (2.73). As discussed in Section 2.3.3, such a coupling can only be achieved if dark energy is sourced by the proper conformal current instead of the energy-momentum current.

The second procedure consists of adding a positive cosmological constant Λ to the left-hand side of Einstein's equation, which is then interpreted as a fundamental constant of nature. However, this procedure is not free of problems either. Owing to the strong equivalence principle, all solutions to the standard Einstein's equations are spacetimes that reduce locally to Minkowski. Since Minkowski is inexorably tied to a vanishing Λ, one is actually adding a vanishing Λ to general relativity. Therefore, the usual course of adding Λ to the left-hand side of Einstein's equation while keeping the spacetime's local kinematics governed by the Poincaré-invariant special relativity is unjustified.

Conversely, in the de Sitter-invariant general relativity, where all solutions to the gravitational field equations are spacetimes that reduce locally to the Sitter, the cosmological term Λ is constitutive and does not need to be added by hand to the left-hand side of the gravitational field equation. Consequently, the de Sitter-invariant Einstein's equation naturally has a solution for a universe with accelerated expansion. Furthermore, since Λ is encoded in the spacetime's local kinematics, it does not appear explicitly in the gravitational field equation, and is no longer required to be constant by the second Bianchi identity. These properties allow an entirely new view of the universe, where some issues of the standard model could find a solution.

There is a feeling today that the current problems of quantum gravity and cosmology will require new physics to be solved. By construction, the de Sitter-invariant approach to cosmology gives rise to deviations concerning the Poincaré-invariant approach, precisely for energies comparable to the Planck energy and at the universe's large scale. Accordingly, it could eventually provide the new physics necessary to tackle those problems.

Acknowledgments

DFL thanks Dalhousie University, Canada, for a Ph.D. scholarship. JGP thanks Conselho Nacional de Desenvolvimento Científico e Tecnológico, Brazil, for a research grant (Contract 312094/2021-3). JRS thanks Conselho Nacional de Desenvolvimento Científico e Tecnológico, Brazil, for a Ph.D. scholarship (Contract 166193/2018-6).

Bibliography

[1] G. Amelino-Camelia, *Doubly Special Relativity*, Nature **418**, 34 (2002); arXiv:gr-qc/0207049.

[2] G. Amelino-Camelia, *Doubly-Special Relativity: Facts, Myths and Some Key Open Issues*, Symmetry **2**, 230 (2010); arXiv:1003.3942.

[3] J. Kowalski-Glikman, *Observer-independent quantum of mass*, Physics Letters A **286**, 391 (2001); arXiv:hep-th/0102098.

[4] J. Magueijo and L. Smolin, *Lorentz invariance with an invariant energy scale*, Phys. Rev. Lett. **88**, 190403 (2002); arXiv:hep-th/0112090.

[5] C. W. Misner, K. S. Thorne and J. A. Wheeler, *Gavitation* (W. H. Freeman, New York, 1973).

[6] J. L. Synge, *Relativity: The General Theory* (Wiley, New York, 1960); in the Preface.

[7] R. Aldrovandi and J. G. Pereira, *An Introduction to Geometrical Physics*, 2nd edition (World Scientific, Singapore, 2016).

[8] R. Sharpe, *Differential Geometry: Cartan's Generalization of Klein's Erlangen Program* (Springer, Berlin, 1997).

[9] D. K. Wise, *MacDowell-Mansouri gravity and Cartan geometry*, Class. Quantum Grav. **27**, 155010 (2010); arXiv:gr-qc/0611154].

[10] R. Aldrovandi, J. P. Beltrán Almeida and J. G. Pereira, *de Sitter special relativity*, Class. Quantum Grav. **24**, 1385 (2007); arXiv:gr-qc/0606122.

[11] S. Cacciatori, V. Gorini and A. Kamenshchik, *Special Relativity in the 21st Century*, Ann. Phys. (Berlin) **17**, 728 (2008); arXiv:gr-qc/0807.3009.

[12] S. W. Hawking and G. F. R. Ellis, *The Large Scale Structure of Space-Time* (Cambridge University Press, Cambridge, 1973).

[13] F. Gürsey, in *Group Theoretical Concepts and Methods in Elementary Particle Physics*, ed. F. Gürsey (Gordon and Breach, New York, 1962).

[14] A. Araujo, H. Jennen, J. G. Pereira, A. C. Sampson and L. L. Savi, *On the spacetime connecting two aeons in conformal cyclic cosmology*, Gen. Rel. Grav. **47**, 151 (2015); arXiv:1503.05005.

[15] S. Coleman, *Aspects of Symmetry* (Cambridge University Press, Cambridge, 1985), Chapter 3.

[16] J. G. Pereira and A. C. Sampson, *de Sitter geodesics: reappraising the notion of motion*, Gen. Rel. Grav. **44**, 1299 (2012); arXiv:1110.0965.

[17] J. G. Pereira and D. F. López, *An Improved Framework for Quantum Gravity*, Universe, **6**, 243 (2020); arXiv:2012.09075.

[18] C. G. Callan, S. Coleman and R. Jackiw, *A New Improved Energy-Momentum Tensor*, Ann. Phys. (NY) **59**, 42 (1970).

[19] R. Aldrovandi and J. G. Pereira, *de Sitter Relativity: a New Road to Quantum Gravity?*, Found. Phys. **39**, 1 (2009); arXiv:0711.2274.

[20] S. Weinberg, *Cosmology* (Oxford Univ. Press, New York, 2008), page 6.

[21] R. Gilmore, *Lie Groups, Lie Algebras, and Some of Their Applications* (Wiley, New York, 1974).

[22] E. Inönü and E. P. Wigner, *On the Contraction of Groups and Their Representations*, Proc. Natl. Acad. Scien. **39**, 510 (1953).

[23] Planck Collaboration, *Planck 2018 results*, A&A **641**, A6 (2020).

[24] P. J. Steinhardt, in *Critical Problems in Physics*, edited by V. L. Fitch and R. Marlow (Princeton University Press, Princeton, 1997).

[25] J. D. Barrow and F. J. Tipler, *The Anthropic Cosmological Principle* (Oxford University Press, Oxford, 1988), page 293.

[26] G. 't Hooft, *Local conformal symmetry: The missing symmetry component for space and time*, Int. J. Mod. Phys. D **24**, 1543001 (2015); arXiv:1410.6675.

[27] A. Einstein, B. Podolsky and Rosen, *Can Quantum-Mechanical Description of Physical Reality Be Considered Complete?*, Phys. Rev. **47**, 777 (1935).

[28] A. G. Riess et al, *Observational Evidence from Supernovae for an Accelerating Universe and a Cosmological Constant*, ApJ **116**, 1009 (1998); arXiv:astro-ph/9805201.

[29] S. Perlmutter, *et al*, *Measurements of Omega and Lambda from 42 High-Redshift Supernovae*, ApJ **517**, 565 (1999); arXiv:astro-ph/9812133.

[30] P. de Bernardis, *et al*, *A Flat Universe from High-Resolution Maps of the Cosmic Microwave Background Radiation*, Nature, **404**, 955 (2000); arXiv:astro-ph/0004404.

[31] I. Sevilla-Noarbe, *et al*, *Dark Energy Survey Year 3 Results: Photometric Data Set for Cosmology*, ApJS **254**, 24 (2021); arXiv:2012.12825.

3

Effects of new physics on the standard model: parameters and vice versa

M. W. Barela, V. Pleitez

Abstract: This note discusses the matter of probing Beyond the Standard Model physics and how, to succeed in this quest, the interpretations of the Standard Model regarding observed phenomena must be utilized with caution. We give several specific examples of why this is necessary and assess general scenarios in which it is specially important. In particular, we call attention to the fact that once the Standard Model (SM) is finally replaced, the parameters of the new theory which embed those of the SM must be re-derived directly from data instead of inherited through their expected relations with those of the SM.

3.1 Introduction

One could say that our understanding of the electroweak interactions among elementary particles evolved through around 117 years, beginning with the discovery of radioactivity (1986) and culminating in that of the Higgs boson (2012). A turning point in this process was the proposal of the formerly called "Weinberg-Salam Model" which was a two lepton families version of what it is now called "electroweak standard model" [1, 2]. As is now known, however, this model was mathematically inconsistent: it featured the so-called triangle anomalies. Because it only possessed leptonic doublets and singlets (including massless neutrinos), it was incapable to cancel the anomaly factor, and, due to the chiral nature of electroweak interactions, could not upgrade the classical gauge symmetry to a quantum one.

From the theoretical point of view, the model could be considered mathematically consistent only when two generations of quarks were included [3] and the strong interaction described by the QCD [4] was properly formulated [5]. Experimentally, these advancements were confirmed when the quark charm c and the asymptotic freedom of the strong interactions were discovered. In that newly formed model, the triangle anomalies cancel out generation by generation, thanks, in particular, to the color degrees of freedom. As an immediate accidental benefit of this development, the old question of why the muon must exist acquired a simple answer: because the model with only three quarks and two leptons is anomalous.

Note that, *at the time*, if the Weinberg-Salam model had been perceived to be anomalous, discarding the model in favour of some consistent alternative instead of predicting additional representation content would be, in principle, a viable position. The experimental observation which was, then, interpreted as the particles which were theorized in that context could have been found to correspond to different theoretical objects. Of course, with our current familiarity with the SM as an unimaginably accomplished fundamental theory, such remarks may sound odd or of little use, but, as we shall argue, it is an important notion to have in mind.

3.2 Examples in the standard model construction

For a further, less drastic thought experiment, consider the discovery of the τ. The first evidence for the existence of a heavy lepton was the observation of the anomalous events [6]

$$e^+ + e^- \to e^+ + \mu^- + \text{misising energy} \tag{3.1}$$

To interpret such events as intermediated by a sequential lepton one must impose a theoretical framework. In particular, it was assumed that the usual weak interaction is the ultimate description of nature, at least in the appropriate scenario. In practice, this amounts to considering that the hypothesized τ decays are mediated only by the W vector boson alone, *i.e.*, that the lepton-W and quark-W vertices have the standard electroweak couplings in the form of the four-fermion effective interactions – and that the physical process may be subsumed to this sole contribution. Decays of the τ through the electromagnetic interaction such as $\tau \to e(\mu) + \gamma$ or through exotic interactions, for instance, are forbidden and irrelevant, respectively. There are additional non general inputs needed for the prediction of the τ decay modes: see, for instance Ref. [7]. The process in Eq. (3.1) may then be interpreted as

$$e^+ + e^- \to \gamma^* \to \tau^+ + \tau^-,$$
$$\tau^+ \to e^+ + \nu_e + \bar{\nu}_\tau, \qquad \tau^- \to \mu^- + \bar{\nu}_\mu + \nu_\tau, \qquad (3.2)$$

being τ a sequential spin-1/2 lepton. The possibility of spin-0 particles was ruled out because the rates of $\tau \to e^- + X$ and $\tau \to \mu + X$, where X are hadrons, are equal within experimental error. Additionally, the $e^+ + e^- \to W^+ + W^-$ channel was ruled out by the energy distribution of the electron and muon [7, 8]. To synthesize, although the process $e^+ + e^- \to \tau^+ + \tau^-$ relies only on precise QED calculations, the τ cannot be detected as a long-lived particle, but must instead be reconstructed from its final-state products which involve weak interactions and undetectable neutrinos produced only by the W vector boson [9, 10].

Indeed, these remarks could be made regarding any particle of the latest generations of the SM or the massive vector bosons. The $W^\pm$, for instance, was discovered in 1983 through identification of its leptonic decay channels: $W^\pm \to e^\pm \nu_e(\bar{\nu}_e)$ in both UA1 and U2 and $W^\pm \to \mu^\pm \nu_\mu(\bar{\nu}_\mu)$ in UA2 [11]. In the theory that replaces the SM, or New Standard Model (NSM), however, a particle that is identifiable with the $W^\pm$ could have exotic decay channels.

The lesson we want to emphasize is that high energy physics is model-loaded. This has not always been necessarily the case. For instance, the masses of the electron and muon were measured isolating the electromagnetic theory, quite generally, and no specific non-Abelian model was assumed. In particular, note that the electromagnetic interaction is the only force to posses a fully classic counterpart. This was not the case of the $\tau, c, b, t, W^\pm, Z^0, H^0$ particles whose masses were interpreted in the context of the standard model. To strengthen the intuition behind these philosophy, let us put forward a few more examples.

A given model is determined by its gauge, accidental symmetries and representation content. This last element implies that the electroweak standard model restricted to two matter generations (2ESM) is, by construction, different from the current three matter generations theory (3ESM). With two generations, the quark sector possesses a single measure of mixture, the so-called Cabibbo angle θ_c [12], related to the unitary mixing matrix by

$$|V_{ud}|^2 + |V_{us}|^2 \equiv \cos^2 \theta_c + \sin^2 \theta_c = 1. \qquad (3.3)$$

In the context of the 3ESM, however, the mixtures are measured by three angles and one physical phase. In this case, the analogous of Eq. (3.3) is

$$|V_{ud}|^2 + |V_{us}|^2 + |V_{ub}|^2 = 1, \qquad (3.4)$$

where, as determined phenomenologically,

$$|V_{ud}|^2 + |V_{us}|^2 \lesssim 1, \quad |V_{ub}|^2 \ll 1. \qquad (3.5)$$

We see that interpreting phenomenology within a different model induce a small but not trivial change in the new analogous parameters. If we had simply embedded the 2ESM into the 3ESM hypothesis, we would obtain $V_{ub} = V_{cb} = V_{tb} = 0$ (and the same for the remaining top parameters). Of course, the new model also introduces a new parameter (a physical phase) which induces strictly new physics (CP violation!). Note, in particular, that the parameter analogous to the Cabibo angle in the new model is altered.

At this point, one could argue that this is all obvious or innocuous. Indeed, a model proposed to replace the SM should reproduce its good predictions and, in one way or another, imply it as an approximation at energy scales of up to around 1 TeV. The theoretical mechanism through which this is usually built-in new models is that of deeming exotic particles to be heavy (after all, the SM accommodates the current measured cross sections without the need for extra particles), and concluding that their effects are completely decoupled [13], or they are weakly interacting. As final consequence, then, the parameters (specially effective ones) in the new model which are derived from parameters of the SM may be evaluated using their known values. Although this should be a fair assumption in a large sector of theory space, it is not a general fact (to start, the decoupling theorem may not guarantee the insignificance of exotic effects in every situation [14, 15], but this is not the only flaw in the argument above).

Another example, of a parameter that should certainly change if new singly charged scalar and/or vector bosons are discovered and appended to the SM context is the mass of the top quark. This would provide a possible explanation as to why its mass seems exaggeratedly large in relation to the other particles masses in the model. Moreover, this would represent additional evidence (which has resisted over 20 years) for the discrepancy of 2.4σ in the muon $g-2$ factor [16].

3.3 Patterns to avoid in the beyond standard model phenomenology

Ultimately, our discussion concerns theoretical occurrences which may cause phenomenological predictions to not apply to the models under consideration. Let us analyse three general patterns of the appearance of this phenomenon. For that, consider the usual interpretation of experimental measurements in the context of exploratory phenomenology, which naturally also applies to the examples already given. In such scenarios, there exists, for instance, a statistically significant upper limit on the cross section of some convenient process. In the ideal scenario, this process isolates an exotic contribution with little competing background. The observation is then cast in the form of a prediction resulting from a minimal effective model, and the upper limit on the cross section is translated into a limit on new physics parameters, such as masses or mixing angles. In this stage, two steps (which are ultimately equivalent) are tacitly implied by the usual procedure: choice of effective model and simplification. As a first example consider the search for a doubly-charged vector boson. The preferred channels for the observability of its effects, in general, involve its interactions with charged leptons. Its form is often assumed to be equivalent to [17, 18, 19]

$$\mathcal{L}_{U\ell\ell} = \sum_a g_{U\ell\ell} \bar{\ell}_a^c \gamma^\mu P_L \ell_a U_\mu^{++} + \text{H.c.}, \quad (3.6)$$

where P_L is the left-handed projector, ℓ_a is a lepton field ($a = e, \mu, \tau$) and $g_{U\ell\ell}$ is an effectively arbitrary perturbative coupling. The interaction above, however, is far from skeptical or model independent. Indeed, the most general relevant interaction allowed by Lorentz invariance, renormalizability and reality of the action is given by [20]

$$\begin{aligned}\mathcal{L}_{U\ell\ell} &= \sum_{b>a} g_{U\ell\ell} \left\{ \bar{\ell}_a^c \gamma^\mu [P_L(V_U)_{ab} - P_R(V_U)_{ba}] \ell_b\, U_\mu^{++} + \bar{\ell}_a \gamma^\mu [P_L(V_U^\dagger)_{ab} \right. \\ &\quad - \left. P_R(V_U^\dagger)_{ba}] \ell_b^c\, U_\mu^{--} \right\} + \sum_a g_{U\ell\ell} \left\{ \bar{\ell}_a^c \gamma^\mu [P_L(V_U)_{aa}] \ell_a\, U_\mu^{++} \right. \\ &\quad + \left. \bar{\ell}_a \gamma^\mu [P_L(V_U^\dagger)_{aa}] \ell_a^c\, U_\mu^{--} \right\} \end{aligned} \quad (3.7)$$

The major difference between this form and that of Eq. (3.6) is the unitary mixing matrix V_U, which, by naturalness principles, cannot be ignored. Moreover, $V_U = 1$ could only be the case for the simplest mass matrices – diagonalizable by orthogonal transformations instead of by biunitary ones – which would imply strong constraints on the mass of the boson $U^{\pm\pm}$.

Notice that, even if the searched reaction involves diagonal interactions, such as the case of $pp \to e^+e^+e^-e^-$ or $pp \to \mu^+\mu^+e^-e^-$, and the $g_{U\ell\ell}$ coupling is left free, there is still an imprecision as the $U\ell\ell$ interaction is not universal and may couple the boson to different flavors with different strength. What we have underlined is that a popular framework for the interpretation of experimental results in the search for the $U^{\pm\pm}$ *definitely* produces inaccurate predictions for the exact parameters of some underlying theory. Of course, such simplifications may represent an acceptable approximation and translate to true, useful constraints, but the risk that it causes harmful distortions is also real.

The second pattern we mentioned may be seen in studies which do not scan over $g_{U\ell\ell}$ and, at least implicitly, assume the 3-3-1 model. Comparing the interaction in Eq. (3.7) with the prediction of the 3-3-1, one obtains $g_{U\ell\ell} = g_{3L}/\sqrt{2}$, where g_{3L} is the $SU(3)_L$ coupling. This is then used as a benchmark, equating g_{3L} to the standard model $SU(2)_L$ coupling g_{2L}^{SM}. This may source theoretical errors by several mechanisms. To start, the 3-3-1 g_{3L} is expected to be equal to g_{2L} at a single matching scale [21], not identically. At the few TeV energies where the relevant process is explored, g_{3L} should be used directly. Its value must be obtained from its running and matching with g_{2L} (this process should involve extra unknown parameters). Additionally, the 3-3-1 coupling g_{2L} is not generically equal to the SM g_{2L}^{SM} at any arbitrary scale, as their running may involve distinct group factors and contributing degrees of freedom.

Once more, the simplification of setting $g_{U\ell\ell} = g_{2L}^{SM}/\sqrt{2}$ may be a good approximation in the LHC era. But what about neutral current or even purely electromagnetic processes at high scales, which, within the 3-3-1 context, involve g_X? This coupling should be related to g_Y carefully (which is rarely accomplished) and, differently from g_{3L}, runs aggressively with energy. As a result, failing to interpret experimental input within the framework one wishes to constrain in a precise manner may again lead to unreliable conclusions.

Finally, the last pattern is even more general and applies to cases discussed before. For the sole sake of simplicity, a new experimental result is usually translated into a requirement on some parameter space through modelling with a single exotic degree of freedom. This relies on the hypothesis of absolute dominance (within expected precision) of the chosen exotic particle with relation to the contribution of other exotic concepts. This is, however, not general and ultimately amounts to a choice of model in which additional particles are absent or have effects which are pushed to sufficiently higher regimes. This usually represents a reasonable benchmark choice and is rarely general, so that, when possible, the extra contributions of a specific model should be assessed simultaneously.

The presence of subdominant, not accounted for, effects, however, can not only strengthen the constraints on masses, for instance, as in the case of the top we discussed – it can also *weaken* it. Indeed, destructive interference effects which overcome the pure contribution of the second particle are possible and allow for smaller masses to become allowed, in principle. It has been explicitly verified, in a model independent analysis over an exotic sector with a doubly charged vector bilepton, a flavor changing neutral scalar and a doubly charged one, that interference with the neutral scalar may weaken the bound on the $U^{\pm\pm}$ by up to 20% [20]. This is another very general way in which disregarding the most complete form of some specific framework may render predictions less useful.

In summary: the ideal phenomenological program, in the sense of the reliability of its results, is one which is framework specific. This is, of course, not possible in every situation, as some theoretical concepts are ubiquitous or, on the contrary, are not known to exist within a specific model. Additionally, to examine some hypothesis in a model independent fashion is not only useful but, sometimes, the obvious preferred choice, as it is impractical to reevaluate each established concept in every analysis. However, the lesson of our discussion is that once some model is actively proven to be a viable replacement of the SM or is under focused consideration, every phenomenological statement should be made within its own context. This means not only that an experimental input must be interpreted through complete parametrization of its physics, but also that values for old parameters (such as the SM g_{2L}, g_Y in the example above) *should not* be carried to the NSM. Instead, the analogous, dependent or parameters which embed the old ones should be rederived by a new investigation of the original phenomenological information.

3.4 Examples in classical physics

In fact, the issues discussed in Sec. 3.2 are not exclusive to quantum field theories. For instance, one could realize, in the context of classical mechanics, that some process is not well described by the conservation of the usual kinetic energy $T = mv^2/2$. One could then go one step further and propose the simple polynomial extension $T = mv^2/2 + \kappa m v^4$ as a new dynamical model, which we could call Refined Newtonian. One would test this against observations and fit the new κ-parameter. Now, suppose, in the thought experiment, that Special Relativity was eventually discovered and found to be a better theory. The κ of Refined Newtonian dynamics is naturally embedded in Special Relativity as a low order parameter in the expansion of γ of $T = mc^2(\gamma-1)$ in powers of v/c. However, $\kappa = 3/8c^2$ is now a calculable factor and its value differs from the one found within the framework of Refined Newtonian theory.

Another example in older physics is the Fresnel drag coefficient, $f = 1 - 1/n^2$, where n is the refraction index of the substance, proposed to explain the negative result of the Arago experiment, the first attempt at measuring the absolute motion of the Earth. According to Fresnel, the ether inside a substance is partly dragged when the substance moves with respect to the exterior ether. If a transparent substance moves with 'absolute' velocity v, the ether within it moves with absolute velocity $v_{\text{drag}} = fv$. This was, at the time, a satisfactory (phenomenological) solution to the conclusion of the Arago experiment. In some sense, this hypothesis could be considered as a 'Refined' Maxwell theory, an extension of it. Only with the appearance of the alternative theory, the theory of special relativity, it was possible to understand the hypothesis of Fresnel [22]. Fresnel's f coefficient appears just as an approximation when $v \ll c$.

Another example is the precession of Mercury orbit. At the end of the XIX century, for explaining that anomaly, there was some proposals which assumed modifications of the Newton Gravitation Law which depended on velocity, but each one predicted a value for the anomaly which was below the observed one would depend on velocity, but the results gave always a value for this anomaly below the observed one. The theory of general relativity (TGR) also provides for such a modification of the Newton law depending on the velocity, but it gives the correct result. That is, it was not enough to propose such a potential depending on the velocity. There was only one, that of the TGR.

3.5 Conclusions

After what was argued above, it would not be surprising if the W boson had a mass that differs from the one obtained in the context of the SM [23], or the Cabibbo angle turns out to be different from the accepted value. The first case could be an evidence in favour of models such as the left-right symmetric ones [24] or of some supersymmetric theories [25]. The second disparity, of the Cabibbo anomaly, in turn, could be explained by the existence of new particles, such as, for instance, leptoquarks [26].

In conclusion, although simplifications – such as single exotic particle lagrangians with no mixing – are understandable and necessary in Beyond the Standard Model physics, we urge phenomenologists to make an effort to precisely define a framework in order to derive and state results. Furthermore, once a viable replacement to the SM is finally confirmed, it should not be seen as an "extension" of it, but as an alternative model altogether, which includes the SM as an approximation. Many of the parameters that were interpreted and fitted in the context of the SM should then be reconsidered. Which model, if any, would be that?

Acknowledgments

MB is grateful to CNPq for the financial support.

Bibliography

[1] S. Weinberg, *A Model of Leptons*, Phys. Rev. Lett. **19**, 1264 (1967).

[2] A. Salam, *Weak and Electromagnetic Interactions*, Conf. Proc. C 680519, 367 (1968).

[3] S. L. Glashow, J. Iliopoulos and L. Maiani, *Weak Interactions with Lepton-Hadron Symmetry*, Phys. Rev. D **2**, 1285 (1970).

[4] What we currently call "the standard model" has been proposed by many theorists and experimental, so it is better to cite a source where the main references appear, for example in Ref [5].

[5] J. L. Rosner, *Resource Letter: The Standard model and beyond*, Am. J. Phys. **71**, 302 (2003); arXiv:hep-ph/0206176.

[6] M. L. Perl, G. S. Abrams, A. Boyarski, M. Breidenbach, D. Briggs, F. Bulos, W. Chinowsky, J. T. Dakin, G. J. Feldman and C. E. Friedberg, *et al. Evidence for Anomalous Lepton Production in e^+e^- Annihilation*, Phys. Rev. Lett. **35**, 1489 (1975).

[7] M. L. Perl, G. J. Feldman, G. S. Abrams, M. S. Alam, A. Boyarski, M. Breidenbach, F. Bulos, W. Chinowsky, J. Dorfan and C. E. Friedberg, *et al. Properties of Anomalous e mu Events Produced in e^+e^- Annihilation*, Phys. Lett. B **63**, 466 (1976).

[8] M. L. Perl, *The Tau Lepton*, Ann. Rev. Nucl. Part. Sci. **30**, 299 (1980).

[9] L. Zani, *Studies on τ decays at Belle II*, arXiv:2307.06598.

[10] I. Adachi *et al.* [Belle-II], *Measurement of the τ-lepton mass with the Belle-II experiment*, arXiv:2305.19116.

[11] L. Di Lella and C. Rubbia, *The Discovery of the W and Z Particles*, Adv. Ser. Direct. High Energy Phys. **23**, 137 (2015).

[12] N. Cabibbo, *Unitary Symmetry and Leptonic Decays*, Phys. Rev. Lett. **10**, 531 (1963).

[13] T. Appelquist and J. Carazzone, *Infrared Singularities and Massive Fields*, Phys. Rev. D **11**, 2856 (1975).

[14] D. Toussaint, *Renormalization Effects From Superheavy Higgs Particles*, Phys. Rev. D **18**, 1626 (1978).

[15] F. Arco, D. Domenech, M. J. Herrero and R. A. Morales, *Non-decoupling effects from heavy Higgs bosons by matching 2HDM to HEFT amplitudes*, arXiv:2307.15693.

[16] D. P. Aguillard *et al.*, [Muon g-2], *Measurement of the Positive Muon Anomalous Magnetic Moment to 0.20 ppm*, arXiv:2308.06230.

[17] G. Corcella, C. Corianò, A. Costantini and P. H. Frampton, *Exploring Scalar and Vector Bileptons at the LHC in a 331 Model*, Phys. Lett. B **785**, 73 (2018); arXiv:1806.04536.

[18] G. Corcella, C. Coriano, A. Costantini and P. H. Frampton, *Bilepton Signatures at the LHC*, Phys. Lett. B **773**, 544 (2017); arXiv:1707.01381.

[19] E. Ramirez Barreto, Y. A. Coutinho and J. Sa Borges, *Vector- and Scalar-Bilepton Pair Production in Hadron Colliders*, Phys. Rev. D **83**, 075001 (2011); arXiv:1103.1267.

[20] M.W. Barela and J. Montaño-Domínguez, *Constraints on exotic particle masses from flavor violating charged lepton decays and the role of interference*, Phys. Rev. D **106**, 055013 (2022); arXiv:2205.08604.

[21] M. W. Barela, *A new analysis on matching conditions and the 331 Landau pole*, arXiv:2305.05066.

[22] P. T. Landsberg, *The Relativistic Theory of the Fresnel Drag Coefficient*, Nature **189**, 654 (1961).

[23] T. Aaltonen *et al.* [CDF], *High-precision measurement of the W boson mass with the CDF II detector*, Science **376**, 170 (2022).

[24] H. Diaz, E. Castillo-Ruiz, O. Pereyra Ravinez and V. Pleitez, *Explicit parity violation in $SU(2)_L \otimes SU(2)_R \otimes U(1)_{B-L}$ models*, J. Phys. G **48**, 085010 (2021); arXiv:2002.03524.

[25] M. C. Rodriguez, *Gauge bosons masses in the context of the Supersymmetric $SU(3)_C \otimes SU(3)_L \otimes U(1)_N$ Model*; arXiv:2205.09109.

[26] M. Kirk, *Cabibbo angle anomalies and a global fit to vector-like quarks*; arXiv:2308.09669.

4

Symmetry breaking and confinement in supersymmetric gauge field theories

C. A. Savoy

Abstract: Recent experiments have settled severe restrictions on supersymmetric completions aimed at solving some fundamental questions beyond the Standard Model of particle physics. Nevertheless, supersymmetry remains a precious tool to understand the behaviour of gauge field theories as much as it augments our insight on the evolution of their different regimes at low and high energies. Two out of many applications of supersymmetry to particle physics are discussed here with an emphasis on some mathematical aspects: spontaneous symmetry breaking and confinement. The important algebraic instrument is the equivalence between the orbits defined on the manifold of complex fields by the action of the group of gauge symmetry and the analytic polynomials that are invariant under this action. It provides a general powerful method to find all symmetry breaking patterns of supersymmetric gauge field theories with fermions and scalars. Confinement, the fact that baryons and mesons are agglomerates of quarks (and gluons) is understood as the effect of very strong gauge interactions being screened inside the composite states. An important theoretical constraint requires the matching between the anomalies of the global Lie symmetries of the theory for the constituting fields at high energies and that of their composites at low energies. This property is related to the existence of the syzygies, algebraic relations among analytic invariants, through a conjecture, as a result of some remarkable attributes of supersymmetric theories.

4.1 Supersymmetry: what for?

Since Ruben was a mathematical physicist, I would like to present here a more mathematical aspect of my own work on applications of supersymmetry to particle physics.

Supersymmetry is an extension of Poincaré algebra. The Coleman-Mandula theorem excludes non-trivial Lie algebra extensions in 4D, but it can be generalized to show that supersymmetries are the unique extensions when the Poincaré algebra is upgraded to superalgebras by the addition of anticommutation relations. One introduces N *spinorial supercharges* Q_A with the anticommutators,

$$\{\bar{Q}_A, Q_B\} = \delta_{AB} \sigma_\mu P^\mu$$

giving the energy and the momenta as "bilinears" of the Q_A. The supercharges have spin $\frac{1}{2}$ and as such they connect a fermion to a boson. Also $N \leq 8$ as we physically assume the spin 2 of the graviton as the highest one (since aligning 8 different Q_A a state can jump from helicity -2 to $+2$) . Indeed, increasing the space symmetry to "super-Poincaré" requires the gravity theory to de promoted to a supergravity theory. Here, I shall not even mention the beautiful properties of extended ($N > 1$) supersymmetry and supergravity – which answer for much of the "what for" in the title – because they lead to more involved, less appealing models when applied to particle physics and field theory. Hence, the discussion below is restricted to one "supercharge".

Now, why so many particle physicists concentrate their theoretical and experimental researches on the quest for supersymmetry for the last 40 years or so? Well, because supersymmetry could be the clue to solve the most important questions beyond the established (effective) field theory of particles, the Standard Model (SM), e.g.,

1. Why the cosmological constant is small (with respect to particle physics scales)

2. Why the Higgs is (relatively) light?

3. Why are the strengths of the three fundamental forces of Nature, apart from gravity, so different?

4. Why is there more matter (quarks, electrons) than antimatter in the universe?

5. What is the dark matter that seems to prevail over the observed matter in the Universe?

Actually, the simplest implementation of supersymmetry into the SM is rather straighforward, one has to add a new boson for each fermion and vice-versa, *i.e.*, one "sparticle" for each known particle: squarks, sleptons, gauginos (gauge fermions), higgsinos (Higgs fermions), plus an additional Higgs-higgsino doublet for anomaly cancelation! Once supersymmetry is broken at some scale $\sqrt{\Lambda M_P}$ (the so-called super-Higgs mechanism), where M_P is the Planck mass), the sparticles get masses roughly $O(\Lambda)$ and disappear at lower energies (but see below!). Amazingly, the supersymmetrized SM suggests an intrinsic solution to each of the above questions provided Λ is around or below 1TeV:

1. Energy is non-negative since $P^0 = |Q|^2$ and the vacuum supersymetry invariance reads $Q|\text{vac}> = 0$, thus zero energy. Conversely, spontaneous supersymetry breaking, $Q|\text{vac}> \neq 0$, implies positive vacuum energy.

2. Radiative corrections to the Higgs mass, mainly from its strong coupling to the top quark, might induce the Higgs mechanism with a light Higgs mass.

3. Running the strength of the three fundamental forces to high energy, with the sparticles included in the Feynman loops, shows that their three couplings seem to become equal at a very high energy, suggesting their unification into a larger gauge symmetry.

4. There are several potential sources of matter-antimatter symmetry breaking in supersymmetric models.

5. An intrinsic parity of the theory ($R = -1$ for sparticles), implies a selection rule and that the lightest sparticle be a stable, massive, weak interacting particle, an elegant dark matter candidate.

Of course, by now and after many a year of experimental and theoretical research, the Large Hadron Collider at CERN has excluded to a large extent supersymmetric particles at the scales needed in the issues above. The end of a dream, for sure, but the countless efforts were all but vain, because in the quest for truth the hard task is often to prove that bewitching ideas are wrong or not present in Nature!

In any case, it brings us back to the question: what for, in particle physics? Well, the supersymetric gauge field theories have nice properties, such as the absence of quadratic divergences, only wave function renormalization (see below), a relationship between fermion and boson interactions and, in a non-perturbative regime, dualities between ultraviolet and infrared theories. Their study may suggest new insights on more realistic analogous models without supersymmetry. In extended supersymmetry there are more constraints and, even being less realistic, they have propelled important work on Feynman amplitudes ($N = 4$) and on divergences in quantum gravity ($N = 8$).

In the following, I shall illustrate the application of supersymmetry to a general study of gauge symmetry breaking, and to discuss the duality and confinement properties of some field theories, concentrating on their algebraic aspects.

4.2 Spontaneous gauge symmetry breaking

A supersymmetric field theory (I discuss here rigid or global supersymmetry, meaningful in the flat space approximation, and I avoid the use of superfields that are not familiar to many physicists) is totally specified by:

- The gauge invariance, with a compact Lie group G, and the corresponding massless gauge bosons and their fermion partners, as well as their gauge couplings to everything else through the introduction of covariant derivatives. I denote the generators of the G-algebra, T^A.

- N supersymmetric multiplets (z^i, ψ^i) with complex scalars and 2-component fermions, respectively, where $\{z^i, \bar{z}^{\bar{\imath}}\}$ are the coordinates on a complex Kahler-manifold whose metrics is given by its Kahler-potential, a real function $K(z^i, \bar{z}^{\bar{\imath}})$, through the derivatives:

$$\partial_i \partial_{\bar{\imath}} K = g_{i\bar{\imath}}(z, \bar{z}), \qquad \partial_i K = \partial K / \partial z^i.$$

The simplest example is $\mathbb{C}^N$ with $K(z^i, \bar{z}^{\bar{\imath}})$ given by $\sum_i z^i \bar{z}^{\bar{\imath}}$. Thus, the Kahler-potential defines all the kinetic terms in the Lagrangian of this sector, which I call hereafter the *matter-Higgs sector* by analogy with the corresponding sectors in Nature. The invariance of the theory under G implies the invariance of $K(z, \bar{z})$ or, more precisely, of the metric.

- The self interactions within the matter-Higgs sector (Yukawa and scalar couplings) are all encoded in an analytic function (usually a polynomial), the superpotential $W(z^i)$ ($W(z)$ for short) that completes the specification of a supersymmetric field theory and whose coefficients fix the couplings. Because of its analyticity, the invariance under G implies its invariance under the complexified G^c, a larger invariance with crucial consequences as stressed below.

A remarkable property of supersymmetric gauge theories is that there is only *wave function renormalization*, which means that only the metrics, *i.e.*, the Kahler-potential, is deformed by radiative corrections, while the analytic superpotential W remains invariant. Therefore, only the Kahler-potential is scale dependent, though this will not affect directly the discussion below.

Let us turn now to the discussion of *gauge symmetry breaking* in supersymmetric gauge theories, namely, when supersymmetry remains unbroken. The point I want to emphasize here is that the determination of all patterns of symmetry breaking of these theories can be systematically performed with a couple of very simple general equations, where analyticity plays a central role.

As a corolary of the energy positiveness, the supersymmetric scalar potential, $V(z^i, \bar{z}^i)$ is non negative and reads:

$$V(z^i, \bar{z}^i) = \sum_i |\partial_i W(z)|^2 + \sum_A (K_i(z,\bar{z}) T^{Ai}_j z^j)^2 \geq 0 \quad (4.1)$$

where the $N \times N$ matrices T^A correspond to the linear (generally reducible) representation of the generators of G for $\{z\}$, the whole matter-Higgs sector. Supersymmetry is preserved if and only if this sum of positive terms vanish in the vacuum, which is then an absolute minimum, hence it is broken only if V is always positive!

We now discuss the conditions for supersymmetric gauge symmetry breaking, when some of the non-singlet scalars z^i do not vanish at a supersymmetric minimum defined by:

$$\partial_i W(z) = 0, \forall i \ (\mathcal{F}) \quad \text{and} \quad K_i(z,\bar{z}) T^{Ai}_j z^j) = 0, \forall T^A \ (\mathcal{D}) \quad (4.2)$$

The first one ($\mathcal{F}$) is a set of N analytic equations while the second ($\mathcal{D}$) are N real equations that are not easy to solve but for N small.

It was pointed out in [1], then completely proved in [2, 3], that the sufficient and necessary condition for ($\mathcal{D}$) is the existence of some *analytic invariant* polynomial J(z) such that

$$\exists J(z) \,|\, \partial_i J(z) T^{Ai}_j z^j = 0 \quad \text{and} \quad \partial_i (J(z) - \lambda K(z,\bar{z})) = 0 \quad (\mathcal{D}) \quad (4.3)$$

where λ is a Lagrange multiplier to keep $K(z,\bar{z})$ fixed. Notice that the invariance of J under G implies the sufficiency, the necessity proof being more involved.

Therefore, once we find these polynomials we define all solutions. Remembering the invariance under G^c to mean $W(G^c z) = W(z)$, where $G^c z$ represents the *orbit* of z, the solutions of ($\mathcal{F}$) extend to the whole orbit, while those of ($\mathcal{D}$) extend only to Gz. Hence, each $V(z,\bar{z}) = 0$ solution defines a pattern of breaking $G \to H \subset G$, where H is its little group, *i.e.*, $Hz = z$, thus of its orbit Gz modulo a transformation of GHG^{-1}. The little groups are ordered according to the relation: $H \subset H'$ provided H is conjugate to a subgroup of G. Similarly G-orbits are ordered according to their little groups. The orbits with the largest little groups are called critical.

The interest of the above theorem is that though non-analytic, ($\mathcal{D}$), just like ($\mathcal{F}$), refer to analytic invariants, which possess interesting properties we now turn to discuss. Given any G and any (generally reducible) representation R of dimension N acting linearly on $\{z\}$, one can find an integrity basis of n analytic invariant polynomials $\{J^a(z)\}$ such that any invariant polynomial in $P(z)$ can be written as a polynomial $\tilde{P}(J^a)$ in these J^a. One can choose this basis so that the J^a are homogeneous, of degree d_a, respectively. However, for N large enough (see below) there can be a number s of algebraic relations among the elements of this basis, called *sygyzies*, that constrain the basis,

$$\tilde{S}_\alpha(J^a) = S_\alpha(z^i) \equiv 0 \qquad \alpha = 1,....,s \qquad (4.4)$$

The values taken by the set $\{J^a(z)\}$ constrained by the syzygies on the z orbits defines a manifold in $\mathbb{C}^n$ of dimension $n-s$. This identification can be shown to be one-to-one. In that sense the algebraic manifold defined by the syzygies is identified with the set of G^c-orbits on the Kahler-manifold.

A very selective corolary, remembering that $\partial J^a/\partial z$ transforms under G like $\bar{z}$, and has the same little group H, is [1]: ($\mathscr{D}$) can be violated by z only for generators in the coset G/H that commute with H; if z is on a critical orbit, the condition is also sufficient, *i.e.*, z is not a supersymmetric minimum of V.

As a consequence, the patterns of the gauge symmetry breaking into its subgroups can be found by identifying those $\{J^a(z)\}$ in the basis that solve ($\mathscr{D}$) above and then by combining the solutions to find all symmetry breaking patterns $G \to H \subset G$. To discuss the complementary condition ($\mathscr{F}$), we first notice that the superpotential $W(z)$ can be written as a polynomial $\tilde{W}(J^a)$, and ($\mathscr{F}$) as

$$\sum_a \partial_a \tilde{W}(J^a) \partial_i J^a = 0 \qquad (4.5)$$

while ($\mathscr{D}$) asks for some $\partial_i J^a \neq 0$. This requires an adjustment of parameters in the superpotendial or the exclusion of some J^a in $\tilde{W}(J^a)$ (unaltered by radiative corrections!). This is sometimes done by invoking some additional global symmetries, discrete or continuous. Indeed, in particle physics models, the (extended) matter-Higgs systems are rich enough to accommodate for global symmetries that I shall call *flavour groups*. This will play a central role in the next section.

In this one, I just wanted to illustrate how life would have been much easier with supersymmetry and its features that have no counterpart in generic non-supersymmetric theories: only wave-function logarithmic scale dependence, a key role of analyticity and, as reviewed below, the deeper insight on the interplay between the effectives theories in the IR and in the UV.

4.3 Confinement and t' Hooft anomaly condition

One of the most striking result on supersymmetric gauge theories is the existence of a new type of duality. This duality relates two apparently different theories in the short distance regime that are described by the same effective theory in the infrared limit [10, 11]. I refer to the literature for the many examples that have been displayed. In this section, I only focus on one aspect of these studies, whose importance arises mostly from the analogy with the theory of strong interactions and the confinement of the elementary fields, the quarks and the gluons.

Therefore, let me first sketch the theory of strong interactions, chromodynamics (QCD). Its local symmetry is $SU(3)$ with the gauge bosons, the *gluons*, interacting with six $SU(3)$-triplets of Dirac fermions, the *quarks*, so that each quark can have three *colours*, as these new quantum numbers have been (historically) called. Gauge couplings are logarithmically energy (or scale) dependent because of quantum corrections, so that, *e.g.*, in a pure gauge model, they decrease at very high energies, where the theory is weakly coupled, asymptotically UV "free", and they increase toward the low energy to become strongly coupled in the IR region. Introducing matter, the interaction with fermions (and scalars) have the opposite effect on the running of the coupling. Adding enough "matter", the behaviour will be reversed. With six quarks, QCD is asymptotically free, perturbative at high energies, while in the IR, conversely, it becomes strongly coupled.

With this large coupling, quarks are trapped inside *baryons* (composite fermions of three quarks) and *mesons* (bosons made out of a quark and an antiquark) which are $SU(3)$-invariant, *i.e.*, *colourless*, combinations. These, so-called, *hadrons* are the composite states we observe in Nature (or rather at labs), and their low energy theory barely refers to QCD (which explains the spectrum, though). The system is described by (perturbative) QCD in the UV, and by an effective theory of hadrons, Chiral Perturbation Theory (CHPT) in the IR. After defining the colourless composites, colours are screened in a sense, but the IR theory is largely dictated by the global, *flavour* symmetries of the UV.

In QCD, the UV flavour theory is called chiral as much as QCD preserves the (massless) quark helicity, and flavour symmetries act only on quarks of either one or the other helicity. The composite hadrons, baryons and mesons will inherit these flavour quantum numbers of their components, and chiral symmetries should be explicit in the confining region, implying, *e.g.*, massless baryons, or they would be spontaneously broken, which is the way we understand the baryon masses at the TeV scale. But then, they are to be non-linearly realized, by the existence of (composite) Goldstone bosons which is how we understand the lightness of the pion and other mesons.

In the previous section the G-invariants were used to establish the catalogue of gauge symmetry breaking vacua; here these polynomials on of scalars fields $\{J^a(z)\}$ are upgraded to composite scalar fields, that together with the corresponding fermionic partners will be the matter states, if and when the original gauge theory flows to a confinement of the gauge interactions. To keep in mind the analogy, we call 'quarks' the $\{z^i\}$, and 'hadrons' the $\{J^a\}$ basis. Notwithstanding this analogy, I must emphasize a fundamental difference enforced by supersymmetry: while mesons are scalar bosons associated to a quark-antiquark pair and baryons are tri-quark fermions, the J^a's are complex scalars, associated to their fermions, $\partial_i J^a \psi^i$'s, from the building rules of supersymmetric field theories.

We must construct the supersymmetric theory of these (G-invariant) states, and preserve the 'flavour' global symmetry with a Lie group F, linearly or non-linearly (if F is broken into a subgroup). Indeed, the quarks are in a representation of $G \times F$ and therefore the $\{J^a\}$ will transform in some representation, in general, non-trivial of F. A supersymmetric effective theory for the 'hadrons' means finding a $K(J^a, \bar{J}^{\bar{a}})$ as well as a $W(J^a)$, both invariant under F. Nevertheless, the existence of supersymmetric vacua with some $J^a \neq 0$ can reduce the flavour symmetry, as discussed below.

A large number of examples have been worked out [4, 5], where the $W(J^a)$ were found through various reasonings that can be found in the literature. An important ingredient is an abelian factor in the flavour group F, always present in supersymmetric models, the R symmetry, because the supersymmetriy generator Q has $R = -1$. The superpotential must have $R = 2$, a strong constraint. One has to take into account the possibility of gauge symmetry breaking in the original theories according to the patterns defined in the previous section. In the absence of a superpotential the condition ($\mathscr{D}$) above defines solutions with new gauge (sub)groups and, correspondingly, new theories have to de studied in the IR.

Here, I would like to emphasize a couple of common properties of these known cases that support a (almost proved) conjecture. Indeed, the connection between a gauge theory with their "quarks", weakly coupled at the UV, and confined by the strong gauge coupling in the IR, wherein an effective theory for their basic gauge invariant "hadrons, is strongly suggested by the mathematical equivalence discussed above. However, this equivalence is true only after the 'syzygies', $S_\alpha = 0$, the algebraic relations amongst $\{J^a(z)\}$, are imposed. The necessary, and generically sufficient, condition for the existence of syzygies is the index μ of the global representation of the z, being larger than the index μ_{adj} of the adjoint representation, where the index is defined by the trace of $\frac{1}{D}\sum_{A=1}^{D}(T^A)^2$ over the representation.

On the physical side we have to comply with the *t' Hooft anomaly condition* [7]. The anomaly of a representation of a Lie algebra is defined by the trace of the symmetric product of any three charges, duly normalized. The condition requires that the anomaly of the flavour group F (or its unbroken subgroup) for the representation of the elementary fields $\{z\}$ be the same as that for the representation of the composite invariants $\{J^a\}$. Anomaly matching is a fundamental general constraint on the definition of the degrees of freedom in the confined phase of an asymptotic free gauge theory. It says that the anomalous couplings of three conserved currents, obtained from the (triangle-) loop of the fermions associated to the z^i and from those associated to the J^a (constrained by the anomalies) are equal.

I would like to point out a stunning relation among anomalies, superpotentials and syzygies, that follows from the following conjecture, which has been verified in many examples and partially proved in general: the anomalies match between these two representations occur if and only if the syzygies derive from an F-invariant polynomial in J^a (superpotential), i.e.,

$$\exists \, \tilde{W}(J^a) \text{ such that } S_a = \partial_a \tilde{W}(J^a) = 0. \qquad (\mathscr{S}) \qquad (4.6)$$

The syzygies are the gradients of $\tilde{W}(J)$. The sufficient condition, the matching of anomalies if there is such $\tilde{W}(J)$, has been proved [8]. Indeed, the non-zero eigenvalues of the symmetric matrix $S_{ab} = \partial_a \partial_b \tilde{W}(J)$ correspond to the J^a eliminated by the syzygies ($\mathscr{S}$) and, from the physical viewpoint, to the mass matrix of the corresponding fermions in a supersymmetric vacua, cf. ($\mathscr{S}$). They break the flavour symmetry to a subgroup of F, $F' \subset F$, and the anomaly matching for F' is warranted by the homeomorphism between the manifold defined by the syzygies and the orbits in z. Notice that the massive fermions do not contribute to the anomalies because they are in a real, i.e. left-right symmetric in terms of chirality, representation of F'.

The proof of the necessity, that amounts to perform a sort of integration of the syzigies, $S_a = 0$, into an invariant $\tilde{W}(J)$, imposing the anomaly matching, has only been given for $\{J^a\}$ in a real representation of F.

Therefore in the supersymmetric IR theory the superpotential has to be $\tilde{W}(J)$, ensuring 't Hooft's matching. The syzygies are also the conditions $\mathscr{F}$ for a supersymmetric vacuum. The mathematical equivalence has a physical counterpart in the anomaly matching, which was very differently proven by 't Hooft who upgraded F to a local symmetry with a small coupling, and argued that the anomaly could not change by the strengthening of the G coupling, then took the limit of vanishing gauge coupling, when the flavour symmetry is just global.

Just as for the relation in the previous section, whose proof was completed by mathematicians after being conjectured by physicists, it would be interesting to have their help to prove or precise the relation discussed above between anomalies (the cubic Casimir invariant) and syzygies. What are the conditions for the syzygies to be the gradient of a (flavour invariant!) analytic polynomial? Notice that the distinction between gauge and global symmetries in the invariants is more a physicist attitude. Also, is the R-symmetry playing an important role as it does in the discussion just below?

It is beyond my scope to further discuss the supersymmetric conditions for confinement. Let me just state a few facts. The characterization is given in terms of the index μ, defined above, of the representation of z as compared to the index of the adjoint representation, μ_{adj}, which control the behaviour of the gauge coupling. The need for a polynomial $\tilde{W}(J)$ that enforces the syzygies, alows for confinement only in models where $\mu = \mu_{\text{adj}}$, $\mu_{\text{adj}} + 1$ and $\mu_{\text{adj}} + 2$.

Non-confining theories, with $3\mu_{\text{adj}} > \mu > \mu_{\text{adj}}$, are expected to have duals. It is generally assumed that these theories, called "electric" flow to an infrared fixed point where they are described by a super-conformal theory. This fixed point describes either an interacting theory in terms of the analytic invariants J_a or it is a free theory in this magnetic phase. Many of these examples of duality have been displayed in the literature.

The general character of these conditions may look surprising, not so much if one knows that the R-parity defined above is promoted to an abelian symmetry, R-symmetry, that the charge of the $\{z^i\}$ depends on μ_{adj}/μ_i, and that $\tilde{W}(J)$ must have $R = 2$, as said above.

4.4 Final remarks

Although I focused more on some mathematical aspects, I have reviewed two issues in field theories constrained by supersymmetry where it is possible to have a better insight on relevant physical features: gauge symmetry breaking and confinement. The evolution, the dynamics of the models can be more easily worked out because of the remarkable properties of supersymmetric theories and many studies have been published, in particular, [10]. For instance, after supersymmetry breaking, the quadratic divergences remain absent, the evolution of the parameters is logarithmic in the scale. Of course, extrapolating the properties of supersymmetric models to analogous non-supersymmetric ones, needs some obvious awareness, but can indeed give some insights into more involved physical phenomena.

In truth, I should also emphasize an important issue that any realistic supersymmetric model should address: global supersymmetry breaking is not an easy task. Indeed, the condition $(\mathscr{D})$ is always satisfied at the origin, $z = 0$, so that a necessary condition is $\partial_i W(0) = M_P \Lambda$, which asks for a linear (G-invariant) term in $W(z)$ and a scale Λ. In some sort, assuming a relatively low scale of supersymmetry breaking to understand the scale of electroweak symmetry breaking is technically valid and elegant, but physically unnatural and epistemologically questionable . Indeed, supersymmetry implies supergravity, where the gravitational coupling gives the fundamental scale, the Planck mass, M_P, and supersymmetric theories should be effective at scales quite below M_P, thus it becomes difficult to understand how the new scales needed in particle physics would be triggered, in particular, the Fermi scale of weak interactions.

Yet, it is worth noticing that in supersymmetric unified theories the unification of the three basic interactions occurs a couple of orders of magnitude below M_P, by their logarithmic evolution with the scale, if supersymmetry is there and its breaking is low enough! Two dreams, supersymmetry and unification that look equally out of the reach of our experiments for the time being and, presumably, in the near future, if they are present in Nature in some other way.

Acknowledgements

I thank the editors for giving me this opportunity to remember the friendship and influence of Ruben in my young years, and to participate in this book that acknowledges his contribution to Brazilian physics. I apologize many unquoted authors, as far as, given the nature of this contribution, I drastically restricted the citations. Thanks to Mario Abud for enlightening discussions.

Bibliography

[1] F. Buccella, J. P. Derendinger, S. Ferrara and C.A. Savoy, Phys. Lett. B **115**, 375 (1982).

[2] C. Procesi and G. W. Schwarz, Phys. Lett. B **161**, 117 (1985).

[3] M. Abud and G. Sartori, Phys. Lett. B **161**, 147 (1985).

[4] N. Seiberg, Nucl. Phys. B **435**, 129 (1995).

[5] T. R. Taylor, G. Veneziano and S. Yankelowiz, Nucl. Phys. B **218**, 493 (1983).

[6] N. Seiberg, Phys. Rev. D **49**, 6857 (1994.

[7] G. Hooft, in G. Hooft *et al.*, editors, *Naturalness, chiral symmetry breaking and spontaneous chiral symmetry breaking*, NATO advanced study, Cargese, France, Plenum, 1980.

[8] G. Dotti and A. V. Manohar, Nucl. Phys. B **518**, 575 (1998).

[9] Ph. Brax, C. Grojean and C. A. Savoy Nucl. Phys. B **561**, 77 (1999).

[10] K. Intriligator and N. Seiberg, Nucl. Phys. B, Proc. Suppl. **45BC**, 1 (1996).

[11] C. Csaki, M. Schmaltz and W. Skiba, Phys. Rev. D **55**, 7840 (1997).

5

A natural QCD infrared cutoff

A. A. Natale

Abstract: We briefly discuss some results obtained recently about dynamical gluon mass generation. We comment that this mass provides a natural QCD infrared cutoff and also implies an infrared finite coupling constant. We also discuss the phenomenological applications of these results and how they can be treated in the context of the so-called Dynamical Perturbation Theory.

5.1 Introduction: Dynamical gluon mass generation

In recent years, following a conjecture proposed forty years ago [1], we have seen a great development in the understanding of the Schwinger mechanism in QCD [2, 3, 4, 5, 6, 7]. In quantum electrodynamics in two space-time dimensions it is relatively simple to verify the presence of the Schwinger mechanism, that is, the presence of a pole in the scalar part of the polarisation of the dimensionless vacuum. In the QCD case such verification is much more sophisticated. This means that a particular sum of diagrams involving propagators and vertices ends up resulting in a dynamical gluon mass. This result obtained through solutions of the Schwinger-Dyson equations (SDE) is strongly confirmed when compared with results obtained from lattice QCD [2]. The observation of a dynamical gluon mass implies the study of the gluon self-energy, that is, the vacuum polarisation, which involves the three-gluon vertex, which in turn has a longitudinally coupled part with a simple pole structure

$$\Gamma^{\text{pole}}_{\alpha\mu\nu}(q,r,p) \propto \frac{q_\alpha}{q^2}\delta_{\mu\nu}C_1(q,r,p) + ... \qquad (5.1)$$

where $C_1(q,r,p)_{q^2\approx 0} = 2q.r\mathbb{C}(r^2) + O(q^2)$.

This pole structure can be related to the scalar function $\mathbb{C}(r^2)$ that can be extracted from lattice QCD data. Without going into details, and directing the reader directly to Ref. [7], this scalar function must be no null if the Schwinger mechanism is operative in QCD, and this was demonstrated with extraordinary accuracy in Ref. [7], as shown in Fig. 5.1.

The former analysis that has been done to determine the existence of a dynamical gluon mass [8] is becoming more and more complex, and it is difficult to imagine that these results, which indicate a natural infrared cutoff in QCD, are going to be easily taken into account in phenomenological applications. However, models that assume massive gluons to understand the infrared QCD behavior began to emerge (see, for instance, Ref. [9, 10]), and they are indicating that if we take into account the existence of this natural cutoff, several infrared QCD calculations are well behaved when treated with perturbative methods [10, 11]. The possibility of an expansion in small parameters as advocated in Ref. [10, 11] is not entirely surprising. The phenomenon of dynamical gluon mass generation is also associated with an infrared fixed point of the coupling constant (α_s) [12], and, although the strong force is proportional to the product of α_s times the gluon propagator, the isolated value of the coupling constant is important *per se*, and there are phenomenological estimates that the infrared value of the coupling constant may not be so large, as will be discussed ahead. The important fact is that these QCD complex and detailed studies come out with an infrared finite gluon propagator and an infrared finite coupling constant.

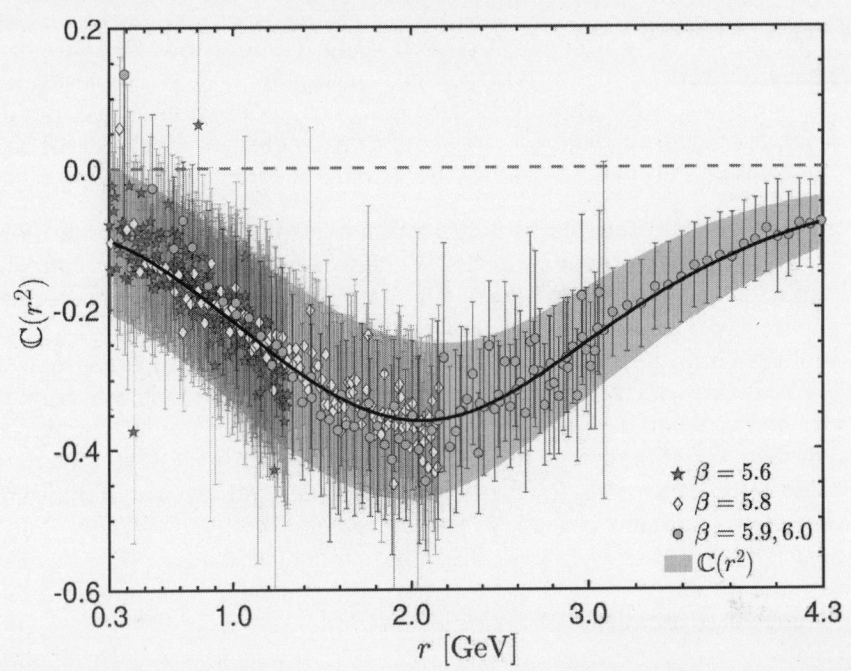

Figure 5.1: $\mathbb{C}(r^2)$ obtained in Ref.[7]. Solid black curve – obtained using central fit forms of lattice QCD of Ref. [13]. The bracketing soft-gray band expresses the uncertainty in this result. Dashed grey line – null result (no Schwinger mechanism)

5.2 Phenomenology with dynamically massive gluons

It is clear that in phenomenological calculations at large energies quarks and gluons are treated as free particles, and usually the latter enters the calculation as a massless particle. Although the perturbative QCD analysis in that energy range works quite well, it would be very interesting if we had a method to treat QCD where both its non-perturbative and perturbative aspects were covered, and a fair amount of work has been done in this direction [14, 15]. Indeed in some phenomenological calculations a gluon mass must be invoked if we are to describe the experimental data. As one example we can recall the hadronic decay of heavy quarkonium like $V = \Upsilon, J/\psi$ that can be measured through the branching ratio $R_V = \Gamma(V \to ggg)/\Gamma(V \to ee)$, which can also provide a measurement of the QCD coupling constant. If the gluon has a dynamical mass (whose value at small momentum will be indicated by m_g) the branching ratio R_V must be changed to $A = R_V \cdot f_3(\eta)$ where

$$f_3(\eta) = \frac{\Gamma(V \to ggg)_{m_g}}{\Gamma(V \to ggg)_{m_g=0}}, \tag{5.2}$$

with $\eta = 2m_g/M_V$ and M_V is the quarkonium mass. The function $f_3(\eta)$ decreases the value of A and is a measure of the effect of the dynamical gluon mass as discussed in Ref. [16]. This effect is even more remarkable in the data of the radiative process $V \to \gamma + X$, where QCD predicts a photon spectrum nearly linear in $z = 2E_\gamma/M_V$ (E_γ is the photon energy). In this case, the photon spectrum does not reach the maximum value of z, indicating a suppression due to the fact that the phase space is occupied by gluons that behave like massive particles [17, 18].

Another example where the dynamical gluon mass plays a fundamental role is in the calculation of hadronic cross sections at high energies in the soft regime, which are dominated by Pomeron exchange. The simplest Pomeron construction in QCD is given by a two-gluon exchange which shows a singularity at $-t = 0$. To solve this problem Landshoff and Nachtmann (LN) suggested that the gluon propagator is intrinsically modified in the infrared region [19]. The LN model was improved with the introduction of dynamically massive gluons in Ref. [20, 21], producing a good description of the elastic differential cross section for pp scattering data at $\sqrt{s} = 53$ GeV. It is clear that the Pomeron component to this cross section should be even more dominant in the LHC regime, where other Reggeon contributions are negligible. A reanalysis of the LN Pomeron model at TeV energies, taking into account the results of dynamical gluon mass generation was performed recently [22], where the scattering amplitude is giving by

$$\mathcal{A}(s,t) = i s^{\alpha_\mathbb{P}(t)} \frac{1}{\tilde{s}_0} \frac{8}{9} n_p^2 [\tilde{T}_1 - \tilde{T}_2], \tag{5.3}$$

with

$$\tilde{T}_1 = \int_0^s d^2k\, \bar{\alpha}\left(\frac{q}{2}+k\right) D\left(\frac{q}{2}+k\right) \bar{\alpha}\left(\frac{q}{2}-k\right) D\left(\frac{q}{2}-k\right) [G_p(q,0)]^2, \tag{5.4}$$

$$\tilde{T}_2 = \int_0^s d^2k\, \bar{\alpha}\left(\frac{q}{2}+k\right) D\left(\frac{q}{2}+k\right) \bar{\alpha}\left(\frac{q}{2}-k\right) D\left(\frac{q}{2}-k\right) G_p\left(q, k-\frac{q}{2}\right) \times$$
$$\left[2G_p(q,0) - G_p\left(q, k-\frac{q}{2}\right)\right]. \tag{5.5}$$

Here $\alpha_\mathbb{P}(t)$ is the Pomeron trajectory, $\tilde{s}_0 \equiv s_0^{\alpha_\mathbb{P}(t)-1}$, $G_p(q,k)$ is a convolution of proton wave functions, and $n_p = 3$ is the number of quarks in the proton. T_1 (T_2) represent the contribution when both gluons attach to the same quark (to different quarks) within the proton, and the coupling $\bar{\alpha}(q^2)$ and gluon propagator $D(q^2)$ are the infrared finite ones that have been obtained in the study of dynamical mass generation that we referred above. In Figs. 5.2 and 5.3, we present the fits for the elastic scattering data obtained in Ref. [22] for the LHC experiments ATLAS and TOTEM, where we use different fits of the dynamical gluon masses obtained in the literature, which are indicated by $m_{log}(q^2)$ and $m_{pl}(q^2)$, and verify that the data is well described by this Pomeron model. The result is dependent on the infrared value of the gluon mass, but still not precise enough to determine the cross section dependence on the formal expression of the dynamical gluon mass with momentum.

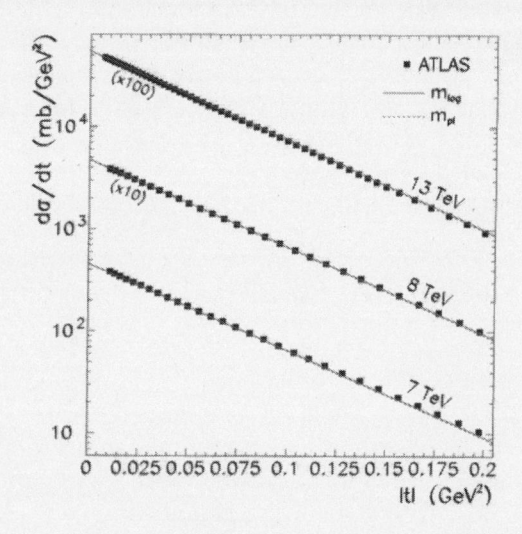

Figure 5.2: Pomeron model description of the pp elastic differential cross section data from ATLAS. The solid and dashed lines show the results obtained using fits of the dynamical gluon mass $m_{log}(q^2)$ and $m_{pl}(q^2)$, respectively.

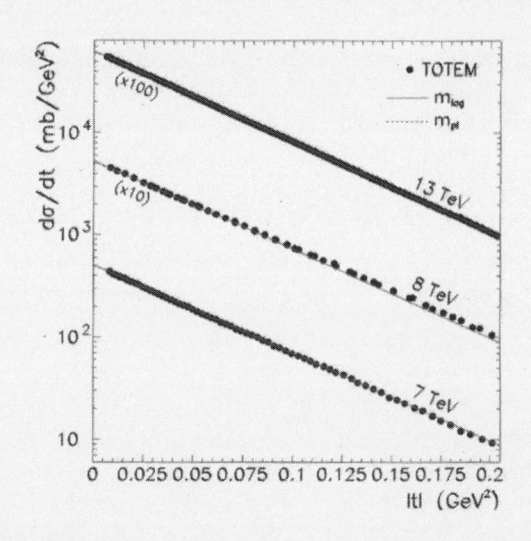

Figure 5.3: Pomeron model description of the pp elastic differential cross section data from TOTEM. The solid and dashed lines show the results obtained using fits of the dynamical gluon mass $m_{log}(q^2)$ and $m_{pl}(q^2)$, respectively.

Looking at the examples we quoted above and others [23], we can say that the consequences of introducing the phenomenon of dynamical mass generation for the gluon cannot be totally neglected in phenomenological calculations. We can say even more: the consideration of these effects in loop calculations (where we have integrations over the whole range of momenta) may even eliminate the existence of the so-called renormalons [24].

5.3 Dynamical perturbation theory

The perturbative description of gauge theory quantities in terms of a coupling constant is of central importance to our understanding of such theories, and thereby of our ability to use them for phenomenology. Much of the current high-energy experimental data needs to be compared with theoretical phenomenological calculations involving various orders of perturbation theory. This means that they can involve QCD calculations at the level of several loops, mixing the non-perturbative part with the perturbative one. The direct calculation of such non-perturbative corrections is in many cases very challenging, and methods like the ones used to compute the dynamical gluon mass (see, for instance, Refs. [4, 6]) have not been introduced into standard phenomenological calculations, and due to its complexity it is possible that it will take a long time to be incorporated into the high energy hadronic phenomenology.

It is interesting that a great interest in non-perturbative effects in quantum field theory has recently arisen in what is described as the resurgence method [25], although this technique is still far from being applied in realistic high energy phenomenological models [26, 27, 28]. Therefore, a simpler method of obtaining phenomenological results, using the fact that we have a natural infrared QCD cutoff (the dynamical gluon mass) and an infrared finite strong coupling constant would be very welcome. One proposal in that direction was formulated many years ago by Pagels and Stokar [29], and was denominated by Dynamical Perturbation Theory (DPT).

DPT is a generalization of perturbation theory, and as stated in Ref.[29] it can be described as follows. Amplitudes that do not vanish in all orders of perturbation theory are given by their free field values. Amplitudes that vanish in all orders in perturbation theory like $\lambda = e^{-1/bg^2}$, as, for example, the dynamical gluon mass that decays with momentum p like $1/p^2$, are retained in the series, in comparison with higher orders like $g^n e^{-1/bg^2}$ with $n > 0$, which can be less important due to the soft behavior of the dressed amplitudes. The use of a dressed gluon propagator and coupling constant, as obtained in solutions of SDE, in the calculations described in Section II is exactly an application of DPT. Note that DPT still assumes a perturbative expansion, and, in favor of this approximation, we can say that there are estimates that the coupling constant g may have a moderate value [30, 31, 32], as well as the fact that models assuming massive gluons admit a well-behaved expansion when compared with results obtained in lattice QCD [10, 11, 33, 34], but it is clear that more studies on this possibility are needed.

5.4 Final remarks

The existence of the Schwinger mechanism in QCD is strongly proven by comparing the results obtained through SDE and those obtained in lattice QCD calculations [2, 7]. The numerical SDE solutions indicating dynamical gluon mass generation are basically performed in the Landau gauge, this solution in other gauges has been discussed in Refs. [1, 4, 35].

The Landau gauge makes the SDE calculations much simpler, remembering that this type of calculation is still quite laborious to be taken into account in phenomenological calculations. At the present time, the practical way to use this information is to use simple fits for the various Green functions, that have been obtained in SDE solutions associated with the Schwinger mechanism, following the DPT proposal. The use of approximate functions in phenomenological calculations is interesting because different phenomenological data depend differently on propagators and vertices. Therefore, the set of experimental data can also serve as a test to determine the functional behavior of the dynamical gluon mass, as well as the coupling constant, whose infrared value is dependent on m_g. The examples of hadronic phenomenology presented in Section II show this different dependence of physical quantities as a function of the gluon propagator and QCD coupling constant.

There are other examples of high energy phenomenology that can be modified when considering the existence of a dynamical gluon mass and infrared finite coupling constant [36, 37, 38]. The presence of an infrared fixed point in QCD [12] can modify the evolution of the coupling constants in the study of grand unification models [39], and it can modify the determination of the conformal region in technicolor or similar theories with many fermions [40]. The effect of dynamically massive gluons also causes different effects on the chiral transition of quarks in the fundamental and adjoint representations [41], and also affects the determination of structure functions at small-x [42].

In this quite brief report we emphasized the existence of the Schwinger mechanism in QCD, how it can modify different observables of hadronic phenomenology, and that the use of the so-called Dynamic Perturbation Theory may be the simplest method to utilize the results of dynamical gluon mass generation.

Acknowledgments

I have benefited from discussions with A. C. Aguilar, E. G. S. Luna and A. Doff.

Bibliography

[1] J. M. Cornwall, Phys. Rev. D **26**, 1453 (1982).

[2] A. C. Aguilar, D. Binosi, J. Papavassiliou, Phys. Rev. D **78**, 025010 (2008).

[3] P. Boucaud, J. P. Leroy, A. Le-Yaouanc, J. Micheli, O. Pene, J. Rodriguez Quintero, Few Body Syst. **53**, 387 (2012).

[4] A. C. Aguilar, D. Binosi, J. Papavassiliou, Front. Phys. China **11**, 111203 (2016).

[5] D. Binosi, Few Body Syst. **63**, 42 (2022).

[6] J. Papavassiliou, Chin. Phys. C **46**, 112001 (2022).

[7] A. C. Aguilar, F. De Soto, M. N. Ferreira, J. Papavassiliou, F. Pinto-Gómez, C.D. Roberts, J. Rodríguez-Quintero, Phys. Lett. B **841**, 137906 (2023).

[8] A. C. Aguilar, A. A. Natale, JHEP **08**, 057 (2004).

[9] M. Peláez, EPJ Web Conf. **274**, 02002 (2022).

[10] M. Peláez, U. Reinosa, J. Serreau, J. Tissier, N. Wschebor, Rept. Prog. Phys. **84**, 124202 (2021).

[11] M. Peláez, U. Reinosa, J. Serreau, J. Tissier, N. Wschebor, Phys. Rev. D **107**, 054025 (2023).

[12] A. C. Aguilar, A. A. Natale, P. S. Rodrigues da Silva, Phys. Rev. Lett. **90**, 152001 (2003).

[13] A. C. Aguilar, F. De Soto, M.N. Ferreira, J. Papavassiliou, J. Rodríguez-Quintero, Phys. Lett. B **818**, 136352 (2021).

[14] M. Ding, C. D. Roberts, S. M. Schmidt, Particles **6**, 57 (2023).

[15] C. D. Roberts, D. G. Richards, T. Horn, L. Chang, Prog. Part. Nucl. Phys. **120**, 103883 (2021).

[16] A. Mihara, A. A. Natale, Phys. Lett. B **482** 378 (2000).

[17] G. Parisi, R. Petronzio, Phys. Lett. B **94**, 51 (1980).

[18] M. Consoli, J. H. Field, Phys. Rev. D **49**, 1293 (1994).

[19] P. V. Landshoff, O. Nachtmann, Z. Phys. C **35**, 405 (1987).

[20] F. Halzen, G. Krein, A. A. Natale, Phys. Rev. D **47**, 295 (1993).

[21] M. B. Gay Ducati, F. Halzen, A. A. Natale, Phys. Rev. D **48**, 2324 (1993).

[22] G. B. Bopsin, E. G. S. Luna, A. A. Natale, M. Peláez, Phys. Rev. D **107**, 114011 (2023).

[23] A. C. Aguilar, A. Mihara, A. A. Natale, Int. J. Mod. Phys. A **19**, 249 (2004).

[24] M. Beneke, Phys. Rept. **317**, 1 (1999).

[25] J. Ecalle, *Les fonctions resurgentes*, v. 1,2, Publ. Math. Orsay, (1981).

[26] I. Aniceto, G. Basar, R. Schiappa, Phys. Rept. **809**, 1 (2019).

[27] M. Marino, Fortsch. Phys. **62**, 455 (2014).

[28] D. Dorigoni, Annals Phys. **409**, 167914 (2019).

[29] H. Pagels, S. Stokar, Phys. Rev. D **20**, 2947 (1979).

[30] J.M. Cornwall, Phys. Rev. D **80**, 096001 (2009).

[31] A. C. Aguilar, A. Mihara, A. A. Natale, Phys. Rev. D **65**, 054011 (2002).

[32] J. D. Gomez, A. A. Natale, Phys. Rev. D **93**, 014027 (2016).

[33] F. Siringo, Phys. Rev. D **107**, 016009 (2023).

[34] F. Siringo, arXiv: 1507.05543.

[35] A. C. Aguilar, D. Binosi, J. Papavassiliou, Phys. Rev. D **95**, 034017 (2017).

[36] E. G. S. Luna, A. F. Martini, M. J. Menon, A. Mihara, A. A. Natale, Phys. Rev. D **72**, 034019 (2005).

[37] E. G. S. Luna, Phys. Lett. B **641**, 171 (2006).

[38] E. G. S. Luna, A. A. Natale, Phys. Rev. D **73**, 074019 (2006).

[39] J. D. Gomez, A. A. Natale, Phys. Lett. B **747**, 541 (2015).

[40] J. D. Gomez, A. A. Natale, Int. J. Mod. Phys. A **32**, 1750012 (2017).

[41] R. M. Capdevilla, A. Doff, A. A. Natale, Phys. Lett. B **728**, 626 (2014).

[42] E. G. S. Luna, A. L. dos Santos, A. A. Natale, Phys. Lett. B **698**, 52 (2011).

6

Describing paths on discrete and finite quantum phase spaces

D. Galetti

In homage to Ruben Aldrovandi

Abstract: It has been shown that a discrete and finite quantum phase space representation of Quantum Mechanics can be constructed for physical systems described by finite-dimensional Hilbert spaces. Those phase spaces that emerge in that description are then represented by finite and discrete lattices constituted of points characterized by two integer labels, each one of them associated with the proper state space quantum number, being the two state spaces connected by a finite Fourier transform. In this sense, the variables used to label the points of the lattice are canonically conjugated by a finite Fourier transform. Here we intend to show how it is possible to describe paths on those finite and discrete phase spaces, and present the mathematical scenario to be used for that aim.

6.1 A brief review of Schwinger's operator bases

Let us consider a finite-dimensional state space obtained by diagonalizing an operator associated with an observable of the physical system of interest. An unitary operator can be constructed out of these state vectors $\{|e_d\rangle\}$ by defining a cyclic relabeling, namely [1]

$$\hat{V}|e_d\rangle = |e_{d-1}\rangle \,,\, d = 1,\ldots,N.$$

where N is the state space dimension, and

$$|e_{N-1}\rangle = |e_1\rangle \,,$$

which implies in the module N arithmetic. The repeated action of $\hat{V}$ defines linearly independent unitary operators such that

$$\hat{V}^k|e_d\rangle = |e_{d-k}\rangle$$

with $d-k$ taken mod N, and

$$\hat{V}^N|e_d\rangle = |e_{d-N}\rangle = |e_d\rangle$$

implying $\hat{V}^N = \hat{1}$. Therefore, the eigenvalues of $\hat{V}$ are given by the complex numbers $v_k = \exp\{2\pi i k/N\}$, with $k = 0,\ldots,N-1$; clearly they are the N roots of unity. Since we now also have the set of eigenvectors of the operator $\hat{V}$, viz. $\{|v_b\rangle\}$, we can construct, in a similar way as we did before, a new reordering unitary operator [1]

$$\hat{U}^l|v_b\rangle = |v_{b+l}\rangle \,.$$

This operator also has period N, i.e., $\hat{U}^N = \hat{1}$ and the same spectrum of eigenvalues, $u_l = \exp\{2\pi i l/N\}$, as $\hat{V}$.

Each unitary operator in both families admit an inverse, and the signals in the eigenvalues are then changed.

As an interesting result emerging out of these constructions, the eigenvectors of $\hat{U}$ are precisely the set of vectors we started with, namely $\{|u_a\rangle\} = \{|e_d\rangle\}$ [1]. Furthermore, the relation between the two families of state vectors is characterized by the finite Fourier coefficients

$$\langle u_a|v_b\rangle = \frac{\omega^{ab}}{\sqrt{N}}$$

and

$$\langle v_b|u_a\rangle = \frac{\omega^{-ab}}{\sqrt{N}},$$

where $\omega := \exp\{2\pi i/N\}$ is a root of unity and the range of the integer labels is $1 \leq a,b \leq N$.

The action of the unitary operators on the state vectors allows us to infer the commutation relation directly; since

$$\hat{V}\hat{U}|v_b\rangle = v_{b+1}|v_{b+1}\rangle = \omega v_b|v_{b+1}\rangle$$

and

$$\hat{U}\hat{V}|v_b\rangle = v_b|v_{b+1}\rangle$$

we have $\hat{V}\hat{U} = \omega\hat{U}\hat{V}$, being the general case

$$\hat{V}^k\hat{U}^l = \omega^{kl}\hat{U}^l\hat{V}^k.$$

The particular set of operators $\hat{V}\hat{U}$ presents some important properties:

- The properties of $\hat{U}$ and $\hat{V}$ exhibit maximum degree of incompatibility and the set of N^2 operators $\hat{S}(l,k) = \frac{\hat{U}^l\hat{V}^k}{\sqrt{N}}$, with $k,l = 0,\ldots,N-1$, constitute an orthonormal and complete operator basis [1].

- Recognizing that there are two Hermitian operators associated with the unitary operators, and that they are canonically conjugated by the finite Fourier transform, the product kl has the dimension of action measured in units of the Planck constant, here taken as $\hbar = 1$ for simplicity.

- A symmetrical version of this basis may be given by

$$\hat{S}_s(l,k) = \omega^{\frac{kl}{2}}\frac{\hat{U}^l\hat{V}^k}{\sqrt{N}}.$$

The labels k and l are those to be associated with the discrete dual variables of a N^2-dimensional finite phase space characterizing the kinematics of the physical system under study.

Additionally, some important features of those operator bases can be immediately verified:

1. $\hat{S}_s(l,k)$ is invariant under the changes $\hat{U} \to \hat{V}$ and $\hat{V} \to \hat{U}^{-1}$, followed by $l \to k$ and $k \to -l$. This property already shows a pre-symplectic character of the operator basis [2, 3].

2. Being $\hat{S}_s(l,k)$ an operator basis we are allowed to decompose, in a direct way, any operator – associated with the dynamical quantities – acting on the states of the physical system, namely

$$\hat{O} = \sum_{l,k=0}^{N-1} O(l,k)\hat{S}_s(l,k),$$

where the coefficients $O(l,k)$ are given by $Tr\left[S_s^\dagger(l,k)\hat{O}\right]$.

3. These operator bases cannot be decomposed into sub-bases when the dimension of the state space, N, is a prime number. In this sense, Schwinger classify the associated space state, in these situations, as characterizing a single degree of freedom [1]. Hereafter, we will only consider state spaces with N a prime number. The cases in which N is a composite number will not be considered here; they deserve a much more elaborated approach.

It is important to emphasize that other operator bases can be constructed out of these Schwinger bases; in particular we must point out those bases proposed in references [2]. Being bases, they can be used in the same way to decompose any operator associated with the dynamical quantities of the physical system of interest; in particular we can decompose Hamiltonians, which govern the time evolution of the system. Those operators, including Hamiltonians, will then be written as particular combinations of the $\hat{U}$ and $\hat{V}$ operators.

6.2 Discrete and finite quantum phase spaces

Discrete phase space approaches for physical systems characterized by a finite-dimensional Hilbert space were initially proposed by Wooters [4], Cohendet et al [5], Galetti and Toledo Piza [2], Galetti and Marchiolli [6], Vourdas [7], Opatrný and co-workers [8], Hakioğlu [9], and many others. Hereafter let us focus on the main properties of a discrete and finite phase space following the approach proposed by [2] and [6].

For simplicity let us consider a physical system with only one degree of freedom characterized by the two sets of orthogonal eigenvectors of the two unitary operators, and consider a new space labeled respectively by the two quantum numbers, i.e.,

$$|u_a\rangle \otimes |v_b\rangle \rightarrow |a;b\rangle \ .$$

Since a and b are discrete and finite (N values), with values ranging from 1 to N (or any complete set of remainders in the extraction of the module N), this space is also finite and discrete, and constitute what we then call the new phase space associated with the physical system. Now, the action of the unitary operators on each site of this new lattice is completely defined by the rules mentioned before, and the cyclic character of those actions indicate that the lattice can also be seen to have the topology of a discrete torus. In this sense, we are not restricted to keep ourselves in the range $1 \leq a, b \leq N$; any finite integer value of a and b are allowed, since we can cyclically go on within the lattice. On the discrete torus this feature corresponds to winding along any of the two directions without any kind of restriction. The mod N arithmetic will then play an essential role in the basic calculations with those operators.

If the physical system under study is characterized by N states (eigenstates of $\hat{U}$ or $\hat{V}$), the corresponding discrete phase space is N^2-dimensional, where the totality of the sites therefore contains all the possible kinematical information related to that physical system.

Such a discrete phase space for a physical system presenting one degree of freedom can be represented by a lattice of points, for instance, when $N = 5$, as in the figure

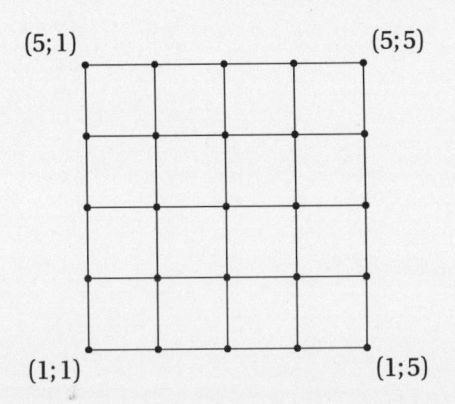

```
(5;1)                    (5;5)
  •----•----•----•----•
  |    |    |    |    |
  •----•----•----•----•
  |    |    |    |    |
  •----•----•----•----•
  |    |    |    |    |
  •----•----•----•----•
  |    |    |    |    |
  •----•----•----•----•
(1;1)                    (1;5)
```

where the labels stand for $(a; b)$. In this way, the set of all discrete phase space points/sites will be henceforth, for simplicity, characterized by the labels $(a; b)$; the lines in the figure only guide the eyes.

Hereafter we will be dealing with paths without any reference to the unitary operators that may generate those discrete phase spaces. Our interest will be only focused on the characterization and on a particular scheme of classifying those paths.

Now, in analogy to the rules of the shifting actions of the unitary operators presented by Schwinger, we will propose a new pair of operators that are also unitary and defined by the shifting rules:

- $\hat{D}^l(a; b) = (a; b + l)$, where $b + l$ is taken as $(b + l)$ (mod N), meaning that the operator $\hat{D}^l$ shifts the labels of a given site $(a; b)$ to $(a; b + l)$ along the horizontal line, not the state vector. Then, this operator is the analogous of the Schwinger $\hat{U}$ operator. In the same way,

- $\hat{C}^k(a; b) = (a + k; b)$, where $a + k$ is also taken as $(a + k)$ (mod N); here the operator $\hat{C}^k$ shifts the labels of a given site $(a; b)$ to $(a+k; b)$ along the vertical line, not the state vector. This operator is the analogous of the inverse of the Schwinger $\hat{V}$ operator.

Concomitantly, the inverse of these operators satisfy the shifting rules:

- $(\hat{D}^{-1})^l(a;b) = (a;b-l)$, and
- $(\hat{C}^{-1})^k(a;b) = (a-k;b)$, with the mod N taken into account.

Therefore, when using products of powers of the $\hat{D}$ and $\hat{C}$ operators, in the sequence of actions determined by the desired monomial, we can start at *any site* of the lattice and arrive at any site to the right and above the starting site (or even to stay at the same site by using the $\hat{I}$ operator). The reverse can be achieved by using the inverse operators. For example, consider the sequence (to be read, as a convention, from right to left)
$$\hat{C}\hat{D}\hat{C}\hat{D}\hat{C}\hat{D};$$
it consists of six shifts. In the same form, we could have the sequence
$$\hat{C}^{-1}\hat{D}^{-1}\hat{C}^{-1}\hat{D}^{-1}\hat{C}^{-1}\hat{D}^{-1}$$
also consisting of six shifts describing a path from some site on the right to another one to the left and below. In the case of a lattice with $N = 5$, the first example can be represented, for the starting site $(a;b) = (1;1)$, as

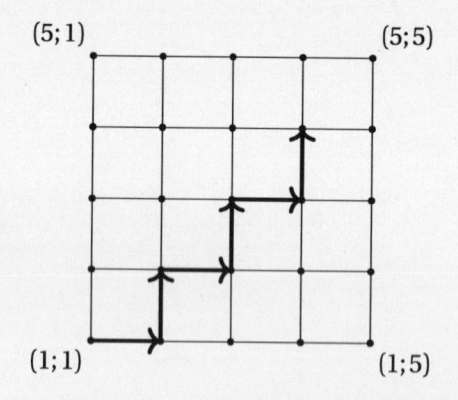

Now, guided by the analogy to the fundamental commutation relation between the unitary Schwinger operators, here we propose a new commutation relation for the new operators:
$$\hat{D}^l\hat{C}^k = p^{kl}\hat{C}^k\hat{D}^l,$$
where p is, for now, an indeterminate, such that any monomial describing a sequence of right-up shifts can be put into another form; for example
$$\hat{C}\hat{D}\hat{C}\hat{D}\hat{C}\hat{D} = p^3\hat{C}^3\hat{D}^3.$$

The crucial point here is that the two paths do not coincide, they are not the same. In other words, the rearrangement due to the commutations introduced a new information embodied in the exponent of the indeterminate p. If we depict the new path we will have

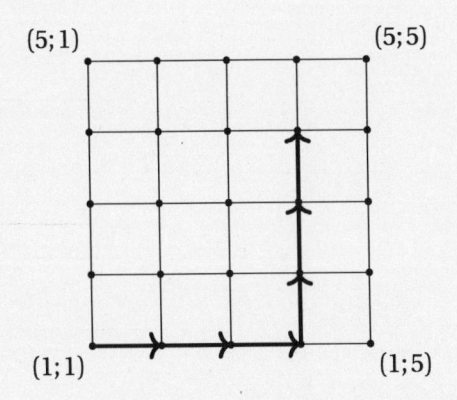

(5;1) (5;5)

(1;1) (1;5)

We immediately recognize that the final site of this new path is exactly the same as the previous one, but the sequence of the steps is different. To interpret what is the physical content embodied in the difference between the two paths, we have to recall two essential mathematical facts.

6.3 A brief review of q-objects

1. Given two variables that do not commute, for example x and y, i.e., $yx = qxy$, with q a parameter commuting with both x and y, then there exists an extension of the usual binomial expression, namely [10, 11]

$$(x+y)^n = \sum_{m=0}^{n} \binom{n}{m}_q x^m y^{n-m},$$

where $\binom{n}{m}_q$ is the so-called q-binomial or Gauss polynomial[1]. To completely describe what the q-binomial is we have to introduce the following notation [11, 12]

- q-integers:
  $(n)_q := \frac{1-q^n}{1-q}$, $(0)_q = 0$, $lim_{q \to 1}(n)_q = n$;
- q-factorial:
  $(n)_q! := \prod_{j=1}^{n} \frac{1-q^j}{1-q}$;

---
[1] For the sake of completeness we note that this non-commutative algebra is at the root of a non-commutative geometry.

- q-numbers:
$$(a)_n = (a;q)_n := (1-a)(1-aq)(1-aq^2)\ldots(1-aq^{n-1}) \;;$$
with
$$(a)_0 = 1 \text{ and } (q)_n = \prod_{j}^{n}(1-q^j) \;.$$

With these notations we have for the q-binomial

$$\binom{n}{m}_q := \frac{(n)_q!}{(m)_q!(n-m)_q!} = \binom{n}{n-m}_q$$

with

$$\binom{n}{0}_q = \binom{n}{n}_q = 1 \;;\; \lim_{q \to 1} \binom{n}{m}_q = \binom{n}{m}.$$

2. From the theory of partitions of integers [11, 13, 14] it is known that the generating function of partitions

$$G(n,m;q) = \sum_{j \geq 0} p(n,m;j) q^j$$

is given by, using the definition of $G(n,m;q)$,

$$\frac{(q)_{n+m}}{(q)_n (q)_m} = \sum_{j \geq 0} p(n,m;j) q^j \;.$$

In this expression $p(n,m;j)$ is the number of partitions of j in at most m parts, being each one $\leq n$, and it is a polynomial of nm degree. Therefore

$$\binom{n+m}{m}_q = \sum_{j \geq 0} p(n,m;j) q^j \;.$$

For instance, for $n = m = 2$ we have

$$\binom{4}{2}_q = p(2,2;0) + p(2,2;1)q + p(2,2;2)q^2 + p(2,2;3)q^3 + p(2,2;4)q^4$$

$$= 1 + q + 2q^2 + q^3 + q^4 \;.$$

6.4 Discrete phase spaces and the q-algebra

Now, with these results, we can establish the correspondence between the paths in the discrete phase space and the q-binomials.

Besides the interpretation of the q-binomial as a way of classifying the partitions of an integer, and noting that still another use of the Gauss polynomials refers to the determination of subspaces of a vector space defined on a finite field [12, 15], it is also possible to use it to determine the area under a path on a lattice, with respect to a reference path [12, 15]. It is this last possibility that we are going to explore hereafter. To that end, and as a fundamental cornerstone of our approach, we will consider the indeterminate, p, appearing in the already mentioned commutation relation,

$$\hat{D}^l \hat{C}^k = p^{kl} \hat{C}^k \hat{D}^l,$$

to belong to the same domain of parameters q that warrant the existence of the Gauss polynomials [15] (if q is a complex number, it cannot be a root of unity), in such a way that for all monomials characterizing paths on a discrete phase space we can now associate a corresponding area with a physical meaning.

For simplicity, let us consider the simple case of spectrum of states with $N = 3$. Studying the simplest possible paths when $N = 3$ and 4 steps, with two $\hat{C}$'s and two $\hat{D}$'s, we have first of all

1. P1: $\hat{C}\hat{C}\hat{D}\hat{D} = \hat{C}^2 \hat{D}^2$; in this case we fix the exponent of q as 0, since there is no commutation. Clearly all other monomials/paths can be put in the form of this first case, viz.:

2. P2: $\hat{C}\hat{D}\hat{C}\hat{D} = q \hat{C}^2 \hat{D}^2$ (one commutation) ;

3. P3: $\hat{D}\hat{C}\hat{C}\hat{D} = q^2 \hat{C}^2 \hat{D}^2$ (two commutations) ;

4. P4: $\hat{C}\hat{D}\hat{D}\hat{C} = q^2 \hat{C}^2 \hat{D}^2$ (also two commutations) ;

5. P5: $\hat{D}\hat{C}\hat{D}\hat{C} = q^3 \hat{C}^2 \hat{D}^2$ (three commutations) ;

6. P6: $\hat{D}^2 \hat{C}^2 = q^4 \hat{C}^2 \hat{D}^2$ (four commutations) .

Now, from the path counting approach we see that the usual binomial gives

$$\binom{2+2}{2} = 6,$$

i.e., there exist six possible paths for combinations of $\hat{C}^2$ and $\hat{D}^2$. On the other hand we see that the obtained exponents (associated with commutations) correspond to the areas defined by the paths with respect to the reference path (taken as zero area). As such, for instance, in the fifth path, namely $\hat{D}\hat{C}\hat{D}\hat{C} = q^3 \hat{C}^2 \hat{D}^2$, there are 3 units of area under that path (with respect to $\hat{C}^2 \hat{D}^2$). In fact, collecting all the paths we have

$$\{q^0 \hat{C}^2 \hat{D}^2, q^1 \hat{C}^2 \hat{D}^2, q^2 \hat{C}^2 \hat{D}^2, q^2 \hat{C}^2 \hat{D}^2, q^3 \hat{C}^2 \hat{D}^2, q^4 \hat{C}^2 \hat{D}^2\},$$

and the sum of all these contributions clearly is

$$(q^0 + q^1 + 2q^2 + q^3 + q^4) \hat{C}^2 \hat{D}^2 = \binom{4}{2}_q \hat{C}^2 \hat{D}^2.$$

Pictorially, we have the six possible paths and the corresponding areas for this example

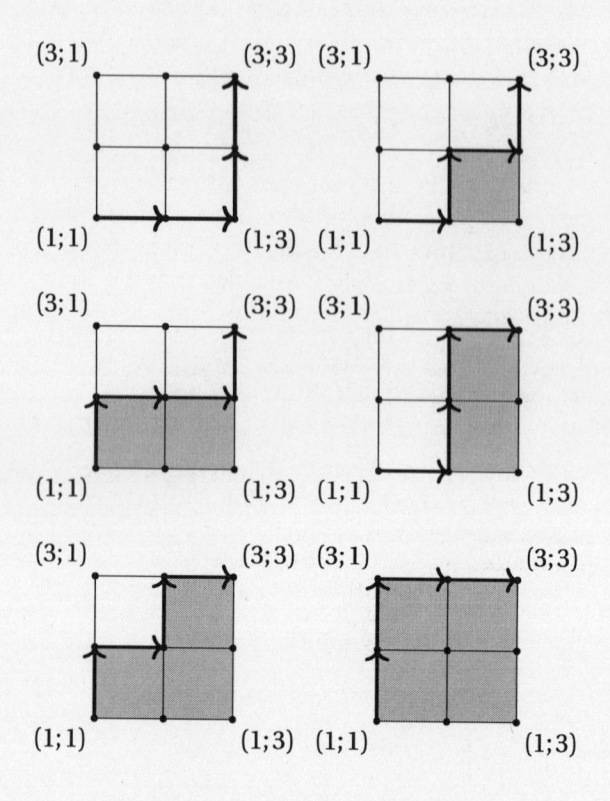

In a general form, considering N = number of sites in one direction and $N-1$ = the associated number of segments/steps, the expression

$$\binom{2(N-1)}{N-1}_q \hat{C}^{N-1} \hat{D}^{N-1}$$

gives the number of all possible paths on the lattice with $N \times N$ sites and with $\hat{C}^{N-1}$ and $\hat{D}^{N-1}$ shifts, as well as the corresponding areas.

Geometrically, we then establish the association for the parameters of a general q-binomial $\binom{n}{m}_q$:

- n = total number of shifts (horizontal + vertical)
- m = number of shifts along the horizontal (or vertical).

The sign of the phase characterizing the area under the path indicates whether the path goes clockwise (positive) or counterclockwise (negative).

Thus far we have been able to only associate paths going right-up with the

Gauss polynomials. These paths, however, do not exhaust all the possibilities. It is immediate to see that there are also the family of all the left-down paths, or mixtures of them. In order to generalize what we have already presented, i.e. to characterize any path on the discrete phase space, associating it with the Gauss polynomials in a simple geometrical form, we need not necessarily to introduce new unitary operators obeying new commutation relations; the work with q-multinomials would then be much more complicated and unclear due to the complexity involved in those different q-commutation relations. For simplicity, and keeping the spirit of the previous approach that deals with only one pair of operators, we will take advantage of the geometrical property of the discrete phase space, namely its toroidal property associated with the cyclic character of the unitary operators. Thus, for example, we can promptly substitute $\hat{C}^{-k}$ by $\hat{C}^{N-k}$; the same for $\hat{D}^{-l}$. Therefore, all paths (even those with mixtures of $\hat{C}^{-k}$ and $\hat{D}^{-l}$) can be put in correspondence with the Gauss polynomials as already described. For this purpose we have to implement an extension of the original discrete (and finite) phase spacein order to accomplish the toroidal property, i.e., we have to add copies of the original phase space such that the new paths described by the new monomials completely extend on them. In this sense, all the paths can be considered to be of the right-up type. Furthermore, it is direct to see that there will be a one-to-one correspondence between the two families of paths, direct and extended respectively.

It is important to emphasize again that any path can be drawn on the original simple discrete phase space, even those with left-down segments. What is proposed here is that any path can be directly associated with the Gauss polynomials, as exposed beforehand, being the advantage of this approach that we can still count the number of unitary cell under paths in a direct and simple way.

Pictorially we have a possible extended phase space for the example of $N = 3$.

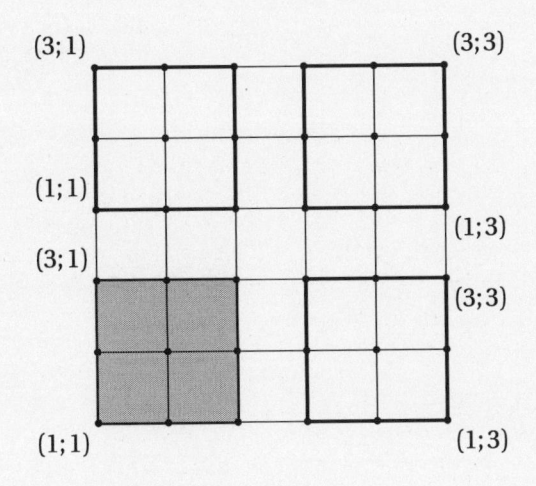

Observe that the original site $(1;3)$ does not coincide with the new site $(1;1)$.

In the simple example of $N = 3$ let us consider the path $P_d = \hat{C}^{-1}\hat{D}^{-1}\hat{C}\hat{D}$ describing a simple counterclockwise loop starting and ending at $(1;1)$ so that $P_d = \hat{1}q^{-1}$. This choice of the origin is arbitrary and was considered for simplicity only; we could have started at any site of the lattice, obeying the cyclic character of the shifts.

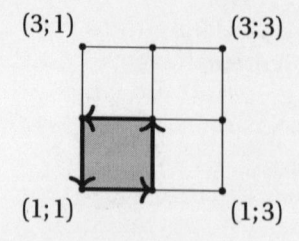

The associated new path reads $P_a = \hat{C}^2\hat{D}^2\hat{C}\hat{D}$, and is depicted in the extended discrete phase space as

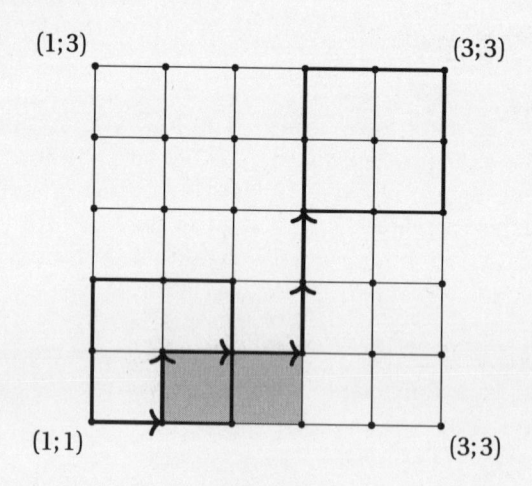

We must observe that in both cases the starting and ending site is $(1;1)$, as it should be.

In what refers to the area enclosed by the path it is important to point that the apparent difference with respect to that obtained in the direct case is due to the fact that, in the extended case, we have to deal with the mod N arithmetic. Therefore, if in the direct case we have

$$P_d = \hat{C}^{-1}\hat{D}^{-1}\hat{C}\hat{D} = \hat{1}q^{-1},$$

in the extended case we will have

$$P_e = \hat{C}^2\hat{D}^2\hat{C}\hat{D} = \hat{C}^3\hat{D}^3 q^2,$$

but it is immediate to see that, besides $\hat{C}^3 = \hat{D}^3 = \hat{I}$, we also have $-1 \equiv 2$ (mod 3). Therefore we conclude that the extended version of the discrete phase space gives the same ending point and the same area mod N enclosed by the path, thus completely characterizing it.

In a general form we can say that the association of the extended paths with the Gauss polynomials is given by

$$(\hat{C}+\hat{D})^M = \sum_{j=0}^{M} \binom{M}{j}_q \hat{C}^j \hat{D}^{M-j},$$

where M must be such that it corresponds to the sum of the total number of steps of the extended path. By its turn, the dimension of the extended discrete phase space will be given by the least number of copies of $N \times N$, being N the dimension of the original state space, such that the new extended path is completely contained inside it. For example, in a simple case of a monomial with 4 operators, namely the path $P_d = \hat{D}\hat{C}^{-t}\hat{D}^{-s}\hat{C}^r$, where N is the dimension of the original state space and $t, s, r \leq N$, the associated extended path will be $P_e = \hat{D}\hat{C}^{N-t}\hat{D}^{N-s}\hat{C}^r$. Then M is given by the sum of the absolute values of the exponents $M = |r| + |N-s| + |N-t| + 1$. Clearly, the case for which the condition $t, s, r \geq N$ is verified can also be treated in a similar way by considering the minimum multiple of N that results in positive exponents of the operators $\hat{D}$ and $\hat{C}$.

Furthermore, since by commuting the operators we get

$$P_e = \hat{C}^{N-t+r}\hat{D}^{N-s+1} q^{N(r+1)} q^{r(1-s)-t},$$

the area under the path (with respect to the reference path) will be given by the exponent of q, viz., $N(r+1) + r(1-s) - t$. Since we have to extract the mod N of this expression, we will end up with an area $A = r(1-s) - t$ integral units of the fundamental cell. For example, if we choose $N = 3, r = 2, s = 1, t = 2$ we would have $\hat{D}\hat{C}^{-2}\hat{D}^{-1}\hat{C}^2 = q^{-2} \Rightarrow A = -2$ for the direct path, while for the extended path we would have $\hat{D}\hat{C}\hat{D}^2\hat{C}^2 = \hat{C}^3\hat{D}^3 q^7$. Since $\hat{C}^3 = \hat{D}^3 = \hat{I}$, we see that $A = 7$. However, we explicitly have, $A = [N(r+1) + r(1-s) - t]$ (mod N), so that $A = [3.3 + 2(1-1) - 2]$ (mod 3) $= -2$, thus confirming our statement.

Closed paths of the form

$$P_c = \underbrace{\hat{D}^{-1}\hat{C}^{-1}\ldots\hat{D}^{-1}\hat{C}^{-1}}_{f}\underbrace{\hat{D}\hat{C}\ldots\hat{D}\hat{C}}_{f}$$

have a distinguished interest in the present context; pictorially it can be seen to represent a closed path enclosing f fundamental unit cells in the discrete phase space. Now, considering one unit cell as having the fundamental area associated with the Planck constant, as we already pointed out, we can conclude that the sequence of operators describing those paths is the discrete quantum analogue of the *ad hoc* Bohr-Sommerfeld quantization rule proposing that, for classical Hamiltonian systems with cyclic variables, the integral of each canonical momentum with respect to its coordinate over a cycle of its motion must be an integer multiple of h, for instance

$$\oint p \, dq = nh.$$

In our *ab initio* discrete approach of the quantum phase space, the counting of cells is the natural process of obtaining the action associated with a transformation – beginning and ending at the same site of the phase space – characterized by a loop. The example given above is the simplest one; any transformation described by a sequence of steps closing a loop will give an integer multiple of the unit cell, and so an integer multiple of the Planck constant due to the inherent complementary role played by the unitary operators.

Finally, it is important to draw attention to the existence of uncertainty relations for unitary operators obeying commutation relations as those presented here [16, 17, 18]. It is then possible to analize the analogue of the Robertson–Schrödinger (RS) [19, 20, 21] uncertainty principle now related to a pair of discrete coordinate and momentum operators, for instance in the Harper model [22], a discrete version of the harmonic oscillator Hamiltonian for continuous variables, as well as its implications for physical systems with periodic boundary conditions. In spite of the great interest in this topic, we refrain from discussing it here.

Bibliography

[1] J. Schwinger, *Quantum Kinematics and Dynamics* (W. A. Benjamin Inc. Publishers, N.Y. 1970).

[2] D. Galetti and A. F. R. de Toledo Piza, Physica **149**, 2676 (1988); Physica A **186**, 513 (1992); Physica A **214**, 207 (1995).

[3] R. Aldrovandi and D. Galetti, J. Math. Phys. **31**, 2987 (1990).

[4] W. K. Wooters, Ann. Phys. **176**, 1 (1987); W. K. Wooters and B. D. Flowers, Ann. Phys. **191**, 363 (1989).

[5] O. Cohendet, P. Combe, M. Sirugue and M. Sirugue-Collin, J. Phys. A **21**, 2875 (1988).

[6] D. Galetti and M. A. Marchiolli, Ann. Phys. **249**, 454 (1996).

[7] A. Vourdas, Phys. Rev. A **41**, 1653 (1990); Rep. Prog. Phys. **67**, 267 (2004).

[8] T. Opatrný, V. Bužek, J. Bajer, and G. Drobný, Phys. Rev. A **52**, 2419 (1995); T. Opatrný, D.-G. Welsch, and V. Bužek, Phys. Rev. A **53**, 3822 (1996).

[9] T. Hakioğlu, J. Phys. A **31**, 6975 (1998).

[10] N. Ya. Vilenkin and A. U. Klimyk, *Representation of Lie Groups and Special Functions: Classical and Quantum Groups and Special Functions* vol.3, (Kluwer Academic Publishers, Dordrecht, 1992).

[11] G. Andrews, *The Theory of Partitions* (Addison-Wesley Publishing Company, Reading, 1976).

[12] V. Kac and P. Cheung, *Quantum Calculus* (Springer Verlag, New York, 2002).

[13] I. P. Goulden and D.M. Jackson, *Combinatorial Enumeration* (Dover Publ. Inc., New York, 1983).

[14] J. Riordan, *Introduction to Combinatorial Analysis* (Dover Publ. Inc., New York, 2002).

[15] P. J. Cameron, *Notes on counting: An introduction to enumerative combinatorics* (Cambridge University Press, Cambridge, 2017).

[16] S. Massar and P. Spindel, Phys. Rev. Lett. **100**, 190401 (2008).

[17] M. A. Marchiolli and M. Ruzzi, Ann. Phys. **327**, 1538 (2012).

[18] M. A. Marchiolli and P. E. M. F. Mendonça, Ann. Phys. **336**, 76 (2013).

[19] W. Heisenberg, Zeits. Physik **43**, 172 (1927).

[20] E. H. Kennard, Zeits. Physik **44**, 326 (1927).

[21] H. P. Robertson, Phys. Rev. **34**, 163 (1929).

[22] P. G. Harper, Proc. Phys. Soc. London A **68**, 874 (1955).

7
Scalar-tensor gravity in Lyra geometry

R. R. Cuzinatto, E. M. de Morais, B. M. Pimentel

Dedicated to Prof. Ruben Aldrovandi, in memoriam.

Abstract: A scalar-tensor theory of gravity based on Lyra manifold is presented. Lyra manifold generalizes the concept of reference frame by including a scale function ϕ. The natural definition of local basis is non-holonomic, its structure constants yielding extra terms in the expression of the connection coefficients which depend on ϕ and its derivatives. The transformation law of tensors fields are modified when compared to the familiar form typical of a Riemannian manifold. The generalized connection is equipped with both curvature and torsion, in principle. Herein we assume a metric compatible four-dimensional torsion-free spacetime. We propose an action for the gravity theory in Lyra spacetime directly inspired in Einstein-Hilbert action of general relativity. The associated Lyra scalar-tensor gravity is dubbed LyST. The field equations are computed by taking variation of the aforementioned action with respect to both the metric tensor and the reference frame scale. These equations present a well-defined Newtonian limit to Poisson's equation with a modified gravitational potential. This consistency check validates the theory for applications in solar-system-scale distances. We then proceed to build the static spherically symmetric solution to LyST. This Lyra-Schwarzschild solution depends on both (an updated version of) the Schwarzschild radius and a new parameter recognized as Lyra radius. The causal structure of Lyra-Schwarzschild metric is analyzed and its dutiful limit to Schwarzschild solution demonstrated.

7.1 Introduction

General relativity (GR) describes the gravitational interaction through a geometric framework based on the hypothesis of a four-dimensional Riemannian manifold, integrability of vector lengths, a torsion-free connection, and a line element built exclusively with the contraction of the metric tensor components with appropriate coordinate differentials [1, 2]. Modified theories of gravity can be built by relaxing these assumptions. An early proposal by Weyl was an attempt to unify gravity and electromagnetism by allowing for changes in the lengths of vectors under parallel transport depending on the gauge potential A_μ [3]. Weyl's theory was rejected as a realistic model when it was pointed out that it would lead to spectral lines emitted by atoms to depend on their past history [4], a fact that is not confirmed by observations. The WIST (Weyl Integrable Space-Time) proposal corrects this problem by demanding the Weyl displacement vector to be irrotational, i.e., $A_\mu = \partial_\mu \sigma$, at the expense of abandoning the interpretation of A_μ as the electromagnetic potential [5, 6].

Lyra was also interested in vector length integrability as a feature of the manifold's geometrical structure [7]. He implemented that in 1951 via the adoption of a gauge function ϕ which would compose a map between reference frames alongside diffeomorphisms. Accordingly, the affine connection Γ related to parallel transports contains two sectors: one of them depending on the metric tensor (and its first-order derivatives), and the second one depending on the scale ϕ (and its first-order derivatives). As a consequence, the curvature tensor formed with this Γ depends explicitly on ϕ; so does the associated torsion tensor. A scale-dependent curvature tensor is one of the differences between Lyra geometry and the (Riemannian) geometry subjacent to the scalar-tensor theory delivered by Brans and Dicke [8].

Lyra launched the geometrical basis for an extended description of gravity but did not delve in physics. Sen was the first to approach the subject in 1957. In fact, in the work [9], he formulated a cosmological model wherein the scale ϕ engenders the redshift of galactic spectral lines. Sen's model included both the scale and the gauge potential A_μ; however, these quantities where constrained, e.g., by the condition $A_\mu = \phi^{-1} \partial_\mu \ln \phi^2$ [10]. This fact yielded the field equation[1]

$$\mathcal{R}_{\mu\nu} - \frac{1}{2} g_{\mu\nu} \mathcal{R} + \frac{3}{2} A_\mu A_\nu - \frac{3}{4} g_{\mu\nu} A_\rho A^\rho = 4\pi G T_{\mu\nu} \tag{7.1}$$

depending explicitly only on A_μ and on the metric tensor—through the contracted objects formed with the Riemann curvature $\mathcal{R}^\rho{}_{\mu\sigma\nu}$ of GR. The constraint between A_μ and ϕ in Sen's proposal introduce a number of consistency problems for the model described by (7.1) and the several applications stemming from it [11, 12, 13, 14, 15, 16]. These inconsistencies are pointed out in [17]; one example is the

---
[1] Model by Sen.

fact that the gauge fixing $\phi = 1$, required to compute Eq. (7.1) from a variational principle, causes $A_\mu = 0$ thus recovering GR and trivializing Sen's attempt towards a modified gravity theory. Sen himself recognized some of the built-in problems of his working hypothesis and tried (alone and with collaborators) to work them off his framework [18, 19]—see also Ref. [20] by other authors. The remedy they found led to the field equation[2]

$$\mathcal{R}_{\mu\nu} - \frac{1}{2} g_{\mu\nu} \mathcal{R} - \frac{3}{2} \frac{1}{\phi^2} \partial_\mu \phi \partial_\nu \phi + \frac{3}{4} g_{\mu\nu} \frac{1}{\phi^2} \partial_\rho \phi \partial^\rho \phi = 4\pi G T_{\mu\nu}, \qquad (7.2)$$

which was proven to be equivalent to a specific incarnation of Brans-Dicke theory [8].

The present work—based on [17]—builds on Sen's seminal ideas of constructing a modified gravity scalar-tensor theory based on Lyra manifold. Herein, however, we do without the gauge potential A_μ (thus eliminating this possible source of inconsistencies), and keep the metric tensor $g_{\mu\nu}$ and the reference frame scale function ϕ as the fundamental geometrical objects of our spacetime proxy. The resulting alternative description of gravitational interaction is dubbed LyST, a shorthand for Lyra Scalar-Tensor theory of gravity.

We begin the journey towards LyST in Section 7.2, where Lyra geometry is formalized. Section 7.3 specifies Lyra spacetime's line element, affine connection, and curvature-based quantities (the torsion tensor is assumed to be null for simplicity). In Section 7.4, we enunciate the action of our gravity theory and derive the field equations thus arriving at LyST. The correct Newtonian limit of LyST is checked in the same section. The internal consistency of our proposal allows us to proceed and study specific solutions of LyST field equations. A first example of such a solution is the generalization of GR's Schwarzschild metric to the context of LyST, called Lyra-Schwarzschild solution; Section 7.5 shows the specific form of this static spherically symmetric line element. It depends on (a generalized version of) the Schwarzschild radius r_S and on the Lyra radius r_L. The causal structure of Lyra-Schwarzschild spacetime is also studied in Section 7.5. Section 7.6 brings our final remarks.

7.2 Lyra geometry

A Lyra differential manifold $\mathcal{M}$ is a topological space of dimension n; it is of the Hausdorff type and second countable [21, 22, 23]. A reference frame in this geometry is given by the triad (U_i, χ_i, Φ_i), where $U_i \subset \mathcal{M}$ is an open subset of $\mathcal{M}$, $\{\chi_i : U_i \to \mathbb{R}^n | n \in \mathbb{Z}_+\}$ is a map parameterizing the coordinates and $\Phi : U_i \to \mathbb{R}^*$ is a scale map.

---

[2] Model by Sen and Dunn.

The choice of a specific reference frame (U,χ,Φ) can be related to a coordinate system x^μ and a scale function ϕ defining the natural basis

$$\mathbf{e}_\mu = \frac{1}{\phi(x)}\partial_\mu. \qquad (7.3)$$

The presence of the scale function therein leads to the non-commutativity of the basis elements

$$[\mathbf{e}_\mu,\mathbf{e}_\nu]=\gamma^\alpha{}_{\mu\nu}\mathbf{e}_\alpha, \qquad \gamma^\alpha{}_{\mu\nu}=\phi^{-2}\left(\delta^\alpha{}_\mu\partial_\nu\phi-\delta^\alpha{}_\nu\partial_\mu\phi\right). \qquad (7.4)$$

The coefficients $\gamma^\alpha{}_{\mu\nu}$ are the structure constants of the Lie algebra respected by the basis. The change of basis between the elements $\mathbf{e}_\mu$ and $\bar{\mathbf{e}}_\mu$ of the reference frames (U,χ,Φ) and $(\bar{U},\bar\chi,\bar\Phi)$ is

$$\bar{\mathbf{e}}_\mu = \frac{\phi(x)}{\bar\phi(\bar x)}\frac{\partial x^\nu}{\partial \bar x^\mu}\mathbf{e}_\nu. \qquad (7.5)$$

Consider a point of a curve $\alpha(t)$ on $\mathcal{M}$; t is the affine parameter along the curve. The tangent vector $\mathbf{v}_{(\alpha)}$ to α at the point $\alpha(0)=P\in\mathcal{M}$ can be represented as

$$\mathbf{v}_{(\alpha)} = v^\mu_{(\alpha)}\mathbf{e}_\mu, \qquad (7.6)$$

which components transform according to:

$$\bar v^\mu_{(\alpha)} = \frac{\bar\phi(\bar x)}{\phi(x)}\frac{\partial \bar x^\mu}{\partial x^\nu}v^\nu_{(\alpha)} \qquad (7.7)$$

The set of all tangent vectors at P form a vector space called the tangent space to $\mathcal{M}$ at P, $\mathbf{T}_P\mathcal{M}$. Similarly, the cotangent space $\mathbf{T}^*_P\mathcal{M}$ is due to all covectors at P,

$$\omega = \omega_\mu \theta^\mu, \qquad (7.8)$$

where the dual basis element θ^μ is defined as

$$\theta^\mu = \phi(x)\mathbf{d}x^\mu \qquad (7.9)$$

in order to fulfill the orthonormality condition $\theta^\nu\circ\mathbf{e}_\mu = \delta^\nu{}_\mu$. Predictably, the covector components transform as follows:

$$\bar\omega_\mu = \frac{\phi(x)}{\bar\phi(\bar x)}\frac{\partial x^\nu}{\partial \bar x^\mu}\omega_\nu. \qquad (7.10)$$

A tensor $\mathbf{W}$ of type (p,q) is a map of p covectors and q tangent vectors onto a real number. This (p,q)-tensor can be expressed on the basis formed by the direct product of p covector basis elements θ^μ and q tangent vector basis elements $\mathbf{e}_\mu$. The transformation rule for the components of such a tensor is

$$\bar{W}^{\alpha_1...\alpha_q}_{\beta_1...\beta_p} = \left[\frac{\bar{\phi}(\bar{x})}{\phi(x)}\right]^{(q-p)} \frac{\partial \bar{x}^{\alpha_1}}{\partial x^{\mu_1}} \cdots \frac{\partial \bar{x}^{\alpha_q}}{\partial x^{\mu_q}} \frac{\partial x^{\nu_1}}{\partial \bar{x}^{\beta_1}} \cdots \frac{\partial x^{\nu_p}}{\partial \bar{x}^{\beta_p}} W^{\mu_1...\mu_q}_{\nu_1...\nu_p} \tag{7.11}$$

under changes of Lyra reference frames.

The definition of lengths and angles in Lyra manifold requires the introduction a $(0,2)$ metric tensor $\mathbf{g}: \mathbf{T}_P\mathcal{M} \times \mathbf{T}_P\mathcal{M} \to \mathbb{R}$ with components

$$g_{\mu\nu} = \mathbf{g}(\mathbf{e}_\mu, \mathbf{e}_\nu). \tag{7.12}$$

The internal product of two vectors will be $\mathbf{g}(\mathbf{u},\mathbf{v}) = g_{\mu\nu}u^\mu v^\nu$, with the frame choice where $\mathbf{u} = u^\mu \mathbf{e}_\mu$, for example. Then, the canonical relation between $\mathbf{T}_P\mathcal{M}$ and $\mathbf{T}^*_P\mathcal{M}$ follows. In fact, the covector components are built as

$$u_\mu = \mathbf{g}(\mathbf{u},\mathbf{e}_\mu) = g_{\mu\nu}u^\nu. \tag{7.13}$$

The length is defined through the curve segment s connecting the points a and b,

$$s = \int_a^b dt\,[\mathbf{g}(\mathbf{v},\mathbf{v})]^{1/2} = \int_a^b dt\,\sqrt{\phi^2 g_{\mu\nu}\frac{dx^\mu}{dt}\frac{dx^\nu}{dt}}. \tag{7.14}$$

The geodesic is the curve connecting a and b that extremizes s. Accordingly, by demanding that the variations of s in (7.14) are null, $\delta s = 0$, we compute the geodesic equation in Lyra manifold:

$$\frac{d^2 x^\mu}{dt^2} + \left\{\begin{array}{c}\mu\\ \rho\sigma\end{array}\right\}\frac{dx^\rho}{dt}\frac{dx^\sigma}{dt} + \frac{1}{\phi}\left[\delta^\mu_{(\rho}\partial_{\sigma)}\phi - g_{\rho\sigma}g^{\mu\nu}\partial_\nu\phi\right]\frac{dx^\rho}{dt}\frac{dx^\sigma}{dt} = 0, \tag{7.15}$$

where

$$\left\{\begin{array}{c}\mu\\ \rho\sigma\end{array}\right\} = \frac{1}{2}g^{\mu\nu}\left(\partial_\sigma g_{\nu\rho} + \partial_\rho g_{\sigma\nu} - \partial_\nu g_{\rho\sigma}\right) \tag{7.16}$$

are the Christoffel symbols and $\delta^\mu_{(\rho}\partial_{\sigma)}\phi = \delta^\mu_\rho \partial_\sigma \phi + \delta^\mu_\sigma \partial_\rho \phi$.

Eq. (7.11) can be used to specify the transformation rule for the metric tensor. Thereby, one computes the transformation rule that the determinant of the of the metric $g = \det(g_{\mu\nu})$ respects:

$$\bar{g} = \left(\frac{\phi}{\bar{\phi}}\right)^{2n}\left|\frac{\partial x}{\partial \bar{x}}\right|^2 g, \tag{7.17}$$

where $n = 4$ is the spacetime dimension. Consequently, the volume $\mathcal{V}$ of a given region in $\mathcal{M}$ will be computed by:

$$\mathcal{V} = \int d^4x\, \phi^4 \sqrt{|g|}. \tag{7.18}$$

The linear connection in Lyra manifold,

$$\Gamma^\lambda{}_{\mu\nu} \mathbf{e}_\lambda \equiv \nabla_{\mathbf{e}_\nu} \mathbf{e}_\mu, \qquad (7.19)$$

is the one participating the definition of the covariant derivative of a vector **v** in the direction of a basis element $\mathbf{e}_\mu$:

$$\nabla_{\mathbf{e}_\nu} \mathbf{v} = \nabla_\nu v^\lambda \mathbf{e}_\lambda \qquad (7.20)$$

with

$$\nabla_\nu v^\lambda = \frac{1}{\phi} \partial_\nu v^\lambda + \Gamma^\lambda{}_{\mu\nu} v^\mu. \qquad (7.21)$$

Notice the presence of the scale accompanying the ordinary derivative in (7.21). At this point, the connection coefficients are not necessarily related to the metric tensor or the Christoffel symbols.

The concept of covariant derivative can be extended to a general (p, q)- tensor **T** as follows:

$$\begin{aligned}\nabla_\sigma T^{\nu_1\ldots\nu_q}_{\mu_1\ldots\mu_p} &= \frac{1}{\phi}\partial_\rho T^{\nu_1\ldots\nu_q}_{\mu_1\ldots\mu_p} + \Gamma^{\nu_1}{}_{\rho\sigma} T^{\rho\ldots\nu_q}_{\mu_1\ldots\mu_p} + \cdots + \Gamma^{\nu_q}{}_{\rho\sigma} T^{\nu_1\ldots\sigma}_{\mu_1\ldots\mu_p} \\ &- \Gamma^\rho{}_{\mu_1\sigma} T^{\nu_1\ldots\nu_q}_{\rho\ldots\mu_p} - \cdots - \Gamma^\rho{}_{\mu_p\sigma} T^{\nu_1\ldots\sigma}_{\mu_1\ldots\rho}.\end{aligned} \qquad (7.22)$$

An self-parallel curve σ on $\mathcal{M}$ is defined as the curve along which the associated tangent vector $\mathbf{v}_{(\sigma)} = v^\mu_{(\sigma)} \mathbf{e}_\mu$ is parallel transported, meaning that the equation $\nabla_{\mathbf{v}_{(\sigma)}} \mathbf{v}_{(\sigma)} = 0$ is satisfied. Expressing the latter in terms of components yields:

$$\frac{d^2 x^\mu}{dt^2} + \left(\phi \Gamma^\mu{}_{\rho\sigma} + \delta^\mu_\rho \nabla_\sigma \phi\right) \frac{dx^\rho}{dt}\frac{dx^\sigma}{dt} = 0, \qquad (7.23)$$

with $\nabla_\nu \phi \equiv \phi^{-1} \partial_\nu \phi$. Eq. (7.15) and (7.23) are different in principle; therefore, geodesic curves and self-parallel curves do not automatically coincide in Lyra manifold.

The curvature tensor associated to the Lyra linear connection is the linear map $\mathbf{R}: \mathbf{T}_P\mathcal{M} \times \mathbf{T}_P\mathcal{M} \times \mathbf{T}_P\mathcal{M} \to \mathbf{T}_P\mathcal{M}$ with components

$$R^\alpha{}_{\mu\nu\beta} = \frac{1}{\phi^2}\partial_\mu\left(\phi\Gamma^\alpha{}_{\beta\nu}\right) - \frac{1}{\phi^2}\partial_\nu\left(\phi\Gamma^\alpha{}_{\beta\mu}\right) + \Gamma^\lambda{}_{\beta\nu}\Gamma^\alpha{}_{\lambda\mu} - \Gamma^\lambda{}_{\beta\mu}\Gamma^\alpha{}_{\lambda\nu}. \qquad (7.24)$$

While curvature is built from second-order covariant derivatives of vectors in $\mathcal{M}$, torsion is an object assembled with a particular combination of first-order covariant derivatives of vectors in $\mathcal{M}$ [21]. In actuality, the torsion related to Lyra connection is the linear map $\tau: \mathbf{T}_P\mathcal{M} \times \mathbf{T}_P\mathcal{M} \to \mathbf{T}_P\mathcal{M}$ with components

$$\tau^\alpha{}_{\mu\nu} = \Gamma^\alpha{}_{\nu\mu} - \Gamma^\alpha{}_{\mu\nu} + \phi^{-2}\left(\delta^\alpha{}_\nu \nabla_\mu \phi - \delta^\alpha{}_\mu \nabla_\nu \phi\right) \qquad (7.25)$$

Notice that Lyra torsion is not only the skew-symmetric part of the connection coefficients due to the last term in (7.25), which is precisely the structure constant $\gamma^{\alpha}{}_{\nu\mu}$ defined in Eq. (7.4).

Clearly, Lyra manifold has a richer geometrical structure than the Riemannian manifold of general relativity, wherein the torsion is null [2]. It is also different from Weitzenböck manifold of teleparallel gravity [13].

7.3 Lyra spacetime

Last section dealt with the geometric structure of Lyra manifold, which is essentially composed by the elements $(\mathcal{M}, \mathbf{g}, \phi, \nabla)$. This can be used as the substrate for a relativistic spacetime. Let us adopt a four-dimensional manifold endowed with a Lorentzian metric signature $(+,-,-,-)$. The line element in this Lyra spacetime will be

$$ds^2 = g_{\mu\nu}(\phi \, dx^{\mu})(\phi \, dx^{\nu}). \tag{7.26}$$

This is an adequate definition of interval because this quantity is invariant both under general coordinate transformations and scale transformations, i.e. reference frame transformations in $\mathcal{M}$.

In this work, we are interested in a direct generalization of GR. Accordingly, we will be inspired by a pseudo-Riemannian spacetime, which is metric compatible and torsion-free. The latter features are compliant with

$$\nabla_{\mathbf{u}} g(\mathbf{v}, \mathbf{w}) = 0 \tag{7.27}$$

and

$$\nabla_{\mathbf{u}} \mathbf{v} - \nabla_{\mathbf{v}} \mathbf{u} = [\mathbf{u}, \mathbf{v}], \tag{7.28}$$

respectively. Herein, $\mathbf{u}$, $\mathbf{v}$ and $\mathbf{w}$ are arbitrary Lyra vectors (cf. discussed in the previous section). By working out all the permutations of (13.25), imposing condition (7.28) and making the choice $\mathbf{u} = \mathbf{e}_{\mu}$, $\mathbf{v} = \mathbf{e}_{\nu}$ and $\mathbf{w} = \mathbf{e}_{\lambda}$, the components of the Lyra connection are expressed univocally in terms of the metric and the scale:

$$\Gamma^{\alpha}{}_{\mu\nu} = \frac{1}{\phi} \begin{Bmatrix} \alpha \\ \mu\nu \end{Bmatrix} + \phi^{-1} \left(\delta^{\alpha}{}_{\nu} \nabla_{\mu} \phi - g_{\mu\nu} \nabla^{\alpha} \phi \right). \tag{7.29}$$

Plugging (7.29) into (7.23) leads to (7.15), thus showing that self-parallel curves and geodesic curves are equivalent in our metric-compatible torsion-free Lyra manifold. The equivalence of affine and metric geodesics is also a feature of GR.

The connection coefficients (7.29) can be substituted into Eq. (7.24) to yield the Lyra curvature tensor components:

$$R^{\alpha}{}_{\mu\nu\beta} = \frac{1}{\phi^2} \mathcal{R}^{\alpha}{}_{\mu\nu\beta} - \frac{2}{\phi} \delta^{\alpha}{}_{[\nu} \nabla_{\beta]} \nabla_{\mu} \phi + \frac{2}{\phi} g_{\mu[\nu} \nabla_{\beta]} \nabla^{\alpha} \phi + \frac{2}{\phi^2} \delta^{\alpha}{}_{[\nu} g_{\beta]\mu} \nabla_{\lambda} \phi \nabla^{\lambda} \phi. \tag{7.30}$$

Here $\nabla_\mu \phi = \phi^{-1} \partial_\mu \phi$. The first term in (7.30) is the curvature tensor evaluated with the Christoffel symbols of GR:

$$\mathscr{R}^\alpha{}_{\mu\nu\beta} = \partial_\nu \left\{ \begin{array}{c} \alpha \\ \mu\beta \end{array} \right\} - \partial_\beta \left\{ \begin{array}{c} \alpha \\ \mu\nu \end{array} \right\} + \left\{ \begin{array}{c} \lambda \\ \mu\beta \end{array} \right\} \left\{ \begin{array}{c} \alpha \\ \lambda\nu \end{array} \right\} - \left\{ \begin{array}{c} \lambda \\ \mu\nu \end{array} \right\} \left\{ \begin{array}{c} \alpha \\ \lambda\beta \end{array} \right\}. \quad (7.31)$$

It is a lengthy but straightforward task to show that the symmetry and skew-symmetry properties of the indices of Lyra curvature tensor $R^\alpha{}_{\mu\nu\beta}$ are completely analogous to those of GR's curvature tensor $\mathscr{R}^\alpha{}_{\mu\nu\beta}$. Moreover, Lyra curvature tensor respects the first Bianchi identity (cyclic permutation of the lower indices add to zero) and the second Bianchi identity (cyclic permutations of the covariant derivative of $R^\alpha{}_{\mu\nu\beta}$ add to zero) [17].

The Lyra equivalent of Ricci tensor is simply $R_{\mu\nu} = R^\alpha{}_{\mu\nu\alpha}$, i.e.

$$R_{\mu\nu} = \frac{1}{\phi^2}\mathscr{R}_{\mu\nu} + \frac{2}{\phi}\nabla_\nu \nabla_\mu \phi + \frac{1}{\phi} g_{\mu\nu} \nabla_\lambda \nabla^\lambda \phi - \frac{3}{\phi^2} g_{\mu\nu} \nabla_\lambda \phi \nabla^\lambda \phi, \quad (7.32)$$

the trace of which, $R = g^{\mu\nu} R_{\mu\nu}$, gives the Lyra curvature scalar:

$$R = \frac{1}{\phi^2}\mathscr{R} + \frac{6}{\phi}\nabla_\lambda \nabla^\lambda \phi - \frac{12}{\phi^2}\nabla_\lambda \phi \nabla^\lambda \phi. \quad (7.33)$$

The analogy with curvature-based objects in GR continues to the Lyra equivalent of Einstein tensor,

$$G_{\mu\nu} = R_{\mu\nu} - \frac{1}{2} g_{\mu\nu} R, \quad (7.34)$$

which obeys $\nabla^\mu G_{\mu\nu} = 0$. Substituting Eqs. (7.32) and (7.33) in Eq. (7.34) gives:

$$G_{\mu\nu} = \frac{1}{\phi^2}\mathscr{G}_{\mu\nu} + \frac{2}{\phi}\nabla_\nu \nabla_\mu \phi - \frac{2}{\phi} g_{\mu\nu} \nabla_\lambda \nabla^\lambda \phi + \frac{3}{\phi^2} g_{\mu\nu} \nabla_\lambda \phi \nabla^\lambda \phi, \quad (7.35)$$

where $\mathscr{G}_{\mu\nu}$ is Einstein tensor in GR.

The above curvature-based objects will be key for building the field equations of the gravitational field in Lyra spacetime. This is the subject of the next section.

7.4 Lyra scalar-tensor gravity

The next logical step, after laying down the geometrical foundations of Lyra spacetime, if to propose a dynamics for the same geometry expected to be sourced by the matter-energy content. This scalar-tensor theory of gravity will generalize general relativity in the sense that the reference frame scale ϕ participates of the description of the interaction alongside the manifold metric $g_{\mu\nu}$. The inspiration for the action integral of LyST comes from GR: we will adopt an Einstein-Hilbert type of action where the Lyra curvature scalar in Eq. (7.33) is the kernel of the integral. The integration element for a four-dimensional spacetime bears the adequate power of the scale for complying with invariance requirements—cf. Eq. (7.18); in fact, it should be $d^4x\,\phi^4\sqrt{-g}$. The last ingredient is the Lagrangian density for the matter fields, which is taken as a function of the matter fields ψ_i themselves, but also depends on the scale function ϕ. Therefore, LyST action reads:

$$S = \int d^4x\,\phi^4\sqrt{-g}\left[\mathscr{L}_m(\psi_i,\nabla\psi_i,\phi,\nabla\phi)\right.$$
$$\left. - \frac{1}{16\pi G}\left(\frac{1}{\phi^2}\mathscr{R} + \frac{6}{\phi}\nabla_\lambda\nabla^\lambda\phi - \frac{12}{\phi^2}\nabla_\lambda\phi\nabla^\lambda\phi\right)\right]. \qquad (7.36)$$

By varying S with respect to $g^{\mu\nu}$, one computes:

$$\mathscr{R}_{\mu\nu} - \frac{1}{2}g_{\mu\nu}\mathscr{R} + 2\phi\nabla_{(\mu}\nabla_{\nu)}\phi + (3-2\phi)g_{\mu\nu}\nabla_\lambda\nabla^\lambda\phi = -8\pi G\phi^2 T_{\mu\nu}, \qquad (7.37)$$

with the stress energy tensor

$$T_{\mu\nu} = -2\frac{\delta\mathscr{L}_m}{\delta g^{\mu\nu}} + g_{\mu\nu}\mathscr{L}_m. \qquad (7.38)$$

Variation of (9.3) with respect to ϕ yields:

$$6\phi\nabla_\lambda\nabla^\lambda\phi - 12\nabla_\lambda\phi\nabla^\lambda\phi + \mathscr{R} = -8\pi G\phi^2 M, \qquad (7.39)$$

where

$$M = -4\mathscr{L}_m - \phi\left(\frac{\partial\mathscr{L}_m}{\partial\phi} - \nabla_\lambda\frac{\partial\mathscr{L}_m}{\partial(\nabla_\lambda\phi)}\right). \qquad (7.40)$$

Finally, variation with respect to the matter fields ψ_i leads to Euler-Lagrange equations:

$$\frac{\partial\mathscr{L}_m}{\partial\psi_i} - \nabla_\lambda\frac{\partial\mathscr{L}_m}{\partial(\nabla_\lambda\psi_i)} = 0. \qquad (7.41)$$

Lyra-Einstein equations could be cast in terms of the Lyra-Einstein tensor $G_{\mu\nu}$ of Eq. (7.34). In fact, when Eqs. (7.32) and (7.33) are used in Eq. (7.37), we are left with $G_{\mu\nu} = 8\pi G T_{\mu\nu}$; precisely the form of Einstein equations of GR. We conclude that LyST gravity is a direct generalization of GR allowing covariance of $G_{\mu\nu}$ and $T_{\mu\nu}$ under both general coordinate transformations and under reference frame scale transformations. This additional feature does not introduce spurious effects as fifth-forces in Solar-system scales because LyST presents a consistent weak-field regime.

The weak field regime—or Newtonian limit—of a gravity theory abides to three basic requirements, viz. (i) non-relativistic motion of test particles (meaning that the spatial components of their four-velocities are negligible); (ii) static gravitational field (so that time derivatives of $g_{\mu\nu}$ and of the LyST scale ϕ are subdominant); and (iii) the gravitational field is almost flat (implying that the metric is a perturbation with respect to Minkowski's and the scale is close to one).

Requirement (ii) reduces the geodesic equation (7.15) to:

$$\frac{d^2 x^\mu}{dt^2} = \frac{1}{2} g^{\mu\nu} \partial_\nu g_{00} + \frac{1}{\phi} g_{00} g^{\mu\nu} \partial_\nu \phi. \qquad (7.42)$$

Requirement (iii),

$$g_{\mu\nu} \approx \eta_{\mu\nu} + h_{\mu\nu} \quad \text{and} \quad \phi \approx 1 + \delta\phi \qquad (7.43)$$

where $h_{\mu\nu} \ll \eta_{\mu\nu}$ and $\delta\phi \ll 1$, plus requirement (i) then bring (7.42) into the classical mechanics' version

$$\ddot{\mathbf{x}} = -\nabla U \qquad (7.44)$$

with the Newtonian potential

$$U = \frac{1}{2} h_{00} + \delta\phi, \qquad (7.45)$$

encompassing the perturbation on the scale. In standard GR, only the first term in (7.45) is present. The LyST version for U absorbs any fifth-force effect on test particles due to the additional degree of freedom ϕ. So much so, that the Poisson equation is recovered in the Lyra version of gravity. In actuality, the trace of Eq. (7.37) can be back substituted into this equation thus yielding:

$$\mathscr{R}_{\mu\nu} + 2\phi \nabla_{(\mu} \nabla_{\nu)} \phi + g_{\mu\nu} \left(\phi \nabla_\lambda \nabla^\lambda \phi - 3 \nabla_\lambda \phi \nabla^\lambda \phi \right) = 8\pi G \phi^2 \left(T_{\mu\nu} - \frac{1}{2} g_{\mu\nu} T \right), \qquad (7.46)$$

which comes down to

$$\mathscr{R}_{00} - \nabla^2 (\delta\phi) = -4\pi G \rho \qquad (7.47)$$

when the weak-field requirements (ii) and (i) are applied. Here we have used that the stress-energy tensor is dominated by the energy density: $T \approx T_{00} = \rho$. On top of that, requirement (iii) demands that

$$\mathscr{R}_{00} \approx -\frac{1}{2} \nabla^2 h_{00}. \qquad (7.48)$$

The latter result is obtained by substituting Eq. (7.43) into Eqs. (7.16) and (7.31)—recall that $\mathscr{R}_{\mu\nu} = \mathscr{R}^\alpha{}_{\mu\nu\alpha}$. Plugging (7.48) into (7.47) leads to the Poisson equation

$$\nabla^2 \left(\frac{1}{2} h_{00} + \delta\phi \right) = \nabla^2 U = 4\pi G \rho. \qquad (7.49)$$

Indeed, the weak field regime of LyST gravity is well defined. This gives us great confidence to explore the solutions to its field equations, Eqs. (7.37), (7.39), and (7.41). In next section, we summarize a simple solution to Eqs. (7.37) and (7.39) with important applications to planetary motion and black hole physics within LyST context.

7.5 Lyra-Schwarzschild solution

The static and spherically symmetric spacetime in LyST gravity is endowed with a metric tensor of the form

$$g_{\mu\nu} = \text{diag}\{\alpha(r), -\alpha^{-1}(r), -r^2, -r^2 \sin^2\theta\} \tag{7.50}$$

and with a reference frame scale of the type

$$\phi = \phi(r). \tag{7.51}$$

Here we use spherical coordinates $\{r, \theta, \varphi\}$. The time dependence is not present; henceforth, a prime denotes differentiation with respect to the radial coordinate r.

Eqs. (7.50) and (7.51) can be substituted into Eqs. (7.37) and (7.39) to give the corresponding LyST field equations in vacuum $(T_{\mu\nu} = M = 0)$:

$$\frac{\alpha'}{\alpha}\frac{\phi'}{\phi} - \frac{1}{\alpha}\frac{1}{r^2} + \frac{1}{r^2} + \frac{1}{r}\frac{\alpha'}{\alpha} + 4\frac{1}{r}\frac{\phi'}{\phi} + 2\frac{\phi''}{\phi} - \left(\frac{\phi'}{\phi}\right)^2 = 0, \tag{7.52}$$

$$-\frac{\alpha'}{\alpha}\frac{\phi'}{\phi} + \frac{1}{\alpha}\frac{1}{r^2} - \frac{1}{r^2} - \frac{1}{r}\frac{\alpha'}{\alpha} - 4\frac{1}{r}\frac{\phi'}{\phi} - 3\left(\frac{\phi'}{\phi}\right)^2 = 0, \tag{7.53}$$

$$-\frac{1}{2}\frac{\alpha''}{\alpha} - 2\frac{\alpha'}{\alpha}\frac{\phi'}{\phi} - \frac{1}{r}\frac{\alpha'}{\alpha} - 2\frac{1}{r}\frac{\phi'}{\phi} - 2\frac{\phi''}{\phi} + \left(\frac{\phi'}{\phi}\right)^2 = 0. \tag{7.54}$$

The combination of Eqs. (7.52) and (7.53) leads to a simple differential equation which solution is

$$\phi(r) = \left(1 - \frac{r}{r_L}\right)^{-1}, \tag{7.55}$$

where r_L is an integration constant dubbed *Lyra radius* for reasons that will be unveiled momentarily. Inserting the above function into Eq. (7.53) and solving the resulting differential equation gives:

$$\alpha(r) = \left(1 - \frac{r_S}{r}\right) \frac{\left(1 - \frac{r}{r_L}\right)^2}{\left(1 - \frac{r_S}{r_L}\right)}. \tag{7.56}$$

At this stage, the quantity r_S is an arbitrary integration constant. However,

$$\lim_{r_L \to \infty} \phi(r) = 1 \quad \text{and} \quad \lim_{r_L \to \infty} \alpha(r) = \left(1 - \frac{r_S}{r}\right), \tag{7.57}$$

which is the result expected from the standard Schwarzschild solution of GR, wherein r_S is the *Schwarzschild radius*. Since Eqs. (7.50), (7.55) and (7.56) obediently recover Schwarzschild metric, we feel justified calling the solution formed by this set of equations the Lyra-Schwarzschild spacetime.

In the context of GR, Schwarzschild radius relates to the geometrical mass $m = GM$ through $r_S = 2m$ [25]. In the context of LyST, the expression of geometrical mass will include both Schwarzschild radius r_S and Lyra radius r_L. In fact, the weak-field regime $\alpha \approx 1 + h_{00}$ and $\phi \approx 1 + \delta\phi$—see Eq. (7.43)—casts Eqs. (7.44) and (7.45) in the form

$$\ddot{r} = -\frac{1}{2}\frac{r_S}{\left(1-\frac{r_S}{r_L}\right)}\frac{1}{r^2} + \frac{3}{2}\frac{r_S}{r_L^2} - \frac{3}{r_L^2}r, \qquad (7.58)$$

where the approximations were taken up to quadratic terms in (r/r_L). The first term on the right-hand side is what is expected from Newtonian mechanics provided that

$$m = \frac{1}{2}\frac{r_S}{\left(1-\frac{r_S}{r_L}\right)} \qquad (7.59)$$

is the mass of the source of the gravitational field. Consistently, the limit $r_L \to \infty$ recovers the usual formula $r_S = 2m$. Interestingly, the equation of motion of a test particle in the Newtonian limit of Lyra-Schwarzschild metric—Eq. (7.58)—brings additional contributions. These second-order effects include a constant repulsive acceleration:

$$a_{\text{rep}} = \frac{3}{r_L^2}\frac{r_S}{2}, \qquad (7.60)$$

and an anti-de Sitter-type attractive term:

$$a_{\text{AdS}} = -\frac{3}{r_L^2}r \qquad (7.61)$$

These additional features are enticing for cosmological applications, which shall be explored in the future. Notice how appealing it is to define the cosmological constant as

$$\frac{\Lambda}{3} = \frac{3}{r_L^2},$$

specially in Eq. (7.61): this would give the typical extra term in Schwarzschild-de Sitter solution [26, 27].

The quantity r_L is an arbitrary integration constant; as such, it could assume either positive or negative values. This leads naturally to two classes of spacetime solutions with different causal structures. The class corresponding to $r_L < 0$ (and $0 < r < \infty$) is either physically meaningless or presents a spacetime diagram for null geodesics that is similar to the one presented by the traditional Schwarzschild metric of GR [17]. For this reason, here we will pay attention to the class of solution where $r_L > 0$ (and $r_S > 0$); this class of spacetime exhibits two singularities. In order to see why, we study the geodesics followed by massless particles. Accordingly, we insert equations (7.50), (7.55), and (7.56) into (7.26), consider radial motion $(d\theta = d\varphi = 0)$, and set $ds^2 = 0$; this leads to the relation

$$\frac{dt}{dr} = \pm\left(1+\frac{r}{r_L}\right)^{-2}\left(1-\frac{2m}{r}+\frac{2m}{r_L}\right)^{-1}, \qquad (7.62)$$

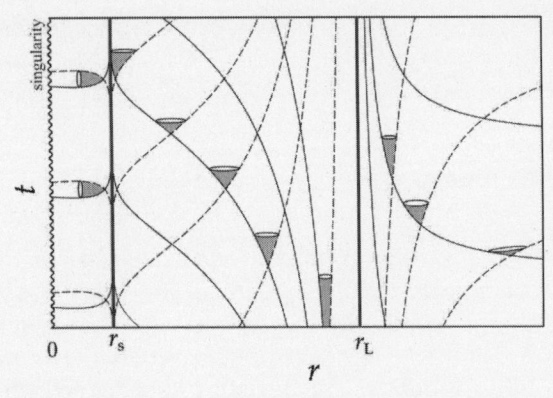

Figure 7.1: Spacetime diagram for null geodesics in Lyra-Schwarzschild spacetime for $r_L > 0$. It is assumed that $r_S < r_L$.

which solution is

$$t_{\pm}(r) = c_1 \pm \left[\frac{r}{\left(1 - \frac{r}{r_L}\right)} + 2m \ln\left(\frac{r}{1 - \frac{r}{r_L}} - 2m\right)\right]. \tag{7.63}$$

From this result, we assess the local light cone structure of Lyra-Schwarzschild metric. The curves with positive (negative) sign are the outgoing (ingoing) null geodesics. The curves built from t_+ (t_-) are the dashed (solid) lines in the diagram of r versus t represented in Fig. 7.1.

The aforementioned singularities of the Lyra-Schwarzschild spacetime for $r_L > 0$ occur at $r = r_S$ and $r = r_L$. The quantity (dt/dr) diverges at these points; this fact explains the pronounced distortions of the light cones in the vicinities of the horizons. Similarly to what happens for the regular Schwarzschild metric of GR, the coordinates r and t switch roles in the region $r < r_S$. Therefore, the singularity at the origin is inevitable. The character of the singularities in Lyra-Schwarzschild spacetime is determined via the Kretschmann scalar $K = R_{\mu\nu\rho\sigma}R^{\mu\nu\rho\sigma}$ which reads–see Eqs. (7.30), (7.55) and (7.56):

$$K = \frac{12 r_S^2}{r^6} \frac{\left(1 - \frac{r}{r_L}\right)^6}{\left(1 - \frac{r_S}{r_L}\right)^2}. \tag{7.64}$$

Notice that: (i) the Kretschmann scalar tends to its pure Schwarzschild version $K = 48m^2/r^6$ in the limit $r_L \to \infty$, as it should; (ii) Eq. (7.64) remains finite at $r = r_S$, so that r_S is a removable singularity; (iii) the Kretschmann scalar approaches zero as $r \to r_L$, and a detailed analysis based on the radial motion of test particles shows that r_L is reached only after an infinite amount of coordinate time. (The latter conclusion is also hinted by the shapes of the light cones around $r = r_L$ in Fig. 7.1.)

The full study of particle and light motion around Lyra-Schwarzschild solution is the subject of others works [23, 28].

7.6 Final remarks

Lyra geometry is endowed with a rich structure encompassing a coordinate-based reference frame with a scale function. The latter is an integral part of maps defined in the manifold. We have explored a connection equipped with non-zero curvature but identically zero torsion. We built the LyST (Lyra-Scalar-Tensor) proposal for a modified gravity framework. The gravitational field is described by both the metric tensor $g_{\mu\nu}$ and the reference scale function ϕ. Their associated field equations are derived from an action inspired in the Einstein-Hilbert action. These field equation accommodate a static spherically symmetric solution dubbed Lyra-Schwarzschild spacetime. It is characterized by a modified version of Schwarzschild radius r_S and by an additional parameter r_L, called the Lyra radius. There are two horizons in Lyra-Schwarzschild spacetime and a central essential singularity. We have shown that the ordinary Schwarzschild metric is also a solution of LyST field equations in the limit of $r_L \to \infty$, in which regime the reference frame scale ϕ is constant. The Newtonian limit of LyST field equations recover Poisson's equation, thus passing the solar system tests in with GR is so successful.

Future works include the detailed study of motion around Lyra-Schwarzschild spacetime [28]. We are also working on the determination of Lyra-FLRW metric; the LyST homogeneous and isotropic metric with applications to cosmology.

Acknowledgements

The authors acknowledge CNPq-Brazil and CAPES-Brazil for financial support.

Bibliography

[1] A. Einstein, *Die Grundlage der allgemeinen Relativitätstheorie*, Ann. Phys. (Berlin) **49**, 769 (1916).

[2] V. De Sabbata and M. Gasperini, *Introduction to Gravitation* (World Scientific, Singapore, 1985).

[3] H. Weyl, *Gravitation und Elektrizität*, Sitzungsberichte der Königlich Preussischen Akademie der Wissenschaften **26**, 465 (1918).

[4] H. F. M. Goenner, *On the History of Unified Field Theories*, Living Reviews in Relativity **7**, 2 (2004).

[5] E. Scholz, *The Unexpected Resurgence of Weyl Geometry in late 20th-Century Physics*. In D. Rowe, T. Sauer, S. Walter (eds), *Beyond Einstein*. Einstein Studies, vol. 14 (Birkhäuser, New York, 2018), pp. 261–360.

[6] C. Romero, J. B. Fonseca-Neto, M. L. Pucheu, *General Relativity and Weyl Geometry*, Class. Quantum Grav. **29**, 155015 (2012); arXiv:1201.1469.

[7] G. Lyra, *Über eine Modifikation der Riemannschen Geometrie*, Mathematische Zeitschrift **54**, 52 (1951).

[8] C. Brans and R. H. Dicke, *Mach's Principle and a Relativistic Theory of Gravitation*, Phys. Rev. **124**, 925 (1961).

[9] D. K. Sen, *A static cosmological model*, Zeitschrift für Physik **149**, 311 (1957).

[10] D. K. Sen, *On Geodesics of a Modified Riemannian Manifold*, Can. Math. Bull. **3**, 255 (1960).

[11] W. D. Halford, *Cosmological Theory Based on Lyra's Geometry*, Austr. J. Phys. **23**, 863 (1970).

[12] K. Bhamra, *A Cosmological Model of Class One in Lyra's Manifold*, Austr. J. Physics **27**, 541 (1974).

[13] A. Beesham, *Friedmann's cosmology in Lyra's manifold*, Astrophys. Spac. Sci. **127**, 355 (1986).

[14] D. R. K. Reddy and R. Venkateswarlu, *Magnetized cosmological model in Lyra manifold*, Astrophys. Spac. Sci. **149**, 287 (1988).

[15] G. P. Singh and K. Desikan, *A new class of cosmological models in Lyra geometry*, Pramana **49**, 205 (1997).

[16] J. K. Singh, *Exact solutions of some cosmological models in Lyra geometry*, Astrophys. Spac. Sci. **314**, 361 (2008).

[17] R. R. Cuzinatto, E. M. de Morais, and B. M. Pimentel, *Lyra scalar-tensor theory: A scalar-tensor theory of gravity on Lyra manifold*, Phys. Rev. D **103**, 124002 (2021); arXiv:2104.06295.

[18] D. K. Sen and K. A. Dunn, *A Scalar-Tensor Theory of Gravitation in a Modified Riemannian Manifold*, J. Math. Phys. **12**, 578 (1971).

[19] J. S. Jeavons, C. B. G. McIntosh, and D. K. Sen, *A correction to the Sen and Dunn gravitational field equations*, J. Math. Phys. **16**, 320 (1975).

[20] W. D. Halford, *Scalar-Tensor Theory of Gravitation in a Lyra Manifold*, J. Math. Phys. **13**, 1699 (1972).

[21] S. Kobayashi and K. Nomizu, *Foundations of Differential Geometry*, Vol. 1 (Wiley-Interscience, New York, 1963).

[22] R. Aldrovandi and J. G. Pereira, An Introduction to Geometrical Physics, 2nd edition (World Scientific, Singapore, 2016).

[23] E. M. de Morais, *Gravitação Escalar-Tensorial na Variedade de Lyra*, PhD Thesis IFT–T.000/99, IFT-UNESP, 2022.

[24] R. Aldrovandi and J. G. Pereira, *Teleparallel Gravity: An Introduction* (Springer, Dordrecht, 2013).

[25] V. P. Frolov and A. Zelnikov, *Introduction to Black Hole Physics* (Oxford University Press, Oxford, 2011).

[26] R. C. Tolman, *Relativity, Thermodynamics, and Cosmology* (Dover, New York, 1987).

[27] R. R. Cuzinatto, B. M. Pimentel, and P. J. Pompeia, *Schwarzschild and de Sitter solutions from the argument by Lenz and Sommerfeld*, Amer. J. Phys. **79**, 662 (2011).

[28] R. R. Cuzinatto, E. M. de Morais, and B. M. Pimentel, *Particle and light motion in Lyra-Schwarzschild spacetime*, in preparation (2023).

8

Braid groups, translation operators and symmetry of Painlevé type equations

H. Aratyn, J. F. Gomes, G. V. Lobo, A. H. Zimerman

Abstract: The affine Weyl group $A_n^{(1)}$ is formulated for $n = 2, 3$ in terms of translation operators defined naturally as basic unit shifts $T_i : v_j \to v_j + \delta_{i,j}$, $i, j = 1, \ldots, n+1$ in a setting of a $n + 1$-dimensional Euclidean space and square roots of products of the neighboring translation operators T_i and T_{i+1} that satisfy fundamental braid group relations. For the case of $n = 2$ we show explicitly that with two general basic requirements, that include braid group relations, such construction will reproduce standard Bäcklund transformations of the extended affine Weyl group structure $A_2^{(1)}$ known to govern the symmetry of Painleveé IV equation.

8.1 Introduction

Bäcklund symmetries of many Painlevé type equations are known to form the affine Weyl groups of type $A_n^{(1)}$. The abelian subgroup of translations that belongs to $A_n^{(1)}$ plays an important role in generating rational solutions of Painlevé equations and in establishing connection between Painlevé equations and discrete Painlevé equations.

We will show here that the extended affine Weyl groups A_n consisting of Bäcklund transformations s_i, $i = 1, 2, \ldots, n+1$, which are symmetries of Painlevé A_n type equations, can be represented as a semi-direct product of the braid group B_{n+2} and the abelian group $\mathcal{T} = \{T_1^{n_1} T_2^{n_2} \ldots T_i^{n_i} | n_i \in \mathbb{Z}, i = 1, 2, \ldots, n+1\}$ of translation operators T_i. Especially, for $n = 3$, the affine extended Weyl group A_3 is obtained by homomorphism from the semidirect product $\mathcal{T} \rtimes B_5$ as explained below in details. The elements of B_5 braid group are square roots $\sigma_i = (T_i T_{i+1})^{1/2}$, $i = 1, 2, 3, 4$ of the product of translation operators.

The square roots σ_i satisfy both braid relations (8.1) and Artin braid relations (8.2) that are fundamental relations of the braid group [1].

Definition 8.1.1. *The braid group B_n is generated by $n - 1$ generators $\sigma_1, \sigma_2, \sigma_3, \ldots, \sigma_{n-1}$ and has "braid" relations:*

$$\sigma_i \sigma_j = \sigma_j \sigma_i, \text{ for } |i - j| \geq 2, \tag{8.1}$$

as well as the so called Artin braid relations:

$$\sigma_i \sigma_{i+1} \sigma_i = \sigma_{i+1} \sigma_i \sigma_{i+1}, \text{ for } 1 \leq i \leq n-1. \tag{8.2}$$

Comparing with relations (8.34) and (8.35) we will see that the square roots of the products of neighboring translation operators $\sigma_i = (T_i T_{i+1})^{1/2}$, $i = 1, 2, 3, 4$, form the B_5 braid group.

For simplicity we will discuss the cases of $n = 2$ and $n = 3$ but expect that the formalism will extend easily to $A_n^{(1)}$ for arbitrary n. We will start first in section 8.2 with a most simple, in this context, example of the affine Weyl symmetry group $A_2^{(1)}$ before proceeding to $A_3^{(1)}$ in section 8.3. The $A_2^{(1)}$ group governs symmetries of Painlevé IV equation. Our discussion will establish an equivalence between formalism based on the Bäcklund transformations regularly denoted in literature [6, 7, 8] by s_i and the one utilizing the translation operators and the square roots of products of the neighboring translation operators that satisfy Artin braid relations (8.2).

In section 8.4 in the context of the 3-dimensional Euclidean space we address the fundamental question of requirements that the square roots $\sigma_i = (T_i T_{i+1})^{1/2}$, $i =$

1, 2, 3 must naturally satisfy to reproduce the well known structure of $A_2^{(1)}$ Bäcklund symmetry transformations:

$$s_i(\alpha_i) = -\alpha_i, \quad s_i(\alpha_{i\pm 1}) = \alpha_{i\pm 1} + \alpha_i, \quad i = 1, 2, 3.$$

It turns out that the only necessary requirements for this to happen are that σ_i squares obviously to $T_i T_{i+1}$ and that it satisfies Artin braid relation (8.2). At the end of the last section we also offer our speculation on a long term objective of the project.

8.2 Translations for $A_2^{(1)}$

We first turn our attention to a simple case of Euclidean three-component vectors (v_1, v_2, v_3), with components v_i that satisfy periodic conditions $v_{i+3} = v_i$, and undergo a simple shift under translation operators T_i, $i = 1, 2, 3$:

$$T_i(v_i) = v_i + 1, \quad T_i(v_j) = v_j, \quad j \neq i. \tag{8.3}$$

Furthermore, there are also two transposition operators s_i, $i = 1, 2$:

$$s_i(v_i) = v_{i+1}, \quad s_i(v_{i+1}) = v_i, \quad s_i(v_{i+2}) = v_{i+2}, i = 1, 2,$$

and an automorphism π:

$$\pi(v_1) = v_2, \quad \pi(v_2) = v_3, \quad \pi(v_3) = v_1 + 1,$$

that can be used to derive the third transformation s_3:

$$s_3(v_3) = v_1 + 1, \quad s_3(v_1) = v_3 - 1, \quad s_3(v_2) = v_2,$$

through the relations $\pi s_i = s_{i+1} \pi$.

All the above transformations form the $A_2^{(1)}$ group of Bäcklund symmetries of Painlevé IV equation (8.8).

We will now show a number of mutual relations that exist between some of these symmetries. One finds namely that the products of translation operators $T_i T_{i+1}$, $i = 1, 2, 3$, acting simply as:

$$(T_i T_{i+1})(v_i) = v_i + 1, \quad (T_i T_{i+1})(v_{i+1}) = v_{i+1} + 1, \quad (T_i T_{i+1})(v_{i+2}) = v_{i+2} \tag{8.4}$$

can be reproduced by the following squares of other symmetry transformations:

$$T_1 T_2 = (\pi s_2)^2, \quad T_2 T_3 = (s_1 \pi)^2, \quad T_3 T_1 = (s_2 \pi)^2. \tag{8.5}$$

Associating, accordingly, the three square roots $(T_i T_{i+1})^{1/2}, i = 1, 2, 3$ with $\pi s_2, s_1 \pi$ and $s_2 \pi$ respectively, we find their actions to be

$$
\begin{array}{c|ccc}
 & v_1 & v_2 & v_3 \\
\hline
(T_1 T_2)^{1/2} & v_2 & v_1 + 1 & v_3 \\
(T_2 T_3)^{1/2} & v_1 & v_3 & v_2 + 1 \\
(T_3 T_1)^{1/2} & v_3 & v_2 & v_1 + 1
\end{array}
\tag{8.6}
$$

Squaring each of the above expressions yields indeed expressions (8.4). The above square root operators satisfy Artin braid relations (8.2) :

$$(T_1 T_2)^{1/2}(T_2 T_3)^{1/2}(T_1 T_2)^{1/2} = (T_2 T_3)^{1/2}(T_1 T_2)^{1/2}(T_2 T_3)^{1/2},$$
$$(T_2 T_3)^{1/2}(T_3 T_1)^{1/2}(T_2 T_3)^{1/2} = (T_3 T_1)^{1/2}(T_2 T_3)^{1/2}(T_3 T_1)^{1/2},$$

etc., which are the only braid relations applying to the case of $n = 2$.

One can pass from the v_i formalism to the α_i formalism with three α_i coefficients defined as

$$\alpha_1 = \sigma(v_2 - v_1), \quad \alpha_2 = \sigma(v_3 - v_2), \quad \alpha_3 = \sigma + \sigma(v_1 - v_3), \tag{8.7}$$

where σ is an arbitrary parameter equal to the sum : $\sum_{i=1}^{3} \alpha_i = \sigma$. This notation was introduced in [2] to enhance the symmetry structure of the underlying Painlevé IV equation given in its symmetric form as :

$$
\begin{aligned}
f_1' &= f_1(f_2 - f_3) + \alpha_1, \\
f_2' &= f_2(f_3 - f_1) + \alpha_2, \\
f_3' &= f_3(f_1 - f_2) + \alpha_3,
\end{aligned}
\tag{8.8}
$$

where $f_i = f_i(z)$ and $' = d/dz$ and $\sum_{i=1}^{3} f_i = \sigma z$.

In the setting of α_i formalism the three translation operators act as:

$$
\begin{aligned}
T_1(\alpha_1, \alpha_2, \alpha_3) &= (\alpha_1 + \sigma, \alpha_2, \alpha_3 - \sigma) \\
T_2(\alpha_1, \alpha_2, \alpha_3) &= (\alpha_1 + \sigma, \alpha_2 - \sigma, \alpha_3) \\
T_3(\alpha_1, \alpha_2, \alpha_3) &= (\alpha_1, \alpha_2 - \sigma, \alpha_3 + \sigma)
\end{aligned}
\tag{8.9}
$$

These actions are illustrated in the Figure 8.1 for $\sigma = 1$, with translations T_1, T_3, T_2 operating along the triangle with vertices at $(\alpha_1, \alpha_2, \alpha_3) = (0, 1, 0), (1, 1, -1)$ and $(1, 0, 0)$, respectively. A similar diagram appeared in [5].

The transformations (8.9) are in agreement with an expression $T_i = r_{i+2} r_{i+1} r_i$, where $r_i = r_{3+i} = s_i$ for $i = 1, 2$ and $r_3 = \pi$ that give translation operators in terms of Bäcklund transformations s_i. More explicitly we have :

$$T_1 = \pi s_2 s_1, \quad T_2 = s_1 \pi s_2, \quad T_3 = s_2 s_1 \pi,$$

These expressions can be reversed. Recalling the relation (8.5) we find from the above expressions that we can write

$$s_i = T_i^{-1}(T_i T_{i+1})^{1/2}, \quad i = 1,2,3$$

reproducing elementary Bäcklund transformations as a product of translation operators with the their square roots satisfying Artin braid relations. As we will confirm in the next section this is a general relation that extends to the higher affine extended Weyl group for $n = 3$.

Due to the presence of parameter σ introduced in equation (8.7) there exist additional automorphisms $\pi_i, i = 1,2,3$ that act on $v_i, i = 1,2,3$ as given below:

	v_1	v_2	v_3	σ
π_1	$-v_2$	$-v_1$	$-v_3+1$	$-\sigma$
π_2	$-v_1-1$	$-v_3$	$-v_2$	$-\sigma$
π_3	$-v_3$	$-v_2$	$-v_1$	$-\sigma$

(8.10)

The automorphisms π_i square to one

$$\pi_i^2 = 1, \quad i = 1,2,3. \tag{8.11}$$

and also satisfy the Artin braid relations

$$\pi_i \pi_j \pi_i = \pi_j \pi_i \pi_j, \quad i \neq j \tag{8.12}$$

They also satisfy the relations

$$\pi_i (T_i T_{i+1})^{1/2} = (T_{i+1} T_{i+2})^{1/2} \pi_{i+2},$$
$$\pi_{i+1} (T_i T_{i+1})^{1/2} = (T_{i+1} T_{i+2})^{1/2} \pi_i,$$
$$\pi_{i+2} (T_i T_{i+1})^{1/2} = (T_{i+1} T_{i+2})^{1/2} \pi_{i+1}.$$

and together with π, s_i of the $A_2^{(1)}$ group form extended Bäcklund symmetries of Painlevé IV equation with parameters α_i that satisfy $\sum_{i=1}^{3} \alpha_i = \sigma$.

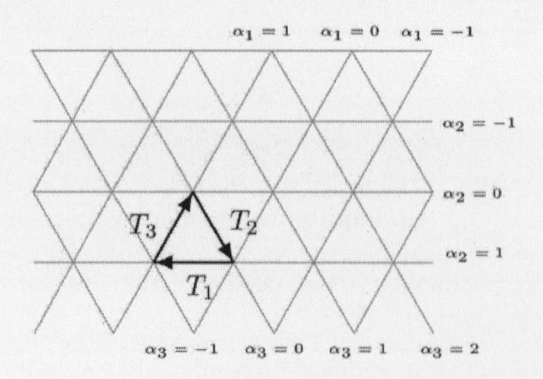

Figure 8.1: Translations: T_1: $(0,1,0) \to (1,1,-1)$, T_2: $(1,0,0) \to (0,1,0)$, T_3: $(1,1,-1) \to (1,0,0)$.

8.3 Translation operators of $A_3^{(1)}$ affine Weyl group

8.3.1 Introducing translation operators and their square roots acting on v_i vectors in the context of $A_3^{(1)}$ group

Consider next the four-component vectors (v_1, v_2, v_3, v_4) defined in an euclidean space that transform under translation operators T_i, $i = 1, 2, 3, 4$ as follows:

$$T_i(v_i) = v_i + 1, \quad T_i(v_j) = v_j, \; j \neq i \tag{8.13}$$

so that e.g. $T_2(v_1, v_2, v_3, v_4) = (v_1, v_2 + 1, v_3, v_4)$. The translation operators commute $[T_i, T_j] = 0$ and therefore e.g. $T_2 T_3(v_1, v_2, v_3, v_4) = (v_1, v_2 + 1, v_3 + 1, v_4) = T_3 T_2(v_1, v_2, v_3, v_4)$.

Can we associate a non-abelian structure to such simple abelian group? Here is an example of doing exactly this. We can define an operator e.g. $(T_2 T_3)^{1/2}$ that acts as

$$(T_2 T_3)^{1/2}(v_1, v_2, v_3, v_4) = (v_1, v_3, v_2 + 1, v_4) \tag{8.14}$$

Acting twice with $(T_2 T_3)^{1/2}$ we then obtain

$$\left((T_2 T_3)^{1/2}\right)^2 (v_1, v_2, v_3, v_4) = (v_1, v_2 + 1, v_3 + 1, v_4),$$

in agreement with the action of the product of translation operators $T_2 T_3$.

Similarly, we also define

$$(T_1 T_2)^{1/2}(v_1, v_2, v_3, v_4) = (v_2, v_1+1, v_3, v_4)$$
$$(T_3 T_4)^{1/2}(v_1, v_2, v_3, v_4) = (v_1, v_2, v_4, v_3+1) \qquad (8.15)$$
$$(T_4 T_1)^{1/2}(v_1, v_2, v_3, v_4) = (v_4, v_2, v_3, v_1+1)$$

to obtain in each case an appropriate action of $T_i T_j$ after squaring the actions of the square-roots.

Common for all these square-root transformations is that they can be expressed by a shift by 1 and transpositions:

$$s_i : v_i \longleftrightarrow v_{i+1}, i = 1, 2, 3, \quad v_j \to v_j, \; j \neq i, i+1. \qquad (8.16)$$

Furthermore we also define

$$s_4(v_1) = v_4 - 1, \; s_4(v_4) = v_1 + 1 \qquad (8.17)$$

as well as an automorphism $\pi(v_i) = v_{i+1}, i = 1, 2, 3$ and $\pi(v_4) = v_1 + 1$ to be able to obtain the same results we have seen above for $(T_i T_{i+1})^{1/2}$ by acting with $s_{i-2} \pi s_i$ on (v_1, v_2, v_3, v_4). This connection between on the one hand $s_{i-2} \pi s_i$ and on the other hand the square root $(T_i T_{i+1})^{1/2}$ will be explained in the next section.

8.3.2 Key results for translation operators within the extended affine Weyl group $A_3^{(1)}$

Introducing $\alpha_i = 2(v_{i+1} - v_i), i = 1, 2, 3$ and $\alpha_4 = 2 + 2(v_1 - v_4)$ leads to identity $\sum_{i=1}^{4} \alpha_i = 2$.

For the transpositions s_i defined in (8.16) and (8.17) it holds that $s_i(\alpha_i) = -\alpha_i$ for all $i = 1, 2, 3, 4$. Consider for illustration s_2. One finds in this case $s_2(\alpha_1, \alpha_2, \alpha_3, \alpha_4) = (\alpha_1 + \alpha_2, -\alpha_2, \alpha_3 + \alpha_2, \alpha_4)$. This is an example of a standard expression for the $A_n^{(1)}$ Bäcklund transformation:

$$s_i : \alpha_i \to -\alpha_i, \alpha_{i-1} \to \alpha_{i-1} + \alpha_i, \alpha_{i+1} \to \alpha_{i+1} + \alpha_i, \; i = 1, 2, ..., n+1, \qquad (8.18)$$

that together with the automorphism $\pi : \alpha_i \to \alpha_{i-1}$ satisfy the the following fundamental relations for all $i = 1, 2, 3, 4$:

$$s_i^2 = 1, \quad s_i s_j = s_j s_i \; (j \neq i, i \pm 1), \quad s_i s_j s_i = s_j s_i s_j \; (j = i \pm 1),$$
$$\pi^4 = 1, \quad \pi s_j = s_{j+1} \pi. \qquad (8.19)$$

In this setting, the four translation operators, $T_i, i = 1, 2, 3, 4$, are given by expression $T_i = r_{i+3} r_{i+2} r_{i+1} r_i$, where $r_i = r_{4+i} = s_i$ for $i = 1, 2, 3$ and $r_4 = \pi$. More explicitly the translation operators $T_1, ..., T_4$ are given by:

$$T_1 = \pi s_3 s_2 s_1, \quad T_2 = s_1 \pi s_3 s_2, \quad T_3 = s_2 s_1 \pi s_3, \quad T_4 = s_3 s_2 s_1 \pi, \qquad (8.20)$$

and satisfy $T_1 T_2 T_3 T_4 = 1$ The inverse T_i^{-1} operators are given by:

$$T_1^{-1} = s_1 s_2 s_3 \pi^3, \quad T_2^{-1} = s_2 s_3 \pi^3 s_1, \quad T_3^{-1} = s_3 \pi^3 s_1 s_2, \quad T_4^{-1} = \pi^3 s_1 s_2 s_3. \qquad (8.21)$$

The operators $T_i, \ldots, T_4$ generate the following translations when acting on the parameters of Painlevé V equation:

$$\begin{aligned}
T_1(\alpha_1, \alpha_2, \alpha_3, \alpha_4) &= (\alpha_1 + 2, \alpha_2, \alpha_3, \alpha_4 - 2), \\
T_2(\alpha_1, \alpha_2, \alpha_3, \alpha_4) &= (\alpha_1 - 2, \alpha_2 + 2, \alpha_3, \alpha_4), \\
T_3(\alpha_1, \alpha_2, \alpha_3, \alpha_4) &= (\alpha_1, \alpha_2 - 2, \alpha_3 + 2, \alpha_4), \\
T_4(\alpha_1, \alpha_2, \alpha_3, \alpha_4) &= (\alpha_1, \alpha_2, \alpha_3 - 2, \alpha_4 + 2),
\end{aligned} \qquad (8.22)$$

As follows from their definitions (8.20), the translation operators commute with Bäcklund transformations s_i for $i = 1, 2, 3, 4$ and automorphism π in the following way:

$$\begin{aligned}
s_i T_i s_i &= T_{i+1}, & s_i T_j &= T_j s_i, & \pi T_i &= T_{i+1} \pi \\
s_i T_i^{-1} s_i &= T_{i+1}^{-1}, & s_i T_j^{-1} &= T_j^{-1} s_i, & j &\neq i, i+1,
\end{aligned} \qquad (8.23)$$

for $i, j = 1, 2, 3, 4$. For example, we find $s_4 T_1 = T_4 s_4$.

We next consider a quartic product of two Bäcklund transformations $s_i s_j$. One can express such products of $s_i s_j$ in the following way

$$T_i T_{i+1} = (s_{i-1} \pi s_{i+1})^2, \qquad (8.24)$$

from which it follows that

$$(T_i T_{i+1})^{1/2} = s_{i-1} \pi s_{i+1}, \qquad (8.25)$$

as illustrated in the following examples.

$$(T_1 T_2)^{1/2} = s_4 \pi s_2, \quad (T_2 T_3)^{1/2} = s_1 \pi s_3$$

There are also the square-roots of the type $(T_i T_{i+2})^{1/2} = s_{i-1} \pi s_i$, for $i = 1$ and $i = 2$ given by

$$(T_1 T_3)^{1/2} = s_4 \pi s_1, \qquad (T_2 T_4)^{1/2} = s_1 \pi s_2.$$

They transform $(\alpha_1, \alpha_2, \alpha_3, \alpha_4)$ as follows

$$\begin{aligned}
(T_1 T_3)^{1/2}(\alpha_1, \alpha_2, \alpha_3, \alpha_4) &= (2 - \alpha_2, -\alpha_1, 2 - \alpha_4, -\alpha_3), \\
(T_2 T_4)^{1/2}(\alpha_1, \alpha_2, \alpha_3, \alpha_4) &= (-\alpha_4, 2 - \alpha_3, -\alpha_2, 2 - \alpha_1),
\end{aligned} \qquad (8.26)$$

which when applied twice successively yield the results for $T_1 T_3$ and $T_2 T_4$ that fully agree with relations (8.22). Moreover for a class of so-called seed solutions of Painlevé V equations with $(\alpha_1, \alpha_2, \alpha_3, \alpha_4) = (a, 1 - a, a, 1 - a)$ [3], the square roots

$(T_i T_{i+2})^{1/2}$ shift the parameter a : $a \to a - (-1)^i$ while maintaining the form of the underlying seed solutions [4].

The following commutation relations can be derived from the definitions (8.25):

$$T_i (T_i T_{i+1})^{1/2} = (T_i T_{i+1})^{1/2} T_{i+1} \tag{8.27}$$

$$T_{i+1}(T_i T_{i+1})^{1/2} = (T_i T_{i+1})^{1/2} T_i \tag{8.28}$$

$$T_j (T_i T_{i+1})^{1/2} = (T_i T_{i+1})^{1/2} T_j, \quad j \neq i, j \neq i+1 \tag{8.29}$$

or in a different form :

$$T_i^{-1} (T_i T_{i+1})^{1/2} = (T_i T_{i+1})^{1/2} T_{i+1}^{-1} \tag{8.30}$$

$$T_{i+1}^{-1}(T_i T_{i+1})^{1/2} = (T_i T_{i+1})^{1/2} T_i^{-1} \tag{8.31}$$

$$T_j^{-1}(T_i T_{i+1})^{1/2} = (T_i T_{i+1})^{1/2} T_j^{-1}, \quad j \neq i, j \neq i+1 \tag{8.32}$$

We also have relations:

$$(T_i T_{i+1})^{1/2} (T_{i+2} T_{i+3})^{1/2} = (T_{i+2} T_{i+3})^{1/2} (T_i T_{i+1})^{1/2}, \tag{8.33}$$

and more generally

$$(T_i T_{i+1})^{1/2} (T_j T_{j+1})^{1/2} = (T_j T_{j+1})^{1/2} (T_i T_{i+1})^{1/2}, \quad j \neq i+1. \tag{8.34}$$

The simple commutation relations (8.34) for $j \neq i+1$ change drastically when we consider the case of $j = i+1$. It turns out that the relevant relations for $(T_i T_{i+1})^{1/2}$ and $(T_{i+1} T_{i+2})^{1/2}$ are cubic and of the form:

$$(T_i T_{i+1})^{1/2} (T_{i+1} T_{i+2})^{1/2} (T_i T_{i+1})^{1/2} = (T_{i+1} T_{i+2})^{1/2} (T_i T_{i+1})^{1/2} (T_{i+1} T_{i+2})^{1/2}. \tag{8.35}$$

One illustrative and simple way to check the above relations is to go back to the space of (v_1, v_2, v_3, v_4) vectors and apply the definitions (8.14) and (8.15) to establish the relation (8.35) in a very simple way.

We recognize in (8.35) the Artin braid relations that are one of two main relations in the definition 8.1.1 of the braid group [1].

We will now discover that the Weyl group $A_3^{(1)}$ of Bäcklund transformations can be realized as a semi-direct product of B_5 braid group augmented with by abelian group $\mathcal{T}$ with four elements T_i, $i = 1, 2, 3, 4$ that satisfy relations (8.27)-(8.29) so that

$$T_i \sigma_i = \sigma_i T_{i+1}, \quad T_{i+1} \sigma_i = \sigma_i T_i, \quad T_j \sigma_i = \sigma_i T_j, \quad |i-j| \geq 2, \tag{8.36}$$

where for brevity we continue to use the symbol σ_i to denote $(T_i T_{i+1})^{1/2}$.

We construct a new group $\mathscr{T} \rtimes B_5$, called the (outer) semi-direct product of $\mathscr{T}$ and B_5:

$$(\mathscr{T} \rtimes B_5) \rtimes (\mathscr{T} \rtimes B_5) \to (\mathscr{T} \rtimes B_5)$$
$$(T_i, \sigma_i) \cdot (T_j, \sigma_j) = (T_i \varphi_{\sigma_i}(T_j), \sigma_i \sigma_j),$$

with respect to homomorphism φ, defined as:

$$\varphi_{\sigma_i}(T_j) = \sigma_i T_j \sigma_i^{-1}. \tag{8.37}$$

It is natural to define a map: $S : (\mathscr{T} \rtimes B_5) \to A_3^{(1)}$ such that

$$S(T_i, \sigma_i) = T_i^{-1} \sigma_i \equiv s_i,$$

thus we have proposed the following expressions for Bäcklund transformation s_i

$$s_i = T_i^{-1}(T_i T_{i+1})^{1/2}, \quad i = 1, 2, 3, 4, \tag{8.38}$$

in terms of translation operators and their square-roots.

It follows that S is a homomorphism that preserves the product "·":

$$S\big((T_i, \sigma_i) \cdot (T_j, \sigma_j)\big) = S\big(T_i \varphi_{\sigma_i}(T_j), \sigma_i \sigma_j\big)$$
$$= (T_i \varphi_{\sigma_i}(T_j))^{-1} \sigma_i \sigma_j = S(T_i, \sigma_i) S(T_j, \sigma_j) = T_i^{-1} \sigma_i T_j^{-1} \sigma_j,$$

with the right hand side that agrees with $(T_i \varphi_{\sigma_i}(T_j))^{-1} \sigma_i \sigma_j$ both for $j = i+1$ and for $j \neq i+1$, since according to equation (8.36)

$$\varphi_{\sigma_i}(T_i^{-1}) = T_{i+1}^{-1}, \quad \varphi_{\sigma_i}(T_{i+1}^{-1}) = T_i^{-1}, \quad \varphi_{\sigma_i}(T_j^{-1}) = T_j^{-1}, \quad |i-j| \geq 2.$$

This just shows that the action of the homomorphism φ_{σ_i} agrees with a "physical" product

$$T_i^{-1} \sigma_i T_j^{-1} \sigma_j = T_i^{-1} (\sigma_i T_j^{-1} \sigma_i^{-1}) \sigma_i \sigma_j.$$

From relations (8.32) we are now able to reproduce a basic property of s_i Bäcklund transformations namely that they square to one:

$$s_i^2 = T_i^{-1}(T_i T_{i+1})^{1/2} T_i^{-1}(T_i T_{i+1})^{1/2}$$
$$= T_i^{-1} T_{i+1}^{-1}(T_i T_{i+1})^{2/2} = 1.$$

Furthermore relations (8.34) allow us to prove

$$s_i s_j = s_j s_i, \quad j \neq i \pm 1,$$

or equivalently that $(s_i s_j)^2 = 1$.

The relations (8.35) are equivalent to

$$s_i s_{i+1} s_i = s_{i+1} s_i s_{i+1}$$

To prove it insert s_i and s_{i+1} from definition (8.38) on both sides of the above equation to obtain $s_i s_{i+1} s_i T_{i+1}^2 T_{i+1}$ on both left hand and right hand side and since the translation operators are invertible they can be removed to leave us with the desired relation.

Thus we can therefore use a "physical" product and furthermore set

$$T_i^{-1} \sigma_i T_i^{-1} \sigma_i = T_i^{-1} (\sigma_i T_i^{-1} \sigma_i^{-1}) \sigma_i^2 = T_i^{-1} T_{i+1}^{-1} \sigma_i^2 = 1,$$

following from $\sigma_i^2 = T_i T_{i+1}$.

8.4 Comments on uniqueness of the square-roots of the product of translations and long term goals of the project

In this section we address the issue of uniqueness of the definition the square-roots of the product of translations. Can we choose the action of $(T_i T_{i+1})^{1/2}$ based solely on basis of requirements of Braid groups relations and recover the correct structure of Bäcklund transformations form the appropriate affine Weyl group. Here we will answer this question in the affirmative carrying out the discussion for simplicity in the setting of $A_2^{(1)}$ group.

Looking back on e.g. equations (8.6) we discover a potential ambiguity in a choice of the square roots $(T_i T_{i+1})^{1/2}$ as there, in principle, could be several candidates for $(T_i T_{i+1})^{1/2}$ that square to $T_i T_{i+1}$ as given in (8.4).

Although we made a consistent choice in selecting the expressions (8.5) based on the Bäcklund transformations s_i, the fundamental question is if there exist other choices for $(T_i T_{i+1})^{1/2}$ than those made in (8.6) that are independent of the form of the Bäcklund transformations s_i and selected solely due to their consistency with the two basic requirements we are imposing:

1) $(T_i T_{i+1})^{1/2}, i = 1, 2, 3$, reproduce the correct expressions (8.4) for $T_i T_{i+1}$

2) $(T_i T_{i+1})^{1/2}, i = 1, 2, 3$, are solutions to Artin braid relations (8.2).

It is easy to find examples of $(T_i T_{i+1})^{1/2}$, which fail one of the above points 1) or 2). For example $(T_i T_{i+1})^{1/2}(v_1, v_2, v_3) = (v_2 + c_2, v_3 + c_3, v_1 + c_1)$, with $c_i, i = 1, 2, 3$ being constants will not square to $T_i T_{i+1}$ and thus fails the requirement 1). Another potential and very simple candidate: $(T_1 T_2)^{1/2}(v_1, v_2, v_3) = (v_1 + 1/2, v_2 + 1/2, v_3)$, $(T_2 T_3)^{1/2}(v_1, v_2, v_3) = (v_1, v_2 + 1/2, v_3 + 1/2)$ etc., will square correctly and thus will satisfy the first requirement but does not satisfy the Artin braid relation and thus fails the requirement 2).

We can address generally the above fundamental question as long as we restrict the choices for $(T_i T_{i+1})^{1/2}$ to be linear of the following form:.

$$(T_1 T_2)^{1/2}(\vec{v}) = (c_1 v_1 + c_2 v_2 + \beta_1, d_1 v_1 + d_2 v_2 + \beta_2, v_3),$$
$$(T_2 T_3)^{1/2}(\vec{v}) = (v_1, n_1 v_2 + n_2 v_3 + \gamma_1, m_1 v_2 + m_2 v_3 + \gamma_2), \ldots.$$

In such case imposing the requirements 1) and 2) still allows the following generalization of the equation (8.6) to

	v_1	v_2	v_3
$(T_1 T_2)^{1/2}$	$v_2 + \beta_1$	$v_1 + \beta_2$	v_3
$(T_2 T_3)^{1/2}$	v_1	$v_3 + \gamma_1$	$v_2 + \gamma_2$
$(T_3 T_1)^{1/2}$	$v_3 + \delta_1$	v_2	$v_1 + \delta_2$

(8.39)

with $\beta_1 + \beta_2 = \gamma_1 + \gamma_2 = \delta_1 + \delta_2 = 1$.

The remaining question is if such $(T_i T_{i+1})^{1/2}$ as given in (8.39) would lead to correct expressions for the Bäcklund transformations s_i? By this we mean, the Bäcklund transformations s_i such that they satisfy the fundamental relations (8.18) with α_i that can then appear as parameters of Painlevé IV equation invariant under $A_2^{(1)}$.

From expressions for translation operators given in relation (8.3) we obtain the following formulas for the Bäcklund transformations s_i as obtained from relation (8.38):

	v_1	v_2	v_3
s_1	$v_2 + \beta_1$	$v_1 + \beta_2 - 1$	v_3
s_2	v_1	$v_3 + \gamma_1$	$v_2 + \gamma_2 - 1$
s_3	$v_3 + \delta_1$	v_2	$v_1 + \delta_2 - 1$

(8.40)

corresponding to $(T_i T_{i+1})^{1/2}$ given in equation (8.39).

The question is if with such generalization it is possible for transformations s_i to satisfy the fundamental relations (8.18). Here we verify that this is the case for $A_2^{(1)}$. For this to happen we need to choose the right basis of α_i parameters. We generalize the expressions (8.7) to

$$\alpha_1 = \sigma(v_2 - v_1) + \sigma \beta_1, \quad \alpha_2 = \sigma(v_3 - v_2) + \sigma \gamma_1, \quad \alpha_3 = \sigma(v_1 - v_3) - \sigma \delta_1 \quad (8.41)$$

We note for completeness that it now holds that $\sum_{i=1}^{3} \alpha_i = \sigma(\beta_1 + \gamma_1 - \delta_1)$.

In this basis it holds that s_i acting as defined in general expressions (8.40) will transform $\alpha_i, i = 1, 2, 3$ according to the fundamental relations (8.18) of $A_2^{(1)}$ transformations.

The above explicit construction of $A_2^{(1)}$ transformations out of basic geometrical objects like translation operators and related square roots of their products leads us naturally to the closing comment about the ultimate objective of our project. Although the principal and initial reason for discovery of Painlevé equations has been their property of having only solutions without any movable critical singularities in the complex plane, a rich geometrical and algebraic structure that has been uncovered in recent decades prompts a question if their origin can be established solely on geometrical grounds. The above example of $A_2^{(1)}$ illustrates well the steps that are likely to be involved in such a project. The natural first step is to define some elementary geometrical objects like basic shifts in Euclidean space that can eventually be also interpreted as elements of an abelian subgroup of an ultimate symmetry group. The extension of this simple abelian structure can then be accomplished by defining, for example, square root operators formed out of products of translations that for consistency need to satisfy fundamental braid group relations. The goal is then to establish both the symmetry groups and corresponding invariant Painlevé type equations out of these simple geometrical considerations.

Acknowledgments

This study was financed in part by the Coordenação de Aperfeiçamento de Pessoal de Nível Superior - Brasil (CAPES) - Finance Code 001 (G.V.L.) and by CNPq and FAPESP (J.F.G. and A.H.Z.).

Bibliography

[1] Ruben Aldrovandi and Roldão Da Rocha Jr., *A Gentle Introduction to Knots, Links and Braids* (World Scientific, Singapore, 2021).

[2] V.C.C. Alves, H. Aratyn, J.F. Gomes and A.H. Zimerman, J. Phys. A: Math. Theor. **53**, 445202 (2020).

[3] H. Aratyn, J.F. Gomes, G.V. Lobo and A.H. Zimerman, *On Rational Solutions of Dressing Chains of Even Periodicity*, Symmetry **15**, 249 (2023).

[4] H. Aratyn, J.F. Gomes, G.V. Lobo and A.H. Zimerman, *Why is my rational Painlevé V solution not unique?*; arXiv:2307.07825.

[5] P. Forrester and N. Witte, *Application of the τ-Function Theory of Painlevé Equations to Random Matrices: PIV, PII and the GUE*, Commun. Math. Phys. **219**, 357 (2001).

[6] M. Noumi, *Painlevé Equations through Symmetry*, in: Translations of Mathematical Monographs, vol. 223, (American Mathematical Society Providence, 2004).

[7] M. Noumi and Y. Yamada, *Affine Weyl Group Symmetries in Painlevé Type Equations*, in: C.J. Howls, T. Kawai and Y. Takei (eds.), *Toward the Exact WKB Analysis of Differential Equations, Linear or Non-Linear*, pp. 245-259 (Kyoto University Press, Kyoto, 2000).

[8] M. Noumi M, *Affine Weyl Group Approach to Painlevé Equations*, Proceedings of the ICM, Beijing 2002, vol. 3, 497; arXiv:math-ph/0304042.

9

Inflationary dynamics in modified gravity models

R. R. Cuzinatto, L. G. Medeiros

Abstract: Higher-order theories of gravity are a branch of modified gravity wherein the geometrodynamics of the four-dimensional Riemannian manifold is determined by field equations involving derivatives of the metric tensor of order higher than two. This paper considers a general action built with the Einstein-Hilbert term plus additional curvature-based invariants, viz. the Starobinsky R^2-type term, a term scaling with R^3, and a correction of the type $R\Box R$. The focus is on the background inflationary regime accommodated by these three models. For that, the higher-order field equations are built and specified for the FLRW line element. The dynamical analysis in the phase space is carried in each case. This analysis shows that the Starobinsky-plus-R^3 model keeps the good features exhibited by the pure Starobinsky inflationary model, although the set of initial conditions for the inflaton field χ leading to a graceful exit scenario is more contrived; the coupling constant α_0 of the R^3 invariant is also constrained by the dynamical analysis. The Starobinsky-plus-$R\Box R$ model turns out being a double-field inflation model; it consistently enables an almost-exponential primordial acceleration followed by a radiation dominated universe if its coupling β_0 takes values in the interval $0 \leq \beta_0 \leq 3/4$. The models introducing higher-order correction to Starobinsky inflation are interesting due to the possibility of a running spectral index n_s, something that is allowed by current CMB observations.

9.1 Introduction

General relativity (GR) currently stands as the canonical theory describing the gravitational interaction. Since its proposition early in the XX century, GR was able to explain and predict a plethora of phenomena in the realms of physics, astrophysics and cosmology. Among them are the examples of gravitational redshift [1], gravitational lensing [2], prediction of existence of black holes [3] and gravitational waves [4], and the description of the universe's large scale evolution [5]. Even so, there are indications that GR is not a definitive theory of gravity. The hints are structural in nature—e.g. the existence of singularities within GR— or particularly related to high-energy regimes: GR can not be trivially quantized [6, 7] and it does not provide a completely consistent description of the primeval universe (around the energy scales related to inflation) [8, 9]. Therefore, it is only natural to propose modification to GR in an attempt to overcome these challenges.

From a purely theoretical point of view, GR is built by considering that gravity is described by a metric-compatible four-dimensional Riemannian manifold, which is endowed with a single rank-2 tensorial field—the metric tensor $g_{\mu\nu}$—, which is invariant under diffeomorphisms, and which exhibits second-order equations of motion (cf. the Lovelock theorem) [10]. Modifications to GR are implemented by relaxing anyone of the aforementioned hypotheses. For instance, Horndeski theories [11] stem from violating the hypothesis that the metric is the only fundamental field: an extra degree of freedom is also assumed. A different pathway is to admit a Riemann-Cartan-type of spacetime substrate, a manifold equipped with an affine connection bearing a non-null antisymmetric sector; in this case, torsion is included as a gravitational entity and the Einstein-Cartan theories are born [12]. Another possibility is to eliminate curvature while keeping a non-null torsion; this is a feature of Weitzenböck manifold and the teleparallel equivalent of general relativity [13, 4, 15, 16, 17, 18].[1] On the other hand, if the fields equations for the metric tensor are allowed to include derivatives of order greater than two— while simultaneously maintaining all the other hypotheses—then the higher-order gravity theories are obtained [19, 20].

Higher-order theories of gravity feature additional terms to the Einstein-Hilbert (EH) action engendering higher-order derivatives in the field equations. Such extra terms in the action may be seen as correction terms, classified according to their typical mass/energy scale. Following this classification, zero-order terms are those counted in units of square mass; they correspond to the curvature scalar R and the cosmological constant Λ in the EH action. First-order corrections to EH action involve term of mass to the fourth power; these are built with the invariants

$$R^2 \quad \text{and} \quad R_{\mu\nu}R^{\mu\nu}. \tag{9.1}$$

---

[1] Regarding the teleparallel framework for gravity, we also point the reader to the contribution by P. J. Pompeia for this book and the references cited in that paper.

It is worth mentioning that the other two possible first-order invariants, $R_{\mu\nu\alpha\beta}R^{\mu\nu\alpha\beta}$ and $\Box R$, do not contribute to the field equations.[2] Second-order terms are corrections to EH action having units of mass to the sixth power; they made up with the following invariants [21]

$$R\Box R, R_{\mu\nu}\Box R^{\mu\nu},$$
$$R^3, RR_{\mu\nu}R^{\mu\nu}, R_{\mu\nu}R^{\nu}{}_{\alpha}R^{\alpha\mu}, \qquad (9.2)$$
$$RR_{\mu\nu\alpha\beta}R^{\mu\nu\alpha\beta}, R_{\mu\alpha}R_{\nu\beta}R^{\mu\nu\alpha\beta}, \text{ and } R_{\mu\nu\alpha\beta}R^{\alpha\beta}{}_{\kappa\rho}R^{\kappa\rho\mu\nu}.$$

Among the various applications of higher-order theories of gravity [22, 23, 24, 25], one class of particular interest is that of inflationary cosmology [26, 27, 28, 29].

In the end of 1979, Alexei A. Starobinsky proposed that quantum gravitational effects, presumably significant in the primordial universe, produce a quasi-de Sitter cosmic dynamics, i.e. an almost-exponential inflationary regime [9, 30]. In fact, A. A. Starobinsky showed that the inclusion of the term R^2 in the EH action is able to generate an early accelerated expansion ending in a radiation-dominated decelerated universe. Starobinsky model is an enormous success: nowadays, it is one of the most promising candidates for realizing the inflationary dynamics. The main reason for this accomplishment is its being a single-parameter model fitting perfectly the most recent observations of the cosmic microwave background radiation (CMB) [31, 32]. Moreover, the theoretical motivation for Starobinsky model is quite robust. In effect, Starobinsky inflation occurs in energy scales of about 10^{15} GeV; in such period the action containing the term R^2 may be considered as part of a higher-order theory expected in the context of quantization of gravity [33].

The main goal of this contribution is to review the basic aspects of the cosmic dynamics predicted by Starobinsky inflation and to study its extension to models containing second-order derivative corrections involving the curvature scalar. Section 9.2 presents a general action integral encompassing the regular EH term, plus Starobinsky R^2-contributions, and the novel higher-order corrections; the field equations for this modified gravity are also derived therein. Section 9.3 summarizes the conditions for inflation in a homogeneous and isotropic background; the field equations are also specified in FLRW spacetime. Subsections 9.3.1, 9.3.2, and 9.3.3 analyse the inflationary dynamics (in the phase space) in three separate models, viz. the original Starobinsky proposal, the model supplementing Starobinsky term with a R^3 contribution, and a higher-order model adding a correction of the type $R\Box R$ to the traditional R^2-term. Section 9.4 brings our final comments.

---

[2]The term $R_{\mu\nu\alpha\beta}R^{\mu\nu\alpha\beta}$ may be written as a linear combination of R^2, $R_{\mu\nu}R^{\mu\nu}$, and the Gauss-Bonnet topological invariant. The term $\Box R$ is explicitly a surface term.

9.2 Fundamentals of the proposed modified gravity models

The most general action presenting up to second order correction to the EH action involving the curvature scalar reads:

$$S = \frac{M_{Pl}^2}{2} \int d^4x \sqrt{-g} \left[R + \frac{1}{2\kappa_0} R^2 + \frac{\alpha_0}{3\kappa_0^2} R^3 - \frac{\beta_0}{2\kappa_0^2} R \Box R \right]. \tag{9.3}$$

Herein κ_0 has units of square mass while α_0 and β_0 are dimensionless parameters. Starobinsky R^2 term introduce the first-order correction to Einstein-Hilbert R term. The last two terms of (9.3) account for all the possible second-order corrections built with the curvature scalar. Parameter κ_0 sets the energy scale for inflation; α_0 and β_0 regulate the deviations from Starobinsky model.

It is convenient to perform a conformal metric transformation and to introduce dimensionless fields as follows:

$$\bar{g}_{\mu\nu} = e^\chi g_{\mu\nu}, \quad \lambda = \frac{R}{\kappa_0} \quad \text{and} \quad e^\chi = 1 + \lambda + \alpha_0 \lambda^2 - \frac{\beta_0}{\kappa_0} \Box \lambda. \tag{9.4}$$

The above allows one to cast (9.3) in the Einstein frame [29]:

$$\bar{S} = \frac{M_{Pl}^2}{2} \int d^4x \sqrt{-\bar{g}} \left[\bar{R} - 3\left(\frac{1}{2} \bar{\nabla}_\rho \chi \bar{\nabla}^\rho \chi - \frac{\beta_0}{6} e^{-\chi} \bar{\nabla}_\rho \lambda \bar{\nabla}^\rho \lambda + V(\chi, \lambda) \right) \right], \tag{9.5}$$

where

$$V(\chi, \lambda) = \frac{\kappa_0}{3} e^{-2\chi} \lambda \left(e^\chi - 1 - \frac{1}{2} \lambda - \frac{\alpha_0}{3} \lambda^2 \right), \tag{9.6}$$

stands for the multi-field potential of our model. The latter is a gravity model described in terms of the metric tensor $\bar{g}_{\mu\nu}$ along with two scalar fields, viz. χ and λ.

The field equations follow from setting to zero the variations of the action (9.5) with respect to the fields $\bar{g}_{\mu\nu}$, χ and λ. Executing this procedure for the metric tensor yields:

$$\bar{R}_{\mu\nu} - \frac{1}{2} \bar{g}_{\mu\nu} \bar{R} = \frac{1}{M_{Pl}^2} \bar{T}_{\mu\nu}^{(\text{eff})}, \tag{9.7}$$

with the effective energy momentum tensor given by

$$\frac{1}{M_{Pl}^2} \bar{T}_{\mu\nu}^{(\text{eff})} = \frac{3}{2} \left(\bar{\nabla}_\mu \chi \bar{\nabla}_\nu \chi - \frac{1}{2} \bar{g}_{\mu\nu} \bar{\nabla}^\rho \chi \bar{\nabla}_\rho \chi \right) +$$
$$- \frac{\beta_0 e^{-\chi}}{2} \left(\bar{\nabla}_\mu \lambda \bar{\nabla}_\nu \lambda - \frac{1}{2} \bar{g}_{\mu\nu} \bar{\nabla}^\rho \lambda \bar{\nabla}_\rho \lambda \right) - \frac{3}{2} \bar{g}_{\mu\nu} V(\chi, \lambda). \tag{9.8}$$

The field equations for the scalar fields are:

$$\bar{\Box}\chi - \frac{\beta_0}{6}e^{-\chi}\bar{\nabla}_\rho\lambda\bar{\nabla}^\rho\lambda - V_\chi = 0, \qquad (9.9)$$

$$\beta_0 e^{-\chi}\left(\bar{\nabla}^\rho\chi\bar{\nabla}_\rho\lambda - \bar{\Box}\lambda\right) - 3V_\lambda = 0. \qquad (9.10)$$

The shorthand notations $V_\chi = \frac{\partial V}{\partial \chi}$ and $V_\lambda = \frac{\partial V}{\partial \lambda}$ were used.

9.3 Inflation on the FLRW background

Generically, inflation may be regarded as an early period of near-exponential accelerated expansion taking place at some point roughly in between 10 MeV and 10^{16} GeV. The motivations for this early vertiginous expansion range from the need to explain the observed flat universe, to the attempt to justify the high degree of homogeneity and isotropy displayed by the CMB, and, more importantly, to predict the causally connected density fluctuations that are correlated to the large-scale structure in the present-day universe [8, 34, 35].

Inflationary cosmology addresses basically three points:

1. Initial conditions leading to the quasi-exponential expansion;

2. The details of the early accelerated regime and its connections with observations;

3. The ending of the accelerated expansion and reheating.

The first point is addressed in two ways. Approach number one is more thorough; it admits a broad range of possible initial conditions in a non-homogeneous and anisotropic spacetime. The second approach to point number 1 is a simplified approach assuming generic initial conditions while the spacetime is restricted to being described by FLRW line element at the background level [36]. Notice that the flatness problem and the problem of generating the primordial fluctuations can be treated via both the above approaches; however, the problem of explaining homogeneity and isotropy can only be addressed by the first, more complete approach. Regardless the approach, a robust inflationary model should be able to produce an accelerated expansion from fairly general initial conditions.

Point number 2 is the most relevant one since it directly connects inflation to observations. In fact, initial fluctuations are generated during the inflationary dynamics; these density perturbations are the very seeds of the universe's large-scale structure. The necessary condition for achieving an inflationary regime accommodating causally connected perturbation is an accelerated expansion:[3]

$$\text{Inflation} \iff \ddot{a} > 0 \iff \frac{d}{dt}(aH)^{-1} < 0.$$

The scale $(aH)^{-1}$ is known as Hubble horizon or Hubble radius; it delimits the region wherein two points are momentarily causally connected. The Hubble radius decreases during inflation allowing quantum fluctuations to exit the the horizon. These initially correlated perturbations are then frozen, and later produce the necessary conditions for structure formation [37] (after horizon crossing at the end of the accelerated period).

Point number 3 addresses the end of the inflationary regime. The particles the eventually populated the primeval universe were diluted to such a degree during the almost-exponential expansion that any hint of a thermalized universe disappears after inflation. Hence, a viable inflationary model should be able to repopulate the universe after its ending, then producing a hot Big Band phase dominated by radiation (ultra-relativistic particles). The period bridging inflation to a radiation-dominated era is called reheating [38, 39].

The three points above can be (partially) studied in a Friedmann-Lemaître-Robertson-Walker (FLRW) background. The homogeneous and isotropic FLRW flat spacetime is described by the line element

$$ds^2 = -dt^2 + a^2(t)(dx^2 + dy^2 + dz^2), \tag{9.11}$$

where $a(t)$ is the scale factor; natural units are assumed: $c = 1$. Specifying the field equations (9.7), (9.9), and (9.10) on the spacetime (9.11), leads to:

$$h^2 = \frac{1}{2}\left(\frac{1}{2}\chi_t^2 - \frac{\beta_0}{6}e^{-\chi}\lambda_t^2 + \bar{V}(\chi,\lambda)\right), \tag{9.12}$$

$$h_t = -\frac{3}{4}\chi_t^2 + \frac{1}{4}\beta_0 e^{-\chi}\lambda_t^2, \tag{9.13}$$

and

$$\chi_{tt} + 3h\chi_t - \frac{\beta_0}{6}e^{-\chi}\lambda_t^2 + \bar{V}_\chi = 0, \tag{9.14}$$

$$\beta_0 e^{-\chi}\left[\lambda_{tt} - (\chi_t - 3h)\lambda_t\right] - 3\bar{V}_\lambda = 0. \tag{9.15}$$

For convenience, the above equations were written in terms of the dimensionless Hubble function h and the dimensionless potential $\bar{V}$:

$$h \equiv \frac{1}{\sqrt{\kappa_0}}\frac{\dot{a}}{a} \quad \text{and} \quad \bar{V}(\chi,\lambda) \equiv \frac{1}{\kappa_0}V(\chi,\lambda). \tag{9.16}$$

---

[3]The Hubble function is defined as usual: $H = \dot{a}/a$, where an overdot denotes differentiation with reespect to the cosmic time t.

Moreover, use is made of the dimensionless time derivative

$$A_t \equiv \frac{1}{\sqrt{\kappa_0}}\dot{A}. \tag{9.17}$$

The following three subsection deal with particular solutions to Eqs. (9.12), (9.13), (9.14), and (9.15).

9.3.1 Starobinsky model

Starobinsky inflation adds the first-order correction to EH action via the term proportional R^2. In this case, S is simplified by taking $\alpha_0 = \beta_0 = 0$. Consequently, the field equation for λ–Eq. (9.15)–becomes a constraint equation given by:

$$\bar{V}_\lambda = 0 \Rightarrow \lambda = e^\chi - 1. \tag{9.18}$$

Inserting (9.18) into Eqs. (9.12), (9.13) and (9.14), leads to:

$$h^2 = \frac{1}{2}\left(\frac{1}{2}\chi_t^2 + \bar{V}^{St}\right), \tag{9.19}$$

$$h_t = -\frac{3}{4}\chi_t^2, \tag{9.20}$$

and

$$\chi_{tt} + 3h\chi_t + \bar{V}_\chi^{St} = 0. \tag{9.21}$$

The χ-related potential $\bar{V}^{St}(\chi)$ for the Starobinsky model (label St) reads

$$\bar{V}^{St}(\chi) = \frac{1}{6}\left(1 - e^{-\chi}\right)^2. \tag{9.22}$$

Notice that Starobinsky inflation is achieved by the dynamics of the scalar field χ alone. This dynamics is obtained from Eqs. (9.19) and (9.21). By taking χ as the variable describing the evolution of the system, one rewrites Eq. (9.21) in the form:

$$\frac{d\chi_t}{d\chi} = \frac{-3\chi_t\sqrt{\frac{1}{4}\chi_t^2 + \frac{1}{2}\bar{V}^{St}} - \bar{V}_\chi^{St}}{\chi_t}. \tag{9.23}$$

The above equation is an autonomous first-order ordinary differential equation; its structure is studied by means of the direction fields related to (χ, χ_t). Fig. 9.1 shows the phase space for system of Eq. (9.23).

There are two noticeable features in 9.1: an approximately horizontal attractor line in the vicinity of $\chi_t \approx 0$ and an accumulation point at the origin.

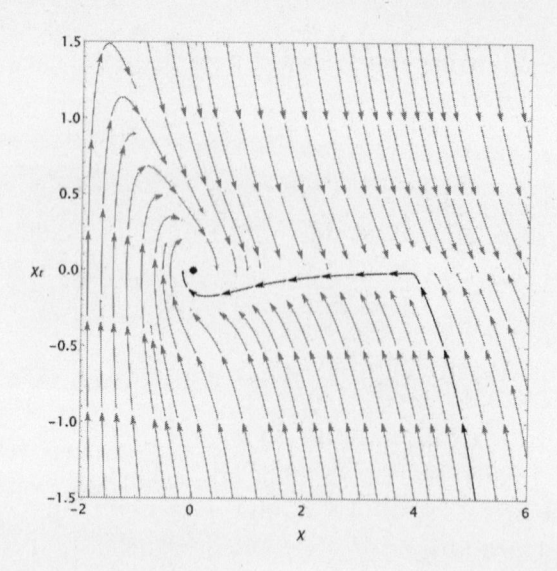

Figure 9.1: Phase space (χ, χ_t) for the inflaton field in Starobinsky model. The black dot corresponds to the accumulation point at $(0,0)$; the black oriented line highlights a possible trajectory in the phase space.

The attractor line realizes an (almost-)exponential expansion regime since $\chi_t^2 \ll \bar{V}^{St}$ ($\chi_t \ll 1$ and $\bar{V}^{St} \sim 1/6$) along this trajectory. In fact, by using these conditions in Eqs. (9.19) and (9.20), we build a slow-roll parameter ϵ satisfying

$$\epsilon = -\frac{h_t}{h^2} = \frac{3\chi_t^2}{\left(\chi_t^2 + 2\bar{V}^{St}\right)} \ll 1. \tag{9.24}$$

The condition $\epsilon \ll 1$ yields the inflationary period because

$$h_t \ll h^2 \Rightarrow h \approx \text{constant} \Rightarrow a(t) \propto \exp\left(\sqrt{\kappa_0} h t\right). \tag{9.25}$$

Moreover, Fig.9.1 makes it transparent that a broad range of initial conditions ($\chi^i > 2$ and χ_t^i arbitrary) set the system towards the attractor line. Starobinsky model is therefore capable of producing an inflationary regime starting from a very general set of initial conditions.[4]

The accumulation point at $(\chi, \chi_t) = (0,0)$ is the point of inflation's end. The dynamics of χ in the vicinity of this point is oscillatory. This means that χ transfers energy to the matter fields it is coupled with while it oscillates coherently about the origin. The process just described is known as pre-heating; it is the initial phase of the reheating, when a large number of matter particles is produced. Since pre-heating is essentially a non-thermal process, a subsequent thermalization stage

---

[4]Starobinsky inflation is an example of the chaotic inflationary scenario [35].

is demanded to lead the universe to a radiation-dominated era where all kinds of matter particles are in thermal equilibrium [40, 41].

In spite of being a preliminar analysis, the above study based on Fig. 9.1 shows that Starobinsky model successfully addresses the three basic points of interest listed at the beginning of Section 9.3. In the next two subsection, it will be checked if that continues to be the case for the models including the R^3- and $R\Box R$-type corrections to Starobinsky inflation.

9.3.2 Starobinsky-plus-R^3 model

A term of the type R^3 can be added to Starobinsky action ($\propto R + R^2$) thus generating the Starobinsky-plus-R^3 model. The inflationary dynamics accommodated by this modified gravity model respects Eqs. (9.19), (9.20), and (9.21) provided that $\bar{V}^{St}$ is generalized to the potential [28]

$$\bar{V}^{\alpha_0}(\chi) = \frac{e^{-2\chi}}{72\alpha_0^2}\left(1 - \sqrt{1 - 4\alpha_0(1 - e^\chi)}\right)\left(-1 + 8\alpha_0(1 - e^\chi) + \sqrt{1 - 4\alpha_0(1 - e^\chi)}\right). \tag{9.26}$$

The potential is real-valued regardless of the value taken by χ under the constraint: $0 \leq 4\alpha_0 \leq 1$.

The phase-space analysis for the Starobinsky-plus-R^3 model is performed along the lines of what was done in Section 9.3.1, by employing Eq. (9.23) with the substitution $\bar{V}^{St} \to \bar{V}^{\alpha_0}$. This leads to Fig. 9.2.

The main difference between the Figs. 9.2 and 9.1 is the appearance of a new critical point

$$P_c = (\chi_c, 0) = \left(\ln\left(4 + \sqrt{3\alpha_0^{-1}}\right), 0\right). \tag{9.27}$$

This critical point is a saddle point that splits the phase space into two distinct regions in regard to the direction field lines. The sector of Fig. 9.2 to the left of the vertical black attractor line yields an inflationary regime ending in the stable accumulation point $(\chi, \chi_t) = (0, 0)$. If the inflaton field χ starts from (χ^i, χ_t^i) in this region, inflation occurs in the usual way: the accelerated expansion subsequently gives off into a decelerated phase with χ oscillating about the origin (potential minimum). On the other hand, the trajectories to the right from the vertical dashed line yield a inflationary dynamics that never ends. In fact, Ref. [28] details how the field χ grows indefinitely in this sector; its dynamics leading to the transition of an initial almost-exponential expansion to the asymptotically accelerated phase of the power-law type $a(t) \sim t^{12}$.

The precise location of the point P_c is sensitive to the value of parameter α_0 accompanying the term R^3 in the action (9.3). The smaller the value of α_0, the greater the value of χ_c. Reassuringly enough, in the (Starobinsky) limit $\alpha_0 \to 0$,

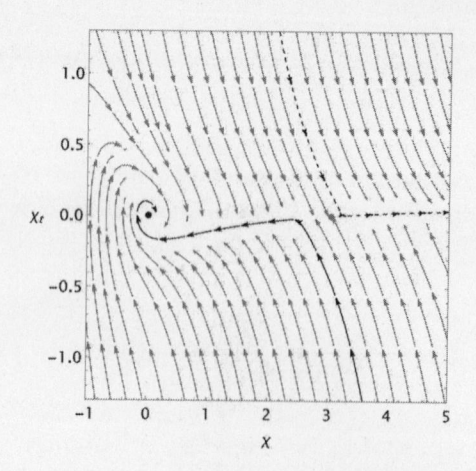

Figure 9.2: Phase-space representation (χ, χ_t) for Starobinsky-plus-R^3 model with parameter $\alpha_0 = 10^{-2}$. The black dot and the gray dot in the plot mark the critical points $(0,0)$ and $(\chi_c, 0)$ where $\chi_c = 3.06$. The black line and the dashed line show two opposite trajectories with respect to the critical point $(\chi_c, 0)$. Source: Ref. [28].

it is $\chi_c \to \infty$, and Fig. 9.2 degenerates into 9.1, as it should. The most notable difference between the Starobinsky-plus-R^3 setup and the standard Starobinsky inflation is the fact that the initial conditions leading to a physically meaningful inflation cannot be chosen arbitrarily.[5] In effect, the greater the value of α_0 the smaller the set of initial conditions (χ^i, χ_t^i) capable of producing an inflationary regime that evolves to a radiation epoch. In this sense, a introduction of the R^3 correction to the Starobinsky model requires some sort of fine tuning in the initial conditions of the inflaton field [28].

9.3.3 Starobinsky-plus-$R\Box R$ model

This section deals with the changes to inflation resulting from the inclusion of a $R\Box R$-type correction to Starobinsky model.

This scenario is called the Starobinsky-plus-$R\Box R$ model; its main distinctive feature with respect to the previous cases (Subsections 9.3.1 and 9.3.2) is the presence of two scalar fields χ and λ that are both responsible for the background dynamics, i.e. wherein a multi-field inflation will be realized. The related phase-space analysis is performed rewriting the second-order equations (9.14) and (9.15) as a system of four first-order equations. Accordingly, by defining

$$\chi_t = \psi \quad \text{and} \quad \lambda_t = \phi \tag{9.28}$$

---

[5]By "physically meaningful inflation" it is meant a primordial accelerated expansion that ends in a radiation-dominated Hot Big-Bang phase.

it results:

$$\chi_t = \psi, \tag{9.29}$$

$$\psi_t = -3h\psi + \frac{\beta_0}{6}e^{-\chi}\phi^2 - \bar{V}_\chi^{\beta_0}, \tag{9.30}$$

$$\lambda_t = \phi, \tag{9.31}$$

$$\beta_0 \phi_t = \beta_0(\psi - 3h)\phi + 3e^\chi \bar{V}_\lambda^{\beta_0}, \tag{9.32}$$

with

$$h = \sqrt{\frac{1}{2}\left(\frac{1}{2}\psi^2 - \frac{\beta_0}{6}e^{-\chi}\phi^2 + \bar{V}^{\beta_0}\right)} \tag{9.33}$$

and

$$\bar{V}^{\beta_0}(\chi,\lambda) = \lim_{\alpha_0 \to 0} \bar{V}(\chi,\lambda) = \frac{1}{3}e^{-2\chi}\lambda\left(e^\chi - 1 - \frac{1}{2}\lambda\right). \tag{9.34}$$

Notice that: (i) the phase space is four dimensional in the higher-order Starobinsky model—it is built with χ, χ_t, λ, and λ_t; (ii) the dimensionless Hubble function h depends explicitly on the parameter β_0—the coupling of the $R\Box R$-term in the action (9.3); and, predictably (iii) the dimensionless potential $\bar{V}^{\beta_0}$ is a double-field quantity.

The autonomous system formed by Eqs. (9.29), (9.30), (9.31), and (9.32) admits a single critical point at the origin:

$$P_0 = (\chi_0, \lambda_0, \psi_0, \phi_0) = (0,0,0,0). \tag{9.35}$$

Eqs. (9.29)—(9.32) can be linearized about point P_0. Thereby, it follows that Lyapunov exponents r_0 related to the stability of the critical point satisfy the algebraic equation

$$\beta_0 r_0^4 + r_0^2 + \frac{1}{3} = 0. \tag{9.36}$$

The solution of Eq. (9.36),

$$r_0 = \pm\sqrt{\frac{-1 \pm \sqrt{1 - \frac{4\beta_0}{3}}}{2\beta_0}}, \tag{9.37}$$

and the analysis of the direction fields in the phase-space, lead to the conclusion that P_0 is a stable fixed point only within the interval

$$0 \leq \beta_0 \leq \frac{3}{4}. \tag{9.38}$$

In fact, any value of β_0 outside the above interval leads to $\text{Re}[r_0] > 0$ for at least one of the four possible r_0 in Eq. (9.37). To put it another way, the equilibrium point P_0 is unstable whenever condition (9.38) is violated. Moreover, it is worth mentioning that the stability of P_0 is a necessary condition for a graceful exit from inflation into a radiation-dominated universe. This result was first published in Ref. [27] and later reanalyzed by [29].

Details about the dynamics of the double-field higher-order Starobinsky inflation are obtained from the numerical analysis of the four-dimensional phase space $(\chi, \chi_t, \lambda, \lambda_t)$. For this end, Eqs. (9.14) and (9.15) are cast into the form:

$$\frac{d\chi_t}{d\chi} = \frac{-3h\chi_t + \frac{\beta_0}{6} e^{-\chi} \lambda_t^2 - \bar{V}_\chi^{\beta_0}}{\chi_t}, \quad (9.39)$$

$$\frac{d\lambda_t}{d\lambda} = (\chi_t - 3h) + \frac{3e^\chi}{\beta_0 \lambda_t} \bar{V}_\lambda^{\beta_0}, \quad (9.40)$$

with h given by Eq. (9.33).

By using Eqs. (9.39) and (9.40), two-dimensional slices of the phase space can be performed, e.g. plots of (χ, χ_t) and (λ, λ_t) are built for fixed values of β_0 and of the remaining dynamical variables. Specifically, the direction fields in the (χ, χ_t) slice are obtained by choosing adequate values for β_0, λ, and λ_t; Fig. 9.1 is representative of the (χ, χ_t) plane thus constructed: it is verified the existence of an attractor line close to $\chi_t \simeq 0$ in the Starobinsky-plus-$R\square R$ model. The attractor line in the (χ, χ_t)-plane is very robust in the sense that it exists for arbitrary values of β_0, λ, and λ_t that are consistent with a physical inflation—i.e. β_0 within the interval in (9.38) and a real-valued h given by Eq. (9.33). On the other hand, the direction fields for the two-dimensional slice (λ, λ_t) are built by fixing the values assumed by β_0, χ, and χ_t; Fig. 9.3 illustrates two such examples of (λ, λ_t)-plane slices.

A joint analysis of Figs. 9.1 and 9.3 indicates that the field χ approaches the attractor line $\chi_t \simeq 0$ simultaneously as the field λ tends to the accumulation point where $\lambda_t \to 0$ and $\lambda \simeq e^\chi$. This attractor trajectory $(\chi, \lambda, \chi_t, \lambda_t) \simeq (\chi, e^\chi, 0, 0)$ in the four-dimensional phase space corresponds to the configuration realizing the inflationary regime. This fact is verified from the first-order approximation slow-roll parameter

$$\epsilon \simeq \frac{4e^{-2\chi}}{(3 - \beta_0 e^\chi)}. \quad (9.41)$$

Internal consistency with the first-order approximations requires $\beta_0 e^\chi$ smaller than (but not to close to) 3. Accordingly, Eq. (9.41) shows that the inflationary regime ($\epsilon \ll 1$) takes place whenever $\chi \gtrsim 2$. Further details on the show-roll regime are available in Ref. [29].

We summarize the analysis of this subsection by stating the three basic conditions that must be satisfied for achieving a physical inflationary regime within the Starobinsky-plus-$R\square R$ model: (1) Parameter β_0 should pertain to the interval of values specified in (9.38); (2) The initial condition for the field χ must comply with $\chi^i \gtrsim 2$; and (3) The dimensionless Hubble function should be well defined, i.e. $h(t) \in \mathbb{R}$, for all trajectories taken by the fields χ and λ.

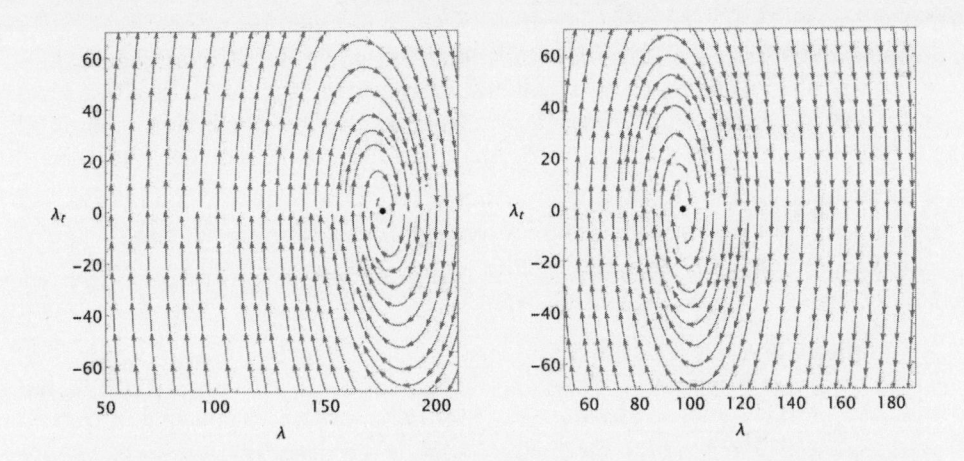

Figure 9.3: Two-dimensional (λ, λ_t)-slices of the four-dimensional $(\chi, \chi_t, \lambda, \lambda_t)$-phase space corresponding to $\beta_0 = 10^{-3}$ and $\chi_t = 0$ with $\chi = 5.18$ (left panel) and $\chi = 4.58$ (right panel). The black dots mark the position of the accumulation points: $(\lambda, \lambda_t) \simeq (177, 0)$ in the left panel; $(\lambda, \lambda_t) \simeq (98, 0)$ in the right panel.

9.4 Final remarks

This article recalls some of the motivations to consider extensions to general relativity for describing the gravitational interaction. A particular branch of modified gravity proposals is chosen as the focus, namely that of higher-order gravity. The latter admits a four-dimensional Riemaniann manifold endowed with a rank-2 metric tensor $g_{\mu\nu}$ which field equations include derivatives of order higher than two (Section 9.1). For this reason, Einstein-Hilbert action (wherein the Lagrangian density is $\mathscr{L}^{\text{EH}} \propto R \sim \partial^2 g$) is generalized into Starobinsky model ($\mathscr{L}^{\text{St}} \propto R + R^2$), and further into the higher-order Starobinsky model ($\mathscr{L}^{\text{HOSt}} \propto R + R^2 + \alpha_0 R^3 + \beta_0 R \Box R$)—cf. Section 9.2. The main scope of the paper was to specify the field equations for $g_{\mu\nu}$ and the extra scalar degree(s) of freedom χ (and λ) for the homogeneous and isotropic FLRW background of non-perturbative cosmology before studying the early-universe inflationary regime allowed within those modified gravity models (Section 9.3).

Three specific examples were scrutinized in Subsections 9.3.1 through 9.3.3. Starobinsky model was taken as the paradigm of successful realization of inflation. Its dynamics was studied carefully in the phase space because of its transparency and for setting the stage for the more complicated models that followed. Starobinsky's inflaton field dynamics follows an attractor line towards an accumulation point for arbitrary general initial conditions (Fig. 9.1). It engenders a quasi-exponential expansion that exits gracefully to a radiation-dominated universe.

The same possibility—that of an inflation ending in a Hot Big-Bang universe—is realized within the Starobinsky-plus-R^3 model (Subsection 9.3.2), albeit for a more restrict set of initial conditions. In fact, besides the accumulation point at the origin of the phase space (χ, χ_t) for the single inflaton field of this model, there is an unstable equilibrium point depending on $\chi_c = \ln\left(4 + \sqrt{3\alpha_0^{-1}}\right)$; the associated trajectories split the phase space into two region, one of those leading to eternal inflation (see Fig. 9.2). In order to tone down this possibility, the parameter α_0 could be constraint to assume small values.

Parameter β_0 typical of the Starobinsky-plus-$R\Box R$ model is also constrained based on similar arguments. However, this case is more evolved partially due to the fact that there are two scalar degrees of freedom (χ and λ) playing the role of the inflaton. The related double-field inflation is achieved by requiring β_0 to take on values within the interval $0 \leq \beta_0 \leq 3/4$. This requirement is based both on the phase-space analysis and on the demand for stability of the critical point at the origin of the four-dimensional space $(\chi, \lambda, \chi_t, \lambda_t)$. Subsection 9.3.3 contains the details of how to slice the phase space into two-dimensional sectors (such as those in Fig. 9.3) leading to these conclusions and to the additional requirement that it should be $\chi^i \gtrsim 2$ for an initial condition leading to a physical inflationary regime.

The constraints on the parameters α_0 and β_0 deduced here stem from a simplistic reasoning based on the backgroung evolution of the field equations. These constraints can be refined by the perturbative treatment of the modified gravity models. This technically sofisticated task is undertaken elsewhere—see e.g. [29, 28, 27]. In fact, the CMB data offers a contour region in a plot of the tensor-to-scalar ratio r in as a function of the scalar tilt n_s [32]. Starobinsky model is highly favored because its prediction for $r = r(n_s)$ for a number of e-folds in the interval $50 \lesssim N \lesssim 60$ respects $r \lesssim 0.01$. Starobinsky-plus-R^3 model [28] and Starobinsky-plus-$R\Box R$ model [29, 27] are also consistent with CMB observations; additionally, they allow for a larger variability of n_s values thus accommodating a greater flexibility for data constraining. This might be consistent with the possibility of a non-null running of n_s in the power spectrum parameterization [31].

Acknowledgements

RRC and LGM are grateful to Ruben Aldrovandi for his supervision, his friendship, the inspiration, and the time they have shared at IFT-UNESP. The authors thank CNPq-Brazil for partial financial support–Grants: 309984/2020-3 (RRC) and 307901/2022-0 (LGM).

Bibliography

[1] S. Weinberg, *Gravitation and Cosmology* (John Wiley & Sons, New York, 1972).

[2] M. Bartelmann, *Gravitational lensing*, Class. Quantum Grav. **27**, 233001 (2010), arXiv:1010.3829.

[3] R. M. Wald, *General Relativity*, (Chicago University Press, Chicago, 1984).

[4] M. Maggiore, *Gravitational Waves*, Vol. 1: Theory and Experiments (Oxford University Press, Oxford, 2008).

[5] T. R. padmanabhan, *Structure Formation in the Universe* (Cambridge University Press, Cambridge, 1993).

[6] R. Utiyama and B. S. DeWitt, *Renormalization of a classical gravitational field interacting with quantized matter fields*, J. Math. Phys. **03**, 608 (1962).

[7] R. P. Woodard, *How far are we from the quantum theory of gravity?*, Rep. Prog. Phys. **72**, 126002 (2009); arXiv:0907.4238.

[8] A. H. Guth, *Inflationary universe: A possible solution to the horizon and flatness problems*, Phys. Rev. D **23**, 347 (1981).

[9] A. A. Starobinsky, *A new type of isotropic cosmological models without singularity*, Phys. Lett. B **91**, 99 (1980).

[10] T. Clifton, P. G. Ferreira, A. Padilla, and C. Skordis, *Modified gravity and cosmology*, Phys. Rep. **513**, 1 (2012); arXiv:1106.2476 .

[11] G. W. Horndeski, *Second-order scalar-tensor field equations in a four-dimensional space*, Int. J. Theor. Phys. **10**, 363 (1974).

[12] A. Trautman, *Einstein-Cartan Theory*. In *Encyclopedia of Mathematical Physics*, edited by J.-P. Francoise, G. L. Naber and S. T. Tsou (Oxford: Elsevier, vol. 2, 2006); arXiv:gr-qc/0606062.

[13] R. Aldrovandi and J. G. Pereira, *Teleparallel Gravity: An Introduction* (Springer, Dordrecht, 2013).

[14] J. G. Pereira and Y. N. Obukhov, *Gauge structure of teleparallel gravity*, Universe **5**, 139 (2019); arXiv:1906.06287.

[15] M. Krššak, R. J. van den Hoogen, J. G. Pereira, C. G. Boehmer, and A. A. Coley, *Teleparallel theories of gravity: illuminating a fully invariant approach*, Class. Quant. Grav. **36**, 183001 (2019); arXiv:1810.12932.

[16] R. Aldrovandi, J. G. Pereira, and K. H. Vu, *Selected topics in teleparallel gravity*, Braz. J. Phys. **34**, 1374 (2004); arXiv:gr-qc/0312008.

[17] R. Aldrovandi, P. B. Barros, and J. G. Pereira, *Gravitation as anholonomy*, Gen. Relat. Grav. **35**, 991 (2003); arXiv:gr-qc/0301077.

[18] V. C. de Andrade, L. C. T. Guillen, and J. G. Pereira, *Gravitational energy-momentum density in teleparallel gravity*, Phys. Rev. Lett. **84**, 4533 (2000); arXiv:gr-qc/0003100.

[19] R. R. Cuzinatto, C. A. M. de Melo, L. G. Medeiros, and P. J. Pompeia, *Gauge formulation for higher order gravity*, Eur. Phys. J. C **53**, 99 (2008); arXiv:gr-qc/0611116.

[20] R. R. Cuzinatto, C. A. M. de Melo, L. G. Medeiros, and P. J. Pompeia, *Scalar-multi-tensorial equivalence for higher order* $f\left(R, \nabla_\mu R, \nabla_{\mu_1}\nabla_{\mu_2} R, \ldots, \nabla_{\mu_1}\ldots\nabla_{\mu_n} R\right)$ *theories of gravity*, Phys. Rev. D **93**, 124034 (2016); arXiv:1603.01563.

[21] Y. Décanini and A. Folacci, *Irreducible forms for the metric variations of the action terms of sixth-order gravity and approximated stress-energy tensor*, Class. Quant. Grav. **24**, 4777 (2007); arXiv:0706.0691.

[22] R. R. Cuzinatto, C. A. M. de Melo, L. G. Medeiros, and P. J. Pompeia, *Observational constraints to a phenomenological $f(R, \nabla R)$-model*, Gen. Relat. Grav. **47**, 29 (2015); arXiv:1311.7312.

[23] G. Rodrigues-da-Silva and L. G. Medeiros, *Spherically symmetric solutions in higher-derivative theories of gravity*, Phys. Rev. D **101**, 124061 (2020); arXiv:2004.04878.

[24] S. G. Vilhena, L. G. Medeiros, and R. R. Cuzinatto, *Gravitational waves in higher-order R^2 gravity*, Phys. Rev. D **104**, 084061 (2021); arXiv:2108.06874.

[25] M. F. S. Alves, L. F. M. A. M. Reis, and L. G. Medeiros, *Gravitational waves from inspiraling black holes in quadratic gravity*, Phys. Rev. D **107**, 044017 (2023); arXiv:2206.13672.

[26] R. R. Cuzinatto, C. A. M. de Melo, L. G. Medeiros, and P. J. Pompeia, $f\left(R, \nabla_\mu R, \nabla_{\mu_1}\nabla_{\mu_2} R, \ldots, \nabla_{\mu_1}\ldots\nabla_{\mu_n} R\right)$ *theories of gravity in Einstein frame: A higher order modified Starobinsky inflation model in the Palatini approach*, Phys. Rev. D **99**, 084053 (2019); arXiv:1806.08850.

[27] R. R. Cuzinatto, L. G. Medeiros, and P. J. Pompeia, *Higher-order modified Starobinsky inflation*, JCAP **02**, 055 (2019); arXiv:1810.08911.

[28] G. Rodrigues-da Silva, J. Bezerra-Sobrinho, and L.G. Medeiros, *Higher-order extension of Starobinsky inflation: initial conditions, slow-roll regime, and reheating phase*, Phys. Rev. D **105**, 063504 (2022); arXiv:2110.15502.

[29] G. Rodrigues-da-Silva and L. G. Medeiros, *Second-order corrections to Starobinsky inflation*, Eur. Phys. J. C **83**, 1032 (2023); arXiv:2207.02103.

[30] A. A. Starobinsky, *Spectrum of relict gravitational radiation and the early state of the universe*, J. Exper. Theor. Phys. Lett. **30**, 682 (1979).

[31] Planck Collaboration, Y. Akrami et al., *Planck 2018 results X. Constraints on inflation*, A & A **641**, A10 (2020); arXiv:1807.06211.

[32] BICEP/Keck Collaboration, P. A. R. Ade et al., *BICEP/Keck XIII: Improved constraints on primordial gravitational waves using Planck, WMAP, and BICEP/Keck Observations through the 2018 Observing Season*, Phys. Rev. Lett. **127**, 151301 (2021); arXiv:2110.00483.

[33] K. S. Stelle, *Renormalization of higher-derivative quantum gravity*, Phys. Rev. D **16**, 953 (1977).

[34] V. Mukhanov, *Physical Foundations of Cosmology* (Cambridge University Press, Cambridge, 2005).

[35] A. D. Linde, *Chaotic inflation*, Phys. Lett. B **129**, 177 (1983).

[36] R. Brandenberger, *Initial conditions for inflation – a short review*, Int. J. Mod. Phys. D **26**, 1740002 (2016); arXiv:1601.01918.

[37] D. Baumann, *Cosmology: Part III Mathematical Tripos*, Lecture Notes (2021). Available at: https://cmb.wintherscoming.no/pdfs/baumann.pdf.

[38] M. A. Amin, M. P. Hertzberg, D. I. Kaiser, and J. Karouby, *Nonperturbative dynamics of reheating after inflation: a review*, Int. J. Mod. Phys. D **24**, 1530003 (2015); arXiv:1410.3808.

[39] K. D. Lozanov, *Lectures on Reheating after Inflation*, Lecture Notes (2019), arXiv:1907.04402.

[40] L. Kofman, A. D. Linde, and A. A. Starobinsky, *Towards the theory of reheating after inflation*, Phys. Rev. D **56**, 3258 (1997); arXiv:hep-ph/9704452.

[41] B. A. Bassett, S. Tsujikawa, and D. Wands, *Inflation dynamics and reheating*, Rev. Mod. Phys. **78**, 537 (2006); arXiv:astro-ph/0507632.

10

The Miles' theory of surface wind-waves in finite depth: a predictive physical model in coastal regions

M. A. Manna

Abstract: This work is a review of recent developments in the Miles' theory of the growth of surface wind waves. In the linear regime, Miles' theory of wave amplification by wind is extended from deep water to the case of finite depth. A depth-dependent wave growth rate γ is derived from the dispersion relation of the wind/water interface. For different values of the dimensionless water depth parameters $\delta = gh/U_1^2$ (h the water depth, g the gravity) and the wave-age parameter $\theta_{fd} = \frac{c}{U_1}$ (U_1 a characteristic wind speed, c the wave phase velocity) a family of wave growth curves of γ in function of θ_{fd} and δ is plotted. The model provides a fair agreement with the data and empirical relationships obtained from the Lake George experiment, as well as with the data from the Australian Shallow Water Experiment. Two major results are obtained: (i) For small wave ages θ_{fd}, the wave growth rates are comparable to those of deep water, and (ii) for large wave ages θ_{fd} a finite-depth limited growth is reached with wave growth rates going to zero.

10.1 Introduction

Surface water waves and their generation by wind is a fascinating problem. The starting point is the Navier-Stokes equations for air and water. This problem is a formidable one for both the physical and the mathematical point of view. Its exactly theoretical solution is impossible so several approximations and assumptions are required in order to obtain particular solutions. The pioneers works are those of Refs.[1, 2] and [3, 4].

The Miles mechanism of wave generation by wind states that waves are produced and amplified through a *resonance phenomenon*. Resonance appears between the wave-induced pressure gradient on the inviscid airflow and the surface waves. The resonant mechanism happens at a critical height where the airflow speed matches the phase velocity of the surface wave. In Jeffrey's and Miles' theories the viscosity is neglected, the water is considered deep and irrotational and the equations of motions are linearized.

Energy and momentum flow continuously from the air to the water. The wave energy density $\mathcal{E}$ for linear surface waves is given by

$$\mathcal{E} = 2\rho_w g \eta_0^2, \qquad (10.1)$$

with ρ_w the water density, g the gravity and η_0 the maximum wave amplitude. However waves may lose energy because of dissipation and in addition energy can be distribute between many models by finite-amplitude four waves interactions. The *action balance equation* has been commonly adopted to represent the temporal and spatial dynamics of these processes. In deep water it reads

$$\frac{\partial}{\partial t}\mathcal{M} + \vec{\nabla}.(\vec{c_g}\mathcal{M}) = S, \qquad (10.2)$$

where $\vec{\nabla}$ is the Laplace operator and $\mathcal{M}$ is *the action density* defined as

$$\mathcal{M} = \frac{\mathcal{E}}{\omega}, \qquad (10.3)$$

with ω the wave frequency and $\vec{c_g}$ the group velocity observed in a frame of reference moving with the wave and the source term S is given by

$$S = S_{in} + S_{nl} + S_{ds}, \qquad (10.4)$$

with S_{in}, S_{nl}, S_{ds} representing (respectively) the effects of the wind imput, non-linear interactions and dissipation due to white capping.

From a theoretical point of view pioneering surface wind-waves growth theories exist since the works of [1, 2], Phillips [5] and [4] until the modern works of [6], [7]. These works were almost focused on the computation of the term S_{in} in (10.4).

Later on numerical approaches were developed in order to calculate S_{nl} and S_{ds} in reference [8].

The coastal region is amongst the most dynamic physical system we can observe on the earth's surface. It results from the nonlinear interaction between ocean waves, currents and sediments. Each one of these actors depend on underlying factors and processes. Ocean waves are created by winds, currents depend on bathymetry and tides, sediments (size, mineralogy, quantity, etc) result from geological and climatic factors.

Extreme wave events in coastal regions (or freak waves events) occur in the presence of wind. This issue, in relation to the forecast of extreme waves, is really challenging the engineering and the physics communities.

In references [9] and [10] the authors investigated the influence of wind on extreme wave events using the sheltering theory. They have shown that extreme events may be sustained longer by the air-flow separation. This mechanism can only be invoked if the wavecrest is steep enough to produce air-flow separation. Otherwise, for a too low steepness parameter $k\eta_0$ (k wavenumber) separation mechanism becomes irrelevant. Moreover, these works were limited to deep water and hence unable to fully describe winds generating near-shore waves where the wave field is influenced by bottom bathymetry. Consequently they are not adequate to correctly describe or forecast wind influence on extreme wave events in the coastal zone. Therefore an extension of Miles' theory of wind-generated monochromatic waves to the case of finite depth under weak or moderate winds (n terms of adequate finite depth parameters) is needed.

In the *finite depth water domaine* the source term reads

$$S = S_{in} + S_{nl} + S_{ds} + S_{bf} + S_{tri}. \tag{10.5}$$

The term S_{in} must be recalculated as he is strongly influenced by the finite depth h, the term S_{bf} represents bottom friction and S_{tri} is triad nonlinear wave interactions.

Theoretical extensions of wave growth to the finite depth domain were done in references [11, 12]. They provided mathematical laws able to qualitatively reproduce features of the fields experiments on growth rate evolution of finite depth wind-waves and supplied a theoretical basis allowing to go beyond the empirical laws. In [12] was studied the wind action on the evolution of a wave-paquet and in [13] the action of a constant vorticity flow on the wave growth γ. In [14] and [15] was studied the evolution in time of a normal Fourier mode k under the coupled action of *weakly nonlinearity, dispersion and anti-dissipation*.

This work is based on these last developments and is devoted to give a review of *l'etat de l'art* in the field. The paper is divided in two parts, given by Section 10.2 and Section 10.3. These sections deal respectively with the linear theoretical laws of growth of surface waves in finite depth, and the pioneering experiments on growth of surface wind-waves. In subsection 10.2.1 we display the model. In subsection 10.2.2 the linear problem in the water domain is study.

Then in subsection 10.2.3, the air domain is coupled with the water domain. The linear problem can be solved at the interface and we derive the linear dispersion relation of wave amplification in finite depth. We introduce dimensionless variables and scalings, to obtain an adequate growth rate. The theoretical linear dynamic is discussed. In subsection 10.3.1 the theoretical laws are compared with both the Young-Verhagen data and plots of empirical relationships from the Lake George experiment and with Donelan's data from the AUSWEX program. In subsection 10.3.2 are exhibited the critical values of wave ages and wavelengths for which the growth rate goes to zero. In subsection 10.3.3 the white-capping influence on the phenomenon is discussed. Finally subsection 10.4 draws the conclusions.

10.2 Wind generated surface waves: the linear regime

10.2.1 The interface problem

We are going to study the stability of an air-water interface. Let the fluid particles be located relatively to a fix rectangular Cartesian frame with origin O and axes (x, y, z), where Oz is the upward vertical direction. We assume translational symmetry along y and we will only consider a sheet of fluid parallel to the xz plane. The plane $z = 0$ characterizes the interface at rest. The perturbed air-water interface will be described by $z = \eta(x, t)$. The water lies between the bottom located at $z = -h$ and the interface $z = \eta(x, t)$. The air occupies the $\eta(x, t) < z < +\infty$ region. We suppose the water as well as the air to be inviscid and incompressible. The unperturbed air flow is a prescribed mean shear flow, only depending on the vertical coordinate z. We assume the dynamic to be linear and disregard the air turbulence.

10.2.2 The linearized water dynamics

In the water domain we consider the Euler equations for finite depth with $u(x, z, t)$ and $w(x, z, t)$ being the horizontal and vertical velocities of the fluid. The continuity equation and the linearised equations of motion for $-h \leq z \leq \eta(x, t)$ read [16]

$$u_x + w_z = 0, \quad \rho_w u_t = -P_x, \quad \rho_w w_t = -P_z - g\rho_w, \qquad (10.6)$$

where $P(x,z,t)$ is the pressure and subscripts in u, w and P denote partial derivatives. The boundary conditions at $z = -h$ and at $z = \eta(x,t)$ are

$$w(-h) = 0, \quad \eta_t = w(0), \quad P(\eta) = P_a(\eta), \tag{10.7}$$

where $P_a(x,z,t)$ is the air pressure evaluated at $z = \eta$. The equation $P(\eta) = P_a(\eta)$ is the continuity of the pressure across the air/water interface. We introduce a reduced pressure defined by

$$\mathbf{P}(x,z,t) = P(x,z,t) + \rho_w g z - P_0, \tag{10.8}$$

where P_0 is the atmospheric pressure. In terms of (10.8) equation (10.6) and the continuity of the pressure across the air/water interface read

$$u_x + w_z = 0, \quad \rho_w u_t = -\mathbf{P}_x, \quad \rho_w w_t = -\mathbf{P}_z, \tag{10.9}$$

$$\mathbf{P}(x,\eta,t) = P_a(x,\eta,t) + \rho_w g \eta - P_0. \tag{10.10}$$

The linear equations system (10.7)-(10.9) can be solved, assuming normal mode solutions as $u = \mathcal{U}(z)\exp(i\theta)$, $w = \mathcal{W}(z)\exp(i\theta)$, $\eta = \eta_0 \exp(i\theta)$, $\mathbf{P} = \mathcal{P}(z)\exp(i\theta)$, with $\theta = k(x - ct)$ where k is the wavenumber, c the phase speed and η_0 is a constant. We obtain

$$\mathcal{W}(z) = \frac{-ikc \sinh k(z+h)}{\sinh kh} \eta_0, \tag{10.11}$$

$$\mathcal{U}(z) = \frac{kc \cosh k(z+h)}{\sinh kh} \eta_0, \tag{10.12}$$

$$\mathcal{P}(z) = \frac{k \rho_w c^2 \cosh k(z+h)}{\sinh kh} \eta_0. \tag{10.13}$$

The phase speed c is unknown in equations (10.11)-(10.13). To determine c we have to consider the boundary conditions (10.10), not yet used, and the continuity of P at $z = \eta$ which yields

$$\rho_w \eta_0 \exp(i\theta)\{c^2 k \coth kh - g\} + P_0 = P_a(x,\eta,t). \tag{10.14}$$

In the single-domain problem $P_a = P_0$ and (10.14) gives the usual expression for c,

$$c^2 = c_0^2 = \frac{g}{k} \tanh(kh). \tag{10.15}$$

In the problem under consideration the determination of c needs the use of the air pressure evaluated at $z = \eta$ i.e., $P_a(x,\eta,t)$

10.2.3 Air profil, linearized air dynamics and the wave growth rate

We consider a steady air flow with a prescribed mean horizontal velocity depending only on the vertical coordinate z: $\vec{U} = U(z)\vec{e_x}$. We choose $U(z)$ to be the logarithmic wind profile

$$U(z) = U_1 \ln(z/z_0), \quad U_1 = \frac{u_*}{\kappa}, \quad \kappa \approx 0.41. \tag{10.16}$$

This is commonly used to describe the vertical distribution of the horizontal mean wind speed within the lowest portion of the air-side of the marine boundary layer (see reference [17]. It can also be justified with scaling arguments and solution matching between the near-surface air layer and the geostrophic air layer [18]. In (10.16)

- u_* is the friction velocity,
- κ the Von Kármán constant
- z_0 the aerodynamic sea surface roughness located just above the interface water/air.

Through this paper, z_0 will be regarded as a constant, independent from the sea state. This approximation was first proposed by [19]

The perturbations to the mean flow $U(z)$ and to the pressure P_a are: $u_a(x,z,t)$, $w_a(x,z,t)$ and $P_a(x,z,t)$ where subscript a stands for *air*. So with $\mathbf{P}_a(x,z,t) = P_a(x,z,t) + \rho_a g z - P_0$, ρ_a the air density, and $U' = dU(z)/dz$ we have the following Euler equations

$$u_{a,x} + w_{a,z} = 0, \tag{10.17}$$
$$\rho_a[u_{a,t} + U(z)u_{a,x} + U'(z)w_a] = -\mathbf{P}_{a,x}, \tag{10.18}$$
$$\rho_a[w_{a,t} + U(z)w_{a,x}] = -\mathbf{P}_{a,z}, \tag{10.19}$$

which must be completed with the appropriate boundary conditions. The first one is the kinematic boundary condition,

$$\eta_t + U(z_0)\eta_x = w_a(z_0). \tag{10.20}$$

Using (10.16) equation (10.20) can be reduced to

$$\eta_t = w_a(z_0). \tag{10.21}$$

Equation (10.21) describes the influence of the surface perturbation on the vertical perturbed wind speed. We assume $\mathbf{P}_a = \mathscr{P}_a(z)\exp(i\theta)$, $u_a = \mathscr{U}_a(z)\exp(i\theta)$, $w_a = \mathscr{W}_a(z)\exp(i\theta)$ and we add the following boundary conditions on $\mathscr{W}_a$ and $\mathscr{P}_a$,

$$\lim_{z \to +\infty} (\mathcal{W}'_a + k\mathcal{W}_a) = 0, \quad \lim_{z \to z_0} \mathcal{W}_a = W_0, \tag{10.22}$$

and

$$\lim_{z \to +\infty} \mathcal{P}_a = 0, \tag{10.23}$$

that is, the disturbance plus its derivative vanish at infinity, the vertical component of the wind speed is enforced by the wave movement at the sea surface and the pressure vanishes at infinity. Using equations (10.17)-(10.19) and (10.23) we obtain

$$w_a(x,z,t) = \mathcal{W}_a \exp(i\theta), \tag{10.24}$$

$$u_a(x,z,t) = \frac{i}{k}\mathcal{W}_{a,z} \exp(i\theta), \tag{10.25}$$

$$P_a(x,z,t) = ik\rho_a \exp(i\theta) \int_z^\infty [U-c]\mathcal{W}_a dz'. \tag{10.26}$$

Eliminating the pressure from the Euler equations we obtain the Rayleigh equation ([20]) $\forall z \setminus z_0 < z < +\infty$ (inviscid Orr-Sommerfeld equation)

$$(U-c)(\mathcal{W}''_a - k^2 \mathcal{W}_a) - U'' \mathcal{W}_a = 0 \tag{10.27}$$

The Rayleigh equation is singular at the critical height $z_c = z_0 e^{c\kappa/u_*} > z_0 > 0$, where $U(z_c) = c$. This model disregards any kind of turbulence, and so that the critical height is set above any turbulent eddies or other non-linear phenomena. In equations (10.24)-(10.27) neither $\mathcal{W}_a(z)$ nor c are known. In order to find c, we have to calculate $P_a(x,\eta,t)$. We obtain

$$P_a(\eta) - P_0 = -\rho_a g \eta + ik\rho_a e^{(i\theta)} \int_{z_0}^\infty [U-c]\mathcal{W}_a dz, \tag{10.28}$$

where the lower integration bound is taken at the constant roughness height z_0 because $\mathcal{W}_a(z) = 0$ for $\eta(x,t) \leq z < z_0$. Finally, using equation (10.21) to eliminate the term $ik\rho_a \exp(i\theta)$ in the equation (10.28), equation (10.14) yields

$$g(1-s) + c\frac{sk^2}{W_0}I_1 - c^2\{\frac{sk^2}{W_0}I_2 + k\coth(kh)\} = 0, \tag{10.29}$$

where $s = \rho_a/\rho_w \sim 10^{-3}$ and the integrals I_1 and I_2 are defined as follow

$$I_1 = \int_{z_0}^\infty U\mathcal{W}_a dz, \quad I_2 = \int_{z_0}^\infty \mathcal{W}_a dz. \tag{10.30}$$

Equation (10.29) is the dispersion relation of the problem. The parameter s is small and (10.29) may be approximated as

$$c = c_0 + sc_1 + O(s^2). \tag{10.31}$$

The explicit form of c_1 is calculated in the next section. Therefore, we can find $\mathcal{W}_a(z)$ by solving the Rayleigh equation with c replaced by c_0, that is to say, of order zero in s The function $\mathcal{W}_a(z)$ is complex and consequently c also i.e.,

$$c = \Re(c) + i\Im(c). \tag{10.32}$$

Its imaginary part $\Im(c)$ gives the growth rate of $\eta(x, t)$ defined by

$$\gamma = k\Im(c), \tag{10.33}$$

so we have

$$\eta(x, t) = \eta_0 \exp^{ik[x-\Re(c)t]} \exp^{\gamma t}. \tag{10.34}$$

We define three dimensionless parameters δ, θ_{dw} and θ_{fd}

$$\delta = \frac{gh}{U_1^2}, \quad \theta_{dw} = \frac{1}{U_1}\sqrt{\frac{g}{k}}, \quad \theta_{fd} = \frac{1}{U_1}\sqrt{\frac{g}{k}} T^{1/2}, \tag{10.35}$$

with $T = \tanh(\frac{\delta}{\theta_{dw}^2})$. The dimensionless parameter δ, for constant U_1, measures the influence of the limit phase velocity $\sqrt{gh}$ on the rate of growth of η, the parameter θ_{dw} is a *theoretical analogous of the deep water wave age* mesuring the relative value of the deep water phase speed in relation to the characteristic wind velocity U_1 and θ_{fd} is a *theoretical analogous of the finite depth wave age*.

Since as a wave "*ages*" it grows longer and as it grows longer it moves faster so the phase velocity c increases. Consequently θ_{fd} will be bigger for older waves and smaller for younger waves.

In order to obtain the growth rate, we introduce the following non-dimensional variables and scalings (hats meaning dimensionless quantities)

$$\frac{U}{U_1} = \hat{U}, \quad \frac{\mathcal{W}_a}{W_0} = \hat{\mathcal{W}}_a, \quad zk = \hat{z}, \quad \frac{c}{U_1} = \hat{c}, \quad \frac{tg}{U_1} = \hat{t}. \tag{10.36}$$

Using (10.35) and (10.36) in equation (10.29) and retaining only the term of order s we obtain $\hat{c}(\delta, \theta_{dw})$,

$$\hat{c} = \theta_{dw} T^{1/2} - \frac{s}{2} \theta_{dw} T^{1/2} + \frac{s}{2} \{T \hat{I}_1 - \theta_{dw} T^{3/2} \hat{I}_2\}. \tag{10.37}$$

The dimensionless growth rate $\hat{\gamma} = \frac{U_1}{g}\gamma$ is,

$$\hat{\gamma} = \frac{s}{2}\left\{\frac{T\Im(I_1)}{\theta_{dw}^2} - \frac{T^{3/2}\Im(I_2)}{\theta_{dw}}\right\}. \tag{10.38}$$

A given set of (δ, θ_{dw}) fixed the γ valued. The unique curve of wave growth rate in deep water is transformed in a *family of curves* indexed by $\delta = gh/U_1^2$, i.e., a curve for each value of δ.

In Figure 10.1 is shown a family of six values of δ against the θ_{fd} parameter:

- small finite wave age θ_{fd} corresponds to short surface waves. This stage represents the initial growth of the wave field near the shoreline of a calm lake,

- as the time proceeds the surface waves reaches moderate θ_{fd} which correspond to mild or moderate wavelengths,

- long waves are found for large θ_{fd}.

Of course, as the wavelengths are increasing, the amplitudes keep on growing. From a physical point of view, this means that Figure 10.1 is a snapshot of the theoretical dynamical development of the wave which is growing in amplitude and wavelength in time:

- at small θ_{fd} the growth rate γ is equal for all values of δ, the limit being the deep water case i.e.; the Miles' curve,

- as θ_{fd} increases, the finite-depth effects begin to appear. The growth rate becomes lower than in the deep water limit, for each value of δ. The growth rates are scaled with δ. For a given θ_{fd}, the bigger the δ the larger the $\hat{\gamma}$. Each δ-curve approaches its own (idealized) *theoretical θ_{fd}-limited growth* as $\hat{\gamma}$ goes to zero. At this stage the wave reaches a final state of linear progressive wave with zero growth. In others words, for a given δ the surface wave does not grow old anymore beyond a determined θ_{fd}.

Our results concern the dimensionless growth rate $\hat{\gamma}$ instead of the β-Miles parameter. We have the following transformation rule between this parameter β and dimensionless $\hat{\gamma}$

$$\beta = \frac{2\hat{\gamma}}{s}\theta_{dw}^3 T^{1/2}, \tag{10.39}$$

where we took β as it is usually defined,

$$\Im(c) = c_0 \frac{s}{2}\beta(\frac{U_1}{c_0})^2. \tag{10.40}$$

Its evolution is shown in Figure 10.2, showing the correct deep water trends, and the new finite depth limits. The effects of depth are critical. β is almost constant for small θ_{fd}, as usual, but it goes dramatically to zero when the depth limit is close.

10.3 Young-Donelan field experiments on growth of surface wind-waves in finite depth

Experiments in Lake George, Australia, described in references [21] and [22] provided the first systematic attempts to understand the physics of wave-wind

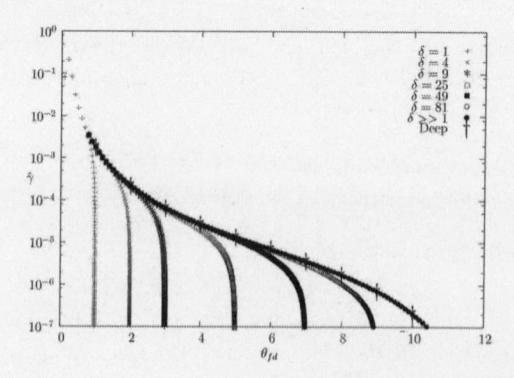

Figure 10.1: Evolution of the growth rate in semi-logarithmic scale. Every curve but the rightmost one correspond to finite depth. From left to right, they match $\delta = 1, 4, 9, 25, 49, 81$. We can observe that for each depth, there is a θ_{fd} limited wave growth. The deep water limit, also computed, corresponds to small θ_{fd} and matches Miles' results.

generation in finite depth water. These papers gave a very complete description of the basin geometry and bathymetry, experimental design, used instrumentation, as well as the adopted scaling parameters. The measurements have confirmed the water depth dependence of the asymptotic limits to wave growth. Young in references [23] and [24] has derived an empirical relation in terms of appropriate dimensionless parameters able to reproduce the experimental data of [21]. Especially the empirical relationship between the fractional energy increase as a function of the inverse wave age, found by in reference [25] (for deep water), was extended to the finite depth domain. Experimental results and empirical laws have shown that, contrary to the deep water case, the wave age at which the growth rate becomes zero is wind-dependent and depth-dependent. So, the point of full development is warped from the deep water case, where it was established in [26]. As a result a growth law against the inverse wave age exists for each value of the wind intensity $U(z)$ and the water depth h.

The evolution of the growth rates is such that at small wave ages growth rates are comparable to the deep water limit, at large wave ages the growth rate is lower in shallow water than in deep water, and beyond a limit wave age, the growth rate vanishes.

10.3.1 Empirical relations versus theoretical laws

Field or laboratory experiments involved measurements of a wind wave train i.e., a *superposition of wave Fourier modes*. The results are commonly given in terms of the observed phase and group speeds C_p, C_g at the peak frequency ω_p.

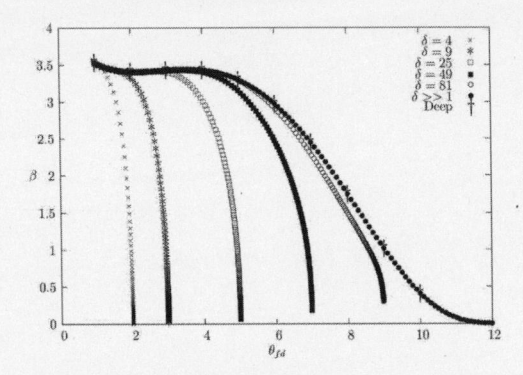

Figure 10.2: Evolution of Miles' coefficient β for several values of the depth. Each curve is plotted with the same Charnock constant $\alpha_c \approx 0.018$. The finite-depth effect is critical, and high value of δ correspond to deep water.

Consequently qualitative comparison between field (or laboratory) observations and theoretical laws can only be done using the phase and group speeds c, c_g and frequency ω of *only one mode* instead of C_p, C_g and ω_p corresponding to a wave pacquet

First of all we are going to show that the theoretical curves for $\hat{\gamma}$ are, *mutatis mutandi*, in good qualitative agreement with the empirical curves of the dimensionless fractional wave energy increase per radian $\hat{\Gamma}$ as a function of the inverse wave age U_{10}/Cp in [23]. In this reference, experimental field data for $\hat{\Gamma}$

$$\hat{\Gamma} = \frac{C_g}{\omega_p} \frac{1}{E} \frac{\partial E}{\partial x}, \tag{10.41}$$

in the finite depth Lake George are adequately represented by the empirical relationship

$$\hat{\Gamma} = A(\frac{U_{10}}{C_p} - 0,83)\tanh^{0.45}(\frac{U_{10}}{C_p} - \frac{1,25}{\delta_Y^{0,45}}), \tag{10.42}$$

with A constant, $\delta_Y = gh/U_{10}^2$ the non-dimensional water depth, U_{10} the wind speed measured at a reference height of 10 m, and C_g and C_p the group and phase speeds of the components at the spectral peak frequency ω_p.

In order to make a qualitative comparison between $\hat{\Gamma}$ curves in function of the inverse wave-age U_{10}/C_p and theoretical $\hat{\gamma}$ curves in function of $1/\theta_{fd}$ we need to write the empirical $\hat{\Gamma}$ in terms of theoretical quantities. So, the following changes are necessary:

$$\text{measured} \quad C_g, C_p, \omega_p \rightarrow \text{theoretical} \quad c_g, c, \omega, \tag{10.43}$$

$$\text{and} \quad \frac{U_{10}C_{10}^{1/2}}{\kappa} = u_*/\kappa = U_1, \tag{10.44}$$

with C_{10} the 10 m drag coefficient defined in [24]. Thus, from the fact that the energy growth rate is two times the amplitude growth rate, that is

$$\Gamma = 2\gamma,$$

and using $2c_g = c(1 + 2kh/\sinh(2kh))$, (10.43), (10.44), (10.36) and the expression of θ_{fd} in (10.35) we obtain

$$\hat{\Gamma} = \frac{\theta_{dw}}{T^{1/2}} \hat{\gamma} [1 + \frac{2\delta}{\theta_{dw}^2 \sinh(\frac{2\delta}{\theta_{dw}^2})}]. \tag{10.45}$$

This expression gives the theoretical equivalent of the empirical $\hat{\Gamma}$ in function of θ_{dw}, δ and $\hat{\gamma}$. The values of $\hat{\gamma}$ for fixed δ's as a function of $1/\theta_{fd}$ are numerically obtained using θ_{fd}, $T = \tanh(\frac{\delta}{\theta_{dw}^2})$ and (10.38). Steps (10.43) and (10.44) transform δ_Y and C_p/U_{10} into δ and θ_{fd} according to

$$\delta_Y = \delta \frac{C_{10}}{\kappa^2}, \tag{10.46}$$

$$\frac{C_p}{U_{10}} = \theta_{fd} \frac{C_{10}^2}{\kappa}. \tag{10.47}$$

In reference [23] the curves of Γ versus U_{10}/C_p have been presented for the δ_Y-intervals. rather than for a single value of δ_Y. The intervals were

$$\delta_Y \in [0.1 - 0.2], \quad \delta_Y \in [0.2 - 0.3], \tag{10.48}$$

$$\delta_Y \in [0.3 - 0.4], \quad \delta_Y \in [0.4 - 0.5]. \tag{10.49}$$

They were determined from the variations in U_{10}, the depth h being nearly constant around 2 m. Consequently we substitute the δ_Y-intervals with δ-intervals using (10.46) and we evaluate the mean value $\overline{\delta}$. For example $\delta_Y \in [0,1 - 0,2]$ is transformed into $\delta = [13, 17 - 26, 35]$ with $\overline{\delta} = 19,76$ in Figure 10.3(a). Figures 10.3(a), 10.3(b), 10.3(c) and 10.3(d) are displaying a fair concordance of the model with the experimental data and plots of empirical laws for Lake George. The agreement improves as $\frac{1}{\theta_{fd}}$ increases.

10.3.2 The critical wave age and the critical wavelength

In Figure 10.4 are plotted, against δ, the critical values of the parameter θ_{fd}^c for which the growth rate γ goes to zero. They obey the relation

$$\theta_{fd}^c = \delta^{\frac{1}{2}}. \tag{10.50}$$

The above relation, found numerically, is coherent with the parameter formulation of θ_{fd} in (10.35). It is indeed a limiting value for θ_{fd} uniquely determined by the water depth. In [26] the author has shown from an empirical relationship (formule (6) in reference above) that $\hat{\Gamma}$ (the growth rate) goes to zero as a function of the inverse wave age U_{10}/C_p for

$$\frac{C_p}{U_{10}} = 0.8 \left(\frac{gh}{U_{10}^2}\right)^{0.45}. \tag{10.51}$$

Using a C_{10} drag coefficient parametrization such as in [27]

$$C_{10} = (0.065 U_{10} + 0.8) 10^{-3}, \tag{10.52}$$

and taking an average $U_{10} = 7\ m/s$ (see [28]), one finds the U_1 to U_{10} relationship

$$U_{10} \approx 28,3\ u_* \approx 11,6\ U_1, \tag{10.53}$$

So, this limiting law reads

$$\frac{C_p}{U_1} = 1,01\ \delta^{0,45}, \tag{10.54}$$

a result in excellent agreement with the theoretical value (10.50).

With θ_{fd}^c we can calculate the corresponding critical wave length λ^c. Using (10.50) in θ_{fd} we obtain

$$\frac{\delta}{\theta_{dw}^2} = \tanh\left(\frac{\delta}{\theta_{dw}^2}\right). \tag{10.55}$$

Relation (10.55) means the wave has entered the shallow water region. In such a limit the range of δ/θ_{dw}^2 is: $0 < \delta/\theta_{dw}^2 < \frac{\pi}{4}$ ([28], [29]). As a result we obtain $\lambda^c = 8h$. For values of λ such that $\lambda > \lambda^c$ the phase velocity is in the long wave limit i.e., $c = \sqrt{gh}$. Consequently, if $\lambda > \lambda_c$ *the wave feels the bottom, the amplitude does not grow anymore, the resonance wind/phase speed ceases, and the wave reaches its utmost state as a progressive plane wave.*

Finally in Figure 10.4 are also represented data from [30], from the Australian Shallow Water Experiment. A fit is also plotted to show the trend. The raw data consists in the water depth h in metres, the friction velocity u_*, the 10 metres wind velocity U_{10} and the ratio of the former with the measured phase speed c_p, U_{10}/c_p. For example, $u_* = 0.44\ m.s^{-1}$ and $h = 0.32\ m$ gives $\delta = 2.7$ and $\theta_{fd} = 1.55$, which gives a small relative error regarding (10.50). All the points give (δ, θ_{fd}) coordinates close to the theoretical limit.

10.3.3 The white-capping dissipation influences

This subsection aims at answering the question: why do the $\hat{\Gamma}$ curves seem to be consistent with the empirical fits of [23], even though bottom friction dissipation S_{bf} and white-capping dissipation S_{ds} are disregarded?

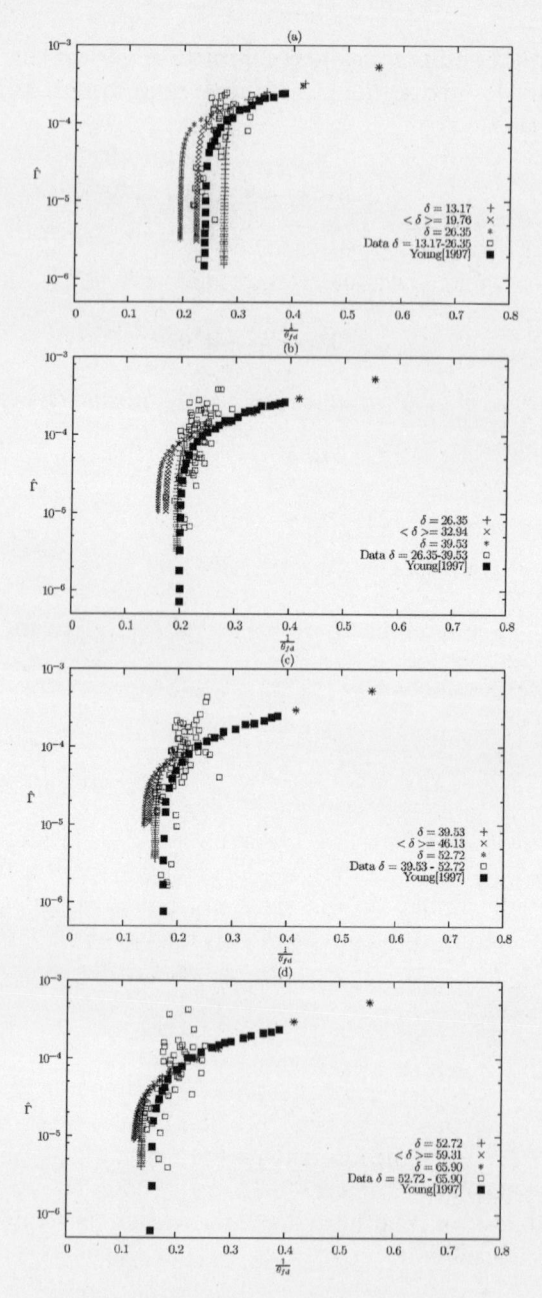

Figure 10.3: Growth rate $\hat{\Gamma}$ as a function of inverse wave age $1/\theta_{fd}$ for several values of the parameter δ. White squares correspond to Lake George experiment data, Black squares correspond to the empirical relationship (eq. (6)) found by [23]. Present results correspond to symbols +, × and ∗. (a): the dataset covers a range of wind speed corresponding to $\delta_Y = 0.1-0.2$, or, using (10.46) $\delta = 13.17-26.35$, and an average value $<\delta>=(13.17+26.35)/2$ is used. (b): same as (a) with $\delta_Y = 0.2-0.3$. (c): same as (a) with $\delta_Y = 0.3-0.4$. (d) : same as (a) with $\delta_Y = 0.4-0.5$.

It is currently admitted that the bottom friction S_{bf} plays a relatively minor role in depth limited growth studies, even though being an important dissipative factor for swell propagating in shallow water (see [27] for more information). Consequently, we do not consider bottom friction in the following analysis. The white-capping dissipation S_{ds} is an important dissipative mechanism since in finite depth conditions, wind waves show significant wave breaking events. Hence, dissipation due to wave breaking S_{ds} is considered to be the dominant dissipative term in finite depth, compared to the deep water case [28, 29]. Now, what can we observe in plots 10.3(a), 10.3(b), 10.3(c) and 10.3(d)?

- For young sea regimes ($1/\theta_{fd}$ large), one can observe in figures 10.3(a), 10.3(b), 10.3(c) and 10.3(d) that the $<\delta>$-curves match the experimental $\hat{\Gamma}_Y$ due to Young (in black squares). Hence, for large value of $1/\theta_{fd}$ we have $\hat{\Gamma} = \hat{\Gamma}_Y$. Small values of θ_{fd} correspond to wave propagating in deep water, for any $<\delta>$. This is in line with Figure 7.1.c in [30] where $S_{ds} \to 0$ for large frequencies.

- For mature or old sea regimes ($1/\theta_{fd}$ small) both curves $\hat{\Gamma}$ and $\hat{\Gamma}_Y$ go to zero. In developed finite depth seas, wave energy (amplitude) evolution becomes depth limited no matter what the value of S_{ds} is. Hence, finite depth-limitation phenomenon prevails.

- For intermediate regimes the $\hat{\Gamma}$ and $\hat{\Gamma}_Y$ curves are similar in shape. Nevertheless, $\hat{\Gamma} > \hat{\Gamma}_Y$ for all the values of $<\delta>$ considered herein. This is in agreement with Figure 7.1.c in [24] where $S_{ds} \lesssim 0$ for intermediate frequencies. Consequently, the wave growth rate $\hat{\gamma}$ ($\hat{\Gamma} = 2\hat{\gamma}$) is overestimated in our model. We can observe in figures 10.3(a), 10.3(b), 10.3(c) and 10.3(d) that the gap between $\hat{\Gamma}$ and $\hat{\Gamma}_Y$ increases as $<\delta>$ decreases, because the white-capping S_{ds} is larger and wider for small kh as we can see in Figure 7.1.c in [30].

10.4 Conclusions

In this review our aim was exclusively focused on the derivation of a linear Miles' theory for waves propagating on finite depth h. We extended the well known Miles' theory to the finite depth context under breeze to moderate winds conditions. We have linearized the equations of motion governing the dynamics of the air/water interface problem in finite depth and have studied the linear instability in time of a normal Fourier mode k. The prediction of exponential growth of wave amplitude (or energy) is well confirmed by field and laboratory experiments (the wind-to-waves energy transfer rates predictions are smaller than the observations, although their order of magnitude is the same).

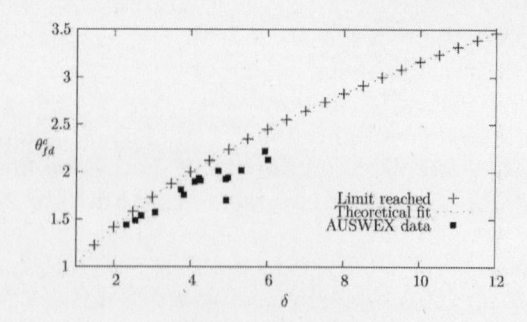

Figure 10.4: Parameter curves corresponding to zero growth rate. The theoretical limit is given by Eq. (10.50). The AUSWEX data are experimental results from [25] (the sea state is fairly close to the finite depth full development).

There are many other parameters that influence the growth of wind-waves in finite depth. For example, wind speed and wind direction variations with time, geometry and bathymetry of the lake, bottom friction, surface drift induced by the air flow, boundary layer turbulence, nonlinear waves interactions, and so on. Taken into account all these phenomena represents a work that cannot be handled analytically, even though numerically. Although our study is a highly idealized, we believe that it may provide a valuable insight about the effect of depth on the mechanism of water wave amplification by wind and be useful in theoretical forecast of wind-wave growth rates in finite depth.

Acknowledgments

The author thanks the organizers for the invitation to contribute to the tribute in memory of Professor Ruben Aldrovandi.

Bibliography

[1] H. Jeffreys, Proc. Roy. Soc. A **107**, 189 (1925).

[2] H. Jeffreys, Proc. Roy. Soc. A **110**, 241 (1926).

[3] J. Miles, J. Fluid Mech. **3**, 185 (1957).

[4] J. Miles, Appl. Mech. Rev. **50-7**, R5 (1997).

[5] O. Phillips, J. Fluid Mech. **2**, 417 (1957).

[6] P. Janssen, J. Phys. Oceanogr. **21**, 1631 (1991).

[7] S. E. Belcher and J.C.R. Hunt, J. Fluid Mech. **251**, 109 (1993).

[8] P. Janssen, *The interaction of ocean waves and wind* (Cambridge University Press, Cambridge, 2004).

[9] C. Kharif, J.-P. Giovanangeli, C. Touboul, L. Grade, and E. Pelinovsky, J. Fluid Mech. **594**, 209 (2008).

[10] J. Touboul and C. Kharif, Phys. Fluids **18**, 108103 (2006).

[11] P. Montalvo, J. Dorignac, M. Manna, C. Kharif, and H. Branger, Coastal Engineering **77**, 49 (2013).

[12] P. Montalvo, R. Kraenkel, M. A. Manna, and C. Kharif, Natural Hazards and Earth System Science **13**, 2805 (2013).

[13] M. A. Manna and A. Latifi, Coastal Engineering **7**, 266 (2021).

[14] M. A. Manna, P. Montalvo, and R. A. Kraenkel, Physical Review E **90**, 013006 (2014).

[15] M. A. Manna and A. Latifi, Fluids **170**, 103976 (2022).

[16] M. Lighthill, *Waves in Fluids* (Cambridge University Press, Cambridge, 1925).

[17] J. Garratt, G. Hess, W. Physick, and P. Bougeault, Boundary-layer meteorology **78**, 9 (1996).

[18] H. Tennekes, Journal of the atmospheric sciences **30**, 234 (1972).

[19] H. Charnock, Quart. J. Roy. Meteorol. Soc. **81**, 639 (1955).

[20] L. Rayleigh, Proc. Lond. Math. Soc. **XI**, 57 (1880).

[21] I. R. Young and L. A. Verhagen, Coastal Eng. **29**, 47 (1996).

[22] I. R. Young and L. A. Verhagen, Coastal Eng. **29**, 79 (1996).

[23] I. Young, Coastal Eng. **32**, 181 (1997).

[24] I. Young, *Wind Generated Ocean Waves* (Elsevier, 1997).

[25] M. A. Donelan, A. V. Babanin, I. R. Young, and M .L. Banner, J. Phys. Ocean. **36**, 1672 (2006).

[26] W. J. Pierson and L. Moskowitz, J. Geophys. Research **69**, 5181 (1964).

[27] J. Wu, J. Geophys. Research **87**, 9704 (1982).

[28] J. D. Fenton, J. Fluid Mech. **94**, 129 (1979).

[29] M. Francius and C. Kharif, J. Fluid Mech. **561**, 417 (2006).

[30] I. Young and A. Babanin, J. Phys. Ocean. **36**, 376 (2006).

11

Field propagators in the interpolating angle and their limiting cases for instant form dynamics (IFD) and light-front dynamics (LFD)

A. T. Suzuki

Abstract: In quantum field theories, the time-ordered products (or vacuum expectation values) of two fields defines the propagator of those fields. Mathematically, this propagator belongs to a class of what is known as the Green's functions and becomes physically important in that this time-ordering makes it possible to introduce the concept of antiparticles. Propagators are the Green's functions of the field operator. The Feynman propagator corresponds to the boson field operators and fermion propagator to the fermion field operators. In this paper we are going to construct both the boson and fermion field propagators in the interpolating angle coordinates and derive from them the corresponding two most important propagators within the perspectives of IFD and LFD as specific angle limits are taken and show how they are distinctly expressed; in particular, how the instantaneous terms in the field propagators do emerge in those limits and how they do cancel out or remain, depending on the limiting angle considered.

11.1 Introduction

Our understanding today of particles and their interactions is that they can be described by the tools of relativistic quantum fields. As quantum mechanical description objects, these fields are expressed in terms of operators that must meet certain criteria to be observable and measurable. Two distinct classes of fields are known to be present in nature, i.e., boson fields, characterized by integer spins and fermion fields, characterized by half-integer spins. As dynamical entities, their interactions are to be described by time evolution operators that connect different space-time points, objects that we call propagators. Independent of the type of fields that we have to deal with in describing different types of particles, the study of relativistic dynamics can be done using different approaches, using different coordinate systems.

A comprehensive study of such relativistic dynamics was pioneered by Dirac in 1949 [32], who considered three possibilities for its description: the instant $(x^0 = 0)$, front $\left(x^+ = (x^0 + x^3)/\sqrt{2} = 0\right)$, and point $\left(x_\mu x^\mu = a^2 > 0, x^0 > 0\right)$ forms. Of these possibilities, we are looking specifically at the first two here: The instant form dynamics (IFD) of quantum field theories is based on the usual equal time $t = x^0$ quantization (here we often assume units such that $c = \hbar = 1$, except when we want to emphasize at particular points), which provides a traditional approach that comes from the nonrelativistic dynamics, and therefore has strong connections with Euclidean space formalism. The equal light-front time $\tau \equiv (t + z/c)/\sqrt{2} = x^+$ quantization yields Dirac's front form dynamics, nowadays more commonly called light-front dynamics (LFD), which works strictly in Minkowski space.

For the IFD, the Minkowski space-time metric $g_{\mu\nu} = (1,-1,-1,-1)$ and all the related properties are implied, namely, spacetime coordinates are given by contravariant four-vectors $x^\mu = (x^0, x^1, x^2, x^3) = (t, x, y, z)$, with covariant four-vectors being $x_\mu = (x_0, x_1, x_2, x_3) = (t, -x, -y, -z)$. The scalar product of two four-vectors being $x \cdot y = g_{\mu\nu} x^\mu y^\nu = x_\mu y^\mu$ and the Poincare invariant length of any four-vector being then $x \cdot x \equiv x^2 = t^2 - \vec{x}^2$. Momentum four-vectors follow the same pattern, $p^\mu = (E, p_x, p_y, p_z) = (E, \vec{p})$, and $p \cdot k = p_\mu k^\mu = E_p E_k - \vec{p} \cdot \vec{k}$; whereas, for the LFD we use the following notations and conventions for the light-front coordinates and momenta [2, 3, 4, 5]: $x^\pm = \frac{1}{\sqrt{2}}(x^0 \pm x^3)$, and $k^\pm = \frac{1}{\sqrt{2}}(k^0 \pm k^3)$. We have therefore the Minkowski space-time metric $g^{\mu\nu} = (+, -, 1, 2)$ given by

$$g^{\mu\nu} = \begin{bmatrix} 0 & 1 & 0 & 0 \\ 1 & 0 & 0 & 0 \\ 0 & 0 & -1 & 0 \\ 0 & 0 & 0 & -1 \end{bmatrix} = g_{\mu\nu}. \tag{11.1}$$

This means that the covariant and contravariant indices of a given vector are related by $a_\pm = a^\mp$, and $a_j = -a^j$ for $(j = 1, 2)$. Then the scalar product of any two vectors becomes $a_\mu b^\mu = a_+ b^+ + a_- b^- + \mathbf{a}_\perp \cdot \mathbf{b}^\perp = a^- b^+ + a^+ b^- - \mathbf{a}^\perp \cdot \mathbf{b}^\perp$, where we use the convenient shorthand $\mathbf{a}_\perp = (a_1, a_2)$ and $\mathbf{a}^\perp = (-a^1, -a^2)$.

For a massive scalar particle, the on-shell condition $k^2 = m^2$ leads to $k^- = \frac{\mathbf{k}_\perp^2 + m^2}{2k^+}$. This dispersion relation is quite remarkable for the following reasons: (a) Even though it is a relativistic energy-momentum relation, it is a linear relation, contrary to the usual quadratic one; (b) The dependence of the light-front "energy" k^- with respect to the transverse momentum $\mathbf{k}^\perp$ is just like the non-relativistic relation. (c) There is a sign correlation between the longitudinal momentum k^+ and the energy k^-; for k^+ positive (negative), k^- is also positive (negative). (d) The dependence of the energy k^- on the momentum components $\mathbf{k}^\perp$ and k^+ is multiplicative and large energy can result from large $\mathbf{k}^\perp$ and/or small k^+. All these simple observations have dramatic consequences into the relativistic physical aspects of particle dynamics.

11.1.1 The interpolating angle coordinates and the "hat" notation

Here, we adopt a convention for the space-time mimicking the light-front coordinates and introduce the interpolating angle [6, 7], as

$$\begin{bmatrix} x^{\hat{+}} \\ x^{\hat{-}} \end{bmatrix} = \begin{bmatrix} \cos\delta & \sin\delta \\ \sin\delta & -\cos\delta \end{bmatrix} \begin{bmatrix} x^0 \\ x^3 \end{bmatrix}; \text{ and } \begin{bmatrix} x^0 \\ x^3 \end{bmatrix} = \begin{bmatrix} \cos\delta & \sin\delta \\ \sin\delta & -\cos\delta \end{bmatrix} \begin{bmatrix} x^{\hat{+}} \\ x^{\hat{-}} \end{bmatrix} \quad (11.2)$$

in which the interpolating angle is allowed to run from 0 through 45° ($0 \le \delta \le \frac{\pi}{4}$.) For the limits

$$\delta \to 0 \implies \begin{cases} x^{\hat{+}} = x^0 \\ x^{\hat{-}} = -x^3. \end{cases} \quad (11.3)$$

$$\delta \to \frac{\pi}{4} \implies \begin{cases} x^{\hat{+}} = \frac{1}{\sqrt{2}}(x^0 + x^3) = x^+ \\ x^{\hat{-}} = \frac{1}{\sqrt{2}}(x^0 - x^3) = x^-. \end{cases} \quad (11.4)$$

We note that the limit for $\delta \to 0$ leads *not* to the usual coordinate x^3, but to the mirrored, "space-symmetric", $-x^3$. This, of course, has to be considered if we want to analyze this particular limit and compare it to the usual IFD result in which the coordinate x^3 plays an important role (e.g. z-component of an orbital angular momentum). Similar definition is valid for the momentum variables $p^{\hat{+}}$ and $p^{\hat{-}}$.

Then the scalar product of any two vectors becomes

$$a_{\hat{\mu}} b^{\hat{\mu}} = (a^{\hat{+}} b^{\hat{+}} - a^{\hat{-}} b^{\hat{-}})\cos 2\delta + (a^{\hat{+}} b^{\hat{-}} + a^{\hat{-}} b^{\hat{+}})\sin 2\delta - a^1 b^1 - a^2 b^2. \quad (11.5)$$

Note that the transverse components of the four vector, namely, 1 and 2 (those who customarily are ascribed to x and y axis respectively), remain unaffected by the interpolating angle.

For shorthandedness and convenience, we define $\mathbb{C} = \cos 2\delta$, $\mathbb{S} = \sin 2\delta$, and $\mathbf{a}_\perp = a^1 \frac{\mathbf{x}}{|\mathbf{x}|} + a^2 \frac{\mathbf{y}}{|\mathbf{y}|}$.

We have therefore the Minkowski space-time metric $g^{\widehat{\mu}\widehat{\nu}} = (\widehat{+}, \widehat{-}, 1, 2)$ with interpolating angle as

$$g^{\widehat{\mu}\widehat{\nu}} = \begin{bmatrix} \mathbb{C} & \mathbb{S} & 0 & 0 \\ \mathbb{S} & -\mathbb{C} & 0 & 0 \\ 0 & 0 & -1 & 0 \\ 0 & 0 & 0 & -1 \end{bmatrix} = g_{\widehat{\mu}\widehat{\nu}}. \qquad (11.6)$$

This means that the covariant and contravariant indices are related by

$$a_{\widehat{+}} = \mathbb{C} a^{\widehat{+}} + \mathbb{S} a^{\widehat{-}} \quad ; \quad a^{\widehat{+}} = \mathbb{C} a_{\widehat{+}} + \mathbb{S} a_{\widehat{-}} \qquad (11.7)$$

$$a_{\widehat{-}} = \mathbb{S} a^{\widehat{+}} - \mathbb{C} a^{\widehat{-}} \quad ; \quad a^{\widehat{-}} = \mathbb{S} a_{\widehat{+}} - \mathbb{C} a_{\widehat{-}} \qquad (11.8)$$

$$a_j = -a^j \quad , \quad (j = 1, 2). \qquad (11.9)$$

11.2 Feynman propagator

The Feynman propagator [8] cast in the general interpolating angle case is

$$\Delta_F(x) = \int \frac{d^2\mathbf{p}_\perp dp_{\widehat{-}} dp_{\widehat{+}}}{(2\pi)^4} \frac{e^{-i(p_{\widehat{+}} x^{\widehat{+}} + p_{\widehat{-}} x^{\widehat{-}} + \mathbf{p}_\perp \mathbf{x}^\perp)}}{\left(\mathbb{C} p_{\widehat{+}}^2 + 2\mathbb{S} p_{\widehat{+}} p_{\widehat{-}} - \mathbb{C} p_{\widehat{-}}^2 - \mathbf{p}_\perp^2 - m^2 + i\varepsilon\right)}, \qquad (11.10)$$

where in the last expression above we have chosen to express all the momentum components (that is, for the integration variables) in terms of the (lower) covariant component indices.

Solving for the quadratic expression in the denominator of the Feynman propagator in order to separate the two distinct poles, we have

$$\Delta_F(x) = \int \frac{d^2\mathbf{p}_\perp}{(2\pi)^2} e^{-i\mathbf{p}_\perp \mathbf{x}^\perp} \int_{-\infty}^{+\infty} \frac{dp_{\widehat{-}}}{(2\pi)} e^{-ip_{\widehat{-}} x^{\widehat{-}}} \int_{-\infty}^{+\infty} \frac{dp_{\widehat{+}}}{(2\pi)} \frac{e^{-ip_{\widehat{+}} x^{\widehat{+}}}}{\mathscr{D}(\mathscr{A}_{\widehat{+}}, \mathscr{B}_{\widehat{+}})}, \qquad (11.11)$$

where $\mathscr{D}(\mathscr{A}_{\widehat{+}}, \mathscr{B}_{\widehat{+}}) \equiv \mathbb{C} (p_{\widehat{+}} - \mathscr{A}_{\widehat{+}} + i\varepsilon')(p_{\widehat{+}} - \mathscr{B}_{\widehat{+}} - i\varepsilon')$. The two poles in $p_{\widehat{+}}$ are $p_{\widehat{+}}^{(a)} = \mathscr{A}_{\widehat{+}} - i\varepsilon'$ and $p_{\widehat{+}}^{(b)} = \mathscr{B}_{\widehat{+}} + i\varepsilon'$ where the real part of the two poles are defined as

$$\mathscr{A}_{\widehat{+}} \equiv -\frac{\mathbb{S} p_{\widehat{-}}}{\mathbb{C}} + \frac{\sqrt{p_{\widehat{-}}^2 + \mathbb{C}(\mathbf{p}_\perp^2 + m^2)}}{\mathbb{C}}, \quad \text{and} \qquad (11.12)$$

$$\mathscr{B}_{\widehat{+}} \equiv -\frac{\mathbb{S} p_{\widehat{-}}}{\mathbb{C}} - \frac{\sqrt{p_{\widehat{-}}^2 + \mathbb{C}(\mathbf{p}_\perp^2 + m^2)}}{\mathbb{C}}, \qquad (11.13)$$

and the imaginary part of the poles is given now by

$$\varepsilon' \equiv \frac{\varepsilon}{2\sqrt{p_-^2 + \mathbb{C}(\mathbf{p}_\perp^2 + m^2)}} \equiv \frac{\varepsilon}{2\mathbb{P}}. \tag{11.14}$$

Since the square root in the above three expressions appears quite often in our calculations, we have introduced the shorthand notation for it as

$$\mathbb{P} \equiv \sqrt{p_-^2 + \mathbb{C}(\mathbf{p}_\perp^2 + m^2)}.$$

From the expressions in Eqs.(11.12) and (11.13), we may analyse the connection between the sign of the energies $\mathcal{A}_\mp$, $\mathcal{B}_\mp$ and the sign of the momentum p_-. Since $\mathbb{C}, \mathbb{S}$ and $\mathbb{P}$ are strictly positive quantities within the interpolation angle $0 \leq \delta \leq \pi/4$, we have that:

* For $p_- = 0$: Clearly for this situation $\mathcal{A}_\mp$ is positive, $(\mathcal{A}_\mp > 0)$, while $\mathcal{B}_\mp$ is negative, $(\mathcal{B}_\mp < 0)$;

* For $p_- < 0$: In this case $\mathcal{A}_\mp$ remains positive, $(\mathcal{A}_\mp > 0)$. On the other hand $\mathcal{B}_\mp$ might be positive only if $\mathbb{S}p_- > \mathbb{P}$. However, this condition cannot be satisfied to make $\mathcal{B}_\mp$ positive, therefore $\mathcal{B}_\mp$ is still negative, $(\mathcal{B}_\mp < 0)$;

* For $p_- > 0$: In this case $\mathcal{B}_\mp$ is clearly negative, $(\mathcal{B}_\mp < 0)$, while $\mathcal{A}_\mp$ continues to be positive, $(\mathcal{A}_\mp > 0)$, because $\mathbb{S}p_- < \mathbb{P}$.

We thus conclude that for any sign, positive or negative, for the momentum component p_-, the pole $\mathcal{A}_\mp$ corresponds to the positive energy solution and $\mathcal{B}_\mp$ to the negative energy solution. Therefore, we may draw the pole structure in the $p_\mp$ complex plane as $\mathcal{A}_\mp - i\varepsilon'$, located in the fourth quadrant, and $\mathcal{B}_\mp + i\varepsilon'$, located in the second quadrant.

In order to perform the integration in the "energy" variable $p_\mp$ in Eq.(11.11) we use the Cauchy residue theorem. We may consider three possibilities:

1) For $x^\mp > 0$: This requires $\mathfrak{Im}\, p_\mp < 0$ for the exponential factor to converge. This means that the semi-circle C_R that closes the contour must be located in the lower half of the complex $p_\mp$ plane and the closed contour encloses the pole $p_\mp = \mathcal{A}_\mp - i\varepsilon'$.

We thus have for this case:

$$\oint \frac{dp_\mp}{(2\pi)} \frac{e^{-ip_\mp x^\mp}}{\mathcal{D}(\mathcal{A}_\mp, \mathcal{B}_\mp)} = \lim_{R \to \infty} \left\{ \int_{-R}^{+R} \frac{dp_\mp}{(2\pi)} \frac{e^{-ip_\mp x^\mp}}{\mathcal{D}(\mathcal{A}_\mp, \mathcal{B}_\mp)} + \int_{C_R} \frac{dp_\mp}{(2\pi)} \frac{e^{-ip_\mp x^\mp}}{\mathcal{D}(\mathcal{A}_\mp, \mathcal{B}_\mp)} \right\} \tag{11.15}$$

The left-hand side of Eq.(11.15) is by Cauchy's theorem equal to $-i\mathrm{Res}(\mathcal{A}_\mp - i\varepsilon')$, where the minus sign is due to the clockwise direction of the closed contour. Since

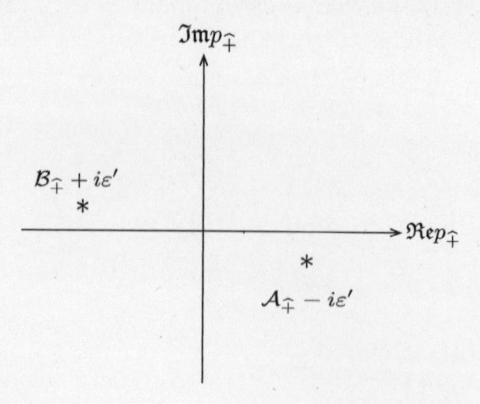

Figure 11.1: The pole structure in the complex plane.

the arc contribution in the limit $R \to \infty$ goes to zero, in this limit we have

$$\int_{-\infty}^{+\infty} \frac{dp_{\hat{\mp}}}{(2\pi)} \frac{e^{-ip_{\hat{\mp}} x^{\hat{\mp}}}}{\mathscr{D}(\mathscr{A}_{\hat{\mp}}, \mathscr{B}_{\hat{\mp}})} = -i \frac{e^{-i\mathscr{A}_{\hat{\mp}} x^{\hat{\mp}}}}{\mathbb{C}(\mathscr{A}_{\hat{\mp}} - \mathscr{B}_{\hat{\mp}})}, \qquad (x^{\hat{\mp}} > 0). \qquad (11.16)$$

We may summarize the foregoing result as (using $2\mathbb{P} = \mathbb{C}(\mathscr{A}_{\hat{\mp}} - \mathscr{B}_{\hat{\mp}})$, see Eq.(11.12) - Eq.(11.14)):

$$\Delta_F^{\mathscr{A}}(x) = -i\theta(x^{\hat{\mp}}) \int \frac{d^2\mathbf{p}_\perp}{(2\pi)^2} e^{-i\mathbf{p}_\perp \mathbf{x}^\perp} \int_{-\infty}^{+\infty} \frac{dp_{\hat{-}}}{(2\pi)} \frac{1}{2\mathbb{P}} e^{-i(p_{\hat{-}} x^{\hat{-}} + \mathscr{A}_{\hat{\mp}} x^{\hat{\mp}})}. \qquad (11.17)$$

2) <u>For $x^{\hat{\mp}} < 0$</u>: This implies that in order to have a converging exponential factor in the integrand, $\Im p_{\hat{\mp}} > 0$. This means that the semi-circle C_R that closes the contour must now be located in the upper half of the complex $p_{\hat{\mp}}$ plane, in a counterclockwise direction. A closed contour in this sense encloses now the pole $p_{\hat{\mp}} = \mathscr{B}_{\hat{\mp}} + i\varepsilon'$. We thus have for this case:

$$\oint \frac{dp_{\hat{\mp}}}{(2\pi)} \frac{e^{-ip_{\hat{\mp}} x^{\hat{\mp}}}}{\mathscr{D}(\mathscr{A}_{\hat{\mp}}, \mathscr{B}_{\hat{\mp}})} = \lim_{R \to \infty} \left\{ \int_{-R}^{+R} \frac{dp_{\hat{\mp}}}{(2\pi)} \frac{e^{-ip_{\hat{\mp}} x^{\hat{\mp}}}}{\mathscr{D}(\mathscr{A}_{\hat{\mp}}, \mathscr{B}_{\hat{\mp}})} + \int_{C_R} \frac{dp_{\hat{\mp}}}{(2\pi)} \frac{e^{-ip_{\hat{\mp}} x^{\hat{\mp}}}}{\mathscr{D}(\mathscr{A}_{\hat{\mp}}, \mathscr{B}_{\hat{\mp}})} \right\} \qquad (11.18)$$

The left-hand side of Eq.(11.18) is by Cauchy's theorem equal to $+i\text{Res}(\mathscr{B}_{\hat{\mp}} + i\varepsilon')$, where the plus sign now is due to the counterclockwise direction of the closed contour. Since the arc contribution in the limit $R \to \infty$ goes to zero, in this limit we now have

$$\int_{-\infty}^{+\infty} \frac{dp_{\hat{\mp}}}{(2\pi)} \frac{e^{-ip_{\hat{\mp}} x^{\hat{\mp}}}}{\mathscr{D}(\mathscr{A}_{\hat{\mp}}, \mathscr{B}_{\hat{\mp}})} = +i \frac{e^{-i\mathscr{B}_{\hat{\mp}} x^{\hat{\mp}}}}{\mathbb{C}(\mathscr{B}_{\hat{\mp}} - \mathscr{A}_{\hat{\mp}})}, \qquad (x^{\hat{\mp}} < 0). \qquad (11.19)$$

In this last expression, we have already dropped the ε' in the result after the $p_{\mp}$ integration, and put an reminder that this result is now valid for the specific case of $x^{\hat{\mp}} < 0$.

As before, we may now summarize the foregoing result as

$$\Delta_F^{\mathscr{B}}(x) = -i\theta(-x^{\hat{\mp}}) \int \frac{d^2\mathbf{p}_\perp}{(2\pi)^2} e^{-i\mathbf{p}_\perp \mathbf{x}^\perp} \int_{-\infty}^{+\infty} \frac{dp_-}{(2\pi)} \frac{1}{2\mathbb{P}} e^{-i(p_- x^{\hat{-}} + \mathscr{B}_{\hat{\mp}} x^{\hat{\mp}})}. \quad (11.20)$$

3) For $x^{\hat{\mp}} = 0$: In this case, the main converging factor in the integrand becomes one, that is, $e^0 = 1$. We have therefore

$$\oint \frac{dp_{\hat{\mp}}}{(2\pi)} \frac{1}{\mathscr{D}(\mathscr{A}_{\hat{\mp}}, \mathscr{B}_{\hat{\mp}})} = \lim_{R \to \infty} \left\{ \int_{-R}^{+R} \frac{dp_{\hat{\mp}}}{(2\pi)} \frac{1}{\mathscr{D}(\mathscr{A}_{\hat{\mp}}, \mathscr{B}_{\hat{\mp}})} + \int_{C_R} \frac{dp_{\hat{\mp}}}{(2\pi)} \frac{1}{\mathscr{D}(\mathscr{A}_{\hat{\mp}}, \mathscr{B}_{\hat{\mp}})} \right\} \quad (11.21)$$

Although for this case the exponential factor in the integrand is absent, the denominator of the integrand has enough powers in $p_{\hat{\mp}}$ to let the arc contribution goes to zero when $R \to \infty$. Therefore, closing the contour from below, that is, with C_R in the clockwise direction, this encloses the pole $p_{\hat{\mp}} = \mathscr{A}_{\hat{\mp}} - i\varepsilon'$ and we get

$$\int_{-\infty}^{+\infty} \frac{dp_{\hat{\mp}}}{(2\pi)} \frac{1}{\mathscr{D}(\mathscr{A}_{\hat{\mp}}, \mathscr{B}_{\hat{\mp}})} = \frac{-i}{\mathbb{C}(\mathscr{A}_{\hat{\mp}} - \mathscr{B}_{\hat{\mp}})} = -\frac{i}{2\mathbb{P}}, \quad (x^{\hat{\mp}} = 0). \quad (11.22)$$

Closing the contour in the counterclockwise direction, we enclose the other pole, $p_{\hat{\mp}} = \mathscr{B}_{\hat{\mp}} + i\varepsilon'$, and we obtain

$$\int_{-\infty}^{+\infty} \frac{dp_{\hat{\mp}}}{(2\pi)} \frac{1}{\mathscr{D}(\mathscr{A}_{\hat{\mp}}, \mathscr{B}_{\hat{\mp}})} = \frac{+i}{\mathbb{C}(\mathscr{B}_{\hat{\mp}} - \mathscr{A}_{\hat{\mp}})} = -\frac{i}{2\mathbb{P}}, \quad (x^{\hat{\mp}} = 0). \quad (11.23)$$

Thus, both circuits yield the same answer, as it should and serve as a check for our results. The result above is consistent with the direct computation of the integral as follows: First partial fraction the denominator, and integrate each ensuing integral within the finite limits $(-R, +R)$. After integration, take the limit $R \to \infty$ to get

$$\frac{1}{2\mathbb{P}} \lim_{R \to \infty} \left\{ \frac{1}{2\pi} \ln(p_{\hat{\mp}} - \mathscr{A}_{\hat{\mp}} + i\varepsilon') \Big|_{-R}^{+R} - \frac{1}{2\pi} \ln(p_{\hat{\mp}} - \mathscr{B}_{\hat{\mp}} - i\varepsilon') \Big|_{-R}^{+R} \right\} = -\frac{i}{2\mathbb{P}},$$

confirming our previous result.

Finally, the overall result for the Feynman propagator is given by the sum of the results in Eqs.(11.17) and (11.20), $\Delta_F(x) = \Delta_F^{\mathscr{A}}(x) + \Delta_F^{\mathscr{B}}(x)$, that is,

$$\Delta_F(x) = -i \int \frac{d^2\mathbf{p}_\perp}{(2\pi)^2} \int_{-\infty}^{+\infty} \frac{dp_{\hat{=}}}{(2\pi)} \frac{1}{2\mathbb{P}} \Big\{ \theta(x^{\hat{+}}) e^{-i(p_{\hat{=}} x^{\hat{=}} + \mathscr{A}_{\hat{+}} x^{\hat{+}} + \mathbf{p}_\perp \mathbf{x}^\perp)}$$

$$+ \theta(-x^{\hat{+}}) e^{-i(p_{\hat{=}} x^{\hat{=}} + \mathscr{B}_{\hat{+}} x^{\hat{+}} + \mathbf{p}_\perp \mathbf{x}^\perp)} \Big\}. \quad (11.24)$$

To derive the fermion propagator we need to apply the Dirac operator on it,

$$S_F(x) = \left(i\gamma^{\hat{+}} \partial_{\hat{+}} + i\gamma^{\hat{=}} \partial_{\hat{=}} + i\gamma^\perp \partial_\perp + m \right) \Delta_F(x), \quad (11.25)$$

where $\Delta_F(x)$ is given by Eq.(11.24). This differential operation on Eq.(11.24) means we have to consider

$$N^A = \left[i\left(\gamma^{\hat{+}} \partial_{\hat{+}} + \gamma^{\hat{=}} \partial_{\hat{=}} + \gamma^\perp \partial_\perp \right) + m \right] \!\Big\{ \theta(x^{\hat{+}}) e^{-i(p_{\hat{=}} x^{\hat{=}} + \mathscr{A}_{\hat{+}} x^{\hat{+}} + \mathbf{p}_\perp \mathbf{x}^\perp)} \Big\}$$

$$N^B = \left[i\left(\gamma^{\hat{+}} \partial_{\hat{+}} + \gamma^{\hat{=}} \partial_{\hat{=}} + \gamma^\perp \partial_\perp \right) + m \right] \!\Big\{ \theta(-x^{\hat{+}}) e^{-i(p_{\hat{=}} x^{\hat{=}} + \mathscr{B}_{\hat{+}} x^{\hat{+}} + \mathbf{p}_\perp \mathbf{x}^\perp)} \Big\}. \quad (11.26)$$

The $\theta(\pm x^{\hat{+}})$ factors will be affected only by the partial differentiation in $\partial_{\hat{+}}$. So, using $\partial_{\hat{+}} \theta(\pm x^{\hat{+}}) = \pm \delta(x^{\hat{+}})$ we have:

$$N^A = \theta(x^{\hat{+}}) e^{-i(p_{\hat{=}} x^{\hat{=}} + \mathscr{A}_{\hat{+}} x^{\hat{+}} + \mathbf{p}_\perp \mathbf{x}^\perp)} \left[\gamma^{\hat{+}} \mathscr{A}_{\hat{+}} + \gamma^{\hat{=}} p_{\hat{=}} + \gamma^\perp \mathbf{p}_\perp + m \right]$$

$$+ i\gamma^{\hat{+}} \delta(x^{\hat{+}}) e^{-i(p_{\hat{=}} x^{\hat{=}} + \mathscr{A}_{\hat{+}} x^{\hat{+}} + \mathbf{p}_\perp \mathbf{x}^\perp)}$$

$$N^B = \theta(-x^{\hat{+}}) e^{-i(p_{\hat{=}} x^{\hat{=}} + \mathscr{B}_{\hat{+}} x^{\hat{+}} + \mathbf{p}_\perp \mathbf{x}^\perp)} \left[\gamma^{\hat{+}} \mathscr{B}_{\hat{+}} + \gamma^{\hat{=}} p_{\hat{=}} + \gamma^\perp \mathbf{p}_\perp + m \right]$$

$$- i\gamma^{\hat{+}} \delta(x^{\hat{+}}) e^{-i(p_{\hat{=}} x^{\hat{=}} + \mathscr{B}_{\hat{+}} x^{\hat{+}} + \mathbf{p}_\perp \mathbf{x}^\perp)}. \quad (11.27)$$

Then the fermion propagator in the general interpolating angle becomes

$$S_F(x) = -i \int \frac{d^2\mathbf{p}_\perp}{(2\pi)^3} \int_{-\infty}^{+\infty} \frac{dp_{\hat{=}}}{2\mathbb{P}} \Big\{ \theta(x^{\hat{+}}) [\gamma^{\hat{\mu}} \mathscr{A}_{\hat{\mu}} + m] e^{-i \mathscr{A}_{\hat{\mu}} x^{\hat{\mu}}}$$

$$+ \theta(-x^{\hat{+}}) [\gamma^{\hat{\mu}} \mathscr{B}_{\hat{\mu}} + m] e^{-i \mathscr{B}_{\hat{\mu}} x^{\hat{\mu}}} \Big\}$$

$$+ \delta(x^{\hat{+}}) \int \frac{d^2\mathbf{p}_\perp}{(2\pi)^3} \int_{-\infty}^{+\infty} dp_{\hat{=}} \frac{\gamma^{\hat{+}}}{2\mathbb{P}} \Big\{ e^{-i \mathscr{A}_{\hat{\mu}} x^{\hat{\mu}}} - e^{-i \mathscr{B}_{\hat{\mu}} x^{\hat{\mu}}} \Big\}, \quad (11.28)$$

where we have introduced the shorthand notation

$$\gamma^{\hat{\mu}}(\mathscr{A}_{\hat{\mu}}, \mathscr{B}_{\hat{\mu}}) \equiv \gamma^{\hat{+}}(\mathscr{A}_{\hat{+}}, \mathscr{B}_{\hat{+}}) + \gamma^{\hat{=}} p_{\hat{=}} + \gamma^\perp \mathbf{p}_\perp$$

$$(\mathscr{A}_{\hat{\mu}}, \mathscr{B}_{\hat{\mu}}) x^{\hat{\mu}} \equiv (\mathscr{A}_{\hat{+}}, \mathscr{B}_{\hat{+}}) x^{\hat{+}} + p_{\hat{=}} x^{\hat{=}} + \mathbf{p}_\perp \mathbf{x}^\perp. \quad (11.29)$$

Observing Eq.(11.28) we note that: (a) *instantaneous terms* in the general interpolating fermion propagator **do not** cancel each other straightaway. In order to see their cancellation, we need to work out the *positive*-energy and *negative*-energy sectors of the propagator and perceive that they can be combined together after changing momentum integration variables from $\mathbf{p}_\perp \to -\mathbf{p}_\perp$ and $p_{\hat{-}} \to -p_{\hat{-}}$ for one of them and **only** after that the "energy" ($p_{\hat{-}}$) integration in the instantaneous term piece results in zero by virtue of the integrand becoming an odd function integrated over the whole range from $-\infty$ to $+\infty$, and (b) since there is **no sign correlation** between the *energies* $\mathcal{A}_{\hat{\mp}}$, $\mathcal{B}_{\hat{\mp}}$ and *transverse momentum* $p_{\hat{-}}$ in the general interpolating angle case, we **cannot** take the light-front limit $\delta \to \pi/4$ directly in Eq. (11.28).

For the interpolating fermion propagator then we have the following conclusions:

1. For all the cases $0 \leq \delta < \dfrac{\pi}{4}$: The instantaneous term that arises from the *positive energy* $\mathcal{A}_{\hat{\mp}}$ propagator and the instantaneous term that arises from the *negative energy* $\mathcal{B}_{\hat{\mp}}$ propagator can be combined together to yield zero and since there is no sign correlation between energies $\mathcal{A}_{\hat{\mp}}$, $\mathcal{B}_{\hat{\mp}}$ and momentum $p_{\hat{-}}$, this combination is made possible by changes in the integration variables from $\mathbf{p}_\perp \to -\mathbf{p}_\perp$ and $p_{\hat{-}} \to -p_{\hat{-}}$ withouth any restriction whatsoever.

2. The limit to **IFD** which is achieved when we let $\delta \to 0$ can be performed without any problem. There are no singularities and the limit can be taken directly from Eq.(11.28).

3. **However** the limit to **LFD** which is achieved when we let $\delta \to \pi/4$, on the other hand, has *singularities* and because there is a *constraint on the signs between energy and momentum* in the light front, changes in the sign of momentum integration from $\mathbf{p}_\perp \to -\mathbf{p}_\perp$ and especially from $p_{\hat{-}} \to -p_{\hat{-}}$ must be carried out with much care and attention. We **must** rearrange Eq.(11.28) in a convenient form **before** taking the limit to the light front $\mathbb{C} \to 0$. In order to implement the sign correlation between transverse momentum and energy, we split Eq.(11.28) using the identity

$$\int_{-\infty}^{+\infty} dp_{\hat{-}} = \int_{-\infty}^{0} dp_{\hat{-}} + \int_{0}^{+\infty} dp_{\hat{-}}. \text{ Then}$$

$$S_{\text{F}}(x) = -i \int \frac{d^2\mathbf{p}_\perp}{(2\pi)^3} \int_{-\infty}^{0} \frac{dp_{\hat{-}}}{2\mathbb{P}} \left\{ \theta(x^{\hat{+}})\mathscr{F}(\mathscr{A}_{\hat{+}}) + \theta(-x^{\hat{+}})\mathscr{G}(\mathscr{B}_{\hat{+}}) \right\}$$

$$+\delta(x^{\hat{+}}) \int \frac{d^2\mathbf{p}_\perp}{(2\pi)^3} \int_{-\infty}^{0} dp_{\hat{-}} \frac{\gamma^{\hat{+}}}{2\mathbb{P}} \left[e^{-i\mathscr{A}_{\hat{\mu}} x^{\hat{\mu}}} - e^{-i\mathscr{B}_{\hat{\mu}} x^{\hat{\mu}}} \right],$$

$$-i \int \frac{d^2\mathbf{p}_\perp}{(2\pi)^3} \int_{0}^{+\infty} \frac{dp_{\hat{-}}}{2\mathbb{P}} \left\{ \theta(x^{\hat{+}})\mathscr{F}(\mathscr{A}_{\hat{+}}) + \theta(-x^{\hat{+}})\mathscr{G}(\mathscr{B}_{\hat{+}}) \right\}$$

$$+\delta(x^{\hat{+}}) \int \frac{d^2\mathbf{p}_\perp}{(2\pi)^3} \int_{0}^{+\infty} dp_{\hat{-}} \frac{\gamma^{\hat{+}}}{2\mathbb{P}} \left[e^{-i\mathscr{A}_{\hat{\mu}} x^{\hat{\mu}}} - e^{-i\mathscr{B}_{\hat{\mu}} x^{\hat{\mu}}} \right], \quad (11.30)$$

where we have introduced the shorthand notation $\mathscr{F}(\mathscr{A}_{\hat{+}}) \equiv [\gamma^{\hat{\mu}} \mathscr{A}_{\hat{\mu}} + m] e^{-i(\mathscr{A}_{\hat{\mu}} x^{\hat{\mu}})}$, and $\mathscr{G}(\mathscr{B}_{\hat{+}}) \equiv [\gamma^{\hat{\mu}} \mathscr{B}_{\hat{\mu}} + m] e^{-i(\mathscr{B}_{\hat{\mu}} x^{\hat{\mu}})}$.

For the **first** two integrals in Eq.(11.30) we do the following change in the integration variables ($\mathbf{p}_\perp \to -\mathbf{p}_\perp$), and ($p_{\hat{-}} \to -p_{\hat{-}}$), which leads to the following symmetry properties $\mathscr{A}_{\hat{+}} \to -\mathscr{B}_{\hat{+}}$, $\mathscr{B}_{\hat{+}} \to -\mathscr{A}_{\hat{+}}$, and $\mathbb{P} \to \mathbb{P}$. Then

$$\mathscr{F}(\mathscr{A}_{\hat{+}}) \to \mathscr{G}(-\mathscr{B}_{\hat{+}}) = [-\gamma^{\hat{\mu}} \mathscr{B}_{\hat{\mu}} + m] e^{+i\mathscr{B}_{\hat{\mu}} x^{\hat{\mu}}} \quad (11.31)$$

$$\mathscr{G}(\mathscr{B}_{\hat{+}}) \to \mathscr{F}(-\mathscr{A}_{\hat{+}}) = [-\gamma^{\hat{\mu}} \mathscr{A}_{\hat{\mu}} + m] e^{+i\mathscr{A}_{\hat{\mu}} x^{\hat{\mu}}}. \quad (11.32)$$

Therefore, our fermion propagator becomes

$$S_{\text{F}}(x) = -i \int \frac{d^2\mathbf{p}_\perp}{(2\pi)^3} \int_{0}^{+\infty} \frac{dp_{\hat{-}}}{2\mathbb{P}} \left\{ \theta(x^{\hat{+}})\mathscr{G}(-\mathscr{B}_{\hat{+}}) + \theta(-x^{\hat{+}})\mathscr{F}(-\mathscr{A}_{\hat{+}}) \right\}$$

$$+\delta(x^{\hat{+}}) \int \frac{d^2\mathbf{p}_\perp}{(2\pi)^3} \int_{0}^{+\infty} dp_{\hat{-}} \frac{\gamma^{\hat{+}}}{2\mathbb{P}} \left[e^{+i\mathscr{B}_{\hat{\mu}} x^{\hat{\mu}}} - e^{+i\mathscr{A}_{\hat{\mu}} x^{\hat{\mu}}} \right],$$

$$-i \int \frac{d^2\mathbf{p}_\perp}{(2\pi)^3} \int_{0}^{+\infty} \frac{dp_{\hat{-}}}{2\mathbb{P}} \left\{ \theta(x^{\hat{+}})\mathscr{F}(\mathscr{A}_{\hat{+}}) + \theta(-x^{\hat{+}})\mathscr{G}(\mathscr{B}_{\hat{+}}) \right\}$$

$$+\delta(x^{\hat{+}}) \int \frac{d^2\mathbf{p}_\perp}{(2\pi)^3} \int_{0}^{+\infty} dp_{\hat{-}} \frac{\gamma^{\hat{+}}}{2\mathbb{P}} \left[e^{-i\mathscr{A}_{\hat{\mu}} x^{\hat{\mu}}} - e^{-i\mathscr{B}_{\hat{\mu}} x^{\hat{\mu}}} \right], \quad (11.33)$$

We observe that now Eq.(11.33) may, by rearranging the terms in a convenient way, be re-written as

$$S_F(x) = -i \int \frac{d^2\mathbf{p}_\perp}{(2\pi)^3} \int_0^{+\infty} \frac{dp_\succ}{2\mathbb{P}} \left\{ \theta(x^{\hat{\mp}})\mathscr{F}(\mathscr{A}_{\hat{\mp}}) + \theta(-x^{\hat{\mp}})\mathscr{F}(-\mathscr{A}_{\hat{\mp}}) \right\}$$

$$+ \delta(x^{\hat{\mp}}) \int \frac{d^2\mathbf{p}_\perp}{(2\pi)^3} \int_0^{+\infty} dp_\succ \frac{\gamma^{\hat{\mp}}}{2\mathbb{P}} \left[e^{-i\mathscr{A}_{\hat{\mu}}x^{\hat{\mu}}} - e^{+i\mathscr{A}_{\hat{\mu}}x^{\hat{\mu}}} \right],$$

$$- i \int \frac{d^2\mathbf{p}_\perp}{(2\pi)^3} \int_0^{+\infty} \frac{dp_\succ}{2\mathbb{P}} \left\{ \theta(x^{\hat{\mp}})\mathscr{G}(-\mathscr{B}_{\hat{\mp}}) + \theta(-x^{\hat{\mp}})\mathscr{G}(\mathscr{B}_{\hat{\mp}}) \right\}$$

$$+ \delta(x^{\hat{\mp}}) \int \frac{d^2\mathbf{p}_\perp}{(2\pi)^3} \int_0^{+\infty} dp_\succ \frac{\gamma^{\hat{\mp}}}{2\mathbb{P}} \left[e^{+i\mathscr{B}_{\hat{\mu}}x^{\hat{\mu}}} - e^{-i\mathscr{B}_{\hat{\mu}}x^{\hat{\mu}}} \right], \quad (11.34)$$

In other words, our original interpolating fermion propagator can be rewritten as the sum $S_F(x) = S_F^A(x) + S_F^B(x)$, with *positive energy* sector given by

$$S_F^A(x) = -i \int \frac{d^2\mathbf{p}_\perp}{(2\pi)^3} \int_0^{+\infty} \frac{dp_\succ}{2\mathbb{P}} \left\{ \theta(x^{\hat{\mp}})[\gamma^{\hat{\mu}}\mathscr{A}_{\hat{\mu}} + m] e^{-i\mathscr{A}_{\hat{\mu}}x^{\hat{\mu}}} \right.$$

$$\left. + \theta(-x^{\hat{\mp}})[-\gamma^{\hat{\mu}}\mathscr{A}_{\hat{\mu}} + m] e^{+i\mathscr{A}_{\hat{\mu}}x^{\hat{\mu}}} \right\}$$

$$+ \delta(x^{\hat{\mp}}) \int \frac{d^2\mathbf{p}_\perp}{(2\pi)^3} \int_0^{+\infty} dp_\succ \frac{\gamma^{\hat{\mp}}}{2\mathbb{P}} \left[e^{-i\mathscr{A}_{\hat{\mu}}x^{\hat{\mu}}} - e^{+i\mathscr{A}_{\hat{\mu}}x^{\hat{\mu}}} \right], \quad (11.35)$$

and *negative energy* sector being

$$S_F^B(x) = -i \int \frac{d^2\mathbf{p}_\perp}{(2\pi)^3} \int_0^{+\infty} \frac{dp_\succ}{2\mathbb{P}} \left\{ \theta(x^{\hat{\mp}})[-\gamma^{\hat{\mu}}\mathscr{B}_{\hat{\mu}} + m] e^{+i\mathscr{B}_{\hat{\mu}}x^{\hat{\mu}}} \right.$$

$$\left. + \theta(-x^{\hat{\mp}})[\gamma^{\hat{\mu}}\mathscr{B}_{\hat{\mu}} + m] e^{-i\mathscr{B}_{\hat{\mu}}x^{\hat{\mu}}} \right\}$$

$$+ \delta(x^{\hat{\mp}}) \int \frac{d^2\mathbf{p}_\perp}{(2\pi)^3} \int_0^{+\infty} dp_\succ \frac{\gamma^{\hat{\mp}}}{2\mathbb{P}} \left[e^{+i\mathscr{B}_{\hat{\mu}}x^{\hat{\mu}}} - e^{-i\mathscr{B}_{\hat{\mu}}x^{\hat{\mu}}} \right]. \quad (11.36)$$

When we take the light-front limit $\delta \to \pi/4$ or $\mathbb{C} \to 0$:

$$p_{\hat{-}} \to p_- = p^+, \qquad \mathbb{P} \to p_{\hat{-}} + \mathcal{O}(\mathbb{C}) = p^+ + \mathcal{O}(\mathbb{C})$$
$$x_{\hat{-}} \to x_- = x^+, \qquad \mathcal{A}_{\hat{\mp}} \to p_{\text{on}}^- + \mathcal{O}(\mathbb{C})$$
$$x_{\hat{\mp}} \to x_+ = x^-, \qquad \mathcal{B}_{\hat{\mp}} \to -\frac{2p^+}{\mathbb{C}} - p_{\text{on}}^- + \mathcal{O}(\mathbb{C})$$

Then the explicit expression for the *positive*-energy part of the fermion propagator in the light-front limit is

$$\begin{aligned}
S_F^A(x) \underset{\mathbb{C} \to 0}{\to} & -i \int \frac{d^2 \mathbf{p}^\perp}{(2\pi)^3} \int_0^{+\infty} \frac{dp^+}{2p^+} \\
& \times \left\{ \theta(x^+)(\gamma^+ p_{\text{on}}^- + \gamma^- p^+ - \boldsymbol{\gamma}^\perp \mathbf{p}^\perp + m) e^{-i(p_{\text{on}}^- x^+ + p^+ x^- - \mathbf{p}^\perp \mathbf{x}^\perp)} \right. \\
& \left. + \theta(-x^+)(-\gamma^+ p_{\text{on}}^- - \gamma^- p^+ + \boldsymbol{\gamma}^\perp \mathbf{p}^\perp + m) e^{+i(p_{\text{on}}^- x^+ + p^+ x^- - \mathbf{p}^\perp \mathbf{x}^\perp)} \right\} \\
& + \delta(x^+) \int \frac{d^2 \mathbf{p}^\perp}{(2\pi)^2} \int_0^{+\infty} \frac{dp^+}{(2\pi)} \frac{\gamma^+}{2p^+} \left\{ e^{-i(p_{\text{on}}^- x^+ + p^+ x^- - \mathbf{p}^\perp \mathbf{x}^\perp)} \right. \\
& \left. - e^{+i(p_{\text{on}}^- x^+ + p^+ x^- - \mathbf{p}^\perp \mathbf{x}^\perp)} \right\}. \quad (11.37)
\end{aligned}$$

This *positive*-energy part is exactly the fermion propagator that is obtained in the direct light-front calculation:

$$\begin{aligned}
S_F = & -\frac{i}{(2\pi)^3} \int d^2 \mathbf{p}_\perp \int_0^{+\infty} \frac{dp^+}{2p^+} \\
& \times \left\{ \theta(x^+) e^{-i(p_{\text{on}}^- x^+ + p^+ x^- - \mathbf{p}_\perp \mathbf{x}_\perp)} (\gamma^+ p_{\text{on}}^- + \gamma^- p^+ - \boldsymbol{\gamma}^\perp \mathbf{p}^\perp + m) \right. \\
& \left. + \theta(-x^+) e^{+i(p_{\text{on}}^- x^+ + p^+ x^- - \mathbf{p}_\perp \mathbf{x}_\perp)} (-\gamma^+ p_{\text{on}}^- - \gamma^- p^- + \boldsymbol{\gamma}^\perp \mathbf{p}^\perp + m) \right\} \\
& + \frac{\gamma^+ \delta(x^+)}{(2\pi)^3} \int d^2 \mathbf{p}_\perp \int_0^{+\infty} \frac{dp^+}{2p^+} \left\{ e^{-i(p_{\text{on}}^- x^+ + p^+ x^- - \mathbf{p}_\perp \mathbf{x}_\perp)} \right. \\
& \left. - e^{+i(p_{\text{on}}^- x^+ + p^+ x^- - \mathbf{p}_\perp \mathbf{x}_\perp)} \right\}. \quad (11.38)
\end{aligned}$$

Note that the last term in the above equation, the instantaneous term[9, 10], is integrated solely over the positive momentum, $0 < p^+ < +\infty$.

Now the *negative*-energy propagator in the light-front limit is

$$\begin{aligned}
S_F^B(x) \underset{\mathbb{C} \to 0}{\to} & -i \int \frac{d^2 \mathbf{p}^\perp}{(2\pi)^3} \int_0^{+\infty} \frac{dp^+}{2p^+} \left\{ \theta(x^+) [-\gamma^\mu \mathcal{B}_\mu + m] e^{+i \mathcal{B}_\mu x^\mu} \right. \\
& \left. + \theta(-x^+) [\gamma^\mu \mathcal{B}_\mu + m] e^{-i \mathcal{B}_\mu x^\mu} \right\} \\
& + \delta(x^+) \int \frac{d^2 \mathbf{p}^\perp}{(2\pi)^3} \int_0^{+\infty} dp^+ \frac{\gamma^+}{2p^+} \left[e^{+i \mathcal{B}_\mu x^\mu} - e^{-i \mathcal{B}_\mu x^\mu} \right], \quad (11.39)
\end{aligned}$$

where $\mathcal{B}_\mu$ exhibits singular behavior as $\mathbb{C} \to 0$:

$$\gamma^\mu \mathcal{B}_\mu = -\gamma^+ \left(\frac{2p^+}{\mathbb{C}} + p^-_{\text{on}}\right) + \gamma^- p^+ - \gamma^\perp \mathbf{p}^\perp, \quad (11.40)$$

$$\mathcal{B}_\mu x^\mu = -\left(\frac{2p^+}{\mathbb{C}} + p^-_{\text{on}}\right) x^+ + p^+ x^- - \mathbf{p}^\perp \mathbf{x}^\perp. \quad (11.41)$$

We should point out here that the light front limit, $\mathbb{C} \to 0$, should be treated with caution for the $\mathcal{B}_{\bar{+}}$ *negative*-energy part of the propagator. As a caveat, just looking at the last expression above, the first term in it, $\frac{2p^+}{\mathbb{C}}$, goes to infinity in this limit for nonzero p^+. It may be finite for $\mathbb{C} \to 0$ if $p^+ \to 0$ also – a reminiscent of the zero mode contribution. However, in this case, when $p^+ \to 0$, it means $p^-_{\text{on}} \to \infty$. This means we were not able to get rid of the divergence; we simply shift from one place to another. So, in the following analysis, we shall consider both of them as leading terms in the study of the light front limit.

In the light-front limit then the *leading terms* of $S_F^B(x)$ part of the fermion propagator are

$$\begin{aligned}S_F^B(x)\Big|_{\text{leading}} &= -i \int \frac{d^2\mathbf{p}^\perp}{(2\pi)^3} \int_0^{+\infty} dp^+ \frac{\gamma^+}{2p^+} \left\{ \theta(x^+)\left(\frac{2p^+}{\mathbb{C}} + p^-_{\text{on}}\right) e^{+i\left(\frac{-2p^+}{\mathbb{C}} - p^-_{\text{on}}\right)x^+} \right.\\ &\quad\left. + \theta(-x^+)\left(\frac{-2p^+}{\mathbb{C}} - p^-_{\text{on}}\right) e^{-i\left(\frac{-2p^+}{\mathbb{C}} - p^-_{\text{on}}\right)x^+} \right\}\\ &\quad + \delta(x^+) \int \frac{d^2\mathbf{p}^\perp}{(2\pi)^3} \int_{-\infty}^{+\infty} dp^+ \frac{\gamma^+}{2p^+} \left\{ e^{+i\left(\frac{-2p^+}{\mathbb{C}} - p^-_{\text{on}}\right)x^+} - e^{-i\left(\frac{-2p^+}{\mathbb{C}} - p^-_{\text{on}}\right)x^+} \right\}. \quad (11.42)\end{aligned}$$

We now rewrite Eq.(11.42) above using the identity:

$$\mp i \left(\frac{2p^+}{\mathbb{C}} + p^-_{\text{on}}\right) e^{\mp i\left(\frac{2p^+}{\mathbb{C}} + p^-_{\text{on}}\right)x^+} = \left(\frac{\partial}{\partial x^+}\right) e^{\mp i\left(\frac{2p^+}{\mathbb{C}} + p^-_{\text{on}}\right)x^+},$$

so that now those terms are expressed as

$$\begin{aligned}S_F^B(x)\Big|_{\text{leading}} &= \int \frac{d^2\mathbf{p}^\perp}{(2\pi)^3} \int_0^{+\infty} dp^+ \frac{\gamma^+}{2p^+} \left[\theta(x^+)\left(\frac{\partial}{\partial x^+}\right) e^{-i\left(\frac{2p^+}{\mathbb{C}} + p^-_{\text{on}}\right)x^+} \right] \quad (11.43)\\ &\quad + \int \frac{d^2\mathbf{p}^\perp}{(2\pi)^3} \int_0^{+\infty} dp^+ \frac{\gamma^+}{2p^+} \left[\theta(-x^+)\left(\frac{\partial}{\partial x^+}\right) e^{+i\left(\frac{2p^+}{\mathbb{C}} + p^-_{\text{on}}\right)x^+} \right]\\ &\quad + \delta(x^+) \int \frac{d^2\mathbf{p}^\perp}{(2\pi)^3} \int_{-\infty}^{+\infty} dp^+ \frac{\gamma^+}{2p^+} \left[e^{-i\left(\frac{2p^+}{\mathbb{C}} + p^-_{\text{on}}\right)x^+} - e^{+i\left(\frac{2p^+}{\mathbb{C}} + p^-_{\text{on}}\right)x^+} \right].\end{aligned}$$

We may re-express the terms containing the derivatives in the integrand using:

$$\theta(\pm x^+)\left(\frac{\partial}{\partial x^+}\right)e^{\mp i\left(\frac{2p^+}{C}+p_{on}^-\right)x^+} = \frac{\partial}{\partial x^+}\left\{\theta(\pm x^+)e^{\mp i\left(\frac{2p^+}{C}+p_{on}^-\right)x^+}\right\}$$
$$\mp \delta(x^+)e^{\mp i\left(\frac{2p^+}{C}+p_{on}^-\right)x^+}. \qquad (11.44)$$

The terms containing the derivatives in the integrand then may be rewritten as

$$\mathfrak{D}_F^B(x)\Big|_{\text{derivatives}} \equiv \frac{\partial}{\partial x^+}\left\{\int\frac{d^2\mathbf{p}^\perp}{(2\pi)^3}\int_0^{+\infty}dp^+\frac{\gamma^+}{2p^+}\theta(x^+)e^{-i\left(\frac{2p^+}{C}+p_{on}^-\right)x^+}\right\}$$
$$- \frac{\partial}{\partial(-x^+)}\left\{\int\frac{d^2\mathbf{p}_\perp}{(2\pi)^3}\int_0^{+\infty}dp^+\frac{\gamma^+}{2p^+}\theta(-x^+)e^{+i\left(\frac{2p^+}{C}+p_{on}^-\right)x^+}\right\}$$
$$- \delta(x^+)\int\frac{d^2\mathbf{p}_\perp}{(2\pi)^3}\int_0^{+\infty}dp^+\frac{\gamma^+}{2p^+}\left[e^{-i\left(\frac{2p^+}{C}+p_{on}^-\right)x^+}\right]$$
$$+ \delta(x^+)\int\frac{d^2\mathbf{p}_\perp}{(2\pi)^2}\int_0^{+\infty}dp^+\frac{\gamma^+}{2p^+}\left[e^{+i\left(\frac{2p^+}{C}+p_{on}^-\right)x^+}\right]. \qquad (11.45)$$

The first two terms in $\mathfrak{D}_F^B(x)\Big|_{\text{derivatives}}$ cancel against each other. We can see this by letting $-x^+ \to y^+$ as follows

$$\frac{\partial}{\partial x^+}\left\{\int\frac{d^2\mathbf{p}_\perp}{(2\pi)^3}\int_0^{+\infty}dp^+\frac{\gamma^+}{2p^+}\theta(x^+)e^{-i\left(\frac{2p^+}{C}+p_{on}^-\right)x^+}\right\}$$
$$-\frac{\partial}{\partial(y^+)}\left\{\int\frac{d^2\mathbf{p}_\perp}{(2\pi)^3}\int_0^{+\infty}dp^+\frac{\gamma^+}{2p^+}\theta(y^+)e^{-i\left(\frac{2p^+}{C}+p_{on}^-\right)y^+}\right\} = 0.$$

Then, finally for the *leading terms* in $S_{\text{F leading}}^B(x)$ we have

$$\begin{aligned}
S_{\text{F leading}}^B(x) &= -\delta(x^+)\int \frac{d^2\mathbf{p}_\perp}{(2\pi)^3} \int_0^{+\infty} dp^+ \frac{\gamma^+}{2p^+}\left[e^{-i\left(\frac{2p^+}{\mathbb{C}}+p_{\text{on}}^-\right)x^+}\right] \\
&+ \delta(x^+)\int \frac{d^2\mathbf{p}_\perp}{(2\pi)^3} \int_0^{+\infty} dp^+ \frac{\gamma^+}{2p^+}\left[e^{+i\left(\frac{2p^+}{\mathbb{C}}+p_{\text{on}}^-\right)x^+}\right] \\
&+ \delta(x^+)\int \frac{d^2\mathbf{p}^\perp}{(2\pi)^3} \int_{-\infty}^{+\infty} dp^+ \frac{\gamma^+}{2p^+}\left[e^{-i\left(\frac{2p^+}{\mathbb{C}}+p_{\text{on}}^-\right)x^+} - e^{+i\left(\frac{2p^+}{\mathbb{C}}+p_{\text{on}}^-\right)x^+}\right]. \\
&= 0. \quad (11.46)
\end{aligned}$$

So the leading term for the *negative*-energy sector of the fermion propagator vanishes away in the light-front limit.

This serendipitous vanishing away of this term on the branch of *negative*-energy sector is what makes the light-front fermion propagator so unique. It means that the positive-energy sector of the fermion propagator in the light-front already carries all the relevant physical information!

That being the case in the LFD, some interesting questions can be raised in this scenario. (a) How do we interpret and introduce antiparticles in this context? (b) Is vacuum trivial in LFD? (c) Does the instantaneous term carry any relevant physical information?

11.3 The fermion propagator in the IFD limit

As our final consideration, we look at the instant form limit, $\delta \to 0$ or $\mathbb{C} \to 1$ and $\mathbb{S} \to 0$ for which we have

$$\begin{aligned}
p_{\hat{\scriptscriptstyle-}} &\to \mathbb{S}p^{\hat{+}} - \mathbb{C}p^{\hat{-}} = -p^{\hat{-}} = -\{p^0 \sin\delta - p^3\cos\delta\} = p^3, \\
p^{\hat{-}} &\to -p^3, \\
x_{\hat{\scriptscriptstyle-}} &\to x^3, \\
x^{\hat{-}} &\to -x^3, \\
x_{\hat{\mp}} &\to x^0, \\
\mathbb{P} &\to \sqrt{(p^3)^2 + \mathbf{p}_\perp^2 + m^2} = \sqrt{\vec{p}^2 + m^2} \equiv \omega_{\vec{p}}, \\
\mathscr{A}_{\hat{\mp}} &\to \omega_{\vec{p}}, \\
\mathscr{B}_{\hat{\mp}} &\to -\omega_{\vec{p}}. \quad (11.47)
\end{aligned}$$

Thus Eq.(11.28) is written in the **IFD** case,

$$S_F(x) \underset{\delta \to 0}{\to} -i \int \frac{d^2 \mathbf{p}^\perp}{(2\pi)^3} \int_{-\infty}^{+\infty} \frac{dp^3}{2\omega_{\vec{p}}}$$
$$\times \{\theta(x^0)[\gamma^0 \omega_{\vec{p}} - \gamma^3 p^3 - \boldsymbol{\gamma}^\perp \mathbf{p}^\perp + m] e^{-i(\omega_{\vec{p}} x^0 - p^3 x^3 - \mathbf{p}^\perp \mathbf{x}^\perp)}$$
$$+ \theta(-x^0)[-\gamma^0 \omega_{\vec{p}} - \gamma^3 p^3 - \boldsymbol{\gamma}^\perp \mathbf{p}^\perp + m] e^{-i(-\omega_{\vec{p}} x^0 - p^3 x^3 - \mathbf{p}^\perp \mathbf{x}^\perp)}\}$$
$$+ \delta(x^0) \int \frac{d^2 \mathbf{p}^\perp}{(2\pi)^3} \int_{-\infty}^{+\infty} dp^3 \frac{\gamma^0}{2\omega_{\vec{p}}} \{e^{-i(\omega_{\vec{p}} x^0 - p^3 x^3 - \mathbf{p}^\perp \mathbf{x}^\perp)}$$
$$- e^{-i(-\omega_{\vec{p}} x^0 - p^3 x^3 - \mathbf{p}^\perp \mathbf{x}^\perp)}\}, \qquad (11.48)$$

By making the change of integration variables in $\mathbf{p}^\perp \to -\mathbf{p}^\perp$ and $p^3 \to -p^3$ and rewriting the measure as $d^3 \vec{p}$, we have

$$S_F(x) \underset{\delta \to 0}{\to} -i \int \frac{d^3 \vec{p}}{(2\pi)^3} \frac{1}{2\omega_{\vec{p}}} \{\theta(x^0)[\gamma^0 \omega_{\vec{p}} - \vec{\gamma} \cdot \vec{p} + m] e^{-i(\omega_{\vec{p}} x^0 - \vec{p} \cdot \vec{x})}$$
$$+ \theta(-x^0)[-\gamma^0 \omega_{\vec{p}} + \vec{\gamma} \cdot \vec{p} + m] e^{+i(\omega_{\vec{p}} x^0 - \vec{p} \cdot \vec{x})}\}$$
$$+ \delta(x^0) \int \frac{d^3 \vec{p}}{(2\pi)^3} \frac{\gamma^0}{2\omega_{\vec{p}}} \{e^{-i(\omega_{\vec{p}} x^0 - \vec{p} \cdot \vec{x})} - e^{+i(\omega_{\vec{p}} x^0 - \vec{p} \cdot \vec{x})}\}$$
$$S_F(x) \underset{\delta \to 0}{=} -i \int \frac{d^3 \vec{p}}{(2\pi)^3} \frac{1}{2\omega_{\vec{p}}} \{\theta(x^0)[\gamma^0 \omega_{\vec{p}} - \vec{\gamma} \cdot \vec{p} + m] e^{-i(\omega_{\vec{p}} x^0 - \vec{p} \cdot \vec{x})}$$
$$+ \theta(-x^0)[-\gamma^0 \omega_{\vec{p}} + \vec{\gamma} \cdot \vec{p} + m] e^{+i(\omega_{\vec{p}} x^0 - \vec{p} \cdot \vec{x})}\}. \qquad (11.49)$$

Finally, Eq.(11.28) is written in the **IFD** limit as,

$$S_F(x) \underset{\delta \to 0}{\to} -i \int \frac{d^3 \vec{p}}{(2\pi)^3} \frac{1}{2\omega_{\vec{p}}} \{\theta(x^0)(\gamma \cdot p_{\text{on}} + m) e^{-i p_{\text{on}} \cdot x}$$
$$+ \theta(-x^0)(-\gamma \cdot p_{\text{on}} + m) e^{+i p_{\text{on}} \cdot x}\}, \qquad (11.50)$$

with the definition $p_{\text{on}}^\mu = (\omega_{\vec{p}}, \vec{p}) = (\omega_{\vec{p}}, p^1, p^2, p^3)$.

We also analyze the **IFD** limit using Eqs.(11.35) and (11.36). From Eq.(11.35) we have

$$S_F^A(x) \underset{\delta \to 0}{\to} -i \int \frac{d^2\mathbf{p}_\perp}{(2\pi)^2} \int_0^{+\infty} \frac{dp^3}{(2\pi)} \frac{1}{2\omega_{\vec{p}}}$$

$$\times \left\{ \theta(x^0)(\gamma^0 \omega_{\vec{p}} - \vec{\gamma} \cdot \vec{p} + m) e^{-i(\omega_{\vec{p}} x^0 - \vec{p} \cdot \vec{x})} \right.$$

$$\left. + \theta(-x^0)(-\gamma^0 \omega_{\vec{p}} + \vec{\gamma} \cdot \vec{p} + m) e^{+i(\omega_{\vec{p}} x^0 - \vec{p} \cdot \vec{x})} \right\}$$

$$+ \delta(x^0) \int \frac{d^2\mathbf{p}_\perp}{(2\pi)^2} \int_0^{+\infty} \frac{dp^3}{(2\pi)} \frac{\gamma^0}{2\omega_{\vec{p}}} \left\{ e^{-i(\omega_{\vec{p}} x^0 - \vec{p} \cdot \vec{x})} - e^{+i(\omega_{\vec{p}} x^0 - \vec{p} \cdot \vec{x})} \right\}. \quad (11.51)$$

Thus, the *positive*-energy part in Eqs.(11.35) is in the **IFD** limit

$$S_F^A(x) \underset{\delta \to 0}{\to} -i \int \frac{d^2\mathbf{p}_\perp}{(2\pi)^2} \int_0^{+\infty} \frac{dp^3}{(2\pi)} \frac{1}{2\omega_{\vec{p}}} \left\{ \theta(x^0)(\gamma \cdot p_{\text{on}} + m) e^{-i p_{\text{on}} \cdot x} \right.$$

$$\left. + \theta(-x^0)(-\gamma \cdot p_{\text{on}} + m) e^{+i p_{\text{on}} \cdot x} \right\}$$

$$+ \delta(x^0) \int \frac{d^2\mathbf{p}_\perp}{(2\pi)^2} \int_0^{+\infty} \frac{dp^3}{(2\pi)} \frac{\gamma^0}{2\omega_{\vec{p}}} \left\{ e^{-i p_{\text{on}} \cdot x} - e^{+i p_{\text{on}} \cdot x} \right\}. \quad (11.52)$$

For the negative energy sector, from Eq.(11.36) we have

$$S_F^B(x) \underset{\delta \to 0}{\to} -i \int \frac{d^2\mathbf{p}_\perp}{(2\pi)^2} \int_0^{+\infty} \frac{dp^3}{(2\pi)} \frac{1}{2\omega_{\vec{p}}}$$

$$\times \left\{ \theta(x^0)(+\gamma^0 \omega_{\vec{p}} + \gamma^3 p^3 + \gamma^\perp \mathbf{p}^\perp + m) e^{+i(-\omega_{\vec{p}} x^0 - p^3 x^3 - \mathbf{p}^\perp \mathbf{x}^\perp)} \right.$$

$$\left. + \theta(-x^0)(-\gamma^0 \omega_{\vec{p}} - \gamma^3 p^3 - \gamma^\perp \mathbf{p}^\perp + m) e^{-i(-\omega_{\vec{p}} x^0 - p^3 x^3 - \mathbf{p}^\perp \mathbf{x}^\perp)} \right\}$$

$$+ \delta(x^0) \int \frac{d^2\mathbf{p}_\perp}{(2\pi)^2} \int_0^{+\infty} \frac{\gamma^0}{2\omega_{\vec{p}}} \left\{ e^{+i(-\omega_{\vec{p}} x^0 - p^3 x^3 - \mathbf{p}^\perp \mathbf{x}^\perp)} \right.$$

$$\left. - e^{-i(-\omega_{\vec{p}} x^0 - p^3 x^3 - \mathbf{p}^\perp \mathbf{x}^\perp)} \right\}, \quad (11.53)$$

After performing the change of variables $p^3 \to -p^3$ and $p_\perp \to -p_\perp$ we get

$$S_F^B(x) \underset{\delta \to 0}{\to} -i \int \frac{d^2\mathbf{p}_\perp}{(2\pi)^2} \int_{-\infty}^{0} \frac{dp^3}{(2\pi)} \frac{1}{2\omega_{\vec{p}}}$$

$$\times \left\{ \theta(x^0)(+\gamma^0 \omega_{\vec{p}} - \vec{\gamma} \cdot \vec{p} + m) e^{-i(\omega_{\vec{p}} x^0 - \vec{p} \cdot \vec{x})} \right.$$
$$\left. + \theta(-x^0)(-\gamma^0 \omega_{\vec{p}} + \vec{\gamma} \cdot \vec{p} + m) e^{+i(\omega_{\vec{p}} x^0 - \vec{p} \cdot \vec{x})} \right\}$$

$$+ \delta(x^0) \int \frac{d^2\mathbf{p}_\perp}{(2\pi)^2} \int_{-\infty}^{0} \frac{\gamma^0}{2\omega_{\vec{p}}} \left\{ e^{-i(\omega_{\vec{p}} x^0 - \vec{p} \cdot \vec{x})} \right.$$
$$\left. - e^{+i(\omega_{\vec{p}} x^0 - \vec{p} \cdot \vec{x})} \right\}. \quad (11.54)$$

Finally, we get for the *negative*-energy part in Eq.(11.36) in **IFD**

$$S_F^B(x) \underset{\delta \to 0}{\to} -i \int \frac{d^2\mathbf{p}_\perp}{(2\pi)^2} \int_{-\infty}^{0} \frac{dp^3}{(2\pi)} \frac{1}{2\omega_{\vec{p}}} \left\{ \theta(x^0)(\gamma \cdot p_{\text{on}} + m) e^{-ip_{\text{on}} \cdot x} \right.$$
$$\left. + \theta(-x^0)(-\gamma \cdot p_{\text{on}} + m) e^{+ip_{\text{on}} \cdot x} \right\}$$

$$+ \delta(x^0) \int \frac{d^2\mathbf{p}_\perp}{(2\pi)^2} \int_{-\infty}^{0} \frac{\gamma^0}{2\omega_{\vec{p}}} \left\{ e^{-ip_{\text{on}} \cdot x} - e^{+ip_{\text{on}} \cdot x} \right\} \quad (11.55)$$

We note that the integration in dp^3 runs from $0 \leq p^3 < \infty$ in Eq.(11.52) and from $-\infty < p^3 \leq 0$ in Eq.(11.55), so that these can be combined together to yield

$$\int \frac{d^2\mathbf{p}_\perp}{(2\pi)^2} \int_{-\infty}^{0} \frac{dp^3}{(2\pi)} + \int \frac{d^2\mathbf{p}_\perp}{(2\pi)^2} \int_{0}^{\infty} \frac{dp^3}{(2\pi)} = \int \frac{d^3\vec{p}}{(2\pi)^3}. \quad (11.56)$$

Thus, the fermion propagator $S_F(x) = S_F^A(x) + S_F^B(x)$ becomes in the **IFD** from Eqs.(11.52) and (11.55)

$$S_F(x) \underset{\delta \to 0}{\to} -i \int \frac{d^3\vec{p}}{(2\pi)^3} \frac{1}{2\omega_{\vec{p}}} \left\{ \theta(x^0)(\gamma \cdot p_{\text{on}} + m) e^{-ip_{\text{on}} \cdot x} \right.$$
$$\left. + \theta(-x^0)(-\gamma \cdot p_{\text{on}} + m) e^{+ip_{\text{on}} \cdot x} \right\}$$
$$+ \delta(x^0) \int \frac{d^3\vec{p}}{(2\pi)^3} \frac{\gamma^0}{2\omega_{\vec{p}}} \left\{ e^{-ip_{\text{on}} \cdot x} - e^{+ip_{\text{on}} \cdot x} \right\}. \quad (11.57)$$

Of course, the $\delta(x^0)$ term in $S_F(x)$ vanishes and the final result is

$$S_F(x) \underset{\delta \to 0}{\to} -i \int \frac{d^3\vec{p}}{(2\pi)^3} \frac{1}{2\omega_{\vec{p}}} \{\theta(x^0)(\gamma \cdot p_{\text{on}} + m)e^{-ip_{\text{on}} \cdot x}$$
$$+ \theta(-x^0)(-\gamma \cdot p_{\text{on}} + m)e^{+ip_{\text{on}} \cdot x}\}. \qquad (11.58)$$

This agrees with the result obtained directly before the splitting into parts A and B.

11.4 Conclusion

We have seen with this explicit calculations from the interpolating angle propagators the light-front form and instantaneous form limits by looking at how different parts of the positive- and negative-energy sectors behave in order to achieve the known results for each form. In particular, for the light-front form case ($\delta \to \pi/4; \mathbb{C} \to 0$), we see how the negative-energy part subtly and fortuitously vanishes away, leaving us only with the positive-sector contribution for the entire fermion propagator, with the conspicuous instantaneous term, the presence of which has been known for a long time. Another thing that we learned in this calculation is that the limit for the LFD cannot be taken straightaway in order to get the result, since we cross singularities in this process. We had to carefully analyze the limit by taking the leading terms close to such singularities.

Bibliography

[1] P. A. M. Dirac, Rev. Mod. Phys. **21**, 392 (1949).

[2] T. W. Chen, Phys. Rev. D **3**, 1989 (1971).

[3] E. Elizalde and J.Gomiz, Il Nuovo Cim. **35**, 367 (1976).

[4] Y. Frishman et al, Phys. Rev. D **15**, 2275 (1977).

[5] M. Sawicki, Phys. Rev. D **44**, 433 (1991).

[6] K. Hornbostel, Phys. Rev. D **45**, 3781 (1992).

[7] C. R. Ji and C. Mitchell, Phys. Rev. D **64**, 085013 (2001).

[8] N. N. Bogoliubov and D. V. Shirkov, *Introduction to the Theory of Quantized Fields*, 3rd edition (John Wiley & Sons, New York, 1980).

[9] J. B. Kogut and D. E. Soper, Phys. Rev. D **1**, 2901 (1970); D. E. Soper, Phys. Rev. D **4**, 1620 (1971); P.P. Srivastava and S. J. Brodsky, Phys. Rev. D **61**, 025013 (1999).

[10] C-R. Ji, Z. Li, B. Ma and A. T. Suzuki, Phys. Rev. D **98**, 036017 (2018).

12

Local versus global subtleties of projective representations

J. M. Hoff da Silva, J. E. Rodrigues

Abstract: In this short review, we pay attention to some subtleties in the study of projective representations, contrasting local to global properties and their interplay. The analysis is exposed rigorously, showing and demonstrating the main necessary theorems. We discuss the implementation of useful algebraic topology tools to characterize representations.

12.1 Introduction

In answering the honorific invitation to contribute with a manuscript to the book *Tribute to Ruben Aldrovandi*, it is our pleasure to start recalling one of his recommendations dating back to 2004 or so, when asked about the physical meaning of a particle. After a long and detailed explanation about the mathematical structure underlying the representation idea and (quite probably) guessing the first author's lack of necessary background, Professor Aldrovandi recommended a "judicious reading of Bargmann's paper" [1]. This short review presents some subtleties of projective representations whose roots can be traced back to this seminal work.

In another seminal work [2], E. P. Wigner provided a consistent approach to representing the Poincarè group in the Hilbert space without even assuming the continuity of the representation but instead demonstrating it. As a result, the very concept of a particle arises firmly supported by the robustness of Wigner's mathematical approach: a particle is an irreducible representation of the Poincaré group, connecting once and for all the spacetime symmetries to the particles it supports. In the process, it could not be less asked from the physical point of view: all the results are obtained from the requirement that quantum physics gives the same results here and there, today and tomorrow, provided the same conditions, i.e., it only requires symmetry for quantum processes. Bargmann's work systematizes some of Wigner's steps concerning group representations to provide general results whose particular cases encompass Lorentz and Poincarè group representations in the Hilbert space. In particular, these two cases follow more simply (although complex) than in the Wigner approach.

The advance of algebraic topology and the usage of some of its tools greatly simplify the process of studying whether a representation is genuine or projective. In this regard, Čech cohomology is particularly useful. When defined upon a continuous manifold, the standard formalism developed by Bargmann is straightforwardly handled with the aid of Čech cohomology elements. However, Bargmann's approach stops being helpful when this is not the case, however, and the group-associated manifold is not topologically trivial. However, elements of Čech cohomology are still helpful to study representations.

This manuscript is organized as follows: starting, in Section II, from the basic concepts underlining the mathematical theory of unitary representations of continuous groups, we move to the idea of local exponents and the demonstration of its differentiability in Section III. The definition of local groups and the conditions under which local results can be claimed valid globally are presented in Section IV. Section V delves into some useful tools from algebraic topology, whose generality and manageability allow interesting connections. In Section VI we conclude.

12.2 Basic background

States Ψ in Quantum Mechanics are equivalence classes, so-called rays, of vectors in a given Hilbert space. Each vector ψ itself is a representative of the class it belongs to, i.e., $\psi \in \Psi$, and each representative of a given ray differs from another representative by a unimodular complex phase. For two representatives $\psi \in \Psi$ and $\phi \in \Phi$, the transition probability of a state Ψ to Φ is given by $|(\psi, \phi)|^2$, and hence the inner product between rays is naturally given by $\Psi \cdot \Phi = |(\psi, \phi)|$. Two descriptions of a given quantum mechanical system are isomorphic if, and only if, there exists a one-to-one correspondence $\Psi \longleftrightarrow \Phi$ between rays preserving transition probabilities: $\Psi_1 \cdot \Psi_2 = \Phi_1 \cdot \Phi_2$. This isomorphism encompasses relevant physical situations as the description of the same quantum phenomena in two distinct inertial frames.

In analogy to vectorial rays, it is possible to define an operator ray, say $\mathcal{U}$, as the set of all operators τU, with $|\tau| = 1$, for a fixed operator U, also called a representative of $\mathcal{U}$. It is due to Wigner [3] a theorem stating that an isomorphic ray correspondence defines a unitary and linear (or anti-unitary and anti-linear) operator. For topological continuous groups G (the standard case for this tutorial review), operators representing group elements belonging to its identity component are necessarily unitary. Besides, the product of two operator rays $\mathcal{U}\mathcal{V}$ is defined as the ray composed by all the products UV with $U \in \mathcal{U}$ and $V \in \mathcal{V}$. Let $a \in G$ be a group element, $\mathcal{U}_a$ its isomorphic ray correspondence, and U_a a representative. From the usual group representation rule $\mathcal{U}_a \mathcal{U}_b = \mathcal{U}_{ab}$ one has $U_a U_b = \omega(a, b) U_{ab}$, with $|\omega(a, b)| = 1$. As it can be seen, selecting new representatives given by $U'_a = \phi(a) U_a$ and $U'_b = \phi(b) U_b$ ($|\phi(a)| = 1 = |\phi(b)|$) we have, from $U'_a U'_b = \omega'(a, b) U'_{ab}$ and using the linearity of the representation, $[\phi(a)\phi(b)\omega(a, b) - \phi(ab)\omega'(a, b)]U_{ab} = 0$ motivating the following definition:

Definition 1. *Two representation factors, $\omega(a, b)$ defined in a neighborhood Σ and $\omega'(a, b)$ defined in Σ' are said equivalent if, in $\Sigma_0 \subset \Sigma \cap \Sigma'$, they are related by*

$$\omega'(a, b) = \frac{\phi(a)\phi(b)}{\phi(a, b)} \omega(a, b). \tag{12.1}$$

For those systems whose group realization can be performed with $\omega = 1$, the representation is said to be genuine, otherwise it is called projective. The theory developed by Bargmann [1] answers quite judiciously whether a given (continuous) group representation is genuine or projective. In order to see the part of this theory relevant for this short review, we shall recall the definition of continuity of a given representation:

Definition 2. *A ray representation of a group G is continuous if the following condition is reached: for every element $a \in G$, every ray Ψ in the Hilbert space, and every $\epsilon \in \mathbb{R}_+^*$, there exists a neighborhood Σ of a in G such that the distance between $\mathcal{U}_a \Psi$ and $\mathcal{U}_b \Psi$ is less than ϵ if $b \in \Sigma$.*

This concept of continuity in this context is profound and brings several deep consequences in representation theory [4]. By now, it is enough to highlight two aspects related to this definition: firstly [1] it refers to the theoretical statement that probability transitions vary continuously with the group element. Secondly, as Wigner proved in 1939 [2], it allows for a special selection of representatives strongly continuous (in the sense of Definition 2), the so-called *admissible representatives*[1]. Let, then, $\{U_a\}$ be an admissible set of representatives of a continuous group G in a given neighborhood Σ of the identity $e \in G$, so that $U_e = 1$ and a, b, and ab are in Σ. Therefore U_{ab} is well defined and belongs to the same ray as $U_a U_b$. Hence $U_a U_b = \omega(a,b) U_{ab}$ and, obviously, $\omega(e,e) = 1$. Moreover, the associative law $(U_a U_b) U_c = U_a (U_b U_c)$ leads to

$$\omega(a,b)\omega(ab,c) = \omega(b,c)\omega(a,bc). \qquad (12.2)$$

It can be shown that the continuity of admissible representatives implies the continuity of $\omega(a,b)$ factors [1, 5]. Now we shall state a few important definitions.

Definition 3. *Every complex and continuous function $\omega(a,b)$ ($|\omega(a,b)| = 1|$) defined for the a, b elements of some neighborhood Σ is a local factor of G defined in Σ if $\omega(e,e) = 1$ and Eq. (19.55) is valid whenever ab and bc belong to Σ.*

Definition 4. *If Σ coincides with G, such that (19.55) is valid in all group, ω is then called factor of G.*

When treating a given projective representation, the reader is probably more familiar with exponential terms. In the next section, we shall delve into this more familiar and easily handled notation (and its consequences).

12.3 Local exponents and differentiability

As mentioned, it is often beneficial[2] to write $\omega(a,b) = e^{i\xi(a,b)}$, $\xi \in \mathbb{R}$, so that the previous definitions can be restated as

Definition 5. *A local exponent of a group G defined in a neighborhood Σ is a real and continuous function $\xi(a,b)$ defined for every a, b of Σ satisfying*

- $\xi(e,e) = 0$, so that $\omega(e,e) = 1$;

- $\xi(a,b) + \xi(ab,c) = \xi(b,c) + \xi(a,bc)$, $ab, bc \in \Sigma$, so that Eq. (19.55) is valid.

---

[1] The theorem stating this possibility was revisited by Bargmann [1]. See also [5] for a broad discussion about this proof.

[2] See a remark on such identification at the beginning of the theorem's (2) proof.

Finally, if Σ coincides with G, ξ is called an exponent of G.

In general, the phases of a projective representation are independent of the physical state upon which it acts [6]. Nevertheless, the proof for this statement needs it is always possible to prepare a physical state represented as the sum of two linearly independent states. This requirement cannot always be accomplished, and, for those systems, the phases can also depend on dynamical labels. We shall keep our notation without referencing this generality by now, but one should bear in mind this additional generality. Now, from Eq. (19.56), taking $\omega = e^{i\xi}$ and $\phi(a) = e^{ix(a)}$, we have

$$\xi'(a,b) = \xi(a,b) + \Delta_{a,b}[x], \tag{12.3}$$

where

$$\Delta_{a,b}[x] := x(a) + x(b) - x(ab). \tag{12.4}$$

If $x(a=e) = 0$ it is fairly simple to see that $\xi'(e,e) = 0$. Besides, from Eq. (12.3),

$$\xi'(a,b) + \xi'(ab,c) = \xi(a,b) + \Delta_{a,b}[x] + \xi(ab,c) + \Delta_{ab,c}[x], \tag{12.5}$$

which, with the aid of the second item of Def. (5), reads

$$\xi'(a,b) + \xi'(ab,c) = \xi(b,c) + \xi(a,bc) + \Delta_{a,b}[x] + \Delta_{ab,c}[x]. \tag{12.6}$$

Finally, noticing that

$$\xi(k,l) = \xi'(k,l) - \Delta_{k,l}[x]$$

and

$$\Delta_{a,b}[x] + \Delta_{ab,c}[x] - \Delta_{b,c}[x] - \Delta_{a,bc}[x] = 0,$$

we arrive at

$$\xi'(a,b) + \xi'(ab,c) = \xi'(b,c) + \xi'(a,bc),$$

that is, all the conditions present in Def. (5) are filled and the following statement can be written: if ξ is a local exponent defined in Σ and $x(a)$ a continuous real function in Σ^2 (a neighborhood consisting of products ab) such that $x(e) = 0$, then ξ' defined by (12.3) is also a local exponent in Σ. All that motivates the following definition:

Definition 6. *Two local exponents ξ and ξ' defined in Σ and Σ', respectively, are equivalent if Eqs. (12.3) and (12.4) are valid in some neighborhood $\Sigma_0 \subset (\Sigma \cap \Sigma')$, where $x(a)$ is a continuous real function defined in Σ^2.*

We observe that the equivalence $\xi \equiv \xi'$ produced by Eq. (12.3) is a formal equivalence relation, i.e., symmetric, reflexive, and transitive.

We shall now pay some attention to an important aspect of this construction, the differentiability of local exponents for continuous groups. Differentiable means a term with continuous partial derivatives of all orders concerning the group elements or coordinates. The proof presented in [1] is an adaptation of a method for approaching some more or less known (at that time) results about Lie groups shown in Ref. [7]. Let us revisit it in detail.

Theorem 1. *In a Lie group every local exponent is equivalent to a differentiable local exponent.*

Proof. As it is well known [8], every Lie group G supports a Haar invariant measure. Let da and $d'a$ denote the left and right invariant measures in G, respectively. Now define two real functions, g and g', diffentiable in Σ, and null everywhere outside $\Sigma' \subset \Sigma$. Besides, the functional form of these functions must respect[3]

$$\int_G g(a)da = 1 = \int_G g'(a)d'a. \tag{12.7}$$

Note that the integrals are trivial in G, being non-null (and equal to 1) only in Σ'.

Define two equivalence relations by

$$\xi'(a,b) = \xi(a,b) + \Delta_{a,b}[x],$$
$$x(a) = -\int_G \xi(a,k)g(k)dk, \tag{12.8}$$

where $a, b \in \Sigma_1$, and

$$\xi''(a,b) = \xi'(a,b) + \Delta_{a,b}[x'],$$
$$x'(a) = -\int_G \xi'(l,a)g'(l)d'l, \tag{12.9}$$

where $a, b \in \Sigma_2 \subset \Sigma_1$. Now take $\Sigma' \subset \Sigma_2$ and consider Eqs. (12.8) starting with $\xi'(a,b) = \xi(a,b) \cdot 1 + \Delta_{a,b}[x]$ writing (in Σ') $1 = \int_G g(k)dk$. Using Eq. (12.4) we have

$$\xi'(a,b) = \int_G \{\xi(a,b) - \xi(a,k) - \xi(b,k) + \xi(ab,k)\}g(k)dk, \tag{12.10}$$

and from the very definition (5), which reproduces Eq. (19.55), we are left with

$$\xi'(a,b) = \int_G \{\xi(a,bk) - \xi(a,k)\}g(k)dk. \tag{12.11}$$

In the first integral, the relabel $k \mapsto b^{-1}k$ produces

$$\int_G \xi(a,bk)g(k)dk \longrightarrow \int_G \xi(a,k)g(b^{-1}k)dk,$$

---

[3]At first sight, this set of requirements may appear too restrictive. That is not the case, however. It is possible to envisage a plethora of functions filling all requirements.

since dk is a Haar measure. Back to Eq. (12.11) we arrive at

$$\xi'(a,b) = \int_G \xi(a,k)\{g(b^{-1}k) - g(k)\}dk. \tag{12.12}$$

The above steps may be followed for Eqs. (12.9) in a similar fashion, resulting in

$$\xi''(a,b) = \int_G \xi'(l,b)\{g'(la^{-1}) - g'(l)\}d'l. \tag{12.13}$$

Finally, inserting Eq. (12.12) into (12.13) leads to

$$\xi''(a,b) = \int_G \int_G \xi(l,k)\{g(b^{-1}k) - g(k)\}\{g'(la^{-1}) - g'(l)\}dkd'l \tag{12.14}$$

and since $\xi''(a,b)$ depends on a and b only via g and g', differentiability of ξ'' is inherited from these two functions. Lastly, since $\xi \simeq \xi''$ the theorem is proved. $\square$

A similar procedure establishes differentiability for x functions, as seen in the sequel.

Lemma 1. *If two differentiable exponents of a Lie group are equivalents, then $\xi' = \xi + \Delta[x]$ in a suitably chosen neighborhood with x differentiable.*

Proof. Since ξ' and ξ are differentiable in a neighborhood, so it is $\Delta[x]$ and η defined by $\eta(a) = \int_G \Delta_{a,k}[x]g(k)dk$, with g defined as in the theorem (1). Now define $\bar{x}(a) = x(a) - \eta(a)$, i.e.

$$\bar{x} = x(a) \cdot 1 - \int_G \{x(a) + x(k) - x(ak)\}g(k)dk. \tag{12.15}$$

Expressing $1 = \int_G g(k)dk$ the expression above reduces to $\bar{x} = \int_G \{x(k) - x(ak)\}g(k)dk$. Now, taking $k \mapsto a^{-1}k$ in the second integral, we are left with

$$\bar{x}(a) = \int_G x(k)\{g(k) - g(a^{-1}k)\}dk, \tag{12.16}$$

showing the dependence of $\bar{x}$ on a through g and evincing the differentiability of $\bar{x}$ and, as a consequence, of x. $\square$

We end this section calling attention to the fact that differentiability implies continuity, a fact to be appreciated in Theorem (3).

12.4 Considerations about the local group and extensions

It is possible to explore further the ray characteristic of a given admissible set of representatives. Operators belonging to $\mathcal{U}_a$ are of the form $e^{i\theta}U_a$, with $\theta \in \mathbb{R}$. Therefore, the representation reads

$$(e^{i\theta}U_a)(e^{i\theta'}U_b) = e^{i(\theta+\theta')}\omega(a,b)U_{ab} = e^{i(\theta+\theta'+\xi(a,b))}U_{ab}, \qquad (12.17)$$

suggesting the following definition:

Definition 7. *Let ξ be a local exponent of G defined in Σ. The local group H is composed by pairs $\{\theta, a\}$, $\theta \in \mathbb{R}$ and $a \in \Sigma^2$, with composition rule given by*

$$\{\theta_1, a\}\{\theta_2, b\} = \{\theta_1 + \theta_2 + \xi(a,b), ab\}. \qquad (12.18)$$

The topological space associated with H is the product $\mathbb{R} \times \Sigma^2$, and its group properties are straightforwardly verified from the definition right above and Def. (5). In particular, the identity element $\bar{e}$ of H is $\bar{e} = \{0, e\}$, while the inverse reads $\{\theta, a\}^{-1} = \{-(\theta + \xi(r, r^{-1}), r^{-1})\}$. There is also a one-parameter subgroup, say C, belonging to the center of G, characterized by elements of the form $\{\theta, e\}$. It can be seen ([1], and [5] for a comprehensive discussion) that $H/C \simeq G$. Take two local exponents, ξ and ξ', defined in Σ. The mapping

$$\varphi: H \to H'$$
$$\{\alpha, a\} \mapsto \varphi(\{\alpha, a\}) = \{\alpha - x(a), a' = a\}, \qquad (12.19)$$

where $x(a)$ is the real function appearing in the equivalence relation (12.4), establish the isomorphism $H \simeq H'$ locally.

In general, given a set of admissible representatives defined in a neighborhood Σ of G, extending it for a set defined everywhere in G is impossible. This observation is crucial: it happens more often than never for the phase of the projective representation to be equivalent to zero locally. However, this is different globally. Topological obstructions in the group manifold may forbid local results to be valid everywhere. We shall now revisit some important theorems to give a flavor of this point.

Theorem 2. *Let G be a connected and simply connected group, ω a group factor, and $\mathcal{U}_a$ a continuous ray representation such that the local factor defined by an adequately chosen set of admissible representatives $\{U_a\}$ coincides with ω em some neighborhood Σ. Then exists an admissible set of representatives $\{U'_a\}$ uniquely determined for the whole group such that $U'_a U'_b = \omega(a,b) U'_{ab}$ and $U_a = U'_a$ in some neighborhood $\Sigma' \subset \Sigma$.*

Proof. Being G connected and simply connected, there is a unique continuous $\xi(a,b)$ function, solution of $e^{i\xi(a,b)} = \omega(a,b) \ \forall a, b \in G$. This is an exponent of

G and implies that H is also a connected and simply connected group. Let $V_{(\theta,a)} = e^{i\theta} U_a$ be the representation of an element $\{\theta, a\} \in H$. The composition law in H is ordinary (not projective), and hence, there exists a strongly continuous (unitary) representation $W(\theta, a)$ of H, which coincides with $V_{(\theta,a)}$ in some neighborhood. Here is the reason: following [9], every element, say a, of a connected group may be written as the product $a = a_1 a_2 \cdots a_n$ of n (finite) elements of a neighborhood. Therefore, $V_a = \Pi_i V_i$, $i = 1, \cdots, n$. Besides, for a simply connected group it is always possible to have $V_{a_1} \cdots V_{a_n} = V_{a'_1} \cdots V_{a'_m}$ if $a_1 \cdots a_n = a'_1 \cdots a'_m$ [9]. Therefore, as the product $V_{a_1} \cdots V_{a_n}$ depends on the element a (and not on the partition itself), from defining $W_a = V_{a_1} \cdots V_{a_n}$ for $a \in \Sigma'$ the group composition property follows straightforwardly (the uniqueness also follows from $a_1 \cdots a_n = a'_1 \cdots a'_m$ and continuity of W's is inherited from V's). Returning to our notation, there is, then, a unitary, continuous representation $W_{(\theta,a)}$ of H coinciding with $V_{(\theta,a)}$ in Σ'.

Now, let $\Sigma' \subset \mathbb{R} \times \Sigma^2$ be such that $|\theta| < k$ in Σ', for a suitable[4] $k \in \mathbb{R}$. For every θ there exists $\beta = \theta/n$, $n \in \mathbb{N}^*$, such that $\{\theta, e\} = \{\beta, e\}^n$, or, in terms of our previous analysis, $W_{(\theta,e)} = (V_{(\beta,e)})^n = e^{i\theta} 1$. Take $U'_a = W_{(0,e)}$ $\forall a$. By means of Eq. (12.18), $\{\theta, a\} = \{\theta, e\}\{0, a\}$, that is $W_{(\theta,a)} = W_{(\theta,e)} W_{(0,a)} = e^{i\theta} U'_a$ and, as a consequence, $U_a = U'_a$ in Σ'. Finally, again with the aid of (12.18) $\{0, a\}\{0, b\} = \{\xi(a,b), ab\}$, i.e., $U'_a U'_b = e^{i\xi(a,b)} U'_{ab} = \omega(a,b) U'_{ab}$. □

Since we are interested in investigating the global validity of local properties, it is only natural to define the next concept.

Definition 8. *An exponent ξ_1 of G is called an extension of ξ if they are equal in some neighborhood.*

The following result asserts that the extensions of local equivalent exponents are also equivalent.

Theorem 3. *Let ξ and ξ' be two equivalent local exponents of a connected and simply connected group G, such that $\xi' = \xi + \Delta[x]$ in some neighborhood, and assume that the exponents ξ_1 and ξ'_1 of G are extensions of ξ and ξ', respectively. Then, $\xi'_1(a,b) = \xi_1(a,b) + \Delta_{a,b}[x_1]$ for every $a, b \in G$, where $x_1(a)$ is continuous in a and $x_1 = x$ in some neighborhood Σ'.*

Proof. It is clear that both exponents ξ'_1 and ξ_1 define two connected and simply connected local groups H'_1 and H_1, respectively, for which the composition rule is given by (12.18). As mentioned, the mapping $\varphi : H_1 \to H'_1$ given by (12.19) establishes a local isomorphism. In the Ref. [9], there is an important result: the mapping φ may be uniquely extended to an isomorphism φ^* of H_1 and H'_1 as a

---

[4] It is possible to refine the neighborhood concept for this proof. However, this approach is enough for our general purposes.

whole (and not only locally) if H_1 is locally connected and simply connected[5], with $\varphi^* = \varphi$ in $\Sigma' \subset \Sigma$.

Of course $\varphi^*(\theta, e) = \{\theta, e\} \, \forall \theta$. Now take $\varphi^*(0, a) = \{-x_1(a), g(a)\}$ where $g(a)$ is to be found. From $\{\theta, a\} = \{\theta, e\}\{0, a\}$, we have $\varphi^*(\theta, a) = \{\theta - x_1(a) + \xi_1'(e, a), g(a)\}$. However, from the general rule $U_a U_b = e^{i\xi(a,b)} U_{ab}$ it is straightforward to see that if, for instance, $a = e$ then $1 U_b = e^{i\xi_1'(e,b)} U_{eb=b}$, forcing the conclusion that[6] $\xi_1'(e, b) = 0$. Therefore $\varphi^*(\theta, a) = \{\theta - x_1(a), g(a)\}$. We can now particularize the neighborhood to Σ' to fix $g(a) = a$ and, then, extend it to all element a. This leads to

$$\varphi^*(0, a)\varphi^*(0, b) = \{-x_1(a), a\}\{-x_1(b), b\} = \{-x_1(a) - x_1(b) + \xi_1'(a, b), ab\},$$

and, on the other hand, $\varphi^*(0, ab) = \{-x_1(ab), ab\}$, from which[7] we arrive at $\xi_1'(a, b) = \xi_1(a, b) + x_1(a) + x_1(b) - x_1(a, b)$ or, for short, $\xi_1'(a, b) = \xi_1(a, b) + \Delta_{a,b}(x_1)$ on the group as a whole. Finally, being x_1 continuous, $x_1 = x$ in Σ' so as to Eq. (12.19) dictates. □

These two theorems are somewhat enough to appreciate the relevance of group topology in the decision between a genuine or projective representation. More often than never, it is possible to show the equivalence between a local exponent to zero in a given neighborhood. Nevertheless, the maintenance of a vanishing local exponent for the whole group requires the group to be connected and simply connected. One must look at the covering group when this is not the case. There is an isomorphism between a given group G and $\tilde{G}/K$, where $\tilde{G}$ is the covering group of G and K is a discrete central invariant subgroup of $\tilde{G}$. If, and only if, G is simply connected, this isomorphism reduces to $G \simeq \tilde{G}$. When G is not simply connected, there is a record, so to speak, of projective representation encoded in K. That is indeed the case, for instance, for the Lorentz and Poincarè groups in more than two dimensions which are doubly (not simply) connected and representations up to a sign are in order.

As can be seen, the standard approach to the study of projective representations involves group theory, topology, and analysis. While precise and robust, it is certainly demanding. In the next section, we shall glance at some help from algebraic topology.

---

[5] Intuitively, for a connected and simply connected group, the local isomorphism may be settled everywhere around the identity element, without any distinction. This is certainly not the case if topological obstructions are in order in the group manifold.

[6] Just as all local exponent: $\xi_1'(e, b) = 0 = \xi_1'(a, e) = \xi_1'(e, e)$.

[7] Along with the fact that $\varphi^*(0, a)\varphi^*(0, b) = e^{i\xi_1(a,b)} \varphi^*(0, ab)$.

12.5 A glance at characterizations coming from algebraic topology

We start introducing the concept of a n–cochain following the exposition of Ref. [10]:

Definition 9. *Let G be a group and M an abelian group, a $(n+1)$–dimensional cochain is a function $\xi(g_0, \cdots, g_n)$ defined on $G \times G \times \cdots \times G$ with values in M.*

The set of all $(n+1)$–cochains forms a group $C^{n+1}(G, M)$ and it is possible to define an operator δ increasing the degree of a given cochain by [11]

$$\delta : C^{n+1}(G, M) \to C^{n+2}(G, M) \qquad (12.20)$$

$$\delta\xi(g_0, \cdots, g_{n+1}) = \sum_{i=0}^{n+1} (-1)^i \xi(g_0, \cdots, \hat{g}_i, g_i g_{i+1}, \cdots, g_{n+1}), \qquad (12.21)$$

where $\hat{g}_i$ stands for suppression of the corresponding (under hat) element. There is still an element of indeterminacy in the expression for $\delta\xi$ concerning the suppression of the last argument factor, but the examples we shall depict will resolve this specific point. The standard nomenclature calls a cochain ξ' by a coboundary of the cochain ξ if $\xi' = \delta\xi$. If $\delta\xi' = 0$, ξ' is called a cocycle. The δ operator satisfies the fundamental property $\delta \circ \delta = 0$. To verify this property, we shall first see how to operate in simple cases for clarity. For degrees 0, 1, and 2 we have, respectively

$$\begin{aligned}
\delta\xi(a, b) &= \xi(ab) - \xi(a), \\
\delta\xi(a, b, c) &= \xi(ab, c) - \xi(a, bc) + \xi(a, b), \\
\delta\xi(a, b, c, d) &= \xi(ab, c, d) - \xi(a, bc, d) + \xi(a, b, cd) - \xi(a, b, c).
\end{aligned} \qquad (12.22)$$

Now it is straightforward to see that $\delta(\delta\xi(a, b, c)) = \delta\xi(ab, c) - \delta\xi(a, bc) + \delta\xi(a, b)$, amounts out to

$$\delta(\delta\xi(a, b, c)) = \xi(abc) - \xi(ab) - \xi(abc) + \xi(a) + \xi(ab) - \xi(a) \qquad (12.23)$$

and, therefore, $\delta(\delta\xi(a, b, c)) = 0$. Note that the first term of (12.23) has been canceled by the first term arising from the application of δ in $\xi(a, bc)$, and the other terms follow the very same rule. Bearing in mind this simple prescription, it is possible to see that

$$\begin{aligned}
\delta\xi(g_0, \cdots, g_{n+1}) = {}&\xi(\hat{g}_0, g_0 g_1, \cdots, g_{n+1}) - \xi(g_0, \hat{g}_1, g_1 g_2, \cdots, g_{n+1}) \\
&+ \cdots + (-1)^{n+1} \xi(g_0, g_1, \cdots, g_n, \hat{g}_{n+1}),
\end{aligned} \qquad (12.24)$$

leading to

$$\begin{aligned}
\delta(\delta\xi(g_0, \cdots, g_{n+1})) = {}&\delta\xi(\hat{g}_0, g_0 g_1, \cdots, g_{n+1}) - \delta\xi(g_0, \hat{g}_1, g_1 g_2, \cdots, g_{n+1}) \\
&+ \cdots + (-1)^{n+1} \delta\xi(g_0, g_1, \cdots, g_n, \hat{g}_{n+1}) = 0.
\end{aligned} \qquad (12.25)$$

The set of all n–dimensional cocycles and the set of all coboundaries of $(n+1)$–dimensional cochains form each one a group, $Z^n(G,M)$ and $B^n(G,M)$, respectively [12]. This fact motivates the following definition.

Definition 10. *The n–th Čech cohomology group, $\check{H}^n(G,M)$, is defined by*

$$\check{H}^n(G,M) = Z^n(G,M)/B^n(G,M).$$

As it is well known, Čech cohomology groups are closely related to the De Rham cohomology groups. This relation gains the status of an isomorphism when the base group manifold is a differential manifold [13], leading to an interesting parallel. In the De Rham cohomology, dealing with exact and closed forms, Poincarè lemma states that every closed form is also exact in a star-shaped domain (i.e., locally). Nontrivial topology engenders global obstructions to this result. Therefore, due to the alluded isomorphism between both cohomologies, this is also the case for Čech cohomology. This fact and the results previously revised in this manuscript help us understand the usefulness of cohomology groups regarding local versus global properties of phase representations. There is, however, an additional bonus: as we have seen, if the group to be represented is not continuous, the theory presented by Bargmann is of little help. However, cochains may still be defined. We shall return to the main line of this manuscript, making explicit the connection between the elements just described and Bargmann's approach.

Consider a ray operatorial representation $U_a U_b = e^{i\xi(a,b)} U_{ab}$. Associativity $(U_a U_b) U_c = U_a (U_b U_c)$ implies

$$\xi(a,b) + \xi(ab,c) = \xi(b,c) + \xi(a,bc), \tag{12.26}$$

just as Definition (5) stays. From Eqs. (12.22), however, we already know that $\delta\xi(a,b,c) = \xi(ab,c) - \xi(a,bc) + \xi(a,b)$ and, therefore, one is forced to conclude that $\xi(b,c) = \delta\xi(a,b,c)$, or generically

$$\xi(a,b) = \delta\xi(c,a,b). \tag{12.27}$$

Thus, the associativity of operators in a possibly projective representation induces a phase factor, which is nothing but a coboundary of a 1–cochain. It shows that we can remove the phase and arrive at a genuine representation if, and only if, $\xi(c,a,b)$ is a coboundary. If this is not the case, i.e., $\xi(a,b)$ is a coboundary which is not a cocycle, then $\check{H}^2(G,M)$ is nontrivial. There is, then, a topological obstruction to the phase elimination, resulting in a projective representation.

We shall finalize pointing out that the survival of a phase in the representation scheme may be accompanied by physical significance. Schwinger showed [14] that the (Weyl) operators realizing Heisenberg algebra do form a complete basis for all unitary operators, describing symmetric operations in the sense of Wigner [2], evincing quantum kinematics, and giving a complete set of physical degrees of freedom in Quantum Mechanics. The Schwinger operators span a $Z_N \times Z_N$ (where Z_N is the cyclic group) discrete representation of Weyl's realization. In Ref. [11], it was shown that in the realm of Schwinger's representation, a fundamental cocycle exists responsible for 1) making the representation globally projective and 2) assigning a pre-symplectic structure in the space state. Within this scope, classical symplectic structure would result from a continuum limit of quantum pre-symplectic structure.

12.6 Concluding remarks

It is possible to assert that the study of group representations in the Hilbert space performs the core of the physical labeling of particles degrees of freedom and furnishes the foundations of investigating quantum kinematics and dynamics. More than a solid mathematical setup to decide whether a representation is genuine, it allows the appreciation of some profound physical results. Apart from the classical and quantum interplay mentioned in the last section, we want to remark on the possibility of frame gauge freedom in Quantum Field Theory as a natural consequence of a (generalized) projective representation Ref. [15]. The analysis performed in Ref. [15] may also be applied to nonrelativistic theories where projective representation depends on time. We shall delve into this generalization to the pre-symplectic structure in Ref. [11] in the near future.

Acknowledgements

JMHS thanks National Council for Scientific and Technological Development (CNPq) for partial financial support (grant No. 307641/2022-8).

Bibliography

[1] V. Bargmann, *On Unitary Ray Representations of Continuous Groups*, Ann. Math. **59**, 1 (1954).

[2] E. P. Wigner, *On Unitary Representations of the Inhomogeneous Lorentz Group*, Ann. Math. **40**, 184 (1939).

[3] E. P. Wigner, *Group theory and its application to the Quantum Mechanics of atomic spectra* (Academic Press, London, 1959).

[4] K-H. Neeb, *Positive energy representations and continuity of projective representations for general topological groups*, Glasgow Math. J. **56**, 295 (2014);

B. Janssens and K-H. Neeb, *Projective unitary representations of infinite dimensional Lie groups*, Kyoto J. Math. **59**, 293 (2019).

[5] J. M. Hoff da Silva and G. M. Caires da Rocha, *Strongly Continuous Representations in the Hilbert Space: A Far-Reaching Concept*, Universe **7**, 285 (2021).

[6] S. Weinberg, *The Quantum Theory of Fields*, Vol. I (Cambridge University Press, New York, 1995).

[7] K. Iwasawa, *On Some Types of Topological Groups*, Ann. Math. **50**, 507 (1949).

[8] R. Raczka and A.O. Barut, *Theory Of Group Representations and Applications* (World Scientific, Singapore, 1986).

[9] L. Pontrjagin, *Topological Groups* (Princeton University Press, Princeton 1939).

[10] A. A. Kirillov, *Elements of the Theory of Representations* (Springer, Berlin, 1976).

[11] R. Aldrovandi and D. Galetti, *On the Structure of Quantum Phase Space*, J. Math. Phys. **31**, 2987 (1990).

[12] M. Nakahara, *Geometry, Topology and Physics*, 2nd ed. (CRC Press, London, 2003).

[13] J. Schwartz, *De Rham's Theorem for Arbitrary Spaces*, Am. J. Math. **77**, 29 (1955).

[14] J. Schwinger, *Unitary Operator Bases*, Proc. Nat. Acad. Scien. **46**, 570 (1960).

[15] J. Wawrzycki, *A generalization of Bargmann's Theory of Ray Representation*, Comm. Math. Phys. **250**, 215 (2004).

13

Teleparallelism, gauge theory and anholonomy: Utiyama's approach.

P. J. Pompeia

Abstract: In the present work, Utiyama's formalism for gauge theory is applied to the translation group. The minimal coupling prescription, composed by two instructions, defines the covariant derivative and establishes that the gauge field is the anholonomic part of the tetrad. The field strength that determines the dynamics of the gauge field can be interpreted as the torsion, showing that the resulting theory describes the gravitational interaction in the context of teleparallel theories.

13.1 Introduction

The invitation to participate in this tribute to Prof. Ruben Aldrovandi is a big honor for me, since I had the opportunity to learn a lot from him. My interaction with Prof. Aldrovandi primarily occurred during my graduate studies at Instituto de Física Teórica – IFT (Institute of Theoretical Physics). When I was finishing my undergraduate course in Physics, I started looking for a place (and an advisor) to do my Master's. I had just attended an introductory course in General Relativity (GR) and I was amazed by the way geometry and Physics were connected in this theory. At the time, although I could follow and reproduce some calculations presented in GR books, the truth is that I did not understand what the calculations actually meant. This intrigued me even more and I decided to pursue the subject in my Master's.

After visiting some institutions, I was accepted at IFT to be advised by Prof. Bruto Pimentel. The subject of my dissertation would be the analysis of the constraints of the Teleparallel Equivalent of General Relativity (TEGR)[1, 2, 3, 4] via Hamilton-Jacobi formalism. Prof. Pimentel suggested that I should take courses on gravitation with Prof. Ruben Aldrovandi and Prof. José Geraldo Pereira and so I did: I attended three courses with them, "Introduction to General Relativity", "Introduction to Cosmology" and "Gravitation Theory: Fields and Tetrads". Each course had its own lecture notes provided by the professors, which I still use nowadays. After the first course, GR started making sense to me – I finally could understand the roles of the metric tensor and the connection, their relation to covariant derivative and curvature and, especially, how the content of matter/energy was associated to curvature via Einstein equations.

The last of the three courses mentioned previously and the studies related to my dissertation opened my mind to new ways of interpreting the gravitational interaction. In TEGR, a topic of research of Profs. Aldrovandi and Pereira at the time, gravitation could also be described in terms of torsion instead of curvature. Besides, it presented an important feature: TEGR could be interpreted as a gauge theory in great similarity with electromagnetism. This was absolutely fascinating for me at that time.

When it seemed like I was finally having a good understanding of how gravity worked, a new perspective emerged. In a talk at IFT, Prof. Aldrovandi spent an hour explaining how gravitation could be seen as anholonomy [5]. Once again, I was not able to comprehend what that meant. At first, it seemed that all that I needed to understand gravity was to learn Riemannian geometry and how curvature and energy were connected; suddenly, curvature could be "replaced" by torsion; now, gravity was anholonomy. At this point, I realized that there was much more yet to be learned and that it would take me a long time to have a broad view of how gravity could be described.

Some time after this talk, I started my PhD, once again under supervision of Prof. Pimentel at IFT. During my PhD, I had the opportunity to learn more about gauge theory, particularly, in the context of Utiyama's approach [6]. In this work, by its turn, Utiyama derives a gravitation theory for the group of Lorentz transformation, showing that GR could be seen as a particular case of his proposal. It was nice to finally understand how some things that were disconnected to me could be stuck together.

Utiyama's formalism for gauge theory is quite appealing, since the structures that usually emerge in gauge theories (covariant derivative, field strength, and so on) can be derived as solutions of a set of equations that follow from the symmetry requirements. This property of Utiyama's approach could be immediately generalized to theories involving Lagrangians depending on second-order of derivatives of the gauge fields [7]. This was pursued by me and three colleagues (also PhD students at IFT[1]), and we ended up making an application to the Lorentz group, obtaining the gauge strucuture of higher-order gravity theory in Riemann manifolds [8]. This work was important to me at the time because it was selected by Prof. Aldrovandi as the theme to be presented in my PhD qualifying exam. Having Prof. Aldrovandi in my qualifying board was a singular situation – on one hand, I was tense because he knew so much about the subject that he could easily make severe criticisms to the work and make questions that I would not be able to answer; on the other hand, precisely for the same reasons, it was a great opportunity for me to see what I still could pursue and learn about the subject. It turned out that the exam was really "smooth" and Prof. Aldrovandi was quite kind and seemed to be satisfied with the results.

After I obtained my PhD, I still had the sensation that something was still missing for me concerning teleparallel theories, gauge symmetry and anholonomy. This gap was finally fulfilled with a group of PhD students at Instituto Tecnológico de Aeronáutica – ITA (Aeronautics Institute of Technology)[2]. We resorted to Utiyama's gauge formalism and considered its application to the translation group in the context of higher order teleparallel theories [9]. Part of the results obtained with these students compose the main part of this work.

An interesting feature of the gauge approach to symmetries associated to spacetime coordinate transformation is that it provides a new perspective for the geometric interpretation of the interaction. Usually, when one studies the gravitational interaction (GR-like, TEGR-like theories, and so on), one chooses a specific spacetime (Riemann, Riemann-Cartan, Weitzenböck, etc.) with a metric, a connection, some additional conditions (metricity condition and/or null torsion and/or null curvature, ...) and uses the geometric entities (metric, tetrad, connection,...) as the elementary fields in the context of a field theory. In the gauge

---

[1] Cássius de Melo, Léo Medeiros e Rodrigo Cuzinatto – the last two were advised by Prof. Aldrovandi.
[2] Elisa Assencio, Reinaldo Caraça and Silas Vilhena.

approach, the starting point is a field theory and the structures that emerge from the symmetry requirements can be interpreted from a geometric point of view.

The aim of this manuscript is to discuss how teleparallelism, gauge theory and anholonomy are naturally connected in the context of the Utiyama's formalism for the translation group. In the next section, a brief summary of Utiyama's approach to gauge theory is presented. Afterwards, the application of this formalism to the translation group is performed. Next, the geometric interpretation of the interaction is discussed, followed by the final remarks.

13.2 Utiyama's approach to gauge theory

The starting point of Utiyama's approach [6] is to consider a physical system described by a set of fields Q^A ($A = 1, 2, \cdots, N$) and an action integral

$$S = \int_\Omega d^4 u \, L\left(Q^A, \partial_\mu Q^A\right)$$

that is invariant under a set of global transformations of the fields. Utiyama considers an infinitesimal transformation described by the bilinear combination

$$\delta Q^A = \epsilon^a I_{(a)\,B}^{\,A} Q^B, \qquad (13.1)$$

where $I_{(a)\,B}^{\,A}$ are the generators of the transformation and ϵ^a ($a = 1, 2, \ldots, n$) are constant parameters. These transformations compose a Lie group, G, meaning that the structure constants $f_{a\,b}^{\ \ c}$, defined by the commutator of the generators,

$$\left[I_{(a)}, I_{(b)}\right]_B^A = f_{a\,b}^{\ \ c} I_{(c)\,B}^{\,A},$$

satisfy the Jacobi identity:

$$f_{a\,b}^{\ \ m} f_{m\,c}^{\ \ l} + f_{c\,a}^{\ \ m} f_{m\,b}^{\ \ l} + f_{b\,c}^{\ \ m} f_{m\,a}^{\ \ l} = 0.$$

The symmetry requirement is manifest by the invariance of the action integral:

$$\delta S = 0. \qquad (13.2)$$

Utiyama then replaces the global transformation group G by a wider group G', where the parameters ϵ^a are replaced by a set of arbitrary functions: $\epsilon^a \to \epsilon^a(u)$. With this new transformation, the invariance is lost. However, the symmetry can be recovered if a new field $A(u)$ is introduced. Then Utiyama aims to answer the following five questions:

"(1) What kind of field, A, is introduced on account of the invariance?

(2) How is this new field A transformed under G'?

(3) What form does the interaction between the field A and the original field Q take?

(4) How can we determine the new Lagrangian $L'(Q,A)$ from the original one $L(Q)$?

(5) What type of field equations for A are allowable?"

When considering the global group G and the linear independence of the parameters ϵ^a, Utiyama concludes that the invariance condition implies:

$$\frac{\partial L}{\partial Q^A} I^A_{(a)\,B} Q^B + \frac{\partial L}{\partial (\partial_\mu Q^A)} I^A_{(a)\,B} \partial_\mu Q^B = 0. \tag{13.3}$$

For the local group, the variation of the Lagrangian becomes:

$$\delta L = \left[\frac{\partial L}{\partial Q^A} I^A_{(a)\,B} Q^B + \frac{\partial L}{\partial (\partial_\mu Q^A)} I^A_{(a)\,B} \partial_\mu Q^B \right] \epsilon^a(u)$$
$$+ \frac{\partial L}{\partial (\partial_\mu Q^A)} I^A_{(a)\,B} Q^B \partial_\mu \epsilon^a(u)$$

If the relation in Eq. (13.3) is assumed to hold even when $G \to G'$, the conclusion is that $\delta L \neq 0$ when ϵ^a is not constant (at least for a general form of L).

In order to reinstate the symmetry, the solution is to introduce a gauge potential A^c_μ (here we take a shortcut in comparison with Utiyama's original proposal), which transforms according to

$$\delta A^c_\mu = \epsilon^a f^{\,c}_{a\,b} A^b_\mu + \partial_\mu \epsilon^c. \tag{13.4}$$

This answers questions (1) and (2) and the proof of this relation is a beautiful part of Utiyama's paper.

The original Lagrangian is then replaced by a new functional, $L(Q^A, \partial_\mu Q^A) \to L'(Q^A, \partial_\mu Q^A, A^a_\mu)$. The symmetry condition and the independence of the parameters ϵ^a and their derivatives lead to the following set of equations:

$$\begin{cases} \frac{\partial L'}{\partial Q^A} I^A_{(a)\,B} Q^B + \frac{\partial L'}{\partial (\partial_\mu Q^A)} I^A_{(a)\,B} \partial_\mu Q^B + \frac{\partial L'}{\partial A^c_\mu} f^{\,c}_{a\,b} A^b_\mu = 0, & (i) \\ \frac{\partial L'}{\partial (\partial_\mu Q^A)} I^A_{(a)\,B} Q^B + \frac{\partial L'}{\partial A^a_\mu} = 0. & (ii) \end{cases} \tag{13.5}$$

A key point to obtain the solutions to these equations [10] is to understand that any function $f(ax - by)$ is a solution to

$$b \frac{\partial f}{\partial x} + a \frac{\partial f}{\partial y} = 0.$$

From this perspective, the solution of equation (ii) in Eq. (13.5) implies that the dependence of the Lagrangian with the gauge field and the derivative of Q^A must be through the combination:

$$D_\mu Q^A = \partial_\mu Q^A - I^{A}_{(c)\,B} Q^B A^c_\mu. \tag{13.6}$$

This object is called *covariant derivative*, and one can prove that it transforms covariantly under the group G'. This result, when used in the first equation of Eq. (13.5), establishes the so-called *minimal coupling prescription*, according to which the ordinary derivative is replaced by the covariant derivative at the Lagrangian level:

$$L(Q^A, \partial_\mu Q^A) \to L(Q^A, D_\mu Q^A).$$

This answers questions (3) and (4).

Finally, Utiyama considers a Lagrangian for the free gauge field $L_0 = L_0(A^a_\mu, \partial_\nu A^a_\mu)$ and assumes that it is gauge invariant. As before, from the independence of ϵ^a and their derivatives, a set of three equations is obtained:

$$\begin{cases} \frac{\partial L_0}{\partial A^c_\mu} f^{c}_{a\,b} A^b_\mu + \frac{\partial L_0}{\partial(\partial_\mu A^c_\nu)} f^{c}_{a\,b} \partial_\mu A^c_\nu = 0, \\ \frac{\partial L_0}{\partial A^a_\mu} + \frac{\partial L_0}{\partial(\partial_\mu A^c_\nu)} f^{c}_{a\,b} A^b_\nu = 0, \\ \frac{\partial L_0}{\partial(\partial_\mu A^a_\nu)} + \frac{\partial L_0}{\partial(\partial_\nu A^a_\mu)} = 0. \end{cases}$$

The solutions to these equations demand the dependence of L_0 with A and its derivative to occur only through the particular combination that defines the *field strength*:

$$F^a_{\mu\nu} = \partial_\mu A^a_\nu - \partial_\nu A^a_\mu - f^{a}_{c\,b} A^c_\mu A^b_\nu,$$

i.e.

$$L_0 = L_0(F^a_{\mu\nu}).$$

This answers question (5).

In his work, Utiyama applies this formalism to $U(1)$, $SU(2)$ and Lorentz groups. In the next section, the translation group is considered and the main results will be presented.

13.3 The translation group

An important feature of Utiyama's approach concerns the underlying spacetime. In principle, there are no restrictions concerning the manifold where the theory is built as long as one can properly define the fields, the derivatives and so on. Utiyama himself noticed the importance of this property to build his gravitational theory for the Lorentz group. He started with a cartesian coordinate system of coordinates x^a and introduced an auxiliary set of curvilinear coordinates u^μ with an invertible map $u^\mu(x^a) \longleftrightarrow x^a(u^\mu)$. The line element, as a scalar and an invariant under coordinate transformations, satisfies the relation:

$$ds^2 = \eta_{ab} dx^a dx^b = g_{\mu\nu} du^\mu du^\nu,$$

where η_{ab} is the Minkowski metric and $g_{\mu\nu} = g_{\mu\nu}(u)$ represents the metric tensor components in the curvilinear coordinates u^μ. Both η_{ab} and $g_{\mu\nu}$ are related by:

$$\begin{cases} g_{\mu\nu}(u) = b^a{}_\mu b^b{}_\nu \eta_{ab}(x), \\ \eta_{ab}(x) = b_a{}^\mu b_b{}^\nu g_{\mu\nu}(u) \end{cases} \quad (13.7)$$

where

$$b^a{}_\mu \equiv \frac{\partial x^a}{\partial u^\mu}, \quad b_a{}^\mu \equiv \frac{\partial u^\mu}{\partial x^a}. \quad (13.8)$$

It is possible to interpret $b^a{}_\mu$ as a tetrad field, in the sense that it connects the Minkowski metric to a general metric in an arbitrary curvilinear coordinate system. This was done by Utiyama when studying the gauge theory for the Lorentz group. However, this tetrad is a trivial one since it actually only represents a change of coordinates – the importance of this result shall be explored later. Utiyama makes a generalization and considers $b^a{}_\mu$ as a set of independent fields. Kibble was likely the first to criticize this generalization [11]. In his opinion, treating $b^a{}_\mu$ as independent fields was something necessary, but there should be a reason for this and this condition should not be imposed by convenience. Kibble then decided to analyze the gauge invariance of the Poincaré group and obtained a class of theories of the Einstein-Cartan type [3, 12].

When considering the translation group, it is immediate to identify the generators of the transformation as the derivatives:

$$\delta Q^A = \epsilon^a \partial_a Q^A.$$

This is indeed the case when a cartesian coordinate system is being used. Note that if one considers curvilinear coordinates with $\delta Q^A = \epsilon^\mu \partial_\mu Q^A$, misleading results may be obtained if, for instance, $u^\mu \to \theta$ represents an angle – in this case the transformation would be a rotation instead of a translation. This shows the importance of considering the two coordinate system (cartesian and curvilinear) when one intends to analyze the translation transformations and describe the physical system in a general coordinate set. The starting point is to consider the global translation in cartesian coordinates:

$$x^a \to x'^a = x^a + \epsilon^a, \quad \delta Q^A = \epsilon^a \delta^A{}_B \partial_a Q^B. \quad (13.9)$$

Using the derivative as the generator of the translation immediately sets the gauge group as abelian, since

$$f_{cb}^{\ a} = 0.$$

This simplifies significantly the analysis and shows a common ground with electromagnetism, that is also associated to an abelian group.

The action integral in curvilinear coordinates is given by

$$S = \int_\Omega d^4u\, L\left(Q^A(u), \partial_\mu Q^A(u), b^a_\mu\right).$$

Note that b^a_μ is explictly declared in the functional dependence of the action integral – its presence is important to allow one to properly address the translation transformations. In particular, it allows one to associate the derivative in curvilinear coordinates with the derivative in cartesian ones by means of the relation:

$$\partial_\mu Q^A = b^a_\mu \partial_a Q^A. \tag{13.10}$$

Since b^a_μ is present in the action, its transformation law has also to be determined. Considering its definition in Eq.(13.8), it is immediate to verify that

$$\delta b^a_\mu \equiv b'^a_\mu - b^a_\mu = \frac{\partial x'^a}{\partial u^\mu} - \frac{\partial x^a}{\partial u^\mu} = \partial_\mu \epsilon^a. \tag{13.11}$$

This is null for a global translation, i.e. ϵ^a = constant $\Rightarrow \delta b^a_\mu = 0$. As a consequence, it plays no role when the global variation of the action/Lagrangian is taken into account:

$$\delta L = 0 \Rightarrow \frac{\partial L}{\partial Q^A} \partial_a Q^A + \frac{\partial L}{\partial \partial_\mu Q^A} \partial_\mu \partial_a Q^A = 0. \tag{13.12}$$

When the global transformation is replaced by the local one, δb^a_μ can no longer be neglected.

Following Utiyama's procedure, G is replaced by G', i.e., $\epsilon^a \to \epsilon^a(u)$, the symmetry is reinstated with the introduction of the gauge field A^c_μ in the action integral,

$$S' = \int_\Omega d^4u\, L'\left(Q^A, \partial_\mu Q^A, h^c_\mu, A^c_\mu\right). \tag{13.13}$$

For the present case, the gauge field transforms as

$$\delta A^c_\mu = \partial_\mu \epsilon^c. \tag{13.14}$$

The variation of the action integral under the assumptions that Eq.(13.12) is valid and that the parameters and their derivatives are independent leads to:

$$\frac{\partial L'}{\partial \partial_\mu Q^A} \partial_c Q^A + \frac{\partial L'}{\partial b^c_\mu} + \frac{\partial L'}{\partial A^c_\mu} = 0. \tag{13.15}$$

Differently from the Eq.(13.5) - (ii), this equation now presents three terms. The proper way to determine the functional dependence of the Lagrangian with $\partial_\mu Q^A, b_\mu^c$ and A_μ^c, is to consider the solution for each possible pair, as if each of them satisfied an equation of their own, i.e.:

$$\begin{cases} \frac{\partial L'}{\partial \partial_\mu Q^A} \partial_c Q^A + \frac{\partial L'}{\partial b_\mu^c} = 0, \\ \frac{\partial L'}{\partial \partial_\mu Q^A} \partial_c Q^A + \frac{\partial L'}{\partial A_\mu^c} = 0, \\ \frac{\partial L'}{\partial b_\mu^c} + \frac{\partial L'}{\partial A_\mu^c} = 0. \end{cases}$$

This means that the dependence of the Lagrangian with the gauge field will not be only through the covariant derivative. The first of these equations stablishes that L' should present a dependence on the combination:

$$V_\mu{}^A \equiv b_\mu^c \partial_c Q^A - \partial_\mu Q^A.$$

This object is clearly null due to Eq.(13.10), therefore it is discarded. The solution to the second equation defines the covariant derivative of the translation group:

$$D_\mu Q^A \equiv \partial_\mu Q^A - A_\mu^c \partial_c Q^A. \tag{13.16}$$

Finally, the solution to the third equation determines that the Lagrangian has dependence with the gauge field through a second object:

$$h_\mu^c \equiv b_\mu^c - A_\mu^c. \tag{13.17}$$

According to Utiyama's procedure, the minimal coupling for the present case establishes the two-steps prescription:

$$\begin{cases} \partial_\mu Q^A \to D_\mu Q^A, \\ b_\mu^a \to h_\mu^a, \\ L\left(Q^A, \partial_\mu Q^A, b_\mu^a\right) \to L\left(Q^A, D_\mu Q^A, h_\mu^a\right). \end{cases}$$

Interestingly, with the definition of h_μ^c, Eq. (13.16) can be expressed as

$$D_\mu Q^A = h_\mu^c \partial_c Q^A, \tag{13.18}$$

and it shows consistency with the prescription for the $b_\mu^a \to h_\mu^a$:

$$\partial_\mu Q^A = b_\mu^a \partial_a Q^A \to h_\mu^a \partial_a Q^A = D_\mu Q^A.$$

The next step of Utiyama's program is the analysis of the Lagrangian for the free gauge field, L_0. The starting point is to define the functional dependence of the Lagrangian, which is chosen as:

$$L_0 = L_0\left(A_\mu^c, \partial_\nu A_\mu^c, b_\mu^c\right).$$

Once again, the presence of b_μ^c is assumed so that the translation transformations can be properly performed. The symmetry equations in the present case read

$$\frac{\partial L_0}{\partial A_\mu^c} + \frac{\partial L_0}{\partial b_\mu^c} = 0, \tag{13.19}$$

$$\frac{\partial L_0}{\partial \partial_\nu A_\mu^c} + \frac{\partial L_0}{\partial \partial_\mu A_\nu^c} = 0. \tag{13.20}$$

These equations are decoupled, which means that they can be solved independently. The solution for Eq. (13.19) requires b_μ^a and A_μ^a appears in L_0 by means of the same object h_μ^a defined previsouly, i.e.

$$h_\mu^a \equiv b_\mu^a - A_\mu^a.$$

The dependence of L_0 with the derivative of the gauge field is set by Eq. (13.20). It leads to the definition of the field strength:

$$F_{\nu\mu}^c \equiv \partial_\mu A_\nu^c - \partial_\nu A_\mu^c. \tag{13.21}$$

The final form of the Lagrangian of the free gauge field is:

$$L_0\left(A_\mu^c, \partial_\nu A_\mu^c, b_\mu^c\right) \to L_0\left(h_\mu^c, F_{\nu\mu}^c\right).$$

This concludes Utiyama's program for the translation group as presented in the previous section.

Up to this point, the approach presented above considers the gauge theory for translation purely from a field theory perspective. Its connection and interpretation from a geometrical point of view is presented in the next section.

13.4 Geometrical interpretation

The key point for the geometrical interpretation of the interaction associated to the gauge group of translation is the minimal coupling prescription, in particular:

$$b_\mu^a \to h_\mu^a.$$

With this prescription, the mapping between the components of tensors in Cartesian and curvilinear coordinates, which was originally established by

$$\mathscr{T}_\mu^\nu(u) = \frac{\partial u^\nu}{\partial x^b} \frac{\partial x^a}{\partial u^\mu} \mathscr{T}_a^b(x) = b_b^{\ \nu} b_\mu^{\ a} \mathscr{T}_a^b(x),$$

is now replaced by the prescription

$$\mathcal{T}^\nu_\mu(u) = h_b^{\ \nu} h^a_{\ \mu} \mathcal{T}^b_{\ a}(x),$$

where $h_b^{\ \nu}$ is defined as the inverse of $h^a_{\ \mu}$, i.e. $h^a_{\ \mu} h_a^{\ \nu} = \delta^\nu_\mu$, $h^a_{\ \mu} h_b^{\ \mu} = \delta^a_b$.

In particular, the metric tensor is mapped according to

$$g_{\mu\nu} = h^a_{\ \mu} h^b_{\ \nu} \eta_{ab}. \tag{13.22}$$

$h^a_{\ \mu}$ plays the role of a tetrad field, but differently from $b^a_{\ \mu}$ in Eq. (13.7), where only the effect of coordinate transformations was considered, here $h^a_{\ \mu}$ brings the contribution of the translation interaction by means of the gauge field. In fact, $b^a_{\ \mu}$ is a gradient, which means that:

$$\partial_\nu b^a_{\ \mu} - \partial_\mu b^a_{\ \nu} = 0.$$

This property is not shared by $h^a_{\ \mu}$:

$$\partial_\nu h^a_{\ \mu} - \partial_\mu h^a_{\ \nu} = \partial_\mu A^a_{\ \nu} - \partial_\nu A^a_{\ \mu} = F^a_{\ \nu\mu} \neq 0.$$

Here is where the concept of anholonomy should be recovered, and it is very opportune to quote Aldrovandi, Barros and Pereira [5]:

"Anholonomy – the property of a differential form which is not the differential of anything, or of a vector field which is not a gradient – is commonplace in many chapters of Physics." The new tetrad $h^a_{\ \mu}$ is composed by two parts, one that is a true gradient – the holonomous part, $b^a_{\ \mu}$, – and another one which is not a gradient and constitutes the anholonomous part, $A^a_{\ \mu}$. The latter describes the interaction associated to the translation group and the "curl" of $h^a_{\ \mu}$ determines the field strength, which is the key ingredient for describing the dynamics of the gauge field (according to the symmetry requirements of the gauge theory).

The second part of the minimal coupling prescription, $\partial_\mu Q^A \to D_\mu Q^A$, allows one to establish the link between the covariant derivative of tensorial objects in curvilinear coordinates, ∇_μ, and the translation group covariant derivative by means of the mapping

$$\nabla_\mu \Phi^\nu = h_a^{\ \nu} D_\mu \Phi^a.$$

This implies that the space-time connection is given by

$$\Gamma^\nu_{\ \mu\rho} \equiv h_a^{\ \nu} \partial_\mu h^a_{\ \rho}. \tag{13.23}$$

This choice is equivalent to setting the absolute parallelism condition,

$$\nabla_\mu h^b_{\ \rho} = \partial_\mu h^b_{\ \rho} - \Gamma^\nu_{\ \mu\rho} h^b_{\ \nu} = 0. \tag{13.24}$$

Interestingly, this implies that the connection is compatible with the metric since

$$\nabla_\rho g_{\mu\nu} = \left(\nabla_\rho h^a_\mu h^b_\nu + h^a_\mu \nabla_\rho h^b_\nu\right)\eta_{ab} = 0. \tag{13.25}$$

In other words, the metric and connection satisfy the metricity condition.

This connection is free of curvature,

$$R_{\nu\mu\beta}{}^\sigma(\Gamma) = 0, \tag{13.26}$$

but presents torsion:

$$T^\nu_{\mu\rho}(\Gamma) \equiv \Gamma^\nu_{\mu\rho} - \Gamma^\nu_{\rho\mu} = h_a{}^\nu\left(\partial_\mu h^a_\rho - \partial_\rho h^a_\mu\right). \tag{13.27}$$

Up to this point, after the introduction of the gauge field, the spacetime in which the interaction takes place is equivalent to a manifold equipped with a metric tensor (defined in terms of the tetrad) and a connection which is compatible with the former. Also, the connection characterizes a manifold with torsion and no curvature. The conclusion is that one has essentially a Weitzenböck spacetime.

Besides, considering that h^a_ρ has an holonomous and an anholonomous parts, only the latter survives in the expression for the torsion, which leads to the identification of the torsion as the field strength itself:

$$T^\nu_{\mu\rho} = h_a{}^\nu F^a_{\mu\rho}.$$

This way, from a geometrical point of view, the dynamics of the gauge field is described by the torsion. The symmetry requirements of gauge theories do not demand a specific form for the Lagrangian of the gauge field – they only establish that the latter is a function of the field strength and, for the translation group, of the tetrad. It means that several theories can be encompassed within this structure. In particular, if one restricts the field equations to be linear in the second derivative of h^a_μ, then the most general class of Lagrangians obtained is the one proposed by Hayashi and Shirafuji in the context of the "new general relativity" [13], which includes TEGR as a particular case. This encloses the analyzis and the imminent conclusion is that the gauge theory for the translation group represents the gravitational interaction in the context of the teleparallel theories of gravity.

13.5 Final remarks

In the present work, it is shown that the application of Utiyama's formalism to the translation group leads to a theory that can be interpreted as a geometric theory in the context of the teleparallel theories of gravity. The minimal coupling prescription is split in two instructions: One determines the covariant derivative; the second shows explicitly that the tetrad field is composed by an holonomous and an anholonomous parts, the latter being essentially the gauge field, which is introduced to restore the symmetry when the local group is taken into account. The split of the tetrad in its two parts also allows one to understand why inertial effects (due to coordinate transformations) and gravitation share a common property – both their effects are linearly combined in the tetrad field. The anholonomous part of the tetrad is the one that composes the field strength, or torsion in its geometric interpretation, and establishes the dynamics of the gravitational field. Since the inertial/coordinate effects vanish in the torsion tensor, one cannot eliminate the dynamics of the gravitational field by a proper choice of coordinates – this is also true in the context of GR (and its modified versions), but in the present analysis, this can be seen more straightforwardly.

This work does not reveal any new structure in comparison with the standard approaches to teleparallel theories, but also no structure is missing as well. This just show that the Utiyama's approach is robust and reliable. One advantage of this formalism lies on its systematicity, allowing its application to very different scenarios/extensions. It brings a different point of view for the construction of the building blocks of gauge interactions. Seeing things from different perspectives is certainly a powerful tool in the proposition of new physical theories. And this is an ability that was instilled in me by Prof. Aldrovandi, to whom I am truly grateful.

Acknowledgments

I appreciate the organizers for inviting me to contribute to this tribute to Prof. Aldrovandi.

Bibliography

[1] R. Aldrovandi, J. G. Pereira, *Teleparallel Gravity: An Introduction* (Springer Netherlands, Dordrecht, (2012).

[2] R. Aldrovandi, J. G. Pereira, K .H. Vu, *Selected Topics in Teleparallel Gravity*, Braz. J. Phys. **34**, 1374 (2004).

[3] R. Aldrovandi, J. G. Pereira, *An Introduction to Geometrical Physics*, 2nd edition (World Scientific, Singapore, 2017).

[4] M. Krššak, R. J. van den Hoogen, J. G. Pereira, C. G. Böhmer, A. A. Coley, *Teleparallel theories of gravity: illuminating a fully invariant approach*, Class. Quant. Grav. **36**, 183001 (2019).

[5] R. Aldrovandi, P. B. Barros, J. G. Pereira, *Gravitation as Anholonomy*, Gen. Rel. Grav. **35**, 991 (2003).

[6] R. Utiyama, *Invariant Theoretical Interpretation of Interaction*, Phys. Rev. **101**, 1597 (1956).

[7] R. R. Cuzinatto, C. A. M. de Melo, P. J. Pompeia, *Second order gauge theory*, Ann. Phys. **322**, 1211 (2007).

[8] R. R. Cuzinatto, C. A. M. de Melo, L. G. Medeiros, P. J. Pompeia, *Gauge formulation for higher order gravity*, Eur. Phys. J. C **53**, 99 (2008).

[9] E. M. B. Assencio, R.S. Caraça, S.G. Vilhena, P. J. Pompeia, *Second-order teleparallel gauge theory*, Class. Quant. Grav. **40**, 205015 (2023).

[10] O. A. Acevedo, R. R. Cuzinatto, B. M. Pimentel, P. J. Pompeia, *Teorias de gauge a la Utiyama*, Rev. Bras. Ens. Fís. **40**, e4302 (2018).

[11] T. W. B. Kibble, *Lorentz invariance and the gravitational field*, J. Math. Phys. **2**, 212 (1961).

[12] R. Aldrovandi, J. G. Pereira, *Gravitation: in search of the missing torsion*, Ann. Fond. Louis de Broglie **32**, 229 (2007).

[13] K. Hayashi and T. Shirafuji, *New general relativity*, Phys. Rev. D **19**, 3524 (1979).

14

The beauty of self-duality

L. A. Ferreira

Dedicated to the memory of Prof. Ruben Aldrovandi

Abstract: Self-duality plays a very important role in many applications in field theories possessing topological solitons. In general, the self-duality equations are first order partial differential equations such that their solutions satisfy the second order Euler-Lagrange equations of the theory. The fact that one has to perform one integration less to construct self-dual solitons, as compared to the usual topological solitons, is not linked to the use of any dynamically conserved quantity. It is important that the topological charge admits an integral representation, and so there exists a density of topological charge. The homotopic invariance of it leads to local identities, in the form of second order differential equations. The magic is that such identities become the Euler-Lagrange equations of the theory when the self-duality equations are imposed. We review some important structures underlying the concept of self-duality, and show how it can be applied to kinks, lumps, monopoles, Skyrmions and instantons.

14.1 Introduction

Topological solitons play a fundamental role in the study of non-linear phenomena in many areas of science. The non-trivial topological structures make them quite stable, and consequently very important in the description of many facets of the theory. Topological solitons appear in a variety of theories ranging from kinks in $(1 + 1)$-dimensions, to vortices in $(2 + 1)$-dimensions, magnetic monopoles and Skyrmions in $(3+1)$-dimensions, and instantons in four dimensional Euclidean spaces. They are relevant for many non-linear phenomena in high energy physics, condensed matter physics and science in general [1, 2, 3].

Among the types of topological solitons there is a class which is special, the so-called self-dual solitons. They are classical solutions of the self-duality equations which are first order differential equations that imply the second order Euler-Lagrange equations of the theory. In addition, on each topological sector there is a lower bound on the static energy, or Euclidean action, and the self-dual solitons saturate that bound. Therefore, self-dual solitons are very stable.

The reason why one performs just one integration to construct self-dual solitons, instead of two in the case of the usual topological solitons, is not linked to dynamically conserved quantities. In all cases where self-duality is known to work, the relevant topological charge admits an integral representation, and so there exists a density of topological charge. As such charge is invariant under any smooth (homotopic) variations of the fields, it leads to local identities, in the form of second order differential equations, that are satisfied by any regular configuration of the fields, not necessarily solutions of the theory. The magic is that such identities become the Euler-Lagrange equations of the theory when the (first order) self-duality equations are imposed.

The concept of generalized self-dualities has been put forward using such an ideas where one can construct, from one single topological charge, a large class of field theories possessing self-dual sectors [4]. In $(1+1)$-dimensions it was possible to construct field theories, with any number of scalar fields, possessing self-dual solitons, and so generalizing what is well known in theories with one single scalar field, like sine-Gordon and $\lambda \phi^4$ models [5, 6]. In addition, exact self-dual sectors were constructed for Skyrme type theories by the addition of extra scalar fields [7, 8, 9, 10], and concrete applications have been made to nuclear matter [11].

In this paper we review those developments in a simple and concise way. The concept of self-duality has been used for a long time in several contexts [12, 13, 14, 15], and we give here the main idea behind the concept of generalized self-duality proposed in [4], and in fact genereralizing it to the case of complex fields. Consider a field theory that possesses a topological charge with an integral representation of the form

$$Q = \frac{1}{2} \int d^d x \left[\mathcal{A}_\alpha \widetilde{\mathcal{A}}_\alpha^* + \mathcal{A}_\alpha^* \widetilde{\mathcal{A}}_\alpha \right] \tag{14.1}$$

where $\mathcal{A}_\alpha$ and $\widetilde{\mathcal{A}}_\alpha$ are functionals of the fields of the theory and their first derivatives only, and where * means complex conjugation, and not transpose complex conjugate. The index α stands for any type of indices, like vector, spinor, internal, etc., or groups of them. The fact that Q is topological means that it is invariant under any smooth (homotopic) variations of the fields. Let us denote the fields by χ_κ, and they can be scalar, vector, spinor fields, and the index κ stands for the space-time and internal indices. We take χ_κ to be real, and so, if there are complex fields, χ_κ stands for the real and imaginary parts of those fields. The invariance of Q under smooth variations of the fields, i.e. $\delta Q = 0$, leads to the identities

$$\frac{\delta \mathcal{A}_\alpha}{\delta \chi_\kappa} \widetilde{\mathcal{A}}_\alpha^* - \partial_\mu \left(\frac{\delta \mathcal{A}_\alpha}{\delta \partial_\mu \chi_\kappa} \widetilde{\mathcal{A}}_\alpha^* \right) + \mathcal{A}_\alpha \frac{\delta \widetilde{\mathcal{A}}_\alpha^*}{\delta \chi_\kappa} - \partial_\mu \left(\mathcal{A}_\alpha \frac{\delta \widetilde{\mathcal{A}}_\alpha^*}{\delta \partial_\mu \chi_\kappa} \right)$$
$$+ \frac{\delta \mathcal{A}_\alpha^*}{\delta \chi_\kappa} \widetilde{\mathcal{A}}_\alpha - \partial_\mu \left(\frac{\delta \mathcal{A}_\alpha^*}{\delta \partial_\mu \chi_\kappa} \widetilde{\mathcal{A}}_\alpha \right) + \mathcal{A}_\alpha^* \frac{\delta \widetilde{\mathcal{A}}_\alpha}{\delta \chi_\kappa} - \partial_\mu \left(\mathcal{A}_\alpha^* \frac{\delta \widetilde{\mathcal{A}}_\alpha}{\delta \partial_\mu \chi_\kappa} \right) = 0 \tag{14.2}$$

By imposing the first order differential equations, or self-duality equations, on the fields as

$$\mathcal{A}_\alpha = \pm \widetilde{\mathcal{A}}_\alpha \tag{14.3}$$

it follows that, together with the identities (14.2), they imply the equations

$$\frac{\delta \mathcal{A}_\alpha}{\delta \chi_\kappa} \mathcal{A}_\alpha^* - \partial_\mu \left(\frac{\delta \mathcal{A}_\alpha}{\delta \partial_\mu \chi_\kappa} \mathcal{A}_\alpha^* \right) + \mathcal{A}_\alpha \frac{\delta \mathcal{A}_\alpha^*}{\delta \chi_\kappa} - \partial_\mu \left(\mathcal{A}_\alpha \frac{\delta \mathcal{A}_\alpha^*}{\delta \partial_\mu \chi_\kappa} \right)$$
$$+ \frac{\delta \widetilde{\mathcal{A}}_\alpha^*}{\delta \chi_\kappa} \widetilde{\mathcal{A}}_\alpha - \partial_\mu \left(\frac{\delta \widetilde{\mathcal{A}}_\alpha^*}{\delta \partial_\mu \chi_\kappa} \widetilde{\mathcal{A}}_\alpha \right) + \widetilde{\mathcal{A}}_\alpha^* \frac{\delta \widetilde{\mathcal{A}}_\alpha}{\delta \chi_\kappa} - \partial_\mu \left(\widetilde{\mathcal{A}}_\alpha^* \frac{\delta \widetilde{\mathcal{A}}_\alpha}{\delta \partial_\mu \chi_\kappa} \right) = 0 \tag{14.4}$$

Note that (14.4) are the Euler-Lagrange equations associated to the functional

$$E = \frac{1}{2} \int d^d x \left[\mathcal{A}_\alpha \mathcal{A}_\alpha^* + \widetilde{\mathcal{A}}_\alpha \widetilde{\mathcal{A}}_\alpha^* \right] \tag{14.5}$$

So, first order differential equations together with second order topological identities lead to second order Euler-Lagrange equations. Note that, if E is positive definite then the self-dual solutions saturate a lower bound on E as follows. From (14.3) we have that $\mathcal{A}_\alpha^2 = \widetilde{\mathcal{A}}_\alpha^2 = \pm \mathcal{A}_\alpha \widetilde{\mathcal{A}}_\alpha$. Note that (14.3) also implies that $\mathcal{A}_\alpha \widetilde{\mathcal{A}}_\alpha^* = \mathcal{A}_\alpha^* \widetilde{\mathcal{A}}_\alpha$. Therefore, if $\mathcal{A}_\alpha \mathcal{A}_\alpha^* \geq 0$, and consequently $\widetilde{\mathcal{A}}_\alpha \widetilde{\mathcal{A}}_\alpha^* \geq 0$, we have that

$$\mathcal{A}_\alpha = \widetilde{\mathcal{A}}_\alpha \quad \rightarrow \quad Q = \int d^d x \, \mathcal{A}_\alpha \mathcal{A}_\alpha^* \geq 0$$

$$\mathcal{A}_\alpha = -\widetilde{\mathcal{A}}_\alpha \quad \rightarrow \quad Q = -\int d^d x \, \mathcal{A}_\alpha \mathcal{A}_\alpha^* \leq 0 \tag{14.6}$$

Therefore we have that

$$E = \frac{1}{2} \int d^d x \, [\mathcal{A}_\alpha \mp \widetilde{\mathcal{A}}_\alpha][\mathcal{A}_\alpha^* \mp \widetilde{\mathcal{A}}_\alpha^*] \pm \frac{1}{2} \int d^d x \, [\mathcal{A}_\alpha \widetilde{\mathcal{A}}_\alpha^* + \mathcal{A}_\alpha^* \widetilde{\mathcal{A}}_\alpha] \geq |Q| \qquad (14.7)$$

and the equality holds true for self-dual solutions, where we have

$$E = \int d^d x \, \mathcal{A}_\alpha \mathcal{A}_\alpha^* = \int d^d x \, \widetilde{\mathcal{A}}_\alpha \widetilde{\mathcal{A}}_\alpha^* = |Q| \qquad (14.8)$$

The splitting of the integrand of Q as in (14.1) is quite arbitrary, but once it is chosen one can still change $\mathcal{A}_\alpha$ and $\widetilde{\mathcal{A}}_\alpha$ by the apparently innocuous transformation

$$\mathcal{A}_\alpha \to \mathcal{A}_\alpha' = \mathcal{A}_\beta \, k_{\beta\alpha}; \qquad \widetilde{\mathcal{A}}_\alpha^* \to (\widetilde{\mathcal{A}}_\alpha')^* = k_{\alpha\beta}^{-1} \widetilde{\mathcal{A}}_\beta^* \qquad (14.9)$$

The topological charge does not change and so it is still invariant under homotopic transformations. Therefore, we can now apply the same reasoning as above with the transformed quantities $\mathcal{A}_\alpha'$ and $\widetilde{\mathcal{A}}_\alpha'$. The transformed self-duality equations are

$$\mathcal{A}_\beta \, k_{\beta\alpha} = \pm \left(k_{\alpha\beta}^{-1}\right)^* \widetilde{\mathcal{A}}_\beta \quad \to \quad \mathcal{A}_\beta \, h_{\beta\alpha} = \pm \widetilde{\mathcal{A}}_\alpha \qquad (14.10)$$

where we have defined the hermitian and invertible matrix

$$h \equiv k \, k^\dagger \qquad (14.11)$$

Together with the transformed identities (14.2), the new self-duality equations (14.10) imply the Euler-Lagrange equations associated to the energy

$$E' = \frac{1}{2} \int d^d x \left[\mathcal{A}_\alpha h_{\alpha\beta} \mathcal{A}_\beta^* + \widetilde{\mathcal{A}}_\alpha h_{\alpha\beta}^{-1} \widetilde{\mathcal{A}}_\beta^* \right] \qquad (14.12)$$

Note that the matrix h, or equivalently k, can be used to introduce new fields in the theory without changing the topological charge Q and therefore its field content.

It is import to note that the new self-duality equations (14.10) will also imply the Euler-Lagrange equations, coming from E', associated to such new fields $h_{\alpha\beta}$. Indeed, if the topological charge does not depend upon these new fields, so does not $\mathcal{A}_\alpha$ and $\widetilde{\mathcal{A}}_\alpha$. Then the Euler-Lagrange equations associated to the fields $h_{\alpha\beta}$ is

$$\mathcal{A}_\alpha \mathcal{A}_\beta^* - \widetilde{\mathcal{A}}_\gamma \, h_{\gamma\alpha}^{-1} h_{\beta\delta}^{-1} \widetilde{\mathcal{A}}_\delta^* = 0 \qquad (14.13)$$

Note that such equations are implied by the self-duality equations (14.10).

In addition, it follows that (14.10) implies $\mathcal{A}_\alpha h_{\alpha\beta} \mathcal{A}_\beta^* = \widetilde{\mathcal{A}}_\alpha h_{\alpha\beta}^{-1} \widetilde{\mathcal{A}}_\beta^* = \pm \mathcal{A}_\alpha \widetilde{\mathcal{A}}_\alpha^* = \pm \mathcal{A}_\alpha^* \widetilde{\mathcal{A}}_\alpha$. Therefore, if $\mathcal{A}_\alpha h_{\alpha\beta} \mathcal{A}_\beta^* \geq 0$, and consequently $\widetilde{\mathcal{A}}_\alpha h_{\alpha\beta}^{-1} \widetilde{\mathcal{A}}_\beta^* \geq 0$, we have that the bound follows in the same way as before

$$E' = \frac{1}{2}\int d^d x \left[\mathcal{A}_\beta k_{\beta\alpha} \mp \left(k_{\alpha\beta}^{-1}\right)^* \tilde{\mathcal{A}}_\beta \right] \left[\mathcal{A}_\gamma^* k_{\gamma\alpha}^* \mp k_{\alpha\gamma}^{-1} \tilde{\mathcal{A}}_\gamma^* \right]$$
$$\pm \frac{1}{2}\int d^d x \left[\mathcal{A}_\alpha \tilde{\mathcal{A}}_\alpha^* + \mathcal{A}_\alpha^* \tilde{\mathcal{A}}_\alpha \right] \geq |Q| \qquad (14.14)$$

We now discuss some examples where such ideas have been applied.

14.2 Multi-field kinks in $(1+1)$-dimensions

Self-dual sectors for theories in $(1+1)$-dimensions, containing just one scalar field, like the sine-Gordon, and $\lambda \phi^4$ models, have been known for quite a long time. The application of the ideas explained in Section 14.1 have lead to the construction of self-dual sectors in theories containing any number of scalar fields in $(1+1)$-dimensions [5, 6]. We consider here theories of real scalar fields. In such case, the relevant topological charge is given by

$$Q = \int_{-\infty}^{\infty} dx \frac{dU}{dx} = \int_{-\infty}^{\infty} dx \frac{\delta U}{\delta \varphi_a} \frac{d\varphi_a}{dx} = U(\varphi_a(x=\infty)) - U(\varphi_a(x=-\infty)).$$
(14.15)

where U is an arbitrary real functional of the real scalar fields φ_a, $a = 1, 2, \ldots r$, but not of their derivatives. Clearly, the density of such a topological charge has the form given in (14.1), and following (14.9) we can split it as (the quantities $\mathcal{A}_\alpha$ and $\tilde{\mathcal{A}}_\alpha$ are real, and so is the matrix k)

$$\mathcal{A}_a \equiv k_{ab} \frac{d\varphi_b}{dx}; \qquad \tilde{\mathcal{A}}_a \equiv \frac{\delta U}{\delta \varphi_b} k_{ba}^{-1}, \qquad (14.16)$$

where k_{ab} is an arbitrary invertible matrix that can be introduced due to the freedom in the splitting. According to (14.10), the self-duality equations are

$$\eta_{ab} \frac{d\varphi_b}{dx} = \pm \frac{\delta U}{\delta \varphi_a}, \qquad \eta = k^T k \qquad (14.17)$$

and so, η_{ab} is an invertible symmetric matrix. In what follows, we shall take η_{ab} to be a constant matrix, and not a matrix containing new fields, as it is allowed by the construction discussed in Section 14.1. It will play the role of a metric in the target space of the scalar fields φ_a.

Following (14.12) the static energy of our theory is

$$E = \int_{-\infty}^{\infty} dx \left[\frac{1}{2} \eta_{ab} \frac{d\varphi_a}{dx} \frac{d\varphi_b}{dx} + V \right], \qquad (14.18)$$

where the potential is given by

$$V = \frac{1}{2} \eta_{ab}^{-1} \frac{\delta U}{\delta \varphi_a} \frac{\delta U}{\delta \varphi_b} \qquad (14.19)$$

Therefore, from the arguments of Section 14.1, it follows that solutions of (14.17) are solutions of the static Euler-Lagrange equations associated to the energy functional (14.18). The quantity U plays the role of a pre-potential. Note that given a choice of pre-potential U one can directly obtain the potential V and so a scalar field theory with a self-dual sector. However, given the potential V it is not in general easy to find the pre-potential U. We shall discuss here the construction of self-dual theories from the choice of pre-potential.

We restrict our discussion to the cases where the scalar fields φ_a, the pre-potential U, and the matrix η_{ab} are real. In addition, we are interested in the cases for which the static energy functional E, given in (14.18), is positive definite. Thus we need to restrict our discussion to cases in which all the eigenvalues of η_{ab} are positive definite. In order for the self-dual solutions of (14.17) to possess finite energy E, we need the energy density to vanish at spatial infinities when evaluated on such solutions, and so, given our restrictions, we require that

$$\frac{d\varphi_b}{dx} \to 0; \qquad \frac{\delta U}{\delta \varphi_a} \to 0; \qquad \text{as} \quad x \to \pm\infty. \qquad (14.20)$$

Thus, the self-duality equations (14.17) should possess constant vacua solutions $\varphi_a^{(\text{vac.})}$ that are zeros of all the first derivatives of the pre-potential, i.e.,

$$\frac{\delta U}{\delta \varphi_b}\bigg|_{\varphi_a = \varphi_a^{(\text{vac.})}} = 0. \qquad (14.21)$$

We then see from (14.19) that such vacua are also zeros of the potential V and of its first derivatives, i.e.,

$$V\left(\varphi_a^{(\text{vac.})}\right) = 0; \qquad \frac{\delta V}{\delta \varphi_b}\bigg|_{\varphi_a = \varphi_a^{(\text{vac.})}} = 0. \qquad (14.22)$$

Moreover, we would like the theories we are constructing to possess various soliton type solutions, and we know that, in general, the total topological charges of such solutions are obtained by additions, under some finite or infinite abelian group, of the charges of the constituent one-solitons. Thus, we would like to have systems of vacua as degenerate as possible. Certainly there are numerous ways of achieving this goal. We shall use a group theoretical approach to the construction of the pre-potentials U, as we now explain.

Consider a Lie algebra $\mathscr{G}$ and let $\vec{\alpha}_a$, $a = 1, 2, \ldots r \equiv \text{rank } \mathscr{G}$, be the set of its simple roots. We use the scalar fields φ_a to construct our basic vector in the root space:

$$\vec{\varphi} \equiv \sum_{a=1}^{r} \varphi_a \frac{2\vec{\alpha}_a}{\vec{\alpha}_a^2}. \qquad (14.23)$$

Next we choose a representation $\mathcal{R}$ (irreducible or not) of the Lie algebra $\mathcal{G}$, and we denote by $\vec{\mu}_k$ the set of weights of $\mathcal{R}$. We take the pre-potential U to be of the form

$$U \equiv \sum_{\vec{\mu}_k \in \mathcal{R}^{(+)}} [\gamma_{\vec{\mu}_k} \cos(\vec{\mu}_k \cdot \vec{\varphi}) + \delta_{\vec{\mu}_k} \sin(\vec{\mu}_k \cdot \vec{\varphi})], \quad (14.24)$$

where the superscript $+$ in $\mathcal{R}^{(+)}$ means that if $\mathcal{R}$ possesses pair of weights of the form $(\vec{\mu}_k, -\vec{\mu}_k)$, we take just one member of the pair. There are several ways of having the pre-potential (14.24) satisfying (14.21), and so the vacuum structure of our theories can be quite complicated. For details see [5]. In order to clarify the aspects of the construction we discuss here and example for the $SU(3)$ group.

14.2.1 An $SU(3)$ example

The rank of $SU(3)$ is two and so we have two fields, φ_1 and φ_2, in this case. We take the matrix η_{ab} to be of the form

$$\eta = \begin{pmatrix} 2 & -\lambda \\ -\lambda & 2 \end{pmatrix}, \qquad \eta^{-1} = \frac{1}{4-\lambda^2} \begin{pmatrix} 2 & \lambda \\ \lambda & 2 \end{pmatrix}, \quad (14.25)$$

where we have introduced a real parameter λ. The eigenvalues of η are $2 \pm \lambda$, and so we have to keep λ in the interval $-2 < \lambda < 2$, to have η positive definite and invertible. The weights of the triplet representation of $SU(3)$ are given by

$$\vec{\mu}_1 = \vec{\lambda}_1, \qquad \vec{\mu}_2 = \vec{\lambda}_1 - \vec{\alpha}_1, \qquad \vec{\mu}_3 = \vec{\lambda}_1 - \vec{\alpha}_1 - \vec{\alpha}_2 \quad (14.26)$$

where α_a, $a = 1, 2$ are the simple roots of $SU(3)$, and $\vec{\lambda}_1$, is the fundamental weights which is the highest weight of the triplet representation. Thus from (14.24) we get the pre-potential as

$$U = \gamma_1 \cos \varphi_1 + \gamma_2 \cos \varphi_2 + \gamma_3 \cos(\varphi_1 - \varphi_2), \quad (14.27)$$

where we have chosen the δ-terms in (14.24) to vanish. The static energy (14.18) now becomes

$$E = \int_{-\infty}^{\infty} dx \left[(\partial_x \varphi_1)^2 + (\partial_x \varphi_2)^2 - \lambda \partial_x \varphi_1 \partial_x \varphi_2 + V(\varphi_1, \varphi_2) \right], \quad (14.28)$$

where the potential (14.19) is given by

$$\begin{aligned} V = \ & [-\gamma_1^2 \sin^2(\varphi_1) + \gamma_1 \sin(\varphi_1)(\gamma_3(\lambda-2)\sin(\varphi_1-\varphi_2) \\ & - \gamma_2^2 \sin^2(\varphi_2) - \gamma_2\gamma_3(\lambda-2)\sin(\varphi_2)\sin(\varphi_1-\varphi_2) \\ & - \gamma_2 \lambda \sin(\varphi_2)) + \gamma_3^2(\lambda-2)\sin^2(\varphi_1-\varphi_2)]/(\lambda^2-4) \end{aligned} \quad (14.29)$$

The self-duality equations (14.17) are now of the form:

$$\partial_x \varphi_1 = \pm \frac{[2\gamma_1 \sin(\varphi_1) + \gamma_2 \lambda \sin(\varphi_2) - \gamma_3(\lambda-2)\sin(\varphi_1-\varphi_2)]}{\lambda^2 - 4}, \quad (14.30)$$

$$\partial_x \varphi_2 = \pm \frac{[\gamma_1 \lambda \sin(\varphi_1) + 2\gamma_2 \sin(\varphi_2) + \gamma_3(\lambda-2)\sin(\varphi_1-\varphi_2)]}{\lambda^2 - 4}.$$

The vacua are determined by the conditions (14.21) which in this case become

$$\frac{\partial U}{\partial \varphi_1}\bigg|_{\varphi_a = \varphi_a^{(\text{vac.})}} = -\gamma_1 \sin(\varphi_1^{(\text{vac.})}) - \gamma_3 \sin(\varphi_1^{(\text{vac.})} - \varphi_2^{(\text{vac.})}) = 0, \quad (14.31)$$

$$\frac{\partial U}{\partial \varphi_2}\bigg|_{\varphi_a = \varphi_a^{(\text{vac.})}} = \gamma_3 \sin(\varphi_1^{(\text{vac.})} - \varphi_2^{(\text{vac.})}) - \gamma_2 \sin(\varphi_2^{(\text{vac.})}) = 0,$$

and these conditions imply that

$$\gamma_1 \sin(\varphi_1^{(\text{vac.})}) = -\gamma_3 \sin(\varphi_1^{(\text{vac.})} - \varphi_2^{(\text{vac.})}) = -\gamma_2 \sin(\varphi_2^{(\text{vac.})}). \quad (14.32)$$

Certainly (14.32) are satisfied if

$$\varphi_a^{(\text{vac.})} = \pi n_a; \quad n_a \in \mathbb{Z}; \quad a = 1, 2; \quad \text{any values of the } \gamma\text{'s}. \quad (14.33)$$

However, we also have the additional vacua, depending upon the particular values of the γ-constants that we are free to choose. For instance, one finds that (14.32) are satisfied if

$$\left(\varphi_1^{(\text{vac.})}, \varphi_2^{(\text{vac.})}\right) = \left(\frac{2\pi}{3} + 2\pi n_1, \frac{4\pi}{3} + 2\pi n_2\right); \quad \gamma_1 = \gamma_2 = \gamma_3 = 1,$$

$$\left(\varphi_1^{(\text{vac.})}, \varphi_2^{(\text{vac.})}\right) = \left(\frac{4\pi}{3} + 2\pi n_1, \frac{2\pi}{3} + 2\pi n_2\right); \quad n_1, n_2 \in \mathbb{Z}. \quad (14.34)$$

14.2.2 A mechanical interpretation of the self-dual solutions

As we have seen in (14.20) and (14.21), the finite energy solutions of the self-duality equations (14.17) have to go to constant vacua solutions for $x \to \pm\infty$. Therefore, each of these solutions connect two vacua of the theory. In order to have a geometric picture of these solutions let us write the self-duality equations (14.17) as

$$\vec{v} = \pm \vec{\nabla}_\eta U; \quad \text{with} \quad (\vec{v})_a = \frac{d\varphi_a}{dx}; \quad (\vec{\nabla}_\eta U)_a = \eta_{ab}^{-1} \frac{\delta U}{\delta \varphi_b}. \quad (14.35)$$

Given the pre-potential U and the metric η_{ab}, which we assume real, constant and positive definite, the η-gradient of U defines curves in the space of $\varphi_1, \ldots, \varphi_r$, with $\vec{\nabla}_\eta U$ being the tangent vector to these curves. The curves never intersect each other, since otherwise $\vec{\nabla}_\eta U$ would not be uniquely defined on a given point in φ-space. They can at most touch each other tangentially, or meet at points where $\vec{\nabla}_\eta U$ vanishes. The self-duality equation is a first order partial differential equation and so a given solution is determined by the values of the fields φ_a at a given point $x = x_0$.

The geometric picture is therefore that of a particle traveling in the φ-space with x-velocity $\vec{v}$, and with the space coordinate x playing the role of time. Therefore, the problem of solving the self-duality equation (14.17) reduces to that of constructing the curves in the φ-space determined by the η-gradient of U. Any particular solution corresponds to a particular curve determined by the initial values $\varphi_a(x_0)$. The finite energy solutions correspond to the curves that start and end at the extrema of the pre-potential U, i.e. at the points where $\vec{\nabla}_\eta U$ vanishes.

Consider now a given curve γ in the φ-space, parameterized by x, i.e. $\varphi_a(x)$, which is a solution of the self-duality equation (14.17), and associated to this curve define the quantity

$$\mathcal{Q}(\gamma) = \int_\gamma dx\, \vec{v} \cdot \vec{\nabla} U = \int_\gamma dx \frac{d\varphi_a}{dx} \frac{\delta U}{\delta \varphi_a} = U(x_f) - U(x_i), \qquad (14.36)$$

where x_f and x_i correspond to the final and initial points respectively, of the curve γ. Note that the tangent vector to this curve is $\vec{\nabla}_\eta U$ and not the ordinary gradient of U, i.e. $\vec{\nabla} U$, since the curve is a solution of the self-duality equations (14.17). From these self-duality equations we see that

$$\mathcal{Q}(\gamma) = \pm \int_\gamma dx\, \eta_{ab} \frac{d\varphi_a}{dx} \frac{d\varphi_b}{dx} = \pm \int_\gamma dx\, \omega_a \left(\frac{d\tilde{\varphi}_a}{dx}\right)^2, \qquad (14.37)$$

where we have diagonalized the matrix η, i.e.

$$\eta = \Lambda^T \eta^D \Lambda; \qquad \Lambda^T \Lambda = \mathbf{1}; \qquad \eta^D_{ab} = \omega_a \delta_{ab}; \qquad \omega_a > 0 \quad (14.38)$$

and have assumed that the eigenvalues of η are all positive, and have defined $\tilde{\varphi}_a = \Lambda_{ab} \varphi_b$. Under the assumption that η is positive definite, one observes that $\mathcal{Q}(\gamma)$ can only vanish if the fields are constant along the whole curve, or in other words, if the curve is just a point. Therefore, the solutions of the self-duality equations cannot start and end on points in the φ-space, where the the pre-potential U has the same value. In fact, there is more to this. As one progresses along the curve, the difference between the value of the pre-potential U at this particular point and at the initial point, only increases in modulus. This means that the curve, that is a solution of the self-duality equations (14.17), climbs the pre-potential U, either upwards or downwards, without ever returning to an altitude that it has already passed through.

14.2.3 A connection with Hamilton-Jacobi equation

For a mechanical system with Hamiltonian $H = H(\varphi_a, p_a, t)$, where φ_a and p_a are the canonical coordinates in phase space, the Hamilton-Jacobi equation is given by

$$H\left(\varphi_a, \frac{\partial S}{\partial \varphi_a}, t\right) + \frac{\partial S}{\partial t} = 0 \qquad (14.39)$$

with S being Hamilton's principal function, which is related to the momenta by

$$p_a = \frac{\partial S}{\partial \varphi_a} \qquad (14.40)$$

The Euler-Lagrange equations associated to the static energy functional (14.18) are given by

$$\eta_{ab} \partial_x^2 \varphi_b = \frac{\partial V}{\partial \varphi_a} \qquad a, b = 1, 2, \ldots r \qquad (14.41)$$

One can interpret such an equation as the Newton equation for a particle, of unit mass, moving in a r-dimensional φ-space with metric η, with time being the x coordinate, and under the action of an inverted potential, i.e.

$$\tilde{V} \to -V \qquad\qquad x \to t \qquad (14.42)$$

Identifying the pre-potential U with Hamilton's principal function up to a sign, i.e. $S \equiv \pm U$, one then gets the relation (14.19) can be written as

$$\frac{1}{2} \eta_{ab}^{-1} \frac{\delta S}{\delta \varphi_a} \frac{\delta S}{\delta \varphi_b} + \tilde{V} = 0 \qquad (14.43)$$

But that is just the Hamilton-Jacobi equation (14.39) for the Hamiltonian

$$H = \frac{1}{2} \eta_{ab}^{-1} p_a p_b + \tilde{V}(q) \qquad (14.44)$$

as we are assuming the that U, and so S, does not depend upon time, i.e. x. In its turn, the self-duality equations (14.17) become just the kinematical relation between momenta and velocities

$$\dot{\varphi}_a = \eta_{ab}^{-1} p_b \qquad (14.45)$$

The Lagragian associated to the Hamiltonian (14.44) is

$$L = \frac{1}{2} \eta_{ab} \dot{\varphi}_a \dot{\varphi}_b - \tilde{V}(\varphi) \qquad (14.46)$$

Note also that the topological charge (14.15) takes the form of an action

$$Q = \pm \int_{-\infty}^{\infty} dt\, p_a \dot{\varphi}_a \qquad (14.47)$$

The Hamilton-Jacobi equation (14.43) (see (14.39)) implies that the Hamiltonian vanishes, i.e.

$$H = 0 \qquad \rightarrow \qquad -2\tilde{V} = \eta_{ab}^{-1} p_a p_b = p_a \dot{\varphi}_a \qquad (14.48)$$

and so we can write

$$Q = \pm \int_{-\infty}^{\infty} dt \left[p_a \dot{\varphi}_a - H \right] \qquad (14.49)$$

The static energy (14.18) becomes

$$E = \int_{-\infty}^{\infty} dt \left[\frac{1}{2} \eta_{ab} \dot{\varphi}_a \dot{\varphi}_b - \tilde{V}(\varphi) \right] = \int_{-\infty}^{\infty} dt \left[H - 2\tilde{V}(\varphi) \right] = \pm Q \qquad (14.50)$$

Therefore, we have a mechanical system of a particle in d dimensions, and the BPS solutions correspond to solutions of such a system where the energy, measured by H, vanishes. The Hamilton-Jacobi equation leads to the equality of the static energy, measured by E, to the topological charge Q. The BPS equation itself is just the kinematical relation between velocities and momenta.

14.3 Lumps in $(2+1)$-dimensions

As an example of a theory with self-dual sector we shall consider the CP^{N-1} model in $(2+1)$-dimensions. CP^{N-1} is the $N-1$ dimensional complex projective space, i.e. the space of all equivalent classes of complex vectors $z = (z_1, z_2, \ldots z_N)$, such that two vectors z and z' are equivalent if $z' = \lambda z$, with λ being a complex number [16, 17]. We shall take the representatives of such classes to be the unit vectors

$$z = (z_1, z_2, \ldots z_N) \qquad\qquad z_a^* z_a = 1 \qquad (14.51)$$

CP^{N-1} is isomorphic to the hermitian symmetric space $SU(N)/SU(N-1) \otimes U(1)$. Indeed, $SU(N)$ acts transitively on the vectors z through its defining N-dimensional representation. As such representation is unitary its action preserves the modulus of the vectors z, and a given vector, let us say $z = (0, 0, \ldots 1)$, is left invariant by $(N-1) \times (N-1)$ unitary matrices, i.e. the subgroup $U(N-1) = SU(N-1) \otimes U(1)$. The isometry subgroup of any other vector z is isomorphic to $SU(N-1) \otimes U(1)$.

The second homotopy group of CP^{N-1} is isomorphic to the integers under addition, i.e. $\pi_2(SU(N)/SU(N-1) \otimes U(1)) = \mathbb{Z}$. The corresponding topological charge has an integral representation given by

$$Q = \frac{1}{2\pi} \int d^2x \, \varepsilon_{\mu\nu} \partial_\mu A_\nu \qquad (14.52)$$

with
$$A_\mu = \frac{i}{2}\left(z^\dagger \partial_\mu z - \partial_\mu z^\dagger z\right) \tag{14.53}$$

and where the integration in (14.52) is on the two dimensional plane (x_1, x_2), which by identifying the spatial infinity becomes isomorphic to S^2. Under the local phase transformation $z \to e^{i\alpha} z$, we have that $A_\mu \to A_\mu - \partial_\mu \alpha$. Introducing the covariant derivative $D_\mu \equiv \partial_\mu + i A_\mu$, we can write (14.52) as

$$Q = \frac{i}{2\pi} \int d^2x\, \varepsilon_{\mu\nu} \left(D_\mu z\right)^\dagger D_\nu z = \frac{1}{4\pi} \int d^2x \left[\left(D_\mu z\right)^\dagger i\varepsilon_{\mu\nu} D_\nu z + \left(i\varepsilon_{\mu\nu} D_\nu z\right)^\dagger D_\mu z\right] \tag{14.54}$$

Following (14.9) we define the quantities

$$\mathscr{A}_\mu^a = \left(D_\mu z\right)_b k_{ba} \qquad \widetilde{\mathscr{A}}_\mu^a = \left(k_{ab}^{-1}\right)^* i\varepsilon_{\mu\nu} \left(D_\nu z\right)_b \tag{14.55}$$

and so, the charge (14.54) can be written in the form (14.1). From (14.10) the self-duality equations are given by

$$\left(D_\mu z\right)_b h_{ba} = \pm i\, \varepsilon_{\mu\nu} \left(D_\nu z\right)_a \tag{14.56}$$

According to (14.12), the energy functional becomes

$$E = \frac{1}{2} \int d^2x \left[\left(D_\mu z\right)_a^* h_{ab} \left(D_\mu z\right)_b + \left(D_\mu z\right)_a^* h_{ab}^{-1} \left(D_\mu z\right)_b\right] \tag{14.57}$$

Note however, that by contracting both sides of (14.56) with $\varepsilon_{\rho\mu}$, one gets

$$\left(D_\mu z\right)_a = \pm i\, \varepsilon_{\mu\nu} \left(D_\nu z\right)_b h_{ba} \tag{14.58}$$

Therefore, (14.56) and (14.58) imply

$$\left(D_\mu z\right)_b \left(h_{ba} - h_{ba}^{-1}\right) = 0 \quad \to \quad h^2 = \mathbb{1} \tag{14.59}$$

But an hermitian matrix can be diagonalized by an unitary transformation, $h = U h_D U^\dagger$, with h_D diagonal. Therefore

$$h^2 = \mathbb{1} \quad \to \quad h_D^2 = \mathbb{1} \tag{14.60}$$

and so the square of the eigenvalues of h have to be unity, i.e. $\lambda_a^2 = 1$. But in order for the energy E, given in (14.57), to be positive definite, we need all the eigenvalues of h to have the same sign. Consequently, we have that

$$h = \mathbb{1} \tag{14.61}$$

In such case, (14.56) reduces to the self-duality equation for the usual CP^{N-1} model [16, 17]

$$\left(D_\mu z\right)_a = \pm i\, \varepsilon_{\mu\nu} \left(D_\nu z\right)_a \tag{14.62}$$

and (14.57) to the energy of the usual CP^{N-1} model

$$E = \int d^2x \, (D_\mu z)^\dagger \, D_\mu z \tag{14.63}$$

In order to construct the self-dual solutions for (14.62), it is better to introduce the complex fields u_a as

$$(u_1, u_2, \ldots u_{N-1}, 1) = \frac{1}{z_N}(z_1, z_2 \ldots, z_{N-1}, z_N) \tag{14.64}$$

One could have divided the vector of complex fields z, by any other component z_a, and the construction would be equivalent. It then follows that the covariant derivative becomes

$$\begin{aligned}(D_\mu z)_\alpha &= z_N \Omega_{\alpha\beta} \, \partial_\mu u_\beta; \qquad \alpha, \beta = 1, 2, \ldots N-1 \\ (D_\mu z)_N &= -z_N \frac{u^\dagger \partial_\mu u}{1 + u^\dagger u}\end{aligned} \tag{14.65}$$

with

$$\Omega_{\alpha\beta} = \delta_{\alpha\beta} - \frac{u_\alpha u_\beta^*}{1 + u^\dagger u}; \qquad \alpha, \beta = 1, 2, \ldots N-1 \tag{14.66}$$

Therefore, the self duality equations (14.62) become

$$\begin{aligned}\left[D_\mu z \mp i\varepsilon_{\mu\nu} D_\nu z\right]_\alpha &= z_N \Omega_{\alpha\beta} \left[\partial_\mu u_\beta \mp i\varepsilon_{\mu\nu} \partial_\nu u_\beta\right]; \qquad \alpha, \beta = 1, 2, \ldots N-1 \\ \left[D_\mu z \mp i\varepsilon_{\mu\nu} D_\nu z\right]_N &= -z_N \frac{u_\beta^*}{1 + u^\dagger u}\left[\partial_\mu u_\beta \mp i\varepsilon_{\mu\nu} \partial_\nu u_\beta\right]\end{aligned} \tag{14.67}$$

Therefore, the self duality equations (14.62) imply that

$$\partial_\mu u_\alpha = \pm i \varepsilon_{\mu\nu} \partial_\nu u_\alpha; \qquad \alpha = 1, 2, \ldots N-1 \tag{14.68}$$

These are Cauchy-Riemann equations for the u-fields. Indeed, the upper sign (+) implies that u is holomorphic, i.e. $u_\beta = u_\beta(w)$, and the lower sign (−) that u is anti-holomorphic, i.e. $u_\beta = u_\beta(w^*)$, where $w = x_1 + i x_2$.

14.4 Monopoles in $(3+1)$-dimensions

We now consider the case of the topological magnetic charge defined by the integral over the three dimensional space $\mathbb{R}^3$

$$Q_M = -\frac{1}{2}\int_{\mathbb{R}^3} d^3x \, \varepsilon_{ijk} \text{Tr}(F_{ij} D_k \Phi) = \int_{\mathbb{R}^3} d^3x \, \text{Tr}(B_i D_i \Phi) \tag{14.69}$$

where $B_i = -\frac{1}{2}\varepsilon_{ijk}F_{jk}$ is the non-abelian magnetic field, $F_{ij} = \partial_i A_j - \partial_j A_i + ie[A_i, A_j] = F_{ij}^a T_a$, is the field tensor, $A_i = A_i^a T_a$, the gauge field, and $\Phi = \Phi_a T_a$, the Higgs field in the adjoint representation of a simple, compact, Lie group G, with generators T_a, $a = 1, 2, \ldots \dim G$. In addition, $D_i* = \partial_i * + ie[A_i, *]$ is the covariant derivative in the adjoint representation of G.

In this case all the fields are real and so, following (14.10) and the results of [18], we introduce the real quantities

$$\mathscr{A}_a \equiv B_i^b\, k_{ba}; \qquad \widetilde{\mathscr{A}}_a \equiv k_{ab}^{-1}(D_i\Phi)^b \qquad (14.70)$$

and so (14.69) can be written as in (14.1). The self-duality equations (14.10) become

$$\frac{1}{2}\varepsilon_{ijk}F_{jk}^b\, h_{ba} = \pm (D_i\Phi)^a \qquad h = k\,k^T \qquad (14.71)$$

with h_{ab}, $a, b = 1, 2, \ldots \dim G$, a symmetric invertible matrix of scalar fields. The equations (14.71) constitute a generalization of the so-called BPS (Bogomolny-Prasad-Sommerfiled) equations [12, 13] for self-dual monopoles. The energy functional (14.12) becomes [18]

$$E_{YMH} = \int d^3x \left[\frac{1}{4} h_{ab} F_{ij}^a F_{ij}^b + \frac{1}{2} h_{ab}^{-1}(D_i\Phi)^a(D_i\Phi)^b\right] \qquad (14.72)$$

We then have a theory with gauge fields A_μ, Higgs field Φ in the adjoint representation of the gauge group G, and $[\dim G(\dim G+1)/2]$ real scalars fields assembled in the real, symmetric and invertible matrix h. The self-duality equations (14.71) imply not only the static Euler-Lagrange equations associated to the gauge and Higgs fields, but also the ones associated to the scalar fields h_{ab}.

The energy (14.72) evaluated on the self-dual solutions of (14.71) is equal to the magnetic charge

$$E_{YMH} = Q_M \qquad (14.73)$$

Under a gauge transformation $A_\mu \to g A_\mu g^{-1} + \frac{i}{e}\partial_\mu g\, g^{-1}$, we have that $F_{\mu\nu} \to g F_{\mu\nu} g^{-1}$ and $D_\mu \Phi \to g D_\mu \Phi g^{-1}$. Therefore, energy (14.72) and the self-duality equations (14.71) are invariant under

$$\begin{aligned} F_{\mu\nu}^a &\to d_{ab}(g) F_{\mu\nu}^b; \qquad (D_\mu\Phi)^a \to d_{ab}(g)(D_\mu\Phi)^b \\ h_{ab} &\to d_{ac}(g) d_{bd}(g) h_{cd} \end{aligned} \qquad (14.74)$$

where $d(g)$ are the matrices of the adjoint representation of the gauge group

$$g\, T_a\, g^{-1} = T_b\, d_{ba}(g) \qquad (14.75)$$

Due to the introduction of the extra scalar fields h_{ab}, the system described above has plenty of self-dual solutions. Using a spherically symmetric ansatz one can show in fact that the usual 't Hooft-Polyakov monopole [19, 20] becomes a self-dual solution with a particular configuration of the h-fields. The system above is also conformally invariant in the three dimensional space $\mathbb{R}^3$. Using an ansatz based on such conformal symmetry one construct solutions with toroidal magnetic fields and vanishing magnetic charge. For more details on such results we refer to [18].

14.5 Skyrmions in $(3+1)$-dimensions

Skyrmions are topological soliton solutions of theories in (3+1)-dimensions with target space being the group $SU(2)$. The three fields in $SU(2)$ are interpreted as the three pions π^+, π^0 and π^-. Such type solutions are interpreted, following a proposal of Skyrme [21, 22], as nuclei and the topological charge plays the role of the baryonic number [1, 2].

The relevant topological charge in this case is given by the integral over the three dimensional space $\mathbb{R}^3$

$$Q_B = \frac{i}{48\pi^2} \int d^3x \, K(U) \, \varepsilon_{ijk} \widehat{\text{Tr}}(R_i R_j R_k) \tag{14.76}$$

with $R_i = i\,\partial_i U \, U^\dagger = R_i^a \, T_a$, $U \in SU(2)$, and $K(U)$ is an arbitrary real functional of the chiral fields U, but not of their derivatives. K can be thought as a deformation of the metric on the target space $SU(2)$. We use the notation $\widehat{\text{Tr}}(T_a T_b) = \delta_{ab}$, with T_a, $a = 1, 2, 3$, being the generators of the Lie algebra of $SU(2)$.

We now discuss some Skyrme type models with exact self-dual sectors. In all cases the fields are real.

14.5.1 The BPS Skyrme model

Following (14.1) we introduce the real quantities

$$\mathcal{A}_\alpha \equiv \frac{\lambda}{24} \varepsilon_{ijk} \widehat{\text{Tr}}(R_i R_j R_k); \qquad \widetilde{\mathcal{A}}_\alpha \equiv K = \mu\sqrt{V} \tag{14.77}$$

where λ and μ are coupling constants, and V plays the role of the potential. Then one observes that (14.77) can be written in the form (14.1). The self-duality equations (14.3) become

$$\frac{\lambda}{24} \varepsilon_{ijk} \widehat{\text{Tr}}(R_i R_j R_k) = \pm\mu\sqrt{V} \tag{14.78}$$

The energy functional (14.5) becomes

$$E = \int d^3x \left[\frac{\lambda^2}{24^2} B_i B_i + \mu^2 V \right] \tag{14.79}$$

with $B_i = \varepsilon_{ijk}\widehat{\mathrm{Tr}}(R_i R_j R_k)$. Such a model was proposed in [23] and has been applied in many contexts including nuclear physics and neutron stars [24, 25, 26]. The solutions of (14.78) have been constructed using a spherically symmetric ansatz, for the potential $V = \mathrm{Tr}(1-U)/2$, and they are of the compacton type, i.e. the fields go zero for a finite value of the radial distance.

14.5.2 A special self-dual Skyrme model

Let us denote

$$A_i = i\widehat{\mathrm{Tr}}(\partial_i U U^\dagger T_3); \qquad H_{ij} = \partial_i A_j - \partial_j A_i = i\widehat{\mathrm{Tr}}([\partial_i U U^\dagger, \partial_j U U^\dagger] T_3) \qquad (14.80)$$

with $U \in SU(2)$. Writing $R_i = i\,\partial_i U U^\dagger = R_i^a T_a$, we have that

$$\varepsilon_{ijk} A_i H_{jk} = 2\varepsilon_{ijk} R_i^1 R_j^2 R_k^3 = -i\frac{2}{3}\varepsilon_{ijk}\widehat{\mathrm{Tr}}(R_i R_j R_k) \qquad (14.81)$$

Taking $K = -4$, we can write (14.76) as

$$Q_B = \frac{1}{4\pi^2}\int d^3x\, A_i B_i \qquad (14.82)$$

with

$$B_i = \frac{1}{2}\varepsilon_{ijk} H_{jk} \qquad (14.83)$$

We now introduce the real quantities

$$\mathscr{A}_\alpha \equiv m_0 f A_i; \qquad \widetilde{\mathscr{A}}_\alpha \equiv \frac{1}{e_0 f} B_i \qquad (14.84)$$

where m_0 and e_0 are coupling constants. Then we can write (14.82), up to a constant, in the same form as (14.1). The self-duality equations (14.3) become

$$m_0 e_0 f^2 A_i = \pm B_i \qquad (14.85)$$

and the energy functional (14.5) becomes

$$E = \frac{1}{2}\int d^3x\left[m_0^2 f^2 A_i^2 + \frac{1}{e_0^2 f^2} B_i^2\right] \qquad (14.86)$$

Such a theory was first proposed in [7] for the case $f = 1$, and then generalized in [8] for an arbitrary real function f. The theory with $f = 1$ does not possess finite energy solutions in $\mathbb{R}^3$ due to an argument by Chandrasekhar [27] in the context of force free fields in magnetohydrodynamics. However, exact solutions have been constructed in [7] for the case where the three dimensional space is the three sphere S^3.

The self-duality equations (14.85) and the energy (14.86) are conformally invariant in $\mathbb{R}^3$, and this fact was used in [8] to build a conformal ansatz based on the toroidal coordinates

$$x^1 = \frac{a}{p}\sqrt{z}\cos\varphi; \qquad x^2 = \frac{a}{p}\sqrt{z}\sin\varphi; \qquad x^3 = \frac{a}{p}\sqrt{1-z}\sin\xi \qquad (14.87)$$

where

$$p = 1 - \sqrt{1-z}\cos\xi \qquad 0 \le z \le 1 \qquad 0 \le \varphi, \xi \le 2\pi \qquad (14.88)$$

Parameterizing the $SU(2)$ group elements as

$$U = \begin{pmatrix} Z_2 & iZ_1 \\ iZ_1^* & Z_2^* \end{pmatrix}; \qquad |Z_1|^2 + |Z_2|^2 = 1 \qquad (14.89)$$

the vector A_i, introduced in (14.80), can be written as

$$A_\mu = \frac{i}{2}\left(Z_a^*\partial_\mu Z_a - Z_a\partial_\mu Z_a^*\right) \qquad (14.90)$$

The conformal ansatz corresponds to

$$Z_1 = \sqrt{F(z)}\,e^{in\varphi} \qquad Z_2 = \sqrt{1-F(z)}\,e^{im\xi} \qquad (14.91)$$

with m and n being integers. The self-duality equations (14.85) are solved by the functions

$$F = \frac{m^2 z}{m^2 z + n^2(1-z)} \qquad f^2 = \frac{2p}{m_0 e_0 a}\frac{|mn|}{[m^2 z + n^2(1-z)]} \qquad (14.92)$$

The energy and the topological charge evaluated on such solutions are

$$E = 4\pi^2 \frac{m_0}{e_0}|mn|; \qquad Q = -mn \qquad (14.93)$$

We then have an infinite number of exact solutions, and they correspond to special types of self-dual Skyrmions with target space $S^3 \equiv SU(2)$. Due to the conformal symmetry the solutions do not have a fixed size. For more details we refer to [8].

14.5.3 A more general self-dual Skyrme model

Using the fact that the quantites $R_i = i\,\partial_i U\,U^\dagger = R_i^a\,T_a$, satisfy the Maurer-Cartan equation

$$\partial_\mu R_\nu - \partial_\nu R_\mu + i\left[R_\mu, R_\nu\right] = 0 \qquad (14.94)$$

we can write the topological charge (14.76), for $K=1$, as

$$Q_B = \frac{i}{96\pi^2}\int d^3x\, \varepsilon_{ijk}\widehat{\text{Tr}}(R_i\,[R_j,R_k]) = -\frac{1}{96\pi^2}\int d^3x\, \varepsilon_{ijk}\widehat{\text{Tr}}(R_i\,(\partial_j R_k-\partial_k R_j))$$

$$= -\frac{1}{48\pi^2}\int d^3x\, \varepsilon_{ijk}R_i^a\,\partial_j R_k^a \equiv -\frac{1}{48\pi^2}\frac{e_0}{m_0}\int d^3x\, \mathscr{A}_i^a\,\widetilde{\mathscr{A}}_i^a \qquad (14.95)$$

where we have introduced the real quantities

$$\mathscr{A}_i^a \equiv m_0 R_i^b\, k_{ba}\,; \qquad\qquad \widetilde{\mathscr{A}}_i^a \equiv \frac{1}{e_0} k_{ab}^{-1}\varepsilon_{ijk}\,\partial_j R_k^b \qquad (14.96)$$

where k_{ab} is some invertible matrix, and m_0 and e_0 are coupling constants. Therefore, the topological charge (14.76), for $K=1$, can be written in the same form as (14.1). The self-duality equations (14.3) become

$$\lambda\, h_{ab}\, R_i^b = \frac{1}{2}\varepsilon_{ijk} H_{jk}^a \qquad \text{with} \qquad \lambda = \pm m_0\, e_0 \qquad (14.97)$$

where $h = k\, k^T$ is a real, symmetric and invertible matrix, and where we have denoted

$$H_{ij}^a = \partial_i R_j^a - \partial_j R_i^a = \varepsilon_{abc}\, R_\mu^b\, R_\nu^c \qquad (14.98)$$

The energy functional (14.5) becomes

$$E = \int d^3x \left[\frac{m_0^2}{2} h_{ab}\, R_i^a\, R_i^b + \frac{1}{4 e_0^2} h_{ab}^{-1} H_{ij}^a\, H_{ij}^b\right] \qquad (14.99)$$

The energy evaluated on the self-dual solutions of (14.97) is given by

$$E = 48\pi^2\, \frac{m_0}{e_0}\, |Q| \qquad (14.100)$$

Such a theory was proposed in [9] and further explored in [10]. The entries of the matrix h_{ab} are considered as six real scalar fields added to the theory. Note that for $h = \mathbb{1}$ the model reduces to the original Skyrme model [21, 22]. The topological charge (14.95) is interpreted, following Skyrme, as the baryon number. More recently such a model was extended by treating a fractional power of the density of the topological charge as an order parameter to describe a fluid of baryonic matter [11]. Such an extension has lead to a very interesting application to nuclear theory. The model describes with quite good accuracy the binding energies per nucleon of more than 240 nuclei, and also the relation between their radii and baryon number.

The important results of [10] are: *i)* the first order self-duality equations (14.97) imply the nine static second order Euler-Lagrange equations associated to fields U and h_{ab}, *ii)* the static Euler-Lagrange equations associated to the fields h_{ab} are equivalent to the self-duality equations, *iii)* given a configuration for the U-fields one can solve the self-duality equations by taking h_{ab} to be

$$h = \frac{\sqrt{\det \tau}}{m_0 \, e_0} \, \tau^{-1}; \qquad \text{with} \qquad \tau_{ab} = R_i^a \, R_i^b \qquad (14.101)$$

So, the fields h_{ab} are spectators in the sense that they adjust themselves to solve the self-duality equations for any configuration of the U-fields. Note that the matrix τ is similar to the Skyrme model strain tensor [1]. For U-field configurations where τ is singular the matrix h_{ab} still solves the self-duality equation but it is not completely determined by U, and have some arbitrary components [10]. The theory (14.99) is conformally invariant in the three dimensional space $\mathbb{R}^3$ and that plays an important role in the properties of the model. Exact solutions to the self-duality equations (14.97) have been constructed in [10] using an holomorphic ansatz, and also a toroidal ansatz based on the conformal symmetry. For more details about these results we refer to [9, 10, 11].

14.6 Instantons in four Euclidean dimensions

As a last example of applications of the methods described in Section 14.1 we just mention the case of instanton solutions of Yang-Mills theory in four Euclidean dimensions. The relevant topological charge in this case is the Pontryagin number

$$Q_{YM} = \int d^4x \, \text{Tr}\left(F_{\mu\nu} \widetilde{F}^{\mu\nu}\right) \qquad (14.102)$$

with $F_{\mu\nu}$ being the filed tensor and $\widetilde{F}_{\mu\nu}$ its Hodge dual, i.e.

$$F_{\mu\nu} = \partial_\mu A_\nu - \partial_\nu A_\mu + i \, e \, [A_\mu, A_\nu]; \qquad \widetilde{F}_{\mu\nu} = \frac{1}{2} \varepsilon_{\mu\nu\rho\sigma} F^{\rho\sigma} \qquad (14.103)$$

and A_μ being the gauge potential for a compact Lie group G. Following (14.1) we denote

$$\mathcal{A}_\alpha \equiv F_{\mu\nu}; \qquad \widetilde{\mathcal{A}}_\alpha \equiv \widetilde{F}_{\mu\nu} \qquad (14.104)$$

The self-duality equations (14.3) become

$$F_{\mu\nu} = \pm \widetilde{F}_{\mu\nu} \qquad (14.105)$$

and the functional (14.5) becomes the Yang-Mills Euclidean action

$$S_{YM} = \frac{1}{8} \int d^4x \, \left[\text{Tr}\left(F_{\mu\nu} F_{\mu\nu}\right) + \text{Tr}\left(\widetilde{F}_{\mu\nu} \widetilde{F}_{\mu\nu}\right)\right] = \frac{1}{4} \int d^4x \, \text{Tr}\left(F_{\mu\nu} F_{\mu\nu}\right) \qquad (14.106)$$

where we have used the fact that $\text{Tr}\left(F_{\mu\nu} F_{\mu\nu}\right) = \text{Tr}\left(\widetilde{F}_{\mu\nu} \widetilde{F}_{\mu\nu}\right)$.

The solutions of (14.105) are the well known instanton solution of Euclidean Yang-Mills theory, and they plays an important role in the structure of the vacua and also on non-perturbative phenomena in Yang-Mills theory [15, 1].

Following (14.9) one could introduce a real, symmetric and invertible matrix h_{ab} into the self-duality equations (14.105) as $F^b_{\mu\nu} h_{ba} = \pm \widetilde{F}^a_{\mu\nu}$, with $F_{\mu\nu} = F^a_{\mu\nu} T_a$, and $\widetilde{F}_{\mu\nu} = \widetilde{F}^a_{\mu\nu} T_a$, and T_a, $a = 1, 2, \ldots \dim G$, being a basis for the Lie algebra of the gauge group G. However, due to arguments similar to those used (14.58)-(14.61), one can show that such a matrix h has to be the unity matrix [28].

Acknowledgements

The author is supported by Fundação de Amparo à Pesquisa do Estado de São Paulo (FAPESP) (contract 2022/00808-7), and Conselho Nacional de Desenvolvimento Científico e Tecnológico - CNPq (contract 307833/2022-4).

Bibliography

[1] N.S. Manton and P. Sutcliffe, *Topological Solitons* (Cambridge University Press, Cambridge, 2004).

[2] Yakov M. Shnir, *Topological and Non-Topological Solitons in Scalar Field Theories* (Cambridge University Press, Cambridge, 2018).

[3] Ya. M. Shnir, *Magnetic monopoles* (Springer, 2005).

[4] C. Adam, L. A. Ferreira, E. da Hora, A. Wereszczynski, and W. J. Zakrzewski, *Some aspects of self-duality and generalised BPS theories*, JHEP **08**, 062 (2013).

[5] L. A. Ferreira, P. Klimas, and Wojtek J. Zakrzewski, *Self-dual sectors for scalar field theories in (1 + 1) dimensions*, JHEP **01**, 020, (2019).

[6] L. A. Ferreira, P. Klimas, A. Wereszczynski, and W. J. Zakrzewski, *Some Comments on BPS systems*, J. Phys. A **52**, 315201, (2019).

[7] L. A. Ferreira and Wojtek J. Zakrzewski, *A Skyrme-like model with an exact BPS bound* JHEP **09**, 097, (2013).

[8] L. A. Ferreira and Ya. Shnir' *Exact Self-Dual Skyrmions*, Phys. Lett. B **772**, 621 (2017).

[9] L. A. Ferreira, *Exact self-duality in a modified Skyrme model*, JHEP **07**, 039 (2017).

[10] L. A. Ferreira and L. R. Livramento, *Self-Duality in the Context of the Skyrme Model*, JHEP **09**, 031 (2020).

[11] L. A. Ferreira and L. R. Livramento, *A False Vacuum Skyrme Model for Nuclear Matter*, J. Phys. G **49**, 115102 (2022).

[12] E. B. Bogomolny, *Stability of Classical Solutions*, Sov. J. Nucl. Phys. **24**, 449 (1976).

[13] M. K. Prasad and Charles M. Sommerfield, *An Exact Classical Solution for the 't Hooft Monopole and the Julia-Zee Dyon*, Phys. Rev. Lett. **35**, 760 (1975).

[14] Alexander M. Polyakov and A. A. Belavin, *Metastable States of Two-Dimensional Isotropic Ferromagnets*, JETP Lett. **22**, 245 (1975).

[15] A. A. Belavin, Alexander M. Polyakov, A. S. Schwartz, and Yu. S. Tyupkin, *Pseudoparticle Solutions of the Yang-Mills Equations*, Phys. Lett. B **59**, 85 (1975).

[16] A. D'Adda, M. Luscher, and P. Di Vecchia, *A 1/n Expandable Series of Nonlinear Sigma Models with Instantons*, Nucl. Phys. B **146**, 63 (1978).

[17] W. J. Zakrzewski, *Low Dimensional Sigma Models* (Adam Hilger, Bristol and Philadelphia, 1989).

[18] L. A. Ferreira and H. Malavazzi, *Generalized self-duality for the Yang-Mills-Higgs system*, Phys. Rev. D **104**, 105016 (2021).

[19] Gerard 't Hooft, *Magnetic Monopoles in Unified Gauge Theories*, Nucl. Phys. B **79**, 276 (1974).

[20] Alexander M. Polyakov, *Particle Spectrum in the Quantum Field Theory*, JETP Lett. **20**, 194 (1974).

[21] T. H. R. Skyrme, *A Nonlinear field theory*, Proc. Roy. Soc. A **260**, 127 (1961).

[22] T. H. R. Skyrme *A Unified Field Theory of Mesons and Baryons*, Nucl. Phys. **31**, 556 (1962).

[23] C. Adam, J. Sanchez-Guillen, and A. Wereszczynski, *A Skyrme-type proposal for baryonic matter*, Phys. Lett. B **691**, 105 (2010).

[24] C. Adam, J. Sanchez-Guillen, and A. Wereszczynski, *A BPS Skyrme model and baryons at large N_c*, Phys. Rev. D **82**, 085015 (2010).

[25] C. Adam, C. Naya, J. Sanchez-Guillen, and A. Wereszczynski, *Bogomol'nyi-Prasad-Sommerfield Skyrme Model and Nuclear Binding Energies* Phys. Rev. Lett. **111**, 232501 (2013).

[26] C. Adam, C. Naya, J. Sanchez-Guillen, R. Vazquez, and A. Wereszczynski, *BPS Skyrmions as neutron stars*, Phys. Lett. B **742**, 136 (2015).

[27] S. Chandrasekhar, *Hydrodynamic and hydromagnetic stability* (Dover, New York, 1981).

[28] H. Malavazzi. *Private communication.*

15

Introducing braids, knots, and links

R. da Rocha

Abstract: Elementary group theory, knots and links are introduced, with the presentation of the braid group generators and free groups. The formulation of a finite number of identical particles in quantum mechanics in this setup is presented and addressed. The Artin's braid groups, braid statistics, and Reidemeister moves are also reported.

15.1 Introduction

Braids, knots, and links have been pervading an increasing interest in the layer between mathematics and physics, since the third last century [1, 2, 3]. Knot theory is an intricate mathematical formalism, related to low-dimensional topology. The formalism of knots was first introduced and developed in 1771 by Vandermonde, who attributed topological features to the geometrical properties of knots [4]. Knots were more formally investigated by Gauss, who introduced in 1833 the Gauss linking integral for computing the linking number associated with two knots. Gauss supervised Listing, whom the 8-knot had been named after, which is also called the Listing's knot. In 1867, motivated by experiments and investigations about toric rings emerging from smoke, developed by Tait, Thomson (namely, Lord Kelvin) proposed the description of atoms by knots of whirl vortexes [5]. Helmholtz had inspired Tait, implementing the foundations of the dynamics of vortexes in inviscid incompressible fluid flows [7, 8]. Maxwell, already a well-established scientist, and a workmate and long-life friend of both Tait and Thomson, also developed a deep interest in knot theory, studying Listing's work on knots. Maxwell, motivated by the applications of the knot theory in electromagnetism, analyzed Helmholtz's manuscripts on vortexes and knots, proposing a physical meaning to the Gauss linking integral, stating a particular case of what today is known as Ampère's law: an electric current induced on a knot yields a magnetic field. The linking number, on the other hand, was proposed to describe the net work done by a charged particle, which moves along a second knot. Maxwell also investigated smoke ring vortexes, modeling them by three Borromean rings.

The keen interest in knot theory is also a consequence of an increasing appreciation of the huge importance and the prominent role of topological and algebraic properties in physical phenomena. On the other hand, it emerges from the discovery of a a rather unanticipated relationship involving knots and algebraic theory, comprising von Neumann operator algebras. Non-commutative geometry naturally arising from those algebras is related to deep mathematical structures defining quantum groups. The chain uniting these concepts involves the solubility of some lattice models in statistical mechanics and the integrability of at first Schrödinger differential equations, both yielding the algebraic condition underlying the Yang-Baxter equation [9]. Braids were first studied by Artin [10] and comprise highly intuitive groups, having an intimate relationship with knots and links. Topologists in the early part of the 20th century, including for instance Dehn and Alexander, studied knots from the knot group point of view, and from invariants appearing in homology theory, such as the Alexander polynomial for the two trefoil knots. Dehn also developed a procedure called Dehn surgery, which relates knots to the 3-manifolds theory, also formulating the Dehn problems in the group theory setup, like the word problem. More precisely, given a 3-manifold whose boundary is made of 2-tori, one can glue in one solid torus by a homeomorphism of its boundary to each of the torus boundary components of the original 3-manifold. There are several inequivalent ways of doing this, in general. This process is called Dehn filling. Dehn surgery on a 3-manifold which contains a link consists of drilling out a tubular neighborhood of the link, together with Dehn filling on all the components of the boundary corresponding to the link. The work of Alexander consisted of a pioneering approach to studying topological invariants of knots and links [11]. Alexander and Briggs in 1926, and independently Reidemeister in 1927, showed that any two-knot diagrams of the same knot, can be related, up to an isotopy, by a sequence of the three fundamental Reidemeister moves [12, 13]. Thereafter, Witten, Thurston, Jones, and Kontsevich discovered and invented subtle relationships between the classification of knots and links and partition functions of models in statistical mechanics and topological quantum field theory (TQFT) as well, through polynomial invariants. New developments on TQFT unlocked novel possibilities, including models of loop quantum gravity and quantum information theory [14, 15, 16, 18, 19, 20, 21, 23, 24, 25, 26]. One of the relationships between knot theory and quantum gravity resides in the Chern–Simons theory and obtaining link invariants, such as the Jones polynomial, from Yang-Mills theory [29, 30]. Also, knot invariants emerge naturally in gravitational physics, in the connection between knot theory and the loop representation of loop quantum gravity. Ref. [27] used generalized the braid group iteratively, producing new braid representations out of any given one. Besides, Ref. [28] linearized the Artin representation of the braid group given by automorphisms of a free group providing a linear faithful representation of the braid group, with important applications to two-dimensional quantum field theory.

Interest in knot theory from the general mathematical community significantly increased after Jones discovered what is currently known as Jones polynomial, in 1984 [31, 32]. It made other relevant knot polynomials be constructed, such as the HOMFLY, the bracket, and the Kauffman polynomials. Thereafter, Witten in 1988 proposed a new setup for investigating the Jones polynomial, using Feynman path integrals and introducing new notions such as TQFT [22]. Witten's approach to the Jones polynomial yielded new invariants for the classification of 3-manifolds. Concomitantly, other approaches resulted in the Witten–Reshetikhin–Turaev invariants and quantum invariants [33]. In the 1980s, Conway introduced a procedure for unknotting knots [34]. After, in the early 1990s knot invariants encoding the Jones polynomial and its generalizations, called the finite-type invariants, were introduced [35, 36, 37]. These invariants, previously described by classical topological tools, were shown by Kontsevich to be a byproduct of integrating certain algebraic structures [38]. From a more applied and practical point of view, the DNA molecule consists of two polynucleotide strands twisted around each other in a double helix, encoding life. It has several twists in it, as it coils around itself [39]. Polynomial invariants have a pivotal prominence to study the knotting and packing/unpacking of the DNA molecule.

In the current language, the word knot is loosely used for proper knots, links, sometimes braids, and even more general weaving patterns. Fig. 15.1 illustrates the torus knots with a different number of crossing and links. The torus knots are an infinity family of prime knots, encoding an intimate relationship between braids and knots. Given two coprime integers p and q, the torus knot $T_{p,q}$ can be engendered by wrapping a closed loop around the surface of a torus such that it encircles it p times along the latitude and q times along the longitude, defined respectively as the short and the long ways around the torus. A torus knot is trivial if and only if either p or q is equal to ± 1. Torus knots are completely characterized by p and q [40]. They are invertible and chiral. The trefoil knot is equivalent to $T_{3,2}$. In Figs. 15.1 and 15.2, some cases are depicted, respectively in two and three dimensions.

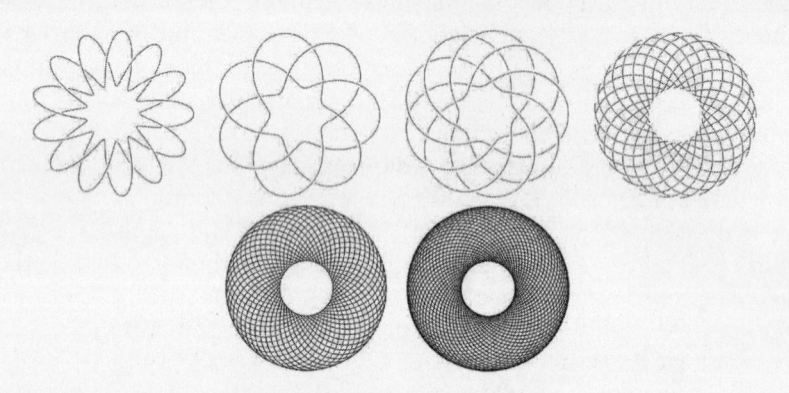

Figure 15.1: Torus knots, with a different number of crossings and links. From left to right: the first plot displays the $T_{2,13}$ torus knot; the second plot is the $T_{3,7}$ torus knot, whereas the third plot regards $T_{5,9}$. The fourth plot shows $T_{11,25}$, the penultimate plot is the $T_{11,25}$ and the last plot illustrates the $T_{41,57}$ torus knot.

Figure 15.2: 3-dimensional torus knots, with different numbers of crossings and links. From left to right: the first plot displays the $T_{2,13}$ torus knot, whereas the second plot regards $T_{3,4}$. The third plot shows $T_{7,10}$ and the fourth plot illustrates the $T_{13,43}$ torus knot.

Knots are closed one-dimensional compact spaces, homeomorphic to loops or families of loops. A is formally defined as any subspace of the Euclidean three-dimensional space E^3 which is topologically equivalent to the circle, which is homeomorphic to a loop. A knot is essentially a circle immersed in E^3, or more technically, a closed curve homeomorphic to the circle. A homeomorphism establishes a topological equivalence between two spaces, being a continuous mapping whose inverse mapping is also continuous. When such a mapping exists between two spaces A and B, all the topological properties of A and B are similar. In particular, A and B have the same dimension. Hence as topological spaces, all knots are topologically equivalent and consist of circles. Two knots, once closed, are equivalent when it is possible to map one to the other by tying and untying, without cutting a strand. The mentioned two knots are distinct when this procedure is not accomplishable. For example, the knot in Fig. 15.3 is trivial, being equivalent to the circle itself, and is called the unknot. However, neither the trefoil nor the 8-knot can be unknotted, and they cannot be transformed into each other.

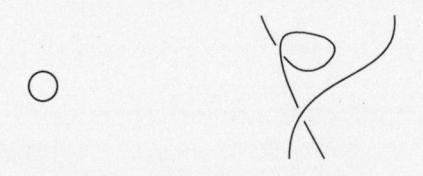

Figure 15.3: The unknot and a trivial knot.

Links are submanifolds of E^3, diffeomorphic to a disjoint union of circles, which compose the link itself. Links can be then seen as collections of knots that can be either interlaced or not. A knot is a link with just one component. Braids are quite well characterized algebraically, as they form groups. They are the best-known weaving patterns, and they permit characterization of links, and therefore knots, as their particular cases. A whole classification of weaving patterns, from carpets to spider webs, therefore results. Braids have many applications in physics. It is thus natural, to begin with them, delving into this fascinating structure.

15.2 Braids and braid groups

Braid groups concern usual braids. One can easily build braids in practice, multiply and invert them, in woven fabrics or even at home with a knitting needle and crochet, which also includes knots and links [41]. Fig. 15.4 displays an example of a 4-braid.

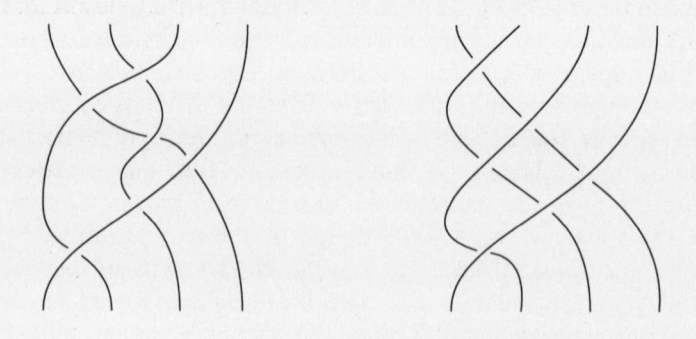

Figure 15.4: Examples of 4-braids.

Given two planes $E^2 \subset \mathbb{R}^3$, with three chosen distinct points on each plane, it suffices to join these points in any way with strings, to come across with a braid. More precisely, let us consider two parallel planes $A, B \subset \mathbb{R}^3$, each one of them containing n distinct points in the sets $\{a_i\}_{i=1}^n$ and $\{b_j\}_{j=1}^n$, respectively. A n-strand braid is a collection of n curves $\{x_k\}_{k=1}^n$ such that 1) each curve x_k has one endpoint, at the set $\{a_i\}$, and another endpoint, at the set $\{b_j\}$; 2) all the x_i are pairwise disjoint; 3) every plane parallel to A and B either intersects each of the x_i at one point or does not intersect at all. Fig. 15.5 depicts some simple threads of 3-strands. Plot 15.5d shows a trivial 3-braid, with no interlacing of strands.

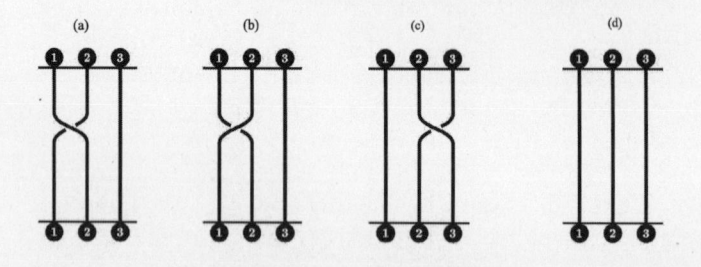

Figure 15.5: Some simple braids of 3-strands.

Both the plots 15.5a and 15.5c illustrate the rudimentary steps of weaving, corresponding to two among the simplest nontrivial braids. By historical convention, strings are considered as going from the top to the bottom. In the drawing the plane E^2 is represented by a line. In the plot 15.5a, the line from the point labeled by 2 to the one labeled by 1 goes down behind that from 1 to 2. Just the opposite occurs in the plot 15.5b. Braids 15.5a and 15.5b are distinct, since they are planar and there should be an additional third dimension for the strings, constituting the braid, either overcross or undercross each other. The trivial braid 15.5d regards the neutral element of multiplication, indicating that the product between it and any other braid yields the same braid. Any braid has an inverse. In particular, the braids 15.5a and 15.5b are straightforwardly verified to be the inverse of each other. Although the very definition of the product between braids, by concatenation, yields associativity, it is non-commutative. One can compare the braid 15.5a to 15.5c; and 15.5d to 15.5b. Any 3-strand braid can be obtained by successive multiplications of the elementary braids 15.5a, 15.5c, and their inverses. Such elementary braids are said to generate the third braid group, denoted by B_3. The procedure of constructing braids as products of elementary braids can be used successively with any arbitrary number of products. Therefore the braid group has infinite order. Braids can be multiplied by downward concatenation. Given two braids A and B, their product AB, denoted here by juxtaposition, is obtained by drawing B below A. Fig. 15.6 shows the product of the previous Fig. 15.5b by itself.

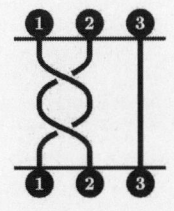

Figure 15.6: Product of the braid 15.5b by itself.

This reasoning can be straightforwardly generalized to the nth braid group, B_n, also known as the Artin braid group, whose elements are braids with n-strands. The elements of the Artin braid group, with group operation given by the composition of braids, are constituted by equivalence classes of n-braids.

It is instructive to compare this point of view, with two copies of the plane E^2 embedded in the Euclidean host space, E^3, to another one, purely restricted to the plane. Let us identify the two planes and consider the braid in Fig. 15.6. Each distinguished point is, ultimately, sent back into itself. Hence, it would appear, at first sight, that it corresponds to the identity, but that is not the case. In fact, the identity element of the B_3 group is represented by 15.5d, and the braid in Fig. 15.6 cannot be unwoven, reducing to it. It can be possible to disentangle it in the E^3 space, nevertheless it cannot be disentangled in E^2. Since every braid is a composition of elementary braids, that would mean that any braid on E^3 can be unbraided, as hair braids, which can be simulated by gluing together their extremities, thereby eliminating one degree of freedom.

Since braids can be unwoven in E^3, the braid group reduces to the symmetric group, and quantum and statistical mechanics in E^3 have the usual formulation. Differences could however appear in the two-dimensional case. Anyhow, from the intrinsic E^2 point of view, what seems to be the identity exhibits infinite possibilities, as it could also be obtained by the composition of any number of the braids in Fig. 15.6. Let us consider again Fig. 15.6, but now as it would be seen when projected on E^2. Entwining in E^3 reduces to oriented exchanges in E^2. The braid 15.5a represents a counterclockwise exchange of points 1 and 2 (Fig. 15.5d). By the braid in Fig. 15.5a, both points come back to their original position. Strings are nevertheless impenetrable and therefore they are forbidden to cross each other. The strings' impenetrability can be simulated by representing each strand by a hole in E^2, a point that is forbidden to any other hole. Repeated multiplication by the braid in Fig. 15.5a leads to paths turning $2, 3, \ldots, n$ times. Each particle sees the others as forbidden points, like holes. All this strongly suggests a relation to the fundamental group of the punctured E^2.

The multiplicity of the identity braid is merely a particular case and would be simply twice the transposition of points 1 and 2. The nth braid group B_n is somehow an extension of the group of permutations, S_n. Mathematicians have several definitions for B_n, the previous configuration space definition allowing, as asserted, the generalization of braid groups on any manifold M. The double exchange of two particles is usually supposed to lead to identity permutation. However, as already discussed, this may be different in two-dimensional spaces. Once defined, a few basic properties regarding braids need then to be exposed, such as what it means for two braids to be equivalent and that braids form a group under the operation of composition, called the Artin braid group. Such a prominent group can be defined using simple generators and relations, presenting relevant algebraic properties.

Permutation groups can be then introduced. Let $C = \{c_1, c_2, \ldots, c_n\}$ be a finite set of n elements, where the c_i are called letters. A permutation of C is a bijection $\phi : C \to C$. The usual notation for a fixed permutation, wherein each c_j is led into some c_{p_j}, reads

$$\begin{pmatrix} c_1 & c_2 & \ldots & c_j & \ldots & c_{n-1} & c_n \\ c_{p_1} & c_{p_2} & \ldots & c_{p_j} & \ldots & c_{p_{n-1}} & c_{p_n} \end{pmatrix}. \tag{15.1}$$

The set of all permutations of the set C constitutes a group, under the operation of composition, i.e., the product, called the nth symmetric group, denoted by S_n. Taking the particular case when $n = 4$, an example of a product in S_4 is given by

$$\begin{pmatrix} a & b & c & d \\ b & d & c & a \end{pmatrix} \begin{pmatrix} a & b & c & d \\ a & c & b & d \end{pmatrix} = \begin{pmatrix} a & b & c & d \\ c & d & b & a \end{pmatrix}. \tag{15.2}$$

Fig. 15.7 shows the product (15.2), where the composition is similar for braid groups. The right action is used to comply with the downward convention for braids.

$$\begin{pmatrix} a & b & c & d \\ c & d & b & a \end{pmatrix} \qquad \begin{pmatrix} a & b & c & d \\ b & d & c & a \end{pmatrix} \qquad \begin{pmatrix} a & b & c & d \\ a & c & b & d \end{pmatrix}$$

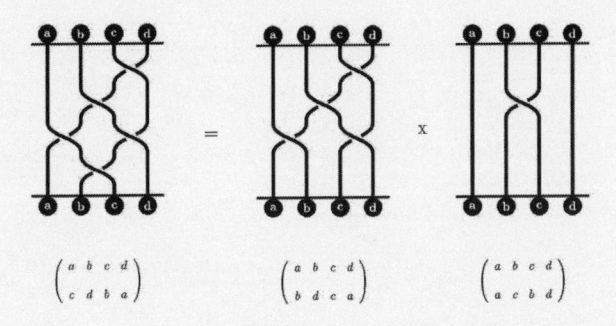

Figure 15.7: An example of permutation product in S_4.

There is a fundamental difference between the braiding and the permutation groups representations. In S_n, strands do not differ between undercrossing and overcrossing. The order, namely the number of elements of S_n, is given by $|S_n| = n!$. A permutation having the special form

$$\begin{pmatrix} c_1 & c_2 & \ldots & c_{r-1} & c_r \\ c_2 & c_3 & \ldots & c_r & c_1 \end{pmatrix} \qquad (15.3)$$

is a cycle of length r, usually denoted by $(c_1, c_2, \ldots, c_r)$. A product of two cycles is not necessarily a cycle. The product of disjoint cycles, defined as cycles with no letter in common, is commutative.

A very important fact consists of every permutation can be written as a product of disjoint cycles. Eq. (15.2) can be written as

$$(a, b, d)(c)(a)(b, c)(d) = (a, c, b, d). \qquad (15.4)$$

It is convenient to attribute a variable t_r to a cycle of length r and indicate the cycle structure of a permutation by the monomial $t_1^{n_1} t_2^{n_2} t_3^{n_3} \ldots t_r^{n_r}$, meaning that there are n_1 1-cycles, n_2 2-cycles, ..., n_r r-cycles. In the example (15.4), the monomial is $t_1^3 t_2 t_3$.

Permutations, P, of the same cycle type, namely, with the same set $\{n_j\}$ of exponents, can be led to each other under the adjoint action, SPS^{-1}, for any element $S \in S_n$. This means that permutations are representatives of conjugate classes. Hence, one same monomial is attributed to all permutations of a fixed class. In this sense, such monomials are invariants of the group S_n. It should be noticed that each class corresponds also to a representation of the group so that there is a monomial for each representation. A polynomial corresponds therefore to a sum over representations.

A cycle of length 2 is a transposition, represented by the cycle (a, b). Every cycle is a composition of transpositions, so that every permutation can be written ultimately as a product of transpositions. Transpositions generate the symmetric group. A basis of a group G is a set of elements $\{b_k\}_{i=1}^n \subset G$ such that any $g \in G$ can be obtained as a product of elements in $\{b_k\}$, called generators of G. Permutations formed by the product of an odd [even] number of transpositions are called odd [even] permutations. Using the notation

$$\begin{pmatrix} 1 & 2 & \ldots & n-1 & n \\ p_1 & p_2 & \ldots & p_{n-1} & p_n \end{pmatrix}, \tag{15.5}$$

one can use the set $\{s_j\}_{j=1}^n$ of elementary transpositions to compose a basis of S_n. The element s_i exchanges only the ith with the $(i+1)^{\text{th}}$ entry, leaving the other ones fixed:

$$s_i = \begin{pmatrix} 1 & 2 & \ldots & i & i+1 & \ldots & n-1 & n \\ 1 & 2 & \ldots & i+1 & i & \ldots & n-1 & n \end{pmatrix}, \tag{15.6}$$

obeying the relations, for all $\{i, j\} \subset \{1, \ldots, n\}$,

$$s_i s_{i+1} s_i = s_{i+1} s_i s_{i+1}, \tag{15.7}$$

$$s_i s_j = s_j s_i, \quad \text{for } |i-j| \geq 2, \tag{15.8}$$

the first of which is pictured in Fig. 15.8, for $n = 4$.

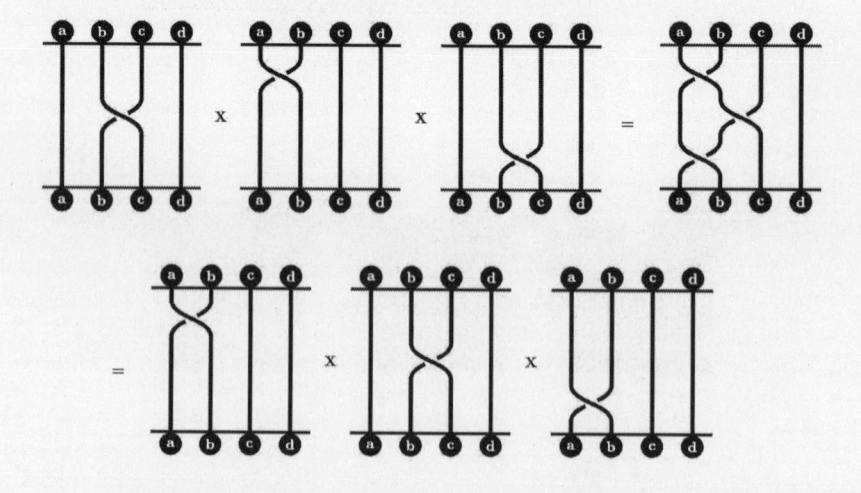

Figure 15.8: Pictorial presentation of the relation $s_1 s_2 s_1 = s_2 s_1 s_2$.

Notice the behavior of the third strand in Fig. 15.8. It has been exchanged twice with the second one and, consequently, it appears as a simple, unmoved strand. This comes from the involutory property

$$s_i s_i = \mathrm{id}, \tag{15.9}$$

typical of transpositions. Indeed, complying with straightforward accessible experiments, braid groups generators satisfy relations (15.7, 15.8), but there is no analog to (15.9) for them. This property means precisely that a pure permutation does not distinguish between a strand going over or under the other. Each elementary permutation s_i is identical to its inverse.

It is sometimes interesting and useful to deal with matrix representations of S_n. The most usual the basis consists of matrices that, when applied to column vectors, simply exchange consecutive entries. For $n = 4$, for instance, one can regard the following representation:

$$s_1 = \begin{pmatrix} 0 & 1 & 0 & 0 \\ 1 & 0 & 0 & 0 \\ 0 & 0 & 1 & 0 \\ 0 & 0 & 0 & 1 \end{pmatrix}, \quad s_2 = \begin{pmatrix} 1 & 0 & 0 & 0 \\ 0 & 0 & 1 & 0 \\ 0 & 1 & 0 & 0 \\ 0 & 0 & 0 & 1 \end{pmatrix}, \quad s_3 = \begin{pmatrix} 1 & 0 & 0 & 0 \\ 0 & 1 & 0 & 0 \\ 0 & 0 & 0 & 1 \\ 0 & 0 & 1 & 0 \end{pmatrix}. \tag{15.10}$$

Another basis is more adequate for use in knot theory. The generators for S_n are given in terms of $(n+1) \times (n+1)$ matrices. In S_4, for example, they read

$$s_1 = \begin{pmatrix} 1 & 0 & 0 & 0 & 0 \\ 0 & 0 & 1 & 0 & 0 \\ 0 & 1 & 0 & 0 & 0 \\ 0 & 0 & 0 & 1 & 0 \\ 0 & 0 & 0 & 0 & 1 \end{pmatrix}, \quad s_2 = \begin{pmatrix} 1 & 0 & 0 & 0 & 0 \\ 0 & 1 & 0 & 0 & 0 \\ 0 & 0 & 0 & 1 & 0 \\ 0 & 0 & 1 & 0 & 0 \\ 0 & 0 & 0 & 0 & 1 \end{pmatrix}, \quad s_3 = \begin{pmatrix} 1 & 0 & 0 & 0 & 0 \\ 0 & 1 & 0 & 0 & 0 \\ 0 & 0 & 1 & 0 & 0 \\ 0 & 0 & 0 & 0 & 1 \\ 0 & 0 & 0 & 1 & 0 \end{pmatrix}. \tag{15.11}$$

These are isomorphic to the matrices appearing in (15.10). Other bases for representations can be obtained from that one by similarity transformations, which do not change the cycle character of any product. The monomial $t_1^{n_1} t_2^{n_2} t_3^{n_3} \ldots t_r^{n_r}$, corresponding to an element of the symmetric group, is invariant under similarities and is a cognizable example of a polynomial invariant. A special basis, which will be useful later on, is obtained from the matrices (15.11) by similarity, induced by a left-lower triangular matrix, denoted here by T, whose non-vanishing elements are equal to 1. For $n = 4$, it reads

$$T = \begin{pmatrix} 1 & 0 & 0 & 0 & 0 \\ 1 & 1 & 0 & 0 & 0 \\ 1 & 1 & 1 & 0 & 0 \\ 1 & 1 & 1 & 1 & 0 \\ 1 & 1 & 1 & 1 & 1 \end{pmatrix}, \tag{15.12}$$

and the new basis is formed by conjugation,

$$s_1' = T s_1 T^{-1} = \begin{pmatrix} 1 & 0 & 0 & 0 & 0 \\ 1 & -1 & 1 & 0 & 0 \\ 0 & 0 & 1 & 0 & 0 \\ 0 & 0 & 0 & 1 & 0 \\ 0 & 0 & 0 & 0 & 1 \end{pmatrix}, \quad s_2' = T s_2 T^{-1} = \begin{pmatrix} 1 & 0 & 0 & 0 & 0 \\ 0 & 1 & 0 & 0 & 0 \\ 0 & 1 & -1 & 1 & 0 \\ 0 & 0 & 1 & 0 & 0 \\ 0 & 0 & 0 & 0 & 1 \end{pmatrix}, \tag{15.13}$$

$$s_3' = T s_3 T^{-1} = \begin{pmatrix} 1 & 0 & 0 & 0 & 0 \\ 0 & 1 & 0 & 0 & 0 \\ 0 & 0 & 1 & 0 & 0 \\ 0 & 0 & 1 & -1 & 1 \\ 0 & 0 & 0 & 0 & 1 \end{pmatrix}. \tag{15.14}$$

It corresponds to a reducible representation, as the last row and column of s_1' and s_2', and the first row and column of s_3', can be excluded with no change to the algebra respected by the generators.

15.3 Identical particles

The symmetric group appears in elementary quantum mechanics of a system of n identical particles. All their coordinates spins, and other quantities are denoted by the collective variable x. Exchanging particles is provided by the action of elements in S_n on x. General permutations are products of elementary transpositions of two particles, each one given by $s_i x$, for some $i \in \{1,\ldots,n\}$. For instance, if $n = 2$ and $x = (r_1, r_2)$, the unique possible exchange reads $(r_2, r_1) = s_1[(r_1, r_2)]$. The states are given by rays in the Hilbert space H of wave functions. More precisely, states are representatives of the equivalence class determined by the equivalence relation between wave functions

$$\psi_1(x) \sim \psi_2(x) \quad \text{if} \quad \psi_2(x) = \lambda \psi_1(x), \qquad \lambda \in \mathbb{C} \setminus \{0\}. \tag{15.15}$$

Equivalence classes for the relation $\sim$ are called projective rays. In quantum mechanics, the projective Hilbert space $P(H)$ of a complex Hilbert space H takes $\lambda = e^{i\eta}$, where η is an arbitrary phase. The physical meaning of the projective Hilbert space is that, in quantum theory, the wave functions ψ and $\lambda\psi$ do represent the same physical state, for any $\lambda \neq 0$. It is conventional to choose a unit norm wave function ψ from the ray, $\langle \psi | \psi \rangle = 1$, in which case it is called a normalized wave function. The unit norm constraint does not completely determine ψ within the ray, since ψ can be multiplied by any unitary λ, corresponding to the U(1) group action, preserving the normalization. No measurement can recover the phase of a ray, and therefore the phase is not an observable in quantum mechanics.

A group symmetry in quantum mechanics yields wave functions to respond to transformations according to a unitary (or anti-unitary) representation of the group. Therefore, under exchanges, the wave function changes through a unitary representation $U(S_n)$ of S_n in the Hilbert space. A permutation P is represented by an operator $U(P)$. The set $\{U(s_i)\}_{i=1}^n$ forms a basis for such a representation and respects conditions corresponding to (15.7) – (15.8). There is, however, an additional condition: as ψ is supposed to have values in a one-dimensional complex space, this representation must be a one-dimensional unitary representation, and consequently only phase factors will appear. In fact, for each $j \in \{1,\ldots,n\}$, one has

$$\psi(s_j x) = U(s_j)\psi(x) = e^{i\varphi_j}\psi(x), \tag{15.16}$$

for same phase φ_j. Eq. (15.7) imposes the equality of all the phases, so that $U(s_j)\psi(x) = e^{i\varphi}\psi(x)$, with the same phase φ for all s_j. Analogously, Eq. (15.8) yields

$$U^2(s_j)\psi(x) = U(s_j^2)\psi(x) = e^{i2\varphi}\psi(x) = \psi(x), \tag{15.17}$$

implying that $e^{i\varphi} = \pm 1$. There are only two one-dimensional representations: the totally symmetric one, related to bosons and with $U(P) = +1$ for every permutation

P; and the totally antisymmetric one, in which fermions find their place, with $U(P) = +1$, when P is even, and $U(P) = -1$, when P is odd. The configuration space for the system of n particles corresponds to the product manifold $M \times M \times \cdots \times M = M^n$. For indistinguishable particles, it consists of the quotient of that by the symmetric group, M^n/S_n, which is a multiply-connected space. In the usual $M = E^3$ case, its fundamental group is $\pi_1(E^{3n}/S_n) = S_n$, being E^{3n} its universal covering.

Notice that the symmetric group S_n is specified, up to isomorphism, by stating that it has $(n-1)$ generators satisfying (15.7) - (15.9). When a group is introduced in this way, by symbols (letters) representing its generators and some equations they must satisfy, this group is said to be given by a presentation.

Let us consider free groups or word groups. Going back to the set $C = \{c_1, c_2, \ldots, c_n\}$, we have called letters the elements c_j and will now call C itself an alphabet. An element with p consecutive times the letter c_j is written as c_j^p and it is called a syllable. A finite string of syllables is a word. The empty word 1 has no syllables. On a given word there are two types of transformations, called elementary contractions. They correspond to the usual manipulations of exponents. By a contraction of the first type, symbols like $c_j^p c_j^q$ are replaced by c_j^{p+q}; by a contraction of the second type, a symbol like c_j^0 is replaced by the empty word 1, or simply dropped from the word. With these contractions, each word can be reduced to its simplest expression, a reduced word. The set $F[A]$ of all the reducible words of alphabet A can be made into a group. The product $u \cdot v$ of two words u and v is just the reduced form of the juxtaposition uv. It is possible to show that this operation is associative and attributes an inverse to every reduced word. The resulting group $F[C]$ is the free group generated by C.

A general group G is called a free group if it has a set $C = \{c_1, c_2, \ldots, c_n\}$ of generators such that G is isomorphic to $F[C]$. In this case, the c_j are the free generators of G. The number of letters is the rank of G. The importance of free groups comes from a theorem, asserting that every group G is a homomorphic image of some free group. This means that a mapping $f : F[C] \to G$ exists, preserving the group operation. A homomorphism, in general, loses something: many elements in $F[C]$ may be taken into the same element of G. To obtain an isomorphism, something else must be implemented, extracting the excess through relations between elements of $F[C]$. Another version of the previous theorem states that every group G is isomorphic to some quotient group of a free group.

A subset N of G is called a subgroup of G if N also forms a group under the binary operation that defines G. The subgroup N is called a normal subgroup if it is invariant under conjugation by elements of G. Namely, a subgroup N is normal in G if and only if $gng^{-1} \in N$, for all $g \in G$ and $n \in N$. The usual notation for this relation is $N \triangleleft G$. Normal subgroups are important because only they can be used to construct quotient groups of the given group. Normal subgroups of G are precisely the kernels of group homomorphisms with domain G, which means that they can be used to classify those homomorphisms. Let us consider a subset $\{r_j\} \subset F[C]$. One builds the minimal normal subgroup R with the r_j as generators. The quotient $F[C]/R$ is a subgroup, corresponding to putting $r_j = 1$. An isomorphism of G onto $F[C]/R$ is a presentation of G. The set C is the set of generators and each r_j is a relator. Each $r \in R$ is a consequence of $\{r_j\}$. Each equation $r_j = 1$ is a relation.

There are two ways in which the symmetric group can be related to free groups: 1) one can think of the generators s_i as letters. Any element of S_n corresponds to a word like $s_1^{q_1} s_2^{q_2} s_3^{q_3} s_4^{q_4} \ldots s_1^{p_1} s_2^{p_2} \ldots$, with Eqs. (15.7) – (15.9) consisting of relations; 2) the letters are elements of the set C and their permutations are automorphisms on the group they constitute.

This may not be the simplest way to introduce S_n, but many groups are only defined through a presentation. Anyhow, this is frequently the better way to introduce discrete groups. It is the case of braid groups.

15.4 Artin classical braids

There are several definitions for the braid group B_n, some of them of great physical interest. Given the interval $I = [0, 1] \subset \mathbb{R}$ and $j \in \{1, 2, \ldots, n\}$, a braid is a family of distinct, non-intersecting, curves $\{\gamma_1, \gamma_2, \ldots, \gamma_n\}$, where the $\gamma_j : I \to E^2 \times I$ are defined in such a way that with

$$\gamma_j(0) = (P_j, 0), \qquad (15.18)$$
$$\gamma_j(1) = (P_{\sigma(j)}, 1), \qquad (15.19)$$

where $\{P_1, \ldots, P_n\}$ are n distinct points in the plane E^2 (one usually assumes $P_j = (j, 0) \in E^2$), and σ is an index permutation. A braid is called a tame braid when its curves have continuous first-order derivatives, namely, when they are of class C^1. Otherwise, the braid is asserted to be a wild braid. The braid group B_n consists now of compositions of path meshes. Those braids corresponding to the identity permutation, as that of Figs. 15.5d and 15.6, are called colored or pure braids. There is a surjective homomorphism of the braid group into the symmetric group,

$$h : B_n \to S_n, \qquad (15.20)$$

sending a braid of n strands to its associated permutation. The center, ker h, of this homomorphism, consists of the subgroup of braids of B_n corresponding to the trivial permutation and is therefore composed of colored (or pure) braids. This homomorphism erases the differences coming from strings that either overcrossing or undercrossing each other. The n-strand braid group consists of equivalence classes of braids, with the composition operation connecting the bottom of the first braid to the top of the second, and subsequently rescales the result to preserve unit length. The trivial braid has n parallel strands, and the inverse of a braid can be thought of as being its mirror image. One can produce a knot or a link by connecting the corresponding top and bottom strands by paths in E^3, yielding a closed braid. For the n-strand group, one can use a basis $\{\sigma_j\}_{j=1}^{n-1}$ of generators which are led by this homomorphism into elementary transpositions, that is, such that $h(\sigma_j) = s_j$. They obey the relations $\sigma_j \sigma_{j+1} \sigma_j = \sigma_{j+1} \sigma_j \sigma_{j+1}$, for $1 \leq i \leq n-2$, and $\sigma_i \sigma_j = \sigma_j \sigma_i$, for $|i - j| > 1$, which can be alternatively used as a definition of the group B_n. Therefore, the braid group is introduced by a presentation. Any generator $\sigma_i \in B_n$ corresponds to exchanging the ith-strand with the $(i+1)^{\text{th}}$-strand. The string starting at i crosses above another one, whereas the remaining strings go just straight.

The group B_1 consists of all braids constructed upon one strand, then consisting of the trivial group itself. Besides, B_2 is constituted by twists of two strands. One can associate a positive sign with a twist in one direction, whereas with a twist in the opposite direction, it is associated a negative sign. Therefore, B_2 is isomorphic to the group of integers, endowed with the addition operation.

The braid group B_3 is given by the presentation $B_3 = \langle s_1, s_2 \mid s_1 s_2 s_1 = s_2 s_1 s_2 \rangle$. Fig. 15.9 illustrates the generators of the braid group B_3.

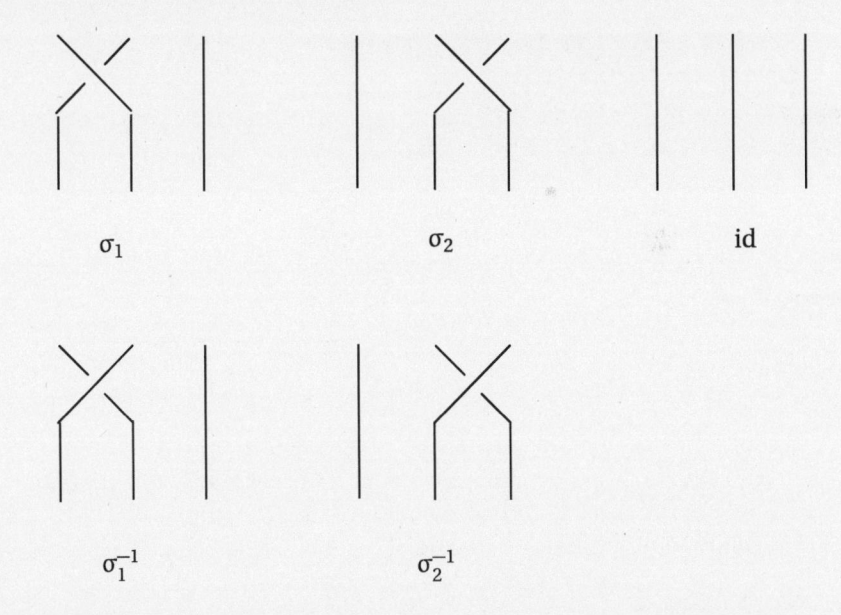

Figure 15.9: Generators $\sigma_1, \sigma_2 \in B_3$, the identity, and their inverses.

Any graph obtained by composing these elementary braids verify automatically the braid relations. Any braid can thus be written as a product of powers of the generators. Hairdos on a head with n hairs are thus encoded in B_n and comprise n-strands. The group B_n has the following presentation:

$$B_n = \langle \sigma_1, \ldots, \sigma_{n-1} \mid \sigma_i \sigma_{i+1} \sigma_i = \sigma_{i+1} \sigma_i \sigma_{i+1}, \sigma_i \sigma_j = \sigma_j \sigma_i \rangle, \qquad (15.21)$$

where in the first group of relations one must observe that the indexes are constrained to $1 \leq i \leq n-2$, whereas the second group of relations is constrained to $|i - j| \geq 2$. The cubic relations, known as the braid relations, play an important role in the theory of Yang–Baxter equations. In general, the braid group B_n generators can be represented by the braiding pattern in Fig. 15.10.

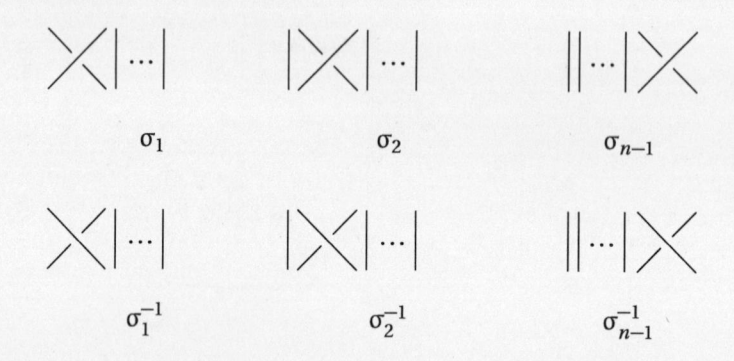

Figure 15.10: The braid group B_n generators.

One calls any sequence of elements $\sigma_i^{\pm 1}$ a braid word. If a braid word contains only elements of type σ_i and no elements of type σ_i^{-1}, then it will be called a positive braid word. If only elements of type σ_i^{-1} exist on a braid word, with no elements of type σ_i, then it is called a negative braid word.

Returning to torus knots, one can realize that the $T_{p,q}$ torus knot is equivalent to the $T_{q,p}$ torus knot, shown by moving the strands on the surface of the torus. Also, the $T_{p,-q}$ torus knot is the mirror image of the $T_{p,q}$ and the $T_{-p,-q}$ torus knot is equivalent to the $T_{p,q}$ torus knot but with reversed orientation [43, 44, 45]. Any $T_{p,q}$ torus knot can be constructed from a closed braid with p strands, with braid word $(\sigma_1 \sigma_2 \cdots \sigma_{p-1})^q$. Fig. 15.11 illustrates some particular cases.

Figure 15.11: Torus knots, with different numbers of crossings and links. From left to right: the first plot displays the $T_{11,7}$ torus knot, whereas the second plot regards $T_{11,-7}$. The third plot shows $T_{-11,-7}$ and the fourth one depicts $T_{-11,7}$.

Braid group generators and the braid statistics can be finally studied. It is worth noticing that, unlike the elementary exchanges of the symmetric group, the square of an elementary braid is not the identity. Going back to quantum mechanics, a basis for a representation of a braid group is given by operators $U(\sigma_j)$ acting on wave functions, according to $U(\sigma_j)\psi(x) = e^{i\varphi}\psi(x)$. However, now there is no constraint enforcing $U(\sigma_j^2) = 1$, so that

$$U^2(\sigma_j)\psi(x) = U(\sigma_j^2)\psi(x) = e^{i2\varphi}\psi(x). \qquad (15.22)$$

Hence, using finite induction, one can straightforwardly prove that

$$U(\sigma_j^k)\psi(x) = e^{ik\varphi}\psi(x), \qquad \forall\, k \in \mathbb{N}. \qquad (15.23)$$

The representation is now, like the group, infinite. It is from the condition $U(\sigma_j^2) = 1$ that the possibilities of values for the phase, for usual n-particle wave functions, are reduced to two. In fact, since twice the same permutation leads to the same state, $U(\sigma_j^2)\psi(x) = \psi(x)$, it yields $e^{i\varphi} = \pm 1$. The two signs correspond to wave functions which are either symmetric or antisymmetric under exchange of particles, when one considers, respectively, bosons or fermions. When statistics are governed by the braid group, as is the case of two-dimensional configuration spaces of impenetrable particles, the phase $e^{i\varphi}$ remains arbitrary and there is a different statistics for each value of φ. Such statistics are called braid statistics.

The absence of the involutory relation (15.9) has, as already asserted, deep consequences. Unlike the elementary exchanges of the symmetric group, the square of an elementary braid is not the identity. In many important applications, however, σ_j^2 differs from the identity in a well-defined way. In the simplest case, σ_j^2 can be expressed in terms of the identity and σ_j, which means that it satisfies a second-order equation like $(\sigma_j - x\,\mathbf{1})(\sigma_j - y\,\mathbf{1}) = 0$, where x and y are numbers and $\mathbf{1} \in B_n$ denotes the identity mapping. In this case, the generators σ_j belong to a subalgebra of the braid group algebra, called Hecke algebra [42]. This is the origin of the so-called skein relations, which are helpful in the calculation of polynomial invariants in knot theory.

Before proceeding, the definition of the loop is essential in what follows. A loop in a topological space X is a continuous function $f : I = [0, 1] \to X$ such that $f(0) = f(1)$. In other words, it is a closed path whose initial point is equal to its end point [46]. A loop can also be seen as a continuous mapping $f : S^1 \to X$, since S^1 can be thought of as a quotient of I under the antipodes identification of 0 with 1. The set of all loops in X is the loop space of X. Up to now, braids living essentially in E^3 have been studied by their diagrams and their projections on the plane E^2. This is more important for knots, whose visualization is more difficult. That is why careful treatment of such projections is necessary. Some equivalences, taken for granted, can be punctiliously codified so that the equivalence between two drawings is obtained thoroughly. Such steps are called Reidemeister moves and are shown in Fig. 15.12, for the $n = 3$ case. A Reidemeister move is any of three local moves on a link diagram. Each move operates on a small region of the diagram and is one of three types.

A Reidemeister type-I move (RI) corresponds to putting or taking out a kink, twisting and untwisting in either direction. A Reidemeister type-II move (RII) consists of sliding a strand over [under] to create [remove] two crossings. It is equivalent to moving one loop completely over another one. They simply straighten the strands. RII is indeed the relation of an elementary braid to its inverse. A Reidemeister type-III move (RIII) corresponds to using the n-strand group, related to sliding a strand across some crossing, or moving a string completely over or under a crossing. Later it will be clear that RIII, ultimately, is the essential content of the Yang-Baxter equation. In accomplishing any Reidemeister move, no other part of the diagram is involved, and a planar isotopy may distort the picture. The numbering that labels the types of moves corresponds to how many strands are involved. For instance, an RII operates on two strands of the diagram, whereas an RIII operates on three strands. Among all Reidemeister moves, RI is the only move that alters the writhe of the diagram. One assumes with each move that the diagram is only locally modified, leaving the rest of the diagram unchanged.

All this may seem trivial in the straightforward examples already presented, but the strict observance of a step-by-step procedure is essential to show the equivalence of intricate weaving patterns. It turns out that rules for only one, two, and three strands suffice to establish an isotopic relationship. The Reidemeister theorem states then that two links are isotopic-equivalent if and only if their diagrams can be obtained from each other by some finite series of RI, RII, and $RIII$ moves represented in Fig. 15.12. In other words, two knots or link diagrams are topologically equivalent if and only if their projections may be deformed into each other by a sequence of RI, RII, and $RIII$ moves and planar ambient isotopies. The main idea of the proof is that piecewise-linearly, one can reduce to the consideration of a few minimal moves on knot diagrams, which one shows can be obtained as a finite sequence of Reidemeister moves [12, 13]. A relevant context wherein the Reidemeister moves play a prominent role is in defining knot invariants. A property of a knot diagram that does not change, under Reidemeister moves, defines an invariant. As none of the Reidemeister moves alters the number of components of a link diagram, the number of components is, therefore, an isotopy invariant. In particular, one can conclude that the Hopf link and the Borromean rings are not isotopic.

Although in principle one can always find a sequence of Reidemeister moves between two equivalent link diagrams, there is no straightforward way of guessing which moves one must implement. A more difficult task consists of distinguishing two different knots using just Reidemeister moves. Knot invariants comprise a more direct way to answer these important questions. A knot invariant is any function of knots that depends only on their equivalence classes. Many important invariants can be defined in this way, including the celebrated Jones polynomial.

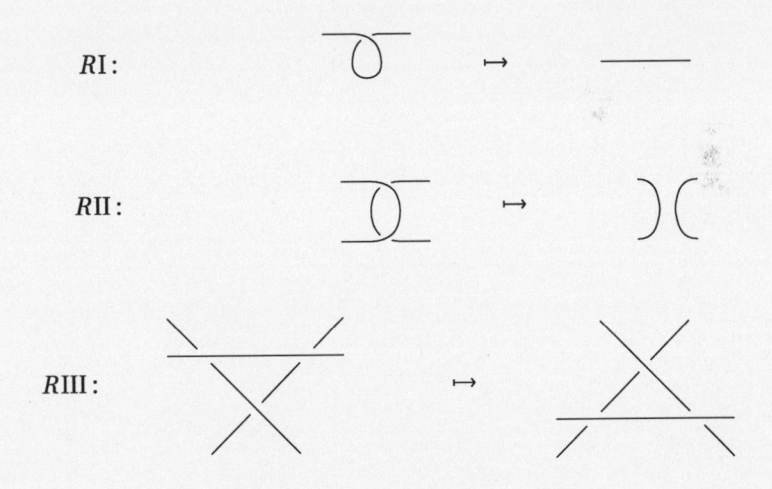

Figure 15.12: Reidemeister moves.

Besides, the two braids in Fig. 15.13 can be led to each other by the composition of the inverse of the first Reidemeister move RI. Subsequently, on the opposite side of the curve with respect to the other curve, after RI itself.

Figure 15.13: Equivalence between braids under RI moves.

Notice that RI and RII are simplifying steps, in the sense that they reduce the number of crossings in the diagram. We will later relate knots and links to braids, upon which Reidemeister moves are also applied. Links are going to be characterized by invariant polynomials, and R-moves (Reidemeister moves) appear as the simplest way to demonstrate the isotopic invariance of a polynomial. Fig. 15.14 illustrates examples of such moves in the context of braids.

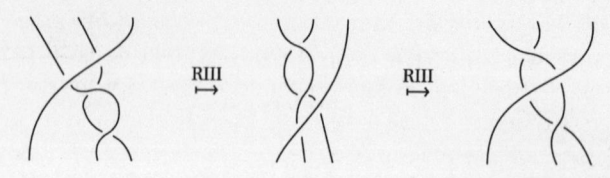

Figure 15.14: Equivalence between braids under RIII moves.

Acknowledgments

RdR is grateful to FAPESP (Grant No. 2021/01089-1 and No. 2022/01734-7) and CNPq (Grant No. 303390/2019-0), for partial financial support.

Bibliography

[1] R. Aldrovandi, R. da Rocha, *A Gentle Introduction To Knots, Links And Braids*, World Scientific, London, 2022.

[2] J. S. Birman, *Recent developments in braid and link theory*, Math. Intell. **13** (1991) 52.

[3] M. F. Atiyah, *The Geometry and Physics of Knots* (Cambridge University Press, Cambridge, 1991).

[4] A. T. Vandermonde, *Remarques sur les problèmes de situation*, Memoires de l'Académie Royale des Sciences (Paris) (1771) 566.

[5] J. J. Thomson, *On the vibrations of a vortex ring, and the action of two vortex rings upon each other*, Phil. Trans. R. Soc. London A **173** (1882) 493.

[6] J. J. Thomson, *A Treatise on the Motion of Vortex Rings* (Macmillan, London, 1883).

[7] D. S. Silver, *Knot Theory's Odd Origins*, American Scientist **94**, 158 (2006).

[8] H. Helmholtz, *Sui movimenti dei liquidi*, Nuovo Cimento **1**, 289 (1869).

[9] J. B. McGuire, *Study of Exactly Soluble One-Dimensional N-Body Problems*, J. Math. Phys. **5**, 622 (1964).

[10] E. Artin, *Theory of braids*, Annals of Math. **48**, 101 (1947).

[11] J. W. Alexander *Topological invariants of knots and links*, Transactions of the American Math. Soc. **30**, 275 (1928).

[12] K. Reidemeister, *Elementare Begründung der Knotentheorie*, Abh. Math. Sem. Univ. Hamburg **5**, 24 (1927).

[13] J. Alexander, G. Briggs, *On types of knotted curves*, Ann. Math. **28**, 562 (1926).

[14] A. Ashtekar, C. Rovelli and L. Smolin, *Weaving a classical geometry with quantum threads*, Phys. Rev. Lett. **69**, 237 (1992).

[15] R. da Rocha, *Holographic entanglement entropy, deformed blue branes, and deconfinement in AdS/QCD*, Phys. Rev. D **105**, 026014 (2022); arXiv:2111.01244.

[16] L. Bonora and A. A. Bytsenko, *Partition Functions for Quantum Gravity, blue Holes, Elliptic Genera and Lie Algebra Homologies*, Nucl. Phys. B **852** 508 (2011); arXiv:1105.4571.

[17] L. Bonora, A. A. Bytsenko and A. E. Goncalves, *Chern-Simons invariants on hyperbolic manifolds and topological quantum field theories*, Eur. Phys. J. C **76**, (2016) 625; arXiv:1606.02554.

[18] I. Kuntz and R. da Rocha, *Spacetime instability due to quantum gravity*, Eur. Phys. J. C **79**, 447 (2019); arXiv:1903.10642.

[19] I. Kuntz and R. da Rocha, *One-loop corrections to η/s in AdS_4/CFT_3*, Nucl. Phys. B **961**, 115265 (2020); arXiv:1909.10121.

[20] I. Kuntz and R. da Rocha, *Transport coefficients in AdS/CFT and quantum gravity corrections due to a functional measure*, Nucl. Phys. B **993**, 116258 (2023); arXiv:2211.11913.

[21] C. Rovelli and L. Smolin, *Knot Theory and Quantum Gravity*, Phys. Rev. Lett. **61**, 1155 (1988).

[22] E. Witten, *Quantum field Theory and the Jones Polynomial*, Comm. Math. Phys. **121**, 351 (1989).

[23] G. P. de Brito, N. Ohta, A. D. Pereira, A. A. Tomaz and M. Yamada, *Asymptotic safety and field parametrization dependence in the $f(R)$ truncation*, Phys. Rev. D **98**, 026027 (2018); arXiv:1805.09656.

[24] R. da Rocha and A. A. Tomaz, *MGD-decoupled blue holes, anisotropic fluids and holographic entanglement entropy*, Eur. Phys. J. C **80**, 857 (2020); arXiv:2005.02980.

[25] R. da Rocha and A. A. Tomaz, *Hearing the shape of inequivalent spin structures and exotic Dirac operators*, J. Phys. A **53**, 465201 (2020); arXiv:2003.03619.

[26] R. da Rocha and A. A. Tomaz, *Holographic entanglement entropy under the minimal geometric deformation and extensions*, Eur. Phys. J. C **79**, 1035 (2019); arXiv:1905.01548.

[27] M. Ludde and F. Toppan, *Matrix solutions of Artin's braid relations*, Phys. Lett. B **288**, 321 (1992).

[28] F. Constantinescu and F. Toppan, *On the linearized Artin braid representation*; arXiv:hep-th/9210020.

[29] J. Baez and J. P. Muniain, *Gauge fields, knots and gravity* Series on Knots and Everything: Volume 4 (World Scientific, London, 1994).

[30] R. Paszko and R. Rocha, *Quadratic gravity from BF theory in two and three dimensions*, Gen. Rel. Grav. **47**, 94 (2015).

[31] V. F. R. Jones, *Index for subfactors*, Invent. Math. **72**, 1 (1983).

[32] V. F. R. Jones, *A polynomial invariant for knots via von Neumann algebras*, Bull. Amer. Math. Soc. **12**, 103 (1985).

[33] V. Turaev, *Quantum invariants of knots and three manifolds*, De Gruyter Stud. Math. **18**, 1 (1994).

[34] J. H. Conway, *An Enumeration of Knots and Links, and Some of Their Algebraic Properties*, In J. Leech (editor), *Computational Problems in Abstract Algebra* (Pergamon Press, Oxford, 1970).

[35] V. A. Vassiliev, *Cohomology of knot spaces*, Adv. Soviet Math. **1**, 23-69 (AMS, Providence, 1990).

[36] J. Birman and X.-S. Lin, *Knot polynomials and Vassiliev's invariants*, Inv. Mathematicae **111**, 225 (1993.

[37] D. Bar-Natan, *On the Vassiliev knot invariants*, Topology **34**, 423 (1995).

[38] M. Kontsevich *Vassiliev's knot invariants*, Adv. Soviet Math. **16**, 137 (1993).

[39] S. Wasserman, J. Dungan, N. Cozzarelli, *Discovery of a predicted DNA knot substantiates a model for site-specific recombination*, Science **229**, 171 (1985).

[40] P. D. Bangert, *Braids and Knots*, in R. Ricca (ed.) *Lectures on Topological Fluid Mechanics*, Lecture Notes in Mathematics (Springer, Berlin, 2009).

[41] J. S. Birman, *Braids, Links, and Mapping Class Groups* (Princeton Univ. Press, Princeton, 1975).

[42] R. Abłamowicz, I. Gonçalves and R. da Rocha, *Bilinear Covariants and Spinor Fields Duality in Quantum Clifford Algebras*, J. Math. Phys. **55**, 103501 (2014); arXiv:1409.4550.

[43] W. B. R. Lickorish, *An introduction to knot theory*, Graduate Texts in Mathematics **175** (Springer-Verlag, New York, 1997).

[44] C. Livingston, *Knot Theory*, The Carus Mathematical Monographs **24** (AMS, Providence, 1993).

[45] A. Kawauchi, *A Survey of Knot Theory* (Birkhäuser, Basel, 1996).

[46] J. F. Adams, *Infinite Loop Spaces*, Annals of Mathematics Studies **90** (Princeton Univ. Press, Princeton, 1978).

16

On Yang-Mills stability bounds and finiteness of the free energy

P. A. Faria da Veiga

Abstract: We report on a joint work with M. O´Carroll. We take the gauge-invariant Yang-Mills (YM) QFT in the imaginary-time functional integral formulation on the finite lattice $\Lambda \subset a\mathbb{Z}^d \subset \mathbb{R}^d$, $d = 2, 3, 4$, $a \in (0, 1]$, with L (even) sites on a side, and with the gauge groups $\mathcal{G} = \mathrm{U}(N), \mathrm{SU}(N)$. The lattice gives an UV regularization of the continuum and Osterwalder-Seiler positivity is verified. To each bond b, we assign a variable U_b from an irrep of $\mathcal{G}$. The physical potentials (gluons) are parameters in the Lie algebra of $\mathcal{G}$. A lattice plaquette p is a minimal square, and $g^2 \in (0, g_0^2]$, $0 < g_0^2 < \infty$, is the gauge coupling. The Wilson lattice partition function $Z_\Lambda^u(a)$ is used, with an action $A_\Lambda(a) = \sum_p A_p$, which is a sum of gauge-invariant plaquette actions $A_p \equiv A_p(a)$, with a multiplicative factor a^{d-4}/g^2. Each A_p has the ordered product of the four U_b, $b \in p$, and $Z_\Lambda(a)$ is given by the integral over the Boltzmann factor $\exp-[A_\Lambda(a)]$, with a product measure over $\mathcal{G}$ Haar measures, one for each b. Formally, in the UV limit $a \searrow 0$, $A_\Lambda(a)$ gives the classical Yang-Mills continuum action. For free b.c., and using scaled fields, we show that the corresponding scaled partition function $Z_\Lambda(a)$ obeys thermodynamic and ultraviolet stable stability bounds (TUV), with constants uniform in L, a and g. Our a priori noncanonical scaling is a field strength renormalization depending on a. Passing to scaled fields does not alter the particle spectrum and makes the Wilson action more regular. With scaled fields, we isolate the UV singularity of the physical, unscaled free energy $f_\Lambda^u(a) = [\ln Z_\Lambda^u(a)]/|\Lambda|$ and show the existence of, at least, subsequential thermodynamic ($L \nearrow \infty$) and UV ($a \searrow 0$) limits of the scaled free energy. To obtain the TUV bounds, the Weyl integration formula is applied to the gauge integral. The CUE and GUE random matrix probability distributions naturally appear. The lower bound on $Z_\Lambda(a)$ results from a new global quadratic upper bound on $A_\Lambda(a)$. Our methods can be coupled with other methods to show existence of QFTs.

16.1 Introduction and the model

Among the most important problems in Physics is to show the mathematical existence and properties of an interacting relativistic quantum field theory (QFT) in spacetime dimension $d = 4$ [1, 2, 3, 4, 5]. Numerous partial results have been derived [4, 6, 7, 8], and Quantum Chromodynamics (QCD), the strong interaction model with quarks, antiquarks and gauge (gluon) fields, and their highly nonlinear dynamics, is considered to be the best candidate for a 4−dimensional QFT which is physically very relevant and mathematically exists. (Its experimental success has already a long history!)

The imaginary-time, Euclidean spacetime in dimension d, classical action of the local gauge-invariant Yang-Mills (YM) model is [1, 4, 5]

$$\begin{aligned}\mathscr{A}_{\text{classical}} &= \sum_{\{\mu<\nu\}} \int_{\mathbb{R}^d} Tr[F_{\mu\nu}(x)]^2 \, d^d x \\ &\equiv \sum_{\{\mu<\nu\}} \int_{\mathbb{R}^d} Tr\{\partial_\mu A_\nu(x) - \partial_\nu A_\mu(x) + ig[A_\mu(x), A_\nu(x)]\}^2 \, d^d x,\end{aligned}$$
(16.1)

where $\mu, \nu = 0, 1, \ldots, (d-1)$, and 0 labels time. A_μ are the gauge fields or vector potentials which are matrices in the Lie algebra of a gauge group $\mathscr{G}$. $F_{\mu\nu}$ is the second order antisymmetric tensor field, $g > 0$ is the gauge coupling and $[\cdot, \cdot]$ denotes the $\mathscr{G}$ Lie algebra commutator.

In the Euclidean spacetime functional integral formulation [4], a QFT is a type of continuous spin classical statistical model, and the YM partition function is given by the path integral of a Boltzmann factor, defined by the exponential of minus the action, and we integrate over all gauge field configurations. As most QFT, this definition is given, first, in a formal way. This is so because it has many singularities. Here, we analyze the short-distance or ultraviolet (UV) singularities of YM. In order to have a well-defined expression for the partition function, we can use a regularization with a discrete Euclidean spacetime such as a finite lattice $\Lambda \subset \mathbb{R}^d$, instead of a continuum spacetime, and consider a Riemann sum approximation to the integral in the action of Eq. (16.1). By doing this, infinities show up due to the unbounded gauge field integration as there is an excess of variables due to local gauge invariance of the action [1, 2, 3, 4].

To avoid this problem, Wilson defined a finite valued finite lattice partition function (see e.g. Ref. [9, 10]). We can take e.g. a finite hypercubic lattice $\Lambda \subset a\mathbb{Z}^d \subset \mathbb{R}^d$, $a \in (0, 1]$, and $L \in \mathbb{N}$ sites on a side. As usual in statistical mechanical lattice models [11, 4, 12, 13], the total number of sites $\Lambda_s = L^d$ plays the role of the volume of Λ, instead of the $\mathbb{R}^d$ volume, i.e. $(aL)^d$. There are a total of $\Lambda_b = dL^{d-1}(L-1)$ bonds in the lattice Λ.

We now define our lattice YM model. For concreteness, we take the gauge group $\mathcal{G}$ to be compact and unitary such as $\mathcal{G} = U(N), SU(N)$, $N \in \mathbb{N}$. (In the sequel, however, we concentrate on $\mathcal{G} = U(N)$ but the results are also valid for $SU(N)$, with minor modifications.) For $d = 2, 3, 4$, we take the finite hypercubic lattice $\Lambda \subset a\mathbb{Z}^d \subset \mathbb{R}^d$, with lattice spacing $a \in (0, 1]$, and $L \in \mathbb{N}$ (L even, for technical reasons) sites on a side. We let $b_\mu(x) = [x, x_\mu^+]$ denote a positively directed *lattice bond* connecting the site/point $x \in \Lambda$ to its nearest neighbor $x_\mu^+ \equiv x + ae^\mu$, where $e^\mu, \mu = 0, 1, \ldots, (d-1)$, is the unitary vector of the μth spacetime direction in Λ.

Next, to each positively oriented bond $b_\mu(x)$ (or, simply, bond), there is a random $\mathcal{G}$ matrix variable. Namely, we assign a unitary matrix U_b from an irreducible representation of $\mathcal{G}$. These are the *bond variables*. The lattice YM model then is a random matrix model, with the integration over field configurations given by a $\mathcal{G}$ Haar integral attached to each Λ bond.

The finite lattice Wilson partition function (see Eq. (16.5) below) is, formally, a well defined regularized version of the continuum spacetime YM model. No infinities show up. Local gauge invariance is verified on the lattice and so is Osterwalder-Schrader-Seiler (OSS) positivity [4, 8]. OSS positivity is essential for the the construction of an underlying quantum mechanical Hilbert space $\mathcal{H}$ for the model. We can also define energy and space component momentum operators acting on $\mathcal{H}$. These operators do commute and their joint spectrum is the energy-momentum or particle spectrum of the model, where we expect to find the particle states corresponding to what is detected in experiments.

Going further, we expect to be able to control of the *thermodynamic limit* $\Lambda \nearrow a\mathbb{Z}^d$ and also the *continuum limit* $a \searrow 0$ of gauge field correlations. If, besides positivity, the other OSS axioms are verified, by the OSS reconstruction theorem, we obtain a continuum, Minkowski spacetime QFT satisfying the Wightman-Haag-Ruelle axioms[4, 5].

In the fundamental work of Balaban (see [14, 15] and Refs. therein), starting with the Wilson plaquette action, finite lattice partition function (see Eq. (16.5) below), for small enough gauge coupling $0 < g \ll 1$, stability bounds [16] for the partition function have been proved, using renormalization group (RG) methods and the heavy multiscale analysis machinery. RG methods in continuum spacetime and using momentum space slices were considered in Ref. [17] to show the UV limit of the YM model, in $d = 4$ with an additional infrared cutoff. The special case of U(1), both the pure-gauge YM action and the coupling with Bose and Fermi fields were treated in Refs. [19, 18, 21, 20]. By applying softer methods, the $d = 2$ YM model was exactly solved in Ref. [22]. Moreover, it is expected that partition function stability bounds of [14, 15] lead to bounds on YM gauge field correlations. However, up to now, in the case of gauge fields, the determination of finite gauge correlations as well as the inclusion of quark/antiquark fields, are still missing and are important open questions. The same can be said about the OSS axioms [4, 5]. Of course, the lack of understanding these gauge models also includes the physically interesting case of spacetime dimension $d = 4$.

In the recent papers [23, 24, 25], Prof. Michael O´Carroll and myself introduced a method performing an a priori QFT renormalization on the lattice. This method is based on a scaling of the physical (original) fields, like a field strength, wavefunction renormalization. This scaling is a-dependent and is noncanonical. It preserves OSS positivity and does not change the decay rates of correlations and, hence, the energy-momentum spectrum of the YM model. After performing the scaling, the new fields are named *scaled fields*. In terms of the scaled fields, the original, physical action is more regular. The scaling may render some models finite and other are smoothed by it and have less singularities. This scaling transformation then corresponds to a partial renormalization. For the free field, the scaling removes the infinities from the free energy and correlations. Correlations become finite *even at coincident points*.

In Refs. [26, 27], using scaled gauge fields, a simple proof of thermodynamic and ultraviolet stable (TUV) stability bounds is given by a direct analysis of the finite lattice physical Wilson partition function $Z(\Lambda, a)$, with free boundary conditions (b.c.) in configuration space, for the model in the lattice Λ. As here, the gauge group was taken to be $\mathcal{G} = \mathrm{U}(N)$, $\mathrm{SU}(N)$, with respective dimensions

$$\delta(N) = N^2 \quad ; \quad \delta(N) = N^2 - 1,$$

but our methods extend to any other compact Lie group.

By the exponential map, the gauge fields A_b are elements of the Lie algebra of $\mathcal{G}$, and we write

$$U_b = \exp(ig a A_b). \tag{16.2}$$

With this parametrization, the fields are the usual physical gauge potentials. The $N \times N$ gluon field matrix A_b, in a suitable basis, is given by

$$A_b = \sum_{c=1}^{\delta(N)} A_b^c \, \theta_c,$$

and has the ordinary gluon fields in its components. Here, for $a = 1, 2, \ldots, N$, we have self-adjoint matrices θ_a denoting the elements of a basis for the self-adjoint matrices of $\mathcal{G}$. These are the Lie algebra generators, normalized by the usual trace condition $\mathrm{Tr}\theta_\alpha \theta_\beta = \delta_{\alpha\beta}$, with a Kronecker delta. With this, if $b \equiv b_\mu(x) = [x, x_\mu^+ \equiv x + ae^\mu]$, then A_b is the gauge field $A_\mu(x)$.

If $p \equiv p_{\mu\nu}(x)$ is a plaquette in the $\mu < \nu$ coordinate plane ($\mu, \nu = 0, 1, \ldots, (d-1)$), and if x denotes the lower left corner of the plaquette, then the sites of Λ taking part in p are vertices of

$$p = p_{\mu\nu}(x): \quad x, \, x_\mu^+, \, x_\mu^+ + ae^\nu, \, x_\nu^+. \tag{16.3}$$

Each plaquette $p \in \Lambda$ is associated with a positive Wilson action A_p involving the trace of the plaquette variable U_p. The variable U_p is given by the ordered product of the four bond variables comprising the four consecutive sides of the plaquette. For the plaquette $p = p_{\mu\nu}(x)$, given above, and using the physical parametrization of Eq. (16.2), we have (the dagger denotes the adjoint!)

$$\begin{aligned} U_p(x) &= \exp[iagA_\mu(x)] \exp[iagA_\nu(x_\mu^+)] \{\exp[iagA_\nu(x)] \exp[iagA_\mu(x_\nu^+)]\}^\dagger \\ &= \exp[iagA_\mu(x)] \exp[iagA_\nu(x_\mu^+)] \exp[-iagA_\mu(x_\nu^+)] \exp[-iagA_\nu(x)]. \end{aligned}$$
(16.4)

Remark 1. *We note that we use the same notation g both for a gauge group element, $g \in \mathcal{G}$, and the gauge coupling parameter $g > 0$, which usually appears as g^2. There should be no confusion!*

From now on, concentrating on the gauge group $\mathcal{G} = U(N)$, we give a schematic description of the model partition function and the stability bounds.

The original, physical model partition function $Z(\Lambda, a) \equiv Z_\Lambda(a)$ is an integral over the Boltzmann factor (exponential of minus the action), with a product measure of $U(N)$ Haar measures (see e.g. Refs. [28, 29, 30]). Namely, we have

$$d\mu(U_b) = \prod_{b \in \Lambda} d\mu(U_b),$$

with a normalized measure for each bond. The finite lattice partition function reads

$$\begin{aligned} Z_\Lambda(a) &= \int \exp\left[-\frac{a^{d-4}}{g^2} \sum_{p \in \Lambda} A_p(U_p)\right] d\mu(U) \\ &\equiv \int \exp\left[-\frac{a^{d-4}}{g^2} \sum_{p \in \Lambda} 2 \Re \operatorname{Tr}(1 - U_p)\right] d\mu(U). \end{aligned}$$
(16.5)

The non-negative Wilson plaquette action $A_p(U_p) \geq 0$ is given by

$$A_p(U_p) = 2 \Re \operatorname{Tr}(1 - U_p) = \|U_p - 1\|_{H-S}^2,$$
(16.6)

where $\|\cdot\|_{H-S}$ means the Hilbert-Schmidt norm

$$\|M\|_{H-S} \equiv [Tr(M^\dagger M)]^{1/2}.$$

The global gauge group $\mathcal{G}_{\text{global}}$ is taken to be the product of a $\mathcal{G} = U(N), SU(N)$ group at each lattice site, namely,

$$\mathcal{G}_{\text{global}} = \prod_{x \in \Lambda} \mathcal{G}_x,$$

where an element of $\mathscr{G}_x$ is an element of $\mathscr{G}$. Respectively, it transforms the bond variables $U_{b_p} \equiv U_{x,x_\mu^+}$ and its adjoint $U_{b_p}^\dagger$ as

$$U_{x,x_\mu^+} \to U_x\, U_{x,x_\mu^+}\, U_{x_\mu^+}^\dagger \quad ; \quad U_{x,x_\mu^+}^\dagger \to U_{x_\mu^+}\, U_{x,x_\mu^+}^\dagger\, U_x^\dagger,$$

Both the plaquette action $A_p(U_p)$ and the total action $\sum_p A_p(U_p)$ are invariant under this *local gauge transformation*.

Understanding that there is a gauge group $\mathscr{G}$ attached to each lattice site x, the action U_p is invariant under the $\mathscr{G}$ local gauge transformation $U_b \to h(x) U_b h(x_\mu^+)$, if $b \equiv [x, x_\mu^+]$ and for any $h(x) \in \mathscr{G}$.

In Eq. (16.5), each plaquette action $A_p(U_p)$ has a prefactor $[a^{d-4}/g^2]$ such that the total action $\sum_{p \in \Lambda} A_p(U_p)$ on the lattice is the Riemann sum approximation to the usual classical action $\mathscr{A}_{classical}$ of Eq. (16.1), with the continuum derivatives being replace by finite difference derivatives on the lattice with spacing $a \in (0, 1]$, i.e. with

$$\partial_\mu^a A_\nu(x) = a^{-1}\left[A_\mu(x + a e^\nu) - A_\mu(x)\right].$$

In the formal continuum limit $a \searrow 0$, $\sum_{p \in \Lambda} A_p(U_p)$ gives the above continuum field, classical action $\mathscr{A}_{classical}$. This important point is verified e.g. in Ref. [3], using the Baker-Campbell-Hausdorff formula. Also, in Eq. (16.5), we take the squared gauge coupling parameter $g^2 \in (0, g_0^2]$, $0 < g_0 < \infty$. We emphasize that the even though we used the physical parametrization of the gauge group bond variable U_b in Eq. (16.4), the partition function defined by Eq. (16.5) is independent of the parametrization. It is also important to call the reader's attention to the fact that the adjoint of the positively oriented bond variable of Eq. (16.4) can be interpreted as associated with the negatively oriented bond. For the plaquette $p = p_{\mu\nu}(x)$, the plaquette action A_p is interpreted as an ordered product of group variables going around the perimeter of the plaquette in a counterclockwise fashion, with a bond variable for a positively oriented traverse and its *adjoint*, for a negatively oriented traverse.

Having defined the model, in the next section we give a description of our results and discuss on how to prove them.

16.2 Our Main Results and Some Steps of the Proofs

Here, we give the statements of our main results in Theorems 1, 2 and 3 below, and present the essential tools for their proofs.

Our stability bound results hold for all g^2 in the range $g^2 \in (0, g_0^2]$, $g_0^2 < \infty$. This is not what happens in other works (see, e.g., [14, 15]), where the restriction to small $g^2 \ll 1$ is needed.

In principle, neglecting all the possible internal degrees of freedom in a more general model (spin, isospin, etc), in our YM lattice model, there are Λ_s sites in Λ, and our system has $\Lambda_b \delta(N)$ degrees of freedom. However, due to gauge invariance of the plaquette actions A_p, in Eq. (16.5), when considering the total number Λ_b of bonds and then the whole set of gauge variables in the lattice Λ, there is an excess of variables. By fixing the gauge, the extraneous gauge variables are eliminated. We sometimes fix the *enhanced temporal gauge*. here, the temporal bond variables are set to the identity (which leads to a trivial gauge integration), as well as some bond variables on the boundary of Λ. The gauged away variables are related to bonds which *do not* form a lattice loop. This guarantees the maximal number of relevant variables is given by $\Lambda_r \approx (d-1)L^{d-1} = (d-1)\Lambda_s/L$, which is roughly the total number of spatial, non-temporal bonds. The remaining bond variables are called *retained bond variables*.

With this, the *effective number of degrees of freedom in our model* is then $[\delta(N)\Lambda_r]$. Below, we use the *volume* Λ_r to define a volumetric free energy. We do not use the physical volume $(aL)^d$ in $\mathbb{R}^d$. By doing so, as there is a finite proportionality between them, and we will neglect any finite additive (d-dependent) constant value of the free energy. This is enough for our purpose in this paper.

For a generic lattice model with partition function $\mathscr{Z}_\Lambda$, when Λ_f degrees of freedom are present, a thermodynamic stability bound is a lower/upper bound on $\mathscr{Z}_\Lambda$ of the form

$$e^{c_\ell \Lambda_f} \leq \mathscr{Z}_\Lambda \leq e^{c_u \Lambda_f}, \qquad (16.7)$$

for some finite 'constants' c_ℓ and c_u independent of Λ_f, and this stability bound is used to control the thermodynamic limit of the free energy

$$f \equiv \lim_{\Lambda \nearrow \mathbb{Z}^d} f_\Lambda \equiv \lim_{\Lambda \nearrow \mathbb{Z}^d} \frac{1}{\Lambda_f} \ln Z_\Lambda,$$

and obtain a finite free energy f for the model.

Here, for the lattice YM model, we are also interested in taking the UV or continuum limit $a \searrow 0$. For this, we also demand c_ℓ and c_u to be uniform in the lattice spacing a. This is what we call a *thermodynamic and UV stable stability bound*, or simply *TUV bound*.

To get our TUV bound, in addition to the original physical, *unscaled* gluon fields which we now denote by A_b^u, with a superscript u, we will also employ local, *scaled gluon fields* $A_\mu(x)$ (without any superscript!) which are related to $A_\mu^u(x)$ by the a-dependent non-canonical scaling transformation

$$A_\mu(x) = a^{(d-2)/2} A_\mu^u(x). \qquad (16.8)$$

Associated with the scaled fields is the *scaled free energy*. In Ref. [27], periodic boundary conditions were also used, as well as free b.c.. Besides the stability TUV bounds on the scaled partition function, the control of the generating functional of gauge field correlations and gauge field correlations were also analyzed and *scaled generating functionals* and *scaled correlations* were introduced as well. Here we will concentrate only at the TUV bound. In [27], in order to allow the reader to get a clear picture of the scaling procedure for gauge fields, we also gave a detailed description on how it works for two models with spin zero scalar fields $\phi(x)$.

As it will be made clear below, the *scaled field quantities have good UV regularity properties* in the lattice spacing a and the gauge coupling g. Our main result is to show the scaled free energy is bounded below and above uniformly in $a \in (0, 1]$, for any finite gauge coupling g^2. This bound is verified by all lattice gauge models defined with the Wilson action. This includes trivial models as well as interacting models in the limit. In Ref. [27], we established a criterium to be satisfied, on the lattice, by asymptotically free model correlations, in terms of their singular behavior in the lattice spacing a.

We now describe how we apply the scaling transformation. For the abelian U(1) case we can define the scaling transformation by the same change of variables of Eq. (16.8), namely

$$A_\mu(x) = a^{(d-2)/2} A_\mu^u(x).$$

In terms of the gauge fields $A_\mu(x)$, the action becomes regular both in g and $a \in (0, 1]$, and the U(1) Haar measure is proportional to the Lebesgue measure.

In the nonabelian case, it is more delicate to implement the scaling. The scaling is performed in each color component $A_\mu^{u,c}$ of the unscaled field A_μ^u by defining

$$A_\mu^c(x) = a^{(d-2)/2} A_\mu^{u,c}(x). \tag{16.9}$$

and the bond variable U_b is parametrized as $U_b = \exp[ig a^{(d-4)/2} A_b]$. The action of the Boltzmann factor for each plaquette becomes also regular. However, the Haar measure is not given in terms of the Lebesgue. The Haar measure does *not* transform by a multiplicative factor. Due to this complexity, the scaling for YM fields does *not* correspond to a change of variables. Below, we show how deal with this problem. The Haar measure for unitary groups is obtained in Refs. [31, 32, 33, 34].

For the case of the gauge groups $\mathcal{G} = \mathrm{U}(N)$, $\mathrm{SU}(N)$, by defining a scaled field partition function by

$$Z_\Lambda(a) \equiv Z(\Lambda, a) = \left(\frac{a^{d-4}}{g^2}\right)^{\delta(N)\Lambda_r/2} Z_\Lambda^u(a), \tag{16.10}$$

with one factor of $\left(\dfrac{a^{d-4}}{g^2}\right)^{1/2}$ for each of the $\delta(N)\Lambda_r$ effective degrees of freedom, $Z_\Lambda(a)$ obeys TUV stability bounds.

In Ref. [27], we considered two types of boundary conditions (b.c.), free and periodic, on the lattice Λ and derived TUV bounds for both cases. The use of periodic b.c. makes it comfortable to use the multiple reflection method [4] to analyze the generating function and correlations. Since here we will only focus on the TUV bound, in order to simplify things, we only take the case of free boundary conditions.

The TUV stability bound on the scaled partition function $Z_\Lambda(a)$ is related to the unscaled, original $Z_\Lambda^u(a)$ as in Eq. (16.10) and obeys the the TUV stability bound (recall $\delta(N) = N^2, (N^2-1)$ is the dimension of the gauge groups U(N) and SU(N))

$$e^{c_\ell \delta(N)\Lambda_r} \leq Z_\Lambda(a) \leq e^{c_u \delta(N)\Lambda_r}, \qquad (16.11)$$

with finite constants c_ℓ and c_u uniform in Λ_r, and for any $a \in (0, 1]$.

Using Eq. (16.10), the proof of the bound of Eq. (16.11) is one of our main results and is stated in the Theorem below.

Theorem 1. *The unscaled partition function $Z_\Lambda^u(a)$ verifies the following stability bound:*

$$z_\ell^{\Lambda_r} \leq Z_\Lambda^u(a) \leq z_u^{\Lambda_r}. \qquad (16.12)$$

Regarding the constants appearing in the above bounds, we have

$$z_u = \int \exp\left[-2(a^{d-4}/g^2)\Re\mathrm{Tr}(1-U)]\right] d\sigma(U). \qquad (16.13)$$

for $U = e^{iX}$, $C^2 = 4N$. Here, U is a single bond variable and $d\sigma(U)$ is its corresponding Haar measure. Also, if $X = \sum_{\alpha=1,\ldots,N^2} x_\alpha \theta_\alpha$ and then

$$\mathrm{Tr}\, X^2 = \sum_{\alpha=1,\ldots,N^2} x_\alpha^2 = \sum_{k=1,\ldots,N} \lambda_k^2,$$

where $\lambda_1, \ldots, \lambda_N$ are the angular eigenvalues of U. Finally, in the upper bound of Eq. (16.12), we have

$$z_\ell = \int \exp\left[-2C^2(a^{d-4}/g^2)(d-1)\mathrm{Tr}\, X^2\right] d\sigma(U). \qquad (16.14)$$

Remark 2. The exponent in the TUV stability bound is the number $\Lambda_b = d(L-1)L^{d-1}$ of bonds. As it will made more transparent below, in both, the upper and lower bound, the same factor $[(a^{d-4}/g^2)^{-N^2/2}]$ is extracted. This factor dominates the a, g^2 dependences. Hence, in the stability bound of Eq. (16.12), the lower and the upper bound present the same singularity in the lattice spacing a, as $a \searrow 0$.

In the sequel, we discuss on the main ideas involved in proving our fundamental results given in Theorem 1. More details are available in Ref. [27] The first point to observe is that the TUV stability bound on the scaled partition function, given in Eq. (16.11), arises from an interesting factorization structure of the bounds on Z_Λ^u, and then on Z_Λ^s. Each factor corresponds to a *single bond single plaquette partition function*. The expressions for the *constants* z_ℓ and z_u involve probability distributions of the circular unitary random matrix and the Gaussian unitary ensembles, CUE [35, 36], and are analyzed in Theorem 2. This analysis leads to the TUV stability bound of Eq. (16.11).

The random matrix ensemble CUE arises naturally in the above context. To go further, and extract the singular behavior of z_ℓ and z_u, the Gaussian unitary random matrix ensemble GUE [35, 36] also shows up. We notice that both z_ℓ and z_u are given by integrals with *class function* integrands. We emphasize that this property was not present for the integrand of the unscaled partition function Z_Λ^u but does hold for the bounds and we recall that a *class function* $f(U)$ on the gauge group $\mathcal{G}$ is constant over each group conjugacy class, i.e. $f(U)$ satisfies the property

$$f(U) = f(VUV^{-1}) \quad , \quad \forall V \in \mathcal{G}.$$

To obtain the lower stability, a new, global quadratic upper bound in the gluon fields, for the positive Wilson plaquette action, is proved. In the plaquette action A_p, writing the plaquette variable U_p in terms of its bond variables, this bound is derived applying the standard trigonometric global bound

$$1 - \cos\theta \leq \theta^2/2 \quad , \quad \theta \in \mathbb{R},$$

to the last equality of Eq. (16.5). Doing this leads directly to a factorized lower bound on the partition function.

For the upper stability bound, we fix what we call the *enhanced temporal gauge* to eliminate the extraneous gauge variable. In this gauge, the temporal (direction) bond variables in Λ are set to the identity (leading to a trivial gauge group integration), as well as certain specified bond variables on the boundary $\partial\Lambda$ of Λ. It is important to remark that the gauged away bond variables involve bonds which *do not* form a lattice loop [4]. This guarantees the maximal number of relevant variables is given by $\Lambda_r \approx (d-1)L^{d-1} = (d-1)\Lambda_s/L$, which is roughly the number of non-temporal (spatial) bonds. These are the *retained bond variables*. The *effective number of degrees of freedom in our model* is then $[\delta(N)\Lambda_r]$. Next, since each plaquette action is positive (they correspond to a Hilbert-Schmidt norm!), we simply set some plaquettes actions to zero in the Boltzmann factor.

For ease of visualization we analyze explicitly here the case with $d = 3$ spacetime dimensions. An upper bound is obtained by discarding all horizontal plaquettes (those orthogonal to the time direction!) from the action, except those with temporal coordinates $x^0 = 1$. We now perform the horizontal bond integration.

Integrate over successive planes of horizontal bonds starting at $x^0 = L$ and ending at $x^0 = 2$. For the $x^0 = 1$ horizontal plane, integrate over successive lines in the $\mu = 2$ direction, starting at $x^1 = L$ and ending at $x^1 = 2$. For each horizontal bond variable, integration appears in only one plaquette. After the integration, in principle, the integral still depends on the other bond variables of the plaquette. However, we can use the left or right invariance of the Haar measure and the remaining integral is independent of the other variables. In this way, we extract a factor z_u. In the total procedure, we integrate over the Λ_r horizontal bonds, so that we extract a factor $z_u^{\Lambda_r}$.

For completeness, we recall that left and right invariance of the single bond Haar measure $d\sigma(U)$. We recall the invariance property (see e.g. [28, 29, 30]): let $f(U)$ be a function of the bond variable $U \in U(N)$ and let $W \in U(N)$. Then,

$$\int_{U(N)} f(U) d\sigma(U) = \int_{U(N)} f(WU) d\sigma(U) = \int_{U(N)} f(UW) d\sigma(U). \qquad (16.15)$$

By the spectral theorem, as U is unitary, there exists a unitary V which diagonalizes U_b, i.e. $V^{-1} U_b V = \mathrm{diag}(e^{i\lambda_1}, \ldots, e^{i\lambda_N})$, $\lambda_j \in (-\pi, \pi]$. The λ_j are called the *angular eigenvalues* of U. Recalling Eq. (16.8), the fundamental relation between scaled gluon fields and the angular eigenvalues is given by the equality

$$\sum_{j=1}^{N} \lambda_j^2 = a^2 g^2 \sum_{c=1}^{\delta(N)} \left|A_b^{u,c}\right|^2 = \frac{g^2}{a^{d-4}} \sum_{c=1}^{\delta(N)} \left|A_b^c\right|^2, \qquad (16.16)$$

which is used to deal with the above quadratic bound on the Wilson action. It is immediate for $\mathcal{G} = U(1)$.

With this, for $\lambda = (\lambda_1, \ldots, \lambda_N)$ and $d\lambda = d\lambda_1 \ldots \lambda_N$, by the Weyl integration formula [72, 28, 29, 30]

$$\int_{U(N)} f(U) d\sigma(U) = \frac{1}{N!} \int_{(-\pi,\pi]^N} f\left(\mathrm{diag}(\lambda_1, \lambda_2, \ldots, \lambda_N)\right) \times \prod_{k,j=1,\ldots,N; k<j} |e^{i\lambda_j} - e^{i\lambda_k}|^2 \frac{d\lambda}{(2\pi)^N}, \qquad (16.17)$$

the N^2-dimensional Haar integration over the $N \times N$ matrix unitary gauge group $\mathcal{G}$ is reduced to an N-dimensional integration over the angular eigenvalues of U. In Eq. (16.17), the measure corresponds to the probability density of the circular unitary ensemble (CUE) and in the bounds on z_u and z_ℓ the probability density for the Gaussian unitary ensemble (GUE). Random matrix theory appears in a natural way in our context (see Refs. [35, 36]).

From the Weyl formula of Eq. (16.17), we see that, even in the case of class functions, the measure $[\prod_{k,j=1,\ldots,N; k<j} |e^{i\lambda_j} - e^{i\lambda_k}|^2 \, d\lambda]$ does not obey

a multiplicative scaling relation under a change of variables transformation. However, for small enough λ_k, scaling λ_k by $(s\lambda_k)$, this measure scales with a factor $s^{\delta(N)}$.

The next Theorem shows bounds on the z_u and z_ℓ factors appearing in Theorem 1.

Theorem 2. Let $C^2 = 4N$. For z_u and z_ℓ appearing in Theorem 1, we have the bounds

$$\begin{aligned} z_u &= \mathcal{N}_C^{-1} \int_{(-\pi,\pi]^N} \exp[-2(a^{d-4}/g^2) \sum_{1 \leq j \leq N}(1-\cos\lambda_j)] \rho(\lambda) \, d^N\lambda \\ &\leq (a^{d-4}/g^2)^{-N^2/2} (\pi/2)^{N^2} \mathcal{N}_G(N) \mathcal{N}_C^{-1}(N) \\ &\equiv (a^{d-4}/g^2)^{-N^2/2} e^{c_u}, \end{aligned} \qquad (16.18)$$

and

$$\begin{aligned} z_\ell &= \mathcal{N}_C^{-1} \int_{(-\pi,\pi]^N} \exp[-2C^2(d-1)(a^{d-4}/g^2) \sum_{1 \leq j \leq N} \lambda_j^2] \rho(\lambda) \, d^N\lambda \\ &\geq (a^{d-4}/g^2)^{-N^2/2} \mathcal{N}_C^{-1}(N)(4/\pi^2)^{N(N-1)/2} [2(d-1)C^2]^{-N^2/2} I_\ell, \\ &\equiv (a^{d-4}/g^2)^{-N^2/2} e^{c_\ell}, \end{aligned} \qquad (16.19)$$

where $I_\ell \equiv I_2(\pi[2(d-1)C^2]^{1/2}/(2g_0))$ and, for $\beta = 2, 4$ and $u > 0$, we have

$$I_\beta(u) = \int_{(-u,u)^N} \exp\left[-(1/2)\beta \sum_{1 \leq j \leq N} y_j^2\right] \hat{\rho}^{\beta/2}(y) \, d^N y, \qquad (16.20)$$

with the weight function $\hat{\rho}(y) = \prod_{1 \leq j < k \leq N}(y_j - y_k)^2$, $I_\beta(u) < I_\beta(\infty) = \mathcal{N}_\beta$, is the normalization constant for the GUE and the GSE probability distributions for $\beta = 2, 4$, respectively. Explicitly, we have $\mathcal{N}_G = [(2\pi)^{N/2} 2^{-N^2/2} \prod_{1 \leq j \leq N} j!]$ and $\mathcal{N}_S = [(2\pi)^{N/2} 4^{-N^2} \prod_{1 \leq j \leq N}(2j)!]$. . The constants c_u and c_ℓ are real and finite, and independent of a, $a \in (0,1]$ and $g^2 \in (0, g_0^2]$, $0 < g_0 < \infty$.

Concerning the existence of the thermodynamic and continuum limits of the scaled free energy we define the scaled partition function by

$$Z_\Lambda(a) = (a^{d-4}/g^2)^{(N^2/2)\Lambda_r} Z_\Lambda^{u,B}(a), \qquad (16.21)$$

and a finite lattice scaled free energy by

$$f_\Lambda(a) = \frac{1}{\Lambda_r} \ln Z_\Lambda(a). \qquad (16.22)$$

Using Theorems 1 and 2, together with the Bolzano-Weierstrass theorem [38], we obtain the additional results given in the next Theorem.

Theorem 3. *The scaled free energy $f_\Lambda(a)$ converges subsequentially, at least, to a thermodynamic limit*

$$f(a) = \lim_{\Lambda \nearrow a\mathbb{Z}^d} f_\Lambda(a).$$

Subsequently, at least subsequentially, it also converges to a continuum limit

$$f = \lim_{a \searrow 0} f(a).$$

Besides, $f(a)$ satisfies the bounds

$$-\infty < c_\ell \leq f^{s,B}(a) \leq c_u < \infty. \tag{16.23}$$

and so does its subsequential continuum limit $f^{s,B}$. The constants c_ℓ and c_u are finite real constants independent of $a \in (0,1]$ and $g^2 \in (0, g_0^2], 0 < g_0 < \infty$.

16.3 Conclusions

We show the boundedness of a scaled free energy of any lattice gauge YM model, defined with the Wilson plaquette action, in spacetime dimension $d = 2, 3, 4$ and using free boundary conditions. The gauge groups $U(N)$ $SU(N)$ are considered, but we can deal with any other compact Lie group as well. The existence of the model free energy also holds in the thermodynamic (infinite volume) limit and the continuum limit, at least in the sense of subsequences. These results do not require adopting a small gauge coupling g^2 but only require $g^2 \in (0, g_0^2], 0 < g_0 < \infty$. In Ref. [27], this result is also extended to the case of periodic boundary conditions, and a similar result is proven for the generating function of plaquette field correlations and the correlations themselves. Besides, it is given a criterium for asymptotic freedom in terms of some correlation singularities in the lattice spacing a, as $a \searrow 0$.

Our methods are based on a priori renormalization, a noncanonical scaling depending on a, and a quite direct analysis of the structure of the Wilson action and the gauge integration procedure. A fundamental tool is to use the Weyl integration formula to produce bounds on the gauge integral. The random matrix distributions of CUE and GUE show up naturally. This method was applied to analyze a bosonic QCD model [39] where the fermionic quark and antiquark fields are replaced by scalar fields. The method can also be coupled to more traditional methods to make further progress in the field.

Acknowledgments

I thank the organizers for the invitation to take part in this celebrational book. I also thank Prof. M. O´Carroll for our long-term collaboration and FAPESP for support in the early stage of this paper.

Bibliography

[1] S. Weinberg, *The Quantum Theory of Fields* (Cambridge University Press, Cambridge, 2005).

[2] T. Banks, *Modern Quantum Field Theory* (Cambridge University Press, Cambridge, 2008).

[3] C. Gattringer, C. B. Lang, *Quantum Chromodynamics on the Lattice: An Introductory Presentation*, Lecture Notes in Physics 788 (Springer, New York, 2010).

[4] J. Glimm, A. Jaffe, *Quantum Physics: A Functional Integral Point of View* (Springer, New York, 1986).

[5] J. Dimock, *Quantum Mechanics and Quantum Field Theory: A Mathematical Primer* (Cambridge University Press, Cambridge, 2011).

[6] V. Rivasseau, *From Perturbative to Constructive Renormalization* (Princeton University Press, Princeton, 1991).

[7] S. J. Summers, *A Perspective on Constructive Quantum Field Theory*, arXiv:1203.3991v2 (2016).

[8] E. Seiler, *Gauge Theories as a Problem of Constructive Quantum Field Theory and Statistical Mechanics*, Lecture Notes in Physics 159 (Springer, New York, 1982).

[9] K. Wilson, in *New Phenomena in Subnuclear Physics*, Part A, edited by A. Zichichi (Plenum Press, New York, 1977).

[10] I. Montvay, G. Münster, *Quantum Fields on a Lattice* (Cambridge University Press, Cambridge, 1997).

[11] K. Huang, *Statistical Mechanics*, 2nd Ed. (Wiley, New York, 1987).

[12] B. Simon, *Statistical Mechanics of Lattice Models* (Princeton University Press, Princeton, 1994).

[13] G. Gallavotti, *Statistical Mechanics: A Short Treatise* (Springer Verlag, Berlin, 1999).

[14] T. Balaban, *Ultraviolet Stability of Three-Dimensional Lattice Pure Gauge Field Theories*, Commun. Math. Phys. **102**, 255 (1985).

[15] T. Balaban, *Large Field Renormalization II. Localization, Exponentiation, and Bounds for the **R** Operation*, Commun. Math. Phys. **122**, 355 (1989).

[16] D. Ruelle *Statistical Mechanics: Rigorous Results* (World Scientific, Singapore, 1999).

[17] J. Magnen, V. Rivasseau, R. Sénéor, *Construction of YM_4 with an Infrared Cutoff*, Commun. Math. Phys. **155**, 325 (1993).

[18] T. Balaban, *(Higgs)$_{2,3}$ in a Finite Volume*, Commun. Math. Phys. **85**, 603 (1982).

[19] B. K. Driver, *Convergence of the $U(1)_4$ Lattice Gauge Theory to its Continuum Limit*, Commun. Math. Phys. **110**, 479 (1987).

[20] J. Dimock, *Nonperturbative Renormalization of Scalar QED in $d = 3$*, J. Math. Phys. **56**, 102304 (2015); *Ultraviolet Regularity of QED in $d = 3$*, J. Math. Phys. **59**, 012301 (2018); *Ultraviolet Stability for QED in $d = 3$*, Ann. Henri Poincaré **23**, 2113 (2022); *Stability for QED in $d = 3$: An Overview*, J. Math. Phys. **63**, 042305 (2022).

[21] C. King, *The $U(1)$ Higgs Model. I. The Continuum Limit. II. The Infinite Volume Limit*, Commun. Math. Phys. **102**, 649 (1986); **103**, 323 (1986).

[22] A. Ashtekar, J. Lewandowski, D. Marolf, J. Mourão, T. Thiemann, *$SU(N)$ Quantum Yang–Mills Theory in Two Dimensions: A Complete Solution*, J. Math. Phys. **38**, 5453 (1997).

[23] M. O'Carroll, *Lattice Scaled Bose Fields and Gauge Interacting Models: Stability and Regularity*, 2018, unpublished.

[24] M. O'Carroll, P. A. Faria da Veiga *Scaled Lattice Fermion Fields, Stability Bounds and Regularity*, J. Math. Phys. **59**, 022301 (2018).

[25] P. A. Faria da Veiga, M. O'Carroll, *Generating Functions for Lattice Gauge Models With Scaled Fermions and Bosons*, Ann. Henri Poincaré **20**, 2323 (2019).

[26] P. A. Faria da Veiga, M. O'Carroll, *On Thermodynamic and Ultraviolet Stability of Yang-Mills*, arXiv:1903.09829v2.

[27] P. A. Faria da Veiga, M. O'Carroll, *On Yang-Mills Stability Bounds and Plaquette Field Generating Function*, 2023, submitted. A former version of this paper is available at arXiv:2005.00899.

[28] D. Bump, *Lie Groups* (Springer, New York, 2000).

[29] B. Simon, *Representations of Finite and Compact Groups* (American Mathematical Society, Providence, 1996).

[30] J. Faraut, *Analysis on Lie Groups: An Introduction* (Cambridge University Press, Cambridge, 2008).

[31] T. J. Nelson, *A Set of Harmonic Functions for the Group $SU(3)$ as Specialized Matrix Elements of a General Finite Transformation*, J. Math. Phys. **8**, 857 (1967).

[32] D. F. Holland, *Finite Transformations of SU(3)*, J. Math. Phys. **10**, 531 (1969); *Finite Transformations and Basis States of SU(N)*, J. Math. Phys. **10**, 1903 (1969).

[33] M. S. Marinov, *Invariant Volumes of Compact Groups*, J. Phys. A: Math. Gen. **13**, 3357 (1980); *Correction to: Invariant Volumes of Compact Groups*, J. Phys. A: Math. Gen. **14**, 543 (1981).

[34] M. Byrd, *The Geometry of SU(N)*, arXiv:physics-9708015, (1997); M. Byrd and E.C.G. Sudarshan, *SU(N) Revisited*, J. Phys. A: Math. Gen. **31**, 9255 (1998).; T. Tilma and E. C. G. Sudarshan, *Generalized Euler Angle Parametrization for SU(N)*, Journal of Physics A: Math. Gen. **35**, 10467 (2002).

[35] M. L. Mehta, *Random Matrices*, 3rd ed. (Elsevier, San Diego, 2004).

[36] P. Deift, *Orthogonal Polynomials and Random Matrices: A Riemann-Hilbert Approach* (AMS, Providence, 2000).

[37] H. Weyl, *Classical Groups: Their Invariants and Representations* (Princeton University Press, Princeton, 1997).

[38] W. Rudin, *Principles of Mathematical Analysis*, 3rd ed. (MacGraw-Hill, New York, 1976).

[39] P. A. Faria da Veiga, M. O'Carroll, *On Thermodynamic and Ultraviolet Stability of Bosonic Lattice QCD Models in Euclidean Spacetime Dimensions $d = 2, 3, 4$*, Rev. Math. Phys. **33**, 2350004 (2023).

17

Nonmetricity and hypermomentum: on the possible violation of Lorentz invariance

Yu. N. Obukhov, F. W. Hehl

Abstract: We outline how the symmetry groups of spacetime are interpreted in a gauge-theoretic approach. Specifically, we focus on the hypermomentum concept and discuss the hyperfluid, that appropriately generalizes the perfect (Euler) fluid of general relativity to the case of continuous media with microstructure. We demonstrate that a possible violation of Lorentz invariance is most adequately understood by means of non-vanishing nonmetricity of a metric-affine geometry of spacetime.

17.1 Introduction

Modern understanding of gravitational phenomena is based on the concepts of spacetime geometry. In a broad sense, the theory of gravity deals with the dynamics of the geometry that arises from the motion of matter. In his paper "Geometry and experience" [1], Einstein advocated to view the geometry as a natural science (actually he had regarded it as the most ancient branch of physics) and summarized this approach in the statement which can hardly be disputed[1]: *"According to the view advocated here, the question whether this continuum has a Euclidean, Riemannian, or any other structure is a question of physics proper which must be answered by experience, and not a question of a convention to be chosen on grounds of mere expediency."*

As is well known, the non-gravitational sector of physics (that encompasses the electromagnetic, weak, and strong interactions) is essentially explained in the framework of a Yang-Mills type gauge-theoretic approach [3, 4, 5]. The latter is based on the fundamental symmetry groups acting in internal spaces. Seeking for an extension of the gauge principle to the gravitational case, one naturally comes from internal symmetries to the 'external' spacetime symmetry groups. Thereby, in the gauge-theoretic paradigm, Einstein's question on an experimental probing of the geometrical structure of spacetime is converted into a question of an experimental determination of the underlying fundamental symmetry of the spacetime.

With this ambitious goal in mind, we have then to think about the appropriate physical tools which are suitable to probe the spacetime geometry. For example, neutral test particles do not feel the presence of electric and magnetic fields, one needs test particles that carry electrical charge. Similarly, exploration of the spacetime structure requires physical matter with adequate "gravitational charges". Remarkably, the nature of such matter is perfectly determined from the gauge-theoretic principles in terms of the Noether currents corresponding to the underlying spacetime symmetry.

It is our pleasure to prepare a paper for the volume devoted to the memory of *Ruben Aldrovandi*, who made important contributions to the development of geometrical methods in physics. He consistently shared Einstein's view, aptly noticing that *"the marriage between geometry and physics is best perceived when we notice that the geometry of Nature is probed by the physical dynamics"* [6]. Both of us were influenced by this remarkable book.

---

[1]The original German text [2] reads: "Die Frage, ob dieses Kontinuum euklidisch oder gemäß dem allgemeinen Riemannschen Schema oder noch anders strukturiert sei, ist nach der hier vetretenen Auffassung eine eigentlich physikalische Frage, die durch die Erfahrung beantwortet werden muß, kein Frage bloßer nach Zweckmäßigkeitsgründen zu wählender Konvention."

17.2 General relativity

The arena of *classical mechanics* is the Galilei-Newton spacetime with the Galilei group as group of motion. Maxwellian *electrodynamics* could not be accommodated in such a spacetime. The group of motion had to be generalized to the Lorentz-Poincaré group residing in the Minkowski spacetime of special relativity. As soon as *gravitation* is taken into account additionally, Einstein demonstrated that the Minkowski geometry of special relativity had to be generalized to the Riemannian geometry of general relativity (GR). This whole development has been conclusively reviewed in Einstein's Princeton lectures of 1921 under the title of "The Meaning of Relativity" [7].

In the context of this development of classical mechanics to electrodynamics and, eventually, to gravity, the Galilei-Newton geometry of spacetime was first generalized to Minkowski geometry of special and then to the Riemannian geometry of GR. Apparently, if spacetime and its underlying group of motion is adapted to more advanced experimental results, the *geometry* of spacetime has to be appropriately generalized. Thus, naively following the course of history, if a spacetime symmetry is violated, Lorentz invariance, for instance, then a more general type of spacetime geometry is expected to unfold.

When Einstein developed general from special relativity, he described matter phenomenologically as a *perfect fluid*, see [7, Eq.(51)]. The dynamics of such a continuous medium is characterized by an average 4-velocity vector field u^i (normalized as $g_{ij}u^i u^j = c^2$) and a scalar energy density field ρ. If necessary, this can be straightforwardly generalized by including elastic stresses. It is a distinguishing feature of GR that there is an intimate relation between the geometry of spacetime and matter. If we denote the matter Lagrangian density of the perfect fluid by $\mathfrak{L}_{\text{mat}} = \sqrt{-g}\, L_{\text{mat}}$, then a variation of the Riemann metric g_{ij} (with $i,j = 0,1,2,3$) yields the covariantly conserved and symmetric energy-momentum tensor σ^{ij} of the perfect fluid, see Hilbert [8]:

$$\sigma^{ij} = \sigma^{ji} = -\frac{2}{\sqrt{-g}} \frac{\delta \mathfrak{L}_{\text{mat}}}{\delta g_{ij}}, \qquad \overset{\{\}}{\nabla}_j \sigma^{ij} = 0. \qquad (17.1)$$

Here $g = \det g_{ij}$, and $\overset{\{\}}{\nabla}$ denotes the covariant derivative with respect to the Riemannian (Levi-Civita) connection

$$\{_k{}^i{}_j\} = \frac{1}{2} g^{il} \left(\partial_j g_{kl} + \partial_k g_{jl} - \partial_l g_{kj} \right). \qquad (17.2)$$

The Noether (canonical) energy-momentum current of the *pressure-less* fluid (= dust) has a particularly simple form

$$\Sigma_k{}^i = u^i \mathcal{P}_k, \qquad \mathcal{P}_k = \frac{\rho}{c^2} u_k, \qquad (17.3)$$

and energy-momentum conservation law (17.1) is supplemented by the angular momentum conservation

$$\Sigma_{[ij]} = 0, \qquad \Sigma_{(ij)} = \sigma_{ij}. \tag{17.4}$$

In the words of Weyl [9, p. 237]: *"The general theory of relativity alone, which allows the process of variation to be applied to the metrical structure of the world, leads to the true definition of energy"*. Accordingly, the properties of matter are directly reflected in the geometry of spacetime—and vice versa. This already gives us an inkling that a possible refined phenomenological description of matter could have implications for the geometry of spacetime in question.

17.3 Metric-affine geometry of spacetime

Already the Galilei-Newton spacetime of classical mechanics carries a metric-affine geometry with a 4-dimensional degenerate metric and a linear connection, see Weyl [9], Havas [10], and, particularly, Kopczyński and Trautman [11, Chap. 3]. This dichotomy of metric g and linear connection Γ runs through the whole of relativistic physics. In general relativity theory, however, the connection is subordinate to the spacetime metric: The Levi-Civita (Christoffel) connection (17.2) can be expressed in terms of the metric and its first derivatives alone, $\Gamma_{kj}{}^i = \{_k{}^i{}_j\}$.

Still, it is worthwhile to mention that Einstein clearly understood the different physical statuses of the metric and connection. Because of the principle of inertia, *"...the essential achievement of general relativity, namely to overcome 'rigid' space (ie the inertial frame), is only indirectly connected with the introduction of a Riemannian metric. The directly relevant conceptual element is the 'displacement field'* (Γ^l_{ik}), *which expresses the infinitesimal displacement of vectors. It is this which replaces the parallelism of spatially arbitrarily separated vectors fixed by the inertial frame (ie the equality of corresponding components) by an infinitesimal operation. This makes it possible to construct tensors by differentiation and hence to dispense with the introduction of 'rigid' space (the inertial frame). In the face of this, it seems to be of secondary importance in some sense that some particular* Γ *field can be deduced from a Riemannian metric..."*, as Einstein formulated[2] in one of his last publications [12], see also Einstein [7, Appendix II] and Schrödinger [14].

Thus, the straightforward generalization of the Riemannian spacetime is the metric-affine spacetime with a (symmetric[3]) metric g_{ij} and an asymmetric linear connection $\Gamma_{ij}{}^k$; we use here Schouten's [13] conventions. In general, these

---

[2]Translation from the German original [12] by F. Gronwald, D. Hartley, and F. W. Hehl.
[3]Einstein as well as Schrödinger used in their unified field theories also an asymmetric metric. Since the antisymmetric part of the metric has no generic geometrical interpretation, we restrict ourselves to its symmetric part. Moreover, they used the metric-affine framework in the context of

geometrical objects are completely independent, and the spacetime geometry is exhaustively characterized by the tensors of *curvature*, *torsion*, and *nonmetricity*, respectively:

$$R_{kli}{}^j := \partial_k \Gamma_{li}{}^j - \partial_l \Gamma_{ki}{}^j + \Gamma_{kn}{}^j \Gamma_{li}{}^n - \Gamma_{ln}{}^j \Gamma_{ki}{}^n, \qquad (17.5)$$

$$T_{kl}{}^i := \Gamma_{kl}{}^i - \Gamma_{lk}{}^i, \qquad (17.6)$$

$$Q_{kij} := -\overset{\Gamma}{\nabla}_k g_{ij} = -\partial_k g_{ij} + \Gamma_{ki}{}^l g_{lj} + \Gamma_{kj}{}^l g_{il}. \qquad (17.7)$$

Here $\overset{\Gamma}{\nabla}$ denotes the covariant derivative with respect to the connection Γ.

A metric-affine space is called a *Riemann-Cartan space* (or a space with a metric-compatible connection), if its nonmetricity is vanishing: $Q_{kij} = 0$. It is called a Riemann space, provided its torsion vanishes additionally: $T_{ij}{}^k = 0$. Then the linear connection reduces to (17.2).

To paraphrase Weyl's statement on the metric and the energy-momentum of matter, we may say that only a metric-affine spacetime which allows the process of the variation to be applied to the affine structure of the world, $\Gamma_{ij}{}^k \to \Gamma_{ij}{}^k + \delta\Gamma_{ij}{}^k$, leads to the true definition of the *hypermomentum* of matter:

$$\Delta^i{}_j{}^k = \frac{\delta L_{\mathrm{mat}}}{\delta \Gamma_{ki}{}^j}. \qquad (17.8)$$

The meaning of this current $\Delta^i{}_j{}^k$ will be discussed below. A fluid with non-vanishing hypermomentum we will call a hyperfluid. We follow here the investigations of Obukhov and Tresguerres [22], see also [23].

17.4 Gauge theories of gravitation as a unifying framework

The interdependence between the fundamental geometrical objects of spacetime, the gravitational field *potentials* (metric and connection) and the physical *sources*[4] of gravity (energy-momentum and hypermomentum currents of matter), can be readily understood in terms of a gauge-theoretic framework for gravity.

Élie Cartan's idea in the early 1920s of *gauging* the (4+6) parameter *Poincaré* (inhomogeneous Lorentz) group with mass m and spin s as the corresponding currents came eventually to fruition by the investigations of Sciama and Kibble [24, 25] during the early 1960s. The simplest gauge theory of gravity is the Einstein-Cartan(-Sciama-Kibble) theory of gravity, an experimentally viable generalization of Einstein's theory. Besides the energy-momentum of matter, also its spin angular

---

a unified theory for gravity and electrodynamics (and possibly meson fields [14]). We, however, opt for a dualistic theory like GR in which matter interacts with the geometry of spacetime.

[4]See also Schwinger's [15] source concept.

momentum acts as source of gravity. The perfect fluid in Einstein's theory is substituted by a spin fluid, see Halbwachs [26, 27].

The Einstein-Cartan theory [28, 29] leads only to minute deviations from general relativity at extremely high matter densities ($\approx 10^{57}$kg/m^3), which may only be relevant in the early cosmos. The corresponding historical and epistemological development is most convincingly described by O'Raifeartaigh [16, Chap. 3] and by Cao [17, Secs. 11.2, 11.3]. The relevant important original papers are reprinted and explained in Blagojević et al.[18].

Encouraged by the successful gauging of the Poincaré group, this concept was extended to the 4-dimensional general affine group $A(4, R) = T(4) \rtimes GL(4, R)$, see [19, 20, 50], and [18, Chap. 9]. Thereby local Lorentz invariance is violated by the emergence of the nonmetricity Q_{kij}, a geometrical object of spacetime. Of course, it is a question to experimental physics whether in some era of the cosmos really a violation of Lorentz invariance emerged. So far no Lorentz violation has been experimentally found. But numerous frameworks have been constructed for the accommodation of such a possible effect.

17.5 Possible violation of Poincaré-Lorentz invariance

The Poincaré group $T(4) \rtimes SO(1,3)$ and the affine group $T(4) \rtimes GL(4,R)$ both embrace the translation group $T(4)$. The latter relates in each case *two* neighboring points of spacetime to each other. Should the translational symmetry be violated, then we expect a fundamental change in the underlying spacetime geometry. In fact, the "square roots" of the 4 translation generators are believed to be complemented by the 4 additional supersymmetry generators of simple supergravity, see [18, Chap. 12]. Thus, there are well-developed methods in supergravity for treating this case. In this article, we will assume that translation invariance is left untouched and we only discuss possible violations of (homogeneous) Lorentz invariance.

The Lorentz group $SO(1,3)$–in contrast to the translation group $T(4)$–acts at one and only one point in spacetime. Accordingly, it is possible to treat Lorentz invariance like an internal symmetry group $U(1), SU(2), SU(3)$ etc. Below, we shall shortly come back to this possibility. If we understand, however, the Lorentz group as an external group–and this corresponds to our present state of knowledge– then the violation of the Lorentz symmetry means that the group $SO(1,3)$ expands to the general linear group $GL(4,R)$: $SO(1,3) \rightarrow GL(4,R)$. Physically, the Lorentz symmetry violation is manifest in that the light cone looses a status of an absolute element. In accordance with the gauge principles, we then find that a nontrivial nonmetricity $Q_{kij} \neq 0$ of spacetime emerges and the Riemann-Cartan geometry is extended to a metric-affine geometry with independent metric g_{ij} and independent connection $\Gamma_{kj}{}^i$.

In the simplest case, we could then use the trace of the nonmetricity, the *Weyl covector* $Q_k := \frac{1}{4} g^{ij} Q_{kij}$ as tool. This seems to be the minimal way to violate (homogeneous) Lorentz invariance. However, such a Weyl-Cartan spacetime, because of its dilation invariance, is expected to be valuable only in the context of massless fields. For massive fields we have to take recourse to the complete nonmetricity, including its trace-free (or deviatoric) part $\nearrow Q_{kij} := Q_{kij} - Q_k g_{ij}$. In 4 dimensions, the 40 component nonmetricity tensor Q_{kij} can be decomposed into four irreducible under the $GL(4, R)$ parts, according to $40 = 16 \oplus 16 \oplus 4 \oplus 4$, see [50, App. B.1].

The metric-affine geometric formalism provides a natural and consistent description of the possible Lorentz symmetry violation. A look at the literature reveals, however, that the latter is mostly described in various non-geometric formulations with the help of non-dynamical Lorentz-violating (LV) tensor fields that may arise from nontrivial vacuum expectation values of appropriate quantum operators, see Mattingly [30], for instance, and Kiefer [31, p. 330]. Such LV tensors may be constructed in terms of a timelike vector field which is introduced as a new element of spacetime structure. Taking into account that gravity is universally interacting with matter, the non-dynamical LV fields are replaced with dynamical tensor fields in Einstein-Aether theories, for specific models see Eling et al [32], Balakin et al [33], and Jacobson [34]. It should be stressed, however, that in these models the spacetime geometry is kept Riemannian, but still a violation of Lorentz invariance is claimed to arise, see the discussions of the Standard Model Extension (SME) overviewed by Bailey [35], Liberati [36], Kostelecky [37], and Heros et al. [38].

The naturalness of such LV mechanisms is an open issue [36], and the origin of an ad hoc Lorentz covariant vector field inducing the Lorentz symmetry violation is unclear. Quite paradoxically, such ad hoc non-geometric structures are still widely used to describe the possible violation of Lorentz invariance, instead of turning to intrinsic geometrical covector fields such as the Weyl field and, more generally, the nonmetricity field in the framework of the metric-affine gravity theory[5].

17.6 Hyperfluid controlled by the energy-momentum and the hypermomentum laws

In order to probe the spacetime structure in the framework of the metric-affine approach with independent metric and connection, one needs the matter with microstructure [50, 41].

---

[5] See, though, the discussion of constraints on the post-Riemannian structures in the LV framework [39, 40].

Historically, the emancipation of the connection structure from its dominance by the metric structure proceeded in several steps: First Voigt (1887) [42], in continuum mechanics, taking certain crystal lattices as a lead, introduced so-called (spin) moment stresses $\tau_{ij}{}^k = -\tau_{ji}{}^k$ as a new concept besides the now asymmetric (force) stresses $\Sigma_{ij} \neq \Sigma_{ji}$. The brothers Cosserat (1909) [43] developed a corresponding classical field theory, see also Truesdell and Toupin [44]. As a result, for the first time the equilibrium conditions for moments, $\partial_k \tau_{ij}{}^k + \Sigma_{[ij]} = 0$, became independent from the corresponding conditions for forces, $\partial_k \Sigma_i{}^k = 0$. Or, 4-dimensionally speaking, angular momentum conservation became independent from energy-momentum conservation.

Further development of the continuous mechanics of media with microstructure [44, 45] resulted in spin fluid models [46, 47], the dynamics of which is satisfactorily described in the framework of the Cosserat approach [43, 26, 27]. The elements of such media are characterized by a *rigid material frame*, representing the degrees of freedom of an intrinsic rotation, or spin, of matter elements, thereby giving rise to a spin density $\mathcal{S}_{ij} = -\mathcal{S}_{ji}$ tensor of the fluid. In contrast to the structureless ideal fluid of GR, such a medium with microstructure is described by *two* Noether currents: the canonical energy-momentum and the spin. For the *pressure-less* case, they read

$$\Sigma_i{}^k = u^k \mathcal{P}_i, \qquad \tau_{ij}{}^k = u^k \mathcal{S}_{ij}. \tag{17.9}$$

The 4-momentum $\mathcal{P}_k \neq \frac{\rho}{c^2} u_k$ is no longer collinear the 4-velocity, and it carries an additional spin-dependent contribution.

The hyperfluid model was developed [22] as a natural extension of the concept of a spin fluid to the case of when matter elements carry a *deformable material frame*, thus adding to the spin the intrinsic dilation and shear degrees of freedom to form the *hypermomentum density* $\mathcal{J}^i{}_j$ of a continuum. The resulting medium with microstructure is then described by the canonical energy-momentum and the hypermomentum (17.8)

$$\Sigma_i{}^k = u^k \mathcal{P}_i, \qquad \Delta^i{}_j{}^k = u^k \mathcal{J}^i{}_j, \tag{17.10}$$

which generalize (again for the *pressure-less* case) the pair of Noether currents (17.9). The spin density is identified with the skew-symmetric part $\mathcal{S}_{ij} = \mathcal{J}_{[ij]}$, whereas the *dilation density* is the trace $\mathcal{J} = \mathcal{J}^i{}_i$, and the symmetric traceless part is the *shear density*.

The consistent variational theory of hyperfluid [23] yields the explicit form of the canonical energy-momentum tensor (17.10) for the case of nontrivial *pressure p*:

$$\Sigma_k{}^i = u^i \mathcal{P}_k - p\left(\delta_k^i - \frac{u_k u^i}{c^2}\right), \tag{17.11}$$

$$\mathcal{P}_k = \frac{\rho}{c^2} u_k - \frac{1}{c^2}(g_{kj} u^l - \delta_k^l u_j) \dot{\mathcal{J}}^j{}_l, \tag{17.12}$$

and the equation of motion of the hypermomentum reads

$$\dot{\mathcal{J}}^i{}_j - \frac{1}{c^2} u^i u_k \dot{\mathcal{J}}^k{}_j - \frac{1}{c^2} u_j u^k \dot{\mathcal{J}}^i{}_k + \frac{1}{c^4} u^i u_j u^l u_k \dot{\mathcal{J}}^k{}_l = 0. \qquad (17.13)$$

Here the dot denotes the substantial derivative along the fluid's flow

$$\dot{\mathcal{J}}^i{}_j := \overset{*}{\nabla}_k(u^k \mathcal{J}^i{}_j),$$

where the modified covariant derivative is defined as

$$\overset{*}{\nabla}_i := \overset{\Gamma}{\nabla}_i - T_{ki}{}^k - \frac{1}{2} Q_{ik}{}^k.$$

The standard Euler-Lagrange machinery yields the conservation laws of the hypermomentum and the energy-momentum, respectively:

$$\overset{*}{\nabla}_j \Delta^i{}_k{}^j = \Sigma_k{}^i - \sigma_k{}^i, \qquad (17.14)$$

$$\overset{*}{\nabla}_i \Sigma_k{}^i = \Sigma_l{}^i T_{ki}{}^l - \Delta^m{}_n{}^l R_{klm}{}^n - \frac{1}{2} \sigma^{ij} Q_{kij}. \qquad (17.15)$$

17.7 Conclusions and outlook

By definition, the Lorentz group consists of transformations of coordinates and frames that does change the spacetime metric with the Minkowski signature $(+,-,-,-)$. From gauge-theoretic principles, we then find the geometry without nonmetricity. However, when the metric loses its status of an absolute element and the Lorentz invariance in broken, the geometric structure of spacetime acquires nontrivial nonmetricity. In other words, the Lorentz symmetry violation and the nonmetricity go hand-in-hand.

Following Einstein, the geometry of spacetime is not fixed by postulates or conventions for the sake of simplicity and convenience, but it should rather be determined from physical observations and experiment. It is sufficient to use structureless test matter to probe the Riemannian geometry. However, one does need to employ test *matter with microstructure* to explore post-Riemannian geometries. Practical advice to experimentalist is as follows: use matter with intrinsic spin to detect torsion, and use matter with intrinsic hypermomentum to detect nonmetricity.

These conclusions are convincingly supported by the analysis of equations of motion of test bodies in post-Riemannian geometries, [48] and [49, 50, 51]. Derived from the most general conservation laws of the Noether currents, the equations of motion may technically look slightly different in different multipolar approximation schemes, but the qualitative conclusion above remains untouched.

Quantum spin dynamics can be effectively used in the search for the torsion manifestations [52, 53, 54]. Still, the study of the quantum hypermomentum dynamics is an open issue, and in the meantime the development of physically feasible classical systems such as the hyperfluid model is of interest. The hyperfluid model attracted considerable attention in the analysis of the dynamics of micromorphic hyperelastic continua [55, 56, 57], whereas in the gravity theory it was mostly used in the cosmological context [58, 59, 60, 61, 62, 63].

An appropriate account for irreversible thermodynamic aspects, more general than those in [64, 65], could pave way to possible applications of the hypermomentum concept and the hyperfluid model ranging from the early cosmology to the heavy ion physics [66]. The hyperfluid could be used as a classical approximation for the study of the quark-gluon plasma dynamics, where the use of a spin fluid (see Beccatini [67] and Biswas et al. [68]) appears to be too restrictive, in our opinion, and an account on the Regge-trajectories-like hadronic excitations is needed.

Acknowledgments

We are grateful to Ingo Müller (Berlin) for useful explanations to 'Extended Thermodynamics.'

Bibliography

[1] A. Einstein, *Geometry and experience*, in: *The Collected Papers of Albert Einstein*. Vol. 7. The Berlin Years: Writings, 1918-1921 (English translation supplement). Translator A. Engel, consultant E. Schucking (Princeton University Press, Princeton and Oxford, 2002), Doc. 52, pp. 208-222.

[2] A. Einstein, *Geometrie und Erfahrung*, Sitzungsber. Preuss. Akad. Wiss. Phys.-math. Klasse **1**, 123 (1921).

[3] L. O'Raifeartaigh, *Group Structure of Gauge Theories* (Cambridge University Press, Cambridge, 1986).

[4] G. Mack, *Physical principles, geometrical aspects, and locality properties of gauge field theories,'* Fortsch. Phys. **29**, 135 (1981).

[5] M. Chaichian and N. F. Nelipa, *Introduction to Gauge Field Theories* (Springer, Berlin, 1984).

[6] R. Aldrovandi and J. G. Pereira, *An Introduction to Geometrical Physics*, 2nd ed. (World Scientific, Singapore, 2017).

[7] A. Einstein, *The Meaning of Relativity*, Princeton Lectures of May 1921, 5th ed. (Princeton Univ. Press, Princeton, 1955).

[8] D. Hilbert, *Die Grundlagen der Physik. (Erste Mitteilung)*, Nachrichten von der Gesellschaft der Wissenschaften zu Göttingen, Math.-Phys. Klasse **1915**, 395 (1915).

[9] H. Weyl, *Space–Time–Matter*, translated from the 4th German edition of 1921 (Dover, New York, 1952).

[10] P. Havas, *Four-dimensional formulations of Newtonian mechanics and their relation to the special and the general theory of relativity*, Rev. Mod. Phys. **36**, 938 (1964).

[11] W. Kopczyński and A. Trautman, *Space-time and gravitation* (PWN, Warsaw, and Wiley, Chichester, 1992).

[12] A. Einstein, Excerpt from the Preface (dated 04 April 1955) in: *Cinquant'anni di Relatività 1905-1955*. M. Pantaleo (ed.) (Editrice Universitaria, Edizioni Giuntine, Florence, 1955).

[13] J. A. Schouten, *Ricci–Calculus. An introduction to tensor analysis and its geometric applications*, 2nd ed. (Springer, Berlin, 1954).

[14] E. Schrödinger, *Space-Time Structure*, reprinted with corrections (Cambridge University Press, London, 1960).

[15] J. Schwinger, *Particles, Sources, and Fields* (Addison-Wesley, Reading, 1970).

[16] L. O'Raifeartaigh, *The Dawning of Gauge Theory* (Princeton University Press, Princeton, 1997).

[17] Tian Yu Cao, *Conceptual Developments of 20th Century Field Theories*, 2nd edition (Cambridge University Press, Cambridge, 2019).

[18] M. Blagojević and F. W. Hehl (eds.), *Gauge Theories of Gravitation: A Reader with Commentaries* (Imperial College Press, London, 2013).

[19] F. W. Hehl, G. D. Kerlick, and P. von der Heyde, *On a new metric affine theory of gravitation*, Phys. Lett. B **63**, 446 (1976).

[20] F. W. Hehl, E. A. Lord, and Y. Ne'eman, *Hypermomentum in hadron dynamics and in gravitation*, Phys. Rev. D **17**, 428 (1978).

[21] F. W. Hehl, J. D. McCrea, E. W. Mielke, and Y. Ne'eman, *Metric-affine gauge theory of gravity: Field equations, Noether identities, world spinors, and breaking of dilation invariance*, Phys. Rept. **258**, 1 (1995).

[22] Yu. N. Obukhov and R. Tresguerres, *Hyperfluid: A model of classical matter with hypermomentum*, Phys. Lett. A **184**, 17 (1993); arXiv:gr-qc/0008013.

[23] Yu. N. Obukhov and F. W. Hehl, *Hyperfluid model revisited*, Phys. Rev. D **108**, 104044 (2023); arXiv.2308.06598.

[24] D. W. Sciama, *The analogy between charge and spin in general relativity*, in: *Recent Developments in General Relativity, Festschrift for L. Infeld* (Pergamon Press, Oxford and PWN, Warsaw, 1962), pages 415-439.

[25] T. W. B. Kibble, *Lorentz invariance and the gravitational field*. J. Math. Phys. **2**, 212 (1961).

[26] F. Halbwachs, *Théorie relativiste des Fluides à Spin*, (Gauthier-Villars, Paris, 1960).

[27] F. Halbwachs, *Lagrangian formalism for a classical relativistic particle endowed with internal structure*, Progr. Theor. Phys. **24**, 291 (1960).

[28] A. Trautman, *The Einstein-Cartan theory*, in: *Encyclopedia of Mathematical Physics*, Eds. J. P. Françoise, G. L. Naber, S. T. Tsou (Elsevier, Oxford, 2006), Vol. 2, page 189 ; arXiv:gr-qc/0606062.

[29] Yu. N. Obukhov, *Poincaré gauge gravity primer*, in: *Modified and Quantum Gravity: From Theory to Experimental Searches on all Scales*, Eds. C. Pfeifer, C. Lämmerzahl, Lect. Notes in Phys. **1017** (Springer, Cham, 2023), pp. 105-143; arXiv:2206.05205.

[30] D. Mattingly, *Modern tests of Lorentz invariance*, Living Rev. Rel. **8**, 5 (2005); arXiv:gr-qc/0502097.

[31] C. Kiefer, *Quantum Gravity*, 3rd ed. (Oxford University Press, Oxford, 2012); arXiv:gr-qc/0502097.

[32] C. Eling, T. Jacobson, and D. Mattingly, *Einstein-Aether theory*, in: *Deserfest: A Celebration of the Life and Works of Stanley Deser*, Center for Theor. Phys., Univ. Michigan, Ann Arbor, USA, 3-5 April 2004, Eds. J. T. Liu, M. J. Duff, K. S. Stelle, and R. P. Woodard (World Scientific, Singapore, 2006), pp. 163-179.

[33] A. B. Balakin and G. B. Kiselev, *Einstein-Yang-Mills-Aether theory with nonlinear axion field: Decay of color aether and the axionic dark matter production*, Symmetry **14**, 1621 (2022); arXiv:2207.04230.

[34] T. Jacobson, *Einstein-aether gravity: A status report*, Proceedings of the conference "From Quantum to Emergent Gravity: Theory and Phenomenology," June 11-15 2007, SISSA; Trieste, Italy; arXiv:0801.1547.

[35] Q. G. Bailey, *Testing gravity in the laboratory*, in *Recent Progress on Gravity Tests: Challenges and Future Perspectives*, editors C. Bambi and A. Cardenas-Avendano; arXiv:2305.06325.

[36] S. Liberati, *Tests of Lorentz invariance: a 2013 update*, Class. Quantum Grav. **30**, 133001 (2013); arXiv:1304.5795.

[37] A. Kostelecky, *Concepts in Lorentz and CPT violation*, in: *CPT and Lorentz Symmetry*, Proc. 9th Meeting on CPT and Lorentz Symmetry, Indiana Univ. Bloomington, USA, 17-26 May 2022, Ed. R. Lehnert (World Scientific, Singapore, 2023), pp. 24-28; arXiv:2210.09824.

[38] C. P. de los Heros and T. Terzić, *Cosmic searches for Lorentz invariance violation*, in: *Modified and Quantum Gravity: From Theory to Experimental Searches on All Scales*, Eds. C. Pfeifer, C. Lämmerzahl, Lect. Notes Phys. **1017** (Springer, Cham, 2023) pp. 241-291; arXiv:2209.06531.

[39] J. Foster, V. A. Kostelecký, and R. Xu, *Constraints on non-metricity from bounds on Lorentz violation*, Phys. Rev. D **95**, 084033 (2017); arXiv:1612.08744.

[40] J. Zhu and B. Q. Ma, *Lorentz violation in Finsler geometry*, Symmetry **15**, 978 (2023); arXiv:2304.12767.

[41] Y. Ne'eman and F. W. Hehl, *Test matter in a space-time with non-metricity*, Class. Quantum Grav. **14**, A251-A260 (1997); arXiv:gr-qc/9604047.

[42] W. Voigt, *Theoretische Studien über die Elasticitätsverhältnisse der Krystalle. I.* Abhandlungen der Königlichen Gesellschaft der Wissenschaften in Göttingen **34**, 3 (1887).

[43] E. Cosserat and F. Cosserat, *Théorie des corps déformables* (Hermann, Paris, 1909); English translation by D. H. Delphenich is available at Neo Classical Physics.

[44] C. Truesdell and R. A. Toupin, *The classical field theories. Encyclopedia of Physics*, Vol. III/1 (Springer, Berlin-Göttingen-Heidelberg, 1960).

[45] G. Capriz, *Continua with microstructure*, Springer Tracts in Natural Philosophy **35** (Springer, Berlin, 1989).

[46] J. Weyssenhoff and A. Raabe, *Relativistic dynamics of spin-fluids and spin-particles*, Acta Phys. Pol. **9**, 7 (1947).

[47] Yu. N. Obukhov and V. A. Korotky, *The Weyssenhoff fluid in Einstein-Cartan theory*, Class. Quantum Grav. **4**, 1633 (1987).

[48] P. B. Yasskin and W. R. Stoeger, em Propagating equations for test bodies with spin and rotation in theories of gravity with torsion, Phys. Rev. D **21**, 2081 (1980).

[49] D. Puetzfeld and Yu. N. Obukhov, *Propagation equations for deformable test bodies with microstructure in extended theories of gravity*, Phys. Rev. D **76**, 084025 (2007); arXiv:0707.2819.

[50] Yu. N. Obukhov and D. Puetzfeld, *Multipolar test body equations of motion in generalized gravity theories*, in: *Equations of Motion in Relativistic Gravity*, Eds. D. Puetzfeld, C. Lämmerzahl, and B. Schutz, Fundamental Theories of Physics **179** (Springer, Cham, 2015), pp 67-119; arXiv:1505.01680.

[51] D. Iosifidis and F. W. Hehl, *Motion of test particles in spacetimes with torsion and nonmetricity*, arXiv:2310.15595.

[52] I. L. Shapiro, *Physical aspects of the space–time torsion*, Phys. Repts. **357**, 113 (2002); arXiv/hep-th/0103093.

[53] W.-T. Ni, *Searches for the role of spin and polarization in gravity*, Rep. Prog. Phys. **73**, 056901 (2010).

[54] Yu. N. Obukhov, A. J. Silenko, and O. V. Teryaev, *Spin-torsion coupling and gravitational moments of Dirac fermions: Theory and experimental bounds*, Phys. Rev. D **90**, 124068 (2014); arXiv:1410.6197.

[55] M. Brocato and G. Capriz, *Spin fluids and hyperfluids*, Theor. Applied Mech. **28-29**, 39 (2002).

[56] G. Capriz and G. Muellenger, *A theory of perfect hyperfluids*, in: *Trends in Applications of Mathematics to Mechanics.* Proceedings of STAMM, Seeheim, Germany, Aachen. Eds. Y. Wang and K. Hutter (Shaker, Aachen, 2005), pp. 85-92.

[57] G. Capriz, *Pseudofluids*, in: *Material Substructures in Complex Bodies: from Atomic Level to Continuum*, Eds. G. Capriz and P. M. Mariano (Elsevier, Amsterdam, 2007), pp. 238-261.

[58] L. L. Smalley and J. P. Krisch, *Fluids with spin and twist*, J. Math. Phys. **36**, 778 (1995).

[59] O. V. Babourova and B. N. Frolov, *Perfect hypermomentum fluid: Variational theory and equations of motion*, Int. J. Mod. Phys. A **13**, 5391 (1998).

[60] D. Puetzfeld and R. Tresguerres, *A cosmological model in Weyl-Cartan spacetime*, Class. Quantum Grav. **18**, 677 (2001).

[61] D. Iosifidis, *Cosmological hyperfluids, torsion and non-metricity*, Eur. Phys. J. C **80**, 1042 (2020).

[62] D. Iosifidis, *The perfect hyperfluid of metric-affine gravity: The foundation*, J. Cosmol. Astropart. Phys. **04**, 072 (2021).

[63] D. Iosifidis, *Non-Riemannian cosmology: The role of shear hypermomentum*, Int. J. Geom. Meth. Mod. Phys. **18**, 2150129 (2021); arXiv:2010.00875.

[64] I. Müller and T. Ruggeri, *Rational Extended Thermodynamics* (Springer, Berlin, 1998).

[65] D. Jou and G. Lebon, *Extended Irreversible Thermodynamics* (Springer, Berlin, 2010).

[66] R. Singh, *Collective dynamics of polarized spin-half fermions in relativistic heavy-ion collisions*, Int. J. Mod. Phys. A **38**, 2330011 (2023).

[67] F. Becattini, *Spin and polarization: a new direction in relativistic heavy ion physics*, Rept. Prog. Phys. **85**, 122301 (2022).

[68] R. Biswas, A. Daher, A. Das, W. Florkowski, and R. Ryblewski, *Boost invariant spin hydrodynamics within the first order in derivative expansion*, Phys. Rev. D **107**, 094022 (2023); arXiv:2211.02934.

18

Agglomeration of local structures as a model of glass formation

R. Kerner

Dedicated to the memory of my dear friend Ruben Aldrovandi

Abstract: We explore a new structural model of alkali-borate glasses inspired by the stochastic matrix metod. In particular, we analyze the dependence of relative proportion of various characteristic clusters on modifier's concentration x. A pure B_2O_3 glass contains according to various estimates from 75% [2] up to 85% [4] of boron atoms inside the boroxol rings, the rest of them in between, linking the boroxol rings via oxygen bonds. Adding the Na_2O modifier creates four-coordinated borons, but the resulting network glass remains totally connected. We study local transformations that lead to creation of new configurations like *tetraborates, pentaborates, diborates*, etc., and set forth a non-linear differential system similar to the Lotka-Volterra equations. The resulting density curves of various local configurations as functions of the alkali concentration x are obtained. The average rigidity is evaluated, enabling us to compute the glass transition temperature $T_g(x)$ for a given value of x.

18.1 Stochastic agglomeration model

The original approach to the geometry of disordered glassy networks was elaborated in the nineties, the leading concept being the growth by agglomeration of small local configurations forming bigger clusters and finally covering the entire bulk of cooling melt, which is observed as *glass transition*. The first models investigated just pairing of single atoms of two or three different kinds, taking into account both their valencies and energy barriers. Such simple models suit quite well chalcogenide covalent network glasses, like $Ge_xSe_{(1-x)}$ or $As_xSe_{(1-x)}$ glasses. The final version of the model, including the stochastic matrix approach, was elaborated by R.K and D.M. dos Santos-Loff, with R.A. Barrio, M. Micoulaut, G. G. Naumis and J.-P. Duruisseau (see e.g. [9], [1], [8]). These glassy compounds, in which selenium is the basic glass former mixed up with arsenic and germanium modifiers are used in the photocopyig devices due to the photoelectric properties of selenium.

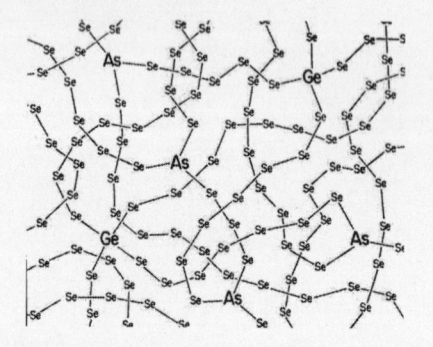

Figure 18.1: Typical ternary $As + Ge + Se$ glassy network

The first models of glass forming by agglomeration of atoms forming covalent bonds were proposed in the nineties (see [10], [11]). No matter how the agglomeration develops in later stages of glass formation from liquid melt, the onset of the process can be fairly well modelled by creation of first doublets, i.e. the smallest clusters made of two atoms only. Already at this stage, the two fundamental thermodynamical functions, energy and entropy, are present. The probabilities of various doublets' creation depends on energy barriers revealing themselves through the corresponding Boltzmann factors, and on entropy through combinatorics of valencies. The first agglomeration model of this kind was introduced in 1988 in a common paper with Dina-Maria dos Santos-Loff [14].

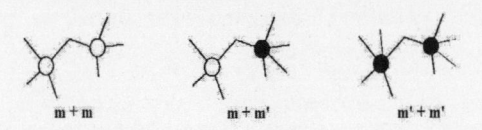

Figure 18.2: Pairing of 4 (m) and 5 (m') valenced atoms

Let us introduce the short-hand notation for three Boltzmann factors related to three energy barriers:

$$e^{-\epsilon} = e^{-\frac{E_{mm}}{kT}}, \; ; e^{-\eta} = e^{-\frac{E_{mm'}}{kT}}, \; ; e^{-\alpha} = e^{-\frac{E_{m'm'}}{kT}}, \qquad (18.1)$$

Supposing that the rate of m-valenced atoms in the hot melt is equal to c and that of the m'-valencced atoms is equal to $(1-c)$, with $0 \leq c \leq 1$, and the energy cost of forming three types of bonds are, respectively, E_{mm}, $E_{mm'}$ and $E_{m'm'}$, we can attribute the following probability factors to three doublets:

$$p_{mm} \simeq c^2 mm e^{-\epsilon}, \quad p_{mm'} \simeq 2c(1-c)e^{-\eta}, \quad p_{m'm'} \simeq (1-c)^2 m'm' e^{-\alpha}. \qquad (18.2)$$

These terms do not add up to 1, as probablilities should. In order to evaluate actual probabilities of finding one of the three possible kinds among all doublets formed, we must divide the terms (18.2) by the normalizing factor, which is their sum:

$$Q = (mmc^2 e^{-\epsilon} + 2mm'c(1-c)e^{-\eta} + m'm'(1-c)^2 e^{-\alpha}). \qquad (18.3)$$

Now we get the genuine probabilities, normed to 1:

$$p_{mm} = \frac{mmc^2 e^{-\epsilon}}{Q}, \quad p_{mm'} = \frac{2mm'c(1-c)e^{-\eta}}{Q}, \quad p_{m'm'} = \frac{m'm'(1-c)^2 e^{-\alpha}}{Q}. \qquad (18.4)$$

(In the example shown in (18.2) the valencies would be $m = 4$ and $m' = 5$). Note the similarity with standard statistical physics: the normalizing factor Q lays the role of the "big sum" Z, and the Boltzmann factors bring the energy content from which the average energy per doublet can be evaluated.

The agglomeration process does not necessarily reproduce the same proportion of m and m' valenced atoms in pairs as it was in the surrounding liquid at higher tempretires, containing mainly single atoms. The issue depends both on energy barriers which may privilege mixing, i.e. the pairs with two different items, or on the contrary, assembling rather similar atoms between themselves avoiding mixing. On the other hand, the combinatorics would privilege mixing, due to the factor 2; finally, relative concentration has also its say. In order to see the direction in which the things evolve, let us compare the concentration of the m-valenced atoms in the set of all doublets. It is easily found to be:

$$c' = \frac{2p_{mm} + p_{mm'}}{2} = \frac{2mmc^2 e^{-\epsilon} + 2mm'c(1-c)e^{-\eta}}{2 \cdot (mmc^2 e^{-\epsilon} + 2mm'c(1-c)e^{-\eta} + m'm'(1-c)^2 e^{-\alpha})} \qquad (18.5)$$

because there are two m-valenced atoms in a (mm) doublet, only one in the (mm') doublet, and none in a $(m'm')$ doublet.

Glasses are extremely homogeneous, which means that departures from average statistics are minimal. In other words, the concentration c observed in doublets should be as close as possible to the average in the surrounding melt, i.e. c' should be equal to c. When written down explicitly, this yields the following equation:

$$c' - c = \frac{mmc^2 e^{-\epsilon} + mm'c(1-c)e^{-\eta}}{mmc^2 e^{-\epsilon} + 2mm'c(1-c)e^{-\eta} + m'm'(1-c)^2 e^{-\alpha}} - c = 0. \qquad (18.6)$$

The denominator in the first term being positive definite, we can multiply by it the whole equation, and after reduction get the following expression for the numerator alone, whose vanishing is enough to satisfy the homogeneity condition (18.6):

$$c' - c \simeq c(1-c)\left[mmce^{-\epsilon} + mm'(1-2c)e^{-\eta} - m'm'(1-c)e^{-\alpha} \right] = 0. \qquad (18.7)$$

Let us follow the assumptions made in ([10]) leading to a simplified model of glass transition, especially for covalent chalcogenide network glasses. For example, in such binary or ternary glasses selenium (Se) is the basic glass former, while the modifiers (As or Ge, or both) can be treated as low-concentration ingredients, which even in not very big amounts increase randomness and hinder cristallization. Choosing the m-valenced atoms as the basic glass former and the m'-valenced ones as the modifier, if the concentration of the latter is low, which means that we assume c close to 1 and $(1-c)$ sufficiently small in order to be able to keep only terms linear in $(1-c)$ and neglect the terms containing $(1-c)^2$. This amounts to neglecting the last term in (18.7) above, i.e. neglecting the rare encounters of two m'-valenced atoms, which leads to the following equation:

$$c(1-c)\left[c\left(mme^{-\frac{E_{mm}}{kT}} - 2mm'e^{-\frac{E_{mm'}}{kT}} + mm'e^{\frac{E_{mm'}}{kT}} \right). \right] = 0. \qquad (18.8)$$

Besides the two obvious solutions, $c_1 = 0$ and $c_2 = 1$ corresponding to pure Se or pure As cases, there is a third solution between 0 and 1,

$$c_3 = \frac{mm'e^{-\frac{E_{mm'}}{kT}}}{2mm'e^{-\frac{E_{mm'}}{kT}} - mme^{-\frac{E_{mm}}{kT}}} \qquad (18.9)$$

Clearly, in order to c_3 represent a probability it must be be less than 1:

$$mm'e^{-\frac{E_{mm'}}{kT}} - mme^{-\frac{E_{mm}}{kT}} \geq 0, \qquad (18.10)$$

which after dividing the whole by mme^{ϵ} leads to the following relation between the activation energies, the glass transition temperature and valencies:

$$\frac{m'}{m} \geq e^{-\frac{E_{mm'} - E_{mm}}{kT}} \qquad (18.11)$$

Taking the logarithm of two sides and multiplying by kT we get the formula which coincides with the definition of free energy variation. However here it does not apply to thermodynamical states, but rather to processes, which are required to be stationary.

$$E_{mm'} - E_{mm} - kT\left[\ln m - \ln m'\right] = \Delta U - T\Delta S \geq 0. \qquad (18.12)$$

The equation (18.9) defines the relation between the glass transition temperature T_g and the modifier concentration c. The derivative dc/dT_g can be inversed and define the slope of the function $T_g(c)$ (dee [10], [17]).

18.1.1 Growth of clusters

The agglomeration modelled as creation of pairs from single atoms is obviously an oversimplification, and can be valid only at the onset of the process. When the temerature of the liquid decreases further on, bigger clusters become stable, leading to an exponential growth of viscosity.

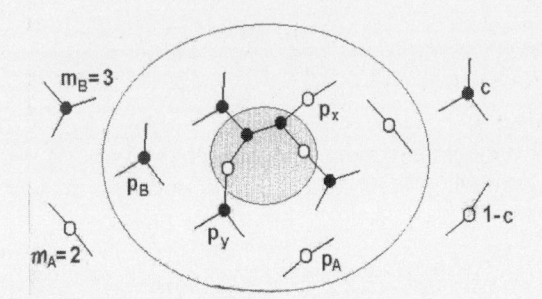

Figure 18.3: A cluster in the As-Se glass, with bulk and rim.

The probabilities constituting the entries of the stochastic matrix will depend on (i) the number of valences of the incoming particle and at the rim site (ii) the concentration of the corresponding species (iii) the binding energies in each case, through Boltzmann factors. These factors will be of three kinds:

$$\circ\!\!-\!\!\circ \iff e^{E_{SeSe}/kT} = e^{-\epsilon},$$
$$\circ\!\!-\!\!\bullet \iff e^{E_{SeAs}/kT} = e^{-\eta},$$
$$\bullet\!\!-\!\!\bullet \iff e^{E_{AsAs}/kT} = e^{-\alpha}.$$

For the one-atom-at-a-time approach, the unnormalized probability factors are shown in the last column. The probability of obtaining state y after one step, starting from state x, is proportional to $3ce^{-\eta}$; that to get y from z, to $3ce^{-\alpha}$; and so on.

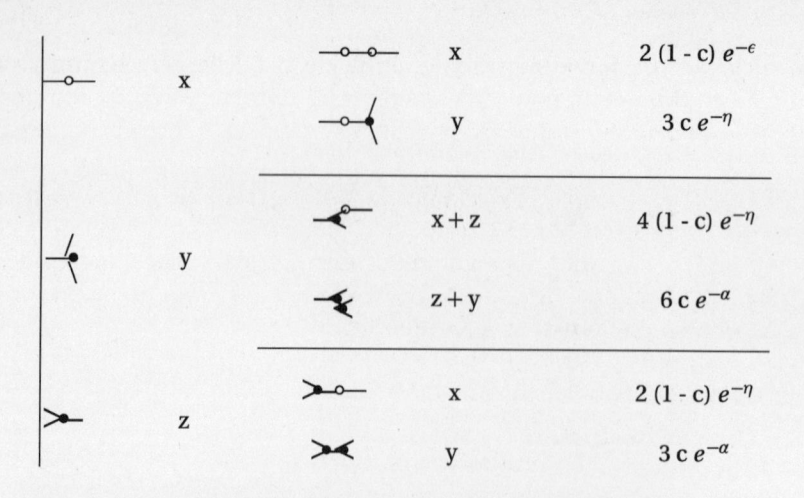

Fig. 5.9 States, steps and matrix entries in the one-bond saturation case.

From that we build up a provisional transition matrix, with not–yet–normalized columns,

$$\begin{pmatrix} 2(1-c)e^{-\epsilon} & 4(1-c)e^{-\eta} & 2(1-c)e^{-\eta} \\ 3ce^{-\eta} & 6ce^{-\alpha} & 3ce^{-\alpha} \\ 0 & 4(1-c)e^{-\eta}+6ce^{-\alpha} & 0 \end{pmatrix}, \quad (18.13)$$

and then proceed to normalize the entries in each column to have their sum equal to 1. To get the stochastic matrix in a simple final form, it will be convenient to introduce the combinations

$$A = \frac{2(1-c)}{2(1-c)+3ce^{\epsilon-\eta}} \; ; \; B = \frac{2(1-c)}{2(1-c)+3ce^{\eta-\alpha}}. \quad (18.14)$$

The transition matrix governing the process takes on the following form:

$$M = \begin{pmatrix} A & \frac{B}{2} & B \\ 1-A & \frac{1-B}{2} & 1-B \\ 0 & \frac{1}{2} & 0 \end{pmatrix}. \quad (18.15)$$

A general state on which M acts is described by a probability distribution $P = (p_x, p_y, 1 - p_x - p_y)$. Matrix M has the eigenvalues $\lambda_1 = 1$; $\lambda_{2,3} = \frac{2A-B-1\mp\sqrt{(2A-B-1)^2-8(B-A)}}{4}$. We can check that, for $A \leq 1$ and $B \leq 1$, the absolute values of λ_2 and λ_3 are smaller then 1. The eigenvector corresponding to the unit eigenvalue, which is

$$v = \frac{1}{3-3A+2B} \begin{pmatrix} 2B \\ 2(1-A) \\ (1-A) \end{pmatrix}, \quad (18.16)$$

will be preserved by higher powers of M, while the other will be progressively damped. Thus, the system evolution will move preferentially along that stable eigenvector, which represents the asymptotic state. We can evaluate relative concentrations of both types of atoms on the rim in this asymptotic state: the average concentration c' is given by the following formula:

$$c' = y + z = \frac{3-3A}{3-3A+2B}. \tag{18.17}$$

Like in the model of doublet creation, let us impose the maximum homogeneity requirement $c' - c = 0$ characterizing glass transition. After substitution of explicit expressions given in (18.14) and after some algebra we can require the numerator of the resulting fraction to vanish, whoch amounts to

$$c' - c = 0 \;\rightarrow\; c(1-c)\left[(27e^{\epsilon-\alpha} - 18e^{\epsilon-\eta})c + 18e^{\epsilon-\eta} - 4\right] = 0. \tag{18.18}$$

The equation (18.18) is similar to the similar condition obtained for the previous model of doublet formation (18.7), and leads to similar conclusions: besides the obvious solutions $c = 1$ and $c = 0$, there is a third one in between, defining the glass transition.

18.2 The alkali-borate glasses

18.2.1 Local structures in pure B_2O_3 glass

The alkali borate glasses, $(1-x)B_2O_3 + xNa_2O$ or $(1-x)B_2O_3 + xLi_2O$ are well known and present an interesting field for theoretical modelling. Typical *structural glasses*, their physical properties are determined by topological and geometrical features characterizing medium-range order, visible in clusters containing up to twenty-odd atoms.

Let us first have a closer look at typical local structures in a pure B_2O_3 network.

The most elementary structures present in the random borate glass network are the boroxol rings and the isolated boron tripods. An example of the amorphous B_2O_3 network is displayed in the following Figure:

We will get a better understanding of the borate glass if we scrutinize the vicinity of any atom beyond its closest neighbors. In particular, larger structural units should include boroxol rings. Let us thus consider the medium-range configurations containing enough information about the boroxol ring content of the network.

Our next step will be the evaluation of respective statistical weights of A and B clusters. According to many data obtained with Raman scattering and NMR, ([5],

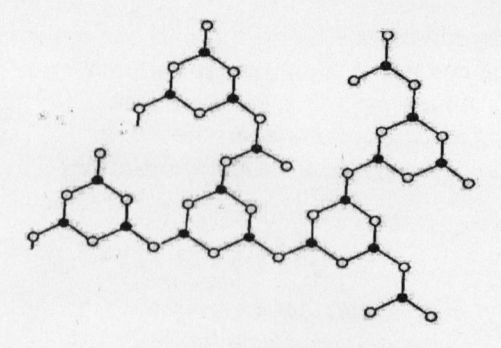

Figure 18.4: Typical clusters present in glassy B_2O_3 network.

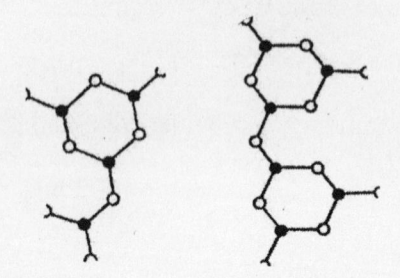

Figure 18.5: Two typical clusters, named A and B

[6], [4]) the proportion of Boron atoms contained in boroxol rings is about 83%. Theoretical predictions vary from 75% to 85% (see [7],[8]).

It is easy to derive the relative frequency of A and B configurations in amorphous B_2O_3 network. Let the probability to find an A-configuration be p, and that of the B configuration $(1-p)$ Then we should have:

$$\frac{3}{4}p + (1-p) = 0.83,$$

which yields the result $p = 0.68$, so close to $66,67\%$ that we shall use the simplest fraction available, and assume the proportion of 2/3 of clusters of A-type and 1/3 of clusters of B-type.

18.2.2 Rigidity and connectivity in pure B_2O_3 network

In order to determine the average rigidity of the B_2O_3 network we shall perform the constraint count. We shall use the classical constraints count (introduced by J.C. Maxwell). We suppose that three covalent bonds around each boron atom represent three angular constraints;

Concerning the two bonds stemming from oxygen, we shall suppose that they represent *one angular constraint* if the oxygen atom is part of the boroxol ring, and *no angular constraint* if the oxygen serves as a bridge between two boroxol rings. We also suppose that all covalent bonds represent *one linear (stretching) constraint each*. Here is the rigidity count for an A and B clusters:

The constraint count in A-cluster gives the following: $4 \times 3 + 3 \times 1 = 15$ angular constraints, and 12 linear (stretching) constraints; $= 27$ constraints for 10 atoms, which gives $2.7 < 3$ constraints per atom. The A configuration is *floppy*

The constraint count in B configuration gives: $6 \times 3 + 6 \times 1 = 24$ angular constraints, and 18 *stretching constraints*; $= 42$ constraints for 15 atoms, which gives $2.8 < 3$ constraints per atom. The B configuration is floppy, too.

The overall constraint count per atom in the network containing 2/3 of A clusters and 1/3 of B clusters is: $(10 \times 2.7 \times (2/3) + 15 \times 2.8 \times (1/3))/(10 \times \frac{2}{3} + 15 \times \frac{1}{3}) = 2.743 < 3$
The pure B_2O_3 random network is *floppy*, its average rigidity defect being $<r> = 2.743 - 3 = -0.257$.

The average rigidity is directly related to the glass transition temperature T_g. Glass transition is not a genuine phase transition in a strict thermodynamical sense; its characteristic features are displayed on the $V - T$ diagram below (left), along with the behavior of specific heat (right).

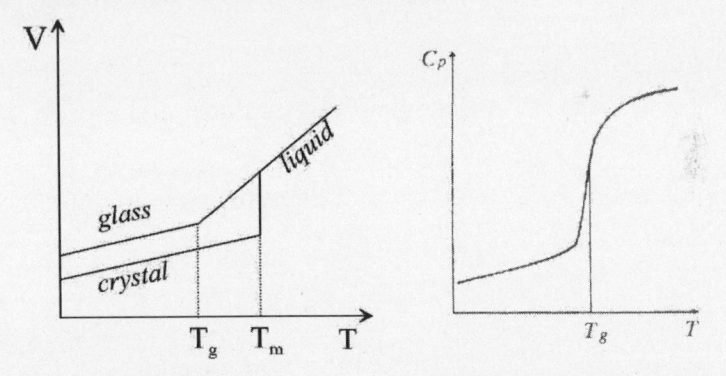

Figure 18.6: Left: Glass transition Right: Specific heat $C_V(x_4)$

The *glass transition temperature* T_g can be identified with the abrupt change in volume, viscosity and specific heat visible in the diagrams above. Unlike the temperature of a genuine phase transition, it often depends on the cooling rate and can vary by dozens of degrees; nevertheless, it is quite well defined for most commonly used glasses. The rate of four-coordinate borons (x_4) with a Na^+ ion and an extra oxygen bond as a function of modifier's density (x_M) (after A.Wright et al., 1995, see [7])

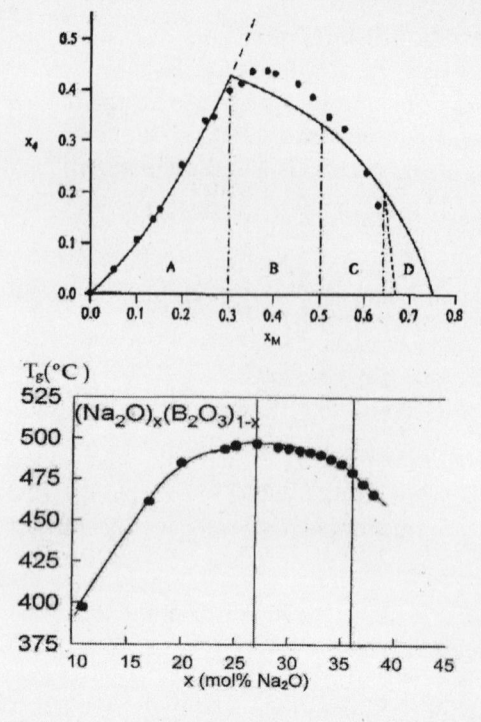

Figure 18.7: Left: 4-coordinate borons, Right: T_g, functions of x_4

A simple model of glassy thermodynamics G.G.Naumis, 2006 ([12]) relates the glass transition temperature T_g with the average number of the so-called *floppy modes* in a given glass.

In his approach to glass transition, G.G. Naumis derived a formula relaying T_g with the density f of *floppy modes* in the vibrational spectrum:

$$T_g(f) = \frac{T_g(f=0)}{1+\alpha f}. \tag{18.19}$$

which can be compared with the Gibbs-Di Marzio phenomenological formula ([13])

$$T_g(r) = \frac{T_g(<r>=2)}{1-\beta(<r>-2)}, \quad \beta = \frac{5\alpha}{2\alpha+6}. \tag{18.20}$$

In covalent glasses, the Gibbs-Di Marzio formula gives the best fit with the value of $\beta = 0.72$. We may try a similar formula as function of the rigidity parameter $<r>$ as follows:

$$T_g(<r>) = \frac{T_g^{iso}}{1-\gamma<r>} \tag{18.21}$$

The best fit for our version of T_g for the alkali-borate glass corresponds to $\gamma = 1.45$, close to 2β of the Gibbs-Di Marzio formula.

18.2.3 Adding the alkali modifier

Adding the alkali modifier results in transformations of local structures. Our aim is to define all such transformations that occur without changing the overall balance of connectivity, i.e. conserving in each case the number of bonds that connect a given cluster (or a couple of clusters) to the surrounding continuous random network.

Local structures are made of atoms with covalent bonds, and ions Na^+ loosely connected to the main network.

Figure 18.8: The graphic representation of three types of atoms present, O, B and Na, and the molecules: the boron oxide B_2O_3 and the sodium oxide Na_2O

Adding the Na_2O modifier results in various transformations of local configurations.

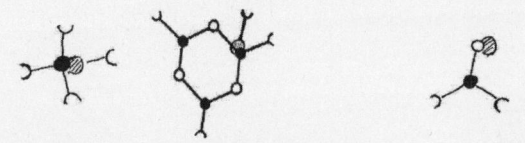

a) A B_4 4-valenced boron and Tetraborate   b) Metaborate

Figure 18.9: Examples of positioning of an Na^+ ion:
a) Transforming a three-valenced boron into B_4 tetracoordinate unit with an extra oxygen bond; local connectivity increases
b) Creating a non-bonding oxygen, i.e. breaking an oxygen bond; the connectivity decreases.

The evolution of rates of local structural units with alkali modifier's concentration x is known due to the data determined via Raman spectroscopy and NMR experimental observations. Our aim is to reproduce the curves of relative abundance of various boroxol groups shown in Figure 18.10.

Let us proceed now to a systematical display of clusters containing the Na^+ ions. Our aim is to find all possible configurations containing one or more Na^+ ions. We shall look for clusters with four external bonds, so that they can replace the configurations A and B without changing the connectivity of the network, i.e. without creating dangling bonds.

Systematics of 4-valenced clusters containing one or more Na^+ ions can be easily established. The calculus of the modifier content x is very simple

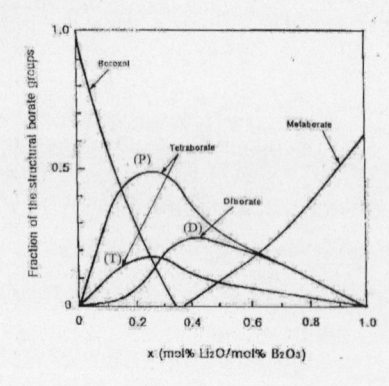

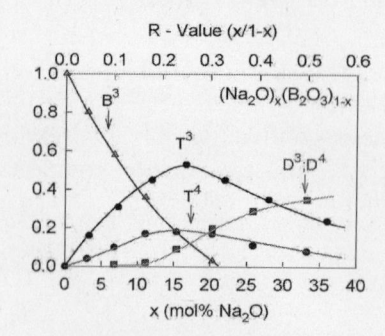

Figure 18.10: The left diagram: $Li_x(B_2O_3)_{(1-x)}$ glass is due to M. Balkanski and M. Massot. The right diagram: $Na_x(B_2O_3)_{(1-x)}$ glass (courtesy of P. Boolchand)

indeed, and is shown explicitly in each particular case. Besides, we shall proceed to the calculus of another important parameter, the *RIGIDITY* of each of the configurations displayed.

The latter is defined as the difference between the mean value of the number of degrees of freedom per atom N_f and the "free" value 3, $r = N_f - 3$ If $r < 0$, the cluster is *floppy (underconstrained)*;

If $r = 0$, the cluster is *isostatic*;

If $r > 0$, the cluster is *rigid (overconstrained)*.

The calculus of rigidity of given configuration is based on the following *constraint count assumptions*:

- Each three-valenced boron atom B_3 creates 3 angular constraints (bond angles $= 120^0$);

- Each tetra-valenced boron atom, B_4, (with an extra oxygen bond) creates 5 angular constraints;

- An oxygen atom inside a boroxol ring creates 1 angular constraint, whereas oxygen bonds out of rings have their angular constraints broken;

- All covalent bonds without exception are equivalent to 1 bond-stretching constraint; finally, the Na^+ ions are not taken into account in the rigidity calculus, their position being not strictly defined.

Structural units with one or two Na^+ ions

Next come clusters with two Na^+ ions and modified connectivity. Adding more of Na_2O leads to multiplication of valences. To keep the connectivity balance,

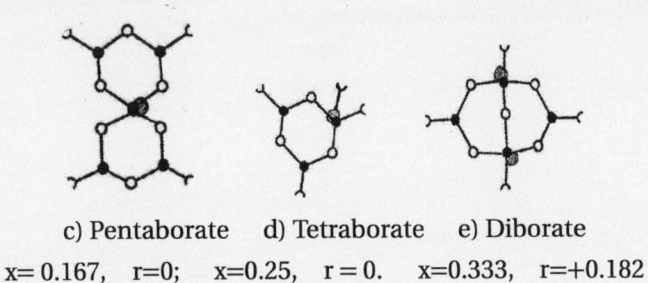

c) Pentaborate   d) Tetraborate   e) Diborate
x= 0.167, r=0;   x=0.25, r=0.   x=0.333, r=+0.182

Figure 18.11: Two important clusters with one Na^+ ion; the first two are isostatic, the third one is overconstrained.

some Na^+ ions break oxygen bonds and remain in the vicinity of one of the oxygens.

f) Dipentaborate   g) Ditetraborate   h) Tetrametaborate
$x = 0.29$ $r = 0.11$ $x = 0.4$ $r = 0.176$ $x = 0.4$ $r = -0.882$

Figure 18.12: Other important clusters with two Na^+ ions. The total connectivity is still $5 + 3 = 8$

When the concentration of Na_2O gets close to 40%, new clusters are formed, containing up to three Na^+ ions.

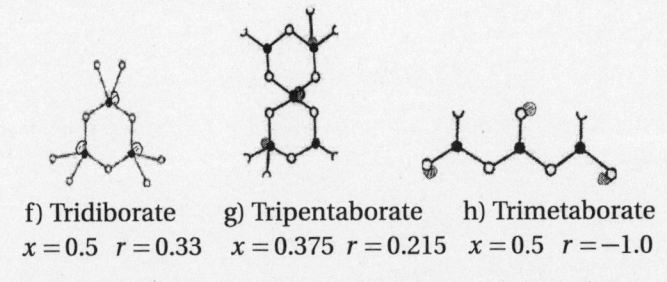

f) Tridiborate   g) Tripentaborate   h) Trimetaborate
$x = 0.5$ $r = 0.33$ $x = 0.375$ $r = 0.215$ $x = 0.5$ $r = -1.0$

Figure 18.13: Other important clusters with three Na^+ ions.

Now we are able to define minimal sets of pure B_2O_3 clusters which can transform into new clusters containing the Na^+ ions in such a way, that the overall connectivity remains unchanged. While comparing many possible reactions of this sort, we shall try to minimize the rigidity variation and maximize the homogeneity of the resulting local structures. Thus, at the onset of modifier's addition, it is reasonable to assume that new local four-valenced configurations should contain no more than one B_4 boron created by one Na^+ ion. Only later, when higher alkali concentrations are attained, configurations containing two or more Na^+ ions start to appear.

We display below consecutive transformations of pairs of local configurations after addition of one Na_2O molecule which after dissociation creates two B_4 four-coordinate borons placed in new local clusters.

Inserting Na_2O with local connectivity conservation results in the following connectivity conserving transformations:

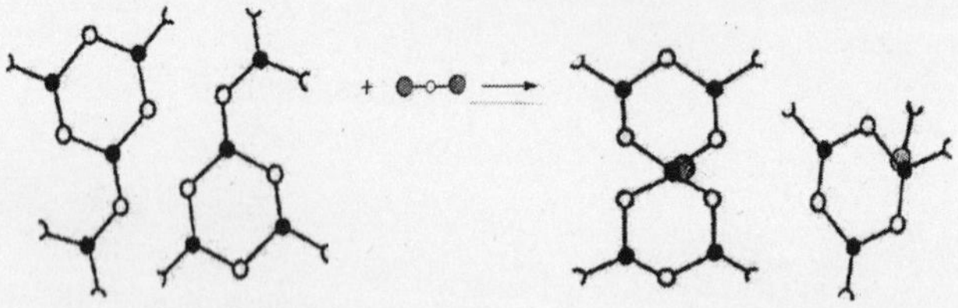

Two A clusters   Pentaborate + Tetraborate

Figure 18.14: Insertion of one Na_2O molecule into a pure amorphous B_2O_3 network. The transformation can be encoded as $2A + Na_2O \rightarrow T + P$.

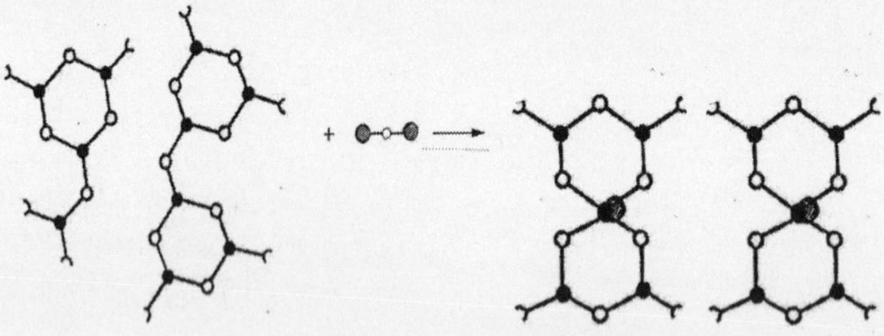

A and B clusters   2 Pentaborates

Figure 18.15: Insertion of one Na_2O molecule into a pure amorphous B_2O_3 network. This transformation can be encoded as $A + B + Na_2O \rightarrow 2P$.

18.3 The Volterra approach

18.3.1 Linear approximation

With the complete set of replacements of local configurations conserving connectivity due to the alkali modifier's addition we can follow the evolution of rates of different local clusters by letting first all A and B configurations initially

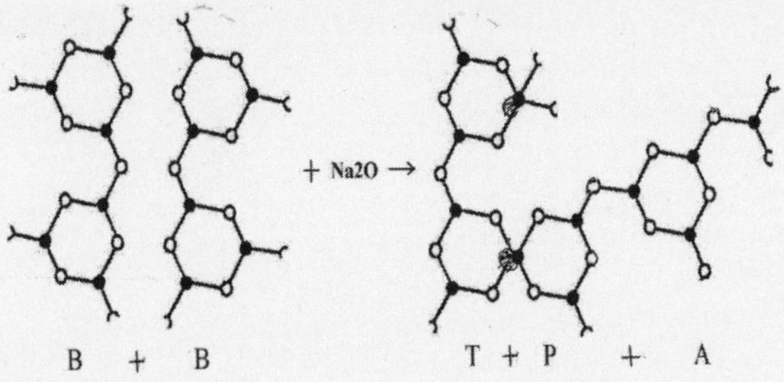

B + B →(+ Na2O) T + P + A

Figure 18.16: Insertion of one Na_2O molecule into a pure amorphous B_2O_3 network. This transformation can be encoded as $B + B + Na_2O \to T + P + A$.

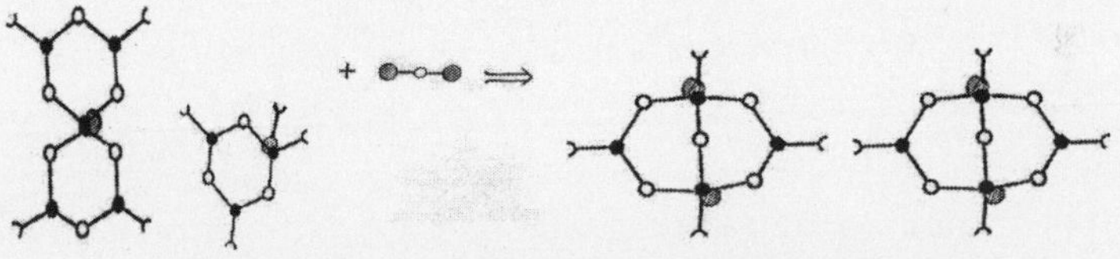

Pentaborate + Tritetraborate ⟹ Two Diborates

Figure 18.17: Insertion of one Na_2O molecule into a $(B_2O_3)_{(1-x)}(Na_2O)_x$ network. This transformation can be encoded as $P + T + Na_2O \to 2D$.

present in a pure B_2O_3 glassy network be transformed into pentaborates and tetraborates. According to the first transformations, the $B = B$ pairs will produce, besides pentaborates and tetraborates, a small amount of A-configurations. This is accredited by experiment, as can be seen in Figure (18.16)

Linear approximations are obtained as follows. First, we start from the pure B_2O_3 network containing 2/3 of A-clusters and 1/3 of B-clusters. Adding an Na_2O molecule leads to three connectivity conserving transformations, each with the appropriate probability: symbolically, we have

$$A + A + Na_2O \to P + T, \text{ with probability } p_A^2 = (2/3)^2 = 4/9,$$

$$A + B + Na_2O \to 2P \text{ with probability } 2p_A p_B = 2 \times (2/3)(1/3) = 4/9, \quad (18.22)$$

$$B + B + Na_2O \to P + T + A, \text{ with probability } p_B^2 = (1/3)^2 = 1/9.$$

The fractions above are normalized to 1, as any probability distribution should. Let us now evaluate relative proportions of new clusters formed after all A and B configuration have undergone transformations shown in (18.22). We have:

$$\tilde{p}_P \simeq p_A^2 + 2p_A p_B + (2/3)p_B^2, \quad \tilde{p}_T \simeq p_A^2 + (2/3)p_B^2, \quad \tilde{p}_A \simeq (2/3)p_B^2. \quad (18.23)$$

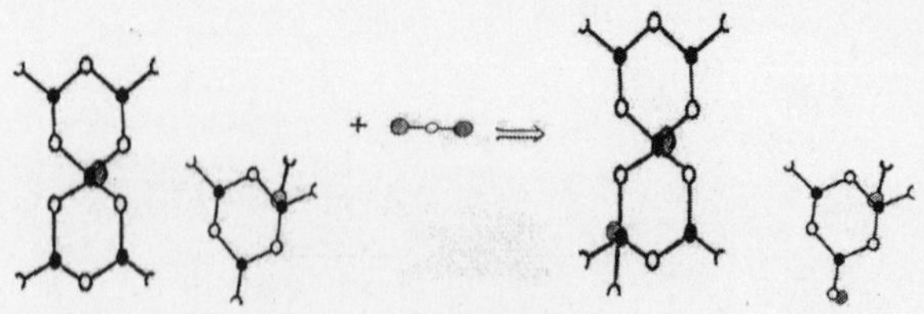

Pentaborate + Tritetraborate   Di-pentaborate + Trimetaborate

Figure 18.18: An alternative reaction to the previous one. This transformation can be encoded as $P + T + Na_2O \to DP + M3$.

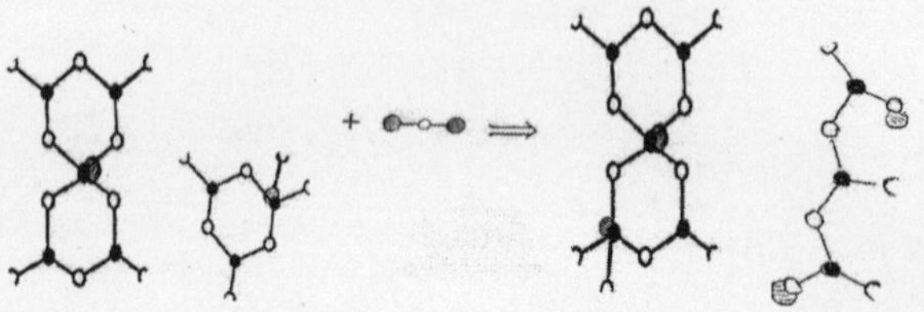

Pentaborate + Tritetraborate   Di-pentaborate + Trimetaborate

Figure 18.19: An alternative reaction to the previous one. This transformation can be encoded as $P + T + Na_2O \to DP + M3$.

The factor (2/3) is necessary to take into account the fact that the pair $B - B$ transforms into three elementary conigurations, and not into two ones like in the cases of the $A + A$ and $A + B$ reactions.

The above expressions are not normalized to 1; in order to do it, we must divide the expressions in (18.23) by their sum. This yields the probability distribution of three types of local clusters, P, T and A at the end of the first stage of transformation caused by the addition of Na_2O alkali modifier.

$$\tilde{p}_P = \frac{13}{21}, \quad \tilde{p}_T = \frac{7}{21}, \quad \tilde{p}_A = \frac{1}{21}. \tag{18.24}$$

Now we can evaluate the alkali molecular rate in this distribution of local configurations. The total number of B_2O_3 molecules in a sample is equal to $\frac{5}{2}\tilde{p}_P + \frac{3}{2}\tilde{p}_T + 2\tilde{p}_A$, which after inserting the numerical values (18.24) gives 90/42; the total number of the Na_2O molecules is given by $\frac{1}{2}\tilde{p}_P + \frac{1}{2}\tilde{p}_T = \frac{20}{42}$ (because a pentaborate or a tetraborate contain one half of the Na_2O molecule). Therefore the molecular content R of Na_2O versus B_2O_3 is equal to $\frac{20}{90} = 22.22\%$, whereas the concentration $<x>$ is $R/(R+1)$ is in this case 18.2%, as shown in 18.20.

The distribution (18.24) of clusters we arrived at may serve as the set of initial conditions for the next transformation stage induced by more incoming Na_2O

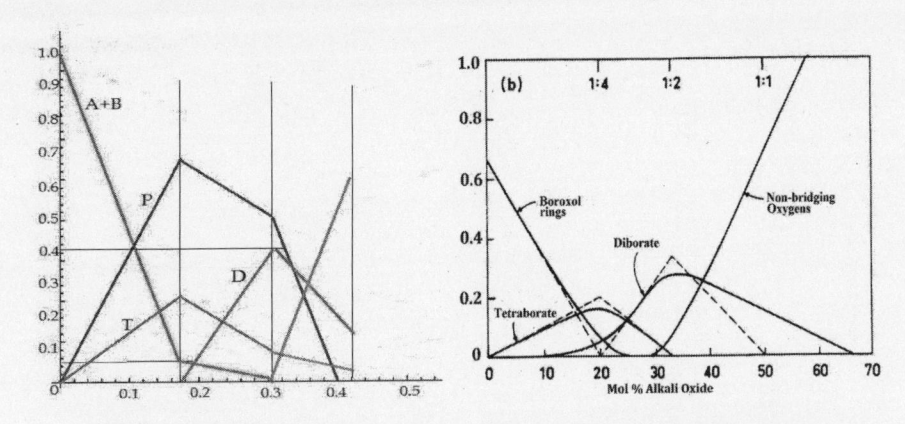

Figure 18.20: Linear approximation (left) versus Raman data (Right)

molecules. The dominant transformations are those of P and T configurations into diborates D, as shown in Figures (18.17, 18.18 and 18.19). The new probability distribution is obtained in the same manner as the previous one, by normalizing the products of probabilities corresponding to pairings $P+P$, $P+T$, $T+T$ etc.

We do not show the calculations here, which are similar to those of the first stage. The resulting distribution is shown in Figure (18.20) and the amounts are now 50% of pentaborates (P), 40% of diborates (D), and the remaining 10% of tetraborates (T). The corresponding Na_2O rate is now $x = 28.8\%$. Similar calculus can be performed for the newt stage, when metaborates (M) start to appear; the results are displayed in Figure (18.20).

18.3.2 The Lotka-Volterra equations

The evolution of various "species" of boroxol clusters with progressive addition of an alkali modifier is similar to the evolution of biological systems with different living organisms, competing for food and space, or even eating each other (predators and preys).

The simplest model is given by two species only, the prey x and the predator y. The evolution of their (relative) numbers can be described as follows:

The prey population $x(t)$ increases at a rate $Ax dt$, proportional to its own number, but is simultaneously killed by predators at a rate $-Bxy dt$;

The predator population $y(t)$ decreases at a rate $-Cy dt$, proportional to its own number, but increases at a rate $Dxy dt$; which leads to the following differential system:

$$\frac{dx}{dt} = Ax - Bxy, \quad \frac{dy}{dt} = -Cy + Dxy. \tag{18.25}$$

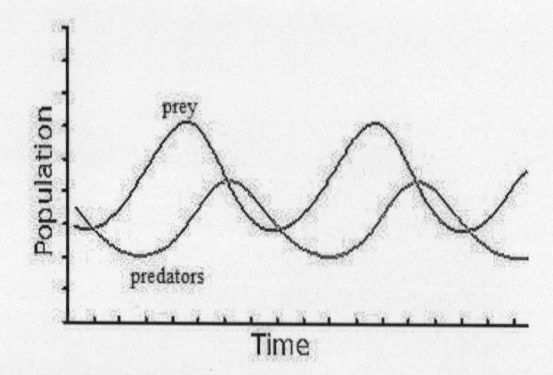

Figure 18.21: *Time evolution of total numbers of prey (upper) and predator (lower) curves.*

The populations display a typical periodic behavior: when the numbers of prey increases, there is more food for predators whose populations increases after some time, too. The more the predators multiply, the less prey is left, so that after some time predators starve, and the pray multiplies again, as can be seen in the Figure (18.21).

18.3.3 Evolution equations for local clusters

The evolution of relative number of local configurations can be described in a similar way, with the time parameter of the biological model being replaced by the modifier concentration x.

In order to establish the system of differential equations of Lotka-Volterra type, let us analyze what happens to the network when a small amount of modifier, Δn molecules, is added to the network with connectivity conservation.

Let us add a small number of molecules Δn to a network containing N clusters of types A, B, P, T, DP, D, M etc., their respective numbers being $N_A, N_B, N_P, N_T, N_{DP}, N_D, N_M$, etc.

The relative probabilities of finding at random a given cluster type are then

$$p_A = N_A/N, \quad p_B = N_B/N, \quad p_P = N_P/N, \text{ etc..}$$

The quantity $\Delta n/N$ corresponds to the variation of the modifier concentration with respect to the initial number of clusters. It can be easily renormalized and replaced by the real molecular concentration Δx in the final formulae

At the onset of modifier addition the equations ruling the first stage of the evolution of clusters' species are established very easily if we neglect all local configurations except the pure boroxol rings and tripods, and the tetraborates and pentaborates, which are the only ones to be produced at the beginning.

The numbers N_A, N_B, N_P and N_T vary as follows:

$$\Delta N_A = -2p_A^2 \Delta n - 2p_A p_B \Delta n, +p_B^2 \Delta n, \quad \Delta N_B = -2p_B^2 \Delta n - 2p_A p_B \Delta n,$$

$$\Delta N_P = p_A^2 \Delta n + 4p_A p_B \Delta n, +p_B^2 \Delta n, \quad \Delta N_T = p_A^2 \Delta n + p_B^2 \Delta n,$$

(The sum of all does not give 0 because $N \neq Const$.)

After dividing by N, we get the equations ruling the probabilities; the expression $\Delta n/N$ cannot be interpreted yet as $\frac{\Delta n}{N_{B_2O_3}} = \Delta \nu$, but can be easily renormalized.

$$\frac{\Delta p_A}{\Delta n} = -2p_A^2 - 2p_A p_B + \frac{2}{3} p_B^2, \quad \frac{\Delta p_B}{\Delta n} = -2p_B^2 - 2p_A p_B,$$

$$\frac{\Delta p_P}{\Delta n} = p_A^2 + 4p_A p_B + \frac{2}{3} p_B^2, \quad \frac{\Delta p_T}{\Delta n} = p_A^2 + \frac{2}{3} p_B^2, \tag{18.26}$$

(The sum of all gives 0 because $\sum_{p_k} p_k = 1$.)

The first evolution stages occur below the 10% of Na_2O concentration. The Na_2O molecules encounter practically only the A and B configurations transforming them into the P and T units. The corresponding reactions are:

$$2A + Na_2O \rightarrow P + T; \quad A + B + Na_2O \rightarrow 2P; \quad B + B + Na_2O \rightarrow A + P + T.$$

After the 10% of Na_2O concentration is reached, the next Na_2O molecules can interact also with the Pentaborates and Tetraborates, according to the reactions shown on the previous slides. Now the evolution equations should take into account more cluster types, according to the following reactions:

$$A + P + Na_2O \rightarrow 3T; \quad A + T + Na_2O \rightarrow D + T;$$

$$B + P + Na_2O \rightarrow A + T + D; \quad B + T + Na_2O \rightarrow D + P;$$

Let us recall the differential system valid at the onset of modifier addition, $\nu = N_{Na_2O}/N_{B_2O_3}$:

$$\frac{\Delta p_A}{\Delta n} = -2p_A^2 - 2p_A p_B + \frac{2}{3}p_B^2, \quad \frac{\Delta p_B}{\Delta n} = -2p_B^2 - 2p_A p_B,$$

$$\frac{\Delta p_P}{\Delta n} = p_A^2 + 4p_A p_B + \frac{2}{3}p_B^2, \quad \frac{\Delta p_T}{\Delta n} = p_A^2 + \frac{2}{3}p_B^2, \qquad (18.27)$$

18.3.4 Continuous limit

Before passing to the continuous limit and forming differential equations, let us express everything exclusively in terms of probabilities and of the unique independent variable, the modifier content x. In order to change from ΔN_A, ΔN_B, etc., into Δp_A, Δp_B, etc., it is enough to divide both sides by the total number of configurations, $N_{total} = N_A + N_B + N_P + N_T + N_D$.

As it is usually done in differential calculus, the ΔN_i and Δn are treated as infinitesimals, so there is no difference which actual values of N_{total} are chosen, the initial or the final ones. Still, we have to express the ratio $\Delta n / N_{total}$ in terms of the differential Δx.

At the moment, on the right-hand side we have got the ratio $\Delta n / N_{total}$; but this can be easily transformed into the quantity $\Delta \nu$ as follows. There is a simple relationship between N_{total}, the total number of local configurations, and N, the total number of $B_2 O_3$ molecules. The total number of $B_2 O - 3$ molecules is given by:

$$N = 2N_A + 3N_B + \frac{3}{2}N_T + \frac{5}{2}N_P + 2N_D,$$

dividing both sides by N_{total}; we get, by definition of configuration probabilities,

$$\frac{N}{N_{total}} = 2p_A + 3p_B + \frac{3}{2}p_{TT} + \frac{5}{2}p_P + 2p_D = <k>, \qquad (18.28)$$

where we note by $<k>$ the *average number of $B_2 O_3$ molecules* per local configuration, so that one can write:

$$N = <k> N_{total}, \quad \text{so that} \quad \frac{\Delta n}{N_{total}} = <k> \frac{\Delta n}{N} = <k> \Delta \nu. \qquad (18.29)$$

Now we can proceed to the continuous limit, dividing by $\Delta \nu$ both sides of the equations (18.26). As an example, let us write down the equation for p_A:

$$\frac{dp_A}{d\nu} = <k> \left(-2p_A^2 - 2p_A p_B - 2p_A p_{TT} - 2p_A p_P + \frac{2}{3}p_B^2 + \frac{2}{3} 2p_B p_P \right), \qquad (18.30)$$

and we remind that $<k> = 2p_A + 3p_B + \frac{3}{2}p_T + \frac{5}{2}p_P + 2p_D$.

The derivation with respect to the variable v can be transformed into the derivation with respect to the variable x using the relation $v = x/(1-x)$; we have

$$\frac{d}{dv} = \frac{dx}{dv}\frac{d}{dx} = \left[\frac{dv}{dx}\right]^{-1}\frac{d}{dx} = (1-x)^2 \frac{d}{dx}. \tag{18.31}$$

Now the first differential equation of (18.26) can be written as follows:

$$\frac{dp_A}{dx} = \frac{<k>}{(1-x)^2}\left(-2p_A^2 - 2p_A p_B - 2p_A p_T - 2p_A p_P + \frac{2}{3}p_B^2 + \frac{2}{3}2p_B p_P\right),$$

and similarly for the four remaning equations.

The explicit form of the Volterra-type system is now

$$\frac{dp_A}{dv} = <k>\left[-2p_A^2 + \frac{2}{3}p_B^2 - 2p_A p_B + 2\frac{2}{3}p_B p_P - 2p_A p_P - 2p_A p_T\right];$$

$$\frac{dp_B}{dv} = <k>\left[-2p_B^2 - 2p_A p_B - 2p_B p_P - 2p_B p_T\right];$$

$$\frac{dp_P}{dv} = <k>\left[p_A^2 + 4p_A p_B + \frac{2}{3}p_B^2 - 2p_B p_P + 2p_B p_T - 2p_A p_P\right]; \tag{18.32}$$

$$\frac{dp_T}{dv} = <k>\left[p_A^2 + \frac{2}{3}p_B^2 - 2p_B p_T + +4p_A p_P + 2\frac{2}{3}p_B p_P - 2p_A p_P\right];$$

$$\frac{dp_D}{dv} = <k>\left[2p_A p_T - 2p_B p_T - 2\frac{2}{3}p_B p_P\right];$$

The initial conditions for our differential system are simple:

$$\overset{o}{p}_A = \frac{2}{3}, \quad \overset{o}{p}_B = \frac{1}{3}, \quad \overset{o}{p}_P = 0, \quad \overset{o}{p}_T = 0, \quad \overset{o}{p}_D = 0, \text{ and so on.}$$

At $x = 0$ we get the value of $<k> = \frac{7}{3}$

Inserting the initial values in the right-hand side, we get the differential system for linear approximation, the solutions of which are simple linear functions displayed below:

$$\overset{1}{p}_A = \frac{2}{3} - \frac{238}{81}x, \quad \overset{1}{p}_B = \frac{1}{3} - \frac{126}{81}x, \quad \overset{1}{p}_P = \frac{266}{81}x, \quad \overset{1}{p}_T = \frac{98}{81}x,$$

They are a bit more precise than those obtained in previous sections, and agree perfectly with initial slopes observed in the experimental data, as shown in Figure 18.22 on the left.

In order to produce the curve corresponding to the abundance of boroxol rings, we should use the probabilities of clusters A and B as follows:

$$p_{rings} = \frac{p_A + 2p_B}{\overset{o}{p}_A + 2\overset{o}{p}_B}.$$

The system (18.32) is too complicated to be solved by hand, but it is a fair game for computer programs like "Maple" or "Mathematica". In our case the "Maple" facility was used, yielding a quite satisfactory result in the interval $0 \leq x \leq 0.4$ Å The resulting curves are displayed in the Figure below (left).

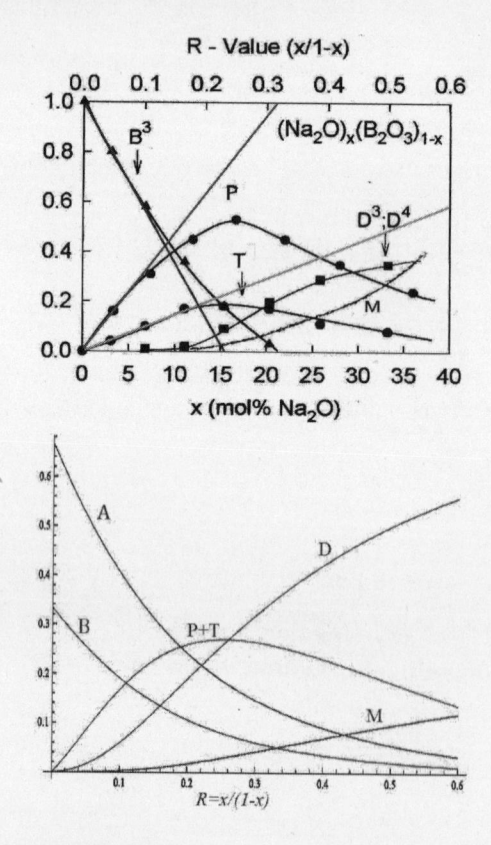

Figure 18.22: Comparison between the experimental data and the solutions of our differential Volterra-type system.

x	p_A	p_B	p_P	p_T	p_D	p_M	$<r>$
0.00	0.67	0.33	0	0	0	0	−0.257
0.08	0.42	0.21	0.28	0.19	0	0	−0.161
0.15	0.267	0.136	0.43	0.17	0	0	−0.104
0.20	0.167	0.083	0.52	0.16	0.07	0.04	−0.082
0.25	0.107	0.05	0.53	0.19	0.09	0.05	−0.045
0.30	0.033	0.017	0.46	0.16	0.17	0.08	−0.094
0.35	0	0	0.43	0.17	0.22	0.18	−0.104
0.40	0	0	0.38	0.16	0.28	0.19	−0.108

Table II: Average rigidity defect $<r>$ for different concentrations of Na_2O. The values calculated averaging from experimental data in (18.10).

We observe that alkali borate glasses $(Na_2O)_x(B_2O_3)_{(1-x)}$ are *floppy* from $x \leq 0.2$, close to *isostatic* in the range $0.2 < x < 0.3$ and floppy again beyond $x > 0.3$.

The average rigidity defect r as function of the alkali modifier concentration can be inserted into the formula for the glass transition temperature T_g introduced in Section 3.2 (formula 18.21) in order to get the curve $T_g(x)$ and compare it with experimental data. The result is shown in the following Figure 18.23.

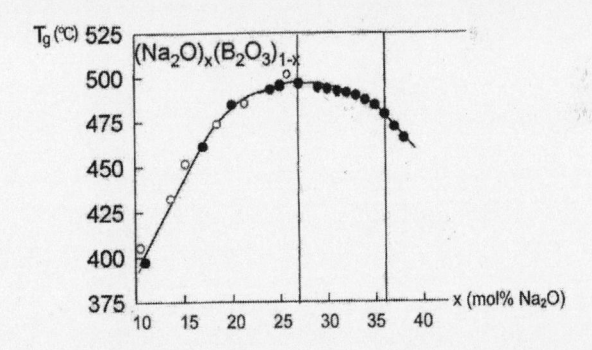

Figure 18.23: Theoretical (white) versus experimental (black) $T_g(x)$.

Bibliography

[1] M. Micoulaut, R. Kerner and D. M. dos Santos-Loff *Statistical modeling of structural and thermodynamical properties of vitreous B_2O_3* J. Phys. Cond. Matter **7**, 8035 (1995). *ibid*, **31**, 323.

[2] A. C. Wright and N. M. Vedishcheva, European Journal of Glass Science and Technology B, **57**, 1 (2016).

[3] A. C. Hannon, R. N. Sinclair and A. C. Wright (1993) *The vibrational modes of vitreous B_2O_3*, Physica A, **201**, 373 (1993).

[4] A. C. Hannon, D. I. Grimley, R. A. Hulme, A. C. Wright and R. N. Sinclair (1994) *Boroxol groups in vitreous boron oxide: new evidence from neutron diffraction and inelastic neutron scattering studies*, Journal of non-crystalline solids, **177**, 299 1994.

[5] P. J. Bray, S.A. Feller, G.E. Jellison Jr, G.E. and Y.H. Yun *B10 NMR studies of the structure of borate glasses*, Journal Non-Crystalline Solids, **38**, 93 (1980).

[6] G. E. Walrafen, S. R. Samanta and P. N. Krishnan) *Raman investigation of vitreous and molten boric oxide* J. Chem. Phys. 113 (1980.

[7] A. C. Wright, N. M. Vedishcheva and B. A. Shakhmatkin "Vitreous borate networks containing superstructural units: a challenge to the random network theory?" J. non-crystalline solids, **192**, 92 (1995).

[8] R. A. Barrio, R. Kerner, M. Micoulaut and G.G. Naumis *Evaluation of the concentration of boroxol rings in vitreous by the stochastic matrix method*, J. Physics: Condensed Matter, **9**, 9219 (1997).

[9] R. A. Barrio, J.-P. Duruisseau and R. Kerner *Structural properties of alkali-borate glasses derived from a theoretical model*, Phil. Magazine B **72**, 535 (1995).

[10] R. Kerner, *Two simple rules for covalent binary glasses*, Physica B: Condensed Matter, **215**, 267 (1995).

[11] R. Kerner and M. Micoulaut, *A theoretical model of formation of covalent binary glasses. I. General setting.* Journal of non-crystalline solids, **176**, 271 (1994).

[12] G. G. Naumis *Variation of the glass transition temperature with rigidity and chemical composition*, Phys. Rev. B **73**, 172202 (2006).

[13] J. H. Gibbs and E. A. Di Marzio *Nature of the glass transition and the glassy state*, J. Chem. Phys. **28**, 373 (1958).

[14] R. Kerner and D. M. dos Santos *Nucleation and amorphous and crystalline growth: A dynamical model in two dimensions*,Phys. Rev. B **34** 858 (1988).

[15] R. Aldrovandi and R. Kerner, *Stochastic Matrix Algebras Applied to Models of Agglomeration and Growth.* In "*New Symmetries and Integrable Models: Proceedings of XIV Max Born Symposium*, Edited by Frydryszak et al. (World Scientific, Singapore, (2000).

[16] R. Aldrovandi, *Special matrices of mathematical physics: stochastic, circulant, and Bell matrices* (World Scientific, Singapore, 2001).

[17] R. Kerner, *Models of Agglomeration and Glass Transition* (Imperial College Press, London, 2007).

[18] R. Kerner and R. Aldrovandi, *Stochastic Matrices as a Tool for Biological Evolution Models*, in *BIOMAT 2009*, Edited by R. Mondaini) (World Scientific, Singapore, 2010).

19

Re-assessing properties of Dirac's equation in presence of Lorentz-symmetry violation

J. P. S. Melo, J. A. Helayël-Neto

Abstract: Our effort in this contribution is to provide physical motivations and a short overview of developments related to the activity known as Lorentz-symmetry violation (LSV) in the context of the so-called Standard Model Extension (SME). Throughout the text, LSV effects in the QED fermionic sector of the SME are studied and discussed. Two interesting aspects regarding a modified Dirac's equation in this scenario stand out: the Klein Paradox and the phenomenon of *Zitterbewegung*.

19.1 Intuitive and general aspects of Lorentz-symmetry violation

Physical arguments point to strong quantum fluctuations of the vacuum at the Planck scale. We refer to this scenario as space-time foam. This means that the vacuum behaves as a dynamical medium that affects the propagation of high-energy particles, yielding, effectively, to the violation of Lorentz symmetry. At a first glance, when hearing about Lorentz-symmetry Violation (LSV), we risk to think of it as a denial of the Theory of Special Relativity, whose underlying symmetry is described by the Lorentz group, $SO(1,3)$.

However, it is essential to clarify that this is not the case. Just as a uniform external magnetic field established in three-dimensional space breaks rotational symmetry, characterized by the group $SO(3)$, some anisotropy in spacetime corresponds to the violation of $SO(1,3)$ symmetry. The entire investigation within the scope of LSV is motivated by the quest to understand the possible origins of spacetime anisotropies present in the quantum vacuum. These origins could potentially indicate new physics beyond the Standard Model.

In fact, in scenarios involving LSV, researchers are also attempting to comprehend the very structure of the quantum vacuum, which exhibits electromagnetic properties such as birefringence, dichroism or some other metamaterial-like optical property. The discussion about a possible scenario characterized by LSV was initially addressed by Dirac in 1951, in a paper where he presented the idea of a new QED with the existence of an ether in the form of a background vector that would establish a preferred direction and investigated whether this vector could reveal the nature of the ultraviolet divergences in quantum field theories [1].

For a long time, and in some cases even today, the renormalization procedure that we implemented to extract finite physical results in quantum field theory was seen as a way to "sweep things under the carpet". However, renormalization has a much deeper physical significance, because it is from this procedure that we construct the renormalization group and arrive at the running coupling, which is essential for describing asymptotic freedom in strong interactions, for example.

It is pertinent to recall here that G. Scharf, in his book "*Finite quantum electrodynamics*", calculates perturbative corrections for QED processes without employing renormalization [2]. To do so, he adopts results from the seventies to handle singular distributions along with an additional criterion, the causality criterion. The most interesting aspect of this approach is that, at a certain point, the author shows that his results perfectly coincide with those obtained via renormalization. Therefore, this indicates that the renormalization procedure for handling divergences in quantum field theory is a sensible scheme if carried out consistently and carefully.

The work by Dirac marks the embryonic discussions that gained consistency with the Superstrings and culminated in the current discussions on LSV. The first revolution of Strings occurred in 1984, and in the era of Superstrings, the first work of V. A. Kostelecký and S. Samuel appeared in 1989. In this work, within the context of open Strings, there are tensor fields that can take nontrivial vacuum expectation values, and these tensor fields condense in the vacuum, breaking Lorentz symmetry [3]. This work serves as the starting point for the next phase of LSV investigation, which is more inspired by String Theory and effective models that attempt to discuss new physical scenarios beyond the Standard Model. Also in 1989, these two authors established phenomenological constraints from String Theory for the context of LSV [4].

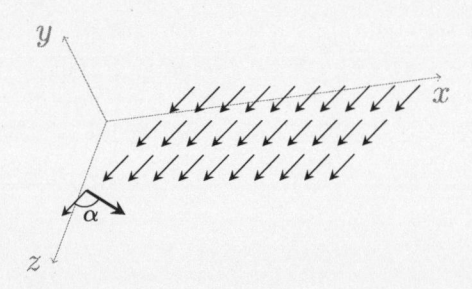

Figure 19.1: The result of a passive Lorentz transformations applied in the initial configuration of Figure 19.2.

In 1990, S. M. Carroll, G. B. Field, and R. Jackiw (CFJ) explored in [5] limits on LSV using a topological model, which is a $(1+3)$D version of the Chern-Simons model in $(1+2)$-D, described by

$$\mathscr{L} \sim \varepsilon_{\mu\nu\kappa\lambda} v^\mu A^\nu F^{\kappa\lambda}. \qquad (19.1)$$

In this expression, A^ν is the photon field, $F^{\kappa\lambda}$ is the electromagnetic field-strength, v^μ is the background vector field that establishes a privileged spacetime direction, altering the Maxwell's equations, and $\varepsilon_{\mu\nu\kappa\lambda}$ is the covariant form of the fully antisymmetric Levi-Civita pseudo-tensor. This model makes use of astrophysical data to estimate the scale of the components of the anisotropy, v^μ, responsible for LSV. Also some important considerations from the modified dispersion relation of the model arise, such as the effect of birefringence emerging. Associated with this modified dispersion relation, there are also two aspects that should be investigated, namely, the potential violation of causality and the stability property of the vacuum. We refer the reader to the reference works [6, 7], where these issues are explored in detail.

Without much delay, between 1997 and 1998, the so-called Standard-Model Extension (SME) was born through a pair of works by D. Colladay and V. A. Kostelecký [8, 9]. The SME incorporates all the characteristics of the usual Standard Model (i.e., the same internal symmetries $SU(3) \times SU(2) \times U(1)$, being free from

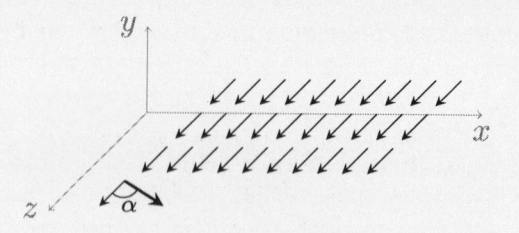

Figure 19.2: A 3D (x, y, z) reference frame and a vector LSV background field in black making an angle α with a expected value indicated by a bold black vector.

higher-order derivatives, and renormalizable) along with General Relativity but considers the possibility of violating Lorentz- and CPT-symmetry. In a sense, Lorentz symmetry remains valid, as the theory behaves normally under rotations or boosts, considering that the so-called passive Lorentz transformations of the observer are performed in the laboratory frame. To better understand that point of view, consider the reference frame in Figure 19.2.

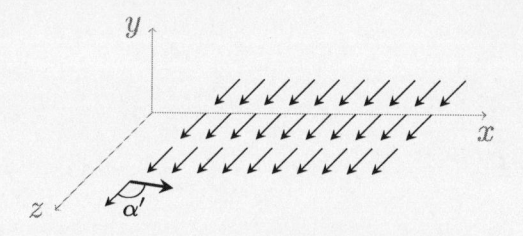

Figure 19.3: The result of an active Lorentz transformations applied in the initial configuration of Figure 19.2.

The coordinates x, y and z are spatial ones and we are not representing the temporal coordinate, ct, just for simplicity. The black arrows represent a vector background field which breaks LS. The bold black arrow represents a expected value describing a non-trivial vacuum state. The angle α is defined between the background and the vacuum state. Whether we perform a passive Lorentz transformation, which just change the reference frame coordinates by rotations and boosts, we can obtain, for example, a new situation described in Figure 19.1. As a result, the angle α does not change due to this transformation and we cannot obtain any information about the LSV background. Also, the covariance of the action is intact and the bold field can have an arbitrary tensor structure. In the SME context, LSV only appears when the fields are rotated or altered with respect to the expected tensor values describing the vacuum state, known as active Lorentz transformations of particles. As before, to better understand it, we can begin again with the Figure 19.2 and then perform an active Lorentz transformation, which consists in keep intact the reference frame and make rotations or boosts in the fields coordinates dependence, as shown in Figure 19.3.

Differently from the result obtained in Figure 19.1, the result of Figure 19.3 changes the initial angle α to another angle α'. This difference of angles reveals the presence of the LSV background. Among the various contemporary approaches to investigate LSV, the SME is the most widely used theoretical framework to study phenomenology from multiple perspectives. The SME incorporates the CFJ model and open new avenues of exploration and demonstrate that there are situations where the effects of LSV can manifest at energy scales accessible in particle accelerators and through current or upcoming astrophysical and cosmological observations.

Experimental and observational searches for these subtle effects have yielded good limits on the parameters that govern LSV. The most recent results are published annually in the so-called "Data Tables for Lorentz and CPT Violation", which, at the time of writing this text, is in its sixteenth version [10]. These searches generally focus on evaluating phenomenologies related to the motion of objects in an anisotropic background, atomic clocks in space, vacuum birefringence of light, spin precession effects, atomic energy level shifts, neutrino physics, modified dispersion relations for high-energy photons, observations of gamma-ray bursts, among others. These investigations aim to explore the subtle effects of LSV and establish constraints on the parameters which characterizing them.

With all this background provided to the LSV, it could be stated that LSV investigation consists of always keeping in mind that LS is an indispensable fact of nature at the scales we know and ask: to what extent can we uphold this symmetry? We have good reasons to believe that it should break at extremely tiny distance scales and also at ultra-high energies. Therefore, in the context of low energies in which we live, we do not expect to observe a complete LSV, but rather its manifestations through very subtle effects, as they can be suppressed by some power of the Planck scale, this is

$$E_P = \sqrt{\frac{\hbar c^5}{G}} \approx 1,22 \times 10^{19} \text{ GeV} \approx 1,96 \times 10^9 \text{ J}. \tag{19.2}$$

The topic of LSV is a pursuit of new physics that goes beyond the Standard Model, with the hope of shedding light on various questions such as: indicating a path towards quantum gravity (String Theory, Loop Quantum Gravity, etc.); addressing the hierarchy problem in gauge theories; understanding the origin of the Higgs boson mass; explaining the asymmetry between matter and antimatter in the universe; resolving the neutron electric dipole moment problem; understanding dark matter; investigating neutrino oscillations and their mass; among others.

19.2 Some aspects of the QED fermionic sector in the SME

In the QED sector of the SME, we have

$$S = \int d^4x \left[\bar{\psi}(i\hbar\Gamma^\mu D_\mu - M)\psi - \frac{1}{4\mu_0}F^{\mu\nu}F_{\mu\nu} \right.$$
$$\left. - \frac{1}{4\mu_0}k_{\mu\nu\lambda\rho}F^{\mu\nu}F^{\lambda\rho} - \frac{1}{2\mu_0}\varepsilon_{\mu\nu\kappa\lambda}v^\mu A^\nu F^{\kappa\lambda} \right], \quad (19.3)$$

where the constant background tensor $k_{\mu\nu\lambda\rho}$ is a CPT-even term, and the total term that contracts with it is commonly referred to as the aether term. The constant background vector k^μ is a CPT-odd term, and the total term that accompanies it is the usual CFJ term. D_μ takes the form of the usual covariant derivative with minimal coupling, and

$$\Gamma^\mu = \gamma^\mu + c^{\mu\nu}\gamma_\nu + d^{\mu\nu}\gamma_\nu\gamma_5 + e^\mu + if^\mu\gamma_5 + \frac{1}{4}g^{\lambda\nu\mu}\Sigma_{\lambda\nu}, \quad (19.4)$$

$$M = mc + a_\mu\gamma^\mu + b_\mu\gamma^\mu\gamma_5 + \frac{1}{4}H_{\mu\nu}\Sigma^{\mu\nu} + m_5\gamma_5, \quad (19.5)$$

with γ^μ and $\gamma_5 = i\gamma^0\gamma^1\gamma^2\gamma^3$ being the usual Dirac matrices obeying the Clifford algebra $\{\gamma^\mu,\gamma^\nu\} = 2\eta^{\mu\nu}$, and $\Sigma^{\mu\nu} = i[\gamma^\mu,\gamma^\nu]/4$. The $c^{\mu\nu}$, $d^{\mu\nu}$, e^μ, f^μ, $c^{\lambda\nu\mu}$, a_μ, b_μ, $H_{\mu\nu}$ and m_5 are all field which can assume expected values describing a non-trivial vacuum state and consequently breaking the invariance under active Lorentz transformations.

In what follows, we will focus on the mass sector, Eq. (19.5), of the Eq. (19.3) considering $H_{\mu\nu} = 0$, $a_\mu = -\xi_\mu$, $b_\mu = -R_\mu$ and $m_5 = -i\zeta$. Therefore, we will work with a modified Dirac equation as follows

$$(i\hbar\gamma^\mu\partial_\mu - mc - i\zeta\gamma_5 - \xi_\mu\gamma^\mu - R_\mu\gamma^\mu\gamma_5)\psi(x) = 0. \quad (19.6)$$

Taking the Fourier transform,

$$\psi(x) = \int \frac{d^4p}{(2\pi\hbar)^4}\psi(p)e^{-ip_\mu x^\mu/\hbar}, \quad (19.7)$$

we can write

$$(p_\mu\gamma^\mu - mc - i\zeta\gamma_5 - \xi_\mu\gamma^\mu - R_\mu\gamma^\mu\gamma_5)\psi(p) = D\psi(p) = 0. \quad (19.8)$$

Where D is a 4×4 matrix with general form given by

$$D = a\mathbb{1} + b\gamma_5 + c_\mu\gamma^\mu + d_\mu\gamma^\mu\gamma_5, \quad (19.9)$$

and we have that the general structure for its inverse can be written in the form of the *ansatz*

$$D^{-1} = x\mathbb{1} + y\gamma_5 + z_\mu\gamma^\mu + w_\mu\gamma^\mu\gamma_5 + t_{\mu\nu}\Sigma^{\mu\nu}. \quad (19.10)$$

This *ansatz* is reasonable assuming that x and y are scalar parameters, and that

$$\Sigma^{\mu\nu} = \frac{i}{4}[\gamma^\mu, \gamma^\nu], \tag{19.11}$$

$$z_\mu = \alpha c_\mu + \beta d_\mu, \tag{19.12}$$

$$w_\mu = \xi c_\mu + \lambda d_\mu, \tag{19.13}$$

$$t_{\mu\nu} = \rho \theta_{\mu\nu} + 2\tau \tilde{\theta}_{\mu\nu}. \tag{19.14}$$

With α, β, ξ, λ, ρ, and τ being real or complex coefficients. And we have, by definition, that

$$\theta_{\mu\nu} \equiv \frac{1}{2}(c_\mu d_\nu - c_\nu d_\mu) \text{ and } \tilde{\theta}_{\mu\nu} = \frac{1}{2}\varepsilon_{\alpha\beta\mu\nu}\theta^{\alpha\beta}. \tag{19.15}$$

That is, $\tilde{\theta}_{\mu\nu}$ is the dual of $\theta_{\mu\nu}$. In this sense, the reasonableness we claim for this ansatz stems from the facts that, firstly, the matrices $1, \gamma_5, \gamma^\mu, \gamma^\mu\gamma_5, \Sigma^{\mu\nu}$ form a set of 16 matrices that constitute a general basis in which any 4×4 matrix can be written, and secondly, the way the coefficients x, y, z_μ, w_μ, and $t_{\mu\nu}$ have been written is committed to reflecting the most general tensorial structure possible to be constructed from the coefficients of D when we seek its inverse.

In this scenario, if we wish to completely determine the inverse D^{-1}, the set of coefficients $x, y, \alpha, \beta, \xi, \lambda, \rho, \tau$ must be determined based on the requirement that

$$DD^{-1} = 1. \tag{19.16}$$

From this requirement and working to simplify the algebra of tensor indices to the fullest extent, we can collect the coefficients of each matrix in the basis 1, γ_5, γ^μ, $\gamma^\mu\gamma_5$, and $\Sigma^{\mu\nu}$. Remembering that the coefficient proportional to the identity must be equal to 1, while those proportional to the other matrices must be equal to zero, we can write a system of eight equations to determine $x, y, \alpha, \beta, \xi, \lambda, \rho, \tau$. This system consists of equations derived from

- Coefficient of 1:

$$ax + by + c^2\alpha + (c \cdot d)\beta - (c \cdot d)\xi - d^2\lambda = 1. \tag{19.17}$$

- Coefficient of γ_5:

$$bx + ay - (c \cdot d)\alpha - d^2\beta + c^2\xi + (c \cdot d)\lambda = 0. \tag{19.18}$$

- Coefficient of γ^μ:

$$c_\mu \to x + a\alpha - b\xi - \frac{i}{2}(c \cdot d)\rho - d^2\tau = 0, \tag{19.19}$$

$$d_\mu \to y + a\beta - b\lambda + \frac{i}{2}c^2\rho + (c \cdot d)\tau = 0. \tag{19.20}$$

- Coefficient of $\gamma^\mu \gamma_5$:

$$c_\mu \to y - b\alpha + a\xi - \frac{i}{2}d^2\rho - (c\cdot d)\tau = 0, \qquad (19.21)$$

$$d_\mu \to x - b\beta + a\lambda + \frac{i}{2}(c\cdot d)\rho + c^2\tau = 0. \qquad (19.22)$$

- Coefficient of $\Sigma^{\mu\nu}$:

This coefficient depends on θ and $\tilde{\theta}$, which, despite being independent, mix different representations of the Lorentz group. Therefore, we can define, in order to explicitly show the distinct representations, that

$$T_{\mu\nu} \equiv \frac{1}{2}\left(\theta_{\mu\nu} + i\tilde{\theta}_{\mu\nu}\right) \in (1,0), \qquad (19.23)$$

$$W_{\mu\nu} \equiv \frac{1}{2}\left(\theta_{\mu\nu} - i\tilde{\theta}_{\mu\nu}\right) \in (0,1). \qquad (19.24)$$

Here, $(1,0)$ and $(0,1)$ are irreducible representations of the Lorentz group. In this framework, θ and $\tilde{\theta}$ are written in a way that

$$\theta = T + W, \qquad (19.25)$$

$$\tilde{\theta} = -iT + iW. \qquad (19.26)$$

So that the coefficients of $\gamma^\mu \gamma_5$ are proportional, independently, to T and W as follows:

$$T \to -2i\alpha - 2i\beta - 2i\xi - 2i\lambda + (a+b)\rho - $$
$$- 2i(a+b)\tau = 0, \qquad (19.27)$$
$$W \to +2i\alpha - 2i\beta - 2i\xi + 2i\lambda + (a-b)\rho + $$
$$+ 2i(a-b)\tau = 0. \qquad (19.28)$$

Solving this system, we find that

$$\begin{cases} x = -\dfrac{a}{b}y = \dfrac{a\left(a^2 - b^2 - c^2 + d^2\right)}{\Delta}, \\ \alpha = \lambda = \dfrac{-\left(a^2 - b^2 - c^2 + d^2\right)}{\Delta}, \\ \xi = -\beta = \dfrac{2(c\cdot d)}{\Delta}, \rho = \dfrac{4ib}{\Delta}, \tau = \dfrac{2a}{\Delta}. \end{cases} \qquad (19.29)$$

where

$$\Delta = \det(D) = \left(-a^2 + b^2 + c^2\right)^2 - 4(c\cdot d)^2 + $$
$$+ 2\left(a^2 - b^2 + c^2\right)d^2 + d^4. \qquad (19.30)$$

These results completely specify both the determinant of D and its inverse D^{-1}, which can be understood as an extended fermionic propagator with Lorentz symmetry violation (LSV) terms. To rescue the result of the modified fermionic dispersion relation (19.8), we take the result (19.30) by identifying $a = -mc$, $b = -i\zeta$, $c_\mu = p_\mu - \xi_\mu$, and $d_\mu = -R_\mu$.

Then, the modified fermion propagator associated with this dynamical equation is

$$iS(p) = i\left\{\left(\slashed{p} - \slashed{\xi} - \slashed{R}\gamma_5 + mc - i\zeta\gamma_5\right)\left[(p-\xi)^2 - m^2c^2 - \zeta^2 - R^2\right]\right.$$
$$- 2\left[(\slashed{p}-\slashed{\xi})\gamma_5 + \slashed{R}\right](p-\xi)\cdot R - 2\zeta\left[(p_\mu-\xi_\mu)R_\nu - (p_\nu-\xi_\nu)R_\mu\right]\Sigma^{\mu\nu}$$
$$\left. - 2mc\,\varepsilon_{\alpha\beta\mu\nu}\left[(p^\alpha-\xi^\alpha)R^\beta - (p^\beta-\xi^\beta)R^\alpha\right]\Sigma^{\mu\nu}\right\}\Delta^{-1}, \quad (19.31)$$

with

$$\Delta = \left[(p-\xi)^2 - m^2c^2 - \zeta^2 + R^2\right]^2 - 4\left\{\left[(p-\xi)\cdot R\right]^2 - m^2c^2 - \zeta^2\right\}. \quad (19.32)$$

The modified dispersion relation comes from the roots of solving Δ for energy in function of linear momenta. This is,

$$\left(p^2 - m^2c^2 - \zeta^2 + \xi^2 + R^2 - 2p\cdot\xi\right)^2 - 4\left[(p\cdot R - \xi\cdot R)^2 - m^2c^2 - \zeta^2\right] = 0, \quad (19.33)$$

in order to obtain $E(\mathbf{p})$.

As a result, we can also obtain the group velocity considering the total differential of it, $d\Delta = (\partial\Delta/\partial E)dE + (\partial\Delta/\partial p_i)dp_i = A\,dE + B\,dp_i = 0$. Then, the $i-th$ component of the group velocity is given by

$$v_i = \frac{\partial E}{\partial p_i} = -\frac{B}{A} = \frac{c_1(p_i - \xi_i) + c_2 R_i}{c_1(E - \xi_0) + c_2 R_0}, \quad (19.34)$$

where $c_1 = (p-\xi)^2 - m^2c^2 - \zeta^2 + R^2$ and $c_2 = -4(p-\xi)\cdot R$.

19.3 The special case with vanishing $R_\mu\gamma^\mu\gamma_5$

In this Section, our discussion will center around the scenario where $R_\mu = 0$. In pursuit of this objective, we will begin by presenting the comprehensive analytical solution to the modified Dirac equations. Subsequently, we will delve into an examination of the Klein's paradox and engage in an in-depth discourse regarding the *Zitterbewegung* phenomenology within this context.

Then, whether $R_\mu = 0$, the Eq. (19.6) assumes the following form

$$\left(i\hbar\gamma^\mu\partial_\mu - mc - i\zeta\gamma_5 - \xi\gamma^\mu\right)\psi(x) = 0. \quad (19.35)$$

In momenta space

$$\left(p_\mu \gamma^\mu - mc - i\zeta\gamma_5 - \xi_\mu \gamma^\mu\right)\psi(p) = 0. \tag{19.36}$$

Particularizing Eq. (19.33) for R_μ trivial, the dispersion relation comes solving it for the energy,

$$E = c\xi_0 \pm c\sqrt{(\mathbf{p}-\boldsymbol{\xi})^2 + m^2c^2 + \zeta^2}. \tag{19.37}$$

Defining effective expression for energy and momentum such as

$$\begin{cases} \mathscr{E} \equiv E - c\xi_0, \\ \mathbf{P} \equiv \mathbf{p} - \boldsymbol{\xi}, \end{cases} \tag{19.38}$$

we can write

$$\mathscr{E} = \pm c\sqrt{\mathbf{P}^2 + m^2c^2 + \zeta^2}. \tag{19.39}$$

Now, whether we consider again the group velocity, we get from (19.34), when R_μ is trivial, the result

$$\mathbf{v} = \frac{c^2(\mathbf{p}-\boldsymbol{\xi})}{(E - c\xi_0)} = \frac{c^2 \mathbf{P}}{\mathscr{E}}. \tag{19.40}$$

The modified fermion propagator in this case is

$$iS(P) = \frac{i(\slashed{p} - \slashed{\xi} + mc - i\zeta\gamma_5)}{(p^2 - 2p\cdot\xi + \xi^2 - m^2c^2 - \zeta^2)}$$
$$= \frac{i(P_\mu \gamma^\mu + mc - i\zeta\gamma_5)}{(P^2 - m^2c^2 - \zeta^2 + i\varepsilon)}, \tag{19.41}$$

where we define an effective four-momentum given by

$$P_\mu \equiv (\mathscr{E}, -\mathbf{P}). \tag{19.42}$$

This propagator is quite similar to usual fermion propagator, with exception of terms proportional to ζ.

The results for the Gordon decomposition and energy-momentum tensor, along with their respective interpretations, remain consistent with those presented in the previous section when we consider R_μ as a trivial parameter. However, we will not utilize them in the subsequent analysis, and this is why we only mention them briefly.

19.3.1 Positive and Negative Energy Solutions

With these remarks in mind, we are now prepared to delve into the study of solutions for the modified Dirac equation defined by Eq. (19.36). Commencing with the solution for positive energies and spin-up $(+s)$ in the laboratory reference frame, this solution takes the following form

$$\psi_+(P,+s) = u(P,+s)e^{-iP_\mu x^\mu/\hbar} = N_+ \begin{pmatrix} 1 \\ 0 \\ \dfrac{c(P_3 - i\zeta)}{\varepsilon + mc^2} \\ \dfrac{c(P_1 + iP_2)}{\varepsilon + mc^2} \end{pmatrix} e^{-iP_\mu x^\mu/\hbar}, \qquad (19.43)$$

where

$$\varepsilon \equiv c\sqrt{\mathbf{P}^2 + m^2 c^2 - \zeta^2}, \qquad (19.44)$$

and N_+ is a normalization coefficient to be determined.

In the case of positive energies and spin-down, $(-s)$, we have

$$\psi_+(P,-s) = u(P,-s)e^{-iP_\mu x^\mu/\hbar} = N_- \begin{pmatrix} 0 \\ 1 \\ \dfrac{c(P_1 - iP_2)}{\varepsilon + mc^2} \\ \dfrac{-c(P_3 + i\zeta)}{\varepsilon + mc^2} \end{pmatrix} e^{-iP_\mu x^\mu/\hbar}, \qquad (19.45)$$

and once again N_- is a normalization coefficient to be determined.

The determination of both N_+ and N_- comes from the exigence of

$$\bar{\psi}_+(P,\pm s)\psi_+(P,\pm s) = 1 \quad \text{and} \quad \bar{\psi}_+(P,\mp s)\psi_+(P,\pm s) = 0.$$

These lead us to write

$$N = N_- = N_+ = \sqrt{\frac{\varepsilon + mc^2}{2mc^2}}. \qquad (19.46)$$

It implies in writing $\psi_+^\dagger(P,\pm s)\psi_+(P,\pm s) = \varepsilon/mc^2$ and $\psi_+^\dagger(P,\mp s)\psi(P,\pm s) = 0$.

In the context of the negative energy solution, where $\mathcal{E} = -\varepsilon$ for both spin states, we find for spin up

$$\psi_-(P,+s) = v(P,+s)e^{iP_\mu x^\mu/\hbar} = N'_+ \begin{pmatrix} \dfrac{-c(P_3 + i\zeta)}{\varepsilon + mc^2} \\ \dfrac{-c(P_1 + iP_2)}{\varepsilon + mc^2} \\ 1 \\ 0 \end{pmatrix} e^{iP_\mu x^\mu/\hbar} \qquad (19.47)$$

and for spin down

$$\psi_-(\mathscr{P},-s) = v(P,-s)e^{iP_\mu x^\mu/\hbar} = N'_- \begin{pmatrix} \dfrac{-c(P_1 - iP_2)}{\varepsilon + mc^2} \\ \dfrac{-c(-P_3 + i\zeta)}{\varepsilon + mc^2} \\ 0 \\ 1 \end{pmatrix} e^{iP_\mu x^\mu/\hbar}. \quad (19.48)$$

Through the requirements of $\bar{\psi}_-(P,\pm s)\psi_-(P,\pm s) = -1$ and $\bar{\psi}_-(P,\mp s)\psi_-(P,\pm s) = 0$, we are able to establish that

$$N = N'_- = N'_+ = \sqrt{\dfrac{\varepsilon + mc^2}{2mc^2}}. \quad (19.49)$$

This is reflected in $\psi^\dagger_-(P,\pm s)\psi_-(P,\pm s) = \varepsilon/mc^2$ and $\psi^\dagger_-(P,\mp s)\psi_-(P,\pm s) = 0$.

19.3.2 Re-assessing the Klein Paradox

To explore the Klein paradox within the context of Eq. (19.35), it is necessary to examine the stationary wave solutions for positive energy and spin-up states, as described by Eq. (19.43). These solutions represent particle configurations moving along the increasing direction of the z axis defined in Figure 19.4. When this is done, the particles will encounter a step potential, resulting in

$$V = V_0 \theta(z) = \begin{cases} 0 & \text{if } z < 0, \\ V_0 & \text{if } z > 0. \end{cases} \quad (19.50)$$

The graphical representation of this potential can be found in Figure 19.4 as well.

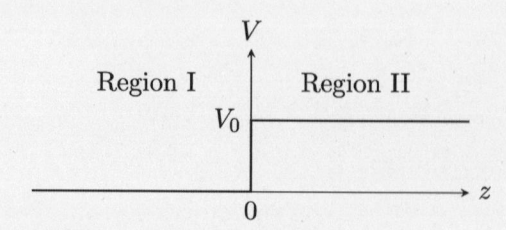

Figure 19.4: Potential $V = V_0\theta(z)$, in which we propose an electron traveling from the left, Region I, to the right, Region II. This potential will assist us in studying the Klein Paradox in the context of the modified Dirac equation (19.35), which we are considering in this section.

Given this physical setup, we must employ a spinor ψ_1 to describe the free particles in Region I traveling to the Region II, which will interact with the potential

$V = V_0$ in $z = 0$. we also need a spinor ψ_1^r to describe particles reflected by the potential in Region I. Last but not least, we should take a spinor ψ_2 which must describe the particles that penetrate the potential and are found in the Region II.

Henceforth, we shall proceed with the perspective we have established for effective energies or momenta, such that ψ_1 possesses a momentum of $\mathbf{P}_1 = P\hat{\mathbf{z}}$, ψ_1^r is associated with a momentum $\mathbf{P}_1^r = -P\hat{\mathbf{z}}$, and ψ_2 carries a momentum of $\mathbf{P}_2 = P'\hat{\mathbf{z}}$. In light of this, it is imperative to express the solutions to the modified Dirac Eq. (19.35) in the form of plane waves

$$\psi_1 = A \begin{pmatrix} 1 \\ 0 \\ \dfrac{-ic\zeta + cP}{\mathcal{E} + mc^2} \\ 0 \end{pmatrix} e^{iPz/\hbar}, \tag{19.51}$$

$$\psi_1^r = B \begin{pmatrix} 1 \\ 0 \\ \dfrac{-ic\zeta - cP}{\mathcal{E} + mc^2} \\ 0 \end{pmatrix} e^{-iPz/\hbar} + D \begin{pmatrix} 0 \\ 1 \\ 0 \\ \dfrac{-ic\zeta + cP}{\mathcal{E} + mc^2} \end{pmatrix} e^{-iPz/\hbar}, \tag{19.52}$$

with dispersions relations which imply in write $Pc = \sqrt{\mathcal{E}^2 - m^2c^4 - \zeta^2 c^2}$, and

$$\psi_2 = C \begin{pmatrix} 1 \\ 0 \\ \dfrac{-ic\zeta + cP'}{(\mathcal{E} - V_0) + mc^2} \\ 0 \end{pmatrix} e^{iP'z/\hbar} + F \begin{pmatrix} 0 \\ 1 \\ 0 \\ \dfrac{-ic\zeta - cP'}{(\mathcal{E} - V_0) + mc^2} \end{pmatrix} e^{iP'z/\hbar}, \tag{19.53}$$

with $P'c = \sqrt{(\mathcal{E} - V_0)^2 - m^2c^4 - \zeta^2 c^2}$. The spinor ψ_r is expressed as a sum of contributions from both spin up and spin down states to accommodate the possibility of a spin-flip resulting from reflection at $z = 0$. Similarly, ψ_2 may also undergo a spin-flip due to its interaction with the potential in Region II. It is worth noting that when $|\mathcal{E} - V_0| < c\sqrt{m^2c^2 + \zeta^2}$, the momentum in Region II becomes imaginary, denoted as $P' = i|P'|$, and the solution exhibits a decreasing exponential behavior, indicating a damped penetration into the potential region. Conversely, in situations where $V_0 > \mathcal{E} + c\sqrt{m^2c^2 + \zeta^2}$, the potential effectively confines the particle, resulting in a real momentum, and leading to oscillatory solutions within Region II.

Now we should require that in $z = 0$ the solutions, inside and outside the potential, ought to be equals,

$$\psi_1(z=0) + \psi_1^r(z=0) = \psi_2(z=0). \tag{19.54}$$

This condition gives rise to the following outcome

$$D = F, \tag{19.55}$$

$$A + B = C, \tag{19.56}$$

$$\frac{(P-i\zeta)D}{\mathcal{E}+mc^2} = -\frac{(P'-i\zeta)F}{\mathcal{E}-V_0+mc^2}, \tag{19.57}$$

$$\frac{P(A-B)-i\zeta(A+B)}{\mathcal{E}+mc^2} = \frac{(P'-i\zeta)C}{\mathcal{E}-V_0+mc^2}. \tag{19.58}$$

The relations (19.55) and (19.57) cannot be satisfied at same time, suggesting $D = F = 0$ and eliminating the spin-flip possibility. Replacing the expressions for Pc and $P'c$ in equality (19.58) and after using the constraint that comes from (19.56), we can write

$$A - B = (\beta - i\alpha)C, \tag{19.59}$$

with

$$\begin{cases} \alpha = \dfrac{c\zeta V_0}{(V_0 - \mathcal{E} - mc^2)(\mathcal{E}^2 - m^2c^2 - \zeta^2)^{1/2}}, \\ \beta = \dfrac{(\mathcal{E}+mc^2)[(\mathcal{E}-V_0)^2 - m^2c^2 - \zeta^2]^{1/2}}{(\mathcal{E}-V_0+mc^2)(\mathcal{E}^2 - m^2c^2 - \zeta^2)^{1/2}}. \end{cases} \tag{19.60}$$

Adding (19.56) with (19.59) and after making (19.56) minus (19.59) we get, respectively,

$$A = (1+\beta - i\alpha)\frac{C}{2}, \tag{19.61}$$

$$B = (1-\beta + i\alpha)\frac{C}{2}. \tag{19.62}$$

From this, we can conclude that

$$\frac{B}{A} = \frac{1-\beta+i\alpha}{1+\beta-i\alpha}, \tag{19.63}$$

$$\frac{C}{A} = \frac{2}{1+\beta-i\alpha}. \tag{19.64}$$

Finally, to fully specify the transmission and reflection coefficients, we ought to consider the current term in the $\hat{\mathbf{z}}$ direction,

$$\begin{aligned}\mathbf{j} &= c\psi^\dagger(z)\gamma^0\gamma^3\psi(z)\hat{\mathbf{z}} \\ &= c\psi^\dagger(z)\begin{pmatrix} 0 & \sigma_3 \\ \sigma_3 & 0 \end{pmatrix}\psi(z)\hat{\mathbf{z}}, \end{aligned} \tag{19.65}$$

in the Dirac representation for gamma matrices with σ_3 being the third Pauli matrix. Consequently, we can show that

$$\begin{cases} \mathbf{j}_1 = AA^* \left(\dfrac{2c^2 P}{\mathcal{E}+mc^2} \right) \hat{\mathbf{z}}, \\ \mathbf{j}_1^r = -BB^* \left(\dfrac{2c^2 P}{\mathcal{E}+mc^2} \right) \hat{\mathbf{z}}, \\ \mathbf{j}_2 = CC^* \left(\dfrac{2c^2 P'}{(\mathcal{E}-V_0)+mc^2} \right) \hat{\mathbf{z}}. \end{cases} \qquad (19.66)$$

Hence, the reflection coefficient shall be

$$R = \frac{|\mathbf{j}_1^r|}{|\mathbf{j}_1|} = \frac{|-BB^*|}{|AA^*|} = \frac{1-2\beta+\beta^2+\alpha^2}{(1+\beta)^2+\alpha^2}, \qquad (19.67)$$

and the transmission coefficient is

$$T = \frac{|\mathbf{j}_2|}{|\mathbf{j}_1|} = \frac{|CC^*|}{|AA^*|} \left| \frac{P'}{P} \left(\frac{\mathcal{E}+mc^2}{\mathcal{E}-V_0+mc^2} \right) \right| = \frac{4\beta}{(1+\beta)^2+\alpha^2}. \qquad (19.68)$$

We can immediately verify that $R+T=1$.

As we demand the case for high barrier, $V_0 > \mathcal{E} + c\sqrt{m^2c^2+\zeta^2}$, we have $\beta < 0$. As a result, the transmission function in this situation is also less than zero, $T < 0$. These results suggest to us that $|\mathbf{j}_1^r| > |\mathbf{j}_1|$. The physical explanation for this phenomenon is the presence of particles moving from Region II to Region I. However, from the very beginning, we have argued that there are no particles in Region II. Therefore, it becomes apparent that the Klein's paradox is occurring within the scenario of the modified Dirac Eq. (19.35).

One commonly suggested solution to this problem is its association with pair production when the inequality $V_0 > \mathcal{E} + c\sqrt{m^2c^2+\zeta^2} > 2c\sqrt{m^2c^2+\zeta^2}$ holds true. This inequality implies that the potential is potent enough to create particle-antiparticle pairs from the vacuum. The difficulty here is in trying to comprehend a multiparticle phenomenon using a simple single-particle wave function. However, it is contended that quantum field theory offers a viable approach for a proper treatment.

19.3.3 Inspecting the *Zitterbewegung*

The term *Zitterbewegung* originates from the German and can be loosely translated into English as referring to a trembling or agitated movement. In our context, *Zitterbewegung* is consistently associated with the hypothesis of a rapid intrinsic oscillation of elementary particles, whose dynamics are governed by the quantum-relativistic wave equation. This concept first emerged in 1928 with G.

Breit and after in 1930 as a direct consequence of the free solutions of the Dirac equation for wave packets, in a work by E. Schrödinger. Schrödinger observed an interference phenomenon between positive and negative energy states, resulting in an electron appearing to oscillate around its classical trajectory at a natural frequency of $\omega = 2mc^2/\hbar$.

In order to reveal the *Zitterbewegung* frequencies in the context of Eq. (19.35) we define a wave packet

$$\Psi(\vec{x},t) = \int \frac{d^3\mathbf{P}}{(2\pi\hbar)^{3/2}} \sqrt{\frac{mc^2}{\varepsilon(\mathbf{P})}} \sum_{\pm s} \left[b(P,s)u(P,s)e^{-iP^\mu x_\mu/\hbar} + d^*(P,s)v(P,s)e^{+iP^\mu x_\mu/\hbar} \right], \quad (19.69)$$

where s carries the spin content, up or down, and the rest of the notation is self explanatory. The normalization condition implies that $\int d^3\mathbf{x}\, \Psi^\dagger(\mathbf{x},t)\Psi(\mathbf{x},t) = 1$ and imposing (19.69) to satisfy it, we can write

$$\int d^3\mathbf{x}\, \Psi^\dagger(\mathbf{x},t)\Psi(\mathbf{x},t) = \int d^3\mathbf{P} \sum_{\pm s} \left[|b(\mathscr{P},s)|^2 + |d(P,s)|^2 \right] = 1, \quad (19.70)$$

where we have used the following definition for the Dirac delta function

$$\int \frac{d^3\mathbf{x}}{(2\pi\hbar)^3} e^{\pm i(\mathbf{P}\pm\mathbf{P}')\cdot\mathbf{x}/\hbar} = \delta^{(3)}(\mathbf{P}\pm\mathbf{P}') \quad (19.71)$$

and the fact that

$$P_0(\mathbf{P}) = \varepsilon(\mathbf{P}) = \varepsilon'(\mathbf{P}')\delta^{(3)}(\mathbf{P}\pm\mathbf{P}') = c\sqrt{(\pm\mathbf{P})^2 + m^2c^2 + \zeta^2} = \varepsilon'(\pm\mathbf{P}) = P_0'(\mathbf{P}). \quad (19.72)$$

to obtain the result (19.70).

To move forward, we define the current

$$J^\mu = c \int d^3\mathbf{x}\, \bar{\Psi}(\mathbf{x},t)\gamma^\mu \Psi(\mathbf{x},t), \quad (19.73)$$

and the i component of the Gordon decomposition:

$$c\bar{\Psi}(\mathbf{x},t)\gamma^i \Psi(\mathbf{x},t) = \frac{1}{2m}\left[\bar{\Psi}\left(\hat{P}^i\Psi\right) - \left(\hat{P}^i\bar{\Psi}\right)\Psi - 2i\hat{P}_\nu\left(\bar{\Psi}\Sigma^{i\nu}\Psi\right) \right], \quad (19.74)$$

We can then write the i component of the current as

$$J^i = \int d^3\mathbf{P} \Bigg\{ \sum_{\pm s} \frac{P^i c^2}{\varepsilon(\mathbf{P})}\left[|b(P,s)|^2 + |d(P,s)|^2\right]$$
$$+ ic \sum_{\pm(s,s')} \left[b^*(-P,s')d^*(P,s)\bar{u}(-P,s')\Sigma^{i0}v(P,s)e^{2iP_0 x_0/\hbar} \right.$$
$$\left. - d(-P,s')b(P,s)\bar{v}(-\mathscr{P},s')\Sigma^{i0}u(P,s)e^{-2iP_0 x_0/\hbar} \right] \Bigg\}. \quad (19.75)$$

The two terms proportional to the exponential in Eq. (19.75) are solutions that depict an interference between positive and negative energy states, a phenomenon referred to as *Zitterbewegung*. These components oscillate with an explicit time dependence at a frequency determined by

$$\omega_z = \frac{2P_0 c}{\hbar} = \frac{2\sqrt{\mathbf{P}^2 + m^2 c^2 + \zeta^2}}{\hbar} > \frac{2c\sqrt{m^2 c^2 + \zeta^2}}{\hbar}. \tag{19.76}$$

We can also investigate *Zitterbewegung* within the framework of the modified Dirac Eq. (19.35) by multiplying it by $-c\gamma^0$ in order to express

$$(i\hbar\partial_t - \xi_0)\psi(x) = \left[c\gamma^0\gamma^i(-i\hbar\partial_i - \xi_i) + \gamma^0 m c^2 + i\gamma^0\gamma_5 c\zeta\right]\psi(x) \tag{19.77}$$

and defining

$$\begin{cases} \alpha^i = \gamma^0\gamma^i, \\ \beta = \gamma^0, \\ \kappa = i\gamma^0\gamma_5, \end{cases} \tag{19.78}$$

this yields the effective Hamiltonian operator

$$H = c\boldsymbol{\alpha}\cdot\mathbf{P} + \beta m c^2 + \kappa c\zeta. \tag{19.79}$$

In the Heisenberg picture the temporal evolution of position is given by

$$\frac{d\mathbf{x}}{dt} = \frac{1}{i\hbar}[\mathbf{x}, H] = c\boldsymbol{\alpha} \tag{19.80}$$

for a constant background. Now, the time evolution of α is given by

$$\frac{d\alpha}{dt} = \frac{1}{i\hbar}[\alpha, H] = \frac{i}{\hbar}\{H, \alpha\} - \frac{2i}{\hbar}\alpha H = \frac{2i}{\hbar}(\mathbf{P} - \alpha H), \tag{19.81}$$

where $\{\beta, \alpha\} = \{\kappa, \alpha\} = 0$. Integrating the result (19.81) with respect to time,

$$\int_{\alpha(0)}^{\alpha(t)} \frac{d\alpha}{\alpha - \frac{c}{H}\mathbf{P}} = -\frac{2iH}{\hbar}\int_{t'=0}^{t'=t} dt', \tag{19.82}$$

we attain

$$\alpha(t) = \left[\alpha(0) - \frac{c}{H}\mathbf{P}\right] e^{-2iHt/\hbar} + \frac{c}{H}\mathbf{P}. \tag{19.83}$$

Taking the Eq. (19.83) to the Eq. (19.80), we arrive at the following result

$$\mathbf{x}(t) = \mathbf{x}(0) + \frac{c}{H}\mathbf{P}t + \frac{i\hbar c}{2H}\left(\alpha(0) - \frac{c}{H}\mathbf{P}\right)\left(e^{-2iHt/\hbar} - 1\right). \tag{19.84}$$

Hence, we find that the motion of a fermionic particle is described by an initial position term followed by a velocity term multiplied by time. This velocity term adopts the shape of the group velocity and is accompanied by an oscillatory component responsible for *Zitterbewegung*. This oscillatory behavior disrupts the typical kinematic structure of the equation of motion. In essence, we observe a fermion oscillating between positive and negative energy states as it traces its classical-type trajectory.

19.4 Concluding comments

To conclude, we would like to recall the the breaking of Lorentz symmetry at the Planck scale takes place in a scenario dominated by supersymmetry, for the latter is broken at energies intermediary between the electroweak and the grand-unification scales. Based on this observation, we point out that a completion of LSV models should be carried out by introducing supersymmetry. The whole set of background bosonic entities present in field-theoretic LSV models could have a microscopic origin from fundamental fermions - actually they may be expressed as fermionic condensates - brought about by supersymmetry. This is the line of investigation we are presently pursuing to connect supersymmetry and LSV breakings and to relate more systematically the fermionic and bosonic modes of LSV models.

Bibliography

[1] P. A. M. Dirac, *Is there an aether?*, Nature **168**, 906 (1951).

[2] G. Scharf, *Finite quantum electrodynamics: the causal approach* (Dover Publications, Mineola, 2014).

[3] V. A. Kostelecký and S. Samuel, *Spontaneous breaking of Lorentz symmetry in string theory*, Phys. Rev. D **39**, 683 (1989).

[4] V. A. Kostelecký and S. Samuel, *Phenomenological gravitational constraints on strings and higher-dimensional theories*, Phys. Rev. Lett. **63**, 224 (1989).

[5] S. M. Carroll, G. B. Field and R. Jackiw, *Limits on a Lorentz- and parity-violating modification of electrodynamics*, Phys. Rev. D **41**, 1231 (1990).

[6] C. Adam and F. R. Klinkhamer, *Causality and CPT violation from an Abelian Chern–Simons-like term*, Nucl. Phys. B **607**, 247 (2001).

[7] A. P. Baêta Scarpelli, H. Belich, J. L. Boldo and J. A. Helayël-Neto, *Aspects of causality and unitarity and comments on vortexlike configurations in an Abelian model with a Lorentz-breaking term*, Phys. Rev. D **67**, 085021 (2003).

[8] D. Colladay and V. A. Kostelecký, *CPT violation and the standard model*, Phys. Rev. D **55**, 6760 (1997).

[9] D. Colladay and V. A. Kostelecký, *Lorentz-violating extension of the standard model*, Phys. Rev. D **58**, 11602 (1998).

[10] V. A. Kostelecký and N. Russel, *Data tables for Lorentz and CPT violation*, arXiv:0801.0287v16.

20

Geodesic analysis, absorption and scattering in the static Hayward spacetime

M. A. A. de Paula, L. C. S. Leite, L. C. B. Crispino

Abstract: We investigate the propagation of massless particles and scalar fields in the background of Hayward regular black holes. We compute the absorption and scattering cross sections and compare our numerical results with some analytical approximations, showing that they are in excellent agreement. We show that some of the absorption and scattering results of Reissner-Nordström black holes can be mimicked by Hayward regular black holes, for appropriate choices of the charge of the two different black holes.

20.1 Introduction

In recent years, experiments testing the strong-field regime have consolidated general relativity (GR) as a robust theory to describe gravity [1, 2, 3, 4]. Despite its achievements, GR also predicts the existence of curvature singularities in the core of the standard black hole (BH) solutions. We may argue that the limitations of Einstein's Theory at the BH center rely on its classical formalism. Therefore, a fully quantum gravity theory, which would successfully combine GR and quantum field theory, could avoid the formation of curvature singularities. Yet, although there have been efforts in this direction (see, e.g., Ref. [5] for a review), a fully successful quantum gravity theory has not been obtained so far.

As an alternative to the standard BH solutions of GR, there are the so-called regular BH (RBH) spacetimes, i.e. (curvature) singularity-free BH geometries. Nonsingular static spacetimes can be obtained by requiring an effective cutoff in the energy density at the BH center, preventing the spacetime metric from diverging at $r = 0$. This can be accomplished by demanding that the spacetime behaves as a de Sitter [6, 7, 8, 9, 10, 11] or Minkowski [12, 13, 14] geometry at the BH core. (For reviews on RBHs and possible physical sources see Refs. [15, 16, 17, 18].)

The Hayward geometry [11] is an example of spacetime which can have no curvature singularities, avoid the mass inflation phenomena [19] (at least from the classical point of view), and can be interpreted as a BH solution sourced by a nonlinear magnetic monopole [20, 21, 22, 23] [1]. Due to these features, the Hayward geometry has gained a lot of attention over the past few years. We can improve our understanding of the Hayward spacetime by investigating how it interacts with surrounding fields. In this context, we can compute for Hayward BHs the absorption and scattering cross sections [a subject which have been extensively studied since the 1960s in several BH scenarios (see, e.g., Refs. [25, 26, 27, 28, 29, 30, 31, 32, 33, 34, 35, 36, 37, 38, 39, 40, 41, 42, 43, 44, 45] and references therein)].

We investigate the absorption and scattering properties of neutral massless test scalar fields in the background of Hayward RBHs. The remainder of this paper is organized as follows. In Sec. 20.2, we introduce the Hayward spacetime as a solution of GR minimally coupled to nonlinear electrodynamics (NED). In Sec. 20.3, we investigate the trajectories of massless particles and also consider the semiclassical glory approximation. The partial wave-analysis is applied in Sec. 20.4 to obtain the absorption and scattering cross sections of the massless scalar field. In Sec. 20.5, we present our main results concerning the absorption and scattering of neutral massless test scalar fields in Hayward spacetime. Our concluding remarks are stated in Sec. 20.6. Throughout this work, we consider natural units, for which $G = c = \hbar = 1$, and signature +2.

---

[1] The Reissner-Nordström solution can also be regarded as a BH solution sourced by a magnetic monopole [24].

20.2 Hayward spacetime

The action associated with the minimal coupling between GR and NED can be written as

$$\mathscr{S} = \frac{1}{16\pi} \int d^4 x \, (R - \mathscr{L}(F)) \sqrt{-g}, \tag{20.1}$$

where R is the Ricci scalar, $\mathscr{L}(F)$ is a gauge-invariant Lagrangian density, and g is the determinant of the metric tensor $g_{\mu\nu}$. The function F is the Maxwell scalar, namely

$$F = F_{\mu\nu} F^{\mu\nu}, \tag{20.2}$$

with $F_{\mu\nu}$ being the standard electromagnetic field tensor. By varying the action (20.1) with respect to $g_{\mu\nu}$, we get

$$G_\mu{}^\nu = T_\mu{}^\nu = 2 \left(\mathscr{L}_F F_{\mu\sigma} F^{\nu\sigma} - \frac{1}{4} \delta_\mu{}^\nu \mathscr{L}(F) \right), \tag{20.3}$$

in which $\mathscr{L}_F \equiv \partial \mathscr{L}/\partial F$. The dynamic field equations of the electromagnetic field are given by

$$\nabla_\mu \left(\mathscr{L}_F F^{\mu\nu} \right) = 0 \quad \text{and} \quad \nabla_\mu \star F^{\mu\nu} = 0, \tag{20.4}$$

where $\star F^{\mu\nu}$ is the dual electromagnetic field tensor.

We consider a static and spherically symmetric line element given by

$$ds^2 = -f(r) dt^2 + f(r)^{-1} dr^2 + r^2 d\Omega^2, \tag{20.5}$$

where $f(r)$ is the metric function to be determined by the field equations (20.3) and $d\Omega^2 = d\theta^2 + \sin^2 \theta \, d\varphi^2$ is the line element of a 2-dimensional unit sphere. In this context, the only non-null components of the electromagnetic field tensor are given by $F_{23} = -F_{32} = Q \sin \theta$, so that the Maxwell scalar is

$$F = \frac{2Q^2}{r^4}. \tag{20.6}$$

The NED model associated with the Hayward spacetime can be written as [20, 21, 23]

$$\mathscr{L}(F) = \frac{12M}{|Q|Q^2} \frac{(Q^2 F/2)^{\frac{3}{2}}}{\left(1 + (Q^2 F/2)^{\frac{3}{4}}\right)^2}, \tag{20.7}$$

where Q and M are the magnetic charge and mass of the central object, respectively. By using the equation $G_0{}^0 = T_0{}^0$, we obtain the Hayward metric function

$$f(r) = 1 - \frac{2M r^2}{r^3 + Q^3}. \tag{20.8}$$

In the chargeless limit ($Q \to 0$), the Hayward metric function reduces to the Schwarzschild one. In Fig. 20.1, we display the Kretschmann scalar invariant, given by

$$K = R_{\mu\nu\sigma\rho} R^{\mu\nu\sigma\rho}, \tag{20.9}$$

where $R_{\mu\nu\sigma\rho}$ is the Riemann tensor, for the Hayward spacetime. Throughout this paper, we consider $Q > 0$, what is sufficient to guarantee the absence of curvature singularities for $r \geq 0$ [46, 47].

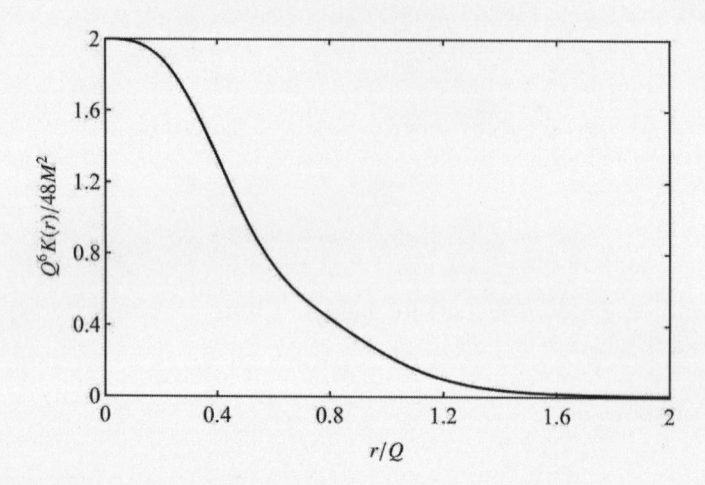

Figure 20.1: Kretschmann scalar invariant of the Hayward spacetime, as a function of r/Q. In the limit $r \to 0$ the scalar is finite and non null, namely $K(r)|_{r=0} = 96M^2/Q^6$.

The line element (20.5), considering the metric function (20.8), describes RBHs when the condition $Q \leq Q_{\text{ext}} \approx 1.0582M$ is satisfied, where Q_{ext} is the extreme charge value. We can obtain Q_{ext} by solving $f(r) = 0$ and $f'(r) = 0$ simultaneously, where $'$ denotes a differentiation with respect to the radial coordinate r. For $Q < Q_{\text{ext}}$, we have two horizons, given by the real roots of $f(r) = 0$. We denote the Cauchy horizon and the event horizon as r_- and r_+, respectively. For $Q = Q_{\text{ext}}$, the two horizons coincide. For its turn, $Q > Q_{\text{ext}}$ leads to horizonless solutions, which is beyond the scope of this work. Moreover, we exhibit our results in terms of the normalized charge, defined as

$$\alpha \equiv \frac{Q}{Q_{\text{ext}}}, \tag{20.10}$$

which facilitates comparisons between different spacetimes. In the Reissner-Nordström (RN) case, Q can represent an electric or magnetic charge, while in the Hayward geometry Q can be identified exclusively as a magnetic charge [20, 21].

For large r, the Hayward metric behaves as

$$f(r) = 1 - \frac{2M}{r} + \frac{2MQ^3}{r^4} + \mathcal{O}\left[\frac{1}{r^5}\right], \tag{20.11}$$

whereas at the core we have

$$f(r) = 1 - \frac{2M}{Q^3}r^2 + \mathcal{O}[r]^5. \tag{20.12}$$

Therefore, the spacetime is asymptotically flat as $r \to \infty$ and has a de Sitter behavior at the center. As occurs in the Bardeen geometry [6, 48], the Hayward spacetime does not satisfy a correspondence with the Maxwell theory for large r since the corresponding NED model (20.7) does not behave as $\mathscr{L}(F) \to F$ for small F. We also point out that the behavior of the Hayward geometry at its center is a common feature of NED-based RBHs that satisfy the weak energy condition [10]. In this context, the energy density of the NED source is maximal and finite at the solution core, preventing it from diverging as $r \to 0$, in contrast with linear electrodynamics.

20.3 Geodesic analysis

In this section, we investigate the propagation of massless particles in Hayward RBH spacetimes. Due to the spherical symmetry of the geometry, we treat the equations of motion in the equatorial plane, i.e., $\theta = \pi/2$, without loss of generality. We recall that in NED models, photons follow null geodesics of an effective metric tensor [49, 50, 51]. Therefore, the classical results discussed in this section apply only for massless particles with nature other than electromagnetic.

20.3.1 Trajectory of massless particles

The classical Lagrangian L that provides the equations of motion of particles in the spacetime (20.5) is given by

$$L = \frac{1}{2} g_{\mu\nu} \dot{x}^\mu \dot{x}^\nu, \tag{20.13}$$

where the overdot corresponds to a differentiation with respect to an affine parameter. For massless particles, we have L = 0. The constants of motion associated with L are given by

$$E = f(r)\dot{t} \quad \text{and} \quad L = r^2 \dot{\varphi}, \tag{20.14}$$

where E and L are the energy and angular momentum of the particle, respectively. Using Eqs. (20.13)-(20.14), and the condition L = 0, we may find a radial equation for massless particles given by

$$\frac{\dot{r}^2}{L^2} = V(r) = \frac{1}{b^2} - \frac{f(r)}{r^2}, \tag{20.15}$$

where $b \equiv L/E$ is the impact parameter. From $\dot{r}|_{r=r_c} = 0$ and $\ddot{r}|_{r=r_c} = 0$, we may find the critical radius r_c of the unstable circular orbit and the critical impact parameter b_c, namely

$$2f(r_c) - r_c f'(r_c) = 0, \tag{20.16}$$

$$b_c = \frac{L_c}{E_c} = \frac{r_c}{\sqrt{f(r_c)}}, \tag{20.17}$$

respectively. In Fig. 20.2, we exhibit some geodesics of massless particles in the background of the Hayward spacetime. We can obtain these trajectories by numerically integrating the radial equation (20.15) and its first derivative. As we can observe, for $b < b_c$, the geodesics are absorbed, while for $b > b_c$ they are scattered. For its turn, the situation $b = b_c$ is related to a geodesic going round the BH in an unstable circular orbit (with radius r_c).

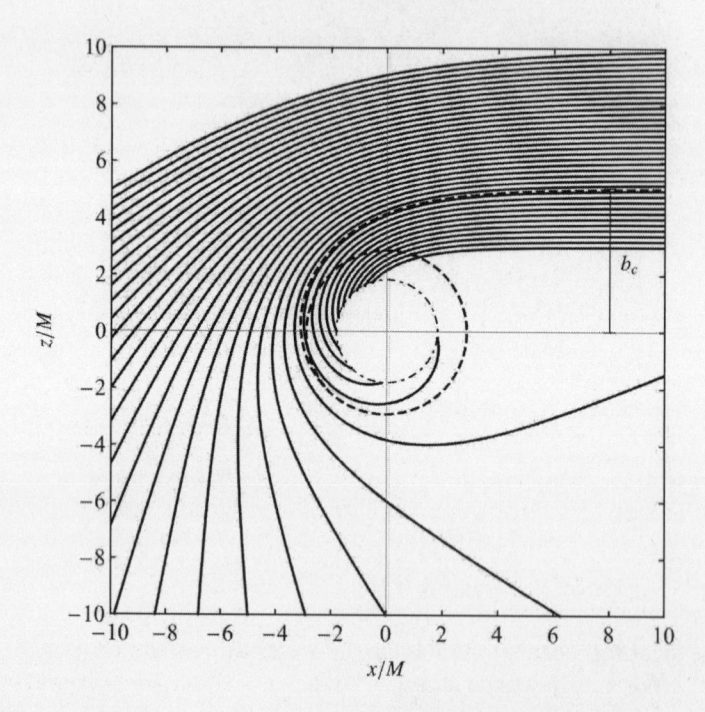

Figure 20.2: Trajectories of massless particles (with nature other than electromagnetic) in a Hayward spacetime with $\alpha = 0.8$, considering distinct impact parameters. The dashed curve is the trajectory associated with the corresponding critical impact parameter, given by $b_c = 5.0685M$, which ends up in an unstable circular orbit with $r_c = 2.8484$. The inner dot-dashed circle is the corresponding event horizon location, namely $r_+ = 1.816M$. The initial conditions are given by $r_{\text{inf}} = 100M$ and $\varphi = \pi - \arctan(3\sqrt{3}/100)$ at $t_0 = 0$.

The classical capture cross section of geodesics, also known as geometric cross section (GCS), is given by [52]

$$\sigma_{gcs} \equiv \pi b_c^2. \tag{20.18}$$

Notice that in the spherically symmetric scenario, the critical impact parameter corresponds to the shadow radius as seen by a distant observer [53, 54]. Therefore, the shape of the shadow can be obtained by the parametric plot of Eq. (20.18). This is illustrated in Fig. 20.3 where we exhibit the shadows of the Hayward spacetime, considering different values of α (and massless particles with nature other than electromagnetic).

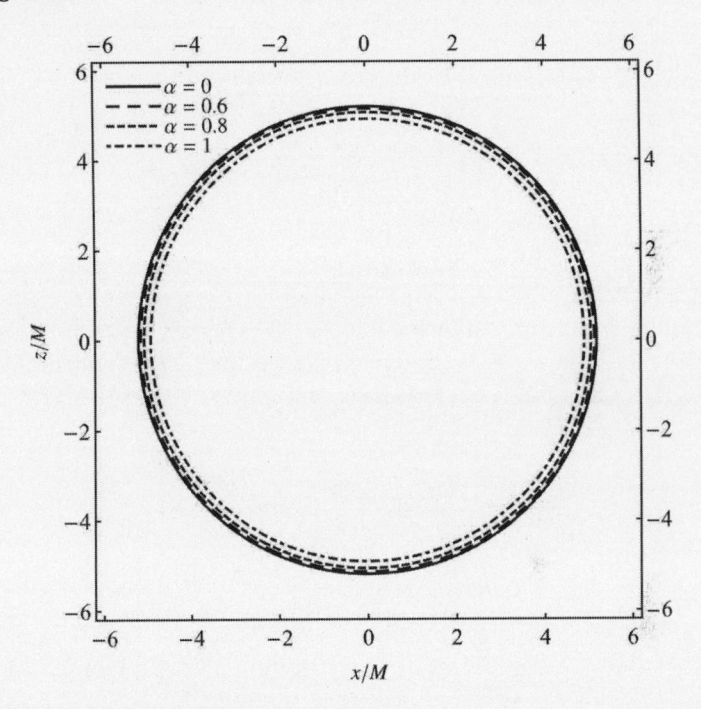

Figure 20.3: Shadows of the Hayward geometry, considering massless particles with nature other than electromagnetic, for distinct values of α. We also consider the Schwarzschild case $\alpha = 0$, for comparison.

At high energies, the absorption cross section (ACS) can be described by a formula known as the sinc approximation, which involves the GCS and the features of null unstable geodesics given by [55, 56]

$$\sigma_{hf} \approx \sigma_{gcs}\left[1 - 8\pi b_c \Lambda e^{-\pi b_c \Lambda}\text{sinc}(2\pi b_c \omega)\right], \tag{20.19}$$

where $\text{sinc}(x) \equiv \sin(x)/x$ and Λ is the Lyapunov exponent related to circular null geodesics [57], namely

$$\Lambda = \sqrt{\frac{L_c^2}{2\dot{t}^2}\left(\frac{d^2V(r)}{dr^2}\right)}\bigg|_{r=r_c}. \tag{20.20}$$

20.3.2 Deflection angle in the weak-field limit

By using the geodesic method, we can obtain an expression for the deflection angle and classical differential SCS in the weak-field limit. The turning point r_0, defined as the radius of maximum approximation of the (massless) particle, for a given value of b, satisfies the condition $\mathcal{U}(r)|_{r=r_0} = 0$, where

$$\mathcal{U}(r) \equiv \frac{dr}{d\varphi} = r^2 \sqrt{\frac{1}{b^2} - \frac{f(r)}{r^2}}. \tag{20.21}$$

Thus, the deflection angle of the scattered massless particle can be written as [58]

$$\Theta(b) = 2 \int_{r_0}^{\infty} \frac{1}{\sqrt{\mathcal{U}(r)}} dr - \pi. \tag{20.22}$$

We can obtain an analytic expression for the deflection angle in the weak field limit by expanding the integrand of Eq. (20.22) in powers of $1/r$. The radius r_0 as a function of b is obtained by solving Eq. (20.17) and expanding the results in powers of $2M/b$. Following these steps, we can find that the weak deflection angle of massless particles in the background of Hayward and RN spacetimes, which are given by

$$\Theta(b)_{\text{H}} = \frac{4M}{b} + \frac{15\pi M^2}{4b^2} + \mathcal{O}\left[\frac{1}{b}\right]^3, \tag{20.23}$$

$$\Theta(b)_{\text{RN}} = \frac{4M}{b} + \frac{3\pi(5M^2 - Q^2)}{4b^2} + \mathcal{O}\left[\frac{1}{b}\right]^3, \tag{20.24}$$

respectively [2]. We see that the charge contributions do not modify the dominant term. Moreover, it can be shown that the charge contributions in the Hayward case will appear only for orders higher than $1/b^3$, due to the asymptotic behavior of the Hayward geometry [cf. Eq. (20.11)].

The classical differential SCS is given by [58]

$$\frac{d\sigma_{\text{cl}}}{d\Omega} = \frac{b}{\sin\theta} \left| \frac{db}{d\Theta} \right|, \tag{20.25}$$

where θ is the scattering angle, which is related to the deflection angle by $\Theta = \theta - 2n\pi$, with $n \in \mathbb{Z}^+$ being the number of times that the massless particle orbits the BH before being scattered to infinity. The classical SCS may be obtained by inverting Eq. (20.22) and inserting $b(\Theta)$ into Eq. (20.25). In the weak field limit, we can use Eqs. (20.23)-(20.24) to obtain the classical differential SCS for small

---

[2] From now on, we will abbreviate Hayward to H in equations and figures, whenever convenient.

scattering angles, which can be expressed as

$$\frac{d\sigma_{cl}^{H}}{d\Omega} = \frac{16M^2}{\Theta^4} + \frac{15\pi M^2}{4\Theta^3} + \mathcal{O}\left[\frac{1}{\Theta}\right]^2, \quad (20.26)$$

$$\frac{d\sigma_{cl}^{RN}}{d\Omega} = \frac{16M^2}{\Theta^4} + \frac{3\pi(5M^2 - Q^2)}{4\Theta^3} + \mathcal{O}\left[\frac{1}{\Theta}\right]^2. \quad (20.27)$$

Similarly to the weak deflection angle, the BH charge does not affect the leading term of the classical differential SCS.

20.3.3 Semiclassical glory

The semiclassical glory approximation can be used to unveil some wave scattering properties near the backward direction, i.e., $\theta = \pi$. In the background of a static and spherically symmetric BH geometry, the glory approximation for scalar waves can be written as [59]

$$\frac{d\sigma_g}{d\Omega} = 2\pi\omega b_g^2 \left|\frac{db}{d\theta}\right|_{\theta=\pi} J_0^2(\omega b_g \sin\theta), \quad (20.28)$$

where ω is the frequency of the scalar wave, b_g is the impact parameter of backscattered rays, and J_0 is the Bessel function of the first kind. Note that exist numerous values of b_g corresponding to multiple values of $\theta = \Theta + 2\pi n$, that result on backscattered null rays. The contributions to the glory scattering come from all the rays scattered near to $\theta \approx 180°$. We know that the main contributions for the glory scattering are provided by the mode $n = 0$ [28, 33, 41]. Therefore, we consider only $n = 0$ in the computation of the glory approximation.

20.4 Partial-wave analysis

In this section, we present the equation that governs the propagation of neutral massless test scalar fields in the background of the setup introduced in Sec. 20.2. We also exhibit the differential SCS and total ACS of massless scalar waves in the background of spherically symmetric BHs.

20.4.1 Massless scalar field

The Klein-Gordon equation that governs the propagation of the neutral massless test scalar field Φ in the background of curved spacetimes reads

$$\frac{1}{\sqrt{-g}}\partial_\mu\left(\sqrt{-g}g^{\mu\nu}\partial_\nu\Phi\right) = 0. \quad (20.29)$$

Within spherical symmetry, we can decompose Φ as

$$\Phi = \frac{1}{r}\sum_{l}^{\infty} C_{\omega l}\Psi_{\omega l}(r)P_l(\cos\theta)e^{-i\omega t}, \qquad (20.30)$$

where $C_{\omega l}$ are coefficients, with ω and l being the frequency and angular momentum of the scalar field, respectively. The function P_l is the Legendre polynomial and $\Psi_{\omega l}$ is the radial function. Using the tortoise coordinate $r_\star$, defined as $f(r)dr_\star = dr$, we can show that $\Psi_{\omega l}$ satisfies

$$\frac{d^2}{dr_\star^2}\Psi_{\omega l} + \left(\omega^2 - V_{\text{eff}}(r)\right)\Psi_{\omega l} = 0, \qquad (20.31)$$

where the effective potential $V_{\text{eff}}(r)$ is

$$V_{\text{eff}}(r) = f(r)\left(\frac{1}{r}\frac{df(r)}{dr} + \frac{l(l+1)}{r^2}\right). \qquad (20.32)$$

In Fig. 20.4, we display the effective potential in the Hayward spacetime for distinct values of α and l. Notice that for $l = 0$, the peak of the effective potential decreases as we increase the α values. However, for $l \geq 1$, the peak presents the opposite behavior. The behavior of the effective potential for $l = 0$ is remarkably different from the well-known (regular) BH solutions.

In Fig. 20.5, we compare the effective potentials in Hayward and RN spacetimes for fixed values of α and l, showing that, outside the event horizon, they typically satisfy

$$V_{\text{eff}}^{\text{RN}} > V_{\text{eff}}^{\text{H}}. \qquad (20.33)$$

The solutions of the Klein-Gordon equation consistent with the absorption/scattering problem are given by

$$\Psi_{\omega l} \sim \begin{cases} T_{\omega l}e^{-i\omega r_\star}, & r_\star \to -\infty\ (r \to r_+), \\ e^{-i\omega r_\star} + R_{\omega l}e^{i\omega r_\star}, & r_\star \to \infty\ (r \to \infty), \end{cases} \qquad (20.34)$$

where $T_{\omega l}$ and $R_{\omega l}$ are complex coefficients, which satisfy

$$|R_{\omega l}|^2 + |T_{\omega l}|^2 = 1. \qquad (20.35)$$

20.4.2 Absorption and scattering cross sections

It is usual to obtain an expression for the total ACS σ as a sum of partial waves contributions σ_l. For that purpose, we expand the scalar field as a sum of

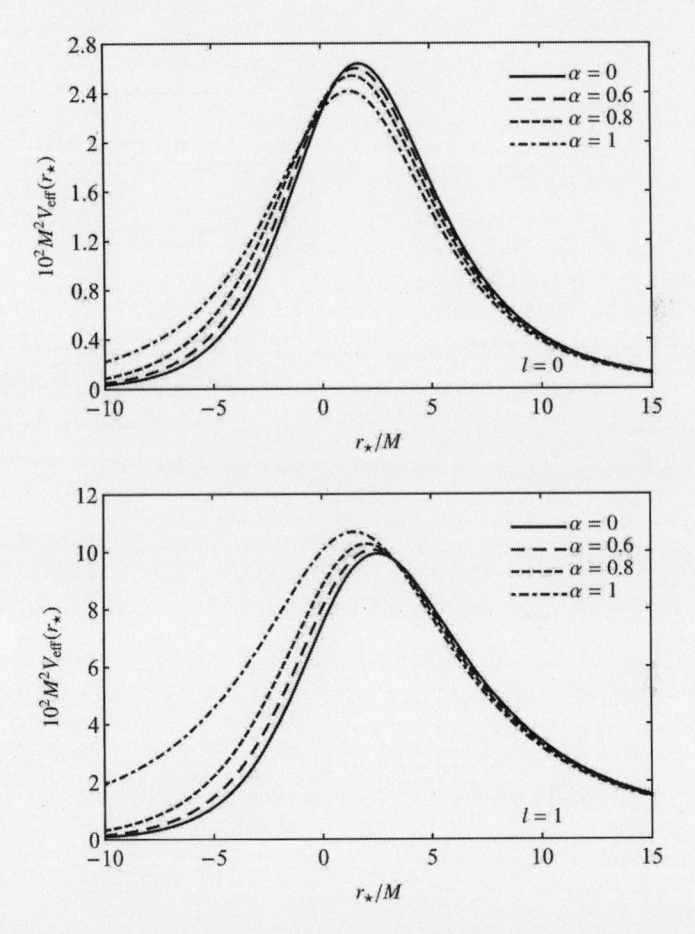

Figure 20.4: Effective potential of massless test scalar fields in the Hayward spacetime, as a function of $r_\star/M$, considering distinct values of α, for $l = 0$ (top panel) and $l = 1$ (bottom panel).

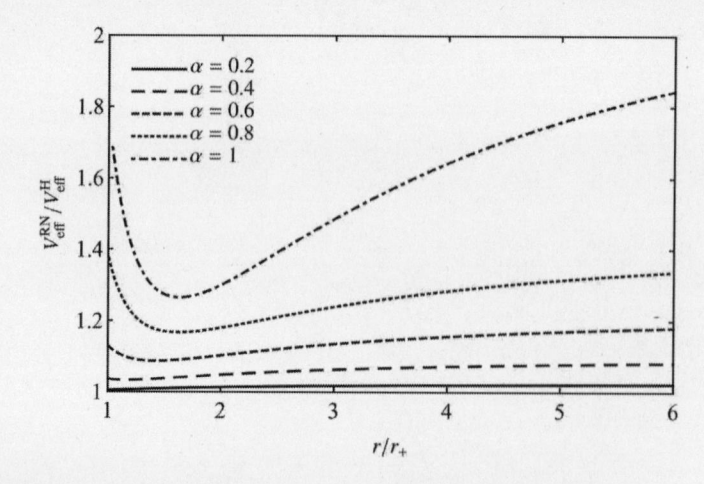

Figure 20.5: Ratio between the effective potential of massless test scalar fields in RN and Hayward spacetimes, as a function of r/r_+, for distinct values of α. Here we consider $l = 0$.

asymptotic plane waves and fix $C_{\omega l}$ with appropriated boundary conditions [60, 30], resulting in

$$\sigma = \sum_{l=0} \sigma_l, \qquad (20.36)$$

where σ_l is given by

$$\sigma_l = \frac{\pi}{\omega^2}(2l+1)\left(1 - |R_{\omega l}|^2\right). \qquad (20.37)$$

For its turn, the differential SCS for static and spherically symmetric spacetimes can be written as [25]

$$\frac{d\sigma}{d\Omega} = |h(\theta)|^2, \qquad (20.38)$$

where $h(\theta)$ is the scattering amplitude given by

$$h(\theta) = \frac{1}{2i\omega} \sum_{l=0}^{\infty} (2l+1)[e^{2i\delta_l(\omega)} - 1]P_l(\cos\theta), \qquad (20.39)$$

with the phase shifts $e^{2i\delta_l(\omega)}$ being defined as

$$e^{2i\delta_l(\omega)} \equiv (-1)^{l+1} R_{\omega l}. \qquad (20.40)$$

20.5 Results

In this section, we present a selection of our results concerning the absorption and scattering cross sections of massless test scalar waves in the background of

Hayward spacetimes. We also compare our numerical results for the Hayward geometry with those obtained in the RN case.

20.5.1 Numerical method

We numerically solve Eq. (20.31) from very close to the event horizon, i.e., $r_{\text{initial}} = 1.001 r_+$, to a region very far from the BH, typically chosen as $r_\infty = 10^3 M$. We then match the numerical solutions with the appropriated boundary conditions given by Eq. (20.34) and compute the reflection coefficient. Moreover, to calculate the absorption and scattering cross sections, we need to perform sums on the angular momentum of the scalar wave. For the absorption case, we typically set $l = 6$, while for the scattering case, we consider $l = 20$. Furthermore, the differential SCS has poor convergence for small values of the scattering angle. We improve the series convergence in this limit using the numerical method developed in Refs. [61, 26].

In Fig. 20.6, we compare our numerical results for the total ACS of massless scalar waves in the Hayward spacetime with some approximations. We can see that in the low-frequency regime, the total ACS tends to the event horizon area, namely

$$\sigma_{\text{lf}} = 4\pi r_+^2, \tag{20.41}$$

as expected [62, 63]. Moreover, in the high-frequency regime, our numerical results oscillate around the GCS [cf. Eq. (20.18)] and the oscillatory pattern is well described by the sinc approximation [cf. Eq. (20.19)], even for moderate frequency values.

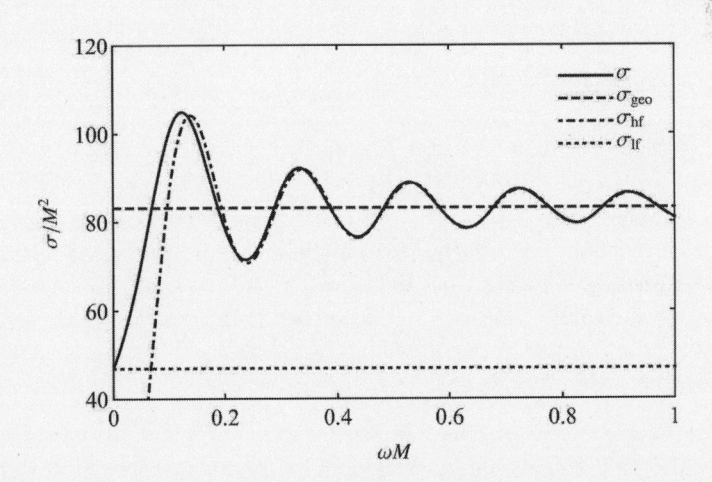

Figure 20.6: Comparison between the analytical approximations and numerical results for the total ACS of massless scalar fields of a Hayward RBH with $a = 0.8$, as a function of ωM.

Analogously, in Fig. 20.7, we compare our numerical results for the differential SCS of massless scalar waves in the Hayward spacetime with some approximations. We can observe that the differential SCS oscillates around the classical differential SCS [cf. Eq. (20.25)] and the oscillatory pattern is well described by the glory approximation [cf. Eq. (20.28)] near the backward direction. We have, therefore, obtained excellent agreement between our numerical results and the approximated analytical ones.

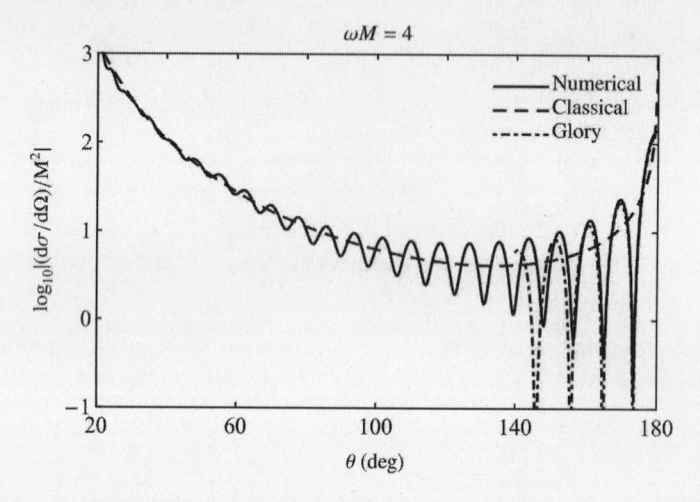

Figure 20.7: Comparison between the numerical and the approximate analytical results for the differential SCS of massless scalar fields in a Hayward RBH with $\alpha = 0.8$, as a function of θ. Here we consider $\omega M = 4$.

20.5.2 Massless scalar absorption

In Fig. 20.8, we show the partial and total ACSs of scalar waves in Hayward spacetimes. As we can see, the total ACS typically decreases as we increase the BH charge. However, for $\alpha^H \gtrsim 0.9658$, the first peak of the total ACS can be larger than in the Schwarzschild case ($\alpha = 0$). This feature can be related to the effective potential. As discussed in Sec. 20.4.1, the height of the potential barrier decreases as we enhance the values of α for $l = 0$. Therefore, massless scalar waves with $l = 0$ are more absorbed in the background of highly charged Hayward spacetimes, in contrast to what happens for $l \geq 1$.

In Fig. 20.9, we compare the total ACSs of massless scalar waves in Hayward and RN spacetimes. As we can see, for the same value of the normalized charge, the total ACS in the Hayward RBH is typically larger than the corresponding one in the RN case. This result is consistent with the analysis presented in Sec. 20.4.1, since the effective potential of the RN BH is always greater than that of the Hayward RBH

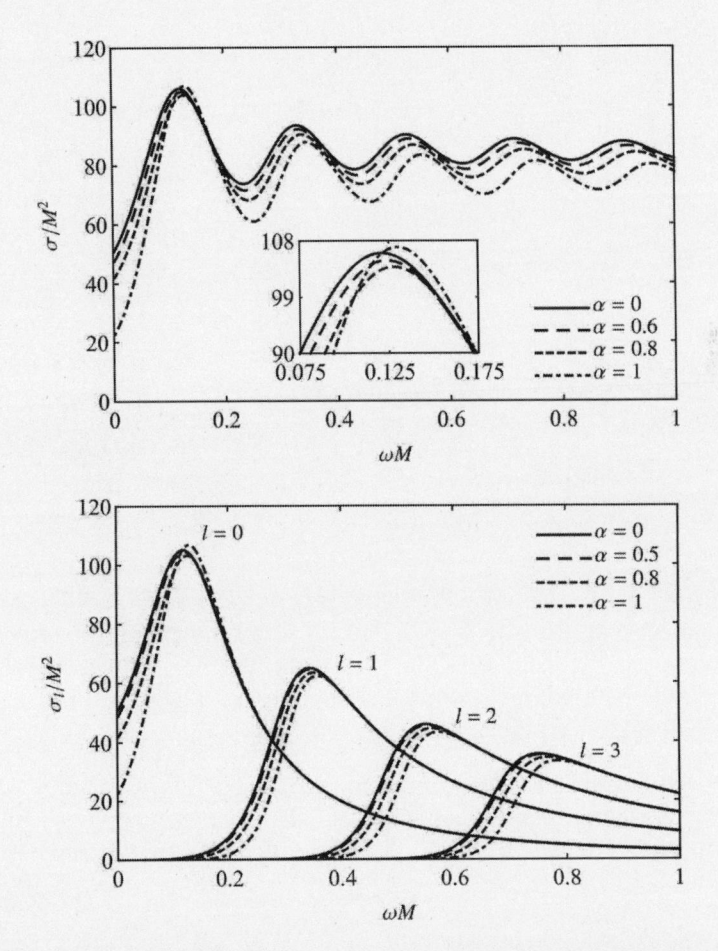

Figure 20.8: Total (top panel) and partial (bottom panel) ACSs of massless scalar fields in the Hayward spacetime, as functions of ωM, considering different values of l and α. The inset in the top panel helps us to visualize the behavior of the total ACS near the first peak.

for the same values of α.

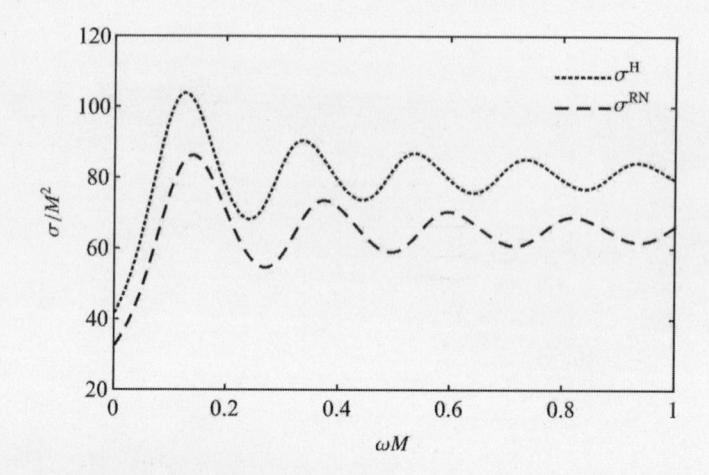

Figure 20.9: Comparison between the total ACSs, plotted as functions of ωM, of massless scalar fields in Hayward and RN spacetimes with $\alpha = 0.8$.

20.5.3 Massless scalar scattering

In Fig. 20.10, we show a selection of our results for the scalar differential SCS in Hayward spacetimes. We can observe that the interference fringe widths get wider as we increase the BH charge, in agreement with the glory approximation [41, 42, 44]. We also notice that, for small scattering angles, the contributions of the BH charge are negligible, as stablished by Eq. (20.26).

A comparison between the scattering spectra of Hayward and RN BHs is presented in Fig. 20.11. For the same α values, the interference fringe widths for the RN spacetime are typically larger than those in the Hayward corresponding case.

20.5.4 Mimicking standard BHs

We have also searched for situations in which the absorption and scattering spectra of Hayward and RN BHs can be very similar. Regarding configurations for which the ACSs are similar, we seek for the values of α that satisfy the following condition: $b_c^H = b_c^{RN}$. On the other hand, in the scattering case, we consider the values of the normalized charges for which the impact parameter of backscattered light rays matches, i.e., $b_g^H = b_g^{RN}$.

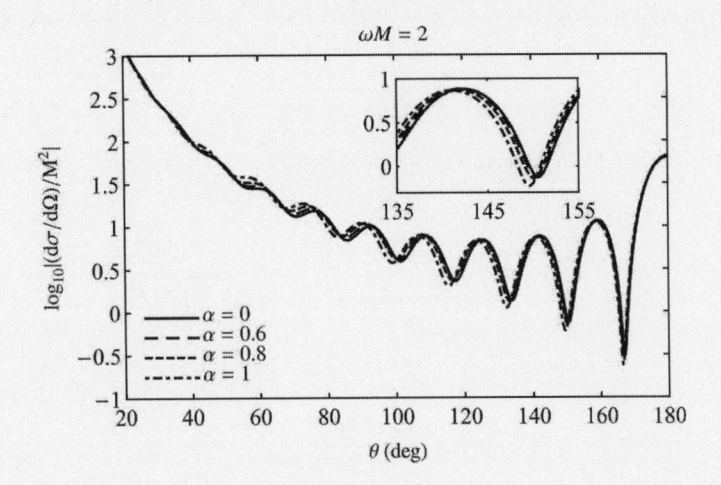

Figure 20.10: Differential SCSs of massless scalar fields in the Hayward spacetime, as a function of θ, considering distinct values of α, for $\omega M = 2$. The inset helps to visualize the differences in the interference fringe widths.

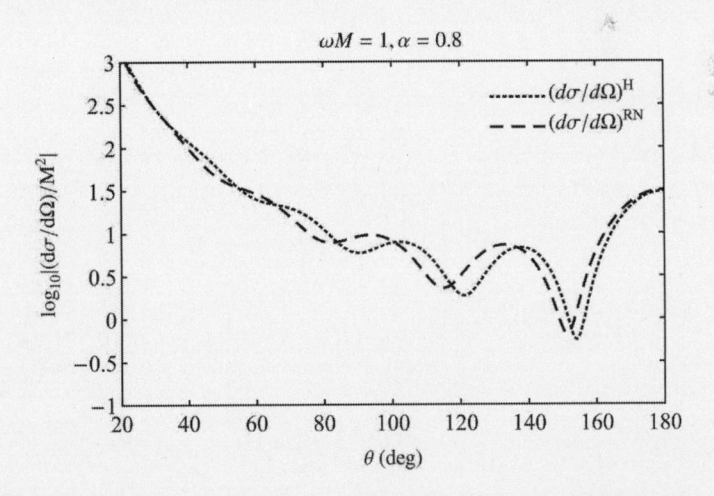

Figure 20.11: Comparison between the differential SCSs of massless scalar fields in Hayward and RN spacetimes with $\alpha = 0.8$, as a function of θ, for $\omega M = 1$.

A situation for which the ACSs of Hayward and RN BHs basically coincide is exhibited in the top panel of Fig. 20.12. Indeed, we can find values of the charge for which the total ACSs can be very similar in the whole frequency range, as long as we consider low-to-moderate values of the normalized charges.

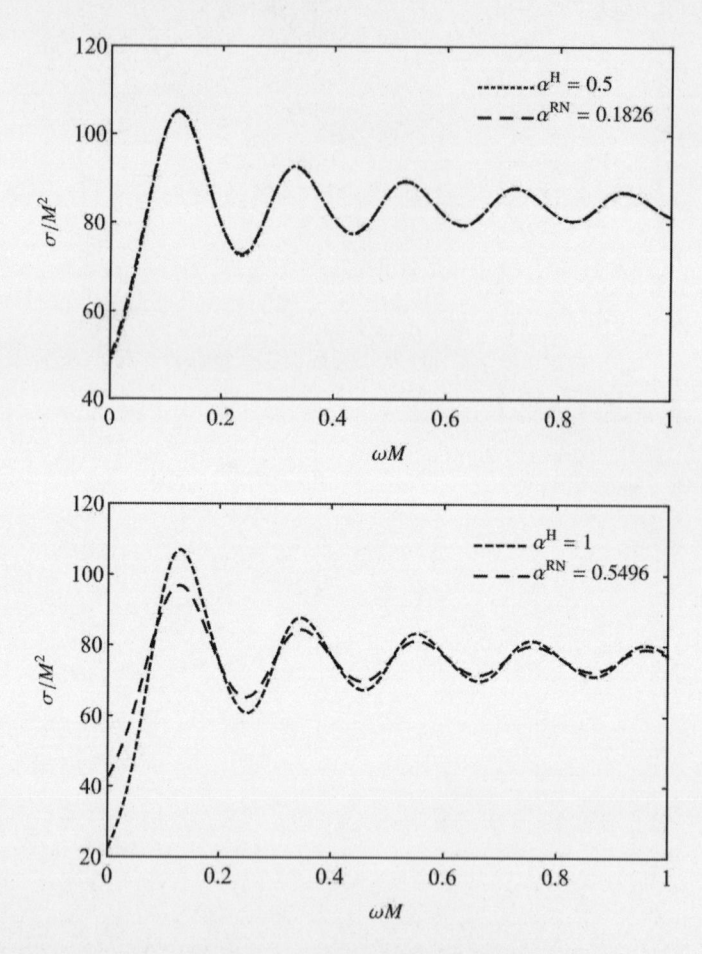

Figure 20.12: Comparison between the total ACSs of massless scalar fields in Hayward and RN spacetimes, as a function of ωM. We have chosen $\alpha^{\mathrm{H}} = 0.5$ and $\alpha^{\mathrm{RN}} = 0.1826$, in the top panel; as well as $\alpha^{\mathrm{H}} = 1$ and $\alpha^{\mathrm{RN}} = 0.5496$, in the bottom panel.

We exhibit, in the top panel of Fig. 20.13, a situation for which the SCSs of Hayward and RN BHs basically coincide. In Fig. 20.13, we show the comparison between the differential SCSs in Hayward and RN spacetimes. For low-to-moderate values of the normalized charges, we can find configurations for which the SCSs are very similar. As we increase the BH charge, keeping $b_g^{\mathrm{H}} = b_g^{\mathrm{RN}}$, the oscillatory profile remains similar, but the differences become more evident.

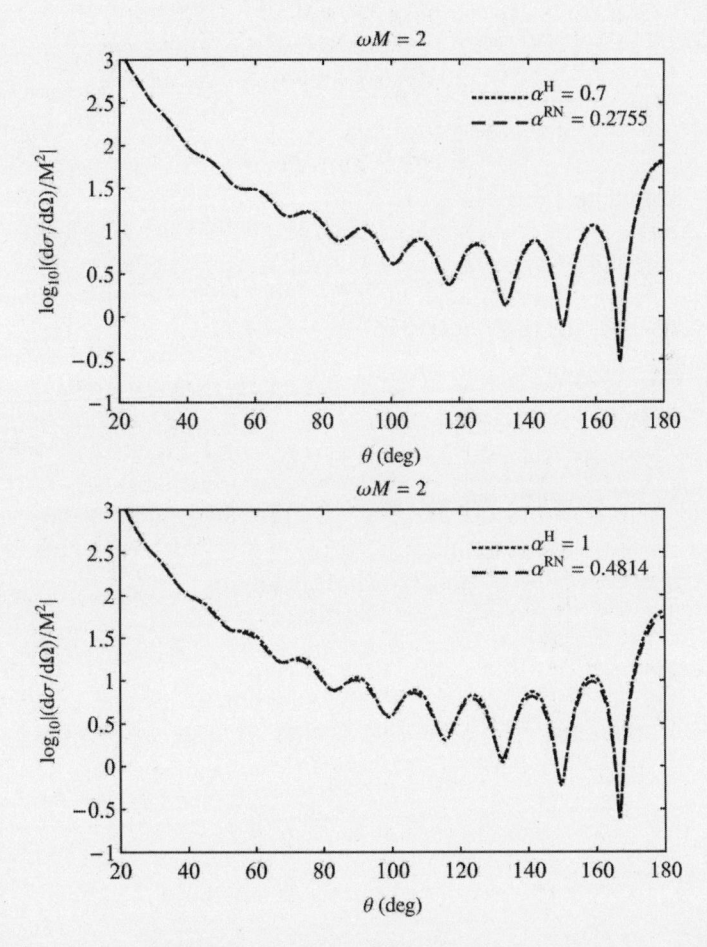

Figure 20.13: Comparison between the differential SCSs of massless scalar fields in Hayward and RN spacetimes, as a function of θ, for $\omega M = 2$. We have chosen $(\alpha^H, \alpha^{RN}) = (0.7, 0.2755)$ (top panel), as well as $(\alpha^H, \alpha^{RN}) = (1, 0.4814)$ (bottom panel).

20.6 Final remarks

We have investigated the absorption and scattering spectra of massless scalar fields in the background of the Hayward RBH solution. We have compared our numerical results obtained for arbitrary values of the frequency and scattering angle of the scalar wave with some analytical approximations, showing that they are in excellent agreement. We have noticed that the interference fringe widths get wider as we increase the RBH charge or decrease the frequency.

Concerning the absorption properties, we have obtained that, although the total ACS typically decreases as we enhance the RBH charge, the first peak (local maximum related to the monopole mode, $l = 0$) of the ACS in the Hayward spacetime can be larger than in the Schwarzschild case, for $a^H \gtrsim 0.9658$, while the local maxima related to $l > 0$ are smaller than those of Schwarzschild, assuming any (positive) value of magnetic charge. This distinctive feature may be related to the behavior of the effective potential.

We also have noticed that it is possible to find configurations for which the absorption and scattering of massless scalar waves in Hayward and RN geometries are very similar. These similarities can be found for general values of the frequency and scattering angle of the scalar wave but are constrained to low-to-moderate values of the BH charges. Our results reinforce that regular and singular BHs can have very similar absorption and scattering properties under certain circumstances, but we might be able to distinguish between them in other scenarios [64].

It is worth mentioning that recently the absorption and scattering properties of massless test scalar fields in Hayward RBH spacetimes were addressed in Ref. [65], but the results obtained there were not sound [66]. Here we provided the correct results.

Acknowledgments

We are grateful to Fundação Amazônia de Amparo a Estudos e Pesquisas (FAPESPA), Conselho Nacional de Desenvolvimento Científico e Tecnológico (CNPq) and Coordenação de Aperfeiçoamento de Pessoal de Nível Superior (CAPES) – Finance Code 001, from Brazil, for partial financial support. MP and LC thank the University of Sheffield, in England, and University of Aveiro, in Portugal, respectively, for the kind hospitality. LL would like to acknowledge IFPA – Campus Altamira for the support. This work has further been supported by the European Union's Horizon 2020 research and innovation (RISE) programme H2020-MSCA-RISE-2017 Grant No. FunFiCO-777740 and by the European Horizon Europe staff exchange (SE) programme HORIZON-MSCA-2021-SE-01 Grant No. NewFunFiCO-

101086251.

Bibliography

[1] B. P. Abbott *et al.* [LIGO Scientific Collaboration and Virgo Collaboration], *Observation of Gravitational Waves from a Binary Black Hole Merger*, Phys. Rev. Lett. **116**, 061102 (2016).

[2] K. Akiyama *et al.* [The Event Horizon Telescope Collaboration], *First M87 Event Horizon Telescope Results. I. The Shadow of the Supermassive Black Hole*, ApJL **875**, L1 (2019).

[3] K. Akiyama *et al.* [The Event Horizon Telescope Collaboration], *First Sagittarius A* Event Horizon Telescope Results. I. The Shadow of the Supermassive Black Hole in the Center of the Milky Way*, ApJL **930**, L12 (2022).

[4] G. Agazie *et al.* [NANOGrav Collaboration], *The NANOGrav 15 yr Data Set: Evidence for a Gravitational-wave Background*, ApJL **951**, L8 (2023).

[5] C. P. Burgess, *Quantum Gravity in Everyday Life: General Relativity as an Effective Field Theory*, Living Rev. Relativ. **7**, 5 (2004).

[6] J. Bardeen, *Non-singular General Relativistic Gravitational Collapse*, in *Proceedings of the International Conference GR5* (Tbilisi, Georgia, U.S.S.R., 1968), p. 174.

[7] I. Dymnikova, *Vacuum nonsingular black hole*, Gen. Relativ. Gravit. **24**, 235 (1992).

[8] A. Borde, *Open and closed universes, initial singularities, and inflation*, Phys. Rev. D **50**, 3692 (1994).

[9] E. Ayón-Beato and A. García, *Regular Black Hole in General Relativity Coupled to Nonlinear Electrodynamics*, Phys. Rev. Lett. **80**, 5056 (1998).

[10] I. Dymnikova, *Regular electrically charged vacuum structures with de Sitter centre in nonlinear electrodynamics coupled to general relativity*, Class. Quantum Grav. **21**, 4417 (2004).

[11] S. A. Hayward, *Formation and Evaporation of Nonsingular Black Holes*, Phys. Rev. Lett. **96**, 031103 (2006).

[12] L. Balart and E. C. Vagenas, *Regular black holes with a nonlinear electrodynamics source*, Phys. Rev. D **90**, 124045 (2014).

[13] H. Culet, *On a Regular Charged black Hole with a Nonlinear Electric Source*, Int. J. Theor. Phys. **54**, 2855 (2015).

[14] A. Simpson and M. Visser, *Regular black holes with asymptotically Minkowski cores*, Universe **6**, 8 (2019).

[15] S. Ansoldi, *Spherical black holes with regular center: a review of existing models including a recent realization with Gaussian sources*, arXiv:0802.0330.

[16] D. P. Sorokin, *Introductory Notes on Non-linear Electrodynamics and its Applications*, Fortsch. Phys. **70**, 2200092 (2022).

[17] L. Sebastiani and S. Zerbini, *Some Remarks on Non-Singular Spherically Symmetric Space-Times*, Astronomy **1**, 99 (2022).

[18] C. Lan, H. Yang, Y. Guo, and Y.-G. Miao, *Regular black holes: A short topic review*, Int. J. Theor. Phys. **62**, 202 (2023).

[19] A. Bonanno, A.-P. Khosravi, and F. Sauressig, *Regular black holes with stable cores*, Phys. Rev. D **103**, 124027 (2021).

[20] Z.-Y. Fan and X. Wang, *Construction of regular black holes in general relativity*, Phys. Rev. D **94**, 124027 (2016).

[21] Z.-Y. Fan, *Critical phenomena of regular black holes in anti-de Sitter spacetime*, Eur. Phys. J. C **77**, 266 (2017).

[22] B. Toshmatov, Z. Stuchlík, and B. Ahmedov, *Comment on "Construction of regular black holes in general relativity"*, Phys. Rev. D **98**, 028501 (2018).

[23] S. H. Mehdipour and M. H. Ahmadi, *Black hole remnants in Hayward solutions and noncommutative effects*, Nuc. Phys. B **926**, 49 (2018).

[24] S. M. Carroll, *Spacetime and Geometry: An Introduction to General Relativity* (Cambridge University Press, Cambridge, 2019).

[25] J. A. Futterman, F. A. Handler, and R. A. Matzner, *Scattering from Black Holes* (Cambridge University Press, Cambridge, England, 1988).

[26] S. Dolan, C. Doran, and A. Lasenby, *Fermion scattering by a Schwarzschild black hole*, Phys. Rev. D **74**, 064005 (2006).

[27] L. C. B. Crispino, E. S. Oliveira, and G. E. A. Matsas, *Absorption cross section of canonical acoustic holes*, Phys. Rev. D **76**, 107502 (2007).

[28] L. C. B. Crispino, S. R. Dolan, and E. S. Oliveira, *Scattering of massless scalar waves by Reissner-Nordström black holes*, Phys. Rev. D **79**, 064022 (2009).

[29] E. S. Oliveira, L. C. B. Crispino, and A. Higuchi, *Equality between gravitational and electromagnetic absorption cross sections of extreme Reissner-Nordström black holes*, Phys. Rev. D **84**, 084048 (2011).

[30] C. L. Benone, E. S. de Oliveira, S. R. Dolan, and L. C. B. Crispino, *Absorption of a massive scalar field by a charged black hole*, Phys. Rev. D **89**, 104053 (2014).

[31] C. F. B. Macedo and L. C. B. Crispino, *Absorption of planar massless scalar waves by Bardeen regular black holes*, Phys. Rev. D **90**, 064001 (2014).

[32] L. C. B. Crispino, S. R. Dolan, A. Higuchi, and E. S. de Oliveira, *Inferring black hole charge from backscattered electromagnetic radiation*, Phys. Rev. D **90**, 064027 (2014).

[33] C. F. B. Macedo, E. S. de Oliveira, and L. C. B. Crispino, *Scattering by regular black holes: Planar massless scalar waves impinging upon a Bardeen black hole*, Phys. Rev. D **92**, 024012 (2015).

[34] C. L. Benone and L. C. B. Crispino, *Superradiance in static black hole spacetimes*, Phys. Rev. D **93**, 024028 (2016).

[35] S. Fernando, *Bardeen–de Sitter black holes*, Int. J. Mod. Phys. D **26**, 1750071 (2017).

[36] P. A. Sanchez, N. Bretón, and S. E. P. Bergliaffa, *Scattering and absorption of massless scalar waves by Born-Infeld black holes*, Ann. Phys. **393**, 107 (2018).

[37] A. Delhom, C. F. B. Macedo, G. J. Olmo, and L. C. B. Crispino, *Absorption by black hole remnants in metric-affine gravity*, Phys. Rev. D **100**, 024016 (2019).

[38] H. C. D. L. Junior, C. L. Benone, and L. C. B. Crispino, *Scalar absorption: Black holes versus wormholes*, Phys. Rev. D **101**, 124009 (2020).

[39] R. B. Magalhães, L. C. S. Leite, and L. C. B. Crispino, *Schwarzschild-like black holes: Light-like trajectories and massless scalar absorption*, Eur. Phys. J. C **80**, 386 (2020).

[40] M. A. A. Paula, L. C. S. Leite, and L. C. B. Crispino, *Electrically charged black holes in linear and non-linear electrodynamics: Geodesic analysis and scalar absorption*, Phys. Rev. D **102**, 104033 (2020).

[41] M. A. A. de Paula, L. C. S. Leite, and L. C. B. Crispino, *Scattering properties of charged black holes in nonlinear and Maxwell's electrodynamics*, Eur. Phys. J. Plus **137**, 785 (2022).

[42] H. C. D. L. Junior, C. L. Benone, and L. C. B. Crispino, *Scalar scattering by black holes and wormholes*, Eur. Phys. J. C **82**, 638 (2022).

[43] M. A. A. de Paula, L. C. S. Leite, and L. C. B. Crispino, *Massless scalar scattering by a charged regular black hole*, Astron. Nachr. **344**, e220115 (2023).

[44] R. B. Magalhães, L. C. S. Leite, and L. C. B. Crispino, *Parametrized black holes: scattering investigation*, Eur. Phys. J. C **82**, 698 (2022).

[45] S. V. M. C. B. Xavier, C. L. Benone, L. C. S. Leite, and L. C. B. Crispino, *Scattering by stringy black holes*, Phys. Rev. D **108**, 084060 (2023).

[46] K. A. Bronnikov and S. G. Rubin, *Black Holes, Cosmology and Extra Dimensions* (World Scientific, Singapore, 2013).

[47] T. Zhou and L. Modesto, *Geodesic incompleteness of some popular regular black holes*, Phys. Rev. D **107**, 044016 (2023).

[48] E. Ayón-Beato and A. García, *The Bardeen model as a nonlinear magnetic monopole*, Phys. Lett. B **493**, 149 (2000).

[49] J. F. Plebański, *Lectures on Non-linear Electrodynamics* (NORDITA, Copenhagen, Denmark, 1970).

[50] S. A. Gutiérrez, A. L. Dudley, and J. F. Plebański, *Signals and discontinuities in general relativistic nonlinear electrodynamics*, J. Math. Phys. **22**, 2835 (1981).

[51] M. Novello, V. A. De Lorenci, J. M. Salim, and R. Klippert, *Geometrical aspects of light propagation in nonlinear electrodynamics*, Phys. Rev. D **61**, 045001 (2000).

[52] R. Wald, *General Relativity* (University of Chicago Press, Chicago, 1984).

[53] P. V. P. Cunha and C. A. R. Herdeiro, *Shadows and strong gravitational lensing: a brief review*, Gen. Relat. Gravit. **50**, 42 (2018).

[54] M. A. A. de Paula, H. C. D. Lima Junior, P. V. P. Cunha, and L. C. B. Crispino, *Electrically charged regular black holes in nonlinear electrodynamics: light rings, shadows and gravitational lensing*, Phys. Rev. D **108**, 084029 (2023).

[55] N. Sanchez, *Absorption and emission spectra of a Schwarzschild black hole*, Phys. Rev. D **18**, 1030 (1978).

[56] Y. Décanini, G. Esposito-Farèse, and A. Folacci, *Universality of high-energy absorption cross sections for black holes*, Phys. Rev. D **83**, 044032 (2011).

[57] V. Cardoso, A. S. Miranda, E. Berti, H. Witek, and V. T. Zanchin, *Geodesic Stability, Lyapunov Exponents and Quasinormal Modes*, Phys. Rev. D **79**, 064016 (2009).

[58] R. G. Newton, *Scattering Theory of Waves and Particles* (Dover Publications, New York, 2013).

[59] R. A. Matzner, C. DeWitt-Morette, B. Nelson, and T.-R. Zhang, *Glory scattering by black holes*, Phys. Rev. D **31**, 1869 (1985).

[60] W. Unruh, *Absorption Cross Section of Small Black Holes*, Phys. Rev. D **14**, 3251 (1976).

[61] D. R. Yennie, D. G. Ravenhall, and R. N. Wilson, *Phase-Shift Calculation of High-Energy Electron Scattering*, Phys. Rev. **95**, 500 (1954).

[62] S. R. Das, G. Gibbons, and S. D. Mathur, *Universality of Low Energy Absorption Cross Sections for Black Holes*, Phys. Rev. Lett. **78**, 417 (1997).

[63] A. Higuchi, *Low-frequency Scalar Absorption Cross Sections for Stationary Black Holes*, Class. Quantum Grav. **18**, L139 (2001); *Addendum*, Class. Quantum Grav. **19**, 599(A) (2002).

[64] E. L. B. Junior, M. E. Rodrigues, and H. A. Vieira, *Is it possible to distinguish between different black hole solutions using the Shapiro time delay?*, Eur. Phys. J. C **81**, 409 (2023).

[65] M.-Y. Wan and C. Wu, *Absorption and scattering of massless scalar wave from Regular Black Holes*, Gen. Relativ. Gravit. **54**, 148 (2022).

[66] M. A. A. de Paula, L. C. dos Santos Leite, and L. C. B. Crispino, *Comment on: "Absorption and scattering of massless scalar wave from Regular Black Holes"*, Gen. Relativ. Gravit. **55**, 73 (2023).

21

On alternative (or modified) theories of gravity

J. C. Fabris

Abstract: A seminar given about 30 years ago by Ruben Aldrovandi motivates this text where some reflexions about constructing theories that modify General Relativity are made. Two particular cases, the Brans-Dicke and Unimodular Gravity ones, are discussed, in a quite qualitative way, showing on how they can address some of the most outstanding problems of General Relativity, specially the transplanckian physics and the cosmological constant problem.

21.1 At that time...

I think it was about 1993, in Paris, in the *Laboratoire de Gravitation et Cosmologie Relativistes*, at that time under the direction of Richard Kerner. Ruben Aldrovandi gave a seminar, that was held at the library of this research unity of the *Université Pierre et Marie Curie* devoted to gravitation, cosmology and other branches of theoretical physical. Aldrovandi began the seminar by asking to the audience how many alternatives have been proposed to General Relativity since the formulation of this geometric theory of gravity. Since nobody tried to answer, he gave an approximative estimation: *more than one thousand*. Later, during his seminar he tried to develop a possible mechanism for avoiding the initial singularity but keeping the accepted framework of the GR and Elementary Particle Physics. At the end, interesting results were displayed, based on the extreme compression of matter, that needed as expected some new ingredients (but not so exotic in principle) to give a complete scenario. Perhaps Ruben wanted to alert that very good results concerning open and challenging problems could be obtained if we keep ourselves in the framework of the known physics, with some extrapolations to extreme situations: in facing a challenge, perhaps no need to throw immediately away the physics we have developed for decades, even if an open view must always be welcome.

Of course, the remark made by Rubem Aldrovandi in his speech in the beginning of the 90's had not the intention to criticize the construction of alternatives to GR. Later, he had made extensive studies in, for exemple, teleparell gravity, an alternative to GR: the gravitational effects in teleparell gravity are given by torsion instead of curvature of a Riemannian manifold. In an article, written by Ruben Aldrovandi and José Geraldo Pereira, published in 2016, the authors write [1]: *This new theory is fully equivalent to general relativity in what concerns physical results, but is deeply different from the conceptual point of view. Its characteristics make of teleparallel gravity an appealing theory, which provides an entirely new way to think the gravitational interaction.*

Teleparalell gravity (see Ref. [2] for a detailed description of this theoretical proposal) may give some new insights for the shortcomings of GR, as the difficulties connected with quantization of the gravitational interaction, preserving otherwise the main achievements of the standard theory of gravity. I understood his remark at that time about the huge number of alternative theories of gravity as an indication that, when studying one or another the important open problem, for example in gravitational physics, one must keep in mind the actual motivations to consider GR as the Standard Theory of Gravity and also the reasons to look for alternatives to this theory.

GR is in principle a very successful theory for the gravitational interaction. It explains de orbits of planets and stars, the deviation of light by massive objects, it predicts the existence of gravitational waves and black holes, besides other compacts objects. However, it contains singularities either inside black holes and at the beginning of the universe. In cosmology, the success in the predictions concerning the primordial nucleosynthesis and of a hot phase in the history of the universe are remarkable. However, without postulating a dark sector for the universe (dark matter and dark energy), it is not possible to understand the present stage of accelerated expansion of the universe, the dynamics of virialized cosmic system and even the formation of the structures in the observed cosmos. All tentative to detect directly the components components of the dark sector have failed until now.

From theoretical side, GR is not easy to quantize. Even if much progress has been obtained in the direction of the construction a consistent quantum theory of gravity, it is clear that to quantize the space-time itself is not an easy task. Teleparalellism may perhaps give a good new path in order to construct a quantum theory of gravity. But, it is still until now an interesting possibility: a concrete quantum theory of gravity has not yet be presented using Teleparalell theory of gravity. Hence, there are reasons to consider viable alternatives to the Standard Theory of Gravity. But, it is important not to loose a general view over the overall scenario, and mainly the success and difficulties of the current Standard Theory of Gravity.

Here, I will make some considerations on two possible alternative theories of gravity, the Brans-Dicke theory (with some unavoidable extension) and the Unimodular Gravity. It is interesting to remember that *alternative theories of gravity* looks an old fashion terminology, perhaps consequence of the social ambiance of the 60's (mainly) and 70's, when contestation of the occidental standard society proliferated from different sides. Today, *modified gravity* seems to be preferred, perhaps because it became important to stress that GR is a consistent theory of gravity, even if there are difficulties here and there. I think that the Brans-Dicke and Unimodular frameworks may be good examples on the different possibilities to construct a theory of the gravitational interaction outside the strict GR context, addressing some important open issues. We will try to show our point of view for this. The focus will be on a qualitative, and incomplete, discussion on the possibilities that are opened when some of the cornerstones of GR are abandoned in favor of a non standard framework.

21.2 The variation of the fundamental constants

The laws of physics make appeal to some characteristics, fundamental constants. These constants simbolizes the domain of physics involved in a given expression. For example, the gravitational coupling constant G indicates that gravitation is, at least, one of the phenomena under consideration. The presence, of $\hbar$ indicates that we have to do with quantum mechanics, the presence of c (velocity of light) to relativistic domain, the Boltzmann constant k_B with thermodynamics. In the General Relativity equations,

$$R_{\mu\nu} - \frac{1}{2} g_{\mu\nu} R = \frac{8\pi G}{c^4} T_{\mu\nu}, \tag{21.1}$$

it appears explicitly G and c. Hence, it is relativistic theory of gravity, while in the Newton's theory of gravity, expressed by the Poisson equation,

$$\nabla^2 \Psi = 4\pi G \rho, \tag{21.2}$$

for the gravitational potential Ψ, only G appears: it is a non-relativistic theory of gravity.

To my knowledge, the only physical expression that contains all these constants is the black hole temperature. For the Schwarzschild black hole, the temperature reads,

$$T = \frac{\hbar c^3}{8\pi G M k_B}. \tag{21.3}$$

We can add to the list of these fundamental constants the electric charge, e. It denotes the presence of electromagnetic interaction. The observations in astrophysics and cosmology are made through the detection of electromagnetic radiation, and in this sense it is important to take into account e in our description. In fact, it appears in the fine structure constant,

$$\alpha = \frac{e^2}{\hbar c} \approx \frac{1}{137}. \tag{21.4}$$

From $\hbar$, G and c, we can construct characteristic unities of length, time and mass:

$$L_P = \sqrt{\frac{G\hbar}{c^3}} \sim 2 \times 10^{-33} \text{ cm}, \tag{21.5}$$

$$T_P = \sqrt{\frac{c^5}{G\hbar}} \sim 5 \times 10^{-44} \text{ s}, \tag{21.6}$$

$$M_P = \sqrt{\frac{\hbar c}{G}} \sim 2 \times 10^{-5} \text{ g}. \tag{21.7}$$

From these expression, we can obtain the Planck energy,

$$E_P = \sqrt{\frac{\hbar c^5}{G}} \sim 2 \times 10^{16} \text{ erg} \sim 1,9 \times 10^{19} \text{ GeV}, \tag{21.8}$$

and the Planck temperature,

$$T_P = \sqrt{\frac{\hbar c^5}{G k_B^2}} \sim 10^{32}\,\text{K}. \tag{21.9}$$

These expressions contains the constant G, $\hbar$ and c and, in this sense, they are considered as characteristics of the regime of a quantum theory of gravity. Their magnitude indicate that we are very far from a direct test of the quantum gravity regime: The maximum energy produced in laboratory (LHC) is about 10 TeV, testing a distance of about 2×10^{-18} cm, with a time scale of 10^{-28} s, and temperature of the order of 10^{17} K. However, some indirect tests of the quantum gravitational regime may be considered, as the power spectrum of scalar perturbations imprinted in the large scale structure of the universe, as well as the power spectrum of the primordial gravitational waves (undetected until now, but with good possibilities to be detected in the near future). The primordial spectrum is determined by the microphysics in the very early universe. Hence, a quantum gravitational phase may leave traces in the primordial spectrum. But the exact determination of this fossils of a quantum gravitational era depends on the specific theory of quantum gravity, which is yet under construction. For some tentatives of obtaining a primordial spectrum in the context of a string effective theory, for example, see Refs. [4, 5].

In the 30's, Dirac considered the hypothesis that the fundamental constants may, in fact, vary with time [6]. The reasoning of Dirac is based on the large number hypothesis, identifying some coincidences in specific numbers obtained with fundamental constants. For example, using c, G and the Hubble constant H_0, we can recover the pion mass:

$$\left(\frac{\hbar^2 H_0}{G c}\right)^{\frac{1}{3}} \sim m_\pi. \tag{21.10}$$

This relation appeared very important at the time Dirac exposed his speculations since the studies of the atomic nucleus was taking form and the strong interaction has been proposed in order to retain the nucleus stable. The strong interaction should be mediated by a massive particle, identified as the pion, with a given mass (140 MeV) corresponding to a typical range for this interaction of the order of the size of the atomic nucleus. In order the relation above not to be a pure coincidence but reflecting a deeper law of Nature, and since the Hubble constant is connected with the age of the universe, c and/or G should depend on time. The choice made by Dirac was that G must be a function of time, such that,

$$G = G_0 \frac{t_0}{t}, \tag{21.11}$$

where t_0 is the present time and G_0 the present value of the gravitational coupling.

Another possibility, it would be to take the velocity of light as depending on time. This hypothesis led to many new proposals connected with a violation of Lorentz symmetry. There are strong constraints on a varying speed of light and, consequently, on the violation of Lorentz symmetry [7, 8]. However, this hypothesis is still not excluded.

Concerning the variation of the gravitational coupling term G, there are very strong observational constraints. The most recent one indicates that the fractional allowed variation of G is of the order of [9],

$$\frac{\dot{G}}{G} \leq 10^{-13} \text{year}^{-1}. \tag{21.12}$$

Since the age of the universe is $T_U \sim 10^{10}$ year, we can, very crudely estimate that the G has varied about a fraction of 10^{-3} during all the cosmic history. This would corresponds to a change in the third decimal case in its value. It is not enough to bring the Planck energy, for example, for a significative lower value.

However, even with this strong observational constraint, the possibility that G is a dynamical quantity may allow some very interesting results: by extrapolating to times near the initial singularity, the variation of G can be more important with far reaching consequences. We will describe in next section how to implement a variation of G in a relativistic theory of gravity, in occurrence the Brans-Dicke theory, and some of its possible consequences, mainly regarding a hypothetical new window to the Planck era and some different views of the Standard Cosmological Model, in particular the expansion of the universe.

21.3 Scalar tensor theories: some curiosities in the Brans-Dicke case

The Dirac proposal of considering G as a function of time has not been followed by a concrete theory incorporating this idea. Further steps to implement a theory of gravity may be traced back to Jordan, at the end of the 40's in the last century, also in an article in the journal Nature [10]. Jordan considered also in this work the possibility of matter creation in an expanding universe.

A consistent, relativistic theory of gravity with a dynamical gravitational coupling has been proposed in the beginning of the 60's by C. Brans and R.H. Dicke, the now called Brans-Dicke (BD) theory [3]. In the BD theory, G is replaced by a dynamical, long interaction scalar field ϕ, such that,

$$G \propto \frac{1}{\phi}. \tag{21.13}$$

A kinetic term for the scalar field is introduced together with a dimensionless coupling parameter ω. No potential related to ϕ term is added, in conformity with the proposal that ϕ is a long interaction scalar field: the presence of a potential term, describing a self-interaction, would lead to an effective mass, shortening the range of the interaction.

In this way, the Einstein-Hilbert Lagrangian,

$$\mathcal{L} = \sqrt{-g}\left\{\frac{R}{16\pi G}\right\} + \mathcal{L}_m(g_{\mu\nu}, \Psi), \tag{21.14}$$

with the matter Lagrangian given by $\mathcal{L}_m(g_{\mu\nu}, \Psi)$, Ψ representing the matter fields, is replaced by

$$\mathcal{L} = \sqrt{-g}\left\{\phi R - \omega\frac{\phi_{;\rho}\phi^{;\rho}}{\phi}\right\} + \mathcal{L}_m(g_{\mu\nu}, \Psi). \tag{21.15}$$

The GR limit must be obtained by imposing ϕ constant but also by considering $\omega \to \infty$. However, in some particular situations, this limit is not so well defined [11, 12]. The observational constraints indicate a very large value for ω, up to $\omega > 40,000$ [13]. In this case, in principle the theory must be essentially indistinguishable from GR. But, we must stress the expression 'in principle".

From the theoretical side, there are some interesting connections of the BD theory with other, perhaps more fundamental, theories. For example, at low energy, the effective action emerging from the string theory, is given by [14],

$$\mathcal{L} = \sqrt{-g}\left\{\phi R + \frac{\phi_{;\rho}\phi^{;\rho}}{\phi}\right\}, \tag{21.16}$$

neglecting matter and gauge fields. This is the BD theory with $\omega = -1$. Of course, this value of ω is in strong disagreement with observations, but we will return to this question below. Also, multidimensional theories, à la Kaluza-Klein, may lead, after reduction to four dimensions, to a BR type action, with

$$\omega = -\frac{(d-1)}{d}, \tag{21.17}$$

d being the number of extra dimensions, $D = 4 + d$. Hence, KK theories [15] with arbitrary dimension may have connection with BD theory with ω varying from 0 ($D = 5$) and -1, which coincides with the effective string action, but under the condition $D \to \infty$. We must quote also that the, today very fashion, $f(R)$ theories may be mapped in a BD-type theory, with $\omega = 0$, but with a potential determined by the form of function $f(R)$ [16]. The presence of the potential, in this case, is in strong contrast with the original purposes of the BD theory, however.

For the moment, let us ignore the observational constraints on ω, and let us explore some aspects of the Brans-Dicke theory. We write first the field equations from the action. They read,

$$R_{\mu\nu} - \frac{1}{2} g_{\mu\nu} R = \frac{8\pi}{\phi} T_{\mu\nu} + \frac{\omega}{\phi^2}\left(\phi_{;\mu}\phi_{;\nu} - \frac{1}{2} g_{\mu\nu}\phi_{;\rho}\phi^{;\rho}\right)$$
$$+ \frac{1}{\phi}\left(\phi_{;\mu}\phi_{;\nu} - g_{\mu\nu}\Box\phi\right), \tag{21.18}$$

$$\Box\phi = \frac{8\pi T}{3 + 2\omega}, \tag{21.19}$$

$$T^{\mu\nu}{}_{;\mu} = 0. \tag{21.20}$$

First of all, a remark on equation (21.20): as in GR, in the BD theory the energy-momentum tensor is conserved since both theories are invariant by general diffeomorphic transformation [17], a property that will be discussed in more details below.

We will now specialize the field equations to the flat Friedmann-Lemaître-Robertson-Walker (FLRW) metric, given by,

$$ds^2 = dt^2 - a(t)^2(dx^2 + dy^2 + dz^2). \tag{21.21}$$

The resulting equations of motion are the following:

$$3\left(\frac{\dot{a}}{a}\right)^2 = \frac{8\pi}{\phi}\rho + \frac{\omega}{2}\frac{\dot{\phi}^2}{\phi^2} - 3H\frac{\dot{\phi}}{\phi}, \tag{21.22}$$

$$\ddot{\phi} + 3H\dot{\phi} = \frac{8\pi}{3 + 2\omega}(\rho - 3p), \tag{21.23}$$

$$\dot{\rho} + 3H(\rho + p) = 0. \tag{21.24}$$

We consider two particular solutions for these equations according the equation of state connecting p and ρ.

- Vacuum state, $p = -\rho$:

$$a \propto t^{\omega + 1/2}, \tag{21.25}$$
$$\phi \propto t^2; \tag{21.26}$$

- Incoherent matter, $p = 0$:

$$a \propto t^{\frac{2 + 2\omega}{4 + 3\omega}}, \tag{21.27}$$
$$\phi \propto t^{\frac{2}{4 + 3\omega}}. \tag{21.28}$$

The solutions above admit a constant scale factor a. For the first case, it occurs for $\omega = -1/2$, while for the second case, this configuration occurs for $\omega = -1$, a value that coincides with the string low energy limit. This does not mean properly a static universe, since the gravitational coupling ϕ is a function of time. In both cases, $\phi \propto t^2$, and the gravitational coupling diverges as $t \to 0$. Hence, in these cases, the Planck energy goes to zero asymptotically. This property may have important consequences for the physics in the primordial universe, affecting for example the features of the initial quantum fluctuations responsible for the primordial spectrum of scalar and tensorial perturbations.

A remark to be made is that these solutions with a constant scale factor are stable as demonstrated in Ref. [18]. For example, for $p = -\rho$, the perturbations on the scalar field, expressed as

$$\lambda = \frac{\delta \phi}{\phi}, \qquad (21.29)$$

$\delta \phi$ being the fluctuation on the (inverse) gravitational coupling, and using the synchronous coordinate condition, reads [18],

$$\lambda = \frac{1}{t}\left\{\int t^{\frac{1-5r}{2}}\left[C_1 J_k(y) + C_2 J_{-k}(y)\right]dy + C_3\right\}, \qquad (21.30)$$

with the definitions,

$$x = t^p, \quad p = 1-r, \quad r = \omega + \frac{1}{2}, \quad y = \frac{kx}{1-r}, \quad q = \frac{4r+3}{2(1-r)}, \qquad (21.31)$$

k being the wavenumber and C_i integrations constants.

For the static scale factor in the case of a vacuum fluid ($p = -\rho$, $\omega = -1/2$), the solution reads (neglecting the fictitious solution represented by the constant C_3),

$$\lambda = \frac{1}{t}\left\{\int t^{\frac{1}{2}}\left[C_1 J_{3/2}(kt) + C_2 J_{-3/2}(kt)\right]dx\right\}. \qquad (21.32)$$

The *static* solution is stable, as it can be verified, for example, by inspecting the asymptotical behavior. The same happens with the static case with $p = 0$, and $\omega = -1$. We must remember that a solution with constant scale factor in GR is unstable.

Of course, we deal here with a fictitious static universe. Even if the scale factor is constant, the gravitational coupling varies. In both cases, $p = -\rho$ and $p = 0$, it varies as $G \propto t^{-2}$. It means that G is a decreasing function of time. Hence, the Planck energy was smaller in the past, approaching zero as $t \to 0$. The time elapsed from this moment until today is finite. In principle, we can have two disconnected branches, one with $-\infty < t < 0$, and another with $0 < t < \infty$. If just one branch is consider, there is no curvature singularities (since a is constant), but there is a geodesic singularity. A bounce-type scenario must be obtained in order to get rid off this geodesic singularity.

Of course, at this level, the above description is just a curiosity. But, it can be brought to a more serious scenario. For example, how to explain the cosmological redshift? We remark that in the gravitational interaction what matters frequently is GM, and the variation of G can be translated into a variation of mass, leading to a change in the spectral lines.

However, there must be a mechanism in order to pass from one cosmological phase to another. We observe a relic of a hot phase, the Cosmic Microwave Background radiation, indicating a radiative dominated phase. Besides this, the observed abundance of helium requires also a hot phase in the past, the existence of structures like galaxies requires the presence of matter with an effective pressure near zero, etc. In order, to implement all these observations in such a scenario, we need to introduce a new ingredient. For example, to pass from a vacuum phase to a matter phase, but keeping the scale factor constant, it is required to change the value of ω from $-1/2$ to -1. This can be achieved by considering ω as a function of time. It is, in some sense, an *epicycle*, but not completely out of sense. Let us describe how it can be obtained.

Our start point is the Bergmann-Wagoner-Brans-Dicke theory, whose Lagrangian in the original Jordan frame is [3, 19]

$$\mathcal{L} = \sqrt{-g}\left\{\phi R - \omega(\phi)\frac{\phi_{;\rho}\phi^{;\rho}}{\phi}\right\} + \mathcal{L}_m(g_{\mu\nu}, \Psi), \tag{21.33}$$

with, as before, the matter Lagrangian given by $\mathcal{L}_m(g_{\mu\nu}, \Psi)$, Ψ representing the matter fields. The novelty is that ω now is a function of ϕ.

The field equations are the following:

$$R_{\mu\nu} - \frac{1}{2}g_{\mu\nu}R = \frac{8\pi}{\phi}T_{\mu\nu} + \frac{\omega(\phi)}{\phi^2}\left(\phi_{;\mu}\phi_{;\nu} - \frac{1}{2}g_{\mu\nu}\phi_{;\rho}\phi^{;\rho}\right)$$
$$+ \frac{1}{\phi}\left(\phi_{;\mu}\phi_{;\nu} - g_{\mu\nu}\Box\phi\right), \tag{21.34}$$

$$\Box\phi = \frac{8\pi T}{3+2\omega(\phi)} - \frac{\omega_\phi}{3+2\omega(\phi)}\phi_{;\rho}\phi^{;\rho}, \tag{21.35}$$

$$T^{\mu\nu}{}_{;\mu} = 0. \tag{21.36}$$

The subscript in ω indicates derivative with respect to ϕ.

Since ω is now a function of the scalar field ϕ, it can change its value, for example, from $-1/2$ to -1. For this we can suppose that,

$$\omega(\phi) = -\frac{1}{2}\tanh\phi - \frac{1}{2}. \tag{21.37}$$

The solutions may differ from those display above, admitting for example $\phi \propto t$, recovering the original proposal of Dirac, $G \propto \frac{1}{t}$. The main point is that the range of scalar field must be $0 < \phi < \infty$. There is one more difficulty to be surmounted: to pass from one phase, dominated by a given fluid to another one, dominated by another fluid, it is necessary that the fluid may depend on ϕ. This can not be achieved here, since the conservation of the energy-momentum tensor, with a constant, scale factor, implies $\rho_i =$ constant for all matter components. At this stage, we can circumvent this problem by rewriting the field equations in the minimally coupled framework through a conformal transformation, such that,

$$g_{\mu\nu} = \phi^{-1} \tilde{g}_{\mu\nu}. \qquad (21.38)$$

In this case, the equations read now,

$$\tilde{R}_{\mu\nu} - \frac{1}{2} \tilde{g}_{\mu\nu} \tilde{R} = 8\pi G \tilde{T}_{\mu\nu} + \frac{\frac{3}{2} + \omega(\phi)}{\phi^2} \left(\phi_{;\mu} \phi_{;\nu} - \frac{1}{2} \tilde{g}_{\mu\nu} \phi_{;\rho} \phi^{;\rho} \right), \qquad (21.39)$$

$$\tilde{\Box} \phi = \frac{8\pi G \phi T}{3 + 2\omega(\phi)} - \left(\frac{\phi \omega_\phi}{3 + 2\omega(\phi)} - 1 \right) \frac{\phi_{;\rho} \phi^{;\rho}}{\phi}, \qquad (21.40)$$

$$\tilde{T}^{\mu\nu}_{;\mu} = -\frac{1}{2} \frac{\phi^{;\nu}}{\phi} \tilde{T}. \qquad (21.41)$$

In these equations, G is the present gravitational coupling and,

$$\tilde{T}^{\mu\nu} = (\tilde{\rho} + \tilde{p}) \tilde{u}^\mu \tilde{u}^\nu - \tilde{g}^{\mu\nu} \tilde{p}, \qquad (21.42)$$

with,

$$\tilde{\rho} = \frac{\rho}{\phi^2}, \quad \tilde{p} = \frac{p}{\phi^2}. \qquad (21.43)$$

In this case it is possible to transit from a phase dominated by a given fluid to another phase dominated by another fluid. But, in order to do this the constancy of the scale factor must be implement in the minimal coupled frame described above, while in the original frame the universe would be fully dynamical, with a varying scale factor: a fully dynamical universe, can be mapped in a universe without expansion.

The reasoning exposed above reveals that it is very challenging to take very far the *curiosity* of having a static scale factor a in a stable cosmological scenario, trying to construct a realistic and complete model. But, at this stage this is not in principle excluded. If this program is, at least partially, successful it may bring new visions on the observational facts like the cosmological redshift, dark energy, initial singularities, etc. Our description above has some similarities (and also some important differences) with the scenario of a universe without (or almost without) expansion proposed by Wetterich [20]. What we have described above is that a theory like the Brans-Dicke may also admit a universe without expansion, even if facing many obstacles to construct a realistic cosmological scenario.

In any case, it may be stressed that, even in its traditional formulation, BD theory may open a window to investigate the transplanckian regime.

21.4 The cosmological constant: a problem?

In the previous section, we have discussed some curious possibilities that emerge from considering the gravitational coupling G as a dynamical quantity. In particular, how to obtain a universe "without expansion" has been considered within one of the most important relativistic theory that incorporates a variable gravitational coupling in a relativistic context, the Brans-Dicke theory. Now, we turn to another recurrent topic in modern cosmology, the presence of the cosmological constant in cosmological models coming from GR. This is frequently considered as one of the most important problem in physics today. But, to which extend this is a problem? We will try to address, at least partially, this question here.

The so-called *cosmological constant problem* has a long history. The first frequently quoted discussion comes from the attempt to construct a static model for the universe by A. Einstein. In cosmology, using the non-flat FLRW metric and a pressureless matter component, the equations governing the evolution of the universe are given by,

$$H^2 + \frac{k}{a^2} = \frac{8\pi}{3}G\rho, \qquad (21.44)$$

$$2\dot{H} + 3H^2 + \frac{k}{a^2} = 0, \qquad (21.45)$$

$$\dot{\rho} + 3H\rho = 0. \qquad (21.46)$$

For a static universe ($H = 0$), these equations are only consistent with $k = 0$ and $\rho = 0$, that is, an empty Minkowski space-time. Inserting a cosmological term, the equations become,

$$H^2 + \frac{k}{a^2} = \frac{8\pi}{3}G\rho + \frac{\Lambda}{3}, \qquad (21.47)$$

$$2\dot{H} + 3H^2 + \frac{k}{a^2} = \Lambda, \qquad (21.48)$$

$$\dot{\rho} + 3H\rho = 0. \qquad (21.49)$$

If the universe is flat ($k = 0$), again there is only trivial solution, but for $k \neq 0$, the solutions become,

$$\frac{2}{3}\Lambda = \frac{8\pi}{3}G\rho, \qquad (21.50)$$

$$\frac{k}{a^2} = \Lambda. \qquad (21.51)$$

For $k < 0$ (open universe), a static universe requires negative mass, but for closed universe ($k > 0$), a positive mass, with a positive cosmological constant, leads to the desired static configuration. Moreover, the universe will have a spherical geometry. Not bad, but this universe is unstable, as it was quickly realized.

This negative result for a static universe does not led to the complete rejection of the cosmological term. In the 30's, Lemaître has revived the cosmological constant for another reasons [21]. At that moment, the density of the universe were estimated (very crudely) by the distribution of galaxies, let us say, only by the detected baryonic matter (The possibility of the existence of a *dark* matter component was only evoked by Zwicky, with very unprecise estimations [22]). After the works of Friedmann, Lemaître and Hubble, the possibility of a static universe has been rejected in favor of dynamical, expanding universe. Using the present data, the baryonic density today is of the order of [23],

$$\rho_{b0} \sim 3,6 \times 10^{-28} \frac{\text{kg}}{\text{m}^3} = 3,6 \times 10^{-31} \frac{\text{g}}{\text{cm}^3}. \qquad (21.52)$$

The subscript 0 indicates the present value.

However, the estimations of the baryonic component were very crude in the 30's, and it was considered the possibility of a universe dominated by baryons only, leading to the Einstein-de Sitter universe. Hence, we can consider the Friedmann's equation,

$$H^2 = \frac{8\pi G}{3}\rho_b. \qquad (21.53)$$

Using that $\rho_b = \rho_{b0} a^{-3}$ we obtain,

$$a = a_0 \left(\frac{t}{t_0}\right)^{2/3}. \qquad (21.54)$$

The age of the universe, today, is given by,

$$t_0 = \frac{2}{3}\frac{1}{H_0}. \qquad (21.55)$$

Using the measured value of H_0, for example obtained from the Cepheid stars,

$$H_0 \sim 70 \frac{\text{km}}{\text{Mpc} \cdot \text{s}}, \qquad (21.56)$$

we obtain an age of the universe of the order of 9,5 billion years, smaller than the age of the globular clusters (the oldest virialized stellar system known), which is of the order of the 13 billion years.

Everything changes if a cosmological constant is added. In this case, the Friedmann equation becomes,

$$H^2 = \frac{8\pi G}{3}\rho + \frac{\Lambda}{3}, \qquad (21.57)$$

Since Λ is a constant, this equation admits the solution (supposing the matter component with the same behavior as before), given by,

$$a(t) = \left(\frac{\Omega_m}{\Omega_\Lambda}\right)^{1/3} \sinh^{2/3}\left\{\frac{3}{2}\sqrt{\Omega_\Lambda}\, t\, H_0\right\}, \qquad (21.58)$$

with

$$\Omega_m = \frac{8\pi G}{3H_0^2}, \qquad (21.59)$$

$$\Omega_\Lambda = \frac{\Lambda}{3H_0^2}, \qquad (21.60)$$

with $\Omega_m + \Omega_\Lambda = 1$.

The Hubble function is given by,

$$H_0 = \left.\frac{\dot{a}}{a}\right|_{t=t_0} \qquad (21.61)$$

where t_0 is the present time. Solving numerically the resulting relation with, for example, $\Omega_\Lambda = 0.7$, we find $t_0 = 13.1$ billion years. This result differs from present estimations (13.8 billion years) because we are ignoring the complete evolution of the. universe. But, this simple analysis show how the introduction of the cosmological constant may solve the *age crisis*.

Hence, the presence of the cosmological constant in the Friedmann equation can solve one of the main problems of the old standard cosmological model based only on the baryonic matter: the incompatibility between the age of the universe and the age of some structures that emerge in the course of the evolution of the cosmos, in occurrence, the globular clusters, as pointed out by Lemaître. Moreover, the introduction of the cosmological constant is very natural. As it was established much later, in the 70's, by Lovelock [24], the most general action constructed out from the curvature tensor, leading to second order differential equations, is given by,

$$I_D = \sum_{n=0}^{[D/2]} c_n \frac{1}{n!} \delta^{[\alpha_1 \alpha_2 \cdots \alpha_{n-1} \alpha_n]}_{[\beta_1 \beta_2 \cdots \beta_{n-1} \beta_n]} R^{\beta_1 \beta_2}{}_{\alpha_1 \alpha_2} \cdots R^{\beta_{n-1} \beta_n}{}_{\alpha_n \alpha_{n-1}}. \qquad (21.62)$$

In this expression D is the dimension of space-time, $[D/2]$ indicates the integer part, and anti-symmetrization in the indices α and β are indicated, while c_n are arbitrary constants. In four dimensions we find,

$$I_4 = \Lambda + c_1 R + c_2 \left(R_{\mu\nu\rho\sigma} R^{\mu\nu\rho\sigma} - 4 R_{\mu\nu} R^{\mu\nu} + R^2 \right). \qquad (21.63)$$

In this expression, c_0 has been identified with the cosmological constant, R leads to the Einstein-Hilbert Lagrangian, and the term connected with c_2 is the Gauss-Bonnet action, which does not contribute to the equation of motions in four dimensions, being a topological term.

The Lovelock invariants reveal that the introduction of the cosmological constant in the gravitational equations are natural. Perhaps, unnatural it would be to ignore it! Of course, it could be argued that nothing predicts the observed value of cosmological constant. But, nothing also previews the value of the gravitational coupling G or other fundamental constant of Nature. Perhaps a complete and consistent quantum theory of gravity may explain this value. However, we are not still there.

Where is the *cosmological constant problem*? An article of 1989 by Weinberg [25] discusses extensively this point. Here, we present our point of view. In an article dated of 1965 [26], Gliner argued that the quantum vacuum should have an equation of state $p = -\rho$, the same equation of state of the cosmological constant, if we interpret the cosmological constant as a fluid. The argument of Gliner is that only this equation of state is invariant by Lorentz transformation, and all inertial observers must *see* the same vacuum state.

In fact, suppose a energy-moment tensor on the form of a perfect fluid,

$$T_{\mu\nu} = (\rho, p, p, p). \tag{21.64}$$

Now perform a Lorentz transformation and impose that the transformed energy-momentum tensor has the same form:

$$T_{\mu'\nu'} = (\rho', p', p', p') = \Lambda^\rho_{\mu'} \Lambda^\sigma_{\nu'} T_{\rho\sigma} = (\rho, p, p, p). \tag{21.65}$$

We may insert the usual Lorentz transformation connecting two inertial observers with a relative motion along the axis x, for simplicity. The solution is $\rho' = -p' = \rho = -p$, that is, the equation of state for a cosmological constant identified as a fluid.

If we have an interpretation of the cosmological constant as a fluid related to the quantum vacuum state, we end with a huge discrepancy. To explain the present accelerated phase of expansion of the universe, we must have a energy density of this fluid, as

$$\rho_\Lambda \sim 10^{-47} \, \text{GeV}^4. \tag{21.66}$$

On the other hand, the theoretical estimations of the vacuum energy density in quantum field theory are quite complex, and perhaps we can not say that we know it for sure, since it depends on many phenomena taking place in this *vacuum state*. Weinberg gives, in the quoted article reference, initally a crude, very simplified estimation (before launching a more deep analysis), based on the vacuum state of an harmonic oscillator, with a cut off given by the Planck frequency:

$$\rho_{vac} = \frac{\hbar}{2} \int_0^{\omega_{Pl}} \omega \frac{d^3\omega}{(2\pi)^3 c^3} = \frac{\hbar}{(2\pi)^2} \frac{\omega_{Pl}^4}{c^3}. \tag{21.67}$$

leading to $\rho_{vac} \sim 10^{71}$ GeV^4. This leads to a discrepancy between the theoretical and observational value of almost 120 orders of magnitudes, considered as the worst discrepancy in all domain of physics. More detailed (and possibly incomplete still) computations and the introduction of new ingredients (like supersymmetry) may lead to less dramatic estimations (perhaps 60, 50 orders of magnitude). However, there is a consensus that the discrepancy is large.

An ideia that came is to *degravitate* the vacuum energy, such that the gravitational effects the vacuum energy are strongly attenuated or even eliminated [27, 28, 29]. But, this is a proposal in construction. There are cosmological models based on a self-interacting scalar field, called quintessence [30], of tachyonic condensate in string theory [31, 32, 33, 34] which give up (in a certain way) the use of the cosmological constant to explain the dark energy. However, these models require a zero (or almost zero) vacuum energy density, quite difficult to explain using the reasoning above. In next section, we discuss another proposal which, in principle, modifies substantially the theory of gravitation, that is, General Relativity, but may give a new view of the problem.

21.5 Unimodular Gravity

General Relativity was proposed as the theory of gravity at the end of 1915. It is based on the idea of identifying the gravitational phenomena as the geometry of the space-time in four dimensions, three spatial and one temporal. It was quickly realized that the new gravitational theory could explain the observed anomalous advanced of the perihelium of Mercury, and in 1919 the predictions for the deflection of light was confirmed during the observations of solar eclipse, made in Sobral (Brazil) and Ilha do Príncipe (Africa). More recently, the detection of gravitational wave and of black holes confirmed two other remarkable predictions of GR. However, these outstanding success of the GR is also followed by many difficulties like the existence of the dark sector in the global content of matter and energy of the universe. The cosmological constant problem discussed in the previous section is one of the aspects of the problem associated to the possible existence of the dark sector.

Soon after the final formulation of the GR theory, one of the first variant (among the more one thousand other proposals that were made since then) of the theory has been proposed. It was called Unimodular Gravity (UG), since it has the same content as GR but with constraint on the determinant of the metric [35, 36, 37]. Originally, it has been imposed that,

$$\det(g_{\mu\nu}) \equiv g = 1. \tag{21.68}$$

This condition must be preserved under general coordinate transformations (diffeomorphisms). Hence, instead of an invariance under general coordinate transformation (general diffeomorphism) under which GR is based, UG is constructed by imposing that the constraint (21.68) is preserved, resulting in the invariance by transverse diffeomorphism [38]. Considering an infinitesimal coordinate transformation,

$$x^\mu \to x^\mu + \xi^\mu, \tag{21.69}$$

while in GR ξ^μ can be kept arbitrary, UG implies,

$$\xi^\mu_{;\mu} = 0. \tag{21.70}$$

Condition (21.68) requires a very restrictive coordinate system in order to be satisfied. For example, in a flat cosmological set, the determinant of the metric, using the lapse function N, is given by,

$$g = Na^3. \tag{21.71}$$

Hence, (21.68) implies, $N = a^{-3}$. In this way, the time coordinate (let us call it θ) is such that the metric is,

$$ds^2 = a^{-6} d\tau^2 - a^2 (dx^2 + dy^2 + dz^2). \tag{21.72}$$

In UG, many classical solutions (like the Schwarzschild one) may also be verified but using non-standard coordinate systems. This restriction can be circumventend by changing (21.68) to,

$$g = \chi, \tag{21.73}$$

where χ is an external function in the sense that it is non-dynamical but allowing, on the other hand, to use a convenient coordinate system.

UG can be implemented through an action as,

$$\mathscr{L} = \sqrt{-g}\left\{R + \zeta(g - \chi)\right\} + \mathscr{L}_m, \tag{21.74}$$

where ζ is a Lagrangian multiplier and χ is an external field, as described above. The resulting equations, after eliminating the Lagrangian multiplier, are

$$R_{\mu\nu} - \frac{1}{4} g_{\mu\nu} R = 8\pi G \left\{ T_{\mu\nu} - \frac{1}{4} g_{\mu\nu} R \right\}. \tag{21.75}$$

These equations are traceless. In comparison to GR, this means that one information (precisely about the trace of the field equations) is lost.

Using the Bianchi identities in equations (21.75), we obtain,

$$\frac{R^{;\nu}}{4} + \frac{8\pi G T^{;\nu}}{4} = 8\pi G T^{\mu\nu}{}_{;\mu}. \tag{21.76}$$

Imposing the conservation of the energy-momentum tensor, the left-hand-side can be integrated, leading to,

$$\frac{R}{4} + \frac{8\pi G T}{4} = \Lambda, \tag{21.77}$$

Λ appearing as an integration constant. Hence, the final equations are,

$$R_{\mu\nu} - \frac{1}{2} g_{\mu\nu} R = 8\pi G T_{\mu\nu} + g_{\mu\nu} \Lambda, \tag{21.78}$$

$$T^{\mu\nu}{}_{;\mu} = 0. \tag{21.79}$$

Hence, the UG equations become formally equivalent to the GR equations in presence of a cosmological constant. However, it is important to remember that Λ in (21.78) appears as an integration constant which, in principle, has no connection with the cosmological constant present in the Lovelock invariant, neither with a cosmological constant associated with a fluid representing the vacuum energy density. In this sense, it is stated generally that the UG at least alleviate the cosmological constant problem.

The previous statement can perhaps be made more clear by considering a self-interacting scalar field with an energy-momentum tensor given by,

$$T_{\mu\nu} = \epsilon \left\{ \phi_{;\mu} \phi_{;\nu} - \frac{1}{2} g_{\mu\nu} \right\} + g_{\mu\nu} V(\phi). \tag{21.80}$$

The parameter ϵ takes value ± 1, representing an ordinary scalar field (positive sign) or a phantom field (negative sign). The cosmological constant is given by the particular case $\phi = $ constant. In UG framework, and using the energy-momentum tensor for a self-interacting scalar field, the field equations are,

$$R_{\mu\nu} - \frac{1}{4} g_{\mu\nu} R = \epsilon \left(\phi_{;\mu} \phi_{;\nu} - \frac{1}{4} g_{\mu\nu} \phi_{;\rho} \phi^{;\rho} \right), \tag{21.81}$$

$$\frac{R_{;\nu}}{4} = \epsilon \left(\phi_{;\nu} \Box \phi + \frac{\phi^{;\rho} \phi_{;\nu;\rho}}{2} \right). \tag{21.82}$$

Remark that the potential $V(\phi)$ has disappeared from the field equations. Moreover, the usual Klein-Gordon equation has been replaced by a more complex structure. If the usual Klein-Gordon equation

$$\epsilon \Box \phi = -V_\phi \tag{21.83}$$

is imposed (which is equivalent to impose the conservation of the energy-momentum tensor), equation (21.87), becomes,

$$\frac{R_{;\nu}}{4} = \epsilon\left(\phi_{;\nu}V_\phi + \frac{\phi^{;\rho}\phi_{;\nu,\rho}}{2}\right). \qquad (21.84)$$

Equation (21.85) can now be integrated, leading to,

$$\frac{R}{4} = \epsilon\left(V(\phi) + \frac{\phi^{;\rho}\phi_{;\rho}}{4}\right) + \Lambda, \qquad (21.85)$$

Λ being again an integration constant. The final equations are,

$$R_{\mu\nu} - \frac{1}{2}g_{\mu\nu}R = \epsilon\left(\phi_{;\mu}\phi_{;\nu} - \frac{1}{2}g_{\mu\nu}\phi_{;\rho}\phi^{;\rho}\right) + g_{\mu\nu}V(\phi) + g_{\mu\nu}\Lambda, \qquad (21.86)$$

$$\epsilon\Box\phi = -V_\phi. \qquad (21.87)$$

Hence, Λ has no (direct at least) relation with $V(\phi)$.

The considerations above show that UG may lead to a new vision on the presence of a cosmological constant in the gravitational equations. All these considerations rely on the conservation of the energy-momentum tensor. However, in UG the conservation of the energy-momentum tensor is not consequence of the theory itself as it happens in GR. In fact, GR is invariant by a general diffeomorphism and this lead to the conservation of the energy-momentum tensor [17]. The energy-momentum tensor is canonically defined from the matter Lagrangian $\mathscr{L}_m$ as,

$$T_{\mu\nu} = -\frac{2}{\sqrt{-g}}\frac{\delta(\sqrt{-g}\mathscr{L}_m)}{\delta g^{\mu\nu}}. \qquad (21.88)$$

Using the matter action,

$$\mathscr{A}_m = \int d^4x \sqrt{-g}\mathscr{L}_m, \qquad (21.89)$$

it results,

$$\delta_g \mathscr{A}_m = \delta_g \int d^4x \sqrt{-g}\mathscr{L}_m = -\frac{1}{2}\int d^4x \sqrt{-g}T_{\mu\nu}\delta g^{\mu\nu}, \qquad (21.90)$$

If $\delta g^{\mu\nu} = \xi^{(\mu;\nu)}$, corresponding to a diffeomorphic transformation, then

$$\delta_\xi \mathscr{A}_m = -\frac{1}{2}\int d^4x \sqrt{-g}T_{\mu\nu}\xi^{\mu;\nu} = \frac{1}{2}\int d^4x \sqrt{-g}T_{\mu\nu}{}^{;\mu}\xi^\nu. \qquad (21.91)$$

Hence, $\delta_\xi \mathscr{A}_m = 0$ implies the conservation of the energy-momentum tensor, $T^{\mu\nu}{}_{;\mu} = 0$. However, UG is invariant by transverse diffeomorphism, and if

$$T^{\mu\nu}{}_{;\mu} = \partial^\nu\Theta, \qquad (21.92)$$

for a given scalar function Θ, we have,

$$\delta_\xi \mathscr{A}_m = \frac{1}{2}\int d^4 x \sqrt{-g}\, T_{\mu\nu}{}^{;\mu}\xi^\nu = \frac{1}{2}\int d^4x \sqrt{-g}\,\Theta_{;\nu}\xi^\nu = \frac{1}{2}\int d^4 x \sqrt{-g}\,\Theta\xi^\nu_{;\nu} = (21.93)$$

without the necessity to have the conservation of the energy-momentum tensor.

There are many discussions in the literature if such possibility of non-conservation of the energy-momentum tensor may be an extra tool to distinguish between GR and UG, at least at perturbative level, see [39, 40] and references therein. Here, we would like to stress that, while the conservation of the energy-momentum tensor implies GR equations in presence of a cosmological constant, the non-conservation of the usual energy-momentum tensor leads to GR equations with a dynamical cosmological term, which can be identified with a dynamical vacuum. This may be connected with interacting models.

Let us take as an example, the equation (21.76), and we identify,

$$\frac{R}{4} + \frac{8\pi G T}{4} = -\Lambda, \qquad (21.94)$$

Λ now being a non-constant function. Hence,

$$8\pi G T^{\mu\nu}{}_{;\mu} = -\Lambda^{;\nu}. \qquad (21.95)$$

The final equations are,

$$R_{\mu\nu} - \frac{1}{2}g_{\mu\nu}R = 8\pi G\, T_{\mu\nu} + g_{\mu\nu}\Lambda, \qquad (21.96)$$

$$T^{\mu\nu}{}_{;\mu} = -\Lambda^{;\nu}. \qquad (21.97)$$

These equations are characteristic of a decaying vacuum theory, with an interaction of matter and the vacuum term.

All these considerations reveal the richness of the UG proposal, leading to many new perspectives to some problems that appear in GR, in particular the *cosmological constant problem*.

21.6 Final remarks

The search for alternative geometrical formulations for the description of the gravitational phenomena has begun almost at the same time General Relativity was proposed. By now, since GR has been proposed, more than one thousand alternative theories to GR have appeared, as Ruben Aldrovandi has emphasized in this speech in the *Laboratoire de Gravitation et Cosmologie Relativistes* about 30 years ago. The terminology has changed, today it is preferred to say *modified gravity* instead of *alternative theories of gravity*, but this profusion of possible new theories of gravity indicates perhaps some aspects of the study of the gravitational phenomena itself, and has a strong contrast with the fate of the newtonian theory, that was essentially the only theory of gravity until the emergence of GR.

The description of gravity as a geometric phenomena, linked with the structure of the space-time itself may be related to, at least, two aspects. The first, the universality of the gravity (absolutely everything is subjected to the gravitational interaction). Describing gravity as the structure of the space-time forcibly implies this universality. Moreover, the appearance of the non-euclidean geometries about 200 years ago, resulting in an infinite numbers of possible, consistent, geometric structures, led to the question "which geometrical structure nature has chosen?", a question that was senseless if just one geometry existed. The GR answer to this was: "Nature has not chosen any *a priori* geometry, it is the matter distribution that creates dynamically the geometrical structure."

Many new geometrical structures emerged, as the non-metricity, torsion, Finsler geometry, etc. Hence, in some sense is natural that many new possible theories of gravity appear, keeping the main cornerstone of the GR theory: Gravity is the structure of the space and time. On the other hand, the quoted remark by Aldrovandi, in my opinion, alert to two main dangers: to forget about the open possibilities still existing without giving up standard physics; the need of a clear motivation when proposing new, still untested, paths deviating from this standard physics. To explore all the possibilities existing in mathematics and physics is important, even crucial in order to open new windows in our comprehension of nature. However, it is important to keep in mind why some still unexplored ways are followed. Aldrovandi and collaborators have considered some important new variant, as the teleparelellism and de Sitter relativity. In this text, we have discussed two other traditional variant: the scalar-tensor gravity theories and the Unimodular Gravity.

The most paradigmatic scalar-tensor theory is the Brans-Dicke one. It implements an idea by Dirac about the possible variation of the the gravitational coupling. Besides giving many different and new predictions compared with GR, the BD theory open an interesting new windows in the strong gravity regime, as it has occurred in the primordial universe, mainly concerning the Planck regime. In fact, a change in the gravitational coupling affects the Planck parameters, like energy, temperature, time and spatial scales. This may imply new important effects even if the BD parameter ω is huge as suggested by experiments and observations. In the present text, we used the BD theory to discuss, quite qualitatively, how a new vision of the dynamics of the cosmic, relating the expansion of the universe, as seen from one frame, to a non-expanding universe but with varying mass of the elementary particles. This may imply in some possible new cosmological scenarios, for example, concerning how to implement an inflationary era.

On the other side, Unimodular Gravity may give new perspectives to the cosmological constant problem. In some sense, UG may lead to *degravitation* of the vacuum energy, but implying at the end in a presence of a cosmological term in the field equations which may be not directly connected with vacuum energy. UG admits a modified energy-momentum tensor conservation law, with respect to the usual conservation law as it appears in GR, that opens new perspective. For example, it may lead naturally to a decaying vacuum state, with an interaction between ordinary matter and the fluid representing the vacuum. One important question is that if the final structure is equivalent to the corresponding structure in GR. Some previous investigation shows that this may happen at perturbative level, but this is not a closed issue. On the other hand, UG may lead to new results at quantum regime.

In spite of the proliferation of *deviations* of the Standard Theory of Gravity, as remarked by Aldrovandi, we think that the proposals discussed here try to keep contact with the concrete problems that physics faces when trying to give a more complete description of Nature, mainly when effects ordinarily originating from quantum field theory are applied to the domain of gravitation.

Acknowledgements

I thank CNPq and FAPES for partial financial support, and the editors for inviting me to contribute to the book in honor of Ruben Aldrovandi.

Bibliography

[1] R. Aldrovandi and J. G. Pereira, Ciência Hoje **55**, 32 (2015). For an English version, see arXiv:1506.03654.

[2] R. Aldrovandi and J. G. Pereira, *Teleparalell Gravity: An Introduction* (Springer, Dordrecht, 2013)

[3] C. H. Brans and R. H. Dicke, Phys. Rev. **124**, 925 (1961).

[4] M. Gasperini, JCAP **12**, 010 (2016).

[5] J. C. Fabris, R. G. Furtado, Patrick Peter and N. Pinto-Neto, Phys. Rev. **D67**, 124003 (2003).

[6] P. A. M. Dirac, Nature **139**, 323 (1937).

[7] S. Liberati, Class. Quantum Grav. **30**, 133001 (2013).

[8] S. Lee, MNRAS **524**, 4019 (2023).

[9] F. Hofmann and J. Müller, Class. Quantum Grav. **35**, 035015 (2018).

[10] P. Jordan, Nature **164**, 637 (1949).

[11] C. Romero and A. Barros, Phys. Lett. A **173**, 243 (1993).

[12] G. Brando, J. C. Fabris, F. T. Falciano and Olesya Galkina, Int. J. Mod. Phys. D **28**, 1950 (2019).

[13] C. M. Will, *Theory and experiment in gravitational physics* (Cambridge University Press, Cambridge, 2018).

[14] J. E. Lidsey, D. Wands and E. J. Copeland, Phys. Rep. **337**, 343 (2000).

[15] D. Bailin and A. Love, Rep. Prog. Phys. **50**, 1087 (1987).

[16] A. De Felice and Sh. Tsujikawa, Liv. Rev. Rel. **13**, 3 (2010).

[17] R. M. Wald, *General Relativity* (Chicago University Press, Chicago, 1984).

[18] J. P. Baptista, J. C. Fabris and S. V. B. Goncalves, Astrophys. Space Sci. **246**, 315 (1996).

[19] R. V. Wagoner, Phys. Rev. D **1**, 3209 (1970).

[20] C. Wetterich, Physics of the Dark Universe **2**, 184 (2013).

[21] G. Lemaître, MNRAS **91**, 490 (1931).

[22] F. Zwicky, Helvetica Physica Acta **6**, 110 (1933).

[23] Planck collaboration, A&A, **641**, A6 (2020).

[24] D. Lovelock, J. Math. Phys. **12**, 498 (1971).

[25] S. Weinberg, Rev. Mod. Phys. **61**, 1 (1989).

[26] E. B. Gliner, ZhTF **49**, 542 (1965). For an English version, see: Sov. Phys. JETP **22**, 378 (1966).

[27] N. Arkani-Hamed, S. Dimopoulos, G. Dvali and G. Gabadadze, *Non-local modification of gravity and the cosmological constant problem*, arXiv:hep-th/0209227.

[28] G. Dvali, S. Hofmann and J. Khoury, Phys. Rev. D **76**, 084006 (2007).

[29] C. de Rham, S. Hofmann, J. Khoury and A. J. Tolley, JCAP **0802**, 11 (2008).

[30] I. Zlatev, L.-M. Wang, and, P. J. Steinhardt, Phys. Rev. Lett. **82**, 896. (1999).

[31] R. Jackiw, *A Particle Field Theorist's Lectures on Supersymmetric, Non-Abelian Fluid Mechanics and d-Branes*, arXiv:physics/0010042.

[32] A. Kamenshchik, U. Moschella and V. Pasquier, Phys. Lett. B **511**, 265 (2001).

[33] J. C. Fabris, S. V. B. Gonçalves and P. S. de Souza, Gen. Rel. Grav. **34**, 53 (2002).

[34] N. Bilič, G. B. Tupper and R. D. Viollier, Phys. Lett. B **535**, 17 (2002).

[35] A. Einstein, *Spielen Gravitationsfelder im Aufber der materiellen Elementarteilchen eine wessentliche Rolle?* (Sizungsberichte der Preussisschen Akad. d. Wissenschaften, 1919). For an English version, see: *Do gravitational fields play an essential part in the structure of the elementary particles of matter?*, in *The principle of relativity*, A. Einstein et. al. (Dover, New York, 1952).

[36] G. P. de Brito, O. Melichev, R. Percacci and A. D. Pereira, JHEP **12**, 90 (2021),

[37] R. Carballo-Rubio, L. J. Garay and G. García-Moreno, Class. Quantum Grav. **39**, 243001 (2022).

[38] J. J. Lopez-Villarejo, JCAP **11**, 002 (2011).

[39] J. C. Fabris, M. H. Alvarenga and H. Velten, Symmetry **15**, 1392 (2023).

[40] C. Gao, R. H. Brandenberger, Y. Cai and P. Chen, JCAP **09**, 021 (2014).

22

Teleparallel gravity, covariance and their geometrical meaning

Martin Krššák

Abstract: We explore the geometrical meaning of teleparallel geometries and the role of covariance in their definition. We argue that pure gauge connections are a necessary ingredient for describing geometry and gravity in terms of torsion and non-metricity. We show the other viable alternative is using the Einstein and Møller Lagrangians, but these are defined through the Riemannian connection coefficients and hence do not involve torsion nor non-metricity. We argue that the teleparallel geometries can be defined on the manifold without introducing any additional structures and that they naturally provide the covariant framework for the Einstein and Møller Lagrangians. We explore some consequences of this viewpoint for the modified theories of gravity as well.

22.1 Introduction

Teleparallel theories of gravity were originally proposed by Einstein in the late 1920s as an attempt for the unified field theory of gravity and electromagnetism [1, 2, 3]. Since 1960s the idea of teleparallelism was revived as an alternative approach to gravity, which found many applications addressing various issues in gravity and cosmology. Among these were the improvements in definitions of gravitational energy-momentum [4, 5, 6, 7], formulation of general relativity as a gauge theory [8, 9, 10], and more recently a plethora of modified gravity theories with the aim to address dark energy and other problems in cosmology [11, 12, 13, 14, 15, 16, 17].

Nevertheless, we face a rather curious situation that even after almost 100 years since the initial formulation, debates persist regarding the very foundations of teleparallel theories of gravity, which primarily revolves around the pure gauge nature of teleparallel connections, due to which these connections can be transformed to zero and hence effectively eliminated from the theory. The main question then concerns whether to consider these pure gauge connections as a fundamental variable of the theory.

If the non-trivial teleparallel connection is utilized, teleparallel theories are covariant and the elimination of the connection is viewed only as a choice of a specific gauge [18, 19, 20, 21, 22, 17]. The other viewpoint is to consider the theory without the teleparallel connection as the fundamental one. Then teleparallel theories are viewed as fundamentally non-covariant [23, 24, 25], and the covariant formulation is considered only as an artificial restoration of covariance using the Stückelberg trick [26, 27, 28, 29, 30]. See [31, 32, 33, 34] for further discussion in the modified case.

Our goal in this paper is to address the origins of the issue of covariance in teleparallel theories of gravity. We first review Einstein's original motivation and his definition of teleparallelism, as well as how teleparallelism was revived starting in the 1960s. We also explain the relationship of these theories to the so-called Einstein and Møller Lagrangians, both of which play important roles in our discussion. Then, we show that there exists a generalization of the original notion of teleparallelism, where teleparallel geometries are viewed as special limiting cases of metric-affine geometries, naturally introducing the pure gauge connections. These two different notions of teleparallelism are then compared, and we demonstrate that when we choose to gauge away the pure gauge connection, we obtain the original Einstein's teleparallelism within the metric affine approach.

Our main argument in this paper is that both approaches are equally suitable for performing calculations and constructing gravitational theories. However, the pure gauge connections are crucial elements to attribute non-trivial geometry to torsion or non-metricity, as without them, torsion and non-metricity are not true tensors. On the other hand, if we view these gauge-fixed geometries as the fundamental definitions of teleparallel theories, we are actually using the coefficients of anholonomy and partial derivatives of the metric to describe the geometry and gravity.

We suggest that this does not actually represent a problem, as long as we do not misidentify these objects as torsion or non-metricity tensors. We argue that describing gravity through the coefficients of anholonomy or partial derivatives of the metric is fully consistent and equivalent to using the Einstein and Møller Lagrangians, and we argue in their favor. However, these Lagrangians are formulated within the Riemannian geometry using the Riemannian connection coefficients and hence have nothing to do with torsion nor non-metricity.

We argue that the actual purpose of teleparallel geometries is to provide a mathematical framework in which the Einstein and Møller Lagrangians are covariant. Therefore, without covariance, teleparallel geometries lose their main purpose. We conclude our paper by a brief discussion of modified teleparallel theories and show how they can be viewed using both approaches.

Notation: To distinguish between four different connections and geometric quantities related to them, we use here an extended notation of [20, 21]. The bare geometric quantities represent quantities related to a general metric-affine connection, while geometric quantities with "∘,•,■" above them are related to the Riemannian, teleparallel, and symmetric teleparallel geometries, respectively. For example, $\Gamma^\rho{}_{\mu\nu}, \overset{\circ}{\Gamma}^\rho{}_{\mu\nu}, \overset{\bullet}{\Gamma}^\rho{}_{\mu\nu}, \overset{\blacksquare}{\Gamma}^\rho{}_{\mu\nu}$ represent the linear connection of the general metric-affine, Riemannian, teleparallel, and symmetric teleparallel geometries, respectively. The Greek indices are used for the components of tensors in the coordinate basis, and the Latin indices for the components in the non-coordinate basis.

22.2 Einstein's teleparallelism and its revival

In order to understand the origins of teleparallel gravity, we will review Einstein's introduction of teleparallelism[1] and the later works that lead to its revival. In the first paper in 1928 [1], Einstein searched for a more general geometrical framework than the standard Riemannian geometry with the metric tensor, which could unify gravity and electromagnetism. He considered replacing the metric tensor by a set of four orthonormal vectors called *vierbeins* or *tetrads*, representing a locally

---

[1] For more details and historical context of Einstein's works on teleparallelism and unified field theory, see [35, 36]. Another useful resource is the English translations of the original works in German and French [37].

inertial reference system, which is related to the metric tensor through

$$g_{\mu\nu} = \eta_{ab} h^a{}_\mu h^b{}_\nu. \qquad (22.1)$$

The tetrad is generally not symmetric and has 16 independent components, in contrast to the 10 components of the metric tensor. It was precisely these additional 6 degrees of freedom in the tetrad that Einstein attempted to link with the 6 components of the Faraday tensor.

To achieve this Einstein has introduced a new geometry defined by the postulate that tetrad vectors do not rotate during the parallel transport. This is in contrast with the Riemannian geometry where the parallel transported vectors do rotate proportionally to the Riemannian curvature. Therefore, Einstein has replaced the Riemannian covariant derivative $\overset{\circ}{\nabla}_\mu$ by a new covariant derivative $\overset{\bullet}{\nabla}_\mu$ defined by the condition of vectors being constant during the parallel transport

$$\overset{\bullet}{\nabla}_\mu h_a{}^\mu = 0. \qquad (22.2)$$

We can straightforwardly solve this condition for the connection coefficients

$$^0\overset{\bullet}{\Gamma}{}^\rho{}_{\nu\mu} = h_a{}^\rho \partial_\mu h^a{}_\nu, \qquad (22.3)$$

where 0 index will explained in Section 22.4. It is straightforward to check that the curvature tensor corresponding to this connection is identically zero, but it is not symmetric, giving rise to the torsion tensor

$$^0\overset{\bullet}{T}{}^\rho{}_{\nu\mu} = {}^0\overset{\bullet}{\Gamma}{}^\rho{}_{\nu\mu} - {}^0\overset{\bullet}{\Gamma}{}^\rho{}_{\mu\nu}, \qquad (22.4)$$

which can be used to describe the geometry of spacetime instead of curvature.

In the second paper [2], Einstein considered an action given by the simplest scalar constructed from torsion

$$\overset{\bullet}{\mathcal{L}}_{1928} = \frac{h}{2\kappa} {}^0\overset{\bullet}{T}{}^\rho{}_{\mu\nu} {}^0\overset{\bullet}{T}_\rho{}^{\mu\nu}, \qquad (22.5)$$

where $h = \det h^a_\mu = \sqrt{-g}$ and $\kappa = 8\pi G/c^4$. Einstein then showed that perturbatively this yields the field equations of vacuum gravity and electromagnetism, where electromagnetic potential was identified with $\phi_\mu = {}^0\overset{\bullet}{T}{}^\nu{}_{\mu\nu}$. Einstein noted that separation of both forces is rather artificial and there is a possible non-uniqueness in the choice of the Lagrangian (22.5). This was followed by a paper by Weitzenböck [38], who pointed out that the connection (22.3) was previously considered in [39], which is why we refer to (22.3) as the *Weitzenböck connection*, and analyzed all possible invariants.

In [3], Einstein considered all torsional invariants and showed that there is an unique combination of three invariants

$$\overset{\bullet}{\mathscr{L}}_{\text{TEGR}} = \frac{h}{2\kappa}\left(\frac{1}{4}{}^0\overset{\bullet}{T}{}^{\rho}{}_{\mu\nu}{}^0\overset{\bullet}{T}_{\rho}{}^{\mu\nu} + \frac{1}{2}{}^0\overset{\bullet}{T}{}^{\rho}{}_{\mu\nu}{}^0\overset{\bullet}{T}{}^{\nu\mu}{}_{\rho} - {}^0\overset{\bullet}{T}{}^{\nu\mu}{}_{\nu}{}^0\overset{\bullet}{T}{}^{\nu}{}_{\mu\nu}\right), \tag{22.6}$$

which leads to the symmetric field equations. Nowadays, we do understand that these symmetric field are not just approximately but fully identical to the Einstein field equations, and that is why we refer to (22.6) as a Lagrangian of the teleparallel equivalent of general relativity (TEGR).

However, Einstein insisted on incorporating electromagnetism into the theory by considering a more general Lagrangian and attempted to include electromagnetism through the difference from (22.6). Einstein then again changed his approach and tried to identify electromagnetism directly with the antisymmetric part of the tetrad in the perturbative expansion [40]. The problems started to appear, mainly due to the fact that Maxwell electromagnetism was never fully realized in these theories beyond some approximations and even Einstein kept changing his opinion how and whether it is realized in his theory. The theory was viewed critically by Eddington, Weyl and mainly Pauli, see [36], and was soon abandoned.

In retrospect, it is easy to see the failure of Einstein's teleparallelism as a consequence of a misguided motivation to identify the extra degrees of freedom of a tetrad with electromagnetism. However, it is important to realize that Einstein's work on teleparallelism involved other important novelties, namely using tetrads instead of the metric tensor and considering other than Riemannian geometries to describe gravity, which should not be automatically dismissed, even if we abandon the idea of a classical unified field theory[2].

In 1960s and 1970s it became clear that Einstein teleparallelism can be a successful theory as long as we consider it as a theory of gravity only, i.e. without any attempt to incorporate electromagnetism. The motivation for this came from two different directions. The first one was Møller's work on the definition of the energy-momentum for gravity and second one came from the gauge approach to gravity by Hayashi, Nakano and Cho.

In order to understand both, it is useful to revisit another idea put forth by Einstein, which goes back to the very early days of general relativity. Almost immediately after introducing general relativity, Einstein became interested in a definition of the energy of gravitational field and considered the Lagrangian [41]

$$\mathscr{L}_{\text{E}} = \frac{1}{2\kappa}\sqrt{-g}g^{\mu\nu}(\overset{\circ}{\Gamma}{}^{\rho}{}_{\sigma\mu}\overset{\circ}{\Gamma}{}^{\sigma}{}_{\rho\nu} - \overset{\circ}{\Gamma}{}^{\rho}{}_{\mu\nu}\overset{\circ}{\Gamma}{}^{\sigma}{}_{\rho\sigma}), \tag{22.7}$$

---

[2]This somewhat resembles another of Einstein's works on the cosmological constant. While the original motivation to make the Universe static was misguided, introduction of the cosmological constant has turned out to be ultimately correct.

from which the gravitational energy-momentum was defined as

$$t^\mu{}_\nu = \mathscr{L}_E \delta^\mu{}_\nu - \partial_\nu g^{\rho\sigma} \frac{\partial \mathscr{L}_E}{\partial_\mu g^{\rho\sigma}}, \qquad (22.8)$$

which became known as the Einstein gravitational energy-momentum pseudo-tensor, and was followed by introduction other similar pseudotensors, e.g. the symmetric one by Landau and Lifshitz [42]. All these pseudotensors have a rather undesirable property that they need to be evaluated in well-behaved coordinate systems, which asymptotically approach the inertial coordinate system [43, 42], but they do give an acceptable definition of the gravitational energy-momentum [44, 45].

The work of Møller [4] was motivated by finding a well-behaved tensorial object to describe the gravitational energy-momentum. His solution was to use tetrads instead of the metric to describe gravity, but tetrads were considered still within the Riemannian geometry. The Møller Lagrangian is expressed in terms of the Ricci coefficients of rotation, see Section 22.3, as [4][3]

$$\mathscr{L}_M = \frac{1}{2\kappa} h \left(\mathring{\omega}^a{}_{ca} \mathring{\omega}^{bc}{}_b - \mathring{\omega}^a{}_{cb} \mathring{\omega}^{bc}{}_a \right), \qquad (22.9)$$

and we can define the Møller energy-momentum complex as

$$\tilde{t}^\mu{}_\nu = \mathscr{L}_M \delta^\mu{}_\nu - \partial_\nu h_a{}^\rho \frac{\partial \mathscr{L}_M}{\partial_\mu h_a{}^\rho}, \qquad (22.10)$$

which was argued to be a tensor with respect to the coordinate transformations and hence was claimed to solve the main problem of Einstein's pseudotensor (22.8).

However, in order to provide a meaningful result, it had to to be supplemented by six conditions on the tetrad

$$\phi_{ab} = 0, \qquad (22.11)$$

where ϕ_{ab} is antisymmetric object constructed from the tetrad and its derivatives. These were originally determined in the weak field limit, and in our notation take the form as $\phi_{ab} = \mathring{\omega}_{acb} \mathring{\omega}^{dc}{}_d$. The problem of finding the well-behaved coordinate system for (22.8) was then turned into a problem of finding six conditions on the tetrad, which was further discussed in [6, 5, 7].

While the starting point of Møller was the Riemannian geometry, and both (22.10) and (22.11) were derived within the Riemannian geometry, at the end of the paper Møller noticed that the condition (22.11) determines the orientation of the tetrads that are fixed throughout the whole spacetime. He argued that this is the case of the Weitzenböck geometry (22.3) and proceeds to discuss Einstein's

---

[3] Møller originally wrote this using the coordinate indexed connection $\mathring{\omega}^\rho{}_{\mu\nu} = h_a{}^\rho h^b{}_\mu h^c{}_\nu \mathring{\omega}^a{}_{bc}$. We will return to this in Section 22.4.

teleparallelism. Therefore, the Møller's work [4] is generally viewed as the first paper since 1930s that acknowledges teleparallelism as a viable theory.

The second motivation to revisit Einstein's teleparallelism came from works on the gauge aspects of gravity. The first paper to discuss gravity as a gauge theory of translations only was by Hayashi and Nakano [8], who argued in its favor over gauging the Lorentz or Poincare groups [46]. They identified the torsion tensor (22.4) as the fields strength of the translational group, but considered a generalized Lagrangian that later became known as *new general relativity* [47]. It was Cho [9] who first argued that it is possible to view general relativity as a gauge theory of translations, if we require the covariance of the field equations, which restricts the form of the translational Lagrangian to the Einstein's teleparallel Lagrangian (22.6).

It is interesting to note that Cho [9] never explicitly mentions Einstein's teleparallelism. He stated that his translational Lagrangian is up to a divergence equivalent to the Einstein Lagrangian, from where it seems that he meant rather an equivalence with the Einstein-Hilbert Lagrangian. The fact that the underlying geometry is the Weitzenböck geometry seems to be first realized by Hayashi in [10], where Hayashi argued against Cho's requirement for the covariant field equations in favor of the generalized Lagrangian [47].

22.3 Metric-affine approach to teleparallel geometries

In the original Einstein's teleparallelism described in the previous section, the distant parallelism condition (22.2) was introduced as a postulate of the new geometry. In this section, we will present a more general viewpoint where teleparallel geometries are viewed as special cases of general metric-affine geometries [18]. Along the way, we will briefly review some elements of differential geometry essential for our discussion. For more details, see [48, 49, 50].

We are interested in studying the geometry of a differentiable manifold $\mathcal{M}$, which is a topological space on which we can define local coordinates. At each point p, we can then define the tangent space and its dual cotangent space, elements of which are vectors and covectors, from where we define then the vector and covector fields. The coordinates define a coordinate basis $\{\partial_\mu\}$ for the vector fields and $\{dx^\mu\}$ for 1-forms or covector fields, which can be written as

$$V = V^\mu \partial_\mu, \qquad \omega = \omega_\mu dx^\mu, \qquad (22.12)$$

where V^μ and ω_μ are components of the vector V and covector ω in the coordinate basis. A general tensor field can be then written in the coordinate basis as

$$X = X^{\mu_1\ldots\mu_p}{}_{\nu_1\ldots\nu_q} \partial_{\mu_1} \otimes \cdots \otimes \partial_{\mu_p} \otimes dx^{\nu_1} \otimes \cdots \otimes dx^{\nu_q}. \qquad (22.13)$$

The tensor fields are invariant under a change of coordinates, and we can determine the transformation properties of tensor components from the knowledge of coordinate basis transformations. Under the coordinate change, $x^\mu \to x^{\mu'}$, the tensor components transform as

$$X^{\mu'\cdots}{}_{\nu'\cdots} = X^{\mu\cdots}{}_{\nu\cdots} \frac{\partial x^{\mu'}}{\partial x^\mu} \cdots \frac{\partial x^\nu}{\partial x^{\nu'}} \cdots, \qquad (22.14)$$

We can consider a more general class of bases by taking 4 independent vectors that we denote h_a, where $a = 1\ldots 4$, and use them as a basis for the vector fields in the tangent space. Equally, we can consider dual covectors h^a as a basis in the cotangent space, $h^a h_b = \delta^a_b$. These basis vectors and covectors can be expressed in the coordinate basis as

$$h^a = h^a_\mu dx^\mu, \qquad h_a = h_a{}^\mu \partial_\mu. \qquad (22.15)$$

If these general basis vectors do not commute, i.e. $[h_a, h_b] \neq 0$, it is not possible to express them in terms of some new coordinates, and we say that h_a is a *non-coordinate basis*. We can then write an arbitrary tensor field in the non-coordinate basis, and obtain a relation between components of a tensor in the coordinate and non-coordinate basis as

$$X^{a\cdots}{}_{b\cdots} = X^{\mu\cdots}{}_{\nu\cdots} h^a_\mu \cdots h_b{}^\nu \cdots \qquad (22.16)$$

In the non-coordinate basis, the components of a tensor are invariant under a coordinate change since h^a_μ transforms as a coordinate covector in the last index. We can instead consider an arbitrary change of basis as

$$h^{a'} = \Lambda^{a'}{}_b h^b, \qquad (22.17)$$

where $\Lambda^{a'}{}_b$ is a general non-singular matrix, i.e. $\Lambda^{a'}{}_b \in GL(4)$. We often write this as $\Lambda^a{}_b$, i.e. $h^{a'} = \Lambda^a{}_b h^b$. The tensor components in the non-coordinate basis do change under (22.17) as

$$X^{a'\cdots}{}_{b'\cdots} = X^{a\cdots}{}_{b\cdots} \Lambda^{a'}{}_a \cdots (\Lambda^{-1})^b{}_{b'} \cdots. \qquad (22.18)$$

As the next step, we introduce the metric tensor on a manifold that allows us to measure distances and angles, leading us to the *Riemannian manifold* $(\mathcal{M}, g)$[4]. The components of the metric tensor in the non-coordinate basis are then

$$g_{ab} = g_{\mu\nu} h_a{}^\mu h_b{}^\nu. \qquad (22.19)$$

The interesting case for us, is the class of orthonormal non-coordinate bases, i.e. the case where we fix the metric in the tangent space to be the Minkowski metric,

---

[4]To be more precise, we are interested in the pseudo-Riemannian or Lorentzian manifolds.

$g_{ab} = \eta_{ab} = \text{diag}(-1,1,1,1)$, which we call the *tetrads*.[5] Then the components of the metric tensor $g_{\mu\nu}$, can be expressed from (22.19) as

$$g_{\mu\nu} = \eta_{ab} h^a{}_\mu h^b{}_\nu, \tag{22.20}$$

which is precisely the relation considered by Einstein (22.1).

We would like to highlight here that it is this restriction to the class of orthonormal non-coordinate bases that allows us to use the tetrad instead of the metric as a fundamental variable[6]. Moreover, this narrows down the transformations of the basis (22.17) to those that preserve the condition of orthonormality, i.e. such transformations that leave the tangent space metric η_{ab} invariant, from where immediately follows that $\Lambda^a{}_b$ must be a local Lorentz transformation, i.e. $\Lambda^a{}_b \in SO(1,3)$.

The last step involves introducing the *covariant derivative* ∇ on the Riemannian manifold $(\mathcal{M}, g)$. This is motivated by the fact that the ordinary partial derivative of a tensor field does not yield a tensor field. To address this, we essentially define the covariant derivative in a way that ensures the resulting object is a tensor field and acts as a derivative. We can characterize the covariant derivative by the connection coefficients, and since we consider both coordinate and non-coordinate bases, it is useful to distinguish between the covariant derivative of components of tensors in different bases, and introduce two kinds of connection coefficients

$$\nabla_\nu X^\rho = \partial_\nu X^\rho + \Gamma^\rho{}_{\mu\nu} X^\nu, \qquad \nabla_\nu X^a = \partial_\nu X^a + \omega^a{}_{b\nu} X^b, \tag{22.21}$$

where we call $\Gamma^\rho{}_{\mu\nu}$ the *linear connection coefficients*, and $\omega^a{}_{b\nu}$ the *spin connection coefficients* [20].

However, it is important to understand that these are merely two different connection coefficients for the same covariant derivative in two different bases. For arbitrary vector fields $X = X^\mu \partial_\mu = X^a h_a$ and $Y = Y^\mu \partial_\mu$, the covariant derivative of a vector in the coordinate basis $\nabla_Y X = (Y^\nu \nabla_\nu X^\mu)\partial_\mu$ must be then same as the covariant derivative of the same vector in non-coordinate basis $\nabla_Y X = (Y^\nu \nabla_\nu X^a) h_a$, which immediately gives us a relation between the linear and spin connection coefficients

$$\Gamma^\rho{}_{\nu\mu} = h_a{}^\rho \partial_\mu h^a{}_\nu + h_a{}^\rho \omega^a{}_{b\mu} h^b{}_\nu. \tag{22.22}$$

The reason why it is useful to keep this distinction between the linear and spin connection coefficients is due to different transformation properties of

---

[5]As is common in the literature, we use the term tetrad for both h^a and h_a, as well as their components.

[6]Note that sometimes this is presented as "differential geometry without a metric" [51], but we should keep in mind that we have the metric η_{ab} in the tangent space, but we keep it fixed and hence non-dynamical.

tensor components in the coordinate and non-coordinate bases, from where the connection coefficients inherit their transformation properties. Under the coordinate change $x^\mu \to x^{\mu'}$, the tensor components transform as (22.14), and hence the linear connection transforms as

$$\Gamma^{\rho'}{}_{\mu'\nu'} = \frac{\partial x^\mu}{\partial x^{\mu'}} \frac{\partial x^\nu}{\partial x^{\nu'}} \frac{\partial x^{\rho'}}{\partial x^\rho} \Gamma^\rho{}_{\mu\nu} - \frac{\partial x^\mu}{\partial x^{\mu'}} \frac{\partial x^\nu}{\partial x^{\nu'}} \frac{\partial^2 x^{\rho'}}{\partial x^\mu \partial x^\nu} \tag{22.23}$$

while the spin connection does transform as a tensor in the last index.

Under the change of non-coordinate basis (22.17), the components of tensors in a non-coordinate basis transform as (22.18), and hence the spin connection transforms as

$$\omega^{a'}{}_{b'\mu} = \Lambda^a{}_c \omega^c{}_{d\mu} \Lambda_b{}^d + \Lambda^a{}_c \partial_\mu (\Lambda^{-1})^c{}_b, \tag{22.24}$$

while the linear connection is invariant under such a change of basis.

In the most general case, both connection coefficients have $4^3 = 64$ independent components. We can characterize the connection in terms of three tensors known as: curvature, torsion and non-metricity. It is again useful to distinguish between working in the coordinate and non-coordinate bases. In the coordinate basis, it is natural to work in terms of the pair $\{g_{\mu\nu}, \Gamma^\rho{}_{\mu\nu}\}$ and we define these three tensors as

$$R^\mu{}_{\nu\rho\sigma} \equiv \partial_\rho \Gamma^\mu{}_{\nu\sigma} - \partial_\sigma \Gamma^\mu{}_{\nu\rho} + \Gamma^\tau{}_{\nu\sigma} \Gamma^\mu{}_{\tau\rho} - \Gamma^\tau{}_{\nu\rho} \Gamma^\mu{}_{\tau\sigma}, \tag{22.25}$$

$$T^\rho{}_{\mu\nu} \equiv \Gamma^\rho{}_{\mu\nu} - \Gamma^\rho{}_{\nu\mu}, \tag{22.26}$$

$$Q_{\rho\mu\nu} \equiv \nabla_\rho g_{\mu\nu}. \tag{22.27}$$

In the non-coordinate basis, it is natural to use the tetrad and the spin connection, i.e. work with the pair $\{h^a{}_\mu, \omega^a{}_{b\mu}\}$, and define these tensors as[7]

$$R^a{}_{b\mu\nu} \equiv \partial_\mu \omega^a{}_{b\nu} - \partial_\nu \omega^a{}_{b\mu} + \omega^a{}_{c\mu} \omega^c{}_{b\nu} - \omega^a{}_{c\nu} \omega^c{}_{b\mu}, \tag{22.28}$$

$$T^a{}_{\mu\nu} \equiv \partial_\mu h^a{}_\nu - \partial_\nu h^a{}_\mu + \overset{\circ}{\omega}{}^a{}_{b\mu} h^b{}_\nu - \overset{\circ}{\omega}{}^a{}_{b\nu} h^b{}_\mu, \tag{22.29}$$

$$Q_{\mu ab} \equiv \nabla_\mu \eta_{ab} = \omega_{ab\mu} + \omega_{ba\mu}. \tag{22.30}$$

The most general geometries with 64 independent components of the connections are known as the *metric-affine geometries* [50]. For the reasons that will be explained in detail in Section 22.5, we primarily focus on three limiting cases defined by taking two of these three tensors to zero.

---

[7] We follow here the formalism used in [20], which differentiates between the two groups of indices explicitly to stress that these tensors are components of the Lie algebra-valued differential forms.

Riemannian connection

The most well-known geometry is the Riemannian or Levi-Civita geometry defined by conditions of vanishing torsion and non-metricity. In the coordinate basis, we solve these conditions to find that the Riemannian linear connection is uniquely determined in terms of the metric tensor as

$$\overset{\circ}{\Gamma}{}^{\rho}{}_{\nu\mu} = \frac{1}{2} g^{\rho\sigma} \left(g_{\nu\sigma,\mu} + g_{\mu\sigma,\nu} - g_{\nu\mu,\sigma} \right). \tag{22.31}$$

In the non-coordinate basis, we find an analogous result that the Riemannian spin connection is determined fully in terms of the tetrad as

$$\overset{\circ}{\omega}{}^{a}{}_{b\mu} = \frac{1}{2} h^{c}{}_{\mu} \left[f_{b}{}^{a}{}_{c} + f_{c}{}^{a}{}_{b} - f^{a}{}_{bc} \right], \tag{22.32}$$

where

$$f^{c}{}_{ab} = h_{a}{}^{\mu} h_{b}{}^{\nu} (\partial_{\nu} h^{c}{}_{\mu} - \partial_{\mu} h^{c}{}_{\nu}), \tag{22.33}$$

are the coefficients of anholonomy. We can then define also $\overset{\circ}{\omega}{}^{a}{}_{bc} = \overset{\circ}{\omega}{}^{a}{}_{b\mu} h_{a}{}^{\mu}$ or $\overset{\circ}{\omega}{}^{\rho}{}_{\nu\mu} = h_{a}{}^{\rho} h^{b}{}_{\nu} \overset{\circ}{\omega}{}^{a}{}_{b\mu}$ that are often called the *Ricci coefficients of rotation*.

Teleparallel connection

The teleparallel connection, occasionally referred as the metric teleparallel connection, is defined by the so-called teleparallel condition, i.e., vanishing curvature, and metric-compatibility. The zero-curvature condition is solved by a pure gauge connection

$$\overset{\bullet}{\omega}{}^{a}{}_{b\mu} = \Lambda^{a}{}_{c} \partial_{\mu} (\Lambda^{-1})^{c}{}_{b}, \tag{22.34}$$

where $\Lambda^{a}{}_{b}$ is a non-singular matrix. The metric compatibility connection then restricts $\Lambda^{a}{}_{b}$ to be a local Lorentz transformation, i.e., $\Lambda^{a}{}_{b} \in SO(1,3)$. The corresponding linear teleparallel connection is then

$$\overset{\bullet}{\Gamma}{}^{\rho}{}_{\nu\mu} = h_{a}{}^{\rho} \partial_{\mu} h^{a}{}_{\nu} + h_{a}{}^{\rho} \overset{\bullet}{\omega}{}^{a}{}_{b\mu} h^{b}{}_{\nu}. \tag{22.35}$$

The crucial relation is the Ricci theorem that allows us relate the teleparallel spin connection (22.34) and the Riemannian spin connection (22.32) as

$$\overset{\bullet}{\omega}{}^{a}{}_{b\mu} = \overset{\circ}{\omega}{}^{a}{}_{b\mu} + \overset{\bullet}{K}{}^{a}{}_{b\mu}, \tag{22.36}$$

where

$$\overset{\bullet}{K}{}^{a}{}_{b\mu} = \frac{1}{2} \left(\overset{\bullet}{T}{}^{a}{}_{\mu b} + \overset{\bullet}{T}{}^{a}{}_{b\mu} - \overset{\bullet}{T}{}^{a}{}_{b\mu} \right), \tag{22.37}$$

is the contortion tensor, and an analogous relation holds for (22.35) and (22.31).

Symmetric teleparallel connection

Analogously to the previous case, we can consider the symmetric teleparallel geometry, where the connection is defined by the teleparallel condition and the condition of being symmetric. This geometry was first considered by Nester and Yo [52] and later explored in [26, 27].

The teleparallel condition has a similar pure gauge-type solution as (22.34) and together with the symmetricity condition determines the symmetric teleparallel linear connection to be given by [27]

$$\overset{\bullet}{\Gamma}{}^{\rho}{}_{\mu\nu} = \frac{\partial x^{\rho}}{\partial \xi^{a}} \frac{\partial}{\partial_{\mu}} \frac{\partial \xi^{a}}{\partial x^{\nu}}, \qquad (22.38)$$

where ξ^{a} are arbitrary four functions. We can then find the analogue of the Ricci theorem (22.36) as

$$\overset{\bullet}{\Gamma}{}^{\rho}{}_{\mu\nu} = \overset{\circ}{\Gamma}{}^{\rho}{}_{\mu\nu} + \overset{\bullet}{L}{}^{\rho}{}_{\mu\nu} \qquad (22.39)$$

where

$$\overset{\bullet}{L}{}^{\rho}{}_{\mu\nu} = \frac{1}{2} \left(\overset{\bullet}{Q}{}^{\rho}{}_{\mu\nu} - \overset{\bullet}{Q}{}_{\mu}{}^{\rho}{}_{\nu} - \overset{\bullet}{Q}{}_{\nu}{}^{\rho}{}_{\mu} \right)$$

is the disformation tensor.

22.4 Einstein's teleparallelism and teleparallel gravity

We can observe that we have in fact two distinct definitions of teleparallel geometries. In the original Einstein's teleparallelism, the geometry is defined by the condition (22.2) that leads to zero curvature. In the covariant or metric-affine approach, we define teleparallel geometry by the condition of zero curvature and obtain a more general teleparallel spin connection (22.34).

It is straightforward to relate both approaches following the fact that the teleparallel spin connection (22.34) is of a pure gauge form, which means that using 22.24 we can always find a local Lorentz transformation that transforms this connection to zero

$$^{0}\overset{\bullet}{\omega}{}^{a}{}_{b\mu} = 0, \qquad (22.40)$$

which is referred as the Weitzenböck gauge [18]. We can consider then the Weitzenböck connection (22.3) as just the universal term in (22.22) responsible for the relation between coordinate and non-coordinate basis, and hence (22.3) is just the linear connection corresponding to the zero spin connection [53], from where should be clear why we added the index 0 in Section 22.2.

This is indeed a subtle difference, but there are serious consequences as far as the mathematical consistency of teleparallel theories is concerned. We can see that the "torsion" in the original Einstein's teleparallelism (22.4) is not actually a tensor, but just the coefficient of anholonomy

$$^{0}\overset{\bullet}{T}{}^{\rho}{}_{\nu\mu} = f^{\rho}{}_{\nu\mu}. \tag{22.41}$$

Our argument is that this represents a serious mathematical consistency problem since non-tensorial quantities are being erroneously called tensors. Nevertheless, despite this problem, (22.41) is sufficient to establish the equivalence between (22.9) and (22.6), by straightforwardly substituting (22.41) into (22.36). We get

$$\overset{\circ}{\omega}{}^{\rho}{}_{\mu\nu} = -{}^{0}\overset{\bullet}{K}{}^{\rho}{}_{\mu\nu}, \tag{22.42}$$

where $^{0}\overset{\bullet}{K}{}^{\rho}{}_{\mu\nu}$ is the contortion (22.37) obtained using (22.41).

However, unlike the actual Ricci theorem (22.36), which makes a sound mathematical statement that a difference between two connections is a tensor, now the Riemannian connection is misidentified with the contortion tensor (22.42). Our main argument in this paper is that we should either use the Riemannian connection or work with the actual teleparallel tensors, but we should never make identifications of the kind (22.42) or (22.41). We do believe that this is actually the source of the confusion about the foundational issues of teleparallel theories.

We note here that in the discussion about whether some object is a tensor or not, the crucial factor is not whether it has Greek or Latin indices, but how it depends on the choice of a basis. For example, objects like $f^{\rho}{}_{\nu\mu}$ or $\overset{\circ}{\omega}{}^{\rho}{}_{\mu\nu}$ are formally "coordinate-tensors", but this is actually irrelevant. These objects are not true tensors since they depend on the choice of a non-coordinate basis in a non-tensorial way. Indeed, these are just the coefficients of anholonomy and Ricci rotation coefficients, and there is no benefit calling them torsion and contortion tensors.

The same applies to the Møller complex (22.10), which is formally a "coordinate-tensor" but depends on the non-coordinate basis in a non-tensorial way. This is why the choice of the tetrad must be fixed using the additional conditions (22.11). We can observe that the Møller Lagrangian (22.9) and complex (22.10) are just straightforward tetrad analogues of Einstein Lagrangian (22.7) and pseudotensor (22.8). The difficulty of finding a well-behaved coordinate system for the Einstein pseudotensor is replaced by finding a well-behaved tetrad for the Møller complex.

On the other hand, the actual teleparallel torsion tensor is

$$\overset{\bullet}{T}{}^{\rho}{}_{\nu\mu} = f^{\rho}{}_{\nu\mu} + \overset{\bullet}{\omega}{}^{\rho}{}_{\nu\mu} - \overset{\bullet}{\omega}{}^{\rho}{}_{\mu\nu}, \tag{22.43}$$

where the presence of the teleparallel spin connection is crucial to make it a proper tensor and hence to be called the torsion tensor. The Lagrangian of teleparallel equivalent of general relativity is then

$$\overset{\bullet}{\mathscr{L}}_{\text{TEGR}} = \frac{h}{2\kappa}\left(\frac{1}{4}\overset{\bullet}{T}{}^{\rho}{}_{\mu\nu}\overset{\bullet}{T}{}_{\rho}{}^{\mu\nu} + \frac{1}{2}\overset{\bullet}{T}{}^{\rho}{}_{\mu\nu}\overset{\bullet}{T}{}^{\nu\mu}{}_{\rho} - \overset{\bullet}{T}{}^{\nu\mu}{}_{\nu}\overset{\bullet}{T}{}^{\nu}{}_{\mu\nu}\right), \tag{22.44}$$

which is a proper scalar (density) under a change of both coordinate and non-coordinate bases.

This brings us to the main question what problems the covariant approach actually solves. The mathematical consistency issues of these theories is indeed solved, i.e. it makes all the objects we refer to as tensors actual tensors. Moreover, it allows us to use arbitrary tetrads and hence avoids the issue of working in the class of preferred tetrads. As we will argue in Section 22.5, both these aspects are realized naturally using only the existing structure on the manifold.

However, it is important to realize that all these features are achieved by determining the spin connection and matching it with the tetrad, what makes the teleparallel gravity computationally equivalent to the Møller approach. While in the the Møller gravity we have to determine a preferred class of tetrads by finding $\Lambda^a{}_b$ that transform to the preferred class from a generic tetrad, in teleparallel gravity we use the same $\Lambda^a{}_b$ to calculate the spin connection (22.34), which we then associate with the tetrad.

The procedure to determine the spin connection is still not fully understood and some unresolved problems remain. The first time the non-trivial spin connection was used in works of Obukhov and Pereira [18, 19], who found it as the asymptotic limit of the Riemannian connection in the Schwarzschild case and demonstrated the regularizing properties on conserved charges. In [21, 54], it was argued that the underlying principle to determine the spin connection should be the finiteness of the action, and that the teleparallel spin connection can be always calculated as

$$\overset{\circ}{\omega}{}^a{}_{b\mu}(h^a_{(\text{r})\mu}), \tag{22.45}$$

where $h^a_{(\text{r})\mu}$ is the reference tetrad, i.e., some tetrad in the Minkowski spacetime that we associate with the "full" tetrad. This follows from a simple observation that in the Minkowski spacetime the most general tetrad is given by a local Lorentz transformation of an inertial tetrad, i.e., the tetrad for which the Riemannian connection (22.32) vanishes, and hence the Riemannian connection of the general Minkowski tetrad is guaranteed to have the pure gauge form (22.34).

It was argued that this method can be viewed as an analogue of the "background subtraction" method of Gibbons and Hawking [55], where we do obtain a finite action using a reference metric as well, i.e. that the teleparallel action is equivalent to the full action including the Gibbons-Hawking boundary term [21]. Recently [56], we have argued that the same result can be achieved in the interior region of a black hole, where we obtain a perfect agreement with the Gibbons-Hawking boundary term even for the asymptotically AdS black holes.

Nevertheless, we still do lack an universal general method of determining spin connection. As it was pointed out in [25], there seems to be some non-uniqueness since multiple tetrads can be associated with the same spin connection, which shows that we lack a completely general principle how to match the reference tetrad with the full tetrad. In particular, this means that the so-called "switching-off gravity" method to determine the reference tetrad in [21, 22, 17] should not be viewed as a general method but rather a tool with a limited use in some special cases [57].[8] However, we should remember that there is an analogous issue in the background subtraction method, which is known to not work in a completely general case, so perhaps one should not expect a too simple solution to a very complex problem of regularization of the gravitational action.

However, we would like to stress here that even if there is some ambiguity in determining the teleparallel spin connection, this is an ambiguity in determining $\Lambda^a{}_b$. Therefore, we have a completely analogous ambiguity in the Møller gravity or the non-covariant teleparallel gravity, where this ambiguity will demonstrate itself through existence of multiple non-equivalent proper tetrads for the same spacetime [57].

We can observe that our discussion essentially goes back to the Einstein Lagrangian (22.7) and represents various reformulations and improvements in dealing with it. The problem of finding the preferred coordinate basis for evaluating the Einstein action (22.7) and pseudotensor (22.8), was recast by Møller into finding a preferred non-coordinate basis for evaluating (22.9) and (22.10). The covariant teleparallel gravity then translates this issue into a question of how to associate the teleparallel spin connection (or a reference tetrad) with the tetrad. We can see the fundamental "law of conservation of difficulty" is indeed at play, and the steps towards improvement are rather incremental. Nevertheless, from this perspective, Møller's work improved the situation by allowing us to use arbitrary coordinates, and the covariant teleparallel gravity is a further improvement that enabled us to use arbitrary tetrads.

22.5 Geometrical significance of teleparallelism

The Riemannian connection is usually seen as the preferred connection on the Riemannian manifold. This follows directly from the fact that it is induced by the metric and hence the Riemannian manifold $(\mathcal{M}, g)$ comes naturally with the Riemannian connection. This property allows us to take Riemannian covariant derivatives without any additional structure and talk about the curvature of the Riemannian manifold or a metric on its own. We would like to show here that teleparallel geometries are equally privileged in the sense that they are defined

---

[8]Another method of determining the spin connection is based on the symmetry arguments, where we require the connection to have the same symmetries as the tetrad [58].

without any additional structure, and that they are fundamentally different from the general metric-affine geometries.

In metric-affine geometries, we cannot meaningfully talk about the curvature of a metric, since curvature is not a property of the metric itself, but rather of the connection (22.25). This means that assigning curvature to any metric is not possible without the connection that is *a priori* independent from the metric. We then have to either work with the pair of variables $\{h^a{}_\mu, \omega^a{}_{b\mu}\}$,[9] or use the Ricci theorem (22.36) to decompose them into the Riemannian connection and the contortion tensor.

There are then two very different school of thoughts how to proceed, as was illustrated in the short but interesting discussion between Weinberg and Hehl [59]. While Weinberg argued that geometry is given by the Riemannian connection and torsion is "just a tensor" that can be treated as an additional (matter) field in the context of general relativity, Hehl contended that torsion is a very specific tensor tied to the very geometric structure of the manifold and translation group. No matter which viewpoint we choose to follow, in generalized geometries like the Einstein-Cartan one, the independent connection does add extra independent degrees of freedom, which represent deviation from the Riemannian geometry and this deviation is expected to be measurable [60].

The situation is different in the case of teleparallel geometries, since the teleparallel torsion is not considered as some additional field to the Riemannian connection or its curvature, but it rather "takes the role of curvature", in the sense that we use it to describe the non-trivial structure of spacetime instead of curvature. This means that unlike the Einstein-Cartan torsion, the teleparallel torsion is measured whenever we observe some effect of curvature in general relativity. The same argument can be made about non-metricity in the symmetric teleparallel case.

Moreover, both teleparallel geometries can be defined on the Riemannian manifold without any additional structure. This naively seems to go against the traditional viewpoint that only the Riemannian connection is defined on the Riemannian manifold, and everything else must be added as an additional structure, but we should keep in mind that the manifold by definition comes with the existence of a basis. Teleparallel geometries can be then considered to be unique geometries where the connection carries information about the basis only. In the case of torsional teleparallel geometry, the connection (22.34) is fully given by local Lorentz transformations $\Lambda^a{}_b$, and in the symmetric teleparallel case, the connection (22.38) is fully given by the choice of coordinates.

---

[9] Or equivalently, with the pair $\{g_{\mu\nu}, \Gamma^\rho{}_{\mu\nu}\}$, depending on whether we use the coordinate or non-coordinate basis. From now on, for simplicity, we focus on the Einstein-Cartan geometry as a representative of metric-affine geometries, and comment only if there is some difference in the case of non-metricity.

Now comes the main difference with the Riemannian case: since the basis is not unique, each choice of a basis yields a different connection. As the torsion (22.29) depends on both the tetrad and connection, each choice of a basis will not only produce a different connection but also a different torsion tensor. Therefore, both the teleparallel connection and torsion are not uniquely determined. This contrasts with the Riemannian case, where all the information about the geometry of the manifold, including the properties of the basis, is encoded in a single quantity—the Riemannian connection.

In teleparallel geometry, we have naturally two quantities and characterize the geometry in terms of both the teleparallel connection and torsion[10]. It is important to realize that together they carry the same information as the Riemannian connection, simply by the virtue of Ricci theorem (22.36), which states that together they give the Riemannian spin connection

$$\overset{\circ}{\omega}{}^a{}_{b\mu} = \overset{\bullet}{\omega}{}^a{}_{b\mu} - \overset{\bullet}{K}{}^a{}_{b\mu}. \qquad (22.46)$$

Therefore, we are guaranteed to not loose any information about the manifold. We can view (22.46) as that each choice of a basis, defines a split of the Riemannian connection into a connection piece that carries information about the basis only and the contortion tensor. As a consequence, we naturally obtain the contortion as a tensorial field strength of gravity[11], and hence the Lagrangian (22.44) is a proper scalar density.

The most important consequence from this viewpoint is that it establishes a relation between the tetrad and teleparallel connection. This is a crucial distinction from metric-affine geometries, where the tetrad and spin connection are fully independent variables. We can now interpret teleparallel geometry as that we first calculate the Riemannian spin connection from the tetrad alone, and then the choice of $\Lambda^a{}_b$ defines its split into the teleparallel connection and contortion (22.46). Consequently, we find that $\Lambda^a{}_b$ in the connection (22.34) and $\Lambda^a{}_b$ used in the torsion (22.43) are the same $\Lambda^a{}_b$, which is equivalent to the statement that the tetrad and teleparallel spin connection are not independent variables.

A completely analogous situations is in the symmetric teleparallel case, where the choice of a basis is related to the choice of the coordinates, and non-metricity plays the role of torsion. Then each choice of the coordinates defines a split of Riemannian linear connection into a symmetric teleparallel linear connection and disformation tensor proportional to the non-metricity. We analogously do have the

---

[10] We can choose to use any of the following equivalent pairs of the variables: torsion and teleparallel connection, tetrad and teleparallel connection, or Riemannian connection and contortion.

[11] Note that in the literature, including [20, 17], it is possible to find a claim that contortion is a purely gravitational strength, i.e. absent of any inertial effects. More careful analysis in our upcoming paper [61], demonstrates that this claim is not entirely correct. However, for our discussion here, it is relevant that contortion is a true tensor.

non-metricity tensor as a true tensorial object that plays the role of a gravitational field strength.

22.6 Conclusions

In recent years, the topic of covariance of teleparallel theories was a subject of various discussions that essentially concern the treatment of the teleparallel spin connection, and whether the so-called Wietzenböck gauge (22.40) is the fundamental definition of teleparallel theories or one should use the non-trivial spin connection. The same kind of discussion can be made in the case of symmetric teleparallel theories, where the question is about the coincident gauge.

We have argued here in favor of the so-called covariant approach to teleparallel gravity theories based on the metric-affine construction presented in section 22.3, where the condition of vanishing curvature results in the pure gauge connection (22.34). The Lagrangians of teleparallel models constructed in this way are invariant under simultaneous local Lorentz transformations of the tetrad and teleparallel spin connection. The main advantage is from the viewpoint of mathematical consistency, as it guarantees that all quantities used in teleparallel theories are actual tensors, and we can perform calculations using an arbitrary basis and avoid working in a preferred class of tetrads.

However, teleparallel gravity requires us to associate the teleparallel connection with each tetrad, which follows from our observation in Section 22.5 that, unlike in the general metric-affine case, in teleparallel geometries the tetrad and spin connection are not independent variables. We can then always find a local Lorentz transformation that transforms the connection to zero and hence effectively eliminate it from the theory and obtain the Weitzenböck gauge. The same local Lorentz transformation that eliminated the connection is now applied to the tetrad and transform it to the preferred class of tetrads.

There are different arguments in favor of the Weitzenböck gauge as the fundamental definition of teleparallelism in the literature. One of them is to follow the original Einstein's definition and postulate teleparallel geometry by the distant parallelism condition (22.2). The other approach is to start with the metric-affine viewpoint, where we do have both the tetrad and spin connection as independent variables, but then argue that since the teleparallel spin connection does not affect the dynamics of tetrads and does not have any field equations in the TEGR case, it can be set to zero [23, 24]. We naturally agree with this possibility, but argue against viewing this as the fundamental definition of teleparallel geometry, which was being asserted recently by Maluf *et. al.* [25].

Another approach is what we will call the Stückleberg viewpoint, where the covariant formulation of teleparallel gravity is viewed as a Stückelberg trick applied to the theory in the Weitzenböck gauge [26, 27, 28, 29, 30][12] While often this viewpoint can be very useful to explore the dynamics of teleparallel theories [28], in the recent paper by Golovnev [30] it was argued that the theory in the Weitzenböck gauge is the fundamental one and the local Lorentz symmetry is "artificially" restored by "introducing" $\Lambda^a{}_b$ as Stückelberg fields.

While the judgment of whether something is artificial or not is ultimately subjective, we find it rather untenable to view $\Lambda^a{}_b$ as something artificially introduced on the manifold. Quite the contrary, the change of a basis is a fundamental concept connected with the very definition of the manifold, which is defined even before we introduce the metric structure. Teleparallel geometry just takes this natural structure present on the manifold and defines the teleparallel connection as an unique connection given by the choice of the basis. We find the argument that the covariance is a fake or artificial symmetry rather misleading since the whole point of the covariant derivative was to make-as the name suggests-the derivative covariant. The covariant derivative is indeed "just" a Stückelbergization of a partial derivative, which, by the same logic, should be then viewed as an artificial concept.

Our argument here is that if we view the covariant formulation as just the artificial restoration of symmetry using the Stückelberg trick, then the Weitzenböck definition of the teleparallelism is the fundamental one and we should indeed de-Stückelbergize our theory. However, then there is no reason to call the coefficients of anholonomy the "teleparallel torsion tensor in the Weitzenböck gauge". Or in the symmetric teleparallel case, where the partial derivative of the metric is identified with the non-metricity tensor

$$^0\dot{Q}_{\rho\mu\nu} = \partial_\rho g_{\mu\nu}, \tag{22.47}$$

to be called the "symmetric teleparallel non-metricity tensor in the coincident gauge".

While it is completely artificial to call the coefficients of anholonomy and partial derivatives of the metric as tensors or view them fundamentally as tensors in some gauge, these are perfectly reasonable non-tensorial quantities, and we can construct theories of gravity in terms of them. We can either use them directly or equivalently consider their linear combinations, (22.32) and (22.31), and work in terms of the Riemannian spin and linear connections.

We choose the latter option and define the "spin connection object"

$$\Omega = \overset{\circ}{\omega}{}^a{}_{ca}\overset{\circ}{\omega}{}^{bc}{}_b - \overset{\circ}{\omega}{}^a{}_{cb}\overset{\circ}{\omega}{}^{bc}{}_a, \tag{22.48}$$

---

[12]We remind here that the Stückelberg trick was used originally in the massive electromagnetism and gravity, where the starting point is the gauge-invariant massless theory. Adding a mass term breaks gauge invariance of the original theory, which is then restored by introducing the Stückelberg fields by hand. In this picture, the gauge symmetry is viewed as an artificial construction where any theory can be made gauge invariant by adding additional fields [62].

and the "linear connection object"

$$\mathbf{G} = \overset{\circ}{\Gamma}{}^\rho{}_{\sigma\mu}\overset{\circ}{\Gamma}{}^\sigma{}_{\rho\nu} - \overset{\circ}{\Gamma}{}^\rho{}_{\mu\nu}\overset{\circ}{\Gamma}{}^\sigma{}_{\rho\sigma}, \tag{22.49}$$

which are both quasi-scalars, i.e. their densities, $h\,\mathbf{\Omega}$ and $\sqrt{-g}\,\mathbf{G}$, do transform by a total derivative term under the change of the non-coordinate and coordinate bases, respectively. It is then guaranteed that a Lagrangian given by a linear function of either of these connection objects will lead to the covariant field equations.

Of course, these are just the Einstein (22.7) and Møller (22.9) Lagrangians, which are fully consistent gravitational Lagrangians. The quasi-invariance of these Lagrangians requires that they must be evaluated in some specific basis to avoid potentially divergent terms, and can be used to calculate the gravitational action that agrees with the standard GHY approach [56].

The main claim of our paper is that there are actually no covariant and non-covariant formulations of teleparallel theories. Only the covariant formulations are the genuinely teleparallel theories, where the geometry and gravity are described in terms of torsion or non-metricity, because only in this case we do actually have the torsion and non-metricity tensors. The reason why the "non-covariant formulations" of teleparallel gravities work and produce correct results in various situations is because the Einstein and Møller Lagrangians work. However, these are defined within the Riemannian geometry and do not use torsion or non-metricity at all.

Our viewpoint is that teleparallel geometries are the proper mathematical frameworks that naturally covariantize the Einstein and Møller Lagrangians. Taking away the covariance then defies their whole purpose and introduces serious mathematical inconsistencies, such as misidentifying the coefficient of anholonomy with the torsion tensor. Of course, these mathematical inconsistencies can be resolved by simply acknowledging that we actually use the Riemannian connections and utilizing the Einstein and Møller Lagrangians.

We do believe that this viewpoint offers an interesting outlook on various modified gravity models. It should be straightforward to see that $f(\overset{\bullet}{T})$ and $f(\overset{\bullet}{Q})$ gravity in the Weitzenböck and coincident gauges are equivalent to $f(\mathbf{\Omega})$ and $f(\mathbf{G})$ gravity theories [63, 34]

$$\mathscr{L}_\Omega = \frac{h}{2\kappa}f(\mathbf{\Omega}), \qquad \mathscr{L}_\mathbf{G} = \frac{h}{2\kappa}f(\mathbf{G}). \tag{22.50}$$

We would like to argue here that this equivalence is trivial and we can actually extend it to all teleparallel modified theories in the Weitzenböck and coincident gauges, and view them as theories with Lagrangians given by various arbitrary contractions of the Riemannian connections with all indices summed over, which are not scalars or invariants in any meaningful sense.

This brings us to the problem of modified teleparallel theories, all of which were constructed based on the claim that the 'torsion scalar' or other index-less objects used in their Lagrangians are some genuinely new teleparallel invariants not attainable within the standard Riemannian geometry [11, 12, 13, 14, 64]. However, if we consider the gauge-fixed theories as fundamental ones, both of these claims are incorrect: these Lagrangians are not invariants or scalars, and it is possible to construct them within the Riemannian geometry using the connection coefficients.

We can then ask the question whether there is any dynamical difference in the covariant approach, i.e. whether covariant $f(\overset{\bullet}{T})$ and $f(\overset{\bullet}{Q})$ differ from $f(\mathbf{\Omega})$ and $f(\mathbf{G})$ in any other way than "just" being their covariant formulations. In the symmetric teleparallel case, the invariance under diffeomorphism symmetry gives us extra 4 equations obtained by variation with respect to ξ^a [27]. However, since these are the field equations for ξ^a, they can be solved by choosing proper ξ^a, i.e. these equations are the conditions on the coordinates and the coincident gauge. In the torsional case, it turns out that the field equations for $\Lambda^a{}_b$ are equivalent to the antisymmetric part of the field equations for the tetrad [32]. Therefore, we can observe that in both torsional and symmetric teleparallel gravity theories, the covariance gives us the field equations that determine a preferred basis. As soon as we determine this preferred basis, these theories are equivalent to their Riemannian connection analogues of the kind of $f(\mathbf{\Omega})$ and $f(\mathbf{G})$ gravity.

The interesting question is whether the covariance could change the number of dynamical degrees of freedom. While in the symmetric teleparallel theories as $f(\overset{\bullet}{Q})$ gravity, the number of degrees of freedom is not fully resolved issue yet [65, 66, 67], the topic is better understood in the case of torsional teleparallel theories. In $f(\overset{\bullet}{T})$ case, it is generally established that the number of propagating degrees of freedom is 5 [68, 69]. Moreover, it was shown that the number of degrees of freedom should not be changed in the covariant formulation [70, 71], which is analogous to the situation in New General Relativity (NGR) case [72]. The NGR result can be easily understood using the perturbative analysis, since the antisymmetric tetrad perturbations $u_{[\mu\nu]}$ and the perturbations of spin connection $w_{\mu\nu}$ appear in the field equations only in the combination $y_{\mu\nu} = u_{[\mu\nu]} - w_{\mu\nu}$, it is possible to made the whole analysis in terms of the symmetric perturbations of the tetrad and $y_{\mu\nu}$ [73]. Since $y_{\mu\nu}$ has the same form and field equations as $u_{[\mu\nu]}$, the number of degrees of freedom is then unchanged in the covariant picture. We would like to suggest here that the only possible way how the number of degrees of freedom could change is if $y_{\mu\nu} = 0$, i.e. if the spin connect degrees of freedom are chosen exactly to counter-balance the Lorentz degrees of freedom of the tetrad.

Acknowledgements

The author would like to thank José G. Pereira for the invitation to submit this work and for his patience during the editorial process. This work was funded through SASPRO2 project *AGE of Gravity: Alternative Geometries of Gravity*, which has received funding from the European Union's Horizon 2020 research and innovation programme under the Marie Skłodowska-Curie grant agreement No. 945478.

Bibliography

[1] A. Einstein, *Riemann-Geometrie mit Aufrechterhaltung des Begriffes des Fernparallelismus*, Sitzber. Preuss. Akad. Wiss. **17**, 217 (1928).

[2] A. Einstein, *Neue Möglichkeit für eine einheitliche Feldtheorie von Gravitation und Elektrizität*, Sitzber. Preuss. Akad. Wiss. **17**, 224 (1928).

[3] A. Einstein, *Einheitliche Feldtheorie und Hamiltonsches Prinzip* , Sitzber. Preuss. Akad. Wiss. **18**, 156 (1929).

[4] C. Møller, *Conservation Laws and Absolute Parallelism in General Relativity*, K. Dan. Vidensk. Selsk. Mat. Fys. Skr. **1** (10), 1 (1961).

[5] C. Pellegrini and J. Plebanski, *Tetrad Fields and Gravitational Fields*, K. Dan. Vidensk. Selsk. Mat. Fys. Skr. **2** (4), 1 (1963).

[6] C. Møller, *Survey of Investigations on the Energy-Momentum Complex in General Relativity*, K. Dan. Vidensk. Selsk. Mat. Fys. Skr. **35** (3), 1 (1966).

[7] C. Møller, *On the Crisis in the Theory of Gravitation and a Possible Solution*, K. Dan. Vidensk. Selsk. Mat. Fys. Skr. **89** (13, 1 (1978).

[8] K. Hayashi and T. Nakano, *Extended translation invariance and associated gauge fields*, Prog. Theor. Phys. **38**, 491 (1967).

[9] Y. M. Cho, *Einstein Lagrangian as the Translational Yang-Mills Lagrangian*, Phys. Rev. D **14**, 2521 (1976).

[10] K. Hayashi, *The Gauge Theory of the Translation Group and Underlying Geometry*, Phys. Lett. B **69**, 441 (1977).

[11] R. Ferraro and F. Fiorini, *Modified teleparallel gravity: Inflation without inflaton*, Phys. Rev. D **75**, 084031 (2007); arXiv:gr-qc/0610067.

[12] R. Ferraro and F. Fiorini, *Spherically symmetric static spacetimes in vacuum f(T) gravity*, Phys. Rev. D **84**, 083518 (2011); arXiv:1109.4209.

[13] E. V. Linder, *Einstein's Other Gravity and the Acceleration of the Universe*, Phys. Rev. D **D81**, 127301 (2010); arXiv:1005.3039. [Erratum: Phys. Rev.D **82**, 109902 (2010)].

[14] C.-Q. Geng, C.-C. Lee, E. N. Saridakis, and Y.-P. Wu, *"Teleparallel" dark energy*, Phys. Lett. B **704**, 384 (2011; arXiv:1109.1092.

[15] Y.-F. Cai, S. Capozziello, M. De Laurentis, and E. N. Saridakis, *f(T) teleparallel gravity and cosmology*, Rept. Prog. Phys. **79**, 106901 (2016); arXiv:1511.07586.

[16] S. Bahamonde, K. F. Dialektopoulos, C. Escamilla-Rivera, G. Farrugia, V. Gakis, M. Hendry, M. Hohmann, J. Levi Said, J. Mifsud, and E. Di Valentino, *Teleparallel gravity: from theory to cosmology*, Rept. Prog. Phys. **86**, 026901 (2023); arXiv:2106.13793

[17] M. Krššák, R. van den Hoogen, J. Pereira, C. Böhmer, and A. Coley, *Teleparallel theories of gravity: illuminating a fully invariant approach*, Class. Quant. Grav. **36**, 183001 (2019); arXiv:1810.12932

[18] Yu. N. Obukhov and J. G. Pereira, *Metric affine approach to teleparallel gravity*, Phys. Rev. D **67**, 044016 (2003); gr-qc/0212080.

[19] T. G. Lucas, Y. N. Obukhov, and J. G. Pereira, *Regularizing role of teleparallelism*, Phys. Rev. D **80**, 064043 (2009); arXiv:0909.2418.

[20] R. Aldrovandi and J. G. Pereira, *Teleparallel Gravity: An Introduction* (Springer, Dordrecht, 2012).

[21] M. Krššák and J. G. Pereira, *Spin Connection and Renormalization of Teleparallel Action*, Eur. Phys. J. C **75**, 519 (2015); arXiv:1504.07683.

[22] M. Krššák and E. N. Saridakis, *The covariant formulation of f(T) gravity*, Class. Quant. Grav. **33**, 115009 (2016); arXiv:1510.08432.

[23] J. W. Maluf, *Hamiltonian formulation of the teleparallel description of general relativity*, J. Math. Phys. **35**, 335 (1994).

[24] J. W. Maluf, *The teleparallel equivalent of general relativity*, Annalen Phys. **525**, 339 (2013); arXiv:1303.3897.

[25] J. Maluf, S. Ulhoa, J. da Rocha-Neto, and F. Carneiro, *Difficulties of Teleparallel Theories of Gravity with Local Lorentz Symmetry*, Class. Quant. Grav. **37**, 067003 (2020); arXiv:1811.06876.

[26] J. Beltrán Jiménez, L. Heisenberg, and T. Koivisto, *Coincident General Relativity*, Phys. Rev. D **98**, 044048 (2018); arXiv:1710.03116.

[27] J. Beltrán Jiménez, L. Heisenberg, and T. S. Koivisto, *Teleparallel Palatini theories*, JCAP **08**, 039 (2018); arXiv:1803.10185.

[28] J. Beltrán Jiménez and K. F. Dialektopoulos, *Non-Linear Obstructions for Consistent New General Relativity*, JCAP **01**, 018 (2020); arXiv:1907.10038.

[29] J. Beltrán Jiménez, L. Heisenberg, and T. S. Koivisto, *The Geometrical Trinity of Gravity*, Universe **5**, 173 (2019); arXiv:1903.06830.

[30] A. Golovnev, *The geometrical meaning of the Weitzenböck connection*; arXiv:2302.13599.

[31] B. Li, T. P. Sotiriou, and J. D. Barrow, *$f(T)$ gravity and local Lorentz invariance*, Phys. Rev. D **83**, 064035 (2011); arXiv:1010.1041.

[32] A. Golovnev, T. Koivisto, and M. Sandstad, *On the covariance of teleparallel gravity theories*, Class. Quant. Grav. **34**, 145013 (2017); arXiv:1701.06271.

[33] C. Bejarano, R. Ferraro, F. Fiorini, and M. J. Guzmán, *Reflections on the covariance of modified teleparallel theories of gravity*, Universe **5**, 158 (2019); arXiv:1905.09913.

[34] M. Blagojević and J. M. Nester, *From the Lorentz invariant to the coframe form of $f(T)$ gravity*; arXiv:2312.14603.

[35] T. Sauer, *Field equations in teleparallel spacetime: Einstein's fernparallelismus approach towards unified field theory*, Historia Math. **33**, 399 (2006); physics/0405142.

[36] H. F. M. Goenner, *On the history of unified field theories*, Living Rev. Rel. **7**, 2 (2004).

[37] D. Delphenich, *Selected papers on teleparallelism*. Available online at: http://www.neo-classical-physics.info/uploads/3/4/3/6/34363841/selected_papers_on_teleparallelism.pdf.

[38] R. Weitzenböck, *Differentialinvarianten in der Einsteinschen Theorie des Fernparallelismus*, Sitzungsber. Preuss. Akad. Wiss. Berlin **26**, 466 (1916).

[39] R. Weitzenböck, *Invariantentheorie* (P. Noordhoff, Groningen, 1923).

[40] A. Einstein, *Auf die Riemann-Metrik und den Fern-Parallelismus gegründete einheitliche Feldtheorie*, Math. Ann. **102**, 685 (1930).

[41] A. Einstein, *Hamilton's Principle and the General Theory of Relativity*, Sitzungsber. Preuss. Akad. Wiss. Berlin (Math. Phys.) **1916**, 1111 (1916).

[42] L. D. Landau and E. M. Lifschits, *The Classical Theory of Fields*. (Pergamon Press, 1975).

[43] A. Einstein, *Der Energiesatz in der allgemeinen Relativitätstheorie*, Sitzungsber. Preuss. Akad. Wiss. Berlin (Math. Phys.) **24**, 154 (1918).

[44] C.-C. Chang, J. M. Nester, and C.-M. Chen, *Pseudotensors and quasilocal gravitational energy momentum*, Phys. Rev. Lett. **83**, 1897 (1999); arXiv:gr-qc/9809040.

[45] C.-M. Chen, J.-L. Liu, and J. M. Nester, *Gravitational energy is well defined*, Int. J. Mod. Phys. D **27**, 1847017 (2018); arXiv:1805.07692.

[46] M. Blagojevic and F. W. Hehl, *Gauge Theories of Gravitation*; arXiv:1210.3775.

[47] K. Hayashi and T. Shirafuji, *New General Relativity*, Phys. Rev. D **19**, 3524 (1979) [Addendum: Phys. Rev. D **24**, 3312 (1982)].

[48] M. Nakahara, *Geometry, topology and physics.* (Taylor & Francis, Boca Raton, 2003).

[49] M. Fecko, *Differential geometry and Lie groups for physicists* (Cambridge University Press, Cambridge, 2011).

[50] F. W. Hehl, J. D. McCrea, E. W. Mielke, and Y. Ne'eman, *Metric affine gauge theory of gravity: Field equations, Noether identities, world spinors, and breaking of dilation invariance*, Phys. Rept. **258**, 1 (1995); gr-qc/9402012.

[51] H. Stephani, D. Kramer, M. A. H. MacCallum, C. Hoenselaers, and E. Herlt, *Exact solutions of Einstein's field equations* (Cambridge University Press, Cambridge, 2003).

[52] J. M. Nester and H.-J. Yo, *Symmetric teleparallel general relativity*, Chin. J. Phys. **37**, 113 (1999); arXiv:gr-qc/9809049.

[53] V. C. de Andrade, L. C. T. Guillen, and J. G. Pereira, *Teleparallel spin connection*, Phys. Rev. D **64**, 027502 (2001); arXiv:gr-qc/0104102.

[54] M. Krššák, *Holographic Renormalization in Teleparallel Gravity*, Eur. Phys. J. C **77**, 44 (2017); arXiv:1510.06676.

[55] G. W. Gibbons and S. W. Hawking, *Action Integrals and Partition Functions in Quantum Gravity*, Phys. Rev. D **15**, 2752 (1977).

[56] M. Krššák, *Bulk Action Growth for Holographic Complexity*; arXiv:2308.04354.

[57] E. D. Emtsova, M. Krššák, A. N. Petrov, and A. V. Toporensky, *On Conserved Quantities for the Schwarzschild Black Hole in Teleparallel Gravity*; arXiv:2105.13312.

[58] M. Hohmann, L. Järv, M. Krššák, and C. Pfeifer, *Modified teleparallel theories of gravity in symmetric spacetimes*, Phys. Rev. D **100**, 084002 (2019); arXiv:1901.05472.

[59] F. W. Hehl, *Note on the torsion tensor*, Physics Today **60** (03), 16 (2007).

[60] Y. Mao, M. Tegmark, A. H. Guth, and S. Cabi, *Constraining Torsion with Gravity Probe B*, Phys. Rev. D **76**, 104029 (2007); arXiv:gr-qc/0608121.

[61] M. Krššák, *work in progress*.

[62] K. Hinterbichler, *Theoretical Aspects of Massive Gravity*, Rev. Mod. Phys. **84**, 671 (2012); arXiv:1105.3735.

[63] C. G. Boehmer and E. Jensko, *Modified gravity: A unified approach*, Phys. Rev. D **104**, 024010 (2021); arXiv:2103.15906.

[64] S. Bahamonde, C. G. Böhmer, and M. Krššák, *New classes of modified teleparallel gravity models*, Phys. Lett. B **775**, 37 (2017); arXiv:1706.04920.

[65] K. Hu, T. Katsuragawa, and T. Qiu, *ADM formulation and Hamiltonian analysis of f(Q) gravity*, Phys. Rev. D **106**, 044025 (2022); arXiv:2204.12826.

[66] K. Tomonari and S. Bahamonde, *Dirac-Bergmann analysis and Degrees of Freedom of Coincident $f(Q)$-gravity*, arXiv:2308.06469.

[67] F. D'Ambrosio, L. Heisenberg, and S. Zentarra, *Hamiltonian Analysis of $f(\mathbb{Q})$ Gravity and the Failure of the Dirac–Bergmann Algorithm for Teleparallel Theories of Gravity*, Fortsch. Phys. **71**, 2300185 (2023); arXiv:2308.02250.

[68] M. Li, R.-X. Miao, and Y.-G. Miao, *Degrees of freedom of $f(T)$ gravity*, JHEP **07**, 108 (2011); arXiv:1105.5934.

[69] M. Blagojević and J. M. Nester, *Local symmetries and physical degrees of freedom in $f(T)$ gravity: a Dirac Hamiltonian constraint analysis*, Phys. Rev. D **102**, 064025 (2020); arXiv:2006.15303.

[70] Y. C. Ong, K. Izumi, J. M. Nester, and P. Chen, *Problems with Propagation and Time Evolution in f(T) Gravity*, Phys. Rev. D **88**, 024019 (2013); arXiv:1303.0993.

[71] D. Blixt, R. Ferraro, A. Golovnev, and M.-J. Guzmán, *Lorentz gauge-invariant variables in torsion-based theories of gravity*, Phys. Rev. D **105**, 084029 (2022); arXiv:2201.11102.

[72] D. Blixt, M. Hohmann, and C. Pfeifer, *Hamiltonian and primary constraints of new general relativity*, Phys. Rev. D **99**, 084025 (2019); arXiv:1811.11137.

[73] M. Hohmann, M. Krššák, C. Pfeifer, and U. Ualikhanova, *Propagation of gravitational waves in teleparallel gravity theories*, Phys. Rev. D **98**, 124004 (2018); arXiv:1807.04580.

23

The geopolitics of artificial intelligence: navigating towards an enlightened tomorrow

S. F. Novaes

> ... "[with AI] the perception of the world will be different, at least as different as between the age of enlightenment and the medieval period, when the Western world moved from a religious perception of the world to a perception of the world on the basis of reason, slowly. This will be faster." (H. Kissinger) [1]

Abstract: This article delves into the evolving landscape of global geopolitics reshaped by artificial intelligence (AI), emphasizing its role as a transformative force in international relations and national competitiveness. It examines the strategic approaches of various countries, highlighting the pioneering Canadian AI model as an exemplar for Brazil. Discussing Brazil's current AI trajectory, the paper underscores the urgent need for a cohesive national AI strategy, focusing on infrastructure, skill development, and ethical considerations. The establishment of the Advanced Institute for Artificial Intelligence (AI2) is presented as a key initiative in bridging academia and industry, fostering digital social innovation, and enhancing Brazil's standing in the global AI domain. The article advocates for Brazil to seize the AI opportunity, aligning AI development with socio-economic growth and national sovereignty, and positions AI as a pivotal element in shaping the future geopolitical landscape.

23.1 Introduction

As Niels Bohr used to say – "it is difficult to make predictions, especially about the 'future'" [2]. Despite Bohr's comment, the epigraph, coming from Kissinger[1], a widely recognized expert in geopolitics, is quite remarkable.

In the arena of global dynamics, AI is not merely a tool but a harbinger of change, promising a future where information and technology transcend traditional geopolitical boundaries. This paper seeks to explore the myriad ways in which AI is redefining the contours of global power.

The ideological differences between these powers may lead to increased technological decoupling and the adoption of a a more self-interested approach of managing AI development. This change causing more competition and less trust between countries, especially in areas like artificial intelligence.

The nations are taking different approaches towards AI R&D, data governance and regulation [3]. The U.S. adopts a more laissez-faire stance, letting companies largely control AI development, with little national data protection policy. The U.S. focuses on reducing regulation to foster innovation and has initiated policies like the CHIPS and Science Act to strengthen parts of the AI supply chain, specially semiconductors, and Executive Orders on AI [4] to maintain technological leadership.

The European Union (EU) is more proactive in data regulation and AI governance, exemplified by the recently approved the first rules for AI in the world by European Parliament, The AI Act (AIA) [5]. These regulations aim to manage AI risks, ensure data protection, and increase competitiveness against U.S. tech firms. The EU is also focused on semiconductor manufacturing through the European Chips Act, aiming to double its global production share by 2030.

China's AI governance is rapidly evolving, guided by the central government. The 2017 national AI strategy and the Personal Information Protection Law (PIPL) are key steps in establishing stricter control over AI and data. China regulates recommender engines to control content in line with government ideologies. The country also focuses heavily on developing its semiconductor industry to achieve AI leadership by 2030 [6].

The future is quite promising. AI will transforme, for the better, education, healthcare, agriculture, manufacturing, entertainment, etc. signifying a transformative shift across various aspects of life and work. In long term, we are very optimistic with the impact of AI in society. We just have be a little cautious in this

---

[1] We must add that Kissinger's influence on U.S. foreign policy over the decades has been marked by intense controversy and widespread criticism, highlighting a tenure characterized by contentious decisions and significant disapproval.

period of interregnum where "the old works no more, the new is not yet born."[2]

23.2 The new geopolitical landscape

AI is reshaping the geopolitical landscape, transitioning from traditional power structures to more agile and influential networks. AI tools are redefining diplomacy, intelligence, and decision-making. These technologies represent a paradigm shift in geopolitics, with their ability to analyze and predict from extensive data sets. This evolution is recalibrating the dynamics of AI-driven diplomacy and intelligence operations.

The U.S., known for its global leadership in AI, fosters innovation with substantial investments and a vibrant AI ecosystem. However, this leadership is increasingly contested by China's rapid advancements in AI. This development suggests that China-U.S. relations are likely to be significantly influenced in the era of AI, marking a critical shift in global technological dynamics and international relations. AI's role in their geopolitical contest carries profound economic and security implications. The Lazard Geopolitical Advisory report [7] offers pivotal insights into AI geopolitics, highlighting the formation of distinct AI ecosystems with nations aligning with either the U.S. or China. Advanced countries like Canada, France, and the UK are poised to use AI to reinforce their positions. Conversely, less developed countries face daunting challenges in AI adoption, including limited infrastructure, financial constraints, a digital divide, a shortage of skilled professionals, and difficulties in establishing effective AI governance.

In the academic realm, China's prominence is increasingly evident. The Chinese Academy of Sciences led the world in AI research publications in 2021, with Tsinghua University, the University of the Chinese Academy of Sciences, Shanghai Jiao Tong University, and Zhejiang University following closely. The Massachusetts Institute of Technology was the highest-ranking U.S. institution, placed tenth globally in AI research output [8, 9]. This trend highlights China's growing influence in AI academia. Meanwhile, other countries like Israel, the UK, Japan, South Korea, and Russia continue to be significant contributors to the global AI research landscape

Chinese entities, such as Tencent, Alibaba, and Huawei, along with research institutes like the Beijing Academy of Artificial Intelligence, and government labs, are excelling past their international counterparts, bolstered by substantial government funding. The Beijing Academy of Artificial Intelligence (BAAI) gains from strategic industry partnerships and considerable computational resources, including Cloudbrain-II — a leading storage system developed by Tsinghua University and Pengcheng Laboratory, topping the 2023 IO500 world ranking

---

[2]After Zygmunt Bauman paraphrasing Antonio Gramsci.

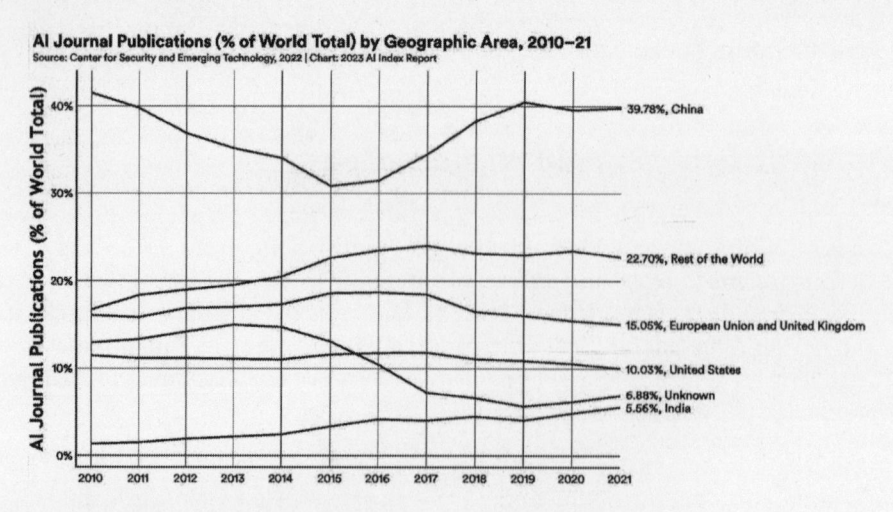

Figure 23.1: AI Journal Publications (% of World Total) by Geographic Area (2010-21) [8].

that evaluates and ranks storage system performance based on bandwidth and metadata performance, making it the most influential benchmark in the field of high-performance computing (HPC) storage.³ This fusion of top-tier expertise and vast computing capabilities enables China to rapidly advance AI research, achieving groundbreaking progress. Consequently, there are growing concerns in the U.S. about China potentially gaining a military advantage, a topic addressed in the RAND 2023 report on AI and geopolitics [10].

The geopolitical significance of a nation will increasingly hinge on its AI capabilities, a fact global leaders are integrating into their strategic considerations. This is underscored by a statement from Russian President Vladimir Putin to students: "Artificial intelligence is the future, not only for Russia but for all humankind ⋯ Whoever becomes the leader in this sphere will become the ruler of the world." [11] This highlights the global race for AI dominance as a key factor in shaping future world leadership.

In the Middle East, AI significantly influences conflicts, shaping diplomatic and economic strategies, as evidenced by Israel's use of technology in Gaza and the U.S.-China technology relations. AI's potential is counterbalanced by risks like misinformation and cybersecurity threats, necessitating the development of regulatory frameworks for ethical compliance and data security. Moreover, AI is transforming the workforce across various sectors, impacting executive decision-making and policy formation.

---

[3]Research SC23 List – IO500, https://io500.org.

The evolving AI landscape necessitates a reassessment of labor market strategies, with an emphasis on cross-national upskilling and updated migration policies. Regulatory initiatives are being spearheaded globally by national governments, international organizations, private sector entities, civil society, and collaborative partnerships. A notable area of concern is the regulation of military AI, particularly autonomous weapons, representing a major challenge in global governance. The development and deployment of these systems by multinational defense companies across national boundaries are prompting a push towards joint global regulation, underlining the competitive and transboundary nature of AI.

23.3 Economic implications of AI

The economic impact of AI is significant, enhancing productivity, innovation, and global market connectivity. However, it also raises issues like job displacement and heightened economic inequality. The early stages of AI adoption could intensify disparities among countries, businesses, and individuals. According to McKinsey Global Institute's simulation [12], companies able to adopt AI quickly ('front-runners') will see a substantial cash flow increase, while late adopters ('laggards') may face a decline in cash flow, leading to a widening economic gap, reaching an estimated 145% difference by the year 2030. Early adopters stand to gain considerable economic and technological advantages.

The adoption of AI will have significant effects on individuals in the workforce. It's poised to widen the gap between high-skill, high-wage jobs and low-skill, low-wage jobs. Many existing roles will evolve, necessitating new skill sets from employees, particularly as routine tasks become automated. The increasing demand for AI, technology, and data literacy skills will require workers to upskill for career progression. Although AI might lead to job displacement in certain areas, it also has the potential to drive economic growth and create new job opportunities, particularly in fields related to AI development and data analysis.

The economic impact of AI on nations is extensive and transformative. It promises enhanced productivity and efficiency across sectors by automating routine tasks and optimizing processes. AI fosters innovation, leading to new products, services, and markets, offering a competitive edge to AI-leading nations. For instance, the McKinsey Global Institute predicts AI could add about US$ 13 trillion to the global economy by 2030.

PricewaterhouseCoopers (PwC) [13] estimates that AI could contribute up to US$15 trillion to the global economy by 2030, potentially increasing global GDP by up to 14% due to the rapid development and adoption of AI technologies. Their analysis suggests that the most significant economic gains from AI will be in China, with an expected increase of 26% in GDP by 2030, and in North America, with a projected rise of 14.5%. These regions could account for nearly 70% of AI's global economic impact.

While AI can streamline global supply chains and public services, it also risks disrupting traditional industries and labor markets. Additionally, AI poses unique challenges for employment, taxation and national security, with strategic advantages for countries investing in AI.

23.4 Ethical and societal considerations

The impact of AI on society is both significant and evolving, encompassing a broad range of applications and implications. AI enhances social interactions, entertainment, and daily life, offering notable advancements in healthcare through improved diagnostics, drug development, and tailored treatments. In education, it enables personalized learning experiences and innovative tools. AI also plays a vital role in environmental conservation and sustainability. However, it presents ethical dilemmas, necessitating the development of new regulations and policies, while also raising substantial privacy and surveillance concerns. Addressing these challenges is crucial to harness AI's full potential for societal benefit.

The ethical dimensions of AI are as crucial as its economic and political impact. A group of relevant players in the arena of AI have written an open letter [14] where they call on all AI labs to immediately pause the training of AI systems. The authors contend that 'AI systems with human-competitive intelligence can pose profound risks to society and humanity'. They raise a few questions: Should we let machines flood our information channels with propaganda and untruth? Should we automate away all the jobs, including the fulfilling ones? Should we develop nonhuman minds that might eventually outnumber, outsmart, obsolete and replace us? Should we risk loss of control of our civilization? In essence, they are depicting a rather bleak, doomsday scenario.

We diverge from this viewpoint. The present time calls not for the imposition of controls, regulations, prohibitions, or restrictions on the development of AI, in its conceptual or tool-based forms. Rather, any form of ethical oversight or restriction should be directed towards the human use of AI tools, ensuring responsible and ethical applications. We must create effective strategies, design a long-term plan, increase the government and private, disseminate AI tools increase the capillarity, and bring academics closer to industry, and above all, train as many people as possible.

It is opportune to make a parallel between the development of Quantum Mechanics and of AI. They share a lot common issues. Quantum Mechanics was created by a small group of European scientist on the middle 20's (Planck, Einstein, Bohr, de Broglie, Born, Dirac, Heisenberg, Pauli, Schrödinger among them). It evolved rapidly, surpassing the bounds of what was thought possible, questioning even the nature of reality. However, no one quite understood well how it worked (and it is still not fully understood!). There was the (real) possibility of exterminating our civilization and this was demonstrated in a practical way with the development of the atomic bomb (unlike AI). It could have uses that would violate our ethical principles, yet, this did not lead to thoughts of hindering its development.

Quantum Mechanics has fundamentally transformed our world, with its applications surpassing all expectations. Without it, numerous essential elements and technologies would not exist. These include semiconductors, which are the backbone of computers and smartphones; lasers and optical communication, critical for internet networks; atomic clocks, vital for precise GPS; medical imaging technologies such as MRI and PET scans; electron microscopy; advances in materials science; cryptography; quantum computing, and more.

The atomic bomb is also a pertinent addition to this list. The Manhattan Project was initiated by President Franklin D. Roosevelt, and it was President Harry S. Truman who ordered the atomic bombings of Hiroshima and Nagasaki. Indeed, such a development would not have been possible without Quantum Mechanics. However, it was the actions of human beings, driven by political ambitions to ensure U.S. geopolitical dominance in the waning days of WWII, that led to its malevolent use.

After the WWII, international agencies were created as a response to the growing concerns and expectations surrounding the discoveries and diverse applications of nuclear technology. The International Atomic Energy Agency (IAEA) was established in 1957, as an autonomous intergovernmental organization, with a core mission to enhance the contribution of atomic energy to the world's peace and well-being. It ensures that the assistance provided by the agency is not used for military purposes. The IAEA, recognized for its efforts,[4] plays a crucial role in contributing to international peace and security, The agency's activities encompass a wide range of nuclear-related issues, including energy production, medical applications, and environmental conservation, ensuring they are addressed safely and securely.

Drawing inspiration from the success of international collaboration, a distinguished group of scientists conceptualized the formation of a European atomic physics laboratory. This initiative aimed to bring together Europe's scientific community and address the mounting costs of nuclear physics research. In 1952, this vision materialized when 11 countries signed an agreement to establish the provisional council of the "Conseil Européen pour la Recherche Nucléaire," (CERN)

---

[4] IAEA and its former Director General, Mohamed ElBaradei, received The Nobel Peace Prize 2005 "for their efforts to prevent nuclear energy from being used for military purposes and to ensure that nuclear energy for peaceful purposes is used in the safest possible way."

tasked with creating a premier institution for fundamental physics research in Europe.

Michael Faraday pioneered the development of the electric motor and established one of the cornerstones of modern physics: the field theory of electromagnetism. On one occasion, when a politician inquired about the practicality of electromagnetism, asking, "What good is it?" Faraday responded, "It is a child who is just born, one cannot say what it will become".[5] Typically, understanding the complete range of applications for a fundamental discovery can take decades. AI is still in its infancy, and it's crucial to nurture its healthy development. Research and Development in the field should continue unabated.

It is imperative to prevent the misuse of AI at all costs. Nonetheless, the emphasis should be on human behavior, especially targeting those who create and misuse algorithms and tools, instead of stifling the advancement of AI. It's the responsibility of governments, judicial systems, and international organizations to ensure the protection of citizens' rights, freedoms, and privacy.

Trusting the 'Big Five' tech companies to self-regulate their AI advancements is both naive and futile. It is suspected that these industry giants could be advancing a doomsday narrative around AI for their own interests. This tactic could pave the way for legislation and restrictions that place an undue burden on smaller companies attempting to compete in the marketplace.

We advocate for the creation of an international agency, modeled on the effective frameworks of IAEA and CERN. This proposed agency would mark a major advancement in fostering the responsible utilization of AI, anchored in a foundation of ethical values. Its inception is envisioned to lead towards a safer, more optimistic future in AI applications, ensuring the development of equitable, secure, and reliable AI systems, ultimately contributing to the betterment of society as a whole.

23.5 The path forward: a Brazilian roadmap

At the dawn of this new era, it is imperative that we approach the future with wisdom, foresight, and a unified dedication to fostering a future that is not only progressive but also inclusive. In this spirit, we propose a strategic roadmap for Brazil. This roadmap is designed to leverage the immense potential of AI in a way that is both beneficial and equitable, aligning seamlessly with the wider goals of global development.

Several nations have already embarked on crafting their national AI strate-

---

[5]A similar aphorism is often attributed to Benjamin Franklin. Moreover, there is some debate regarding the underlying motivation for Faraday's use of this statement (see Ref. [15]).

gies [16], setting the stage for comprehensive technological advancement. Inspired by these global initiatives, Brazil, under the auspices of the Ministry of Science, Technology, and Innovations, began crafting its own national AI blueprint in 2021. This endeavor, known as the Brazilian AI Strategy (Estratégia Brasileira de Inteligência Artificial, EBIA) [17], represents a significant milestone in Brazil's technological journey. It complements a series of related technology initiatives, including the Brazilian Strategy for Digital Transformation (E-Digital) and the General Data Protection Law (LGPD).

Uniquely, the EBIA stands as the first federal strategy in Brazil with a specific focus on AI. Its purpose extends beyond mere policy formation; it aims to serve as a cornerstone, guiding and influencing a range of other initiatives and strategies related to AI. This strategic approach signifies Brazil's commitment to not only embracing AI but also steering its development in a direction that benefits both the nation and the global community at large.

The Bill 2.338/2023, proposed by the President of the Senate, incorporates several progressive aspects including a human rights-oriented approach, risk classification of AI systems, and a governance structure that is risk-based. Key features of this proposed governance include stringent human supervision of high-risk AI systems, ensuring it goes beyond mere formalities; the implementation of governance measures in public administrations; and the requirement for Algorithmic Impact Assessments (AIA) prior to deploying high-risk AI systems.

However, the crux of Brazil's challenge in AI advancement lies not in the quantity of its legislative measures, but in the timeliness and strategic execution of these policies. Despite nearly 90 bills concerning AI regulation proposed in the Chamber of Deputies and Federal Senate, Brazil's journey to becoming an AI leader requires a different approach. The nation must pivot from a predominantly legislative focus to establishing and implementing both short-term and long-term strategic priorities that vitalize AI research and development.

This strategy must be comprehensive, extending beyond increasing federal investments in AI. It should include the development of synergistic partnerships with the private sector, aiming for equitable cost-sharing and resource allocation in AI R&D. Additionally, the strategy should focus on widespread dissemination of AI technologies across various sectors, thereby enhancing their accessibility and impact.

Moreover, forging stronger links between academia and industry is imperative. This collaboration is key to driving innovative advancements and practical AI applications. Equally important is the emphasis on training and upskilling the Brazilian workforce. By equipping them with the necessary skills and knowledge, Brazil can effectively prepare for an AI-driven future. Such a multifaceted approach will not only enhance Brazil's AI capabilities but also solidify its position as a significant player in the global AI landscape.

We advocate that Brazil look to Canada as an exemplary model in the realm of AI development. Canada's AI strategy, widely acclaimed for its progressive and innovative approach, has catapulted the country to the forefront of AI research and innovation. Mirroring Canada's trajectory could be highly beneficial for Brazil, especially considering their comparable territorial sizes and GDPs. Canada's success in becoming a global AI powerhouse offers valuable insights for Brazil.

Canada's pioneering move in March 2017 to launch the Pan-Canadian Artificial Intelligence Strategy – the first national AI strategy of its kind – is particularly noteworthy. This strategy, emphasizing increased funding for AI research, the attraction and retention of top talent, and fostering collaboration among key AI research hubs, has been instrumental in positioning Canada as an attractive hub for AI investment and scholarly advancement. Such strategic focus has not only elevated Canada's status in AI globally but also underscored the critical role of national AI policies.

By adopting a similar approach, Brazil could significantly enhance its standing in the AI domain. This would involve prioritizing increased investment in AI research, nurturing a talented workforce in the field, and encouraging collaborative efforts across various sectors. Emulating Canada's model could pave the way for Brazil to become a significant player in the global AI landscape, mirroring Canada's success while adapting the strategy to Brazil's unique context and needs.

The Canadian AI Strategy represents a multi-faceted approach to advancing AI. Central to this strategy was an initial strategic investment of CAD 125 million, aimed at bolstering AI research and attracting top talent. This funding was crucial in establishing premier research institutes like the Alberta Machine Intelligence Institute (Amii) in Edmonton, the Vector Institute in Toronto, and MILA in Montreal. These institutions have become leaders in AI research, delving into areas such as machine learning, deep learning, computer vision, and ethical AI.

A significant element of Canada's strategy is its global engagement in AI. Canada actively participates in international AI discussions, fostering worldwide collaboration in both research and policy development. The strategy's emphasis on attracting world-class researchers is complemented by competitive funding and resources, nurturing an environment conducive to cutting-edge AI R&D.

Moreover, the strategy is designed to encourage cross-sector collaboration, encompassing academia, industry, and government. This collaborative ethos not only accelerates AI research but also its practical application across diverse sectors. A key goal is leveraging AI to spur economic growth and innovation, impacting areas ranging from healthcare to transportation. Crucially, the Canadian approach to AI policy is holistic, taking into account the social, ethical, legal, and economic implications of AI. This comprehensive perspective ensures that AI development aligns with broader societal values and needs.

The Canadian Artificial Intelligence Framework for Regulation (CAIFR) is pivotal in steering Canada's AI governance. While it is not directly responsible for administering the Pan-Canadian Artificial Intelligence Strategy, CAIFR plays a vital role in ensuring that AI development and deployment in Canada align with societal values, legal norms, and are conducive to innovation and growth in the AI sector.

CAIFR serves as a critical platform for dialogue, bringing together diverse stakeholders such as government bodies, AI developers, businesses, and the public. This collaboration fosters a comprehensive understanding of AI's impact and guides the development of effective strategies.

Significant contributions to Canada's AI R&D also come from both global and Canadian tech companies. These entities, ranging from large multinationals to emerging startups, not only provide essential funding but also partner with academic institutions for research, creating a vibrant ecosystem for AI innovation.

The Canadian government, through agencies like the Canadian Institute for Advanced Research (CIFAR), the National Research Council of Canada (NRC), and Innovation, Science and Economic Development Canada (ISED), also plays a fundamental role in supporting AI development through funding and policy initiatives.

Moreover, CAIFR's involvement in shaping international AI standards and practices highlights its global perspective. Keeping pace with rapid technological advancements in AI is another crucial aspect of CAIFR's role, ensuring that regulatory frameworks remain relevant and effective amidst the evolving landscape of AI technology.

Brazil faces a crucial juncture in its AI journey, marked by the absence of a specific, cohesive AI strategy. To progress effectively, Brazil must establish clear coordination and governance mechanisms for AI development. This includes a continuous assessment of AI's impact on employment and education policies, as well as integrating AI tools into the productive process.

A strategic focus should be placed on leveraging Brazil's competitive advantages. This involves developing an industrial base that is attuned to new technologies, investing in professional training, retaining talent, and addressing ethical and regulatory issues associated with AI.

However, Brazil must confront several challenges to realize this vision. These include improving infrastructure, bridging the digital divide, addressing resource constraints, closing the skill gap in AI and data science, ensuring data accessibility, and developing robust regulatory and policy frameworks. Addressing these challenges will necessitate targeted strategies, international collaboration, and substantial investments in education, infrastructure, and regulation.

The urgency for Brazil to act is paramount. Establishing effective coordination and governance for AI will facilitate a more regular and productive exchange of experiences and insights. Additionally, crafting a national AI policy will enhance transparency and accountability in public investments in AI. Such steps are imperative for Brazil to harness the full potential of AI and establish itself as a significant player in the global AI landscape.

In recognition of these needs, the Advanced Institute for Artificial Intelligence (AI2)[6] has been established as a private, non-profit Institute of Science and Technology. Functioning as a hub of AI expertise, AI2 brings together specialists from 19 universities and research institutes. Our mission is to bridge the gap between academia and the private sector, facilitating a seamless interaction that addresses real-world AI demands. By simplifying legal and bureaucratic barriers, we enable more efficient collaboration. AI2 places a strong emphasis on digital social innovation, focusing on socioeconomic impact projects that aim to draw the attention of policymakers to the strategic dimensions of AI. A key area of our work is training and upskilling, for which we have launched the Hybrid Residency program [18]. This innovative program combines a variety of trainings – including software engineering, data science, and advanced machine learning – with the development of proof of concepts (PoCs) that meet industrial needs. Designed to be both inclusive and scalable, our program has achieved notable success, evidenced by the high employment rates of our alumni. Furthermore, the program has encouraged several partner companies to invest in their own in-house AI teams. This not only benefits the participants but also strengthens the local AI community, showcasing the direct impact of our initiatives.

Artificial intelligence now stands at the forefront of global technological competition, poised to shape the future. Recognized as a pivotal force in driving competitiveness and safeguarding national security, AI has become a strategic priority for leading developed nations. In this rapidly evolving scenario, Brazil faces a critical juncture. It's imperative that Brazil seizes this historical opportunity in AI development. Failure to do so risks not only lagging in scientific and technological progress but also bears significant socioeconomic repercussions, including impacts on national security and sovereignty. Embracing AI is no longer a choice but a necessity for Brazil to maintain its relevance and influence on the international stage.

23.6 Conclusion

As we stand at the precipice of a transformative era powered by Artificial Intelligence, it is crucial for nations like Brazil to embrace this technological evolution. The journey of AI, exemplified by leaders like Canada, offers a beacon for countries aiming to harness AI for societal betterment. For Brazil, this means not

---

[6]https://advancedinstitute.ai

only adopting AI but integrating it into various sectors, ensuring it contributes to economic growth, societal welfare, and national security. The Advanced Institute for Artificial Intelligence (AI2) is a testament to Brazil's potential in shaping its AI future. By focusing on training, innovation, and international cooperation, Brazil can turn the challenges of today into the milestones of tomorrow. The future of AI is bright, promising a world where technology and human ingenuity converge to create unprecedented opportunities and solutions for global challenges.

Acknowledgement

We would like to express our gratitude to Raphael Cóbe for the insightful discussions which have significantly contributed to this work. This article was partially produced with the assistance of the language model tool ChatGPT, version 4.0 [19]. The editing process, however, was entirely conducted by the author.

Bibliography

[1] H. Kissinger, *Henry Kissinger's Last Crusade: Stopping Dangerous AI*, Time Magazine, 5th November issue (2021).

[2] l. G. Mencher, *On the Social Deployment of Science*, Bulletin of the Atomic Scientists **27**, 10 (1971).

[3] B. C. Larsen, *The Geopolitics of AI and the Rise of Digital Sovereignty*, Brookings Institution (2023).

[4] The White House, *Executive Order on the Safe, Secure, and Trustworthy Development and Use of Artificial Intelligence* (2023).

[5] European Council (Press Release), *Artificial Intelligence Act: Council and Parliament Strike a Deal on the First Rules for AI in the World* (2023).

[6] China Association for International Science and Technology Cooperation, *Next Generation Artificial Intelligence Development Plan Issued by State Council* (2017).

[7] Lazard's Geopolitical Advisory group, *The Geopolitics of Artificial Intelligence*, Lazard (2023).

[8] AI Index Steering Committee, *Artificial Intelligence Index Report 2023*, Stanford Institute for Human-Centered Artificial Intelligence (2023).

[9] A. Acharya and B. Dunn, *Comparing U.S. and Chinese Contributions to High-Impact AI*, Center for Security and Emerging Technology (2022).

[10] B. Pavel, et al., *AI and Geopolitics: How Might AI Affect the Rise and Fall of Nations*, RAND Corporation (2023)

[11] J. Vincent, *Putin says the nation that leads in AI "will be the ruler of the world"*, The Verge (2017).

[12] J. Bughin, et al., *Notes from the AI Frontier: Modeling the Impact of AI on the World Economy*, McKinsey Global Institute (2018).

[13] A. S. Rao and G. Verweij, *Sizing the Prize*, PricewaterhouseCoopers (2017).

[14] Y. Bengio et al., *Pause Giant AI Experiments: An Open Letter* (2023).

[15] I. B. Cohen, *Faraday and Franklin's "Newborn Baby"*, Proceedings of the American Philosophical Society **131**, 2, 177-182 (1987).

[16] R. M. O. Cobe, L. G. Nonato, S. F. Novaes, and J. A. Ziebarth, *Rumo a uma Política de Estado para Inteligência Artificial*, Revista USP, **124**, 37-48 (2020).

[17] Ministry of Science, Technology, and Innovations, *Estratégia Brasileira de Inteligência Artificial* (in Portuguese) (2021).

[18] F. Leno da Silva et al., *Rumo a uma Política de Estado para Inteligência Artificial*, Proceedings of the AAAI Conference on Artificial Intelligence **35**, 17, 15640-15646 (2021).

[19] OpenAI, ChatGPT (2023).

24

Necessary steps for looking at time as multidimensional

Francisco Caruso

Abstract: In the History of Ideas, a succession of philosophical and scientific achievements, concerning the concept of space and its dimensionality, were essential to contribute, after a long period, to the theoretical possibility of thinking physical time with more than one dimension. Meanwhile, such a progress brought with it the expectation that one can either understand the role of dimensionality in the World or disclose how certain physical phenomena depend on it. Some of these issues are sketched throughout the text, as well as those remarkable moments in the History of Science when important contributions were made in order to give a satisfactory answer to the following inescapable question: – How many dimensions does time have?

It is a pleasure to dedicate this work to Ruben Aldrovandi, knowing that friends will live forever in the multiple dimensions of individual and collective memories.

24.1 Introduction

In a certain sense, the project aimed at explaining time dimensionality has to do with the attempt to derive the experience of time from perception of brief intervals. This is similar to the effort of relating human's knowledge of space to the laws of visual perception [1], as briefly reviewed in Sections 24.2 and 24.3. In this way, we are led to believe in common sense, *i.e.*, that space has three dimensions and time has one.

The idea of a fourth space dimension had a significant revival with the studies of several mathematicians in the 16th and 17th centuries. The first speculations of new dimensions in space are mentioned in Section 24.4, as a result of two tendencies: the dissemination of a geometric description of Nature and advances in the field of Geometry by figuring higher-dimensional spaces.

For completeness, in the sequel, it is mentioned how the problem of space dimensionality has been approached in modern physics, starting from Kant's conjecture (Section 24.5). Non-Euclidean geometries have also an important influence in the study of higher-dimensional spaces (Section 24.6). After this, the fourth dimension began to be seen as a time-like component of the new space-time concept introduced by Einstein in Physics (Section 24.7). In Section 24.8, it is stressed how metric spaces play important role in the modern discussion of space-time dimensionality. A few examples of multidimensional time are sketched out in Section 24.9, and some concluding remarks are given in Section 24.10.

24.2 Prelude to an one-dimensional time

Perhaps the origin of the unidimensional character of time can be traced back to the abandonment of the cyclical time, diffused in the Classical Greek thought. Such a conception was actually developed in the Stoic theory of the *eternal return* of the same cosmic cycles. From its dawn, Christianity, admitting the beginning of Creation, abandons this cyclical conception and adopts a linear time, whose end would be linked to sublimation in a higher sphere, the *Final Judgment*. More specifically, it was Augustine of Hippo, also known as Saint Augustine, who presented the first philosophical theory of time, based on a specific origin (the crucifixion of Christ) and on the conviction that time is measured by human consciousness of the "rectilinear" movement of history, irreversible and unrepeatable [2].

In his book *On Genesis*, written eight years before the *Confessions*, Augustine views *time* as a creature of God, and so time exists before human consciousness and, in this sense, is *objective*. However, in his *Confessions*, he views time also as a phenomenon of human consciousness, which is clearly a *subjective* account of time [3]. Indeed, corroborating the second conception, we must remember his consecrated answer to the question: What, then is time? – "If no one asks me, I know; if I want to explain to a questioner, I do not know." [4]. This dichotomy between objectivity and subjectivity will always permeate studies about time.

Throughout history, time has been treated from different points of view, which can be generically associated to its cosmological, gnosiological and ethical-religious meanings. The last two categories involve concepts considered intrinsic to mankind. They correspond, respectively, to a phenomenological, subjective or idealistic perception of time, opposed to ethical, moral and religious conceptions.

A typical example of the use of perception, intended as an attempt to explain the dimensionality of time, can be found in Whitrow's book *The Natural Philosophy of Time*, where the author devotes three pages to the possibility of time being multidimensional [5]. His brief presentation of the theme revolves around two points, namely: the issue of prior knowledge and the reversal of perspective. The first is linked to the capacity of dreaming, while the second refers to the possibility of seeing a simple drawing of a cube in a moment in one perspective, and soon after in another one. The conclusion to which he is led is that there is no compelling reason why time should have more than one dimension. In his words [6]:

> Moreover, it is difficult to believe that our system of physics, based on the concept of a unidimensional time variable, could be as successful as it is if in fact we inhabit a world in which time had two or more dimensions. Consequently, although it has not been possible to prove the physical time must necessarily be restricted to one dimension, there appears to be no reason so far for doubting that it is.

Throughout this essay, the focus is narrowed on the scientific meaning of time, leaving aside other aspects related to its cosmological significance, such as those involving mythology and philosophy.

24.3 More than three space dimensions was not acceptable in the Classical Greek Philosophy

The first step in the history of the fourth dimension was actually an attempt to deny its existence. Indeed, the impossibility of a fourth dimension was actually sustained by Aristotle of Stagira. In effect, in his *De Caelo*, which consists of Four Books, he treats this impossibility just right in the first paragraph of Book 1, saying, in summary, that [7]:

> A magnitude if divisible one way is a line, if two ways a surface, and if three a body. Beyond these there is no other magnitude, because the three dimensions are all that there are, and that which is divisible in three directions is divisible in all.

In this same paragraph, the Stagirite continues giving a cosmological justification of this number three by appealing to its divinization, sustained by the Pythagoreans. Quoting him,

> For, as the Pythagoreans say, the universe and all that is in it is determined by the number three, since beginning and middle and end give the number of the universe, and the number they give is a triad. And so, having taken these three from nature as (so to speak) laws of it, we make further use of the number three in the worship of the Gods.

Such kind of identification between the tri-dimensionality of space and God's will is recurrent in the history of science. Johannes Kepler, for example, asseverated that three is exactly the number of dimensions due to the Holly Trinity [8, 9].

The second necessary (but not sufficient) step towards the fourth dimension has to do with the systematization of the geometric knowledge in Ancient Greece, as detailed in [10].

Some centuries later, the Greek astronomer Claudius Ptolemy, in his (lost) book *On Distance*, published in 150 a.C., would have giving a "proof" about the impossibility of the fourth dimension, based on the very fact that it is impossible to draw a fourth line perpendicular to three mutually perpendicular lines. This is indeed not a proof, but rather reinforce that one is unable to visualize the fourth dimension from which one cannot conclude about its non existence.

To the best of our knowledge, speculations and new ideas about the existence of a fourth dimension had to wait for the middle of the 16th century to be strengthened, when a more propitious intellectual atmosphere is found, as shown in [10].

For the moment, it is relevant to stress that the two greater synthesis of the Classical Greek Philosophy – the Aristotelian and the Euclidean – considered impossible the existence of more than three spatial dimensions.

24.4 New speculations about the fourth dimension

The idea of a new spatial dimension was revived by the studies of several mathematicians in the 16th and 17th centuries. Indeed, the Italian physicist, philosopher, mathematician and physician Ge(i)rolamo Cardano and the French mathematician François Viète considered such "additional" dimension in their researches on quadratic and cubic equations. The same did the French mathematician and physicist Blaise Pascal in his study named *Traité des trilignes rectangles et le leurs onglets* [11], when, generalizing his "triligne" from the plane to the space and beyond, he wrote: "*The fourth dimension is not against the pure Geometry.*"

During the 18th century, the theme of the fourth dimension was treated again from a different perspective, *i.e.*, by associating it to *time* no more to *space*. We are talking about the contribution of the French mathematician Jean le Rond d'Alembert and his proposal in the entry "Dimension" wrote for the *Encyclopédie ou Dictionnaire Raisonné des Sciences, des Arts, et de Métiers*, published between 1751 and 1772, by Denis Diderot and himself.

Time was considered also as a fourth dimension by the Italian-French mathematician and astronomer Joseph-Louis Lagrange, in his books *Mécanique Analytique*, de 1788, and *Théorie des Fonctions Analytiques*, de 1797. Later, Lagrange says something like: One can consider the Mechanics as a Geometry in four dimensions and the Analytical Mechanics as an extension of the Analytical Geometry, developed by Descartes in his book *La Géométrie*, published in 1637 [12].

In the beginning of the 19th century, more specifically in 1827, in the book *Der Barycentrische Calcul*, the German mathematician Augustus Ferdinand Möbius rejected the existence of the fourth dimension when he observed that geometrical figures cannot be superimposed in three dimensions since they are the mirror images of themselves [13]. Such a superposition, however, could happen just in a four dimensional space but, "*since, however, such a space cannot be thought about, the superposition is impossible*" [12].

The fourth dimension was also proposed by the German physicist and mathematician Julius Plücker in his book entitled *System der Geometrie des Raumes*, published in 1846, in which he affirms that planes are nothing but collections of lines, as the intersection of them results in points. Following this idea, Plücker said that if lines are fundamental elements of space, then space is four-dimensional, because it is necessary four parameters to cover all the space with lines. However, this proposal was rejected because it was seen as metaphysics. In any case, it was quite clear for many mathematicians that the three-dimensional Geometry had to be generalized [14].

It is important to stress that before, in 1748, and later, in 1826, the Swiss physicist and mathematician Leonhard Euler and the French mathematician Augustine Louis Cauchy, respectively, tried to represent lines in space. In 1843, the English mathematician Arthur Cayley had developed the Analytical Geometry in a n-dimensional space, taking the theory of determinants (name due to Cauchy) as a tool. In the next year, the German mathematician Hermann Günter Grassmann published the book *Die Lineale Ausdehnungslehre, ein neuer Zweig der Mathematik*, in which he thought on a n-dimensional Geometry, stimulated by the discovery of the quaternion, announced by the Irish mathematician and physicist Sir William Rowan Hamilton, in 1843 [15, 12].

Actually, the conjectures about the fourth dimension acquired more soundness from the development of the so-called non-Euclidean Geometries in the 19th century [16]. Let us now summarize how it happened.

24.5 Kant's conjecture and beyond

At this point, it is convenient to go back in time to summarize Kantian original contribution to the problem of space dimensionality, due to its impact on almost all the modern discussion about this issue.

In his precritical period, Kant speculated that space dimensionality could be related to a particular physical law, namely the Newtonian gravitational force. In a nutshell, this fruitful conjecture was settled down in the framework of a philosophical debate concerning the causal explanation of the World, which, at that time, demanded him and other scholars to take a stance on the well-known problem of *body-soul* interaction. From a metaphysical point of view, three possibilities of *causation* where admitted with the aim of clarifying how causes are related to their effects: occasionalism, pre-established harmony and the *influxus physicus*. The young Kant positioned himself in favor of the third option, which means to accept that the interaction among bodies and soul should have a physical cause. He was trying to provide a foundation for the metaphysics of nature, understanding that its task is to discover the inner force of things, the first causes of the law of motion and the ultimate constituents of matter. In order to grasp the Newtonian influence on the young Kant, it is enough to recall what is written in the Preface to the first edition of Newton's *Principia*:

> [...] for the whole burden of philosophy seems to consist in this – from the phenomena of motions to investigate the forces of nature and then from these forces to demonstrate the other phenomena.

In doing so, the young Kant, in his Ph.D. thesis, advanced a very fruitful conjecture: that a physical law should depend on space dimensionality [17]. However, now it is well known that he could not actually prove it [18, 19]. The result of his analysis refers, actually, to the dimensionality of the *extension*, not *space*.

Albeit the basic idea of somehow relating dimensionality to the gravitation law was abandoned during the critical period of Kantian philosophy [20], it is still, unquestionably, a milestone in the contemporary discussion of this essential attribute of space. Frustrated for not achieving the expected result in his thesis, Kant, in his critical period, admits the *a priori* nature of space an time. Thereby, their dimensionalities do not have to be explained. A fragment, published in his *Opus Postumum* [21], reveals that the mature Kant revisited the theme of *dimensionality*, including that of time. Ironically, only the following fragment survived: "*The quality of space and time, for example, that the first has three dimensions and the second, only one, are principles that (...)*".

From the physical point of view, a deeper comprehension of Kant's conjecture can only be reached by means of the concept of *field*. Following Paul Ehrenfest, it was through the solution of the Laplace-Poisson equation for planetary motion in n-dimensional Euclidean space that one can prove, straightforwardly, the relation between the exponent of the Newtonian potential (through which Newtonian gravitational force is determined) and the dimensionality of space is established.

A systematic scientific investigation inspired on Kant's conjecture began indeed with the seminal contributions of Ehrenfest [22, 23]. His basic idea to shed light on the problem of space dimensionality was that one must try to identify particular aspects of a physical phenomenon, called by him "singular aspects", which could be used to distinguish the Physics in three-dimensional space from that in D-dimensions. Formally, what he did to carry on this project was to postulate that the form of a differential equation – which usually describes a physical law in a three-dimensional space – is still valid for an arbitrary number of dimensions [24]. Therefore, the explanation of space dimensionality is based on a *causa formalis* (the form of the equation), while, in the framework of the original Kant's idea, it elapse from a *causa efficiens* (the gravitational force). Once the general solution of such an equation could be found, he required that it should be a stable solution. As an example, Ehrenfest assumed the motion of a planet under a central force, associated with the Newtonian gravitational potential, to be still described by the Laplace-Poisson equation, keeping the same power of the Laplacian operator Δ and making the number of coordinates change from 3 to D. In this way, he sustained to prove space to be three-dimensional. Actually this is not the case. An epistemological criticism of this attempt to prove that space has 3 dimensions was made in Ref. [25].

This argument was also applied to the description of atomic orbits generated by a Coulomb-like potential, which is formally equivalent to the Newtonian one. In this case, it was showed that there is no bound state for hydrogen atom when $D \geq 5$.

Although Ehrenfest's approach to the problem of dimensionality, as Kant's conjecture, did not comply to prove what was originally proposed, proved to be a fertile idea. Frank Tangherlini, for example, in 1963, was the first to formally treat the problem of the hydrogen atom from the point of view of Schrödinger equation [26]. His article inspired several others with subtle differences [27]-[32].

Many other physical phenomena were used in attempt to disclose the threefold nature of space. One can cite some examples of physical phenomena that depend on the number of dimensions of space in which they take place: neutron diffraction [25], the Casimir effect [33, 34], the stellar spectrum [35] and the cosmic background radiation [36]. In the totality of these works – as in all others dealing with the problem of space dimensionality – *time* is assumed to have just one dimension. Thus, even though it is known that a particular physical event in fact occurs in *space-time*, one is actually discussing and imposing limits or constraints on the dimensionality of space alone, as is done, for example, in Ref. [37]. This is, however, a limited strategy to address the problem.

In fact, this limitation should not cause astonishment. The reason is that any discussion of the dimensionality of space or time, following Ehrenfest's general idea, *i.e.*, searching for the singularities that the physical laws may present in relation to a particular number of dimensions, always strikes at an important point: the very fact that such laws are always theoretically or empirically determined without any kind of *a priori* questioning about the dimensionality of space or time. Indeed, all natural law have been conceived admitting space to be three-dimensional and time to have just one dimension. It is as if these constraints were a fact of Nature, an unquestionable truth. This criticism is attenuated in the light of a recently published new proposal [38].

In the case of time, this kind of prejudice seems to be even more ingrained in the scientific community, as suggested, for example, by the reference made earlier to Whithrow [5].

The sensitive experiences of temporal ordering and that time has one dimension seem so intertwined that, in fact, the literature on the problem of temporal dimensionality is incomparably smaller than dealing with the analogous characteristic of space. one can even query whether the very concept of causality on has inherited does not depend on having such relations as true.

So, in what experimental facts or in what other basic concepts should one who is interested in justifying that time is unidimensional, or even prove that it can be multidimensional, be based upon? This theme should be treated elsewhere.

24.6 The new background of non-Euclidean geometries

In 1795, Euclid's Postulate number 5 (Book I) was enounced by the English mathematician John Playfair as follow: Through a given point only one parallel can be drawn to a given straight line. This is known as the *Parallel Postulate* [39, v. 1, p. 220].

The Parallel Postulate started to be criticized by the German mathematician and physicist Johann Carl Friedrich Gauss – who invented the concept of curvature –, in the last decade of the 18th century, when he tried to demonstrate it by using Euclidean Geometry. In effect, in 1792, when he was fifteen years old, he wrote a letter to his friend, the German astronomer Heinrich Christian Schumacher, in which he discussed the possibility of having a Logical Geometry where the Parallel Postulate could not hold. In 1794, he conceived a new Geometry for which the area of a quadrangular figure should be proportional to the difference between 360° and the sum of its internal angles. Later, in 1799, Gauss wrote a letter to his friend and Hungarian mathematician Wolfgang Farkas Bolyai saying that he had tried, without success, to deduce the Parallel Postulate from other postulates of Euclidean Geometry [40].

During the 19th century, Gauss continued the discussion with friends on the plausibility of the existence of a Non-Euclidean Geometry. So, around 1813, he developed what he initially called Anti-Euclidean Geometry, then Astral Geometry and, finally, Non-Euclidean Geometry. He was so convinced about the existence of this new Geometry that he wrote a letter, in 1817, to his friend and German astronomer and physician Heinrich Wilhelm Matthäus Olbers, stressing the physical necessity of such a Geometry as follow [12, p. 871]:

> I am becoming more and more convinced that the [physical] necessity of our [Euclidean] geometry cannot be proved, at least not by human reason nor for human reason. Perhaps in another life we will be able to obtain insight into the nature of space, which is now unattainable. Until then we must place geometry not in the same class with arithmetic, which is purely a priori, but with mechanics.

Seven years later, in 1824, answering a letter from the German mathematician Franz Adolf Taurinus about a demonstration he did that the sum of the internal angles of a triangle cannot be neither greater nor smaller than 180°, Gauss wrote that there was not geometrical rigor in that demonstration because, in spite of the fact that the "metaphysicists" consider the Euclidean Geometry as the truth, this Geometry is incomplete. The "metaphysicists" quoted by Gauss were the followers of Kant, who wrote, in 1781, in his *Kritik der reinen Vernunft* [41], more precisely in its first chapter entitled Transcendental Doctrine of Elements what follows: a) Space is not a concept which has been derived from outward experiences; b) Space then is a necessary representation *a priori*, which serves for the foundation of all external intuitions; c) Space is represented as an infinite given quantity; d) Space has only three dimensions; d) (...) possibility of geometry, as a synthetic science *a priori*, becomes comprehensible [42].

While we owe to Gauss the discovery of Non-Euclidean Geometry, he did not have the courage to publish his discoveries. Indeed, in a letter sent to a German friend and astronomer Friedrich Wilhelm Bessel, in 1829, Gauss affirm that he probably would never publish his findings in this subject because he feared ridicule, or, as he put it, he feared the clamor of the Boetians, a figurative reference to a dull-witted Greek tribe [12, p. 871].

In his research on the existence of a Non-Euclidean Geometry, Gauss figured out hypothetical "worms" that could live exclusively in a bi-dimensional surface, as other "beings" could be able to live in spaces of four or more dimensions [43]. It is interesting to mention that, trying to verify his theory, Gauss and his assistants measured the angles of a triangle formed by the peaks of three mountains, Brocken, Hohehagen and Inselsberg, which belong to the Harz Mountais, in Germany. The distance between two of them were 69,85 and 197 km, respectively. The sum of the internal angles of this triangle was 180° and 14",85. This result frustrated Gauss since the error were within the errors associated to the instruments he used to measure the angles [12, 40].

Independently of Gauss, the Russian Nikolay Ivanovich Lobachevski and the Hungarian János Bolyai (son of Wolfgang) mathematicians, in 1832, demonstrated the existence of triangles which sum of the internal angles are less than 180° [44, 45].

The German mathematician Georg Friedrich Bernhard Riemann, after the presentation of his *Doktoratsschrift*, in December 1851, in Göttingen University, about the Fourier series and what is now know as Riemannian surfaces, started to prepare himself to become *Privatdozent* of this same University. So, at the end of 1853, he presented his *Habilitationsschrif* together with three topics for the *Habilitationsvortrag*. For his surprise, Gauss choose the third topic entitled "Über die Hypothesen, welche der Geometrie zu Grunden liegen" ("On the Hypothesis that are on the Base of Geometry"), where he demonstrated the existence of triangles of which the sum of its internal angles could be greater than 180°. This topic was timidly presented by Riemann in June of 1854, but it caused a deep impact on Gauss, because it was a concrete expression of his previous ideas about a Non-Euclidean Geometry (today, Riemannian Geometry) that he was afraid to publish, as previously mentioned. Riemann's metrical approach to Geometry and his interest in the problem of congruence also gave rise to another type of non-Euclidean geometry. We are talking about a new geometry that cames out not by the rejection of parallel axioms, but rather by its irregular curvature.

It is important to remember that those geometries, today generically know as Non-Euclidean Geometries [46, 47] influenced physical thought in 19th century [48]. They are consequences of the observation that the relaxation of the Parallel Postulate could give rise to two new interpretations. One, in the Hyperbolic Geometry of Bolyai-Lobachevsky [49], for which, from a point outside a line, an infinite number of parallels can be drawn, and the second, in the Spherical Geometry of Riemann, where from a point outside a line, no parallel can be drawn to it [12, 50].

Two specific areas of philosophical debate were the initial source of a *sui generis* public interest in the non-Euclidean geometries and in the geometry in higher dimensions: the nature of the geometric axioms and the structure of our space [51]. As time went on, a expressive interest of the general public fell on the nature of the space and the number of its dimensions. A historical record of this fact can be found in the accurate bibliography prepared by Duncan Sommerville, a Scottish mathematician and astronomer [52]. This history is well documented in the interesting book of Linda Henderson, historian of art [51]. According to her, everything started with a movement to popularize n-dimensional spaces and non-Euclidean geometries in the second half of the 19th century. A whole literature was developed [52] around philosophical and mystical implications in relation to spaces of larger dimensions, easily accessible to a public of non-specialists; in particular, about the imagination of a fourth dimension, long before Minkowski's work and Einstein's Special Relativity and the Cubism. The popularization of these ideas contributed, as carefully analyzed in Ref. [51], to a revolution in Modern Art and, in particular, was fundamental to the Cubism, an artistic movement contemporary to Einstein's Special Relativity, where also use was made of non-Euclidean geometry, namely Minkowski's space-time.

24.7 The fourth dimension as time-like component of the new space-time concept in Physics

As shown in Ref. [10], it was Riemann who generalized the concept of Geometries, by introducing the definition of metric, that defines how one can calculate the distance between two points, given by (in nowadays notation)

$$ds^2 = \sum_{i,j} = g_{ij} dx^i dx^j; \qquad (i,j = 1,2,3)$$

where g_{ij} is the metric tensor of Riemann. In the case of flat spaces and rectilinear coordinates (x, y, z),

$$g_{ij} = (e_i, e_j) = \delta_{ij}$$

where δ_{ij} is the Kronecker delta, e_i ($i = 1, 2, 3$) are the vector-basis of a particular coordinate system and the notation (e_i, e_j) means the scalar product between the two vectors.

Thus, the distance can be written as

$$ds^2 = \sum_{i,j} = \delta_{ij} dx^i dx^j = dx^2 + dy^2 + dz^2$$

known as the Euclidean metric. This definition is straightforwardly extended to higher n-dimensional spaces just doing $i, j \to \mu, \nu = 1, 2, 3, \cdots n$.

The Riemann work about Non-Euclidean Geometry (which easily allows the existence of more dimensions than the usual three), was soon recognized and flourish in all Europe, with eminent scientists propagating his ideas to the general public. For example, the German physicist and physiologist Hermann Ludwig Ferdinand von Helmholtz considered Gauss' worms leaving now in a Riemannian surface (on a sphere). However, in his book entitled *Popular Lectures of Scientific Subjects*, published in 1881, he warned that it is impossible to represent (to visualize) the fourth dimension, because (...) such a representation is so impossible how it should be a color representation for someone born blind [36, p. 29].

From now on, let us summarize the route of the assimilation of such ideas in Physics.

The success of Newtonian mechanical World view will be put to the test, at first, by the study of heat made by the French mathematician and physicist Jean-Baptiste Joseph Fourier.

The propagation of heat will be described by a partial differential equation and no longer by an ordinary differential equation, as in the case of Newtonian mechanics. It is the beginning of valuing the *causa formalis* over the *causa efficiens* as the basis of the causal explanatory system in Physics, intrinsic to Newton's system [53]. It is the beginning of the description of Physics by Field Theories [54]. Later, in the second half of 19th century, also electromagnetism will reaffirm this trend [55].

The discovery of electromagnetic waves by the German physicist Heinrich Rudolf Hertz will give Maxwell's theory a new status. Nevertheless, Maxwell theory remains a phenomenological theory not able to predict, for example, the interaction of light with matter. One of the first attempts to develop a classical interpretive theory capable of explaining the interactions of electromagnetic fields with matter dates from 1895 and is due to the Dutch physicist Hendrik Antoon Lorentz, who combines the Electromagnetism and Classical Mechanics with an atomistic model of matter, the so-called Drude-Lorentz model,[1] and initially develops a Newtonian Classical Electrodynamics, known as Lorentz Electrodynamics.

---

[1] The model according to which the physical world would be composed of ponderable matter, electrically charged mobile particles and ether, such that electromagnetic and optical phenomena would be based on the position and movement of these particles.

Soon after the electron discovery, this elementary particle gains a prominent place in theoretical physics [56]. In fact, as we have already mentioned, Lorentz will dedicate himself to include the interaction of this particle with the electromagnetic fields. As is well known, Lorentz Electrodynamics, despite some initial success, failed in correctly describe such kind of interaction. This problem will be solved just with the advent of Quantum Electrodynamics [57]. From a conceptual point of view, Einstein attributed the weakness of Lorentz theory to the fact that it tried to determine the interaction phenomena by a combination of partial differential equations and total differential equations, a procedure that, in his opinion, is obviously not natural.

In 1888, the English Mathematician Oliver Heaviside showed that the electric field ($\vec{E}$) of a moving electric charge (with velocity v) differ from that ($\vec{E}_o$) of a stationary charge as indicated below [58]:

$$\vec{E}_o = \frac{kq}{r^2}\hat{r} \quad \Rightarrow \quad \vec{E} = \frac{kq}{r^2}\gamma\left[\frac{1-\beta^2}{1-\beta^2\sin^2\theta}\right]^{3/2}\hat{r}$$

where $\beta = v/c$ and $\gamma = (1-\beta^2)^{-1/2}$. So, we can see that, in the direction of motion ($\theta = 0$), the electric field behaves like

$$\vec{E}_\parallel = \frac{1}{\gamma^2}\frac{kq}{r^2}\hat{r}$$

Therefore, this result was interpreted by Heaviside as a contraction of the electrostatic field.

This result was published in 1889 and it was discussed by Heaviside, the British physicist Oliver Lodge and the Irish physicist George FitzGerald [59]. Inspired on this result, FitzGerald proposed that the objects contract along their line of flight. Independently, Lorentz came to the same idea in 1892 (see footnote in Ref. [60]). This is the origin of Lorentz-FitzGerald contraction, involving the γ factor.

Pre-Minkowskian applications of non-Euclidean geometry in Physics weren't many and they were reviewed in Ref. [61].

Now, we would like to stress that, although Lorentz demonstrated, in 1904, that time is related to tri-dimensional space through the relations known as Lorentz Transformations (LT) [62], it was only the Russian-German mathematician Hermann Minkowski who understood [63] that the LT represent a kind of rotation in a 4-dimensional flat space having coordinates (x_1, x_2, x_3, x_4), with a metric (measurement of the distance between two points in this space) defined by:

$$ds^2 = \sum_{\mu,\nu}^{4} g^{\mu\nu}dx_\mu dx_\nu = dx_1^2 + dx_2^2 + dx_3^2 + dx_4^2$$

where $g^{\mu\nu} = \delta^{\mu\nu}$ is the four-dimensional Kronecker delta, $x_1 = x$, $x_2 = y$, $x_3 = z$, $x_4 = ict$, and $i = \sqrt{-1}$.

This expression is known as the Minkowskian metric, or pseudo-Euclidean metric, due to the fact that it can be negative. Note that, to avoid the use of $\sqrt{-1}$, the mathematicians defined a signature for $g_{\mu\nu}$, such that the indices μ and ν can assume the values 1, 2, 3, 4 $(+,+,+,-)$ with $x^4 = ct$, or 0, 1, 2, 3 $(+,-,-,-)$ with $x^0 = ct$, where $\pm$ means ± 1 only on the main diagonal of the metric tensor [16].

In his seminal paper of 1905 about the Electrodynamics of Moving Bodies, Einstein was able to derive LT without having to resort to ether by postulating the constancy of light velocity in the vacuum, *i.e.*, assuming it does not depend on the velocity of the moving body [64, 65].

For Lorentz, the local time (t') introduced in the coordinate transformations between inertial references, would be just an auxiliary parameter necessary to maintain the invariance of the laws of Electromagnetism, as stated at the end of the second edition of his *Theory of Electrons* [66, p. 321]:

> If I had to write the last chapter now, I should certainly have given a more prominent place to Einstein's theory of relativity (...) by which the theory of electromagnetic phenomena in moving systems gains a simplicity that I had not been able to attain. The chief cause of my failure was my clinging to the idea that the variable t alone can be considered as the true time and that my local time t' must be regarded as no more than an auxiliary mathematical quantity. In Einstein's theory, on the contrary, t' plays the same part as t; if we want to describe phenomena in terms of x', y', z', t' we must work with these variables exactly as we could do with x, y, z, t.

On the other hand, the conception and interpretation of Lorentz's transformations as a geometric transformation in a pseudo-Euclidean space of dimension 4, for Minkowski, was only possible thanks to Einstein's assertion, as quoted in a meeting of scientists in 1908, in Cologne [67, p. 82]:

> But the credit of first recognizing clearly that the time of the one electron is just as good as the time of the other, that t and t' are to be treated identically, belongs to A. Einstein.

However, another point made clear by Einstein is that for him the introduction of time as a fourth explicit coordinate in the transformations of inertial reference systems derives from the principle of relativity. In his words [68, p. 365]:

> It is a widespread error that special theory of relativity is supposed to have, to a certain extent, first discovered, or at any rate, newly introduced, the four-dimensionality of the physical continuum. This, of course, is not the case. Classical mechanics, too, is based on the four-dimensional continuum of space and time. But in the four-dimensional continuum of classical physics the subspaces with constant time value have an absolute reality,

independent of the choice of the reference system. Because of this [fact], the four-dimensional continuum falls naturally into a three-dimensional and a one-dimensional (time), so that the four-dimensional point of view does not force itself upon one as *necessary*. The special theory of relativity, on the other hand, creates a formal dependence between the way in which the spatial coordinates, on the other hand, and the temporal coordinates, on the other, have to enter into natural laws.

24.8 The role of metric space in the problem of space-time dimensionality

It is important to highlight the fact that a significant part of the arguments justifying the dimensionality of space depends on the existence of a metric space [25]. This fact refers to the notion of distance in a n dimensional manifold, which is traditionally based on the homogeneous quadratic differential form

$$ds^2 = g_{\mu\nu}dx^\mu dx^\nu$$

in which the μ and ν indexes assume the values $0, 1, 2, 3, \cdots (n-1)$. This formula is ultimately an arbitrary choice, since, in fact, there are no logical arguments excluding *a priori* other forms of the type ds^4, ds^6, $ds^8 \cdots$. At this point it is important to remember that, in 1920, Ehrenfest presented the conjecture that the exponent 2 of the quadratic form in the previous equation for the line element could be related to the dimensionality of space [22] but, to the best of our knowledge, such a conjecture has not yet been demonstrated. Some consequences, such as a possible relation of this conjecture with Fermat's theorem, is discussed in Ref. [25]. Moreover, the fact that many of the fundamental equations of physics involve second-order spatial derivatives (Newton's equation, d'Alembert's wave equation, Schrödinger's equation *etc.*) may also be related to three-dimensionality of space. We will return to this point later.

As already mentioned, it was the development of non-Euclidean geometries in the nineteenth century [68] that allowed, well before the Theory of Relativity, the first speculations about a fourth dimension and what it would be. Among them we can quote that of Hinton [69, 70].

Other aspects of the problem of reality (or not) of a fourth dimension, related to perception and philosophy, were treated by Whitrow [5]. However, from the point of view of physics, it is the metric of Minkowski's geometry that can be easily generalized to any number of spatial and temporal dimensions. For μ and ν

ranging from 0 to 3 ($n = 4$), we have the metric

$$g^{\mu\nu} = \begin{pmatrix} + & 0 & 0 & 0 \\ 0 & - & 0 & 0 \\ 0 & 0 & - & 0 \\ 0 & 0 & 0 & - \end{pmatrix}$$

For any number of space-time dimensions n, the new array $g^{\mu\nu}$ will have dimensions $n \times n$. In his famous book *The Mathematical Theory of Relativity*, Arthur Stanley Eddington ponders that such a choice (a sign + and three −) specifies the world in a way that we could hardly have predicted from first principles [71]. Why does space-time have one and not another signature? It reminds us, then, of the English astrophysicist, without citing the reference, that Hermann Weyl expresses this "special" character by stating that space has dimensions [72]. However, a careful reading of his works shows that this would be the total number of space-time dimensions that ensures the scale invariance of Maxwell's Classical Electromagnetism, but with the time-dimensionality fixed at 1.

Back to Eddington's book, he examines another interesting question: whether the universe can change its geometry. In particular, one wonders if in some remote region of space or time one could have a metric of the type

$$g^{\mu\nu} = \begin{pmatrix} - & 0 & 0 & 0 \\ 0 & - & 0 & 0 \\ 0 & 0 & - & 0 \\ 0 & 0 & 0 & - \end{pmatrix}$$

Its answer is negative and the argument is that, if such a region exists, it must be separated by a surface of the region in which the metric signature is $(+,-,-,-)$, so that, for a side of the separation surface, there is

$$ds^2 = c_1^2 dt^2 - dx^2 - dy^2 - dz^2$$

while, on the other side,

$$ds^2 = -c_2^2 dt^2 - dx^2 - dy^2 - dz^2$$

The transition, in this case, could only take place through a surface on which

$$ds^2 = 0 dt^2 - dx^2 - dy^2 - dz^2$$

Therefore, the (fundamental) velocity c of light would be null [71],

> Nothing could move on the surface of separation between the two regions and no influence can pass from one side to another. The supposed ulterior region is not in any space-time relationship with our universe – which is a somewhat pedantic way of saying that it does not exist.

It is now known that in the classical theories of Gravitation there can be no local changes in the space-time topology without considering quantum fluctuations [73]. The case of a hypothetical world of dimensions 2 + 2 is also briefly discussed by the author. The possibility of a universe in which time can be two-dimensional is still dealt with in another posthumously published book by Eddington [74].

In 1970, Dorling developed an essentially kinematic argument showing that [75]

> the extreme [maximum] property of time-type geodesics in an ordinary space-time is a necessary condition for the existence of stable particles. This maximum property would fail if time were multidimensional.

According to this author, for a multidimensional time, the proton and the electron would not be stable. Not even the photon! In addition, it proposes that objections that occur at speeds greater than that of light and for a multidimensional time may be related. This opens up a possibility of studying *tachyons* in universes with a greater number of time-type coordinates. This is because the only essential difference between time and space (and between the corresponding time-type or space type geodesics) in a Minkowski geometry is the difference in their dimensionality.

Also worthy of note is the work of Mirman [76], in which he defends the thesis that the space-time signature seems to be related to the measurement process and, if there is more than one dimension of the time type, the extra dimensions do not would be observable. The question of measurement seems to us to be a central point in this whole discussion of the number of dimensions, whether of space or of time.

Any measurement process depends not only on the definition of an observer but also on some physical laws. Often what is done to discuss the problem of the dimensionality of space is to generalize the functional form of a differential equation that describes a law of physics in a space R^3 (which – it is always necessary to remember – has been established without any kind of questioning about the three-dimensionality of space) for a space R^n, but keeping the order of the differential equation. Thus, when discussing planetary stability based on Newtonian gravitation in spaces of arbitrary dimensions what is done is to generalize the Poisson equation as follows:

$$\nabla^2_{(3)}\phi = \frac{\partial^2}{\partial x_1^2} + \frac{\partial^2}{\partial x_2^2} + \frac{\partial^2}{\partial x_3^2} = 4\pi\rho \;\Rightarrow\; \nabla^2_{(n)}\phi = \frac{\partial^2}{\partial x_1^2} + \frac{\partial^2}{\partial x_2^2} + \cdots + \frac{\partial^2}{\partial x_n^2} = 4\pi\rho$$

From this we find the general solution of a generalized equation, and assuming a hypothesis (justified only by arguments of anthropic nature [77]) that it similarly describes the same physical phenomenon of the case $n = 3$, we discuss the mechanical stability of this new solution. The epistemological limitations of this method were extensively discussed in Ref. [25] (See also Ref. [38]).

Here, the aim of the paper is achieved.

24.9 Giambiagi and Bolini on multidimensional time

Since this paper is not aimed to review what has been done on multidimensional time, the scope of this small Section is just highlights the original and inspiring contribution of Giambiagi and Bollini for discussing space and time dimensionality, following Ehrenfest's Ansatz.

At this point we would like to recall some works by the dear and late friend Juan José Giambiagi, who, with Guido Bollini, developed in 1972 the famous method of dimensional regularization [78, 79], admitting that the dimensionality of space-time is a real number given by $\nu = 3 + 1 - \epsilon$.

J.J. (as he was known among friends) worked with different collaborators on the problem of dimensionality of space and time in a very open way without any kind of prejudice [80]-[90]. In these seminal works of 1972, Bollini & Giambiagi showed for the first time (as far as we know) that a small fluctuation imposed *ad hoc* to the dimensionality of space-time is at the basis of a method capable of controlling divergences arising in calculating certain physical quantities in gauge field theories. Therefore, they have shown that the dynamics in a field theory can also depend crucially on the number of space-time dimensions.

In the following articles, in very general terms, Giambiagi and collaborators place particular emphasis on the study of the generalized d'Alembert wave equation and its relation to the Huygens principle. What is important for the scope of this essay is to draw attention to the fact that they do so in a much more general way than the generalization of the above-mentioned Poisson equation, with increasing sophistication for each article, even allowing new potencies for the d'Alembert operator, $\Box$. The fact that the properties of the wave equations strongly depend on the spatial dimensions is not new and had already been noted by Ehrenfest [22, 23], Henri Poincaré [91] and Jacques Hadamard [92]. The argument that spatially three-dimensional worlds seem to have a unique and very peculiar combination of properties that guarantee the processing and propagation of signals via electromagnetic phenomena can be found in [93], but it is worth emphasising that this argument is built on the general perception that time has one dimension.

Motivated by new developments in Gravitation and Supersymmetry Theories, Giambiagi seeks to free himself from this "prejudice" and will study, in several of the articles already cited here, from the point of view of Mathematical Physics, solutions for different dimensions of equations involving operators $\Box$, $\Box^{1/2}$, $\Box^2$, $\Box^3$, $\Box^\alpha$, for a temporal coordinate, initially [86], and then in a space-time with $(p + q)$

dimensions [88, 89, 90], where

$$\Box = \frac{\partial^2}{\partial t_1^2} + \frac{\partial^2}{\partial t_2^2} + \cdots + \frac{\partial^2}{\partial t_q^2} - \frac{\partial^2}{\partial x_1^2} - \frac{\partial^2}{\partial x_2^2} - \cdots - \frac{\partial^2}{\partial x_p^2}$$

And the solutions analyzed are those that depend only on the variables

$$t = \sqrt{t_1^2 + t_2^2 + \cdots + t_q^2} \quad \text{e} \quad r = \sqrt{x_1^2 + x_2^2 + \cdots + x_p^2}$$

It is easy to see that the epistemological nature of an eventual linkage of these results, showing that only the power $\alpha = 1$ of the $\Box$ operator and a four-dimensional space-time would ensure the propagation of electromagnetic waves without problems of loss of information and without reverberations [93], would be very different from the already known result. Other more recent contributions in this field of Mathematical Physics can be found in Refs. [94, 95].

24.10   Concluding remarks

All these works offer a substantial range of results that deserve to be analyzed from an epistemological point of view, and not only from the formal perspective, according to which the multiplicity of spatial and temporal dimensions is only a mathematical possibility to be explored and investigated. Perhaps this kind of inquiry into some of these results may shed light on how much our perception and the formal adoption of one-dimensional time on the one hand and the functional forms of physical laws on the other are intertwined. Or perhaps, the scenario is intrinsically more limited, as expressed by Weinstein'a quotation: "[theories with multiple spatial and temporal dimensions] serve to broaden our minds in the sense of what may be physically possible."

Bibliography

[1] W. Friedman. *About Time: inventing the fourth dimension*. Cambridge, Massachusetts: The MIT Press (1990), p. 6.

[2] J. N. Julião. Time and History by St. Augustine. *Veritas* **63** (2), pp. 408-435 (2018).

[3] W. A. Hernandez. St. Augustine on Time. *International Journal of Humanities and Social Science* **6** (6), pp. 37-40 (2016).

[4] Augustine. *The Confessions*. Ed. M. P. Foley. Indianapolis: Hackett Publishing Company (2006).

[5] G. J. Whitrow. *The Natural Philosophy of Time*. Oxford: University Press, second edition (1980), pp. 368-70.

[6] *Idem*, p. 370.

[7] J. Barnes, (Ed.): *The Complete Works of Aristotle*. The revised Oxford Translation, Princeton: Princeton University Press, volume 1, p. 447 (1984).

[8] W. Pauli. The influence of Archetypal Ideas on the Scientific Theories of Kepler. *In* C. G. Jung & W. Pauli: *The Interpretation of Nature and the Psyche*. Japan: Ishi Press International, 2012.

[9] C. G. Jung. *O Homem e seus Símbolos*. Rio de Janeiro: Editora Nova Fronteira, p. 307 (1992).

[10] J. M. F. Bassalo, F. Caruso and V. Oguri. The Fourth Dimension: From its spatial nature in Euclidean geometry to a time-like component of non-Euclidean manifolds. *Revista Brasileira de Ensino de Física* **43** (2021) e20210034.

[11] B. Pascal. *ØEuvres*. Paris: Lefrève Libraian (1819), v. 5, p. 260-298.

[12] M. Kline. *(Mathematical Thought from Ancient to Modern Times*. Oxford: Oxford University Press (1972).

[13] A. F. Möbius. *Der barycentrische Calcul, ein neues Hülfsmittel zur anaytischen Behandlung der Geometrie*. Leipzig: Barth (1827).

[14] H. P. Manning. *Geometry of Four Dimensions*. New York: The Macmillan Company (1914).

[15] C. B. Boyer. *A History of Mathematics*. New York: John Wiley and Sons (1968).

[16] F. Caruso. Ensaio sobre a Dimensionalidade do Tempo. *Tempo Brasileiro* **195**, pp. 83-90 (2014).

[17] J. Handyside (Ed.). *Kant's inaugural dissertation and the early writings on space*. Chicago: Open Court (1929), reprinted by Hyperion Press (1979), pp. 11-15.

[18] F. Caruso & R. Moreira. Sull'influenza di Cartesio, Leibniz e Newton nel primo approccio di Kant al problema dello spazio e della sua dimensionalità (in Italian). *Epistemologia (Genova, Italia)* **21** (1998) 211-224.

[19] F. Caruso & R. Moreira. "On Kant's first insight into the problem of space dimensionality and its physical foundations". *Kant-Studien* **106** (2015) 547-560.

[20] G. G. Brittan Jr. *Kant's Theory of Science*. Princeton: Princeton University Press (1978).

[21] E. Kant. *Opus Postumum – passage des principes métaphysiques de la science de la nature à la physique*. Translation, presentation and notes by F. Marty. Paris, Presses Universitaire de France (1986), p. 131.

[22] P. Ehrenfest. In what way does it become manifest in the fundamental laws of physics that space has three dimensions? *Royal Netherlands Academy of Arts and Sciences (KNAW)* **20** (1917) 200. Reprinted in M. J. Klein (Ed.). *Paul Ehrenfest – Collected Scientific Papers*. Amsterdam: North Holland Publ. Co. (1959), p. 400.

[23] P. Ehrenfest. Welche Rolle spielt die Dreidimensionalität des Raumes in den Grundgesetzen der Physik? *Annalen der Physik* **61** (1920) 440.

[24] F. Caruso & R. Moreira, *Causa efficiens* versus *causa formalis*: origens da discussão moderna sobre a dimensionalidade do espaço (in Portuguese). *Scientia (Unisinos)* **4** (1994) 43-64.

[25] F. Caruso & R. Moreira Xavier. On the Physical Problem of Spatial Dimensions: An Alternative Procedure to Stability Arguments. *Fundamenta Scientiae* **8** (1988) 73.

[26] F. R. Tangherlini. Schwarzschild Field in n Dimensions and the Dimensionality of Space Problem. *Nuovo Cimento* **27** (1963) 636-651.

[27] L. Gurevich and V. Mostepanenko. On the existence of atoms in n-dimensional space. *Physics Letters A* **35** (1971) 201.

[28] K. Andrew and J. Supplee. A hydrogenic atom in d-dimensions. *American Journal of Physics* **58** (1990) 1177.

[29] C. G. Bollini, J. J. Giambiagi & J. S. Helman. Study of wave equations involving iterated Laplacian and potential $r^{-\beta}$ by the $1/N$ method. *Chemical Physics Letters* **175** (1990) 130.

[30] M. A. Shaqqor and S. M. AL-Jaber. A Confined Hydrogen Atom in Higher Space Dimensions. *Internation Journal of Theoretical Physics* **48** (2009) 2462.

[31] F. Caruso, J. Martins and V. Oguri. On the existence of hydrogen atoms in higher dimensional euclidean spaces. *Physics Letters A* **377** (2013) 694.

[32] F. Caruso, J. Martins, L. D. Perlingeiro & V. Oguri. Does Dirac equation for a generalized Coulomb-like potential in $D+1$ dimensional flat space–time admit any solution for $D \geq 4$? *Annals of Physics* **359** (2015) 73.

[33] F. Caruso, N. P. Neto, B. F. Svaiter & N. F. Svaiter. Attractive or repulsive nature of Casimir force in D-dimensional Mikowski spacetime. *Physical Review D* **43** (1991) 1300-1306.

[34] F. Caruso, R. De Paola & N.F. Svaiter. Zero point energy of massless scalar field in the presence of soft and semihard boundary in D dimensions. *International Journal of Modern Physics A* **14** (1999) 2077-2089.

[35] F. Caruso & R. Moreira. Space dimensionality: what can we learn from stellar spectra and from the Mössbauer effect. *In*: R. B. Scorzelli, I. Souza Azevedo & E. Baggio Saitovitch (Eds.), *Essays on Interdisciplinary Topics in Natural Sciences Memorabilia: Jacques A. Danon*, Gif-sur-Yvette/Singapore: Éditions Frontières, pp. 73-84 (1997).

[36] F. Caruso & V. Oguri. The Cosmic Microwave Background Spectrum and a Determination of Fractal Space Dimensionality. *Astrophysical Journal* **694** (2009) 151-153.

[37] B. Müller & A. Schäfer. Improved bounds on the dimension of space-time. *Physical Review Letters* **56** (1986) 1215-1218.

[38] F. Caruso; V. Oguri & F. Silveira. Still learning about space dimensionality: From the description of hydrogen atom by a generalized wave equation for dimensions $D \geq 3$. *American Journal of Physics* **91** (2023) 153–158.

[39] Euclid. *The Thirteen books of Euclid's Elements*. New York: Dover (1956).

[40] M. Kaku. *Introduction to Superstrings and M-Theories*. Berlin: Springer-Verlag (1999).

[41] I. Kant. *Kritik der reinen Vernunft*. English translation in *Great Books of the Western World*, vol. 39. Chicago: Encyclopædia Britannica, Inc. (1993).

[42] Kant, I.: *idem*, pp. 24-25.

[43] J. J. Silvester. A Plea for the Mathematicians. *Nature*, v. 1, p. 238 (1869).

[44] N. I. Lobachevsky. Géométrie imaginaire. *Journal für die Reine und Angewandte Mathematik*, v. 17, p. 295 (1837).

[45] J. Bolyai. *Absoluten Geometrie*. B.G. Teubner, Leipzig (1832). Indeed, Bolyai first announced his discoveries in a 26 pages appendix to a book by his father, the Tentamen, published in (1831).

[46] E. Beltrami. Saggio di interpretazione della geometria non-euclidea. *Giornale di Matematiche*, VI, pp. 284-322 (1868).

[47] G. Loria. *Il passato e il presente delle principali teorie geometriche. Storia e bibliografia*, fourth edition. Padova: Cedam (1931).

[48] R. Martins. The influence of non-Euclidean geometries in 19th century physical thought (in Portuguese). *Revista da Sociedade Brasileira de História da Ciência*, v. 13, pp. 67-79 (1995).

[49] J. Milnor. Hyperbolic Geometry: The first 150 Years. *Bulletin of The American Mathematical Society* (New Series) v. 6, n. 1, pp. 9-24 (1982).

[50] R. Bonola. *Geometrías No Euclidianas*. Buenos Aires: Espasa-Calpe Argentina (1951).

[51] L. D. Henderson. *The Fourth Dimension and Non-Euclidean Geometry in Modern Art*. Princeton: New Jersey, Princeton University Press (1983).

[52] D. M. Y. Sommerville. *Bibliography of Non-Euclidean Geometry including the Theory of Parallels, the Foundations of Geometry and Space of n Dimensions*. St. Martin's Lane, London: Harrison & Sons (1911).

[53] F. Caruso & R. Moreira Xavier. *Causa efficiens versus causa formalis*: origens da discução moderna sobre a dimensionalidade do espaço físico. *Cadernos de História e Filosofia da Ciência*, Série 3, **4**, n. 2, p. 43-64, jul.-dez. (1994).

[54] R. Moreira Xavier. Bachelard e o livro do calor: o nascimento da Física Matemática na época da rearticulação causal do Mundo. *Revista Filosófica Brasileira* **6**, p. 100-113 (1993).

[55] F. Caruso & V. Oguri. *Física Moderna: Origens Clássicas e Fundamentos Quânticos*. Second edition, Rio de Janeiro: Editora LTC (2016).

[56] J. Z. Buchwald. *From Maxwell to microphysics*. Chicago: Chicago University Press (1985).

[57] F. Caruso & V. Oguri. A estranha teoria da luz. *Ciência e Sociedade* **4**, n. 2, pp. 12-17 (2016).

[58] O. Heaviside. Electromagnetic waves, the propagation of potential, and the electromagnetic effects of a moving charge. Reproduced in *Electrical Papers*, v. 2, pp. 490-499 (1894).

[59] J.J. Gray (Ed.). *The Symbolic Universe: Geometry and Physics 1890-1930*. New York: Oxford University Press (1999).

[60] H. A. Lorentz. Versuch einer Theorie der elektrischen und optischen Erscheinungen in betwegten Körper, Leiden: Brill. Reproduced in *Collected Papers*, v. 5, pp. 1-137.

[61] S. Walter. The non-Euclidean style of Minkowskian relativity. In *The Symbolic Universe: Geometry and Physics 1890-1930, op. cit.*, pp. 91-127 (1999).

[62] H. A. Lorentz. Electromagnetic phenomena in a system moving with any velocity smaller than that of light. *Proceedings Acad. Sc. Amsterdam* **6**, p. 809 (1904).

[63] H. Minkowski. Die Grundgleichungen für die elektromagnetischen Vorgänge in bewegten Körpen. *Königlich Gesellschaft der Wissenschaften zu Göttingen Nachrichten, Mathematisch-Physikalische Klasse*, p. 53 (1908).

[64] A. Einstein. Zur Elektrodynamik bewegter Körper. *Annalen der Physik*, Ser. 4, **17**, pp. 891-921 (1905). Portuguese Translation in J. Stachel (Org.): *O ano miraculoso de Einstein: cinco artigos que mudaram a face da Física*. Rio de Janeiro: Ed. UFRJ (2001).

[65] T. S. Miller. *Albert Einstein's Special Theory of Relativity; Emergence (1905) and early interpretation (1905-1911)*. Massachusetts: Addison-Wesley (1981).

[66] H. A. Lorentz. *The Theory of Electrons and its applications to the phenomena of light and radiant heat*. Leipzig: Teubner (1909).

[67] H. Minkowski. Raum und Zeit. *Physikalische Zeitschrift*, v. 20, pp. 104-111 (1909) or Space and Time. A Translation of an Address delivered at the 80th Assembly of German Natural Scientists and Physicians, at Cologne, 21 September (1908).

[68] M. Jammer. *Concepts of Space: The History of Theories of Space in Physics*. New York: Dover (1993).

[69] C. H. Hinton. *What is the fourth dimension?*. London: Allen und Unwin (1887).

[70] C. H. Hinton. *Speculations on the Fourth Dimension: Selected Writings of Charles H. Hinton*, New York: Dover (1980).

[71] A. S. Eddington. *The Mathematical Theory of Relativity*. Cambridge: University Press (1923), p. 25.

[72] H. Weyl. Gravitation und Elektrizität. *Sitzungsberichte der Königlich Preußischen Akademie der Wissenschaften zu Berlin*, p. 465-480 (1918). Eine neue Erweiterung der Relativitätstheorie. *Annalen der Physik* **59**, pp. 101-133 (1919). See also his *Space, Time, Matter*. New York: Dover (1952), pp. 282-825.

[73] See, for exemple, J. Martin, N. Pinto-Neto & I. Damião Soares. Green functions for topology change. *Journal of High Energy Physics* **3** (2005) 60, and references therein.

[74] A. S. Eddington. *Fundamental Theory*. Cambridge: University Press (1946), p. 126.

[75] J. Dorling. The dimensionality of time. *American Journal of Physics* **38** (1970) 539-540.

[76] R. Mirman. Comments on the dimensionality of time. *Foundations of Physics* **3** (1973) 321-333.

[77] F. Caruso. A note on space dimensionality constraints relied on anthropic arguments: Methane structure and the origin of life. *In* M. S. D. Cattani; L. C. B. Crispino; M. O. C. Gomes & A. F. S. Santoro (Eds.) *Trends in Physics: Festschrift in homage to Prof. José Maria Filardo Bassalo*, São Paulo: Livraria da Física (2009), pp. 95-106.

[78] C. G. Bollini & J. J. Giambiagi. Dimensional Regularization: The Number of Dimensions as a Regularizing Parameter. *Nuovo Cimento B* **12** (1972) 20-26.

[79] C. G. Bollini & J. J. Giambiagi. Lowest order 'divergent' graphs in ν-dimensional space. *Physics Letters B* **40** (1972) 566-568.

[80] C. G. Bollini & J. J. Giambiagi. Supersymmetric Klein-Gordon equation in d-dimensions. *Physical Review D* **32** (1985) 3316-3318.

[81] C. G. Bollini & J. J. Giambiagi. Lagrangian Procedures for Higher order field equation. *Revista Brasileira de Física* **17** (1987) 14-30.

[82] C. G. Bollini & J. J. Giambiagi. Higher order equations of Motion. *Revista Mexicana de Física* **36** (1990) 23-29.

[83] C. G. Bollini & J. J. Giambiagi. Huyghens' Principle in $(2n+1)$ Dimensions for Nonlocal Pseudodifferential Operator of the Type $\Box^\alpha$. *Nuovo Cimento A* **104** (1991) 1841-1844.

[84] C. G. Bollini, J. J. Giambiagi & O. Obregón. Are some physical theories related with a specific number of dimensions?. In A. Feinstein & J. Ibáñez (Eds.), *Recent Developments in Gravitation* (Proceedings of Spanish Conference on Gravitation), Singapore: World Scientific (1992), p. 103.

[85] C. G. Bollini & J. J. Giambiagi. Criteria to Fix the Dimensionality Corresponding to Some Higher Derivative Lagrangians. *Modern Physics Letters A* **7** (1992) 593-599.

[86] C. G. Bollini & J. J. Giambiagi. "Arbitrary Powers of d'Alembertians and the Huygens' Principle", *Journal of Mathematical Physics* **34** (1993) 610-621.

[87] J. J. Giambiagi. "Relations Among Solutions for Wave and Klein-Gordon Equations for Different Dimensions", *Nuovo Cimento B* **109** (1994) 635-644.

[88] W. Bietenholz & J. J. Giambiagi. "Solutions of the Spherically Symmetric Wave Equation in $p+q$ dimensions", *Journal of Mathematical Physics* **36** (1995) 383-397.

[89] C. G. Bollini, J. J. Giambiagi, J. Benitez & O. Obregón. "Which is the Dimension of Space if Huygens' Principle and Newtonian Potential are Simultaneously Satisfied?", *Revista Mexicana de Física* **39**, suplemento n. 1, (1993) S1-S6.

[90] J. J. Giambiagi. "Wave Equations with multiple times: Classical and Quantum Solutions", *preprint* CBPF-NF-055 (1995).

[91] H. Poincaré. *Dernières Pensées*. Paris: Flammarion (1917).

[92] J. Hadamard. *Lectures on Cauchy's problem in linear partial differential equations*. New Haven: Yale University Press (1923).

[93] J. D. Barrow, Dimensionality. *Philosophical Transactions of the Royal Society of London A* **310** (1983) 337-346.

[94] W. Craig & S. Weinstein. On determinism and well-posedness in multiple time dimensions. *Proceedings of the Royal Society A* **465** (2009) 3023–3046.

[95] S. Weinstein, Multiple time dimensions. `arXiv:0812.3869v1` (2008).

PERSONAL TESTIMONIES

1
O casarão da rua Pamplona

F. Caruso

A Ruben Aldrovandi, parte dessa memória viva.

A *casa é uma das maiores forças de integração para os pensamentos, as lembranças e os sonhos do homem. Nessa integração, o princípio de ligação é o devaneio*, nos ensina Gaston Bachelard. Hoje, sonhando acordado, lembrei-me do Casarão da Rua Pamplona, 145, em São Paulo, onde funcionou durante décadas o Instituto de Física Teórica. Nele, eu sentia essa força de integração, sem, entretanto, conseguir verbalizá-la. Visitei-o muito menos do que gostaria, mas ele me marcou com boas lembranças e deixou saudades. A casa em si me foi simpática desde a primeira vista. Tinha muitas semelhanças com o casarão no qual estudei francês na minha juventude, no bairro da Tijuca, no Rio de Janeiro. Ambos eram espaços de cultura, pensamentos e de troca de ideias, cercados de uma beleza arquitetônica encantadora.

Figure 1.1: Fotografia antiga do casarão da Rua Pamplona 145, no qual o IFT funcionou de 1952 até 2010. Fonte: Fundação IFT.

Com o tempo, aprendi a conhecer seus rumores e cheiros. O chão de madeira dos espaços comuns invariavelmente se ressentia de ser pisado e retrucava, resmungando, como se fossem rangidos humanos entre os dentes.

Logo na entrada da casa, havia o cheiro do cigarro que o Sr. Antônio sempre mantinha entres os dedos e a boca. Minha chegada só era completa quando, após percorrer o terreno em aclive que separava o casarão do ingresso principal da rua, ouvia de "Seu" Antônio, sentado no abrigo do pequeno alpendre da entrada, um aconchegante "bom dia" ou "boa tarde". Como foi difícil chegar um dia e me dar conta de que ele havia partido!

Havia também o odor de fumo de cachimbo próximo à sala do caro Ruben Aldrovandi – com quem gostava de conversar sobre livros, a Biblioteca do IFT, sobre Heisenberg e Dirac –, o aroma de chá na proximidade da sala de meu grande amigo, pai e irmão mais velho Bruto Pimentel. Sua alma franciscana se refletia na simplicidade de seu espaço, vizinho ao escritório do Prof. Abraham Hirsz Zimerman. Algumas vezes, Bruto e eu íamos visitar o amigo Diógenes Galetti no segundo andar, percebendo, às vezes, um perfume de café nos corredores. Mas, naquele casarão, meu cheiro preferido, inegavelmente, era o da ótima biblioteca que havia sido formada com dedicação e amor pelo Prof. Jorge Leal Ferreira, que, infelizmente, não tive a oportunidade de conhecer pessoalmente. A biblioteca, que podia ser usada com toda liberdade, era o maior patrimônio daquele casarão; ousaria dizer, sua alma.

Frequentemente, ia almoçar com Bruto na pizzaria da própria Rua Pamplona. Por mais que estivesse disposto a experimentar outras coisas, invariavelmente, me rendia à pizza de escarola com alho.

Poucas casas me fizeram me sentir tão bem. Talvez sob inspiração do Prof. Paulo Leal Ferreira, que era um *gentleman*, o clima era de simplicidade, cordialidade, camaradagem e liberdade de pensamento. Agora vejo que era evidente o papel integrador do devaneio de dois irmãos que ousaram fundar um Instituto de Física privado em um país como o nosso.

Em algum momento, aquele pequeno grupo coeso e amigo começou a crescer, a crescer e o casarão ficou pequeno no imaginário de alguns. Estou convencido que a cultura brasileira dificulta a existência de grandes instituições. A dimensão do casarão era compatível com a dimensão do quadro de pesquisadores de então e com aquela do devaneio inovador e contagiante dos irmãos Leal Ferreira.

A mudança da sede do IFT foi inevitável, dizem, e assinalou o fim de uma época, o fim de um sonho, o fim de um modo de ser fazer Ciência. Disso sinto pena, do resto, só saudades.

2

Ruben: O início de uma grande amizade

A. Santoro

Quando cheguei na França, em Paris, fui direto para um hotel no Boulevard Saint Michel, na esquina com uma rua bem movimentada, dia e noite, por reserva de um amigo da Universidade de Brasilia, Levi. Este era um hotel baratíssimo, que ficava próximo ao rio Sena. Lugar maravilhoso, cheio de vida e muita gente andando por todos os lugares. Notava-se, ainda, lembranças do movimento de 1968. Na rua ao lado, ficava uma livraria permanentemente cheia principalmente de latinos, incluindo brasileiros, muitos fugidos da ditadura. Ficamos lá poucas semanas até que, ao visitarmos o Salmeron, ficamos sabendo de um Hotel perto de seu apartamento próximo ao Boulevard Arago, Hotel Arago, mais barato ainda. Assim, nos mudamos para ele porque o dinheiro era curto e ainda não tinha recebido a bolsa francesa que, na época, era de 750 Francos (125 US$). Claudio, meu irmão, estava na casa do Salmeron procurando emprego pela Europa. Salmeron me apresentou o Ruben que, na época, era casado com Sueli, que fazia astrofísica.

Um dia, eu e Claudio fomos a procura de apartamento para alugar, e já então contava com a vinda de João e Moacyr, meus colegas de trabalho. Marcamos com Ruben para passar em seu apartamento para conversar. Ruben na mesma hora nos convidou para almoçar. Aceitamos. Muito tempo depois, com um grau de amizade bem grande, fomos jantar com Ruben e Sueli, eu e Beth e nos divertimos muito ao relembrar este almoço com Claudio e Ruben. Rimos muito ao lembrar desse dia que almoçamos em sua casa quando o Ruben esqueceu que mal tinha comida para ele. E saímos de lá, eu e Claudio, comentando que havia sido muito esquisito o almoço que mal tinha comida para uma pessoa. Mas, fora isso, foi muitíssimo agradável o ambiente de amizade com o qual imediatamente nos acolheu e a solidariedade com dois "exilados".

Achamos um apartamento umas duas estações de Metrô depois do lugar em que Ruben morava (Bourg la Reine), em Fresnes. Moacyr, João e Tereza, eu e Beth fomos morar no novo apartamento, um duplex. Mas durou pouco tempo porque poucos meses depois de estarmos no novo apartamento, João se separou de Tereza e tivemos que entregar o apartamento e cada um foi para um lugar diferente.

Eu e Beth achamos um apartamento ao lado do edifício onde morava o Ruben. Ali ficamos alguns anos. Foi muito agradável e aproveitamos para aprofundar nossa amizade. Ruben, a cada dia que passava, se tornava um irmão. Partilhei muitas histórias com ele sobre o que ocorria comigo e o terrível curso que estava fazendo. Foi um período muito rico de amizade, conversas sobre tópicos de Física interessantes. Ele tinha uma cultura científica muito grande. Falávamos sobre os mais diversos tópicos da Física e isto me ajudava muito a pensar na Física que fazia. Quando ele terminou seu doutorado, voltou para o Brasil e mudei para um apartamento em Cachan, uma estação de metrô de distância na linha de Sceaux, que ia até Orsay e que frequentei durante todo meu primeiro ano na França.

Ruben fazia Física Teórica, muita matemática. Quando me contava seu trabalho parecia que estava falando de uma grande sinfonia. Uma segunda paixão dele era a música. Era rigoroso e apaixonado pelo que fazia. Tinha dois amigos/colegas de faculdade e de IFT (Instituto de Física Teórica): Ennio Candotti e Carlos Savoy. Ennio Candotti estava na Itália, com quem desenvolvi uma grande amizade e continuamos amigos até o presente. E Savoy vivia na França e por lá ficou.

No período em que eu estava na França, descobri que Salmeron havia traçado um plano profissional para mim e tinha arranjado tudo. Eu teria que ir para o IFT me juntar ao Ruben para lá fazer um grupo de fenomenologia. Mas eu tinha compromissos com o Rio de Janeiro, em particular, com o CBPF, o que não se enquadrava nos planos de Salmeron. Havia uma longa história com Mario Novello com quem já tinha não só uma grande amizade, iniciada em Brasília, como uma história de trabalho também.

Eu ia muito a São Paulo para dar seminários no IFT e, poucas vezes, na USP. Com a chegada de Carlos Escobar para o IFT, iniciei uma longa colaboração em Fenomenologia e depois, com nossa mudança para a Física Experimental, procurei Ruben que ficou entusiasmado com a possibilidade de criar um grupo de Física de Altas Energias no IFT. Novamente foi colocado na ordem do dia minha transferência para São Paulo. Fui várias vezes lá para discutir essa possibilidade e ele frequentemente me hospedava em seu apartamento quando já estava casado com a Ana Lucia. Havia alguns recém doutores no IFT que se entusiasmaram também para fazer Física Experimental. Sergio Novaes, então, tomou a decisão e começamos uma colaboração no Fermilab já na proposta de construir detectores *Roman Potes* para observação do fenômeno difrativo no Tevatron. Ruben era um entusiasta da ideia e nos incentivava muito.

Figure 2.1: Esta foto da capa do livro de Leonardo da Vinci foi tirada no apartamento de Rubem, de sua estante de livros de Física e de cultura geral.

Ruben era um apaixonado pelo IFT e por tudo que representava o casarão da Rua Pamplona. De fato, havia uma presença mágica dos irmãos Leal Ferreira, cujo pai, José Hugo Leal Ferreira, foi o fundador do IFT.

A paixão de Ruben pelos livros era emocionante assim como o carinho que tinha pela biblioteca do Instituto. Ele tinha um orgulho muito grande de pertencer àquela instituição e tratava a biblioteca como um filho seu. Ele era muito respeitado pela comunidade científica, era um amigo com quem eu podia discutir Física e problemas institucionais e sociais. Isto tudo nos aproximava bastante. Depois da primeira rodada do Tevatron, e depois da descoberta do Quark Top pelo DZero e pelo CDF, voltei a pensar em fazer física difrativa nas energias do Tevatron. Foi um período muito rico de trabalho na Física Experimental. Também foi quando fizemos uma colaboração muito grande com o LNLS. E foi neste projeto que o grupo do IFT deu início ao trabalho na Física Experimental.

Figure 2.2: Estas duas fotos também foram tiradas no dia que estava investigando junto com ele, na estante dos livros de Rubem e falamos sobre história da Física e problemas que nos interessavam na época, como as simetrias e as violações de simetrias na Física. Ruben era de uma de gentileza ímpar, solidário e generoso.

Relendo o livro de Óptica *Principles of Optics – Electromagnetic Theory of Propagation, Interference and Diffractions of Light*, de Max Born e Emil Wolf, edição da Pergamon Press, na introdução do capítulo VIII, encontramos a seguinte sentença: "*The first reference to diffraction phenomena appears in the work of Leonardo Da Vinci (1452 -1519)*". Fiquei intrigado porque não havia nenhuma referência que pudesse consultar e ver como foi a observação de Leonardo. Comentei com Ruben que, prontamente, me mostrou um livro sobre Leonardo Da Vinci em sua estante. Comecei a procurar no livro e achei um artigo que deixou tudo muito claro. *Leonardo Da Vinci: An Artabras Book*, Reynal and Co., New York, em cujo capítulo "Leonardo Optics", de Domenico Argentieri, p. 405, 414, 415, encontra-se a indagação: "Era Leonardo familiarizado com a difração?". Para mim foi muito interessante verificar que a difração foi primeiramente observada por Leonardo Da Vinci. Falei com alguns amigos e colegas sobre o fato de isso nunca ser mencionado nos livros de Física, no capítulo de óptica. Neste dia, em que fotografei o livro da foto acima, foi muito emocionante para mim porque naquela ocasião descobri a referência que procurava para completar a pouca informação que tinha dos dados históricos da descoberta do fenômeno da difração.

Quando no experimento Dzero, do qual fazia parte, descobrimos o Quark Top, ele vibrou tanto quanto nós que trabalhávamos no experimento. Assim, foi lá no IFT, no casarão da Rua Pamplona, que, no dia 24 de maio de 1995, fiz um seminário sobre nossa descoberta, "Quark Top no Experimento Dzero" a convite do Ruben. Nessa ocasião, falei sobre a descoberta de 17 eventos que nos permitiu medir a massa de 199 GeV, diferente do previsto pelo Modelo Padrão, mas, sabe-se agora que as medidas estão em torno de 170 GeV. Depois, fomos comer uma pizza juntamente com Bruto e com todos os colegas e amigos do IFT.

Eu fiz questão de fazer um artigo de memórias pois Ruben era como um irmão para mim e eu gostava muito de nossa amizade e companheirismo. É muito difícil substituir a vontade de abraçá-lo por algumas palavras que ele não vai poder ouvir. Mas minha lembrança é a de um forte abraço, meu caro amigo. Saudades, Ruben.

3
Lembranças / Remembrances

C. A. Savoy

In 1964, Ruben and I graduated together in Physics from USP and we both joined the Instituto de Física Teórica with an assistantship. At the beginning, we were six members there: Paulo Leal Ferreira and five assistants preparing a PhD! Gradually the other few members were back from the US and the atmosphere was really pleasant, like a big family, in that old house in Rua Pamplona. Even before, in 1963, we had enjoyed our first summer school, in Mexico: as undergraduate students, we were not in the list of IFT people applying to CNPq for travel grants, yet, we looked elsewhere and found an Itamaraty (Foreign Affairs) department and wrote a handwritten letter asking for support; the answer came soon, in a very nice envelope and special paper, telling us they did not supported this kind of activity, but CNPq did, so they had sent our request directly there. As a result, we immediately got our grants, even before the other members of the IFT! Latter, in 1967, we both went to a summer school in Santiago and I remember our discussions about the democratic state and the freedom reigning there at that time – only for a few more years!

During this period, we talked about a variety of subject, but seldom on our research since we worked on quite different subjects from the beginning. However, I remember and quote here, two Ruben statements about PhD: "I don't need advisors to give me ideas, I need them to give me the skills to develop my own!" and "I have chosen to work on cosmology because it encompasses many fields of physics." Eventually, along our lives, cosmology and particle physics have almost coalesced, perhaps we would have now many common interests!

In January 1968, we both went to Europe to start our PhD's, Ruben to ICTP, in Trieste, and me to Padua. Not quite far! After a couple of months, he called me: " Come here by the first train, and you'll see what you'll see!". I did and found a very big conference with a lot of old people. In my way toward a seat next to Ruben's, an old man had to stood up and he gently smiled. Ruben told me: "The nice old guy you have just disturbed is Dirac, the one speaking is Heisenberg, and there you see Fock, Salam, Lifchtz, Weinberg... and you are not dreaming! The year after, Ruben moved to Orsay to work under the supervision of Omnès, then I went to Geneva. He invited me a few times to his apartment in Paris XVème and we spent happy days visiting the marvelous town. It is a real pleasure to remember these days of our youth when our thoughts were driven by our dreams!

At the end of his PhD, Ruben went back to IFT, where he spent his whole career and contributed so much to the growth and evolution of the Instituto, as you all know. I got married to a french physicist and eventually moved permanently to Saclay. In the last 50 years or so, we met only a couple of times and just for the time to exchange a few words. We were so close friends, yet life is life!

4

Some Words of Gratitude

L. A. Ferreira

It is really an honour and a privilege to be invited to contribute to this volume dedicated to the memory of Prof. Ruben Aldrovandi. The reasons are manifold. Ruben was a skilled and gifted theoretical physicist who gave important contributions for many areas of physics like particle physics, field theory, gravitation, gauge theories, statistical mechanics, dynamical systems, etc. Besides that, he was well educated in some important areas of mathematics like topology, differential geometry and algebra. With his solid knowledge and superb intuition in physics and mathematics, he contributed to the education of a great number of young physicists in Brazil.

In particular, I benefited a lot from his post-graduated courses, seminars, and innumerable formal and informal conversations with him, specially around the coffee table at the Institute de Física Teórica (IFT) in São Paulo. That table was close to our pigeon holes (mail boxes), which in the eighties, nineties, and even later, we had to visit at least once a day. It worked as some sort of common room, and thanks specially to Ruben it was quite active. The daily informal coffee conversations could be about everything, from the latest interesting problems in physics to the science funding problems, passing through literature, music, history, politics, etc. He loved books, and was a compulsive reader. He used to read a book that he liked many times, to find nuances he missed in the first readings. He also played the piano, and loved listening to many kinds of music, specially classical music. So, talking to him was really a great pleasure.

But Ruben was also a great and dedicated administrator. He was the scientific director of IFT for many years, and played an important role in the history of it. IFT started in the fifties as a foundation outside the university. Like many research institutions of that type, it had instabilities in its funding. The situation came to a point where the future of IFT was in jeopardy. Ruben was the director when an opportunity came to join the Universidade Estadual Paulista (UNESP). He took that opportunity very seriously and helped saving our institute, by merging the IFT/Foundation with what was then called the IFT/UNESP. I must say I got my first job as a faculty member during that transition thanks to the new funding IFT got from UNESP, and I, like many others, owed a lot to Ruben. Thanks to that transition, Brasil still has nowadays one of the best theoretical physics institutes in the world. The Brazilian physics community is happy and proud of it, and Ruben has played an important role in that.

For all those reasons the present volume is a well deserved and hearty homage to Ruben. We all miss him.

5

A personal tribute to Ruben

P. A. Faria da Veiga

The article presented in the book's first part is my modest contribution dedicated to the memory of the late Professor Ruben Aldrovandi. In my very beginning as a theoretical particle physicist, working on renormalization theory and Quantum Chromodynamics, before I decided to become a more mathematical physicist, Ruben taught me an introductory course on Quantum field theory. He was the owner of a vast knowledge and a wonderful professor. He was also a wise and respectful colleague at Instituto de Física Teórica, now part of Universidade Estadual Paulista (UNESP), a true master. For many of us, above all, he was a great source of inspiration. It was lucky and a great pleasure for me to have my path crossed with his.

6
Breves palavras sobre o professor Ruben Aldrovandi

V. C. de Andrade

Generoso e inspirador, esse era o professor Ruben Aldrovandi. Era sempre um momento esperado do dia ir ao antigo casarão do IFT, ainda localizado na av. Pamplona, em São Paulo, encontrar todos do grupo de pesquisa na sala do Professor Ruben, reunidos em torno dele, sempre com seu cachimbo pujante, perfumando a sala e ouvir seu riso modesto, com os olhos sob a lente grossa dos óculos, muito atentos, enquanto discutia os temas da matemática e física, visceralmente ligados, com uma naturalidade e clareza que só conseguem os grandes cientistas. Sempre saíamos de lá com a certeza de que estávamos no rumo certo, e que a Física Teórica impulsionaria para sempre nossas vidas.

Ruben era, em sua essência, um pensador autônomo e crítico. Não seguia os caminhos ortodoxos, aqueles que todos seguem e que certeiramente vão render os frutos científicos esperados pela métrica da avaliação vigente. Ele simplesmente fazia por amar e por ver total sentido, enquanto nos esforçávamos para acompanhar seus complicados raciocínios matemáticos.

Além de grande pesquisador, Ruben foi atuante na formação de cientistas. Seus orientandos tornaram-se figuras fundamentais em sua vida. O querido professor José Geraldo Pereira, que tive a honra de ter como orientador de doutorado e a grande amiga Ana Lúcia Barbosa, companheira de estudos e colaboradora em nosso grupo de pesquisa, foram orientados pelo professor Ruben, e levam até hoje seu DNA acadêmico, compartilhando sua postura e olhar diferenciados sobre a ciência.

A sabedoria do professor Ruben era tanta, que transbordava em seus livros, nas suas aulas e seminários. Mas nas conversas mais próximas, quando podíamos perguntar sem receio, o mundo se revelava na geometria diferencial, na teoria de campos, nas teorias alternativas para a Relatividade, no sonho das teorias unificadas. Levo desses momentos um sólido conhecimento que transmito aos meus estudantes até hoje.

Ainda no início do mestrado, ao estudar pelo livro clássico do Ruben e José Geraldo, An Introduction to Geometrical Physics, compreendi pela primeira vez a teoria de grupos, fibrados, espaços topológicos, assim como os conceitos de conexões, derivadas covariantes, geodésicas e toda a riqueza da estrutura riemanniana, de maneira bastante especial. Fiquei fascinada com a afirmação do Ruben, em um dos encontros, de que é possível existir mais de uma conexão para um determinado espaço-tempo, definindo diferentes propriedades geométricas. Com isso abriu-se em minha mente a possibilidade de se sair da Relatividade Geral, com curvatura e torção nula, definida ad hoc, e pensar em outras possibilidades de construção geométrica para a descrição da Gravidade. Posteriormente, me encantei com o princípio variacional inverso, com o roteiro para se obter a Lagrangiana de um modelo a partir de suas equações de campo, o que inevitavelmente resultava na discussão sobre o que seria de fato mais fundamental. Ruben apresentava com maestria esses e outros temas. Estudar os fundamentos de teorias se tornou para mim o que há de mais belo na pesquisa científica, e inclusive hoje extrapolo para outras áreas, ao incluir as humanidades.

Realizei meu segundo estágio pós-doutoral com prof. Ruben, após retornar da França, no período da vida atribulado e maravilhoso, que foi a maternidade, e dele tive a empatia e compreensão que me impulsionaram para seguir com firmeza a carreira científica e a contornar as adversidades. Também dele tive apoio além do campo profissional, para o início da minha vida acadêmica profissional na Universidade de Brasília. Seu humanismo e amizade marcaram meu modo de ser professora.

Duas palavras expressam meu sentimento pelo professor Ruben: respeito e admiração.

Agora restam boas lembranças, muitas saudades. E uma vontade de voltar à sua sala do casarão, na Rua Pamplona, Antigo IFT, ver pela janela de vidro as equações diferenciais no quadro branco e sentir o perfume do cachimbo. Com sorte, ouvir seu riso tímido entremeado por palavras sábias sobre alguma questão fundamental da Física.

7

Ruben Aldrovandi: the French Connection

R. Kerner

My first acquaintance with Ruben Aldrovandi goes back to late seventiesn when he was on preparing his doctoral thesis in France, working at the Institute of High Energy Physics at the Paris-XI University in Orsay under the guidance of Roland Omnès. In fact, upon leaving Brazil, Ruben moved to Trieste, where he began a PhD under Christian Fronsdal. However, after attending a seminar by R. Omnès, he decided to move to France to work under his direction, changing the subject quite radically. The French system at that time comprised two doctoral titles, the "small one" called "Doctorat du troisième cycle", and the final one, much more important, corresponding to the German "Habilitationsschrift", called "Doctorat d'Ètat". which was Ruben's case. The thesis, entitled "La coalescence dans le modèle d'univers symétrique", was defended in 1973.

During Ruben's stay in France we met several times, usually at theoretical and mathematical physics seminars organized at Collège de France, in École Normale, or in Orsay, at the Paris-XI University. We discussed sometimes after a seminar, but rather casually. Already then I was impressed by his perfect mastership of French language and a vast knowledge of French literature and history.

When Ruben returned to São Paulo, our contacts ceased for about a decade. But when in 1993 I visited Brazil for the first time participating at a workshop on theoretical physics at the CNPq in Rio de Janeiro, Ruben invited me to visit his Institute at 145 rua Pamplona in São Paulo, and give a talk at the seminar. I spent a week in Ruben's company, delighted by his kind hospitality, discovering common taste not only in science, but also in music and literature. And we became real friends since then.

Our friendship flourished mostly during the two last years of XX-th century, 1998 – 2000, when Ruben and his wife Ana Lucia Barbosa spent two years in Paris, in the Laboratoire de Gravitation et Cosmologie Relativistes which I was directing from 1991 till 2002. Ana Lucia was on a post-doctoral visit, while Ruben was on sabbatical leave of absence from IFT. Very soon they became an integral part of our resarch group, appreciated by all its members. Those were the times when nobody objected smoking a pipe in the office, especially the excellent aromatic tobacco brands he was using.

Ruben also impressed me by his knowledge of French and Italian food and wines. Many a time we would have lunch at the Italian restaurant cmose to the University, on the Rue des Écoles street, with my brazilian PhD student Roberto Colistete Jr., followed by walks through the Jardin des Plantes. We spoke French, although from time to time switched to Portuguese which I wanted to practice, too. Strolling through the Latin Quarter with Ruben, I admired how perfectly he was acquainted with every corner there, as an accomplished Parisian.

During Ana Lucia and Ruben's stay in my Lab, another friend of mine, Dmitry V. Gal'tsov from the Moscow State University, spent three months there, too, as an invited professor. Ana Lucia's PhD thesis concerned the Yang-Mills fields, so it was quite natural that we started to work together and produced a common paper devoted to a non-abelian generalization of the Born-Infeld non-linear electrodynamics.

While continuing his research on teleparallel gravity, which he led since many years with his friend and collaborator José G. Pereira, Ruben was writing a new book on various matrices used in mathematical physics, which appeared in in 2001 under the title "Special matrices of mathematical physics: stochastic, circulant, and Bell matrices", edited by the World Scientific. By one of those happy coincidences that occur sometimes in our scientific development, I was working at that time on models of agglomeration and glass transition, with my friends Rafael Barrio of Mexico and Jean-Paul Duruisseau from my Paris-VI University, and our former PhD students Matthieu Micoulaut (Paris) and Gerardo G. Naumis (Mexico) who spent a year in my Lab as a post-doctoral visitor; several papers were published in common in various journals between 1996 and 2001.

Ruben got interested in our stochastic matrix approach to the glass forming problem, and incorporated it in his excellent book on matrices. Moreover, we wrote a paper together which he presented in September 1999 at the theoretical physics workshop in Karpacz, Poland. He produced a beautiful figure showing the agglomeration of two kinds of atoms – Se and As to be precise – on the rim of a cluster already formed, and used it as illustration for the cover of his book. I am using the same figure, conceived by Ruben back in 1999, in the article on modelling structural network glasses like chalcogenides and borates, contained in the second part of this volume.

Having observed how Ruben worked on his book gave me enough inspiration to consider writing my own book on "Model's of Agglomeration and Glass Transition" which was edited by the Imperial College Press in 2007. One of the chapters of that book contains the discussion on stochastic matrices borrowed from Ruben's book.

After Ruben and Ana Lucia departure we continued to keep in touch. Ruben visited Paris again in 2002 when he participated in the 24th International Colloquium on Group Theoretical Methods in Physics. It was a wonderful occasion to meet again, in the company of many common friends from around the world. At the conference, Ruben presented a paper co-authored with Ana Lucia, on the algebraic skeleton of space-time. Since then I visited São Paulo and met Ruben and Ana Lucia twice, in 2004 and in 2007. I was invited again to give a talk at the same charming building more than half-century old, and met Ruben's colleagues. We spent some time together walking through the streets of São Paulo, and in the evening shared meals in good restaurants. I was also invited to Ruben's home and tried his piano. Ruben played piano much better than me, his favorits being Bach and Mozart.

The last paper we authored together was published in 2010, in the Proceedings of the Biomat Conference in Rio de Janeiro. We exchanged mails and kept contact during Ruben's illness, on which he would not comment being very stoical and keeping rather silent on his ordeal. His passing away left me full of sorrow and sadness, and I miss him badly. Writing this text had a soothing effect on me, because it revived the memory of happy times spent together.

Let these modest lines be a tribute to Ruben and to our everlasting friendship.

8

Ruben: a personal tribute

S. F. Novaes

Ruben Aldrovandi played a pivotal role throughout my academic and professional journey, starting as my first advisor during my Scientific Initiation in 1978. His guidance was instrumental during the challenging times of my Master's and he stepped in as an invaluable mentor during my Ph.D. when my official advisor transitioned from theoretical to experimental high energy physics.

Post my Postdoc in Berkeley, as the director of the Instituto de Física Teórica (IFT), he was instrumental in securing my position as a Researcher at IFT. Two decades later, he supported my own transition from theoretical to experimental high energy physics, including my tenure at Fermilab.

More than an academic mentor, Ruben was a close friend and a person of remarkable cultural breadth, admired for his extensive knowledge across diverse fields. He had a unique scientific journey, starting with his Ph.D. (*Doctorat d'État*) with Roland Omnès at Université de Paris XI. Returning to Brazil in 1973, he brought with him the essence of Paris in his mind and soul. I have always sensed a certain ambivalence about his return to Brazil, a decision he seemed to have made out of a sense of social responsibility rather than personal preference.

Throughout his academic career, his publications – be the articles or books – were often collaborative efforts, featuring his students as co-contributors. Ruben's approach to research and publishing was unique. He deliberately chose unconventional and less trendy subjects that captivated him.

Ruben Aldrovandi's legacy extends far beyond the scientific domain; his profound influence on the personal and professional lives of those he worked with, including myself, is profound and enduring.

9

Ruben: uma pequena biografia

A. L. Barbosa, com colaboração de E. Gausmann

> "... Ali lembranças contentes
> Na alma se representaram;
> E minhas cousas ausentes
> Se fizeram tão presentes
> Como se nunca passaram ... "
>
> Luís Vaz de Camões em *Babel e Sião*.

É sem dúvida um imenso prazer escrever sobre Ruben. Ao início temi que uma saudade avassaladora me atingisse. Bem, a saudade que me invade todos os dias não se tornou maior, senti foi uma grande alegria ao ver que a lembrança de Ruben traz uma avalanche de boas histórias e recordações.

A obra que ele deixou na Física muitos conhecem, então, por sugestão de Evelise, escrevo uma pequena biografia desse homem incrivelmente inteligente e sensível, o homem além da Física.

Vamos lá! Ruben Aldrovandi nasceu nas primeiras horas do dia 13 de janeiro de 1942 em Piracicaba, São Paulo. Nasceu no dia 13 por teimosia, segundo ele afirmava, já que as freiras da maternidade tentaram adiantar o parto para que ele não nascesse num dia com número 13.

De família Metodista, Ruben já sabia ler aos quatro anos de idade; segundo ele, essa exigência de leitura precoce era uma das qualidades dos protestantes: a necessidade de poder ler a Bíblia o quanto antes.

Figure 9.1: Ruben com 2 anos.

Iniciou seus estudos no Grupo Escolar de Piracicaba, instituição com bom ensino. Apesar de sempre ser o melhor aluno da sala, não tinha direito aos prêmios (medalhas) no final dos anos letivos. O pai, Sr. José, ao perguntar ao então diretor da escola o motivo da discriminação com Ruben, soube que, à época, a escola tinha um forte viés católico e anti-protestante. Ruben foi então para o Colégio Piracicabano, escola de ensino fundamental e médio fundada em 13 de setembro de 1881 pela missionária estadunidense Martha Watts, sendo a primeira instituição metodista de ensino do Brasil.

O corpo docente do Piracicabano era composto, na área de ciências exatas e biológicas, por professores e cientistas que também lecionavam na Escola Superior de Agricultura Luiz de Queiroz (ESALQ), em Piracicaba; em disciplinas como inglês, francês e espanhol os professores eram nativos, normalmente missionários. Assim havia o "terrível" inglês da professora escocesa Pamela McPhaden e o vocabulário do professor português com seus falsos cognatos, que por vezes causavam certo mal-estar. Já para as aulas de música, Piracicaba fornecia seus renomados músicos.

Ruben falava de uma Piracicaba onde ele podia ver, da janela de seu quarto, dourados subindo o rio. Uma cidade pequena com forte veia cultural e que pretendia, em eterna disputa com Campinas, ser a "Atenas Paulista".

Nas horas em que não estava no colégio, Ruben jogava futebol (chutava com a esquerda), lia muito, ouvia música clássica (estudou violino durante uns meses) e dedicava-se ao laboratório de química que ele próprio montou no andar debaixo da casa da família, usando o dinheiro da mesada que recebia dos pais. Os materiais, os produtos químicos, assim como a maior parte de seus livros e discos, Ruben adquiria no Rio de Janeiro, onde passava anualmente férias, frequentando a Livraria Leonardo da Vinci, entre outras, no centro da então capital federal. O Rio de Janeiro era sempre a escolha para as férias pois, sua mãe, Sra. Nice, era carioca.

Na infância e na adolescência Ruben teve permissão de seu pai para somente frequentar o culto Metodista em ocasiões especiais. Todavia, assistia com rigor às aulas da Escola Dominical, onde tornou-se amigo do professor Warwick Kerr, que mais tarde seria o primeiro diretor científico da Fapesp (1962). Kerr aconselhou-o a se dedicar à leitura da Bíblia. Quando Ruben terminou a leitura, escolheu afastar-se da instituição religiosa.

Durante a adolescência Ruben decidiu que seria cientista. Uma análise do currículo proposto pela faculdade de Agronomia da ESALQ parecia indicar ser essa instituição o caminho ideal. Todavia, já no primeiro ano do curso de Agronomia, descobriu que não era aquilo que procurava, prestou novo vestibular, agora para Física na USP. Na época, o curso de Física funcionava na Faculdade de Filosofia, Ciências e Letras, localizada na Rua Maria Antônia. Nessa rua Ruben residiu até 1963, ano em que seus pais se mudaram para São Paulo (o pai fora eleito deputado estadual pela UDN), a partir de então passa a morar com eles no Bairro de Perdizes.

É durante o período de graduação na USP que Ruben faz sua primeira visita ao

Instituto de Física Teórica (IFT) na rua Pamplona. Num almoço com Warwick Kerr, conversando sobre os rumos que queria dar para sua vida científica, recebeu do amigo, e então diretor científico da Fapesp, o conselho de procurar o Instituto da Pamplona (Warwick desenhou, em um guardanapo, um mapa para Ruben chegar ao IFT). Foi ao Instituto, gostou do que viu e tornou-se aluno de iniciação científica, juntamente com seus colegas Ennio Candotti e Carlos Savoy. É no IFT que conhece seu grande amigo Jorge Leal Ferreira (irmão de Paulo Leal Ferreira), uma mente brilhante, segundo Ruben.

Ruben graduou-se na USP em 1964. Após a formatura, Sr. José, preocupado com o futuro do filho, disse-lhe que a "brincadeira de cientista havia acabado" e que abriria para Ruben uma agência de carros importados, para que ele fosse o gerente.

Figure 9.2: Ruben na colação de grau em 1964.

Felizmente para nós todos que o conhecemos, Ruben quis seguir a carreira de cientista e pouco tempo depois comunicou ao pai que estava empregado como professor no Instituto de Física Teórica. Em 1968, tirando licença do cargo de professor, partiu para a França onde fez Doctorat en Sciences na Universidade de Paris – XI, sob orientação do Prof. Roland Omnès, sendo o título da tese "La Coalescence dans le Modèle d'Univers Symétrique". Retornou ao Brasil em 1974.

Ruben voltou à França para três períodos sabáticos nos anos 1982-1983, 1990-1991 e 1998-2000, sendo o primeiro deles na Universidade de Paris - XI e os outros dois na Université Pierre et Marie Curie ou Université Paris VI.

Entre maio de 1984 e agosto de 1990, Ruben foi diretor do Instituto de Física Teórica. Período este muito conturbado para o IFT e ao qual muito se dedicou no esforço de salvar o Instituto que sofria grave risco de ser fechado devido à decisão da Finep de não mais financiar o IFT. É possível aferir o grau de dificuldades que Ruben enfrentou como diretor do Instituto pela queda do número de suas publicações no período, a tão amada pesquisa foi temporariamente colocada em segundo plano. O acordo feito com a Unesp em 1987 acabou sendo a melhor solução, com a Universidade ficando responsável pelo pagamento dos professores e funcionários. Já a Fundação Instituto de Física Teórica manteve sua independência ficando com o acervo da biblioteca e o casarão. A Fundação existe até hoje em sua sede no endereço da Rua Pamplona, 145, e Ruben nunca deixou de trabalhar pela manutenção e pelo progresso da Fundação. No ano de 1988 a produção científica de Ruben já apresentou sensível melhora. E em 1990 ele pôde partir para um ano sabático na França.

Ruben era sem dúvida apaixonado pelo Instituto de Física Teórica. Narrava com entusiasmo a história da Fundação IFT (1951), com o Engenheiro José Hugo Leal Ferreira[1] como primeiro presidente e seus amigos generais progressistas, os cientistas alemães e japoneses que vieram, a famosa carta de recomendação escrita por Heisenberg para alguns dos cientistas alemães, a família Leal Ferreira, o casarão e sua contínua transformação para poder receber mais pessoas, o pé de café no terreno, o primeiro computador, a biblioteca, os funcionários, o porteiro e amigo Seu Antônio e os colegas cientistas.

Foi na volta de seu ano sabático, em 1991, que conheci Ruben Aldrovandi. Eu estava no último semestre da graduação em física e procurava um orientador para o mestrado. Cheguei até ele por indicação de uma colega de turma que fizera uma entrevista com ele e estava positivamente impressionada. O primeiro grande diferencial de Ruben era a educação com a qual recebia os candidatos a uma pós-graduação, e mais, o respeito e a boa vontade que ele mostrava ao conversar conosco. Um homem a frente do seu tempo, sem dúvida. Para nós, meninas já calejadas pelo machismo reinante à época, conhecer um professor que estivesse disposto a conversar de forma civilizada e nos orientar, era realmente algo extraordinário. Desisti do mestrado que eu faria com um professor da instituição na qual me formei e iniciei o mestrado com Ruben no IFT.

E todo um universo de possibilidades se abriu nos meus estudos, todo um mundo repleto de conhecimentos e de temas interessantes.

Ruben era muito exigente e as tarefas eram trabalhosas; mas a situação era realmente boa, pois não procurávamos um mestrado fácil, procurávamos boa formação e respeito. E Ruben tinha tudo isso para oferecer a seus alunos.

Um outro ponto importante a ser destacado era que a formação oferecida por Ruben não era superficial, não bastava saber calcular, tinha-se que saber o quê se calculava e para que se calculava. Assim, as reuniões eram longas e as

---

[1]Agradeço a José Geraldo Pereira pelos apontamentos sobre a história do IFT

exposições dos cálculos eram pacientemente assistidas por ele. Sempre houve espaço para discussões, exposições de ideias, questionamentos, discordâncias e concordâncias.

Ruben muito bem aceitava se nós apontássemos algum engano em algum de seus cálculos, inclusive nos incentivava a fazer isso, esperava de nós dedicação ao trabalho e *feedback*. Não era para aceitarmos, sem análise, tudo que ele dissesse ou o que calculasse. Ele estava preocupado em formar cientistas e não meros calculadores que aceitassem tudo o que viesse da "instância superior".

Tampouco exigia produção louca de artigos ou que colocassem o nome dele em artigos dos quais não participara. Tratava todos os alunos com consideração, independentemente de quem fossem seus orientadores.

Aos poucos via-se a maravilha de poder perguntar para Ruben sobre assuntos de física que não fossem relativos a alguma disciplina que ele estivesse ensinando no momento. Podia-se, por exemplo, tirar uma dúvida de Mecânica Quântica, a qualquer tempo. Falando em Mecânica Quântica, que primor aquela apostila de Ruben sobre Teoria de Campos! A parte da introdução das matrizes Gama era magnífica, clara e completa; esse texto, felizmente, hoje se encontra na apostila "An Elementary Introduction to Classical Fields," escrita em coautoria com José Geraldo Pereira.

Falando em matrizes Gama, não posso deixar de contar que, ainda estudante, ao participar de uma das escolas do centro de Física em Trieste, Ruben abordou Dirac em um dos corredores e lhe fez uma pergunta sobre quantização. Contava Ruben que Dirac, parou, pensou um pouco e respondeu gentilmente.

Figure 9.3: Ruben em Florença, 1998.

Nas reuniões de trabalho com Ruben, além de Física, também recebíamos uma boa dose de cultura.

É impressionante que a mesma pessoa que fazia pesquisa de tão alto nível e escrevia livros, conseguisse tempo para ser tão culta, como era o caso de Ruben. Literatura, história, cinema, arte, música, filosofia, psicanálise, religião e pelo que mais se possa imaginar, Ruben passou. Tinha uma grande paixão por história. Na virada do século Ruben dedicou um bom tempo ao estudo dos métodos de datação arqueológica nos livros de Colin Renfrew. Nas duas primeiras décadas do século XXI, voltou recorrentemente às leituras sobre suas queridíssimas Mesopotâmia e Suméria nas obras de Jean Bottéro e de Samuel Noah Kramer, entre outros. Não eram estudos superficiais, era uma busca de conhecimento e compreensão, e quem estivesse ao seu lado tinha o privilégio de ouvir o que ele aprendia. Seu interesse por arqueologia Ruben podia compartilhar com a filha Cibele, artista plástica e arqueóloga!

Para contar um pouco mais sobre Ruben, faço uma divisão em duas áreas de seu maior interesse fora da física: literatura e música.

Literatura

Proponho-me aqui a listar os autores e as obras que Ruben mais citava, o que permite mostrar o quanto ele se dedicava a leitura. Quem sabe essa lista possa servir como fonte de inspiração para algum leitor.

Durante anos Ruben estudou o idioma chinês e seus ideogramas. Apaixonado pela cultura chinesa, em especial pela poesia, chegou a traduzir poemas de Li Po. Apreciava também a poesia de Tu Fu.

Conhecia bastante sobre Zen Budismo e praticou meditação durante certo tempo. Aqui, um autor que Ruben mencionava era Allan Watts.

Suas leituras eram bem variadas, lia autores nacionais e estrangeiros; os estrangeiros, sempre que possível, lia no idioma original. Nos idiomas inglês, francês, espanhol e italiano era fluente. Quanto ao alemão, perdeu a fluência ao longo dos anos, mas preservou a leitura; uma das últimas edições da Odisseia que Ruben adquiriu, era em alemão.

Ruben leu várias vezes a Odisseia e tinha uma coleção de edições da obra, com diferentes tradutores em diferentes idiomas. Decorou os primeiros versos em grego e às vezes os declamava. Também leu a Ilíada, mas preferia a Odisseia.

Outra coleção era a de Bíblias, em idiomas variados, versões protestantes e versões católicas, assim como um exemplar da Vulgata (tradução latina da Bíblia feita por São Jerônimo 340-420, que foi declarada a versão oficial da Igreja romana pelo Concílio de Trento). Essa dedicação ao estudo da Bíblia, entre os protestantes, contrasta-se fortemente com a proposta católica, pelo menos na minha época, em que se conhecia os textos bíblicos apenas durante a missa, nos trechos que constavam no "folheto".

Distraía-se muito lendo romances policiais, em especial as obras de Agatha Christie. Com o tempo, leu também Arthur Connan Doyle, Ruth Rendell, Ellis Peters, Peter Beresford Ellis, Michael Innes e Alexander McCall Smith.

Muito antes que virasse moda, Ruben lera O Hobbit e Os Senhor dos Anéis. Até tentou ler Harry Potter, mas não gostou.

Apreciava as obras dos franceses Victor Hugo, Balzac, Gustave Flaubert (Salambô),[2] Marcel Proust, Maurice Druon (Les Rois Maudits), André Gide (Thésée); da australiana Colleen McCullough, da belga Marguerite Yourcenar (Mémoires d'Hadrien) e muito mais.

Quanto aos autores italianos, Ruben leu Dante Alighieri, Dino Buzzati (Il deserto dei Tartari), Italo Calvino, Umberto Ecco, Italo Svevo, Carlo Emilio Gadda (Quer Pasticciaccio Brutto de Via Merulana), para citar os mais comentados.

Ruben apreciava muito o livro Manuscrit Trouvé à Saragosse do polonês Jan Potocki, escrito originariamente em francês. Outra obra muito querida por ele era Le Maître et Marguerite de Mikhail Boulgakov.

Adorava Don Quijote de la Mancha. Era um apaixonado pelas obras de Borges, Bioy Casares, García Marques e pelo livro Rayuela do argentino Cortázar.

Não posso deixar de mencionar os autores de língua inglesa: William Shakespeare, Christopher Marlowe, John Donne, Emily Brontë, Jane Austen, Wilkie Collins, T.S. Elliot e Lawrence Durrel.

Dentre os autores nacionais Ruben gostava muitíssimo da obra de Gonçalves Dias, em especial dos poemas, I Juca Pirama, A Tempestade e Canção do Tamoio, os quais recitava com certa frequência. Outro poeta favorito era Camões, vários de seus sonetos Ruben sabia de cor e recitava com entusiasmo.

Música

Vejo Ruben e a ciência que ele tanto amava como um único ente. Ao estudar a Plena Consciência no Budismo lembrei-me de Ruben que, com a Física, com a Matemática e com a Música, formava um só "ser". Ou, dizendo de outra forma, não era necessário um esforço consciente para Ruben fazer pesquisa de alto nível, isso estava nele, as ideias que surgiam eram sempre boas, ótimas ou brilhantes. Era assim também a relação entre Ruben e o piano, bastava ouvir poucas vezes uma música, talvez até uma vez somente, para que ele a tocasse no piano sem o uso de partitura.

Ao falar de Ruben e música temos vários caminhos a percorrer.

Música religiosa. Durante o período de graduação Ruben estudou órgão com um professor que era responsável pelo órgão de uma igreja católica que ficava no

---

[2] Coloco entre parênteses os títulos das obras favoritas.

bairro do Pari. Quem o apresentou a esse professor, foi seu primo César, irmão do poeta Mauro Gama. Tocar boa música requer, além do conhecimento musical, domínio da mecânica do instrumento. O órgão do Pari tinha vários teclados e, segundo Ruben, era um bom órgão. Sua facilidade em tocar o instrumento fez com que o professor lhe desse a incumbência de tocar em algumas missas dos domingos. Ruben constatou assim, que a maioria dos padres errava os tempos e ele precisava fazer correções enquanto tocava, o que foi um grande aprendizado. Segundo contava, os templos protestantes usavam órgãos elétricos, por isso tinha que frequentar uma igreja católica. Explicava que a manutenção desses instrumentos sempre foi muito onerosa de tal forma que muitos órgãos foram desativados no mundo todo.

À época em que estudou, só podia se tocar nas igrejas católicas músicas de compositores católicos, assim a famosa marcha nupcial de Mendelssohn, compositor de origem judaica cuja família se convertera ao luteranismo, não era tocada em casamentos. Às vezes o professor permitia que Ruben tocasse composições de autores não católicos, como Johann Sebastian Bach. Ruben dizia que, devido à doutrina protestante proibir imagens, seus fiéis dedicavam-se à música e o faziam com excelência, coisa que quase inexistia na música católica; eu, mesmo sendo católica, senti-me obrigada a concordar...

Ruben, de tempos em tempos, voltava aos Hinos Protestantes; conservava o livro que era usado nos cultos; os hinos eram numerados e, durante o culto, o pastor comunicava aos fiéis o número daquele que seria cantado; comportamento totalmente diferente do que ocorria nas missas, em que as músicas, correntemente desconhecidas dos fiéis, vinham nos folhetos distribuídos no início das missas. Aprendi com Ruben que, do ponto de vista musical, os protestantes eram bem mais inclusivos que os católicos, já que com o tempo todos aprendiam as músicas que eram cantadas.

Música clássica. O compositor favorito de Ruben era Johann Sebastian Bach, com destaque para a obra Paixão segundo São Mateus, em particular a gravação de Otto Kemplerer. Ruben também tocava no piano, no teclado, ou mesmo no cravo, as Cantatas de Bach e outras obras do autor. No seu repertório incluíam-se também outros autores como:[3] Schubert (Ave Maria), Beethoven, Cesar Franck (o autor católico de Panis Angelicus), Brahms (a maravilhosa Berceuse), Puccini (Nessum Dorma, O Mio Babinno Caro), Haendel (Ombra mai Fu), Grieg (Peer Gynt, Suite No. 1 Op. 46), Verdi, e muito mais.

Música brasileira. Ruben trazia consigo a influência da boa música caipira que permeava o Brasil de sua infância: Cabocla Teresa, Tristeza do Jeca, Saudades do Matão (a favorita de seu pai), Piracicaba que eu Adoro Tanto, para citar algumas. Não posso deixar de citar aqui Erotides de Campos, compositor da Ave Maria de

---

[3] Incluo aqui uns exemplos dos quais consigo me lembrar, mas que de forma nenhuma esgotam o vasto conhecimento musical de Ruben.

Piracicaba, aliás, Sr. Umberto Aldrovandi, avô paterno de Ruben, que era músico, entre outras coisas, chegou a tocar junto com Erotides. Ruben tocava todas essas canções no piano. Pelo rádio, Ruben teve acesso à efervescente onda de boa música brasileira das décadas de 30 a 60 e seus grandes compositores e intérpretes: Noel Rosa, Silvio Caldas, Lupicínio Rodrigues, Pixinguinha, Ismael Silva, Ataulpho Alves, Orlando Silva, Cartola, Sinhô, Nelson Gonçalves, Ângela Maria, Dolores Duran, Alaíde Costa, Nelson Cavaquinho, Humberto Teixeira, Catulo da Paixão Cearense, Luiz Gonzaga, entre outros.

Já na década de 60, Ruben frequentava, junto com os colegas, o programa musical de auditório apresentado por Elis Regina no Teatro da Record na Avenida Brigadeiro Luís Antônio, 411 (o teatro ainda está lá, apesar de não mais pertencer à Record). Lá ouviu muita música boa! Ruben contava que, certo dia, Elis Regina trouxe ao palco um rapaz muito tímido para se apresentar, quando o cantor e compositor começou a tocar violão e cantar as pessoas se entreolhavam admiradas com o que ouviam. O jovem era Chico Buarque em início de carreira! Ruben contou que Chico, nessa época, ainda frequentava a faculdade de Arquitetura e havia levado, por segurança, uma claque composta por seus amigos de graduação, o que, segundo Ruben, não foi necessário pois o público ovacionou o jovem promissor!

Ruben admirava muito a obra de Chico Buarque, tanto letra quanto música. Considerava Chico um grande poeta. Adorava Elis Regina, com algumas ressalvas a escolha do repertório. No piano tocava "Quem te viu, quem te vê", "Retrato em Branco em Preto", "Com açúcar e com afeto", "A Banda", e outras. Pode parecer óbvio tudo isso, mas não é. Vejamos um comentário de Ruben sobre a letra de "Quem te viu, quem te vê": é incrível que ele (Chico) tenha conseguido colocar em uma letra ideias tão contrastantes como "noites de gala" e "mestre-sala".

Era muito interessante poder pedir a Ruben que tocasse músicas que estivessem ou não estivessem em seu repertório. Caso ele não conhecesse a música, bastava cantarolá-la ou mostrá-la em alguma gravação, que ele em seguida reproduzia no teclado. Era impressionante!

As composições de Ruben. Ruben além de tocar compunha canções; compunha para as pessoas queridas, para os amigos, para a Natureza e para musicar poemas. As composições eram de tipos variados, ou seja, poderiam ser marchinhas, valsas, toadas, berceuses, samba-canção, entre outros; a escolha dependia do tema e da pessoa homenageada. Essas músicas foram inicialmente gravadas em fitas cassete; com o progresso dos aplicativos para música, Ruben gravou suas composições usando o aplicativo Cubase. Infelizmente, entre as atualizações de versões tanto do aplicativo quanto do computador, esses documentos sofreram danos e ficaram inacessíveis, segundo disse Ruben. Mas, tenho um extrato de uma partitura de uma composição da segunda metade da década de 90, cujo fac-símile está na Figura 4.

Fato muito feliz da vida de Ruben foi poder compartilhar sua paixão pela música com seu filho Leonardo Aldrovandi, pianista, compositor e poeta.

Figure 9.4: Fac-símile de um extrato de composição de Ruben.

Pessoas

Ruben era extremamente sociável. Conversava sobre os mais variados assuntos com os mais variados tipos de pessoas.

Cumpre dizer que acreditava muito na humanidade. Jamais desistiu das pessoas. Nunca o vi planejando algo contra qualquer pessoa ou quaisquer de seus possíveis desafetos. Ruben talvez fosse sincero demais, mas era sobretudo confiável. Uso, para descrever a ética que vi em Ruben, o poema abaixo, escrito pelo cubano José Martí, que Ruben citava e recitava:

> *Cultivo una rosa blanca*
> *en junio como en enero*
> *para el amigo sincero*
> *que me da su mano franca.*
>
> *Y para el cruel que me arranca*
> *el corazón con que vivo;*
> *cardo ni ortiga cultivo;*
> *cultivo la rosa blanca.*

Referia-se com muito respeito, admiração e carinho a seus grandes amigos Alberto Santoro e Ennio Candotti; falava deles tão frequentemente que, quando

Ruben os apresentou para mim, parecia que eu já os conhecia há muito tempo e, obviamente, os tinha também em grande conta.

Ruben tinha grande consideração por seus ex-alunos Sandra Padula e Sérgio Novais (iniciação científica), Roberto Kraenkel, Gerson Francisco, Luciene Pontes, Rodrigo Cuzinato, Léo Medeiros, Vanessa Andrade e Roldão da Rocha, para citar os mais comentados.

Em relação a José Geraldo, que além de ex-aluno era o grande parceiro da física e das publicações, Ruben o considerava como um irmão.

Figure 9.5: Com José Geraldo em 2018

Mencionava também com alegria e respeito o queridíssimo casal Roberto e Sônia Salmeron, o maestro Cláudio Santoro, o orientador Roland Omnès, o colega Sèrge Caser, o matemático Chaim Samuel Honig, o geólogo Paulo Milton B. Landim, "Seu" Antônio e os físicos e colegas Diógenes Galetti, Gehard Bund, Mário Novello, Miguel Manna, Richard Kerner, Jerôme Gariel, Luiz Agostinho Ferreira, Adriano Natale, Juan Carlos Montero, Alfredo Suzuki, Francisco Caruso, Bruto Pimentel, Lauro Tomio, Vicente Pleitez, e muitas outras pessoas, cuja ausência dos nomes aqui deve ser atribuída somente a falhas em minha memória, não à falta de consideração por parte de Ruben.

Falso Epílogo

Aqui coloquei muitas informações com o intuito de dar uma idéia de quão rico era o mundo de Ruben e do quanto me lembro dele ao passar pelas coisas boas e dignas de atenção nesse mundo.

Falar sobre Ruben é sempre denso, positiva e agradavelmente denso! Por isso é falso o epílogo, por não caberem tantas histórias em um só texto. Tudo continua!

Seja na leitura, seja nos filmes, seja nas músicas, não há um só dia que não traga Ruben à minha memória. Ao ler o livro de Ruy Castro A noite do meu bem – a história e as histórias do samba-canção, em cada página eu encontrei Ruben nos cantores e compositores que ele citava. Ler esse livro em sua em sua companhia, seria diversão garantida.

Encontro Ruben também nas árvores que ele tanto amava e gostava de abraçar. Um entusiasta do bairro Bela Vista, Ruben vibraria com as recentes descobertas arqueológicas em torno da antiga sede da Escola de Samba Vai-Vai: o quilombo do Saracura.

Digo mesmo que Ruben pertence à classe das pessoas que o mundo precisava que existissem. Ruben, que enchia nossa alma com tantas histórias, com tantas ideias e conhecimento, é uma presença eterna porque fez germinar em muitos que o conheceram a curiosidade pelas ciências, exatas e humanas.

Ruben, o amor, o amigo, a alegria, o otimismo e muito mais qualidades que, provavelmente, não tenhamos percebido naquela alma tão complexa e sensível. Encerro aqui esse texto com a última foto que tiramos juntos e com um verso de Ricardo Reis (Fernando Pessoa) que acredito bem descrever a postura de Ruben diante da vida.

> *Para ser grande, sê inteiro: nada*
> *Teu exagera ou exclui.*
> *Sê todo em cada coisa. Põe quanto és*
> *No mínimo que fazes.*
> *Assim em cada lago a lua toda*
> *Brilha, porque alta vive.*

Figure 9.6: Com Ana Lucia em 28/12/2021.